Cultural Tapestry

CULTURAL TAPESTRY
Readings for a Pluralistic Society

FAUN BERNBACH EVANS
University of Southern California

BARBARA GLEASON
City College, City University of New York

MARK WILEY
California State University, Long Beach

HarperCollins *Publishers*

Sponsoring Editor: Patrica A. Rossi
Project Coordination, Cover Design: York Production Services
Cover Art: Murray Gibson. Tower of Knowledge (1989). Wool and silk,
13.5″×7′. Photograph courtesy of John Dean
Production Manager: Michael Weinstein
Compositor: York Production Services

About the Cover
The diptych shows the Tower of Babel and the Tree of Life. The two
images are enclosed in a mosaic border that represent the diverse cultures
of the world. Building the biblical Tower of Babel spread the peoples over
the face of the earth and led to misunderstanding and distrust among
various cultures. The tower is being destroyed and the boundary is
disintegrating giving hope of a renewed global understanding.

For permission to use copyrighted material, grateful acknowledgment is
made to the copyright holders on pp. 609–615, which are hereby made part
of this copyright page.

Library of Congress Cataloging-in-Publication Data
Cultural tapestry: readings for a pluralistic society / [edited by]
  Faun Bernbach Evans, Barbara Gleason, Mark Wiley,
      p. cm.
    ISBN 0-673-46428-8 (student ed.).—ISBN 0-673-46609-4 (teacher ed.)
    1. Ethnicity. 2. Pluralism (Social sciences). I. Evans, Faun
Bernbach. II. Gleason, Barbara. III. Wiley, Mark.
GN495.6.C85 1992
305.8—dc20   91-14789
                                                            CIP

92 93 94 9 8 7 6 5 4 3 2

Contents

Preface

WHY A MULTICULTURAL READER?

In short, a cultural reader like ours reflects the times and conditions in which we live. Our society is composed of a broad spectrum of ethnically and linguistically diverse people, a diversity that is potentially both our greatest resource and one of our greatest sources of discord. The diversity of our people need not, however, create differences that keep us apart and cause conflicts among us. Instead our differences can be shared, understood, and built upon, thus strengthening our social bonds. Yet this hypothetical strengthening requires some sort of metaphorical substance, some kind of glue to combine and hold the fragments together. Is there such a metaphorical substance, a basis for unity that all of us can accept without forfeiting what we believe to be most vital in our respective backgrounds? *Cultural Tapestry* is a multichordal response to this question.

It is difficult to imagine what "American culture" in the United States is like. In many ways it seems a protean beast, appearing differently according to the desire of the gazer. We might imagine our culture to be like a never-ending movie whose plot is always twisting in new directions, breaking up into a host of subplots, and adding characters to a kaleidoscope of shifting scenes. In this movie we also need to realize that multiculturalism is not reducible to ethnic, linguistic, or racial differences. Rather our multiculturalism includes all of those elements that contribute to the quality of the environments we inhabit and to how we perceive who we are—both individually and collectively—and to how we see ourselves fitting in or not fitting in with those surrounding us. Moreover, multiculturalism in our society means that certain themes, important since the late fifteenth century, reappear and become significant in new ways. Such themes as immigration; community life; our concern for our cities and farms; for education and family life; and for the sometimes blatant, but more often subtle, forms of prejudice that have been an unfortunate part of our history, are all perennial subjects needing our vigilant attention.

We do not want to turn our backs and deny the more disturbing aspects of our pluralistic society. This serves no one's interests and prevents the potential for understanding the complex problems that divide us. In our book, therefore, we do not present only a spectrum of views on multiculturalism or only a diversity of voices speaking from various ethnic backgrounds. Instead we have sought to provide more coherent contexts for some of the important dilemmas and issues affecting each of us to some degree. We hope our thematic divisions create a fabric palpable enough that the texture and interrelatedness of our common concerns is readily perceivable.

A multicultural society can mean a blurring of clear boundaries among previously distinct groups. It can also mean a desire to reinforce and solidify those boundaries, creating identities that distinguish you from me, one community from another. Or it could mean the tension felt in our lives as each of us tries to negotiate an identity, crossing and recrossing those boundaries daily, sometimes succeeding, sometimes failing to incorporate the richness of this cultural tapestry.

We have designed this anthology to be used for writing classes. As writing teachers ourselves, we also understand the need for our students to learn to read and write in particular ways sometimes referred to today as "academic discourse." We believe our book will help students achieve this particular form of literacy. However, we also believe that students using this book can learn both about the society they compose and about themselves as composers.

We are also aware that our book is not exhaustive: There is much more to be said and debated concerning who we are, where and how we live, and where we are going. But *Cultural Tapestry* provides an opportunity for students and teachers to work together to understand our society's unique situation. It is an opportunity that we hope will open dialogue between college students and non-college students, between those in the workplace and those performing community work, and, in the end, between those who care about the quality of our lives and those who cannot yet imagine what that quality might be like. This dialogue would be a rhetoric nurtured in the relative tranquility of the academy but would also be a rhetoric that can help students develop into involved citizens who feel quite comfortable dirtying their hands in the labor of the world.

USING THE TEXT

As members of the academic community we all routinely encounter a variety of discourse forms—textbooks and works from various disciplines, syllabi, class notes, exams and quizzes; and the noncurricular too, including school newspapers, political pamphlets, and advertisements. However, we also participate in a larger society, one comprising many subcultures and subcommunities where other discourse forms serve specific communicative functions. We sometimes write personal letters, keep journals or diaries, write letters to editors or to prospective employers. We also read magazines, newspapers, and other materials related to our personal interests. Hence we are continually engaged with forms of literacy distinct from academia and forms that no doubt will play a role in our ongoing education beyond college.

It is with these considerations that we approached the task of selecting readings for this anthology. We attempted to include works that not only helped to provide a wide range of genres but also spoke to the expanding cultural diversity of the United States. From the hundreds of selections reviewed, approximately 80 were chosen. Among these offerings we have included a variety of essay types—the scholarly, the general audience form found in magazines, the personal, and the autobiographical. We have also included some journalism, short fiction, and poetry. It was not our aim, however, to represent every single ethnic group. But we have made a concerted effort, though, to balance the readings so that many different voices speak.

Although each selection has been placed into one of the nine thematic chapters, we think you will find that there is much overlap among the chapters. For example, although "The Library Card" by Richard Wright has been chosen for Chapter 7 ("Prejudice and Oppression"), one might also see the relationship of this piece to the theme of Chapter 6 ("Teaching and Learning"). Or one could connect "Seven Amish Farms" by Wendell Berry in Chapter 4 ("Our Environments") with issues presented in Chapter 3 ("Community Life"). We hope, then, that you will view the chapter themes as entries into a cultural conversation and not necessarily as discrete entities unto themselves.

In attempting to facilitate this cultural conversation, we offer at the end of each reading selection discussion questions and writing assignments, which we have segmented into three separate groupings. The section called "Talking about the Text" includes questions intended to prompt engagement with the content and rhetoric of the specific text just read. Those questions under the heading "Exploring Issues" are geared toward fostering discussion of a broader and more intertextual nature. Finally, the "Writing Assignments" suggestions offer a range of writing tasks intended to generate critical thinking and personal involvement with the issues. Interviews, personal narratives, expository, analytical, and argumentative essays, and synthesis and research projects represent this range of assignments.

One exception to this format are the poems we have woven throughout our text. We have decided to let the poems stand on their own without our questions in order to encourage students and teachers to respond in whatever mode seems appropriate. Usually the poems complement one of the other selections in some way, so they could be discussed in the context of these related readings. But that's your choice to make.

Closing each of the nine chapters is a feature called "Extended Writing Assignments." Every effort was made to compose these assignments so that they encourage making connections between and among the readings from any one specific chapter and sometimes across chapter themes as well. Because we know the chapter readings and the companion questions can serve only as entries into the various issues presented in this text, we have designed many of these assignments as opportunities for further research and synthesis. For instance, the selection "We Are Outcasts" by Monica Sone might provoke some students to investigate the internment of Japanese Americans by the U.S. government during World War II. Or the essays by Mike Rose and Diane Ravitch might prompt some to develop individual theories of American education based upon a synthesis of their own research.

In addition to the discussion questions and writing assignments, we have also provided each reading with a biographical gloss on the author and any background information pertinent to that reading selection. We have done this in order to supply more context for the selections, a context that is filled out more with the introductory essays beginning each chapter. These chapter introductions also attempt to identify key issues and to frame questions readers can pursue in their subsequent reading. While the apparatus of *Cultural Tapestry* lends itself to a variety of composition class settings from basic writing to argumentation and research-based courses, we likewise see this text as a viable supplement to cultural studies and social science course syllabi.

HOW WE ORGANIZED THE TEXT

We begin *Cultural Tapestry* with the chapter entitled "Living in a Multicultural Society." In this chapter we have included readings that will not only draw your attention to the pluralistic nature of the United States but will also specify many of the central themes developed more fully in later chapters. Although each of the nine chapters covers a variety of topics, many of the readings within chapters sometimes complement and sometimes contrast with one another. The chapter themes all address questions we think are of particular importance to our multicultural society, and Chapter 1 establishes a point of departure for this evolving cultural conversation.

Chapter 2, "Facing New Worlds," attempts to incorporate the subjects of immigration and assimilation, but the readings in this chapter extend the concept of "new worlds" by considering other kinds of transitions and adjustments many of us must make when encountering divergent modes and forms of living. So, for instance, while Pete Hamill explores the world of Mexican laborers attempting to cross over into the United States, Terry Galloway depicts the struggles of a young girl who gradually loses her hearing and must learn to adjust to living in a new world of silence.

While Chapter 2 probes the self's confrontation with different worlds, Chapter 3 focuses on "Community Life." Here the nature of community is explored as well as the conflicts that arise both within and between communities. We offer a few descriptive accounts of community life; however, other readings focus on conflicts as well as possible solutions to community disruptions.

In Chapter 4, "Our Environments," we look at where we live. The questions framing this chapter are: How do we influence and how are we influenced by the environments within which we dwell? Ecological topics as well as contrasts between urban and agrarian environments are treated here. From a general concern for environments, we move in Chapter 5 to the immediate environment of family life and our personal growth within it. The changing nature of the family along with the tensions this change generates is examined from a variety of perspectives.

Although Chapter 5 includes readings such as Garrison Keillor's "Chicken," which dramatizes the way family life can shape one's informal education, Chapter 6, "Teaching and Learning," foregrounds issues related to more formal educational concerns. Literacy, the diversity of our student populations and methods of teaching these students, and ideas about education beyond the classroom are some of the topics considered here. We hope that the readings included will invite a critical assessment of all of our personal educational experiences by both students and teachers.

Chapter 7 addresses a subject vital to any discussion of cultural pluralism, for diversity, unfortunately, often breeds prejudice. The first selection by Peter Rose, entitled "Prejudice," provides a theoretical backdrop for the subject. Later selections fill out the concept of prejudice through personal accounts, reinforcing the need all of us should feel to begin contemplating the roots of prejudice and its tenacious nature.

Related to the theme of prejudice and oppression is Chapter 8's theme dealing with media representations. In "Images of Ourselves: Media and the Arts" the power of the media to influence the way we think and act allows the potential for the media to perpetuate oppression, often through its blind depictions of the people who live and work in this society. Moreover, the media also exerts a tremendous power in determining the content of our culture. Consequently, the readings in this chapter are intended to investigate the relationship between media and what we imagine our "culture" to be.

Chapter 9, "Harvesting Our Differences," concludes this anthology. The readings in this final chapter have been selected and arranged in order to address a core question guiding our conception of this entire anthology: Given that we live in a multicultural society, how do we harvest our differences and learn to live amicably amid our conflicts? One important way is for each of us to begin talking, listening, and responding to one another. It is our sincere hope that *Cultural Tapestry* will help promote constructive communication.

A project such as this could never have been undertaken without the help of others. We would like to thank Robert A. Schwegler for his valuable assistance as a special consultant for HarperCollins. We owe a special debt of gratitude to our editor, Patricia Rossi, and her assistant, David Munger, for their guidance through the complexities of publication and for their constant support and attention to detail. We would also like to acknowledge the many professionals who contributed to research and production; we are especially grateful to Angela Gladfelter and the copy editors at York Production Services and to Beth Wollar and Ann Stypuloski. For their care in preparing an instructor's manual, we thank Catherine Adamowicz, Stephen Mathis, and Philip Auger.

We would like to express our gratitude to the colleagues across the country whose expert commentary helped us create this book: Patrick Bizzaro, East Carolina University; Carol Brown, Michigan Technological University; Stanley J. Kozikowski, Bryant College; Barbara Ladd, University of North Carolina—Chapel Hill; Stephen Mathis, University of Rhode Island; J. Christopher McCarthy, Los Angeles Harbor College; Lisa J. McClure, Southern Illinois University; Sarah Morgan, Park College; and John J. Ruszkiewicz, University of Texas.

There are many friends, colleagues, and family members who made very tangible contributions to this work: Anil from Krishna Copy Center, Betty Bamberg, Erwin and Cathy Bernbach, Marc and Doris Bernbach, Jack Blum, John Gaines, John Holland, Mary Ann Bruns, Chris Evans, David Fine, George and Virginia Gleason, Laura Gutierrez, Shirley Brice Heath, Ann Humes, Katie Kelly, Seena and Andrew Monagan, Gary Nagy, Paul O'Connell, David Peck, Sandra Pucci, Sally Skapinsky, Helen Sprinkle, Sharon Ulanoff, William Wallis, Andrea White, Robin Wiley, and W. Ross Winterowd. We gratefully acknowledge the support and interest of everyone who helped to bring this work to completion.

Finally, we would like to express our gratitude to our families for their generosity and encouragement and to all of our students—past, present, and future.

Faun Bernbach Evans
Barbara Gleason
Mark Wiley

Introduction: Forming a Community of Readers and Writers

One generation of teachers has somehow got to bring through one generation of students who will have thoughts we have not had before.

James Moffett

From "Censorship and Spiritual Education," in Andrea A. Lunsford, Helene Moglen, and James Slevin, eds. *The Right to Literacy*, (New York: MLA, 1990), 118.

To borrow a line from an old rock song of the sixties, "thinking is the best way to travel." However, not knowing what the original writer specifically meant by *thinking*, we are, nevertheless, appropriating the idea as a motto to introduce you to our book. The kind of work required of you in college involves a great deal of thinking, thinking that you may not be used to doing because it is focused thinking, deep thinking, consistent thinking. It is thinking that happens as you read and write, thinking, that if you are persistent and disciplined enough, will take you beyond where you presently are—intellectually and emotionally—and put you in a place where, we hope, you will be a little bit smarter, a little bit wiser, and more experienced in how you perceive your world.

This book that you presently hold is designed to help you along in this journey. We have chosen and arranged the diverse selections in a way we believe will move and sometimes provoke you to expand your horizons. We have, of course, loaded the dice. Our text comprises specific themes and subjects that we feel are directly relevant to our times and to the society we live in. Moreover, in addition to the content, the form and style of the selections will help you develop the ways of thinking, reading, and writing crucial to achieving the academic literacy that is essential to your education.

We see, then, an important relationship involving thinking, reading, and writing. A writing course is also a reading course, but, obviously, nothing will happen in such a course unless you are thoroughly immersed in your reading and writing. You cannot write well unless you also read well, and reading well means reading critically and becoming involved in the text to the same degree that the writer is involved. This does not mean that you must intuit what is in the writer's mind, but it does mean that you must work to develop an engaged and coherent response to another writer. Such an intellectual engagement with another writer forces you to immerse yourself in the world of textuality through continuous acts of reading and writing. In short, you must develop an ability to respond—a "responsibility," if you will, which requires your active participation and diligence.

When we sit down and begin reading, we are entering a world alien from the familiar world of our everyday activities. This can be simultaneously exciting and frightening, for like any adventure we embark upon, we do not know what awaits us. We may be amused, informed, or even bullied by what we encounter. We may also be bored or confused, entertained or challenged, and even disturbed or shocked. Yet one thing is certain: No matter what we read, if we sincerely give ourselves over to the writing, let ourselves become engaged by the unfolding of a narrative, intrigued by the intricacies of a line of reasoning in an argument, informed by the marshaling of facts supporting a claim, or surprised by the insightful reflections of the personal essay, then we will each respond in some fashion. And this is precisely the place to begin your work as a critical reader as you begin to formulate your response to what you have read.

Even though you may be thinking only about your response, you are actually already engaging in a form of writing. You are focusing your thinking, and you are beginning to respond in a more structured and elaborated fashion than you would be doing in ordinary, informal conversations. Indeed, allow us to add another metaphor to the previous one depicting reading as embarking on a journey. You might see your responses as entering a special kind of "conversation" with another writer, a "conversation" with its own special rules and conventions.

You know, of course, from your experience that when we are conversing with another, both parties are aware that they are speaking about the same subject. When we begin reading, however, we possess few clues as to the writer's subject and perspective. We do, though, predict what might unfold, and we read to verify or modify those predictions as we deem necessary. This kind of reading requires our attention and active participation. For instance, here is the title and the first three paragraphs from Adrienne Rich's autobiobraphical essay found in Chapter 9:

"Split at the Root: An Essay on Jewish Identity"

> For about fifteen minutes I have been sitting chin in hand in front of the typewriter, staring out at the snow. Trying to be honest with myself, trying to figure out why writing this seems to be so dangerous an act, filled with fear and shame, and why it seems so necessary. It comes to me that in order to write this I have to be willing to do two things: I have to claim my father, for I have my Jewishness from him and not from my gentile mother; and I have to break his silence, his taboos; in order to claim him I have in a sense to expose him.
>
> And there is, of course, the third thing: I have to face the sources and the flickering presence of my own ambivalence as a Jew; the daily, mundane anti-Semitisms of my entire life.
>
> These are stories I have never tried to tell before. Why now? Why, I asked myself sometime last year, does this question of Jewish identity float so impalpably, so ungraspably around me, a cloud I can't quite see the outlines of, which feels to me to be without definition?

Your response here might question the meaning and implications of the title. What does Rich mean by being "split at the root"? And how has this split identity possibly affected her life? These twin questions could guide your reading of Rich's entire essay, reading her in order to find satisfactory answers to your questions. As you read through the initial paragraphs, the vagueness of the title begins to accrue a specific content and direction. We discover three things Rich feels she must do: Two of them have something to do with her relationship to her father; the other with her ambivalence toward her Jewishness. As a reader you might want to mark these passages and return to them later to see if Rich has fulfilled her promises to us about what she claims she must do.

You might also read this passage as a strategy Rich employs to frame her subject. You might ask yourself why Rich starts off by telling us how difficult it is to write what she feels she must. Why, for example, is composing this essay going to be "so dangerous an act"? Or you might underline the metaphor she uses to describe the question of her Jewish identity. What does it mean to feel one's identity as a "cloud around" oneself, a cloud "without definition"? Would Rich know who she was if she defined this cloud? And would defining this "cloud" for oneself really be sufficient for finding one's identity? Or is that part of Rich's dilemma, that even trying to define this impalpable, ungraspable cloud will not necessarily remove it from around her?

As a reader you will have to pay attention to find out what Rich does mean. If you are interested in answering these questions, after your first reading you will probably need to go back to certain passages that strike you as clues to the answers you seek. In reading critically, you will possibly have marked these passages as you went along, thinking that you might want to reconsider them later as you learn more about Rich, the challenge she sets herself, and her way of meeting it.

You may be satisfied, or you may be disappointed by what you find out. Or you may still be confused and need to reread and rethink what Rich is saying.

Or you may find that you understand why Rich feels that composing an essay about finding one's identity is such a dangerous act, but you then might want to question the implications. Is this danger true for all Jewish people seeking their identity? Does it necessarily have to be this way? What are the complicating factors in Rich's life that might make her story unique? Conversely, what is it about Rich's situation that is applicable to others', regardless of ethnicity or gender?

These latter questions open up new territory for a reader. You can read across texts, finding others that treat this theme of identity. How do they compare? How do they differ? In developing your response, you are also filling it out and informing it with others' views. You are broadening your frame of reference and trying to fit the conversation you are having with Rich into a wider one incorporating more voices. But beware! As more people enter your conversation, you must realize the tendency for all the talk to drift to other topics. You may forget what you started off talking about and wind up discussing subjects far removed from your original purposes and not having any idea how you got there. If you try to write a response like this that drifts from topic to topic, your readers will not be able to follow your line of reasoning or follow the associations and connections you make between and among various ideas and experiences.

So you need some kind of compass to help you set a course through your reading, and then use your writing as a way of charting that course as you proceed. Sometimes a well-formed question serves best as a reliable guide, a question broad enough to allow for a variety of responses but focused enough to set a direction and to allow you to enter other texts and read them according to your purposes. For example, after reading Rich's essay you may want to write an essay exploring the identity problems that daughters experience because of their fathers, problems accentuated when you consider the role of ethnicity in such relationships. We can break this problem down into two questions: (1) What are some of the effects—both good and bad—that fathers have in shaping how their daughters perceive themselves? (2) How does one's ethnicity complicate these father-daughter relationships?

Next, you have to find other texts dealing with this topic. An obvious place to begin would be the chapter on "Family Life," and certainly, just going by titles alone, Maxine Hong Kingston's "The American Father" would be the place to begin. Kingston's story, however, is fiction, so you have to be careful about the conclusions you draw and the claims you make based on fictional accounts. Another possible source to help you answer your guiding questions might be Kit Yuen Quan's "The Girl Who Wouldn't Sing" from Chapter 1. You must bear in mind, though, that your initial question(s) may shift. Consequently you may be reading for different purposes as your exploration progresses. Maybe you want to broaden your topic to consider the need for anyone to find his or her identity. In this case you may want to read Alice Walker's essay in Chapter 1 or Amy Tan's two fictional pieces in other chapters. The key here is to be aware of when you shift focus and when you are asking different questions from your originals. Otherwise you'll get confused and so will your readers.

Obviously there are no guarantees that your search will always be successful. Who you invite into your circle of conversation depends as much on your own interests, curiosity, and imagination as it does on anybody else telling you what you "ought to read" and respond to. So to help you in this sometimes bewildering process, you might keep a reading journal. This is a sound practice because you can keep a running record both of what you have read as well as of your reactions to what these other writers have said. A reading journal can function for readers and writers not so much as a guide, but as a place where you can record and explore what you discover in your reading. You may simply record main ideas, for instance, so you have an understanding of a writer's argument. For example, as you read Shelby Steele's essay, you might record this sentence as Steele's main argument concerning race relations in America: "Power defines their relations, and power requires innocence, which, in turn, requires racism and racial division."

This may or may not be Steele's thesis; you would naturally have to read his entire essay to make this judgment. But regardless of what you decide, you can explore Steele's claim by pursuing what he means by *innocence* and the relationships between power and innocence and between innocence and racism he sets up in his claim. You can also record in your journal the way Steele explains how this "innocence" is portrayed by both whites and blacks. You can record his examples and then explore how relevant and valid you think they are. Is Steele's treatment of *The Cosby Show* accurate, for example? And is his analysis of Cosby's actions toward white society valid?

There are any number of possible responses a reader and writer could make, depending on one's purposes. In one of our writing classes where we used Steele's essay, a student wrote that "Steele's description of what happens in class discussions when racial issues are brought up is exactly what happened in our class when we started talking about his essay." This student's response could serve as the occasion for her to pursue this topic more elaboratively and formally. She might even pursue this topic from a different angle by asking, "What is appropriate subject matter for a writing class?" And follow this question with others: "Are there some subjects that are taboo for class discussions? If so, is race one of them? If not, how should such a discussion proceed?"

This same writer may find that her initial questions branch out to encompass a wider frame, with her original essay topic on classroom discussions of race metamorphosing into an essay exploring a question concerning the content of a college education. This is one of the questions that frames our Chapter 5; a reader will find more material there as well as in Diane Ravitch's essay in Chapter 9.

Certainly a writer may also want to hear other voices not included in this book. Thus further outside research will be in order. Moreover, as readers bring their past experiences to inform their present readings of texts, so writers draw upon what they know in shaping their responses. When you read a poem like Langston Hughes's "Harlem" or an article like Sue Horton's on mothers and their sons who are gang members, your experience or lack of experience with life in Harlem or with gangs influences your understanding of these texts.

Yet, even if we have no experience of gang life, it does not mean we cannot comprehend the plight of some of these families threatened by gang culture. In fact, one of the best reasons to read is because it offers us experiences we might not encounter otherwise. Indeed, as our reading progresses, we are also composing our own intellectual autobiographies of sorts, because what we read exerts its own powerful influence on what we know and think about the world. Another kind of "reading" you can do this semester is to monitor your personal encounters with texts—whether rewriting them or reading them. Perhaps in writing your literacy autobiography you might uncover particular attitudes you hold toward the written word as well as understand why you write and read the way you presently do.

In any event, we think that the more you pay attention to what you read and to how you read and to how you are responding to what you read, you will discover two things: You will discover that you simply have more to say in your essays; and second, that you will have more options in the way you say what you believe needs saying. To be perfectly honest, however, these abilities require patience and time to develop. But they can be helped along by sharing your responses with others in your class. Each of us is limited in what we know and what we perceive. This is one of the essential facts about being human, so it is not to be lamented. Instead, one might see this limitation as an opportunity to create and to celebrate community in the classroom. For it is precisely in the classroom where readers and writers can enrich and deepen their personal perspectives through sharing them publicly with others. The writing course you are taking now can become the occasion in which private conversations between readers and texts and between writers and their developing texts receive immediate responses from others.

In this environment you can help and be helped to develop expertise as readers and writers. Additionally, as a participant in this kind of nurturing community, you will learn more and feel more satisfied in the process. By the end of this school term, we hope that you feel better informed and generally more critical as a reader of texts and of the worlds around you. We think you will be, but we also hope that you continue in your personal education and that you go on to "have thoughts we have not had before."

Cultural Tapestry

Chapter
1

Living in a Multicultural Society

Visitors to the United States can find almost every culture and ethnicity represented here, though certainly not in every city or state. Some cities, such as New York and Los Angeles, are widely recognized for their diversity, whereas other cities (and even some states) are relatively homogeneous. Moreover, cultural differences may not stop with ethnicity: people also identify with the "cultures" of work, the "culture" of a particular region, or the "culture" of women. In this extended sense of the term, any group of people with shared understandings encoded in language/behavior may be considered a type of "culture."

In this chapter, we invite you to consider what it means to live in a multicultural society, both for yourself and for others. While some of the authors in this section raise issues and direct our attention to controversies, others describe their personal experiences of coping in a complex and often challenging social environment. If you live in a large urban area, you probably already know about the blending of cultural styles and attitudes that Ishmael Reed describes in "The World Is Here." But even if you live in the suburbs or in a less populous area, you undoubtedly have some awareness of your own ethnicity and of some particular culture of which you feel a part. This sense of belonging may be to a general notion of "American culture" but may also include Texas culture or Jewish culture or the culture of rock 'n' roll.

We suggest that you begin by reflecting on the meanings of *ethnicity* and *culture*, a topic addressed by Michael Novak in "The New Ethnicity." This initial consideration of culture and of cultures will pave the way for your reading about the specific concerns of Asian Americans as they are described by Ronald Takaki in "From a Different Shore." In a more personal vein, Maria Mullinaux explores the integration of her various heritages by describing her many grandmothers, including a grandmother from England and a Cherokee grandmother "whose children crossed her from the family Bible."

In their respective essays, Alice Walker and Kit Yuen Quan continue the theme of cultural heritage, adding to this the dimensions of biculturalism and bilingualism. Whereas for Walker it is necessary to find a way back to her African-American heritage, for Quan the issue is one of finding her own voice as the daughter of Chinese immigrants. Walker focuses on living in two cultures while Quan describes her experiences with English as a second language.

In two essays that follow those, Deborah Tannen and Barbara Myerhoff invite us to consider an expanded notion of "culture" by focusing on the cultures of men and women, on the one hand, and the "culture" of our older generations on the other. In "Talk in the Intimate Relationship: His and Hers," Tannen suggests that because they are socialized differently, men and women actually exist in different social worlds, a condition that is reflected in communication styles. Although Myerhoff's essay does not explicitly define a "culture" of older people, her description of a community of elderly Jewish residents suggests a "culture" of people concerned with common issues and customs. We encourage you to view Myerhoff's film, *Number Our Days,* in conjunction with reading this excerpt from her book by the same name.

After having considered some of the issues and reflected on some actual experiences of multicultural lifestyles, we ask that you turn to the theme that perhaps best defines us as a nation: immigration. In "The American Dream and the Politics of Inclusion," Mario Cuomo argues that we must continue to open our doors to immigrants, that modern day immigrants are no different from our forebears, and that each new wave of immigrants revitalizes and strengthens our nation. After you read this essay, we would like for you to evaluate your own position on an open door policy on immigration. How do you feel about such a policy? Do you have any concerns that our population may actually be too diversified already? And, finally, how do you feel about living in a nation of many peoples? Do you feel enriched by the experience of meeting people from vastly different backgrounds? We hope that you *do* feel so enriched and that the reading selections in this book will enable you to reflect further on your past experiences as well as on many important issues related to this theme.

Reading 1

The World Is Here

Ishmael Reed

Ishmael Reed, the editorial director of Yardbird Press, is a contributing writer to the *New York Times,* the *Los Angeles Times, Black Words,* and *Ramparts.* Among his many books are *Flight to Canada, Mumbo Jumbo,* and *Writin' Is Fightin',* from which the following essay is excerpted. In this essay, Reed presents a portrait of our multicultural society and suggests that the United States is a microcosm of the entire world, a blending of cultural styles and attitudes in ways that are uniquely American. While reading this essay, we invite you to consider the degree to which your own communities reflect Reed's portrait of our society as a cultural tapestry.

At the annual Lower East Side Jewish Festival yesterday, a Chinese woman ate a pizza slice in front of Ty Thuan Duc's Vietnamese grocery store. Beside her a Spanish-speaking family patronized a cart with two signs: "Italian Ices" and "Kosher by Rabbi Alper." And after the pastrami ran out, everybody ate knishes.

(*New York Times,* 23 June 1983)

On the day before Memorial Day, 1983, a poet called me to describe a city he had just visited. He said that one section included mosques, built by the Islamic people who dwelled there. Attending his reading, he said, were large numbers of Hispanic people, forty thousand of whom lived in the same city. He was not talking about a fabled city located in some mysterious region of the world. The city he'd visited was Detroit.

A few months before, as I was leaving Houston, Texas, I heard it announced on the radio that Texas's largest minority was Mexican American, and though a foundation recently issued a report critical of bilingual education, the taped voice used to guide the passengers on the air trams connecting terminals in Dallas Airport is in both Spanish and English. If the trend continues, a day will come when it will be difficult to travel through some sections of the country without hearing commands in both English and Spanish; after all, for some western states, Spanish was the first written language and the Spanish style lives on in the western way of life.

Shortly after my Texas trip, I sat in an auditorium located on the campus of the University of Wisconsin at Milwaukee as a Yale professor—whose original work on the influence of African cultures upon those of the Americas had led to his ostracism from some monocultural intellectual circles—walked up and down the aisle, like an old-time southern evangelist, dancing and drumming the top of the lectern, illustrating his points before some serious Afro-American intellectuals and artists who cheered and applauded his performance and his mastery of information. The professor was "white." After his lecture, he joined a group of Milwaukeeans in a conversation. All of the participants spoke Yoruban, though only the professor had ever traveled to Africa.

One of the artists told me that his paintings, which included African and Afro-American mythological symbols and imagery, were hanging in the local McDonald's restaurant. The next day I went to McDonald's and snapped pictures of smiling youngsters eating hamburgers below paintings that could grace the walls of any of the country's leading museums. The manager of the local McDonald's said, "I don't know what you boys are doing, but I like it," as he commissioned the local painters to exhibit in his restaurant.

Such blurring of cultural styles occurs in everyday life in the United States to a greater extent than anyone can imagine and is probably more prevalent than the sensational conflict between people of different backgrounds that is played up and often encouraged by the media. The result is what the Yale professor, Robert Thompson, referred to as a cultural bouillabaisse, yet members of the nation's present educational and cultural Elect still cling to the notion that the United States belongs to some vaguely defined entity they refer to as "Western civilization," by which they mean, presumably, a civilization created by the people of Europe, as if Europe can be viewed in monolithic terms. Is Beethoven's Ninth Symphony, which includes Turkish marches, a part of Western civilization, or the late nineteenth- and twentieth-century French paintings, whose creators were influenced by Japanese art? And what of the cubists, through whom the influence of African art changed modern painting, or the surrealists, who were so impressed with the art of the Pacific Northwest Indians that, in their map of North America, Alaska dwarfs the lower forty-eight in size?

Are the Russians, who are often criticized for their adoption of "Western" ways by Tsarist dissidents in exile, members of Western civilization? And what of the millions of Europeans who have black African and Asian ancestry, black Africans having occupied several countries for hundreds of years? Are these "Europeans" members of Western civilization, or the Hungarians, who originated across the Urals in a place called Greater Hungary, or the Irish, who came from the Iberian Peninsula?

Even the notion that North America is part of Western civilization because our "system of government" is derived from Europe is being challenged by Native American historians who say that the founding fathers, Benjamin Franklin especially, were actually influenced by the system of government that had been adopted by the Iroquois hundreds of years prior to the arrival of large numbers of Europeans.

Western civilization, then, becomes another confusing category like Third

World, or Judeo-Christian culture, as man attempts to impose his small-screen view of political and cultural reality upon a complex world. Our most publicized novelist recently said that Western civilization was the greatest achievement of mankind, an attitude that flourishes on the street level as scribbles in public restrooms: "White Power," "Niggers and Spics Suck," or "Hitler was a prophet," the latter being the most telling, for wasn't Adolph Hitler the archetypal mono-culturalist who, in his pigheaded arrogance, believed that one way and one blood was so pure that it had to be protected from alien strains at all costs? Where did such an attitude, which has caused so much misery and depression in our national life, which has tainted even our noblest achievements, begin? An attitude that caused the incarceration of Japanese-American citizens during World War II, the persecution of Chicanos and Chinese Americans, the near-extermination of the Indians, and the murder and lynchings of thousands of Afro-Americans.

Virtuous, hardworking, pious, even though they occasionally would wander off after some fancy clothes, or rendezvous in the woods with the town prostitute, the Puritans are idealized in our schoolbooks as "a hardy band" of no-nonsense patriarchs whose discipline razed the forest and brought order to the New World (a term that annoys Native American historians). Industrious, responsible, it was their "Yankee ingenuity" and practicality that created the work ethic. They were simple folk who produced a number of good poets, and they set the tone for the American writing style, of lean and spare lines, long before Hemingway. They worshiped in churches whose colors blended in with the New England snow, churches with simple structures and ornate lecterns.

The Puritans were a daring lot, but they had a mean streak. They hated the theater and banned Christmas. They punished people in a cruel and inhuman manner. They killed children who disobeyed their parents. When they came in contact with those whom they considered heathens or aliens, they behaved in such a bizarre and irrational manner that this chapter in the American history comes down to us as a late-movie horror film. They exterminated the Indians, who taught them how to survive in a world unknown to them, and their encounter with the calypso culture of Barbados resulted in what the tourist guide in Salem's Witches' House refers to as the Witchcraft Hysteria.

The Puritan legacy of hard work and meticulous accounting led to the establishment of a great industrial society; it is no wonder that the American industrial revolution began in Lowell, Massachusetts, but there was the other side, the strange and paranoid attitudes toward those different from the Elect.

The cultural attitudes of that early Elect continue to be voiced in everyday life in the United States: the president of a distinguished university, writing a letter to the *Times*, belittling the study of African civilizations; the television network that promoted its show on the Vatican art with the boast that this art represented "the finest achievements of the human spirit." A modern up-tempo state of complex rhythms that depends upon contacts with an international community can no longer behave as if it dwelled in a "Zion Wilderness" surrounded by beasts and pagans.

When I heard a schoolteacher warn the other night about the invasion of the American educational system by foreign curriculums, I wanted to yell at the television set, "Lady, they're already here." It has already begun because the world is here. The world has been arriving at these shores for at least ten thousand years from Europe, Africa, and Asia. In the late nineteenth and early twentieth centuries, large numbers of Europeans arrived, adding their cultures to those of the European, African, and Asian settlers who were already here, and recently millions have been entering the country from South America and the Caribbean, making Yale Professor Bob Thompson's bouillabaisse richer and thicker.

One of our most visionary politicians said that he envisioned a time when the United States could become the brain of the world, by which he meant the repository of all of the latest advanced information systems. I thought of that remark when an enterprising poet friend of mine called to say that he had just sold a poem to a computer magazine and that the editors were delighted to get it because they didn't carry fiction or poetry. Is that the kind of world we desire? A humdrum homogenous world of all brains but no heart, no fiction, no poetry; a world of robots with human attendants bereft of imagination, of culture? Or does North America deserve a more exciting destiny? To become a place where the cultures of the world crisscross. This is possible because the United States is unique in the world: The world is here.

QUESTIONS FOR "THE WORLD IS HERE" BY ISHMAEL REED

Talking About the Text

1. Reed claims that a "blurring of cultural styles" is actually more common than "the sensational conflict between people of different backgrounds that is played up and often encouraged by the media." What are some recent examples of racial or cultural conflict that have been played up by the media? Why would the media focus on events such as these?

2. At the beginning of this essay, there is a quote from the *New York Times*. What purpose(s) does this quote serve? Why does Reed use this descriptive passage when he could state his point directly?

Exploring Issues

1. Why would some people advocate "monoculturalism"? Examples of monoculturalists given here are Adolph Hitler and the American Puritans. Consider these two cases: what are the consequences of living in a monocultural society? What would be the advantages and disadvantages of living in a society such as this? Can you think of other examples of monocultural societies?

2. Some Americans fear foreigners and foreign influences on American institutions and "the American way of life." The word for this type of fear is *xenophobia*. Can you think of some specific reasons why Americans might fear foreign influences in the United States? Do you feel these fears are justified? Why or why not?

Writing Assignments

1. Reed argues that we are by nature a multicultural society, a microcosmic representation of many cultures and ethnicities from all over the world. Write an essay in which you discuss the potential advantages and/or disadvantages of living in such a society. What do we gain from living side by side with people of various religions, races, and cultures? What are the potential problems with this situation? Use your own community as the context for your discussion. Describe people, places, and events in your community to illustrate your general ideas.

2. In his essay, Reed argues that here in the United States there is a "blurring of cultural styles in everyday life." Consider your own environment—local language, music, TV, film, magazines, newspapers, and advertising. Do you find a number of cultural styles represented? Go to a local restaurant, store, library, or other public place, and observe the environment there. Notice the people, the signs, the furniture, the architecture, and the artwork in these environments. Look for signs of different cultures and cultural styles. Take notes on your observations. Use these notes to write an essay in which you focus on the cultural styles evident in the place you observed.

Reading 2

The New Ethnicity

Michael Novak

Michael Novak has been a resident scholar at the American Enterprise Institute since 1978. He is the author of several books and essays, including *The Rise of the Unmeltable Ethnics, The American Vision, The Spirit of Democratic Capitalism,* and *Moral Clarity in the Nuclear Age.* In the following essay, Novak begins with a discussion of the concepts of "culture" and "ethnicity" and then continues with his argument that, despite the homogenizing forces of modernism, people all over the world are reestablishing their sense of individual ethnicity and cultural heritage. Novak believes this heightened sense of cultural awareness to be important—both for the individual's sense of self, and for the politics of world affairs.

Ethnicity is a baffling reality—morally ambivalent, paradoxical in experience, elusive in concept. World travelers observe that cultures differ from one another in mores and manners. Diplomats recognize that even the simplest gestures, words, or behaviors may signal multiple meanings. Nearly everyone recognizes that culture affects the subjectivity of individuals as well as their outward behavior. Culture shapes sensibility and perception, expectation and imagination, aspiration and moral striving, intellect and worldview. Yet it cannot be said that most highly educated persons are well prepared to account for the multicultural experiences available to them in the present age. Our theories about cultural differences and ethnic nuances are not as deep, broad, or subtle as our experience. Some philosophical distinctions may, therefore, be useful in charting this fascinating but treacherous terrain.

"Culture" is not an easy concept, since so many institutions, rituals, and practices contribute to its shaping. Its ramifications are sweeping, subtle, and often unarticulated. Its effects upon us often lie below the threshold of words or even of consciousness. The culture that has shaped us shapes our way of experiencing and perceiving, of imagining and speaking, so deeply that it is very difficult to think our way outside it. It teaches us what to regard as relevant and what to count as evidence; it provides our *canons* of relevance and evidence. We are not "products" of a culture in the way that objects are produced by a machine. Indeed, we must make conscious and voluntary efforts if we intend to appropriate our culture wholly, to go to its depths and to master its multiple possibilities. Cultures are freely elaborated by human beings; they lie, as the German philosophers were wont to say, in the realm of freedom, and the variety of human cultures on this planet is testimony to the capacities of human liberty over and above the necessities of nature. An individual passing over from his or her native culture into a culture quite different may experience "culture shock"; may, that is, come into a set of presuppositions, expectations, criteria for perception and evaluation and behavior so different as to undermine much that was previously taken for granted.

The concept of "ethnicity" has traditionally been seen as somewhat narrower than, although related to, the concept of culture. From earliest times, distinctive social groups found themselves living under the shaping influence of a common culture. In a sense, what made such social groups distinctive were the prior shaping influences of diverse cultures. Yet one could speak of a new overarching culture—Mesopotamian, Greek, Roman—within which the concept of ethnicity pointed to less all-embracing cultural influences. It is useful to note that within a concept like "Western culture," for example, quite dramatic, pervasive, and persistent sources of cultural distinctiveness have remained vital. In philosophy, to choose but one example, there are quite different creative impulses, presuppositions, methods, standards, and criteria manifested in different ethnic traditions: German, French, British, Italian, Spanish, American. In literature, theology, and in the arts it is possible simultaneously to discern characteristics that justify the notion both of a wider shared culture— Western culture—and of particular, original, and vital sources of differentiation. Humanists have not so often used the word "ethnic" to describe these differences (until recently, the word has had a ring more proper to the social sciences). From early Latin times, the tendency has rather been to speak of *nationes* (as at the University of Paris in the 12th century), not in the modern political sense but rather in a pervasive cultural sense, signifying the existence of divergent cultural entities.

It is important, then, to recognize that any humanist wishing to work out a full theory of ethnicity may find many already cherished texts in which, under other names, a tradition of giving cultural differences their due weight has been observed. Among such texts would be Alexis de Tocqueville's *Democracy in America* (1835), Ralph Waldo Emerson's *English Traits* (1856), George Santayana's *The German Mind* (originally titled *Egotism in German Philosophy*, 1939), and many others. More recent writings include Luigi Barzini's *The Italians* (1964), Jacques Maritain's *Reflections on America* (1958), and Hedrick Smith's *The Russians* (1976).

A major watershed in our thinking about ethnicity seems to have been reached in the period after World War II. As a result of the growth of international communication and of a worldwide infrastructure of technology and commerce, human beings almost everywhere have become more aware of cultures not their own. It was long imagined that the creation of "one world" would bring with it many homogenizing tendencies, based on the imperatives of universal "reason" and science and on the standardization of technological artifacts (from Coca-Cola to Shell, from transistors to computers). It was also imagined that the managers and intellectuals who operated the new international systems would create a cadre of leaders, or even perhaps a new managerial class spread around the globe, who would be almost equally at home in the urban technical environments of London, Tokyo, New York, Berlin, Rio de Janeiro, and Calcutta. The same methods, the same problems, and (roughly) the same living conditions, it was imagined, would accompany them wherever they went. Indeed, such eventualities have come to pass, largely as expected, as a result of many homogenizing influences. Political ideals—"liberation," "equality," "national sovereignty"— have crossed virtually all the world's frontiers. So have rock music and movies, jeans and automobiles.

Simultaneously, however, the late 20th century has also been marked by a resurgence of ethnic consciousness. In the Soviet Union since about 1950 the Jewish community has become increasingly conscious of its special identity and increasingly public in its self-consciousness—an attitude seen also among the ethnic Germans, Ukrainians, and other peoples of the U.S.S.R. In Great Britain, the Scots and the Welsh have demanded greater autonomy, as have the French Canadians in Canada. In Africa, Latin America, Asia, and many other places throughout the world the self-consciousness of cultural bodies has been similarly heightened. There appear to be four components of this new self-consciousness, and in examining them, it is important to pause long enough to see clearly what is new in this "new ethnicity."

The new cultural self-consciousness is, first of all, post-tribal, arising in an era in which almost every culture has been obligated to become aware of many others. In contrast to the isolation of ancient times, each culture has met at least some of the others in actual experience, and many others via the media.

Secondly, the new ethnicity arises in an era of advanced technology. This technology paradoxically liberates certain energies for more intense self-consciousness, even as it binds many cultures together in standardized technical infrastructures. The communications media, for example, are neutral with respect to cultural differences. In the techniques required to operate them and in some of their internal imperatives (scientific knowledge, technical control, precision, order) they are clearly homogenizing in effect. On the other hand, the *content* of what the media express is necessarily received by audiences affected by cultural memory, cultural differences, and distinctive cultural aspirations. Communicators who had heretofore taken their own cultural identity for granted—because it was so much a part of their daily reality that they hardly needed to be aware of it—have become more sharply aware of their own distinctive tastes, needs, and hopes in using these media. They commonly find that they must become more analytical, articulate, and self-conscious about their own distinctive voice and viewpoint.

Thirdly, the new ethnicity arises in an era of intense centripetal and homogenizing forces. Great technical power has become centered in the apparatus of the state, in the central agencies of communication, and in the central distributors of technology. These new forces call into being countervailing forces, but are themselves so powerful that a wider range of diversity can be tolerated.

These new forces also generate rebellion against "mindless" and "soulless" modernism. This rebellion represents a fourth condition for the emergence of the new ethnicity—namely, a certain discrediting of the supposed moral superiority of the modern. For some generations now, high political and moral status has accrued to all things modern, enlightened, and up to date. The forces of habit, custom, and tradition have been on the defensive. Now that the fully modern type of man or woman is everywhere more visible among us, however, the secular, pragmatic style of the proponents of modernization has lost its halo and has begun to reveal serious moral flaws. In casting about for a posture that promises a higher degree of wisdom, nobility, and relevance to ordinary people, many leaders have begun to look again at the moral sources of their traditional cultures. For most, the choice is not simply dichotomous—either traditional or modern. Rather, the status of inherited wisdom has risen, while that of the modern has slipped. In order to be evaluated, this inherited wisdom, now at last to be taken more seriously, has first to be more clearly known. Thus, the examination of "roots" has attracted both scholarly and popular attention. It is probable that a general law is here being observed: in times of moral perplexity and crisis, a reappropriation of the past, a search for renewal, gains impetus. In China there have been profound cultural cross-currents, in the United States the Bicentennial renewal, and in other cultures the drive toward cultural or national awakening; all these exhibit a strong moral dimension, fed by dissatisfaction with a merely modern morality.

In a word, peoples in every part of the world, to the surprise of those who anticipated the power only of homogenizing tendencies, are becoming both more aware of others and also more aware of their own distinctive cultural identity. A heightened cultural awareness, coupled with demands for its appropriate political expression, has made of the new ethnicity a major factor in world affairs—perhaps even one of the major sources of political energy in our era.

QUESTIONS FOR "THE NEW ETHNICITY" BY MICHAEL NOVAK

Talking About the Text

1. How does Novak differentiate between "ethnicity" and "culture"?
2. What does Novak mean by "the new ethnicity"?

Exploring Issues

1. Why do you think some people may need/wish to reclaim their ethnic or cultural origins? What are the psychological and/or social consequences of reclaiming ethnic or cultural origins?
2. Novak claims that "in times of moral perplexity and crisis" people seek answers in the past, in "inherited wisdom." After reading Alice Walker's essay in this chapter, consider how Walker may be an example of someone who is seeking inherited wisdom in times of moral perplexity.

Writing Assignments

1. Describe an experience you have had in learning about another culture or ethnic group in the United States. What group did you learn about? How did you learn about this group? Describe your experience in detail and discuss the ways in which this experience influenced your understanding of yourself and of others.
2. Write an essay in which you explain why you may or may not wish to know more about your own ethnicity and how this knowledge may be useful or problematic for you. In other words, what are the potential rewards and the potential problems in developing a strong sense of one's own ethnic identity?

Reading 3

From a Different Shore

Ronald Takaki

Ronald Takaki, the grandson of immigrant plantation laborers from Japan, is professor of Ethnic Studies at the University of California at Berkeley. Takaki has authored several books, including *Iron Cages: Race and Culture in Nineteenth-Century America* and *Strangers from a Different Shore: A History of Asian Americans,* from which this excerpt is taken. Here, Takaki discusses the valuable contributions that Asian Americans have made to the development of the United States and then argues that official U.S. histories often diminish (or ignore) these contributions. Takaki also argues that U.S. history should be "re-visioned" to include Asian Americans and, by extension, all ethnic groups whose histories "burst with the telling."

In Palolo Valley on the island of Oahu, Hawaii, where I lived as a child, my neighbors had names like Hamamoto, Kauhane, Wong, and Camara. Nearby, across the stream where we caught crayfish and roasted them over an open fire, there were Filipino and Puerto Rican families. Behind my house, Mrs. Alice Liu and her friends played mah-jongg late into the night, the clicking of the tiles lulling me to sleep. Next door to us the Miuras flew billowing and colorful carp kites on Japanese boys' day. I heard voices with different accents, different languages, and saw children of different colors. Together we went barefoot to school and played games like baseball and *jan ken po.* We spoke pidgin English. "Hey, da kind tako ono, you know," we would say, combining English, Japanese, and Hawaiian: "This octopus is delicious." As I grew up, I did not know why families representing such an array of nationalities from different shores were living together and sharing their cultures and a common language. My teachers and textbooks did not explain the diversity of our community or the sources of our unity. After graduation from high school, I attended a college in a midwestern town where I found myself invited to "dinners for foreign students" sponsored by local churches and clubs like the Rotary. I politely tried to explain to my kind hosts that I was not a "foreign student." My fellow students and even my professors would ask me how long I had been in America and where I had learned to speak English. "In this country," I would reply. And sometimes I would add: "I was born in America, and my family has been here for three generations."

Indeed, Asian Americans have been here for over 150 years. Resting on benches in Portsmouth Square in San Francisco's Chinatown, old men know their presence in America reaches far into the past. Wearing fedora hats, they wait for the chilly morning fog to lift; asked how long they have been in this country, they say: "Me longtime Californ'." Nearby, elderly Filipinos—*manongs*—point to the vacant lot where the aging International Hotel had once offered these retired farm workers a place to live out the rest of their lives. They remember the night the police came to evict them and the morning the bulldozers obliterated a part of their history. In the California desert town of El Centro, bearded and gray-haired men wearing turbans sit among the fallen leaves on the grounds of the Sikh temple. One of them describes what life was like in California decades ago: "In the early days it was hard. We had a hell of a time. We had to face a lot of narrow mindedness."[1]

Asian Americans are diverse, their roots reaching back to China, Japan, Korea, the Philippines, India, Vietnam, Laos, and Cambodia. Many of them live in Chinatowns, the colorful streets filled with sidewalk vegetable stands and crowds of people carrying shopping bags; their communities are also called Little Tokyo, Koreatown, and Little Saigon. Asian Americans work in hot kitchens and bus tables in restaurants with elegant names like Jade Pagoda and Bombay Spice. In garment factories, Chinese and Korean women hunch over whirling sewing machines, their babies sleeping nearby on blankets. In the Silicon Valley of California, rows and rows of Vietnamese and Laotian women serve as the eyes and hands of production assembly lines for computer chips. Tough Chinese gang members strut on Grant Avenue in San Francisco and Canal Street in New York's Chinatown. In La Crosse, Wisconsin, welfare-dependent Hmong sit and stare at the snowdrifts outside their windows. Holders of Ph.D.'s, Asian-American engineers do complex research in the laboratories of the high-technology industries along Route 128 in Massachusetts. Asian Americans seem to be ubiquitous on university campuses: they represent 11 percent of the students at Harvard, 10 percent at Princeton, 16 percent at Stanford, 21 percent at MIT, and 25 percent at the University of California at Berkeley. From Scarsdale to the Pacific Palisades, "Yappies"—"young Asian professionals"—drive BMWs, wear designer clothes, and congregate at continental restaurants; they read slick magazines like *AsiAm* and *Rice*. "I am Chinese," remarks Chester in David Hwang's play *Family Devotions*. "I live in Bel Air. I drive a Mercedes. I go to a private prep school. I must be Chinese."[2]

Recently Asian Americans have become very visible. While Asians have constituted a majority of Hawaii's people for nearly a century, they have become populous elsewhere in the country. Three hundred thousand Chinese live in New York City—the largest Chinese community outside of China. Describing the recent growth of New York's Chinatown, the *New York Times* observed in 1986: "With new arrivals squeezing in at a rate of nearly 2,000 a month, the district spread north through what was once a Jewish section on the Lower East Side and west across Little Italy, turning Yiddish into Mandarin and fettucine into won tons." Meanwhile, Flushing in Queens has become a "suburban" Chinatown, the home of 60,000 Chinese; resident Eileen Loh observed: "We are changing the face of Flushing." On the other side of the continent, Monterey Park in southern California has come to be called the "Chinese Beverly Hills." About a fourth of San Francisco's population is Asian, and Asians represent over 50 percent of the city's public-school students. In Los Angeles, there are 150,000 Koreans, and the Olympic Boulevard area between Crenshaw and Hoover has been designated Koreatown. Nearby, in an adjacent county, a new Vietnamese community has also suddenly appeared. "Along Garden Grove Boulevard in Orange County," the *New York Times* reported in 1986, "it is easier to lunch on pho, a Vietnamese noodle soup with beef, than on a hamburger." In California, Asian Americans represent nearly 9 percent of the state's population, surpassing blacks in number.[3]

Today Asian Americans belong to the fastest-growing ethnic minority group in the United States. In percentage, they are increasing more rapidly than Hispanics (between 1970 and 1980 the Hispanic population increased by 38 percent, compared to 143 percent for the Asian population). The target of immigration exclusion laws in the nineteenth and early twentieth centuries, Asians have recently been coming again to America. The Immigration Act of 1965 reopened the gates to immigrants from Asia, allowing a quota of 20,000 immigrants for each country and also the entry of family members on a nonquota basis. Currently half of all immigrants entering annually are Asian. The recent growth of the Asian-American population has been dramatic: in 1960, there were only 877,934 Asians in the United States, representing a mere one half of one percent of the country's population. Twenty-five years later, they numbered over five million, or 2.1 percent of the population, an increase of 577 percent (compared to 34 percent for the general population). They included 1,079,000 Chinese, 1,052,000 Filipinos, 766,000 Japanese, 634,000 Vietnamese, 542,000 Koreans, 526,000 Asian Indians, 70,000 Laotians, 10,000 Mien, 60,000 Hmong, 161,000 Cambodians, and 169,000 other Asians. By the year 2000, Asian Americans are projected to represent 4 percent of the total U.S. population.[4]

Yet very little is known about Asian Americans and their history. In fact, stereotypes and myths of Asians as aliens and foreigners are pervasive in American society. During Lieutenant Colonel Oliver North's testimony before the joint House-Senate committee investigating the Iran-Contra scandal in 1987, co-chair Senator Daniel Inouye became the target of racial slurs: some of the telegrams and phone calls received by the committee told the senator he should "go home to Japan where he belonged." But Senator Inouye was born in the United States and had been awarded a Distinguished Service Cross for his valor as an American soldier during World War II. The belief that Americans do not include people with Asian ancestries is usually expressed more innocently, more casually. A white woman from New Jersey, for example, once raved to William Wong of the *Oakland Tribune* about a wonderful new Vietnamese restaurant in her town: "We were there the other night and we were the only Americans there." Wong noted with regret: "She probably meant the only white people."[5]

But her remark reveals a widely shared assumption in American culture— one that reflects and is reinforced by a narrow view of American history. Many existing history books give Asian Americans only passing notice or overlook them altogether. "When one hears Americans tell of the immigrants who built this nation," Congressman Norman Mineta of California recently observed, "one is often led to believe that all our forebearers came from Europe. When one hears stories about the pioneers going West to shape the land, the Asian immigrant is rarely mentioned."[6]

Sometimes Asian pioneers are even excluded from history. In 1987, the editor of *The Californians*, a popular history magazine published in San Francisco, announced the "Pioneer Prize" for the best essay submitted on the "California pioneers." "By 'pioneers,' " the editor explained, "we mean those Americans and Europeans who settled permanently in California between 1823 and 1869 (the year the transcontinental Central Pacific was completed)." But actually, the "pioneers" also included Asians: thousands of them helped to build the very transcontinental railroad referred to in the magazine's announcement, and many settled permanently in California. Many classics in the field of American history have also equated "American" with "white" or "European" in origin. In his prizewinning study, *The Uprooted*, Harvard historian Oscar Handlin presented—to use the book's subtitle—"the Epic Story of the Great Migrations That Made the American People." But Handlin's "epic story" completely left out the "uprooted" from lands across the Pacific Ocean and the "great migrations" from Asia that also helped to make "the American people." Eurocentric history serves no one. It only shrouds the pluralism that is America and that makes our nation so unique, and thus the possibility of appreciating our rich racial and cultural diversity remains a dream deferred. Actually, as Americans, we come originally from many different shores—Europe, the Americas, Africa, and also Asia.[7]

We need to "re-vision" history to include Asians in the history of America, and to do so in a broad and comparative way. How and why, we must ask, were the experiences of the various Asian groups—Chinese, Japanese, Korean, Filipino, Asian Indian, and Southeast Asian—similar to and different from one another? Crossnational comparisons can help us to identify the experiences particular to a group and to highlight the experiences common to all of them. Why did Asian immigrants leave everything they knew and loved to come to a strange world so far away? They were "pushed" by hardships in the homelands and "pulled" here by America's demand for their labor. But what were their own fierce dreams—from the first enterprising Chinese miners of the 1850s in search of "Gold Mountain" to the recent refugees fleeing frantically on helicopters and leaking boats from the ravages of war in Vietnam? Besides their points of origin, we need to examine the experiences of Asian Americans in different geographical regions, especially in Hawaii as compared to the mainland. Time of arrival has also shaped the lives and communities of Asian Americans. About one million people entered between the California gold rush of 1849 and the Immigration Act of 1924, which cut off immigration from Asian countries, and, after a hiatus of some forty years, a second group numbering about three and a half million came between 1965 and 1985. How do we compare the two waves of Asian immigration?

To answer our questions, we must not study Asian Americans primarily in terms of statistics and what was done to them. They are entitled to be viewed as subjects—as men and women with minds, wills, and voices. By "voices" we mean their own words and stories as told in their oral histories, conversations, speeches, soliloquies, and songs, as well as in their own writings—diaries, letters, newspapers, magazines, pamphlets, placards, posters, flyers, court petitions, autobiographies, short stories, novels, and poems. Their voices contain particular expressions and phrases with their own meanings and nuances, the cuttings from the cloth of languages.

For a long time, Asians in this country were not allowed to tell their stories, sometimes even to talk. In Maxine Hong Kingston's novel *China Men*, Bak Goong goes to Hawaii, where he is told by a foreman that laborers are not permitted to talk while working. "If I knew I had to take a vow of silence," he says to himself, "I would have shaved off my hair and become a monk." In the cane fields, he hears the boss shout: "Shut up. Go work. Chinaman, go work. You stay go work. Shut up." He is not even supposed to scream when he feels the sting of the whip on his shoulder. After work, resting in the camp away from the ears of the foreman, Bak Goong tells his fellow workers: "I will talk again. Listen for me." Among themselves they curse the white man on horseback: "Take—that—white—demon. Take—that. Fall—to—the—ground—demon. Cut—you—into—pieces. Chop—off—your—legs. Die—snake." Then, one day, the workers dig a wide hole and they flop on the ground "with their faces over the edge of the hole and their legs like wheel spokes." Suddenly their words come tumbling out: "Hello down there in China!" "Hello, Mother!" "I've been working hard for you, and I hate it." "I've become an opium addict." "I don't even look Chinese anymore." "I'm coming home by and by." "I'm not coming home." The men had, Kingston writes, "dug an ear into the world, and were telling their secrets."[8]

Today we need to fill the shouting holes, to listen to the Bak Goongs of the past and learn their secrets. Their stories can enable us to understand Asians as actors in the making of history and can give us a view from below—the subjective world of the immigrant experience. Detained at the Angel Island Immigration Station in San Francisco Bay, Chinese immigrants carved over a hundred poems on the walls of the barracks. One of them wrote:

I used to admire the land of the Flowery
    Flag as a country of abundance.
I immediately raised money and started my
    journey.
For over a month, I have experienced enough
    wind and waves. . . .
I look up and see Oakland so close by. . . .
Discontent fills my belly and it is difficult for
    me to sleep.
I just write these few lines to express what is
    on my mind.[9]

We need to know what was on the "minds" of the people. As scholars of a new social history have noted recently, so much of history has been the story of kings and elites, rendering invisible and silent the "little people." An Asian American told an interviewer: "I am a second generation Korean American without any achievements in life and I have no education. What is it you want to hear from me? My life is not worth telling to anyone." Similarly, a Chinese immigrant said: "You know, it seems to me there's no use in me telling you all this! I was just a simple worker, a farmworker around here. My story is not going to interest anybody." But others realize they are worthy of scholarly attention. "What is it you want to know?" an old Filipino immigrant asked a researcher. "Talk about history. What's that . . . ah, the story of my life . . . and how people lived with each other in my time."

Ay, manong
your old brown hands
hold life, many lives
within each crack
a story.[10]

NOTES

1. Leonard Greenwood, "El Centro's Community of Sikhs Dying Out," *Los Angeles Times*, December 28, 1966.
2. West Coast premiere of David Hwang's *Family Devotions*, San Francisco State University, February 1987.
3. Albert Scardino, "Commercial Rents in Chinatown Soar as Hong Kong Exodus Grows," *New York Times*, December 25, 1986; Douglas Martin, "Living in Two Worlds: Chinese of New York City," *New York Times*, February 19, 1988; Mark Arax, "Asian Influx Alters Life in Suburbia," *Los Angeles Times*, April 5, 1987; Robert Reinhold, "Flow of 3d World Immigrants Alters Weave of U.S. Society," *New York Times*, June 30, 1986.
4. Data from Cary Davis, Carl Haub, and JoAnne Willette, *U.S. Hispanics: Changing the Face of America*, a publication of the Population Reference Bureau, vol. 38, no. 3 (June 1983), p. 8; Robert W. Gardner, Bryant Robey, and Peter C. Smith, *Asian Americans: Growth, Change, and Diversity*, a publication of the Population Reference Bureau, vol. 40, no. 4 (October 1985), pp. 2, 3, 5, 7, 8.
5. William Wong, "Racial Taunts of Inouye Are a Chilling Reminder," *East/West*, July 23, 1987.
6. Congressman Norman Mineta, from the Foreword, in Timothy J. Lukes and Gary Y. Okihiro, *Japanese Legacy: Farming and Community Life in California's Santa Clara Valley* (Cupertino, Calif., 1985).
7. *The Californians*, May/June 1987, p. 5; Oscar Handlin, *The Uprooted: The Epic Story of the Great Migrations That Made the American People* (New York, 1951).
8. Maxine Hong Kingston, *China Men* (New York, 1980), pp. 100, 101, 102, 114, 117.
9. Mr. Yip, in Him Mark Lai, Genny Lim, Judy Yung (eds.), *Island: Poetry and History of Chinese Immigrants on Angel Island, 1910–1940* (San Francisco, 1980), p. 136; poem, ibid., p. 40. "Flowery Flag" is a reference to the United States. For the need

to study the excluded as well as the excluders, see Roger Daniels, "Westerners from the East: Oriental Immigrants Reappraised," *Pacific Historical Review*, vol. 35 (1966), pp. 373–383, and "American Historians and East Asian Immigrants," *Pacific Historical Review*, vol. 43 (1974), pp. 449–472.

10. Interview with Jean Park (pseudonym), Prologue of "The Autobiography of a Second Generation Korean American," in Christopher Kim, "Three Generations of Koreans in America," Asian American Studies 199 paper, University of California, Berkeley, 1976, pp. 42–44; interview with Suen Hoon Sum, in Jeff Gillenkirk and James Matlow, *Bitter Melon: Stories from the Last Rural Chinese Town in America* (Seattle, 1987), p. 56; interview with Filipino immigrant in Virgilio Menor Felipe, "Hawaii: A Pilipino Dream," M.A. thesis, University of Hawaii, 1972, Prologue, p. iii; Virginia Cerenio, "you lovely people," in Joseph Bruche, *Breaking Silence: An Anthology of Contemporary Asian American Poets* (Greenfield Center, N.Y., 1983), p. 11.

QUESTIONS FOR "FROM A DIFFERENT SHORE" BY RONALD TAKAKI

Talking About the Text

1. In this essay, Ronald Takaki begins with a description of his childhood experiences in a multicultural environment. What are some other ways in which Takaki might have begun his essay? Why do you think he chose to open the essay with a narrative of childhood experiences? What purpose(s) does this serve?

2. Takaki asserts that "we must not study Asian Americans primarily in terms of statistics and what was done to them. They are entitled to be viewed as subjects—as men and women with minds, wills, and voices." Takaki then refers us to some events in *China Men* and quotes two poems by Asian immigrants. What effect(s) do these passages have on you as a reader? How would your reading experience be different if Takaki cited research conclusions and statistics?

Exploring Issues

1. Takaki states that we need to " 're-vision' history to include Asians in the history of America." Do you agree that Asians have been excluded from American histories? Are there other groups that have also been excluded in this way? What are some possible benefits from rewriting histories? Could there be any reasons to *not* rewrite our histories?

2. Takaki asserts that Asian immigrants deserve to have their own voices heard rather than being discussed as victims and objects of research. Why might it be important for us to know the subjective experiences of immigrants?

3. In his reference to *China Men,* Takaki illustrates very concretely the ways in which immigrants' voices were silenced. We can see this same silencing effect illustrated in "The Girl Who Wouldn't Sing" by Kit Yuen Quan. How was Quan's voice silenced? How did she rediscover her voice (and her identity)? Can you think of other cases of a people whose voices were silenced? How was this accomplished?

Writing Assignment

Read Quan's and Walker's essays in this chapter. These are examples of histories presented in the voices of real people, one the child of immigrants and the other an African American. Write a discussion of the potential benefits (and perhaps the potential problems) of including these and other similar essays in the history books of high school and college students.

Reading 4

All My Grandmothers Could Sing Most Died Young

Maria Mullinaux Lemon

Maria Mullinaux writes fiction and poetry in Lincoln, Nebraska, where—as Maria Lemon—she owns and operates a public relations and writing agency. Mullinaux is also the editor of a child advocacy magazine, *Speaking for Children.* In this selection from her poetry, Mullinaux expresses complex feelings about being a woman—feelings sometimes manifested as fear and hatred of her own mother, a woman who could look "so small, frail, frightened." At the same time, Mullinaux articulates a growing appreciation of the women in her family, of the hardships they have endured, and of the ways in which her own sense of self is enhanced by her knowledge of all her many grandmothers—"English, Irish, Norman French, Scots, Dutch, Cherokee, Seminole, Vikings, Monguls, Africans, a long circling arc of woman after woman."

From them my mother got her clear,
bell-like, three-octave soprano,
her perfect pitch, and—perhaps—
her striving to make do,
to bear up well. Though how
at times she cringes
till her voice sputters, cracks—
that did not come from them.
I would say this to you now,
since for another year
she and my father have gone home,
but I have just told you
I would not be like her,
and something in your quick "Don't worry,"
its pat hurry to be said and done,
provokes me, etches
the foul taste of betrayal on my tongue.

I have always betrayed her
with that wish.
Blamed her
for the cast I wore at two
when it was my father,
believing it was love made him hang on,
had heard the snapping at the wrist
and still did not let go.
Blamed her
for our moving house to house
when he would not let her work
to help him pay the rent.
Blamed her
for the hand-me-down
black patent Sunday shoes,
the remade clothes,
my sisters' fights at Christmas,
the Red Sox' refusal to let women pitch,
old sayings about fools and shrews,
the smallness of my breasts,
all broken promises, and all bad weather.

I would say now, she was frightened,
not unkind. She is so small, so old.
Last night she said
the ladies at the church still tell her
she is wonderfully preserved,
and the young ones
still ask her to sing for them.

"My mother," she began.
But her hands, useless
against some invisible,
forced strangulation,
fluttered to her throat
as they always have done
when she has spoken of her past,
and she took up her sewing,
spoke, instead, of my father's mother,
her flaming Irish hair,
how nothing was left of her
but father's memory of her beauty,
how she had birthed fourteen.
Eleven lived.
"You have her hair and eyes,"
she told me.
I should have answered, No,
they are not Ruth Hester Ann's,
my hair and eyes are yours,
and my small feet and hands and breasts,
the way my eyebrows grow, my nose.
But such things never pass between us.

She worked her stitches
closely and exactly,
spellbinding me
with stories of my father's grandmother—
the tall, proud one from England,
the lady whose firm voice
kept on and on
until her husband freed his slaves—
and father's grandfather's mother,
the young Cherokee whose children
crossed her from the family Bible
and with their children marched
to Florida against the Seminoles,
piling treachery on treachery,
generation to generation
dark faced, dark haired, pretending
with their blue eyes that she had never been.

At this her voice cracked again. So much betrayal.
I had heard it all before,
but through my father's eyes.
And as a child, as a young woman,
I gloried with him

for the second son turned Huguenot
and banished from his Norman heritage,
for the Vikings before him,
the farmers, slave-owners,
abolitionists, preachers,
socialists who came after,
all of them misspending youth in drunken frenzy,
as he himself had done,
then finding a good woman,
carving something from earth,
from flesh,
from sweat and blood.
I had not once asked
whose earth,
whose sweat and blood,
nor once imagined
the brown, black, white, red, yellow
women they had pillaged
to carry water,
cook meat, and bear their children.

I watched her sew, glad
my father had gone out.
She was embroidering forget-me-nots
and autumn leaves together
on a wide sash for my sister's daughter's wedding,
each leaf meticulously edge-rusted gold,
each blossom shading blue to blue
from its raised center.
Did my Cherokee grandmother
spend her nights this way,
working the thread and needles
of a white man's wife?
She knew dyes, roots,
seeds, leaves, chants.
Did she forget, bear up, make do?
Was she cast off
for her songs,
her gatherings,
her dark anger when her husband
bought his first, second,
thirtieth dark-skinned, dark-eyed slave?
I have seen the cabin where she lived,
have walked the boards remaining
from the quarters by the creek.
I will never know her name.

I should tell you,
had my father been with us,
he would have said
my mother's mother grew insane
as she grew old,
that she wandered from the house
and they would find her sitting on some curb,
her long wide skirt not long or wide enough
to hide the laces of her hightopped shoes,
the thick worn stockings
she would not replace or go without.
Poor Lou Verna, he would say; a pity.
My mother's silence while he spoke,
so much betrayal, so much discounting
what she would tell me when we were alone,
her mother's long dark auburn hair
which she would let her daughters comb,
her simple Quaker hymns,
her laugh until,
nine days into her widowhood,
her sons sold house, fields,
horses, implements,
the four-post bed,
her geese, chickens, china,
the extra dressing gowns—
sold everything,
took all the sale had brought,
then shared her and her two still infant daughters
among them as cheap household labor.
I did not deserve their beatings,
she would say, I could not escape
except by going with your father,
and her hands would flutter to her throat
and she would look so small, frail, frightened,
determined only to make do, bear up, endure,
that as a child I listened thinking nothing
but that I would not be like her,
would shun her, cling to men,
shun all women as carriers of some plague.
And last night I was glad she said goodnight
and did not tell me of her past again.

If I spoke these things,
surely you would tell me
it was not my father's fault,
my fear and hatred and betrayal of her.

Would even say he would have disapproved
and begged me not to blame the innocent.
He is a good man, has always been
patient, giving, kind,
and how many times have I told you
he raised me as if I were no daughter, but a son,
tempted me to pitch, to ride,
to dream adventures and tall tales,
to stand my ground,
refusing to make do,
shouting I would not bear
what no man should bear at all.
You would not see
how his patience,
how his care and pity
stole her daughters from her
any more than you would understand my anger
that you tell me not to worry,
I will not be like her.

She has gone now,
but before my father takes her home,
they will have stopped
to see her younger sister,
and she will go house to house
to praise all her long-lived brothers
in a high-pitched, childish voice,
as if she had forgiven,
had forgotten how her own mother,
sitting on low curbs,
muttering, listed over and again
the names of all her children,
searching for some sense
beyond the chaos of those
seventeen hard birthings.
I would rather she had killed her brothers
than know how she visits them.

I must tell you, it is true,
I would not be like her,
but you must not assume
the wish stops there.
It is a wish to claim
what she would not have given up
had it not been taken from her:
her pride, her courage, her anger,
the lost Quaker songs, the chants,

the roots, leaves, berries, tapestries,
the plows and hoes and spinning wheels,
the four-post beds, the eider down,
combs, brushes, silks,
carved ships and painted walls,
the wines, the bells and candles
and the meat and water,
books and herstories and lost names
and sweat and blood—
would claim them,
claim them until around me
I feel the eyes of all my grandmothers,
hear their singing,
English, Irish, Norman French,
Scots, Dutch, Cherokee, Seminole,
Vikings, Mongols, Africans,
a long circling arc
of woman after woman
side by side,
not the least surprised
that after all these years
not caring I had never seen them,
I have finally noticed, hear them,
know them for who, for what they are.

Reading 5

The Unglamorous but Worthwhile Duties of the Black Revolutionary Artist, or of the Black Writer Who Simply Works and Writes

Alice Walker

Alice Walker is the author of many essays and books. Perhaps best known for her Pulitzer prize-winning novel, *The Color Purple,* Walker has also authored *Meridian, The Temple of My Familiar,* and *The Third Life of Grange Copeland.* In the following essay, Walker examines her gradual awakening to a cultural heritage that largely had been ignored by her college teachers of the 1960s. Taking this self-analysis a step further, Walker then explores the effects that her awakening has had on her development as a writer during a period of rapid social change here in the United States.

When I came to Sarah Lawrence in 1964, I was fleeing from Spelman College in Atlanta, a school that I considered opposed to change, to freedom, and to understanding that by the time most girls enter college they are already women and should be treated as women. At Sarah Lawrence I found all that I was looking for at the time—freedom to come and go, to read leisurely, to go my own way, dress my own way, and conduct my personal life as I saw fit. It was here that I wrote my first published short story and my first book, here that I learned to feel what I thought had some meaning, here that I felt no teacher or administrator breathing down my neck.

I thought I had found happiness and peace in my own time.

And for that time, perhaps, I had. It was not until after I had graduated and gone south to Mississippi that I began to realize that my lessons at Sarah Lawrence had left crucial areas empty, and had, in fact, contributed to a blind spot in my education that needed desperately to be cleared if I expected to be a whole woman, a full human being, a black woman full of self-awareness and pride. I realized, sometime after graduation, that when I had studied contemporary writers and the South at this college—taught by a warm, wonderful woman whom I much admired—the writings of Richard Wright had not been studied and that instead I had studied the South from Faulkner's point of view, from Feibleman's, from Flannery O'Connor's. It was only after trying to conduct the same kind of course myself—with black students—that I realized that such a course simply cannot *be* taught if *Black Boy* is not assigned and read, or if "The Ethics of Living Jim Crow" is absent from the reading list.

I realized further that when I had been yearning, while here, to do a paper on pan-Africanism in my modern world history class, my Harvard-trained teacher had made no mention of W. E. B. Du Bois (who attended Harvard too, in the nineteenth century), no doubt because he had never heard of him.

I also realized that I had wasted five of my hard-to-come-by dollars one semester when I bought a supposedly "comprehensive" anthology of English and American verse which had been edited by a Sarah Lawrence faculty member. A nice man, a handsome one even, who had not thought to include a single poem by a black poet. I believe this man, who *was* really very nice, did not know there *were* black poets, or, if he did, believed like Louis Simpson that "poetry that is identifiably Negro is not important." I've yet to figure out *exactly* what that means, but it sounds ugly and has effectively kept black poets out of "comprehensive" anthologies, where the reader would have the opportunity to decide whether their poems are "important" or not.

I began to feel that subtly and without intent or malice, I had been miseducated. For where my duty as a black poet, writer, and teacher would take me, people would have little need of Keats and Byron or even Robert Frost, but much need of Hughes, Bontemps, Gwendolyn Brooks, and Margaret Walker.

So for the past four years I've been in still another college. This time simply a college of books—musty old books that went out of print years ago—and of old people, the oldest old black men and women I could find, and a college of the young; students and dropouts who articulate in various bold and shy ways that they believe themselves to be without a valuable history, without a respectable music, without writing or poetry that speaks to them.

My enrollment in this newest college will never end, and for that I am glad. And each day I look about to see what can and should be done to make it a bigger college, a more inclusive one, one more vital and long living. There are things our people should know, books they should read, poems they should know by heart. I think now of *Black Reconstruction* by Du Bois, of *Cane* by Jean Toomer, of *Mules and Men* by Zora Neale Hurston. Ten years ago, the one copy of *Black Reconstruction* that could be found in Atlanta was so badly battered and had been pasted back together so many times that a student could check it out of the library for only thirty minutes, and was then not allowed to take it outside the reading room. *Cane* by Jean Toomer and *Mules and Men* by Zora Neale Hurston I found tucked away behind locked doors in the library of Lincoln University. Knowing both books were out of print at the time, I Xeroxed them and stole somebody's rights, but it was the least I could do if I wanted to read them over and over again, which I did.

Today it gives me pleasure to see a Black Students' Association at Sarah Lawrence. That must mean there are many black students to pay dues. When I was here there were six of us and none of us was entirely black. Much has clearly changed, here as in the rest of the country. But when I look about and see what work still remains I can only be mildly, though sincerely, impressed.

Much lip service has been given the role of the revolutionary black writer but now the words must be turned into work. For, as someone has said, "Work is love made visible." There are the old people, Toms, Janes, or just simply old people, who need us to put into words for them the courage and dignity of their lives. There are the students who need guidance and direction. Real guidance and real direction, and support that doesn't get out of town when the sun goes down.

I have not labeled myself yet. I would like to call myself revolutionary, for I am always changing, and growing, it is hoped for the good of more black people. I do call myself black when it seems necessary to call myself anything, especially since I believe one's work rather than one's appearance adequately labels one. I used to call myself a poet, but I've come to have doubts about that. The truest and most enduring impulse I have is simply to write. It seems necessary for me to forget all the titles, all the labels, and all the hours of talk and to concentrate on the mountain of work I find before me. My major advice to young black artists would be that they shut themselves up somewhere away from all debates about who they are and what color they are and just turn out paintings and poems and stories and novels. Of course the kind of artist we are required to be cannot do this. Our people are waiting. *But there must be an awareness of what is Bull and what is Truth*, what is practical and what is designed ultimately to paralyze our talents. For example, it is unfair to the people we expect to reach to give them a beautiful poem if they are unable to read it.

And so, what is the role of the black revolutionary artist? Sometimes it is the role of remedial reading teacher. I will never forget one of the girls in my black studies course last year at Jackson State. All year long she had been taught by one of the greatest black poets still living: Margaret Walker. I took over the class when Miss Walker was away for the quarter. We were reading "For My People" and this girl came to the section that reads:

> Let a new earth rise. Let another world be born. Let a bloody peace be written in the sky. Let a second generation full of courage issue forth, let a people loving freedom come to growth, let a beauty full of healing and a strength of final clenching be the pulsing in our spirits and our blood. Let the martial songs be written, let the dirges disappear. Let a race of men now rise and take control!

"What do you think?" I asked the girl. (She had read the poem very well.) She shook her head. "What is the matter?" I asked. She said, "Oh, these older poets! They never write poems that tell us to fight!" Then I realized that she had read the poem, even read it passionately, and had not understood a word of what it was about. "What is a 'martial song' "? I asked. "What is a disappearing dirge?" The girl was completely thrown by the words.

I recall a young man (bearded, good-looking), a Muslim, he said, who absolutely refused to read Faulkner. "We in the revolution now," he said, "We don't have to read no more white folks." "Read thine enemy," I prodded, to no avail. And this same young man made no effort, either, to read Hughes or Ellison or McKay or Ernest Gaines, who is perhaps the most gifted young black writer working today. His problem was that the revolutionary rhetoric so popular today had convinced him of his own black perfection and of the imperfection of everybody and everything white, but it had not taught him how to read. The belief that he was already the complete man had stunted this young man's growth. And when he graduates from college, as he will, he will teach your children and mine, and still not know how to read, nor will he be inclined to learn.

The real revolution is always concerned with the least glamorous stuff. With raising a reading level from second grade to third. With simplifying history and writing it down (or reciting it) for the old folks. With helping illiterates fill out food-stamp forms—for they must eat, revolution or not. The dull, frustrating work with our people is the work of the black revolutionary artist. It means, most of all, staying close enough to them to be there whenever they need you.

But the work of the black artist is also to create and to preserve what was created before him. It is knowing the words of James Weldon Johnson's "Negro National Anthem" and even remembering the tune. It is being able to read "For My People" with tears in the eyes, comprehension in the soul. It is sending small tokens of affection to our old and ancient poets whom renown has ignored. One of the best acts of my entire life was to take a sack of oranges to Langston Hughes when he had the flu, about two weeks before he died.

We must cherish our old men. We must revere their wisdom, appreciate their insight, love the humanity of their words. They may not all have been heroes of the kind we think of today, but generally it takes but a single reading of their work to know that they were all men of sensitivity and soul.

Only a year or so ago did I read this poem, by Arna Bontemps, "The Black Man Talks of Reaping":

I have sown beside all waters in my day.
I planted deep within my heart the fear
That wind or fowl would take the grain away.
I planted safe against this stark, lean year.

I scattered seed enough to plant the land
In rows from Canada to Mexico.
But for my reaping only what the hand
Can hold at once is all that I can show.

Yet what I sowed and what the orchard yields
My brother's sons are gathering stalk and root,
Small wonder then my children glean in fields
They have not sown, and feed on bitter fruit.

It requires little imagination to see the author as a spiritual colossus, arms flung wide, as in a drawing by Charles White, to encompass all the "Adams and the Eves and their countless generations," bearing the pain of the reaping but brooding on the reapers with great love.

Where *was* this poem in all those poetry anthologies I read with eager heart and hushed breath? It was not there, along with all the others that were not there. But it must, and will, be always in my heart. And if, in some gray rushing day, all our black books are burned, it must be in my head and I must be able to drag it out and recite it, though it be bitter to the tongue and painful to the ears. For that is also the role of the black revolutionary artist. He must be a walking filing cabinet of poems and songs and stories, of people, of places, of deeds and misdeeds.

In my new college of the young I am often asked, "What is the place of hate in writing?" After all we have been through in this country it is foolish and in any case useless to say hate has no place. Obviously, it has. But we must exercise our noblest impulses with our hate, not to let it destroy us or destroy our *truly precious heritage*, which is not, by the way, a heritage of bigotry or intolerance. I've found, in my own writing, that a little hatred, keenly directed, is a useful thing. Once spread about, however, it becomes a web in which I would sit caught and paralyzed like the fly who stepped into the parlor. The artist must remember that some individual men, like Byron de la Beckwith or Sheriff Jim Clark, should be hated, and that some corporations like Dow and General Motors should be hated too. Also the Chase Manhattan Bank and the Governor of Mississippi. However, there are men who should be loved, or at least respected on their merits, and groups of men, like the American Friends, who should not be hated. The strength of the artist is his courage to look at every old thing with fresh eyes and his ability to re-create, as true to life as possible, that great middle ground of people between Medgar Evers's murderer, Byron de la Beckwith, and the fine old gentleman John Brown.

I am impressed by people who claim they can see every person and event in strict terms of black and white, but generally their work is not, in my long-contemplated and earnestly considered opinion, either black or white, but a dull, uniform gray. It is boring because it is easy and requires only that the reader be a lazy reader and a prejudiced one. Each story or poem has a formula, usually two-thirds "hate whitey's guts" and one-third "I am black, beautiful, strong, and almost always right." Art is not flattery, necessarily, and the work of any artist must be more difficult than that. A man's life can rarely be summed up in one word; even if that word is black or white. And it is the duty of the artist to present the man *as he is*. One should recall that Bigger Thomas was many great and curious things, but he was neither good nor beautiful. He was real, and that is sufficient.

Sometimes, in my anger and frustration at the world we live in, I ask myself, What is real and what is not? And now it seems to me that what is real is what is happening. What is real is what did happen. What happened to me and happens to me is most real of all. I write then, out of that. I write about the old men that I knew (I love old men), and the great big beautiful women with arms like cushions (who would really rather look like Pat Nixon), and of the harried fathers and mothers and the timid, hopeful children. And today, in Mississippi, it seems I sometimes relive my Georgia childhood. I see the same faces, hear the same soft voices, take a nip, once in a while, of the same rich mellow corn, or wine. And when I write about the people there, in the strangest way it is as if I am not writing about them at all, but about myself. The artist then is the voice of the people, but she is also The People.

QUESTIONS FOR "THE UNGLAMOROUS BUT WORTHWHILE DUTIES OF THE BLACK REVOLUTIONARY ARTIST, OR OF THE BLACK WRITER WHO SIMPLY WORKS AND WRITES" BY ALICE WALKER

Talking About the Text

1. What is Walker's attitude toward her former teachers and her education?
2. From reading this essay, what can you surmise about Alice Walker as a person? Is she someone you might admire? Why or why not?
3. Why does Walker place so much emphasis on reading, both for her students and for herself? What purpose does reading serve for Walker and for her students?
4. What do you think Walker means when she says "The artist then is the voice of the people, but she is also The People"?

Exploring Issues

1. Consider some of the potential problems that could result from a student's *not* learning about his or her own cultural identity in the regular school curriculum. How might this affect one's sense of self?
2. To what degree have you learned about African-American traditions in your own educational experience? Do you feel that this is important? Compare your experiences with those of your classmates. Has American education changed since 1971, when this essay was written?

Writing Assignments

1. In this essay, Alice Walker discusses several "duties" that she has as a "black revolutionary artist." Examine Walker's specific descriptions of these duties; then write an essay in which you interpret and define Walker's use of the term *black revolutionary artist*.
2. Write an essay in which you explore and discuss the following statement: African-American history and culture should be included in the curricula of all public schools in the United States. If you wish, you may write an argument *for* or *against* this idea.

Reading 6

The Girl Who Wouldn't Sing

Kit Yuen Quan

This essay originally appeared in a volume of prose and poetry entitled
*Making Face, Making Soul: Haciendo Caros: Creative and Critical
Perspectives by Women of Color,* edited by Gloria Anzaldua (Aunt Lute
Foundations Books, P.O. Box 410687, San Francisco, CA 94141). In this
intensely personal account of her struggles with language, Kit Yuen Quan
relates some of her encounters with both English and Chinese. Having
rejected her Chinese culture and language for many years, Quan finds her
way back to her self by embracing the culture and language of her ancestors.

It was really hard deciding how to talk about language because I had to go
through my blocks with language. I stumble upon these blocks whenever I have
to write, speak in public or voice my opinions in a group of native English
speakers with academic backgrounds. All of a sudden as I scramble for words, I
freeze and am unable to think clearly. Minutes pass as I struggle to retrieve my
thoughts until I finally manage to say something. But it never comes close to
expressing what I mean. I think it's because I'm afraid to show who I really am.
I cannot bear the thought of the humiliation and ridicule. And I dread having to
use a language that has often betrayed my meaning. Saying what I need to say
using my own words usually threatens the status quo.

People assume that I don't have a language problem because I can speak
English, even when I ask them to take into account that English is my second
language. This is the usual reaction I have gotten while working in the feminist
movement. It's true that my language problems are different from those of a
recent immigrant who cannot work outside of Chinatown because she or he
doesn't speak enough English. Unlike my parents, I don't speak with a heavy
accent. After twenty years of living in this country, watching American television and going through its school system, I have acquired adequate English
skills to function fairly well. I can pass as long as I don't have to write anything
or say what I really think around those whom I see as being more educated and

articulate than I am. I can spend the rest of life avoiding jobs that require extensive reading and writing skills. I can join the segment of the population that reads only out of necessity rather than for information, appreciation or enlightenment.

It's difficult for people to accept that I believe I have a literacy problem because they do not understand the nature of my blocks with language. Learning anything new terrifies me, especially if it involves words or writing. I get this overwhelming fear, this heart-stopping panic that I won't understand it. I won't know how to do it. My body tenses up and I forget to breathe if there is a word in a sentence that I don't know or several sentences in a paragraph containing unfamiliar words. My confidence dwindles and I start to feel the ground falling from under me. In my frustration I feel like crying, running out or smashing something, but that would give me away, expose my defect. So I tune out or nod my head as if there is nothing wrong. I've had to cover it up in order to survive, get jobs, pass classes and at times to work and live with people who do not care to understand my reality.

Living with this fear leaves me exhausted. I feel backed against a wall of self-doubt, pushed into a corner, defeated, unable to stretch or take advantage of opportunities. Beyond just being able to read and write well enough to get by, I need to be able to learn, understand, communicate, to articulate my thoughts and feelings, and participate fully without feeling ashamed of who I am and where I come from.

When I first arrived in San Francisco from Hong Kong at age seven and a half, the only English I knew was the alphabet and a few simple words: cat, dog, table, chair. I sat in classrooms for two to three years without understanding what was being said, and cried while the girl next to me filled in my spelling book for me. In music class when other kids volunteered to go up in front of the class to play musical instruments, I'd never raise my hand. I wouldn't sing. The teacher probably wondered why there were always three Chinese girls in one row who wouldn't sing. In art class, I was so traumatized that I couldn't be creative. While other kids moved about freely in school, seeming to flow from one activity to the next, I was disoriented, out of step, feeling hopelessly behind. I went into a "survivor mode" and couldn't participate in activities.

I remember one incident in particular in the fourth grade during a kickball game. I had just missed the ball when Kevin, the class jock, came running across the yard and kicked me in the butt. Had I been able to speak English, I might have screamed my head off or called for the teacher, but I just stood there trying to numb out the pain, feeling everyone's eyes on me. I wasn't sure it wasn't all part of the game.

At home I spoke the sam yup dialect of Cantonese with my parents, who were completely unaware of the severity of my problems at school. In their eyes I was very lucky to be going to school in America. My father had had only a high school education before he had to start working. And we children would not have had any chance to go to college had we stayed in Hong Kong. We had flown over the Pacific Ocean three times between the time I was seven and a half and eight and a half because they were so torn about leaving their home to resettle in a foreign country and culture. At the dinner table after a day of toiling at their jobs and struggling with English, they aired their frustrations about the racism and discrimination they were feeling everywhere: at their jobs, on the bus, at the supermarket. Although they didn't feel very hopeful about their own lives, they were comforted by the fact that my brother and I were getting a good education. Both my parents had made incredible sacrifices for my education. Life would be easier for us, with more opportunities and options, because we would know the language. We would be able to talk back or fight back if need be. All we had to do was study hard and apply ourselves. So every day after school I would load my bag full of textbooks and walk up two hills to where we lived the first few years after we landed here. I remember opening each book and reading out loud a paragraph or two, skipping over words I didn't know until I gave up in frustration.

My parents thought that by mastering the English language, I would be able to attain the Chinese American dream: a college education, a good-paying job, a house in the suburbs, a Chinese husband and children. They felt intimidated and powerless in American society and so clung tightly to me to fulfill their hopes and dreams. When I objected to these expectations using my limited Chinese, I received endless lectures. I felt smothered by their traditional values of how a Chinese girl should behave and this was reason enough not to learn more Chinese. Gradually language came to represent our two or more opposing sets of values. If I asserted my individuality, wanted to go out with my friends, had opinions of my own, or disagreed with their plans for me, I was accused of becoming too smart for my own good now that I had grown wings. "*Cheun neuih*, stupid girl. Don't think you're better than your parents just because you know more English. You don't know anything! We've eaten more salt than you've eaten rice." Everything I heard in Chinese was a dictate. It was always one more thing I wasn't supposed to do or be, one more way I wasn't supposed to think. At school I felt stupid for not knowing the language. At home I was under attack for my rebellious views. The situation became intolerable after I came out to my parents as a lesbian.

When I ran away from home at sixteen, I sought refuge in the women's community working part-time at a feminist bookstore. I felt like I had no family, no home, no identity or culture I could claim. In between hiding from my parents and crashing at various women's houses, I hung out in the Mission playing pool with other young dykes, got high, or took to the streets when I felt like I was going to explode. Sometimes at night I found myself sitting at the counter of some greasy spoon Chinese restaurant longing for a home-cooked meal. I was lonely for someone to talk to who could understand how I felt, but I didn't even have the words to communicate what I felt.

At the bookstore, I was discovering a whole other world: women, dykes, feminists, authors, political activists, artists—people who read and talked about what they were reading. As exciting as it all was, I didn't understand what people were talking about. What was political theory? What was literary criticism? Words flew over my head like planes over a runway. In order to communicate with other feminists, most of whom were white or middle class or both, educated, and at least ten years older than me, I had to learn feminist rhetoric.

Given my uprooted and transplanted state, I have a difficult time explaining to other people how I feel about language. Usually they don't understand or will even dispute what I'm saying. A lot of times I'll think it's because I don't have the right words, I haven't read enough books, or I don't know the language. That's how I felt all the time while working at a feminist bookstore. It wasn't only white, educated people who didn't understand how I felt. Women of color or Third World women who had class privilege and came from literary backgrounds thought the problem was more my age and my lack of political development. I often felt beaten down by these kinds of attitudes while still thinking that my not being understood was the result of my inability to communicate rather than an unreceptive environment.

Even though feminist rhetoric does give me words to describe how I'm being oppressed, it still reflects the same racist, classist standards of the dominant society and of colleges and universities. I get frustrated because I constantly feel I'm being put down for what I'm saying or how I talk. For example, in a collective meeting with other women, I spoke about how I felt as a working class person and why I felt different from them. I told them they felt "middle class" to me because of the way they behaved and because of the values they had, that their "political vision" didn't include people with my experience and concerns. I tried to say all of this using feminist rhetoric, but when I used the term "working class," someone would argue, "You can't use that term. . . ." Because they were educated they thought they owned the language and so could say, "You can't use 'middle class,' you can't use 'working class,' because nowadays everybody is working class and it's just a matter of whether you're poor or comfortable." They did not listen to the point I was trying to make. They didn't care that I was sitting there in the circle stumbling along, struggling to explain how I felt oppressed by them and the structure and policies of the organization. Instead of listening to why I felt that way, they invalidated me for the way I used language and excluded me by defending themselves and their positions and claiming that my issues and feelings were "personal" and that I should just get over them.

Another example of my feeling excluded is when people in a room make all sorts of literary allusions. They make me feel like I should have read those books. They throw around metaphors that leave me feeling lost and confused. I don't get to throw in my metaphors. Instead of acknowledging our different backgrounds and trying to include me in the discussion, they choose to ignore my feelings of isolation. I find that among feminists, white and colored, especially those who pride themselves on being progressive political activists with credentials, there's an assumption that if a person just read more, studied more, she would find the right words, the right way to use them, and even the right thoughts. A lot of times my language and the language of other working class, non-academic people becomes the target of scrutiny and criticism when others don't want to hear what we have to say. They convince themselves we're using the wrong words: "What definition are you using?" "What do you mean by that?" And then we get into debate about what was meant, we get lost in semantics and then we really don't know what we're saying.

Why should I try to use all of these different words when I'm being manipulated and suppressed by those whose rhetoric is more developed, whether it's feminist, academic, or leftist?

Those of us who feel invisible or misunderstood when we try to name what is oppressing us within supposedly feminist or progressive groups need to realize that our language is legitimate and valid. It comes from our families, our cultures, our class backgrounds, our experiences of different and conflicting realities. And we don't need to read another book to justify it. If I want to say *I'm working class*, I should be able to *say* I'm working class without having to read or quote Marx. But just saying that I'm working class never gives me enough of the understanding that I want. Because our experiences and feelings are far too complex to be capsulized in abstractions like "oppression," "sexism," "racism," etc., there is no right combination of these terms which can express why we feel oppressed.

I knew that I needed to go some place where some of my experiences with language would be mirrored. Through the Refugee Women's Program in the Tenderloin district of San Francisco, I started to tutor two Cambodian refugee girls. The Buth family had been in the U.S. for one and a half years. They lived, twelve people to a room, in an apartment building on Eddy Street half a block from the porno theaters. I went to their home one evening a week and on Sundays took the girls to the children's library. The doorbells in the building were out of order, so visitors had to wait to be let in by someone on their way out. Often I stood on their doorsteps watching the street life. The fragrant smell of jasmine rice wafting from the windows of the apartment building mixed with the smell of booze and piss on the street. Newspapers, candy wrappers and all kinds of garbage swept up by the wind colored the sidewalks. Cars honked and sped past while Asian, Black and white kids played up and down the street. Mothers carrying their babies weaved through loose gatherings of drunk men and prostitutes near the corner store. Around me I heard a medley of languages: Vietnamese, Chinese, Cambodian, English, Black English, Laotian.

Sometimes, I arrived to find Yan and Eng sitting on the steps behind the security gate waiting to let me in. Some days they wore their school clothes, while on other days they were barefooted and wore their traditional sarongs. As we climbed the stairs up to their apartment, we inhaled fish sauce and curry and rice. Six-year-old Eng would chatter and giggle but Yan was quieter and more reserved. Although she was only eight years old, I couldn't help but feel like I was in the company of a serious adult. I immediately identified with her. I noticed how, whenever I gave them something to do, they didn't want to do it on their own. For example, they often got excited when I brought them books, but they wouldn't want to read by themselves. They became quiet and withdrawn when I asked them questions. Their answer was always a timid "I don't know," and they never asked a question or made a request. So I read with them. We did everything together. I didn't want them to feel like they were supposed to automatically know what to do, because I remember how badly that used to make me feel.

Play time was the best part of our time together. All the little kids joined in and sometimes even their older brothers. Everybody was so excited that they forgot they were learning English. As we played jigsaw sentences and word concentration and chickens and whales, I became a little kid again, except this time I wasn't alone and unhappy. When they made Mother's Day cards, I made a Mother's Day card. When they drew pictures of our field trip to the beach, I sketched pictures of us at the beach. When we made origami frogs and jumped them all over the floor, I went home and made dinosaurs, kangaroos, spiders, crabs and lobsters. Week after week, I added to my repertoire until I could feel that little kid who used to sit like the piece of unmolded clay in front of her in art class turn into a wide-eyed origami enthusiast.

As we studied and played in the middle of the room surrounded by the rest of the family who were sleeping, nursing, doing homework, playing cards, talking, laughing or crying, Yan would frequently interrupt our lesson to answer her mother. Sometimes it was a long conversation, but I didn't mind because English was their second language. They spoke only Cambodian with their family. If they laughed at something on television, it was usually at the picture and not at the dialogue. English was used for schoolwork and to talk to me. They did not try to express their thoughts and feelings in English. When they spoke to each other, they were not alone or isolated. Whether they were living in a refugee camp in the Philippines or in Thailand or in a one-room apartment on Eddy Street, they were connected to each other through their language and their culture. They had survived war, losing family members, their country and their home, but in speaking their language, they were able to love and comfort each other. Sitting there on the bamboo mat next to the little girls, Eng and her younger sister Oeun, listening to their sweet little voices talking and singing, I understood for the first time what it was like to be a child with a voice and it made me remember my first love, the Chinese language.

While searching for an address, I came across a postcard of the San Francisco-Oakland Bay Bridge. I immediately recognized it as the postcard I had sent to my schoolmate in Hong Kong when I first got here. On the back was my eight-and-a-half-year-old handwriting.

In English it says:

Dear Kam Yee, I received your letter. You asked if I've been to school yet. Yes, I've already found a school. My family has decided to stay in America. My living surroundings are very nice. Please don't worry about me. I'm sorry it has taken so long for me to return your letter. Okay lets talk some more next time. Please give my regards to your parents and your family. I wish you happiness. Signed: Your classmate, Yuen Kit, August 30th.

The card, stamped "Return To Sender," is postmarked 1970. Although I have sketchy memories of my early school days in Hong Kong, I still remember the day when Kam Yee and I found each other. The bell rang signaling the end of class. Sitting up straight in our chairs, we had recited "Goodbye, teacher" in a chorus. While the others were rushing out the door to their next class, I rose from my desk and slowly put away my books. Over my left shoulder I saw Kam Yee watching me. We smiled at each other as I walked over to her desk. I had finally made a friend. Soon after that my family left Hong Kong and I wrote my last Chinese letter.

All the time that I was feeling stupid and overwhelmed by language, could I have been having the Chinese blues? By the time I was seven, I was reading the Chinese newspaper. I remember because there were a lot of reports of raped and mutilated women's bodies found in plastic bags on the side of quiet roads. It was a thrill when my father would send me to the newsstand on the corner to get his newspaper. Passing street vendors peddling sweets and fruit, I would run as quickly as I could. From a block away I could smell the stinky odor of *dauh fuh fa*, my favorite snack of slippery, warm, soft tofu in sweet syrup.

Up until a year ago, I could only recognize some of the Chinese characters on store signs, restaurant menus and Chinese newspapers on Stockton and Powell Streets, but I always felt a tingle of excitement whenever I recognized a word or knew its sound, like oil sizzling in a wok just waiting for something to fry.

On Saturdays I sit with my Chinese language teacher on one of the stone benches lining the overpass where the financial district meets Chinatown and links Portsmouth Square to the Holiday Inn Hotel. We have been meeting once a week for me to practice speaking, reading and writing Chinese using whatever material we can find. Sometimes I read a bilingual Chinese American weekly newspaper called the East West Journal, other times Chinese folk tales for young readers from the Chinatown Children's Library, or bilingual brochures describing free services offered by non-profit Chinatown community agencies, and sometimes even Chinese translations of Pacific Bell Telephone inserts. I look forward to these sessions where I reach inward to recover all those lost sounds that once were the roots of my childhood imagination. This exercise in trying to use my eight-year-old vocabulary to verbalize my thoughts as an adult is as scary as it is exhilarating. At one time Chinese was poetry to me. Words, their sounds and their rhythms, conjured up images that pulled me in and gave me a physical sense of their meanings. The Chinese characters that I wrote and practiced were pictographs of water, grass, birds, fire, heart and mouth. With my calligraphy brush made of pig's hair, I made the rain fall and the wind blow.

Now, speaking Chinese with my father is the closest I have felt to coming home. In a thin but sage-like voice, he reflects on a lifetime of hard work and broken dreams and we slowly reconnect as father and daughter. As we sit across the kitchen table from one another, his old and tattered Chinese dictionary by his side, he tells me of the loving relationship he had with his mother, who encouraged him in his interest in writing and the movies. Although our immigrant experiences are generations apart and have been impacted differently by

American culture, in his words I see the core of who I am. I cannot express my feelings fully in either Chinese or English or make him understand my choices. Though I am still grappling with accepting the enormous love behind the sacrifices he has made to give me a better life, I realize that with my ability to move in two different worlds I am the fruit of his labor.

For 85 cents, I can have unlimited refills of tea and a *gai mei baau* at The Sweet Fragrance Cafe on Broadway across from the World Theatre. After the first bite, the coconut sugar and butter ooze down my palm. Behind the pastry counter, my favorite clerk is consolidating trays of walnut cupcakes. Pointing to some round fried bread covered with sesame seeds, she urges the customer with "Four for a dollar, very fresh!"

Whole families from grandparents to babies sleeping soundly on mothers' backs come here for porridge, pastries and coffee. Mothers stroll in to get sweets for little ones waiting at home. Old women carrying their own mugs from home come in to chat with their buddies. Workers wearing aprons smeared with pig's blood or fresh fish scales drop in for a bite during their break. Chinese husbands sit for hours complaining and gossiping not unlike the old women in the park.

A waitress brings bowls of beef stew noodles and pork liver porridge. Smokers snub out their cigarettes as they pick up their chopsticks. The man across from me is counting sons and daughters on the fingers of his left hand: one son, another son, my wife, one daughter. He must have family in China waiting to immigrate.

The regulars congregate at the back tables, shouting opinions from one end of the long table to the other. The Chinese are notorious for their loud conversations at close range that can easily be mistaken for arguments and fights until someone breaks into laughter or gives his companion a friendly punch. Here the drama of life is always unfolding in all different dialects. I may not understand a lot of it, but the chuckling, the hand gestures, the raising of voices in protest and in accusation, and the laughter all flow like music, like a Cantonese opera.

Twenty years seems like a long time, but it has taken all twenty years for me to understand my language blocks and to find ways to help myself learn. I have had to create my own literacy program. I had to recognize that the school system failed to meet my needs as an immigrant and that this society and its institutions doesn't reflect or validate my experiences. I have to let myself grieve over the loss of my native language and all the years wasted in classrooms staring into space or dozing off when I was feeling depressed and hopeless. My various activities now help to remind me that my relationship with language is more complex than just speaking enough English to get by. In creative activity and in anything that requires words, I'm still eight years old. Sometimes I open a book and I still feel I can't read. It may take days or weeks for me to work up the nerve to open that book again. But I do open it and it gets a little easier each time that I work through the fear. As long as there are bakeries in Chinatown and as long as I have 85 cents, I know I have a way back to myself.

QUESTIONS FOR "THE GIRL WHO WOULDN'T SING" BY KIT YUEN QUAN

Talking About the Text

1. When she was growing up, Kit Yuen Quan had opportunities to speak both Chinese and English. What associations did Quan make with Chinese and what associations with English? How did these associations affect her development as a language user?
2. Quan resented her feminist associates' attempts to control her language use. Why would they have attempted to control Quan's language? What might they have gained by this action? How might they have responded to Quan's objections if she had confronted them directly?

Exploring Issues

1. Quan believes that the U.S. "school system failed to meet . . . [her] needs as an immigrant and that this society and its institutions doesn't reflect or validate . . . [her] experiences." In the United States today, there are many others for whom English is a second language. Do you feel that American schools have any special obligations to students such as Quan? If so, what are these obligations? If not, why not?
2. Quan's parents felt that by learning English, Quan would find access to the "Chinese American Dream: a college education, a good paying job, a house in the suburbs, a Chinese husband and children." Is there anything ambiguous or contradictory about this version of the American Dream? How *might* learning English affect Quan's attitudes toward education, work, and family?

Writing Assignments

1. Interview a second language speaker who has attended school in the United States for at least two years. Ask this person about all sorts of experiences with language learning, language use, reading, and writing. Try to find out about the difficulties this person has had with language and with literacy, and also discover some of the ways in which this person has dealt with these difficulties. Write a report in which you describe the person you interviewed, the interview itself, and what you learned from this experience.
2. Read Alice Walker's essay in this chapter. Then, construct a dialogue between Quan and Walker. Imagine questions they might ask each other and issues they might wish to discuss. What would these two women say to each other about their respective educations in the United States?

Reading 7

Talk in the Intimate Relationship: His and Hers

Deborah Tannen

Deborah Tannen is a professor of linguistics at Georgetown University. In addition to her scholarly writing, Tannen has authored two popular books on language use. The following essay, which appears as a chapter in the first book, *That's Not What I Meant,* received such a strong response that Tannen developed her discussion of men's and women's communication styles into a second book, entitled *You Just Don't Understand.* In this excerpt, Tannen argues that men and women belong to different "cultures" in that they have different expectations of relationships and different styles of actual conversations that, she claims, are representative of the ways that men and women often communicate. We invite you to test these scenarios by reflecting on your own personal experiences in communicating with men and women.

Male-female conversation is cross-cultural communication. Culture is simply a network of habits and patterns gleaned from past experience, and women and men have different past experiences. From the time they're born, they're treated differently, talked to differently, and talk differently as a result. Boys and girls grow up in different worlds, even if they grow up in the same house. And as adults they travel in different worlds, reinforcing patterns established in childhood. These cultural differences include different expectations about the role of talk in relationships and how it fulfills that role. . . .

HE SAID/SHE SAID: HIS AND HER CONVERSATIONAL STYLES

Everyone knows that as a relationship becomes long-term, its terms change. But women and men often differ in how they expect them to change. Many women feel, "After all this time, you should know what I want without my telling you." Many men feel, "After all this time, we should be able to tell each other what we want."

These incongruent expectations capture one of the key differences between men and women. . . . Communication is always a matter of balancing conflicting needs for involvement and independence. Though everyone has both these needs, women often have a relatively greater need for involvement, and men a relatively greater need for independence. Being understood without saying what you mean gives a payoff in involvement, and that is why women value it so highly.

If you want to be understood without saying what you mean explicitly in words, you must convey meaning somewhere else—in how words are spoken, or by metamessages. Thus it stands to reason that women are often more attuned than men to the metamessages of talk. When women surmise meaning in this way, it seems mysterious to men, who call it "women's intuition" (if they think it's right) or "reading things in" (if they think it's wrong). Indeed, it could be wrong, since metamessages are not on record. And even if it is right, there is still the question of scale: How significant are the metamessages that are there?

. . . Metamessages are a form of indirectness. Women are more likely to be indirect, and to try to reach agreement by negotiation. Another way to understand this preference is that negotiation allows a display of solidarity, which women prefer to the display of power (even though . . . the aim may be the same—getting what you want). Unfortunately, power and solidarity are bought with the same currency: Ways of talking intended to create solidarity have the simultaneous effect of framing power differences. When they think they're being nice, women often end up appearing deferential and unsure of themselves or of what they want.

When styles differ, misunderstandings are always rife. As their differing styles create misunderstandings, women and men try to clear them up by talking things out. These pitfalls are compounded in talks between men and women because they have different ways of going about talking things out, and different assumptions about the significance of going about it.

The rest of this [*discussion*] illustrates these differences, explains their origins in children's patterns of play, and shows the effects when women and men talk to each other in the context of intimate relationships in our culture.

WOMEN LISTEN FOR METAMESSAGES

Sylvia and Harry celebrated their fiftieth wedding anniversary at a mountain resort. Some of the guests were at the resort for the whole weekend, others just for the evening of the celebration: a cocktail party followed by a sitdown dinner. The manager of the dining room approached Sylvia during dinner. "Since there's so much food tonight," he said, "and the hotel prepared a fancy dessert and everyone already ate at the cocktail party anyway, how about cutting and serving the anniversary cake at lunch tomorrow?" Sylvia asked the advice of the others at her table. All the men agreed: "Sure, that makes sense. Save the cake for tomorrow." All the women disagreed: "No, the party is tonight. Serve the cake tonight." The men were focusing on the message: the cake as food. The women were thinking of the metamessage: Serving a special cake frames an occasion as a celebration.

Why are women more attuned to metamessages? Because they are more focused on involvement, that is, on relationships among people, and it is through metamessages that relationships among people are established and maintained. If you want to take the temperature and check the vital signs of a relationship, the barometers to check are its metamessages: what is said and how.

Everyone can see these signals, but whether or not we pay attention to them is another matter—a matter of being sensitized. Once you are sensitized, you can't roll your antennae back in; they're stuck in the extended position.

When interpreting meaning, it is possible to pick up signals that weren't intentionally sent out, like an innocent flock of birds on a radar screen. The birds are there—and the signals women pick up are there—but they may not mean what the interpreter thinks they mean. For example, Maryellen looks at Larry and asks, "What's wrong?" because his brow is furrowed. Since he was only thinking about lunch, her expression of concern makes him feel under scrutiny.

The difference in focus on messages and metamessages can give men and women different points of view on almost any comment. Harriet complains to Morton, "Why don't you ask me how my day was?" He replies, "If you have something to tell me, tell me. Why do you have to be invited?" The reason is that she wants the metamessage of interest: evidence that he cares how her day was, regardless of whether or not she has something to tell.

A lot of trouble is caused between women and men by, of all things, pronouns. Women often feel hurt when their partners use "I" or "me" in a situation in which they would use "we" or "us." When Morton announces, "I think I'll go for a walk," Harriet feels specifically uninvited, though Morton later claims she would have been welcome to join him. She felt locked out by his use of "I" and his omission of an invitation: "Would you like to come?" Metamessages can be seen in what is not said as well as what is said.

It's difficult to straighten out such misunderstandings because each one feels convinced of the logic of his or her position and the illogic—or irresponsibility—of the other's. Harriet knows that she always asks Morton how his day was, and that she'd never announce, "I'm going for a walk," without inviting him to join her. If he talks differently to her, it must be that he feels differently. But Morton wouldn't feel unloved if Harriet didn't ask about his day, and he would feel free to ask, "Can I come along?," if she announced she was taking a walk. So he can't believe she is justified in feeling responses he knows he wouldn't have.

MESSAGES AND METAMESSAGES IN TALK BETWEEN . . . GROWN UPS?

These processes are dramatized with chilling yet absurdly amusing authenticity in Jules Feiffer's play *Grown Ups*. To get a closer look at what happens when men and women focus on different levels of talk in talking things out, let's look at what happens in this play.

Jake criticizes Louise for not responding when their daughter, Edie, called her. His comment leads to a fight even though they're both aware that this one incident is not in itself important.

> JAKE: Look, I don't care if it's important or not, when a kid calls its mother the mother should answer.
> LOUISE: Now I'm a bad mother.
> JAKE: I didn't say that.
> LOUISE: It's in your stare.
> JAKE: Is that another thing you know? My stare?

Louise ignores Jake's message—the question of whether or not she responded when Edie called—and goes for the metamessage: his implication that she's a bad mother, which Jake insistently disclaims. When Louise explains the signals she's reacting to, Jake not only discounts them but is angered at being held accountable not for what he said but for how he looked—his stare.

As the play goes on, Jake and Louise replay and intensify these patterns:

> LOUISE: If I'm such a terrible mother, do you want a divorce?
> JAKE: I do not think you're a terrible mother and no, thank you, I do not want a divorce. Why is it that whenever I bring up any difference between us you ask me if I want a divorce?

The more he denies any meaning beyond the message, the more she blows it up, the more adamantly he denies it, and so on:

> JAKE: I have brought up one thing that you do with Edie that I don't think you notice that I have noticed for some time but which I have deliberately not brought up before because I had hoped you would notice it for yourself and stop doing it and also—frankly, baby, I have to say this—I knew if I brought it up we'd get into exactly the kind of circular argument we're in right now. And I wanted to avoid it. But I haven't and we're in it, so now, with your permission, I'd like to talk about it.
> LOUISE: You don't see how that puts me down?
> JAKE: What?
> LOUISE: If you think I'm so stupid why do you go on living with me?
> JAKE: *Dammit! Why can't anything ever be simple around here?!*

It can't be simple because Louise and Jake are responding to different levels of communication. As in Bateson's example of the dual-control electric blanket with crossed wires, each one intensifies the energy going to a different aspect of the problem. Jake tries to clarify his point by overelaborating it, which gives Louise further evidence that he's condescending to her, making it even less likely that she will address his point rather than his condescension.

What pushes Jake and Louise beyond anger to rage is their different perspectives on metamessages. His refusal to admit that his statements have implications and overtones denies her authority over her own feelings. Her attempts to interpret what he didn't say and put the metamessage into the message makes him feel she's putting words into his mouth—denying his authority over his own meaning.

The same thing happens when Louise tells Jake that he is being manipulated by Edie:

LOUISE: Why don't you ever make her come to see you? Why do you always go to her?

JAKE: You want me to play power games with a nine year old? I want her to know I'm interested in her. Someone around here has to show interest in her.

LOUISE: You love her more than I do.

JAKE: I didn't say that.

LOUISE: Yes, you did.

JAKE: You don't know how to listen. You have never learned how to listen. It's as if listening to you is a foreign language.

Again, Louise responds to his implication—this time, that he loves Edie more because he runs when she calls. And yet again, Jake cries literal meaning, denying he meant any more than he said.

Throughout their argument, the point to Louise is her feelings—that Jake makes her feel put down—but to him the point is her actions—that she doesn't always respond when Edie calls:

LOUISE: You talk about what I do to Edie, what do you think you do to me?

JAKE: This is not the time to go into what we do to each other.

Since she will talk only about the metamessage, and he will talk only about the message, neither can get satisfaction from their talk, and they end up where they started—only angrier:

JAKE: That's not the point!

LOUISE: It's *my* point.

JAKE: It's hopeless!

LOUISE: Then get a divorce.

American conventional wisdom (and many of our parents and English teachers) tell us that meaning is conveyed by words, so men who tend to be literal about words are supported by conventional wisdom. They may not simply deny but actually miss the cues that are sent by how words are spoken. If they sense something about it, they may nonetheless discount what they sense. After all, it wasn't said. Sometimes that's a dodge—a plausible defense rather than a gut feeling. But sometimes it is a sincere conviction. Women are also likely to doubt the reality of what they sense. If they don't doubt it in their guts, they nonetheless may lack the arguments to support their position and thus are reduced to repeating, "You said it. You did so." Knowing that metamessages are a real and fundamental part of communication makes it easier to understand and justify what they feel.

"TALK TO ME"

An article in a popular newspaper reports that one of the five most common complaints of wives about their husbands is "He doesn't listen to me anymore." Another is "He doesn't talk to me anymore." Political scientist Andrew Hacker noted that lack of communication, while high on women's lists of reasons for divorce, is much less often mentioned by men. Since couples are parties to the same conversations, why are women more dissatisfied with them than men? Because what they expect is different, as well as what they see as the significance of talk itself.

First, let's consider the complaint "He doesn't talk to me."

THE STRONG SILENT TYPE

One of the most common stereotypes of American men is the strong silent type. Jack Kroll, writing about Henry Fonda on the occasion of his death, used the phrases "quiet power," "abashed silences," "combustible catatonia," and "sense of power held in check." He explained that Fonda's goal was not to let anyone see "the wheels go around," not to let the "machinery" show. According to Kroll, the resulting silence was effective on stage but devastating to Fonda's family.

The image of a silent father is common and is often the model for the lover or husband. But what attracts us can become flypaper to which we are unhappily stuck. Many women find the strong silent type to be a lure as a lover but a lug as a husband. Nancy Schoenberger begins a poem with the lines "It was your silence that hooked me,/ so like my father's." Adrienne Rich refers in a poem to the "husband who is frustratingly mute." Despite the initial attraction of such quintessentially male silence, it may begin to feel, to a woman in a long-term relationship, like a brick wall against which she is banging her head.

In addition to these images of male and female behavior—both the result and the cause of them—are differences in how women and men view the role of talk in relationships as well as how talk accomplishes its purpose. These differences have their roots in the settings in which men and women learn to have conversations: among their peers, growing up.

GROWING UP MALE AND FEMALE

Children whose parents have foreign accents don't speak with accents. They learn to talk like their peers. Little girls and little boys learn how to have conversations as they learn how to pronounce words: from their playmates. Between the ages of five and fifteen, when children are learning to have conversations, they play mostly with friends of their own sex. So it's not surprising that they learn different ways of having and using conversations.

Anthropologists Daniel Maltz and Ruth Borker point out that boys and girls socialize differently. Little girls tend to play in small groups or, even more common, in pairs. Their social life usually centers around a best friend, and friendships are made, maintained, and broken by talk—especially "secrets." If a little girl tells her friend's secret to another little girl, she may find herself with a new best friend. The secrets themselves may or may not be important, but the fact of telling them is all-important. It's hard for newcomers to get into these tight groups, but anyone who is admitted is treated as an equal. Girls like to play cooperatively; if they can't cooperate, the group breaks up.

Little boys tend to play in larger groups, often outdoors, and they spend more time doing things than talking. It's easy for boys to get into the group, but not everyone is accepted as an equal. Once in the group, boys must jockey for their status in it. One of the most important ways they do this is through talk: verbal display such as telling stories and jokes, challenging and sidetracking the verbal displays of other boys, and withstanding other boys' challenges in order to maintain their own story—and status. Their talk is often competitive talk about who is best at what.

FROM CHILDREN TO GROWN UPS

Feiffer's play is ironically named *Grown Ups* because adult men and women struggling to communicate often sound like children: "You said so!" "I did not!" The reason is that when they grow up, women and men keep the divergent attitudes and habits they learned as children—which they don't recognize as attitudes and habits but simply take for granted as ways of talking.

Women want their partners to be a new and improved version of a best friend. This gives them a soft spot for men who tell them secrets. As Jack Nicholson once advised a guy in a movie: "Tell her about your troubled childhood—that always gets 'em." Men expect to *do* things together and don't feel anything is missing if they don't have heart-to-heart talks all the time.

If they do have heart-to-heart talks, the meaning of those talks may be opposite for men and women. To many women, the relationship is working as long as they can talk things out. To many men, the relationship isn't working out if they have to keep working it over. If she keeps trying to get talks going to save the relationship, and he keeps trying to avoid them because he sees them as weakening it, then each one's efforts to preserve the relationship appear to the other as reckless endangerment.

QUESTIONS FOR "TALK IN THE INTIMATE RELATIONSHIP: HIS AND HERS" BY DEBORAH TANNEN

Talking About the Text

1. Notice that Tannen uses subtitles in her text. Why do you think she uses them? How would your reading experience be different if Tannen did *not* use subtitles?

2. Tannen claims that women are more tuned in to "metamessages" than men are. What does Tannen mean when she makes this claim? Do you agree with her? Why or why not?

3. Tannen illustrates her claim with references to people (e.g., Sylvia and Harry), to a play called *Grown Ups,* and to Jack Kroll's commentary on Henry Fonda (as the strong, silent type). Notice that we don't know whether the first people Tannen refers to (Sylvia and Harry) are real or fictitious. Notice also that no transcripts of actual dialogue are used as evidence. Do you find Tannen's examples adequate and convincing? Would you find transcripts of actual recorded speech more convincing? Why or why not?

Exploring Issues

1. Do you think it is possible to characterize men's and women's communication styles without taking into account other factors such as personality, ethnicity, native region, social class, profession, age, and so on? That is, do you feel comfortable with generalizations about all men and all women? Why or why not?

2. Suppose that we accept some of the generalizations that Tannen makes about men's and women's communication. What is the importance of knowing about these differences in communication styles? How might we use this knowledge to improve our lives?

3. Can you think of people whom you know (or know of) who do *not* communicate in the ways that Tannen's theory would predict? Choose one example of such a person and try to explain why this person might differ from the general style that Tannen's theory would predict.

Writing Assignments

1. For a period of five days, pay close attention to communication situations in which men and women are involved. Try to notice some of the differences in the ways men and women communicate. Consider whether people respond to literal meanings or to metamessages. Describe some of these different situations you observe in a notebook. At the end of five days read through your notes and highlight important passages. Then, write a report in which you describe your observations and make some generalizations of your own about men's and women's communication styles.

2. Consider Tannen's thesis that men and women live in different "cultures." Take into account the ways girls and boys are socialized, their behaviors, their expectations, their roles as family members, their work lives, and so on. Decide whether you agree or disagree with Tannen on this issue, and write an argument in defense of your position. Use Tannen's text and your own life experiences as sources of evidence for your argument.

Reading 8

"So what do you want from us here?"

Barbara Myerhoff

Barbara Myerhoff was a professor of visual anthropology at the University of Southern California. The author of many professional articles and books, Myerhoff may be best remembered for her study of an elderly Jewish community in Venice, California. This study was presented in a film that won the Academy Award for Best Documentary Film in 1977 and in a book by the same name, *Number Our Days*. The following excerpt from this book may be read as both an anthropological investigation and as Myerhoff's personal quest for her own cultural identity.

Every morning I wake up in pain. I wiggle my toes. Good. They still obey. I open my eyes. Good. I can see. Everything hurts but I get dressed. I walk down to the ocean. Good. It's still there. Now my day can start. About tomorrow I never know. After all, I'm eighty-nine. I can't live forever.

Death and the ocean are protagonists in Basha's life. They provide points of orientation, comforting in their certitude. One visible, the other invisible, neither hostile nor friendly, they accompany her as she walks down the board-walk to the Aliyah Senior Citizens' Center.

Basha wants to remain independent above all. Her life at the beach de-pends on her ability to perform a minimum number of basic tasks. She must shop and cook, dress herself, care for her body and her one-room apartment, walk, take the bus to the market and the doctor, be able to make a telephone call in case of emergency. Her arthritic hands have a difficult time with the buttons on her dress. Some days her fingers ache and swell so that she cannot fit them into the holes of the telephone dial. Her hands shake as she puts in her eyedrops for glaucoma. Fortunately, she no longer has to give herself injections for her diabetes. Now it is controlled by pills, if she is careful about what she eats. In the neighborhood there are no large markets within walking distance. She must take the bus to shop. The bus steps are very high and sometimes the driver objects when she tries to bring her little wheeled cart aboard. A small boy whom she has befriended and occasionally pays often waits for her at the bus stop to help her up. When she cannot bring her cart onto the bus or isn't helped up the steps, she must walk to the market. Then shopping takes the better part of the day and exhausts her. Her feet, thank god, give her less trouble since she figured out how to cut and sew a pair of cloth shoes so as to leave room for her callouses and bunions.

Basha's daughter calls her once a week and worries about her mother living alone and in a deteriorated neighborhood. "Don't worry about me, darling. This morning I put the garbage in the oven and the bagels in the trash. But I'm feeling fine." Basha enjoys teasing her daughter whose distant concern she finds somewhat embarrassing. "She says to me, 'Mamaleh, you're sweet but you're so *stupid.*' What else could a greenhorn mother expect from a daughter who is a lawyer?" The statement conveys Basha's simultaneous pride and grief in having produced an educated, successful child whose very accomplishments drastically separate her from her mother. The daughter has often invited Basha to come and live with her, but she refuses.

> What would I do with myself there in her big house, alone all day, when the children are at work? No one to talk to. No place to walk. Nobody talks Yiddish. My daughter's husband doesn't like my cooking, so I can't even help with meals. Who needs an old lady around, somebody else for my daughter to take care of? They don't keep the house warm like I like it. When I go to the bathroom at night, I'm afraid to flush, I shouldn't wake anybody up. Here I have lived for thirty-one years. I have my friends. I have the fresh air. Always there are people to talk to on the benches. I can go to the Center whenever I like and always there's something doing there. As long as I can manage for myself, I'll stay here.

Managing means three things: taking care of herself, stretching her monthly pension of three hundred and twenty dollars to cover expenses, and filling her time in ways that have meaning for her. The first two are increasingly hard and she knows that they are battles she will eventually lose. But her free time does not weigh on her. She is never bored and rarely depressed. In many ways, life is not different from before. She has never been well-off, and she never expected things to be easy. When asked if she is happy, she shrugs and laughs. "Happiness by me is a hot cup of tea on a cold day. When you don't get a broken leg, you could call yourself happy."

Basha, like many of the three hundred or so elderly members of the Aliyah Center, was born and spent much of her childhood in one of the small, predominately Jewish, Yiddish-speaking villages known as *shtetls,* located within the Pale of Settlement of Czarist Russia, an area to which almost half the world's Jewish population was confined in the nineteenth century.[1] Desperately poor, regularly

---

[1]The term *shtetl* is surrounded by considerable confusion. Some writers have used it to refer to the territorial units in which Jews lived outside of cities in nineteenth-century Eastern Europe. Of those who stress the territorial dimension, some refer to shtetls as villages, settlements, and towns. Others, Irving Howe for example, prefer that it be preserved for units smaller than towns. Some writers mean shtetl to refer to the legally organized communities in Eastern Europe governed by

terrorized by outbreaks of anti-Semitism initiated by government officials and surrounding peasants, shtetl life was precarious. Yet a rich, highly developed culture flourished in these encapsulated settlements, based on a shared sacred religious history, common customs and beliefs, and two languages—Hebrew for prayer and Yiddish for daily life. A folk culture, *Yiddishkeit*, reached its fluorescence there, and though it continues in various places in the world today, by comparison these are dim and fading expressions of it. When times worsened, it often seemed that Eastern Europe social life intensified proportionately. Internal ties deepened, and the people drew sustenance and courage from each other, their religion, and their community. For many, life became unbearable under the increasingly reactionary regime of Czar Alexander II. The pogroms of 1881–1882, accompanied by severe economic and legal restrictions, drove out the more desperate and daring of the Jews. Soon they were leaving the shtetls and the cities in droves. The exodus of Jews from Eastern Europe swelled rapidly until by the turn of the century, hundreds of thousands were emigrating, the majority to seek freedom and opportunity in the New World.

Basha dresses simply but with care. The purchase of each item of clothing is a major decision. It must last, should be modest and appropriate to her age, but gay and up-to-date. And, of course, it can't be too costly. Basha is not quite five feet tall. She is a sturdy boat of a woman—wide, strong of frame, and heavily corseted. She navigates her great monobosom before her, supported by broad hips and thin, severely bowed legs, their shape the heritage of her malnourished childhood. Like most of the people who belong to the Aliyah Center, her early life in Eastern Europe was characterized by relentless poverty.

Basha dresses for the cold, even though she is now living in Southern California, wearing a babushka under a red sun hat, a sweater under her heavy coat. She moves down the boardwalk steadily, paying attention to the placement of her feet. A fall is common and dangerous for the elderly. A fractured hip can mean permanent disability, loss of autonomy, and removal from the community to a convalescent or old age home. Basha seats herself on a bench in front of

---

Jewish regulatory organs known as *kehilla*. Many use it to signify a particular way of life or state of mind, equating shtetl with Yiddishkeit. Much of the confusion stems from the fact that the most widely read work on the subject, *Life Is With People: The Culture of the Shtetl* by Mark Zborowski and Elizabeth Herzog, is a valuable though seriously flawed work, as Barbara Kirshenblatt-Gimblett has pointed out. The book is an ethnography based on reconstructed materials rather than first-hand observations, and is generally agreed to be overly general, idealized, and static. Since its appearance three decades ago, many authors have used the term shtetl very broadly: to signify contemporary Jewish ghettoes in the New World, life in the Pale of Settlement in the Old World, and all manifestations of immigrant cultures historically based on Eastern European life, regardless of enormous regional and national variations.

Center old people also used the term shtetl to refer to their childhood culture, whether they had lived primarily in cities in Eastern Europe or not. They too idealized these memories and generalized about them, minimizing internal and external variations in the culture. Nevertheless, I have adopted their usage, employing the word to mean their childhood experiences, memories, and the culture of Yiddishkeit. To distinguish between the elders' recollections and actual experiences was not my purpose, nor was it possible. Rather I wished to render their interpretation of their past and present lives.

the Center and waits for friends. Her feet are spread apart, well-planted, as if growing up from the cement. Even sitting quite still, there is an air of determination about her. She will withstand attacks by anti-Semites, Cossacks, Nazis, historical enemies whom she conquers by outliving. She defies time and weather (though it is not cold here). So she might have sat a century ago, before a small pyramid of potatoes or herring in the marketplace of the Polish town where she was born. Patient, resolute, she is a survivor.

Not all the Center women are steady boats like Basha. Some, like Faegl, are leaves, so delicate, dry, and vulnerable that it seems at any moment they might be whisked away by a strong gust. And one day, a sudden wind did knock Faegl to the ground. Others, like Gita, are birds, small and sharp-tongued. Quick, witty, vain, flirtatious, they are very fond of singing and dancing. They once were and will always be pretty girls. This is one of their survival strategies. Boats, leaves, or birds, at first their faces look alike. Individual features are blurred by dentures, heavy bifocals, and webs of wrinkles. The men are not so easy to categorize. As a group, they are quieter, more uniform, less immediately outstanding except for the few who are distinctive individuals, clearly distinguishable as leaders.

As the morning wears on, the benches fill. Benches are attached back to back, one side facing the ocean, one side the boardwalk. The people on the ocean side swivel around to face their friends, the boardwalk, and the Center.

Bench behavior is highly stylized. The half-dozen or so benches immediately to the north and south of the Center are the territory of the members, segregated by sex and conversation topic. The men's benches are devoted to abstract, ideological concerns—philosophical debate, politics, religion, and economics. The women's benches are given more to talk about immediate, personal matters—children, food, health, neighbors, love affairs, scandals, and "managing." Men and women talk about Israel and its welfare, about being a Jew and about Center politics. On the benches, reputations are made and broken, controversies explored, leaders selected, factions formed and dissolved. Here is the outdoor dimension of Center life, like a village plaza, a focus of protracted, intense sociability.

The surrounding scene rarely penetrates the invisible, pulsing membrane of the Center community. The old people are too absorbed in their own talk to attend the setting. Surfers, sunbathers, children, dogs, bicyclists, winos, hippies, voyeurs, photographers, panhandlers, artists, junkies, roller skaters, peddlers, and police are omnipresent all year round. Every social class, age, race, and sexual preference is represented. Jesus cults, Hare Krishna parades, sidewalk preachers jostle steel bands and itinerant musicians. As colorful and flamboyant as the scene is by day, it is as dangerous by night. Muggings, theft, rape, harassment, and occasional murders make it a perilous neighborhood for the old people after dark.

Farther up the boardwalk other elderly Jews stake out their territory on benches and picnic tables used for chess, pinochle, poker, and Mah-Jongg. The Center members do not regard them as "serious" or "cultured" people, while they, in turn, consider the Center elderly too political or religious, too inclined to be "joiners," for their taste. Still other old Jews periodically appear on the boardwalk selling Marxist periodicals, Socialist tracts, collecting money for Mexican laborers, circulating petitions to abolish capital punishment. For them, the Center people are too politically conservative. All the elderly Jews in the neighborhood are Eastern European in origin. All are multilingual. Hebrew is brought out for punctuating debates with definitive learned points, usually by the men. Russian or Polish are more used for songs, stories, poems, and reminiscences. But Yiddish binds these diverse people together, the beloved *mama-loshen** of their childhood. It is Yiddish that is used for the most emotional discussions. Despite their ideological differences, most of these people know each other well, having lived here at the beach for two and three decades.

Signs of what was once a much larger, more complete Yiddish ghetto remain along the boardwalk. Two storefront synagogues are left, where only a few years ago there were a dozen. There is a delicatessen and a Jewish bakery. Before there were many kosher butcher stores and little markets. Only three Jewish board-and-care homes and four large hotels are left to house the elderly. The four thousand or so elderly Jews in the neighborhood must find accommodations in small, rented rooms and apartments within walking distance of the Center. A belt, roughly five miles long and a mile wide, constitutes the limits of the effective community of these Eastern European immigrants, nearly all of whom are now in their middle eighties and up. Several special organizations in the area meet some of their present needs—a secular senior citizen club operated by the city, an outreach city- and state-funded social service center, a women's private political-cultural club, a hot-meals-for-the-elderly service held at a local school. At the edge of the community, still within walking distance of the Center, are several expensive apartments and board-and-care homes (known as "residential facilities"); these accommodate the handful of members who are relatively well-off.

A decade ago, census figures suggest that as many as ten thousand elderly Eastern European Jews lived in the neighborhood. Then Yiddish culture flourished. Groups such as the Workmen's Circle, Emma Lazarus Club, women's philanthropic and religious organizations, various Zionist and Socialist groups were plentiful. Poetry and discussion groups often met in people's homes. There was a dance hall and a choral society. Then, it was said that the community had "the *schonste*† Yiddishkeit outside of New York." Around thirty years ago, Jews from all over the country began to immigrate to the beach community, particularly those with health problems and newly retired. Seeking a benign climate, fellow Jews, and moderately priced housing, they brought their savings and small pensions and came to live near the ocean. Collective life was and still is especially intense in this community because there is no automobile traffic on the boardwalk. Here is a place where people may meet, gather, talk, and stroll, simple but basic and precious activities that the elderly in particular can enjoy here all year round.

*Mother tongue.
†Most beautiful.

In the late 1950s, an urban development program resulted in the displacement of between four and six thousand of these senior citizens in a very short period. It was a devastating blow to the culture. "A second Holocaust," Basha called it. "It destroyed our shtetl life all over again.* Soon after the urban development project began, a marina was constructed at the southern end of the boardwalk. Property values soared. Older people could not pay taxes and many lost their homes. Rents quadrupled. Old hotels and apartments were torn down, and housing became the single most serious problem for the elderly who desperately wanted to remain in the area. While several thousand have managed to hang on, no new members are moving into the area because of the housing problem. Their Yiddish world, built up over a thirty-year period, is dying and complete extinction is imminent. Perhaps it will last another five or at the most ten years. Whenever a Center member leaves, everyone is acutely aware that there will be no replacements. The sense of cultural doom coincides with awareness of approaching individual death. "When I go out of here, it will be in a box or to the old folks' home. I couldn't say which is worse," Basha said. "We've only got a few more years here, all of us. It would be good if we could stay till the end. We had a protest march the other day, when they took down the old Miramar Hotel. I made up a sign. It said, 'Let my people stay.' "

Yet the community is not a dreary place and the Center members not a depressed group. The sense of doom, by some miraculous process, functions to heighten and animate their life. Every moment matters. There is no time for deception, trivia, or decorum. Life at the Center is passionate, almost melodramatic. Inside, ordinary concerns and mundane interchanges are strangely intense, quickly heating to outburst. The emotional urgency often seems to have little to do with content. This caldronlike quality is perhaps due to the elders' proximity to death and the realization that their remaining days are few. They want to be seen and heard from, before it is too late. Fiercely, they compete with each other for limited supplies of time and attention. Perhaps it is due to the members' extreme dependence on each other; though strongly attached, they are ambivalent about living so closely with others brought into contact with them more by circumstance than choice. Perhaps it is because these elderly people enjoy the strong flood of energy and adrenaline released in intense interactions, assuring them that they are still alive and active.

In spite of its isolation, the beach community is well-known in the city, primarily because of its ethnic distinctiveness and longevity. It is small, stable, cohesive, delimited, and homogeneous in terms of the people's cultural and historical background, an urban ghetto—closed, encapsulated, and self-contained. Relations between the older beach citizens and the broader urban and Jewish worlds are attenuated and episodic. Periodically, various charitable organizations and synagogues offer the Center services and aid, for it is well-known that the majority of old people are isolated and living on small, fixed incomes, below national poverty levels. But Center folk are not easy people to help.

*The word *Holocaust*, referring in this setting to Hitler's destruction of six million Jews, mostly Eastern European, was not used casually by these people.

Pride and autonomy among them are passions. They see themselves as givers, not takers, and devote enormous effort toward supporting others more needy than they, particularly in Israel. These elders, with few exceptions, are cut off from their family and children. From time to time, relatives visit them or take them back to their homes for holidays or to spend the night, but on a day-to-day basis, the old people effectively are on their own. They miss their family but cherish their independence.

As the numbers of such people shrink and the neighborhood changes, the Aliyah Center becomes more and more important to its members. Sponsored by a city-wide philanthropic Jewish organization, it is maintained as a day center that emphasizes "secular Judaism." Officially, about three hundred members pay dues of six dollars a year, but these figures do not reflect the actual importance of the Center to the community. Many more use it than join, and they use it all day, every day. The Center is more halfway house than voluntary association, making it possible for hundreds of people to continue living alone in the open community, despite their physical and economic difficulties. Daily hot meals are provided there, and continuous diverse programs are offered—cultural events, discussions, classes of all kinds, along with social affairs, religious ceremonies, celebrations of life crises, anniversaries, birthdays, memorials, and occasional weddings. The gamut of political and social processes found in larger societies are well-developed in Center life. Here is an entire, though miniature, society, a Blakeian "world in a grain of sand," the setting for an intricate and rich culture, made up of bits and pieces of people's common history.

Center culture is in some respects thin and fragile, but its very existence must be seen as a major accomplishment, emerging spontaneously as a result of two conditions that characterize the members: continuities between past and present circumstance, and social isolation. Several marked similarities existed between the circumstances of members' childhood and old age. They had grown up in small, intimate Jewish communities, cohesive, ethnocentric, surrounded by indifferent and often hostile outsiders. Previously, in Eastern Europe, they had been marginal people, even pariahs, as they were now. They had strong early training in resourcefulness and opportunities to develop sound survival strategies. Then, as now, they had been poor, politically impotent, and physically insecure. Then, as now, they turned to each other and their shared Yiddishkeit for sustenance, constituting what Irving Howe has called a "ragged kingdom of the spirit."[2] It was not a great shock for these people to find themselves once more in difficult circumstances, for they had never given up their conviction that life was a struggle, that gains entailed losses, that joy and sorrow were inseparable. They knew how to pinch pennies, how to make do, and how to pay attention to those worse off than they and thereby feel useful and needed. They had come to America seeking another life and found that it, too, provided some fulfillments, some disappointments. And thus, they were now not demoralized or helpless.

---

[2]Irving Howe, *The World of Our Fathers*, p. 8.

Their culture was able to emerge as fully as it did because of the elders' isolation from family and the outside world, ironically, the very condition that causes them much grief. Yet, by this separation, they were freed to find their own way, just as their children had been. Now they could indulge their passion for things of the past, enjoy Yiddishkeit without fear of being stigmatized as "not American." With little concern for public opinion, with only each other for company, they revitalized selected features of their common history to meet their present needs, adding and amending it without concern for consistency, priority, or "authenticity." It had taken three decades for this culture to develop to its present state of complexity, now a truly organic, if occasionally disorderly and illogical amalgam of forms and sentiments, memories and wishes, rotating around a few stable, strong symbols and premises. Claude Lévi-Strauss had used the word *bricolage*[3] to describe the process through which myths are constructed in preliterate societies. Odds and ends, fragments offered up by chance or the environment—almost anything will do—are taken up by a group and incorporated into a tale, used by a people to explain themselves and their world. No intrinsic order or system has dictated the materials employed. In such an inelegant fashion does the *bricoleur* or handyman meet his needs.

Center culture was such a work of bricolage. Robust and impudently eclectic, it shifted and stretched to meet immediate needs—private, collective, secular, and sacred. Thus, when a Center Yiddish History class graduated, a unique ceremony was designed that pasted together the local event with an analogous, historical counterpart, thereby enlarging and authenticating the improvised, contemporary affair. And the traditional Sabbath ceremony was rearranged to allow as many people as possible to participate—making speeches, singing songs, reading poems, taking into account the members' acute need for visibility and attention. Among them, two or even three women instead of one were required to light the Sabbath candles—one singing the blessing in Hebrew, one in Yiddish, one putting the match to the wick. Similarly, Center folk redefined the secular New Year's Eve, holding their dance a full day and a half before the conventional date, since this made it possible for them to get home before dark and to hire their favorite musicians at lower rates. These improvisations were entirely authentic. Somehow midday December 30 became the real New Year's Eve and the later, public celebration seemed unconvincing by comparison. In all this no explicit plan or internal integration could be detected. Cultures are, after all, collective, untidy assemblages, authenticated by belief and agreement, focused only in crisis, systematized after the fact. Like a quilt, Center life was made up of many small pieces sewn together by necessity, intended to be serviceable and to last. It was sufficient for the people's remaining years.

The vitality and flexibility of the Center culture was especially impressive in view of the organization's meager budget. Enough money was available only to pay for a few programs and the salary of the director, Abe, who had devoted

---

[3]Claude Lévi-Strauss, *The Savage Mind*, p. 17.

himself to these elderly people for fourteen years. Sometimes he was a surrogate son, sometimes a worrying, scolding, protecting parent to them. Thirty years younger than most members, Abe was a second-generation American, from the same background as they. A social worker by training, he watched over the elders' health, listened to their complaints, mediated their quarrels, teased and dominated them when they lost heart, and defended them against external threats, insisting to them and the outside world that they survive. Without his dedication, it was unlikely that they would have been able to continue for so long and so well, living alone into advanced old age in an open, inhospitable setting.

I sat on the benches outside the Center and thought about how strange it was to be back in the neighborhood where sixteen years before I had lived and for a time had been a social worker with elderly citizens on public relief. Then the area was known as "Oshini Beach." The word *shini* still made me cringe. As a child I had been taunted with it. Like many second-generation Americans, I wasn't sure what being a Jew meant. When I was a child our family had avoided the words *Jew* and *Yid*. We were confused and embarrassed about our background. In public we lowered our voices when referring to "our people" or "one of us." My grandparents had also emigrated from an Eastern European shtetl as young people. Like so many of the Center folk, they, too, wanted their children to be Americans above all and were ashamed of being "greenhorns." They spoke to my parents in Yiddish and were answered in English. None of the children or grandchildren in the family received any religious education, yet they carried a strong if ambivalent identity as Jews. This identity took the form of fierce pride and defensiveness during the Holocaust, but even then did not result in any of us developing a clear conception of how to live in terms of our ethnic membership.

I had made no conscious decision to explore my roots or clarify the meaning of my origins. I was one of several anthropologists at the University of Southern California engaged in an examination of Ethnicity and Aging. At first I planned to study elderly Chicanos, since I had previously done fieldwork in Mexico. But in the early 1970s in urban America, ethnic groups were not welcoming curious outsiders, and people I approached kept asking me, "Why work with us? Why don't you study your own kind?" This was a new idea to me. I had not been trained for such a project. Anthropologists conventionally investigate exotic, remote, preliterate societies. But such groups are increasingly unavailable and often inhospitable. As a result, more and more anthropologists are finding themselves working at home these days. Inevitably, this creates problems with objectivity and identification, and I anticipated that I, too, would have my share of them if I studied the Center folk. But perhaps there would be advantages. There was no way that I could have anticipated the great impact of the study on my life, nor its duration. I intended to spend a year with them. In fact, I was with them continuously for two years (1973–1974, 1975–1976) and periodically for two more. In the beginning, I spent a great deal of time agonizing about how to label what I was doing—was it anthropology or a personal quest? I never fully resolved the question. I used many conventional anthropological methods and asked many typical questions, but when I had finished, I found my descriptions did not resemble most anthropological writings. Still, the results of the study would certainly have been different had I not been an anthropologist by training.

Sitting in the sun and contemplating the passing parade on the boardwalk that morning in 1973, I wondered how I should begin this study. At eleven-thirty the benches began to empty as old people entered the Center for a "Hot Kosher Meal—Nutritious—65¢," then a new program provided by state and private funds. Inside there was barely enough room to accommodate between 100 and 150 people who regularly ate there. The Center was only a simple, shabby hall, the size of a small school auditorium, empty except for a tiny stage at one end with a kitchen behind it, and a little area partitioned off at the other end, used for a library and office. The front window was entirely covered by hand-lettered signs in Yiddish and English announcing current events:

TODAY AT 2:00
Jewish History Class.—Teacher, Clara Shapiro
Very educational.

SUNDAY AT 1:00
Special Event: Films on Israel
Refreshments. Come. Enjoy.

MONDAY AT 3:00
Gerontology Class.—Teacher, Sy Greenberg.
Informative. Bring your questions.

TUESDAY AT 10:00
Rabbi Cohen talks on Succoth.
Beautiful and enlightening.

Over the front door hung another handmade sign, written and painted by one of the members: "To the extent that here at the Center we are able to be ourselves and to that extent Self feels good to us." The walls were adorned with pictures of assorted Yiddish writers, scholars, and Zionists. Two large colored photographs of the Western Wall in Jerusalem and of Golda Meir hung above a bust of Moshe Dayan. Seniors' arts and crafts were displayed in a glass case. Their paintings and drawings hung along one wall, depicting shtetl scenes and household activities associated with sacred rituals—the lighting of the Sabbath candles, the housewife baking the Sabbath loaf, a father teaching his children their religious lessons, and the like. Portraits of rabbis, tailors, scholars hung there, too, along with symbols of Jewish festivals and holidays— a papier-mâché *dreidel,* and cardboard *menorah,* a *shofar.** A large, wooden Star of David illuminated by a string of Christmas tree lights was prominently displayed. Framed certificates of commendation and thanks from Israeli recipi-

---

*A dreidel is a top used for a Chanukah game; a menorah is the branched candelabra also used for Chanukah; a shofar is the Ram's Horn blown on the Jewish New Year.

ents of the elders' donations hung alongside photographs of kibbutzim children to whom the Center elders had contributed support. The wall opposite bore a collective self-portrait in the form of a room-length mural, designed and painted by the members, portraying their common journey from the past to the present in several colorful, strong, and simple scenes: a picture of a boatload of immigrants arriving at Ellis Island, a shtetl marketplace, a New York street scene, a shtetl street scene, and a group of picketers bearing signs, "Better Conditions First," "We Shall Fight for Our Rights," "Power and Justice for the People," and one that simply said, "Protest Treatment." The last sequence rendered the elders at present, seated on benches along the boardwalk and celebrating the Sabbath inside the Center. Over the small stage, the line from the Old Testament was lettered, "Behold How Good It Is for Brethren to Dwell Together in Unity," and opposite, a prominent placard that read, "Cast Me Not Out in My Old Age But Let Me Live Each Day as a New Life." More than decoration, these visual displays were the people's icons, constituting a symbolic depiction—the group's commentary on itself—by reference to its sources of identity, in particular, its common history. This use of symbols pointed to a community that was highly conscious of itself and its own distinctive ideology.

I followed the crowd inside and sat at the back of the warm, noisy room redolent with odors of fish and chicken soup, wondering how to introduce myself. It was decided for me. A woman sat down next to me who I soon learned was Basha. In a leisurely fashion, she appraised me. Uncomfortable, I smiled and said hello.

"You are not hungry?" she asked.

"No, thank you, I'm not," I answered.

"So, what brings you here?"

"I'm from the University of Southern California. I'm looking for a place to study how older Jews live in the city."

At the word *university*, she moved closer and nodded approvingly. "Are you Jewish?" she asked.

"Yes, I am."

"Are you married?" she persisted.

"Yes."

"You got children?"

"Yes, two boys, four and eight," I answered.

"Are you teaching them to be Jews?"

"I'm trying."

"So what do you want with us here?" asked Basha.

"Well, I want to understand your life, find out what it's like to be older and Jewish, what makes Jews different from other older people, if anything. I'm an anthropologist and we usually study people's cultures and societies. I think I would like to learn about this culture."

"And what will you do for us?" she asked me.

"I could teach a class in something people here are interested in—how older people live in other places, perhaps."

"Are you qualified to do this?" Basha shot me a suspicious glance.

"I have a Ph.D. and have taught in the university for a number of years, so I suppose I am qualified."

"You are a professor then? A little bit of a thing like you?" To my relief, she chuckled amiably. Perhaps I had passed my first rite of entrance into the group.

"Faegl, Faegl, come here!" Basha shouted to a friend across the room. Faegl picked her way neatly over to where we were sitting. She was wiry and slight as Basha was heavy and grand. "Faegl, sit down. Faegl, this here is——What did you say your name was? Barbara? This is Barbara. She is a professor and wants to study us. What do you think of that?"

"Why not? I wouldn't object. She could learn a lot. Are you Jewish?" Faegl leaned past Basha and carefully peered at me over her bifocals.

Basha accurately recited my qualifications and family characteristics. Faegl wasted no time. She moved over to sit next to me and began her interrogation.

"So you are an anthropologist. Then you study people's origins, yes? Tell me, is it true that human beings began in Africa once upon a time?"

"Many scholars think so," I answered.

"Ha! And once upon a time this country belonged to the Indians. That's right?" she went on.

"Yes, certainly," I answered.

"Now a lot of people don't think it's right that we took away from them the country just because we were stronger, yes?"

"Yes." I was growing wary, sensing an entrapment.

Faegl continued systematically. "So this business about putting all the Arabs out of Israel because we said we had our origins there, maybe that's not right either? It is not so simple, is it?"

"No, no. Certainly it is not simple," I answered.

"So Bashaleh, what do you say now?" Faegl asked her. "She's a professor and she says maybe it's not right. Like I told you, even from the Arabs we can't take away the land."

Basha looked at me closely while Faegl waited.

"You don't believe in *Eretz Yisroel?*"* she asked me. "You are some kind of anti-Semite?"

QUESTIONS FOR "SO WHAT DO YOU WANT FROM US HERE?" BY BARBARA MYERHOFF

Talking About the Text

1. This text is an excerpt from a long report by an anthropologist. This sort of report is called an *ethnography.* Judging from this excerpt, what do you think an ethnography *does?* What is the anthropologist's purpose in writing the report?

*The land of Israel; the Promised Land.

2. How does Myerhoff's purpose differ from that of traditional anthropologists? What does she mean when she wonders if this is "anthropology or a personal quest"?
3. What are some of the specific problems that these elderly people face?

Exploring Issues

1. What does this case study suggest about the idea of American society as a "melting pot"? Have these people "melted" into American culture? Explain your answer with specific references to the text.
2. Some people claim that rather than being a "melting pot," the United States is actually a "salad bowl." What do these two metaphors suggest about American culture, and which one applies best to the situations described by Myerhoff in this excerpt from *Number Our Days?*
3. What are some positive aspects of living in a closely knit ethnic community such as the one described in this excerpt? Are there any problems associated with this lifestyle?
4. Can we consider people aged 65 and older to constitute a "culture" in some extended use of that term? Why or why not?

Writing Assignments

1. Drawing on your own knowledge of a specific ethnic community (e.g., Chinese, Italian, or other), write an essay in which you explore the positive and negative aspects of maintaining ethnic communities such as the one described by Barbara Myerhoff. Describe the community with which you are familiar and use this case to illustrate your general ideas.
2. Write an essay in which you explore some of the issues associated with aging. Draw on the text for ideas, but consider also the people you know, such as elderly relatives and neighbors. Use description and narration to develop your essay; that is, describe people and narrate events that illustrate your general ideas.

Reading 9

The American Dream and the Politics of Inclusion

Mario Cuomo

Mario Cuomo is a Democrat and the current governor of the state of New York. The son of Italian immigrants, Cuomo writes about American immigrants from a very personal perspective, arguing that we must maintain an open door policy on immigration and recognize the strengths that immigrants can bring to a relatively young nation.

With all the high points and low points, expansions and contractions this astounding country of ours has experienced in the last 210 years, one theme in our history has been constant; one thread has tied together more than two centuries of striving: the struggle to include.

For the past 210 years we have taken the unprecedented boast of our Declaration of Independence—the promise of equality, life, liberty and the pursuit of happiness—and struggled to extend it to every American. That challenge and opportunity have always been there, driving events in period after period of our history. It is there in the first lines of the Declaration of Independence—in the idea that governments are created to secure those basic elements of what we now call the American dream for every citizen. This might be called the "politics of inclusion."

It is a politics that never divides but unites; that never rejects but embraces; that never stoops to playing one side against another—group against group, state against state, region against region. The politics of inclusion rejoices with those who have earned success but is forever taking up the cause of those who are not yet included—the outsider, the immigrant, the oppressed. It is forever reminding those of us who already possess some share of the American dream that the dream is not yet fulfilled, the promise of our founding fathers not yet complete, until everyone has been included.

What I have discovered is that each individual's effort to fulfill the American dream is essentially the story of millions of Americans, whether they came here by way of Plymouth Rock or Galveston, Ellis Island or the Los Angeles airport. It was, in some ways, my own story too. And that makes me marvel at this amazing place, America, all over again. Like millions of others, I am privileged to be a first-generation American. My mother and father came to this country more than 60 years ago with nothing but their hopes—without education, skills or wealth. The opportunity given them here to lift themselves through hard work enabled them to raise a family. My mother lived to see her youngest child become chief executive of one of the greatest states in the greatest nation in the only world we know.

Like millions of other children of immigrants, I know the strength that immigrants can bring. I know the richness of a society that allows us to enjoy a whole new culture without requiring us to surrender the one into which our parents were born. I know the miraculous power of this place that helps people rise up from poverty to security, and even affluence, in the course of a single lifetime. With generations of other children of immigrants, I know about equality and opportunity and unity, in a special way.

I don't think the view of America from South Jamaica, Queens, the New York City neighborhood where I grew up, was much different from the view available in any of the hundreds of neighborhoods throughout the country where immigrants of every nationality began their pursuit of the American dream. I would guess that in each place there was, and is, the same aching to belong—the sense that we could be a part of this place, if we wanted to work hard enough, and the knowledge that indeed we would have to work very hard because our people weren't born to this place, this land. And I think I know how hard it was, and still is, for children going to school where the dominant language was not the language of their home, where the words sounded hard-edged and tight compared to the rolling, rounded rhythms of their father's and mother's tongue—whether that language was Italian, Spanish, Russian or Chinese.

I think I know, because that language sounded so different for me from the world of words of South Jamaica's "Italian blocks," where passion, pride and powerlessness all lived together, and people talked with their hands and hearts.

And I know how, from time to time, all this can be challenged by the misguided, by the shortsighted and the unkind, by contempt that masks itself as humor, by all the casual or conscious bigotry that must keep the American people vigilant. We have heard such voices again recently: Italians are not politically popular, they say. Or Catholics will have a problem. Or more generally, he has an "ethnic problem."

We hear the familiar word "wop" again. "We oftentimes refer to people of Italian descent as 'wops,' " one public figure recently proclaimed unabashedly. Now, given the unbroken string of opportunity and good fortune provided me by this great country, I might simply have ignored these references. I could easily have let the words pass as inconsequential. But the words took on significance because they were heard far beyond my home or my block or even my state. They were heard by others who remembered times of their own when words stung and menaced them and their people.

Cruel words that wound an entire people raise a question about our fundamental system of American values. Are there really so many who have never heard the sweet sound of reason and fairness? Do so many not understand the beauty and power of this place that they could make of the tint of your skin, the sex you were born to or the vowels of your name an impediment to progress in this land of opportunity?

I don't believe most Americans share in this divisive point of view, so I publicly requested a response to the voice of division. "It is the voice of ignorance," I claimed, "and I challenge you to show me otherwise." In no time at all the answer came back from the American people. As if in unison, people from across the nation responded the same way: "Of course it's wrong to judge a person by the place where his forebears came from. Of course that would violate all that we stand for, fairness and common sense. It shouldn't even have been brought up. It shouldn't even have been a cause for discussion."

I agree. It should not have been. But it was. And the discussion is now concluded, with the answer I was sure of and the answer I am proud of as an American, the answer Abraham Lincoln would have given: You will rise or fall on your merits as a person and the quality of your work. All else is distraction. Lincoln believed, with every fiber of his being, that this place, America, could offer a dream to all people, different from any other in the annals of history. It was a place more generous, more compassionate and more inclusive than any other. No one better understood our sturdiness, the ability of most of us to make it on our own given the chance. But at the same time, no one knew better the idea of family, the idea that unless we helped one another, there were some who would never make it.

One person climbs the ladder of personal ambition, reaches his dream and then turns—and pulls the ladder up. Another reaches the place he has sought, turns and reaches down for the person behind him. It was that process of turning and reaching down, that commitment to keep lifting people up the ladder, that defined the American character, stamping us forever with a mission that reached even beyond our borders to embrace the world.

As individuals, as a people, we are still reaching up, for a better job, a better education, even for the stars. What other people on Earth have ever claimed a quality of character that resided not in a way of speaking, dressing, dancing or praying, but in an idea? What other people on Earth have ever refused to set the definitions of their identity by anything other than that idea?

No, we have not learned quickly or easily that the dream of America endures only so long as we keep faith with the struggle to include. We cannot rest until the promise of equality and opportunity embraces every region, race, religion, nationality and class, until it includes "the penniless beginner" and the "poor man seeking his chance."

We reached out—hesitantly at times, sometimes only after great struggle— but always we reached out, to include impoverished immigrants, the farmers and the factory workers, women, the disabled. To all those whose only assets were their great expectations, America found ways to meet those expectations—and to create new ones. We provided the opportunities for generations of hardworking people to move into the middle class and beyond.

We created a society as open and free as any on Earth. Always, we have extended the promise. We have moved toward our declared purpose as a people: "to form a more perfect union," to overcome all that divides us because we believe the ancient wisdom that Lincoln believed—"A house divided against itself cannot stand."

Step by step, our embrace grows wider, our beliefs stronger. What do we believe? We believe most of all in mutuality: the sharing of benefits and burdens; a recognition that we are—all of us—bound to one another in need and in opportunity. I reject the preaching that we must accept new limitations—that America can no longer afford to include everyone. And I reject the belief that what was possible for the Cuomos and the families of newcomers 10 generations before them is no longer possible now.

I reject the idea that America has used herself up in the effort to help outsiders in, and that now she must sit back exhausted, watching people play the cards fate has dealt them. It would be a desecration of our belief and an act of ingratitude to end the struggle for inclusion because it is over for some of us. We have no right to be content, to close the door to others now that we are safely inside.

We must, instead, continue to live the truth, to go forward, painful step by painful step, enlarging the greatness of this nation with patient confidence in the ultimate justice of the people.

QUESTIONS FOR "THE AMERICAN DREAM AND THE POLITICS OF INCLUSION" BY MARIO CUOMO

Talking About the Text

1. In the title of his essay, Cuomo links two major concepts, the "American Dream" and the "politics of inclusion." What is the "American Dream" and what does Cuomo mean by the "politics of inclusion"? How does Cuomo link these two concepts?
2. Would you judge Cuomo's primary rhetorical purpose to be one of *informing* or one of *persuading* his readers? On what basis can you make this judgment?
3. Why does Cuomo emphasize his personal history as a first-generation American? How does this affect Cuomo's persuasiveness as a writer?
4. How does Cuomo's essay compare with "Along the Tortilla Curtain" by Pete Hamill? In what sense do Cuomo and Hamill agree? What are some differences in the ways that these two authors approach the subject of immigration?

Exploring Issues

1. Why would Cuomo and others find immigration to be an *issue?* Why do some people wish to limit the number of immigrants who come to the United States? Why does Cuomo disagree with these people?
2. In his essay, Cuomo refers to Abraham Lincoln's hope that in the United

States of America "you will rise or fall on your merits as a person and the quality of your work." Do you believe that this is true for all people in the United States today? Why or why not?

Writing Assignments

1. Talk to some people who are themselves immigrants to the United States. Ask them about their reasons for emigrating, their visions of the American Dream, and their opinions about individual success in the United States. Write an essay in which you describe the people you interviewed, the discussions you had with them, and some conclusions you can draw as a result of these interviews.

2. Imagine that you had to leave the United States (for economic, political, or personal reasons). Write an essay in which you explain which country you would choose to immigrate to and why. Include in your essay a discussion of some of the problems you might encounter in immigrating to that particular country.

CHAPTER 1 EXTENDED WRITING ASSIGNMENTS

1-1. Write an essay in which you explore some of the issues and/or problems associated with the "American Dream." Before you begin writing your essay, do the following suggested prewriting assignments.
   a. Write down your own (preliminary) definition of the American Dream.
   b. Read some or all of the following texts:
      "The Girl Who Wouldn't Sing" by Kit Yuen Quan
      "The American Dream and the Politics of Inclusion" by Mario Cuomo
      "Along the Tortilla Curtain" by Pete Hamill
      "What Happened to the Family?" by Jerrold Footlick and Elizabeth Leonard
      "True Blue" by Lynn Darling
      "I Have a Dream" by Martin Luther King, Jr.
   c. Identify some issues related to the American Dream and list them from most to least important.

1-2. Obtain a copy of a currently used high school textbook on American history. Keeping in mind Ronald Takaki's claim about the representations of minorities in our histories, examine this book carefully for the ways in which minorities are represented. How do the authors deal with the histories of minorities in the United States? Are there special chapters or subheadings used to cue readers? How are women represented? In your written report, provide a brief outline of the entire book and explain how the histories of certain minorities (e.g., Chinese Americans) are presented. If you see some obvious gaps, explain what you find missing and why it would be important to include this information. Consider also the tone—that is, the authors' stance—toward particular minorities. Finally, examine the extent to which minorities are allowed to speak for themselves—in their own voices (in long quotations, poems, songs, and stories).

Chapter
2

Facing New Worlds

*C*onfronting change and making transitions involve risk and a fair degree of discomfort, but these experiences can also create opportunities for growth and a heightened awareness of self and others. Having faced the challenge of a new school, a new town, or a new job, we can each recall the uneasy feeling of being a "new kid on the block," a "greenhorn," of not knowing quite how to respond to unfamiliar people and circumstances. Although change and growth are universally present in human cultures, the opportunities are multiplied in a society as ethnically diverse and technologically advanced as ours. Not only have we welcomed new immigrants, but we have also welcomed advances in technology that have radically transformed our society; we now have easy access to other people and places, but we also have changing perspectives on our roles and responsibilities within our own society. In fact, we are all continually facing new worlds as we struggle to adapt to a culture that is virtually defined by change.

In this chapter, we invite you to compare your own experiences with those of others who confront new cultures and new social or personal situations. As you will undoubtedly discover, not all change is for the better; the people represented in these stories and essays often face dilemmas and hardships that you and I will never experience. In coming to understand the experiences of others, you may discover opportunities to confront your own attitudes and beliefs. For example, while you may not have met an undocumented U.S. resident, the news media has certainly given all of us ample opportunity to form negative opinions and stereotypes of "illegal aliens"; while reading some of the selections in this chapter, you may wish to consider your own views of others as well as their views of you.

We begin the chapter with an experience familiar to all: initial encounters with the world of work and choices about jobs and careers. With his own brand of wry humor, Russell Baker takes us back to his childhood and his struggles with an ambitious mother. In this autobiographical essay, Baker describes his feelings about selling magazines as an entry to the world of business. In a more sobering account of adolescence, "I'm Listening As Hard As I Can," Terry Galloway describes her painful transition from the hearing world to the world of the deaf. Here we discover the effects that a physical handicap can have on the personal and social development of a young woman.

While the stories of Russell Baker and Terry Galloway are autobiographical and therefore intensely personal, the case of Edmund Perry is represented from the perspective of a journalist. In "The Two Worlds of Edmund Perry," Robert Sam Anson traces the events that led up to the death of Eddie Perry, a young black student from Harlem who attended school in a predominantly white preparatory school. Here, we discover the difficulties faced by a young black who is given a chance to "assimilate" into Anglo culture. In this case, the attempt to shift in and out of acutely different social worlds appears to have contributed to the death of a young man whose life was filled with promise.

Shifting social roles are also examined by Ellen Goodman in her essay, "The New Middleground." No longer content with the traditional definitions of male and female roles, many women are accepting new challenges while seeking a psychological distance from "feminism" and the women's movement. Through a series of interviews, Goodman uncovers the bases for some of these ambivalent attitudes. Another, very important type of transitional experience is that of the newly arrived immigrant here in the United States. Why are so many people still seeking to settle here? What motivates them and what do they actually find on arrival? Pete Hamill examines the experiences and aspirations of those who cross the border illegally in "Along the Tortilla Curtain." In response to those who fear the influx of Hispanics and Hispanic cultures to the United States, or the "browning of America," Hamill argues that undocumented workers take on jobs that most others decline and therefore provide essential services for the maintenance of our economy.

After considering the issue of immigration on this general basis, you may examine the lives of individuals who have come to this country, all fictional characters meant to represent the experiences of real people. In "Where Do You Sleep?" Frank X. Gaspar portrays a man visiting a border town and observing the border crossings that occur there routinely. In "One Holy Night," Sandra Cisneros introduces a young Mexican woman who discovers her own sexuality and confronts the prospect of motherhood. And in "The Mambo Kings," Oscar Hijuelos describes the adventures of two young Cubans who hope to find fame and fortune as musicians in New York City.

Each of the selections in this chapter provides a glimpse of the inner conflicts or the social realities of people confronting new experiences and new environments. As you read these essays and stories, you may identify with some kinds of transition more than with others. However, we often learn most from that which is least familiar. Even those experiences that we have not actually had ourselves may provide occasions for self-reflection and for deeper insight into our own lives and our own worldviews.

Reading 10

From *Growing Up*

Russell Baker

Russell Baker is a nationally acclaimed journalist whose "Observer" column
has appeared in *The New York Times* since 1962. He has won the George
Polk Award for commentary, the Pulitzer prize for distinguished commentary,
and the 1983 Pulitzer Prize for biography for *Growing Up,* from which the
following selection is taken. In this chapter of *Growing Up,* Baker describes
his introduction to the world of work, some related difficulties, and his
discovery of writing as a potential career.

I began working in journalism when I was eight years old. It was my mother's
idea. She wanted me to "make something" of myself and, after a level-headed
appraisal of my strengths, decided I had better start young if I was to have any
chance of keeping up with the competition.

The flaw in my character which she had already spotted was lack of "gumption." My idea of a perfect afternoon was lying in front of the radio rereading my
favorite Big Little Book, *Dick Tracy Meets Stooge Viller.* My mother despised
inactivity. Seeing me having a good time in respose, she was powerless to hide
her disgust. "You've got no more gumption than a bump on a log," she said.
"Get out in the kitchen and help Doris do those dirty dishes."

My sister Doris, though two years younger than I, had enough gumption
for a dozen people. She positively enjoyed washing dishes, making beds, and
cleaning the house. When she was only seven she could carry a piece of short-
weighted cheese back to the A&P, threaten the manager with legal action, and
come back triumphantly with the full quarter-pound we'd paid for and a few
ounces extra thrown in for forgiveness. Doris could have made something of
herself if she hadn't been a girl. Because of this defect, however, the best she
could hope for was a career as a nurse or schoolteacher, the only work that
capable females were considered up to in those days.

This must have saddened my mother, this twist of fate that had allocated all
the gumption to the daughter and left her with a son who was content with Dick
Tracy and Stooge Viller. If disappointed, though, she wasted no energy on self-
pity. She would make me make something of myself whether I wanted to or not.
"The Lord helps those who help themselves," she said. That was the way her
mind worked.

She was realistic about the difficulty. Having sized up the material the Lord had given her to mold, she didn't overestimate what she could do with it. She didn't insist that I grow up to be President of the United States.

Fifty years ago parents still asked boys if they wanted to grow up to be President, and asked it not jokingly but seriously. Many parents who were hardly more than paupers still believed their sons could do it. Abraham Lincoln had done it. We were only sixty-five years from Lincoln. Many a grandfather who walked among us could remember Lincoln's time. Men of grandfatherly age were the worst for asking if you wanted to grow up to be President. A surprising number of little boys said yes and meant it.

I was asked many times myself. No, I would say, I didn't want to grow up to be President. My mother was present during one of these interrogations. An elderly uncle, having posed the usual question and exposed my lack of interest in the Presidency, asked, "Well, what *do* you want to be when you grow up?"

I loved to pick through trash piles and collect empty bottles, tin cans with pretty labels, and discarded magazines. The most desirable job on earth sprang instantly to mind. "I want to be a garbage man." I said.

My uncle smiled, but my mother had seen the first distressing evidence of a bump budding on a log. "Have a little gumption, Russell," she said. Her calling me Russell was a signal of unhappiness. When she approved of me I was always "Buddy."

When I turned eight years old she decided that the job of starting me on the road toward making something of myself could no longer be safely delayed. "Buddy," she said one day, "I want you to come home right after school this afternoon. Somebody's coming and I want you to meet him."

When I burst in that afternoon she was in conference in the parlor with an executive of the Curtis Publishing Company. She introduced me. He bent low from the waist and shook my hand. Was it true as my mother had told him, he asked, that I longed for the opportunity to conquer the world of business?

My mother replied that I was blessed with a rare determination to make something of myself.

"That's right," I whispered.

"But have you got the grit, the character, the never-say-quit spirit it takes to succeed in business?"

My mother said I certainly did.

"That's right," I said.

He eyed me silently for a long pause, as though weighing whether I could be trusted to keep his confidence, then spoke man-to-man. Before taking a crucial step, he said, he wanted to advise me that working for the Curtis Publishing Company placed enormous responsibility on a young man. It was one of the great companies of America. Perhaps the greatest publishing house in the world. I had heard, no doubt, of the *Saturday Evening Post?*

Heard of it? My mother said that everyone in our house had heard of the *Saturday Post* and that I, in fact, read it with religious devotion.

Then doubtless, he said, we were also familiar with those two monthly pillars of the magazine world, the *Ladies Home Journal* and the *Country Gentleman.*

Indeed we were familiar with them, said my mother.

Representing the *Saturday Evening Post* was one of the weightiest honors that could be bestowed in the world of business, he said. He was personally proud of being a part of that great corporation.

My mother said he had every right to be.

Again he studied me as though debating whether I was worthy of a knighthood. Finally: "Are you trustworthy?"

My mother said I was the soul of honesty.

"That's right," I said.

The caller smiled for the first time. He told me I was a lucky young man. He admired my spunk. Too many young men thought life was all play. Those young men would not go far in this world. Only a young man willing to work and save and keep his face washed and his hair neatly combed could hope to come out on top in a world such as ours. Did I truly and sincerely believe that I was such a young man?

"He certainly does," said my mother.

"That's right," I said.

He said he had been so impressed by what he had seen of me that he was going to make me a representative of the Curtis Publishing Company. On the following Tuesday, he said, thirty freshly printed copies of the *Saturday Evening Post* would be delivered at our door. I would place these magazines, still damp with the ink of the presses, in a handsome canvas bag, sling it over my shoulder, and set forth through the streets to bring the best in journalism, fiction, and cartoons to the American public.

He had brought the canvas bag with him. He presented it with reverence fit for a chasuble. He showed me how to drape the sling over my left shoulder and across the chest so that the pouch lay easily accessible to my right hand, allowing the best in journalism, fiction, and cartoons to be swiftly extracted and sold to a citizenry whose happiness and security depended upon us soldiers of the free press.

The following Tuesday I raced home from school, put the canvas bag over my shoulder, dumped the magazines in, and tilting to the left to balance their weight on my right hip, embarked on the highway of journalism.

We lived in Belleville, New Jersey, a commuter town at the northern fringe of Newark. It was 1932, the bleakest year of the Depression. My father had died two years before, leaving us with a few pieces of Sears Roebuck furniture and not much else, and my mother had taken Doris and me to live with one of her younger brothers. This was my Uncle Allen. Uncle Allen had made something of himself by 1932. As salesman for a soft-drink bottler in Newark, he had an income of $30 a week; wore pearl-gray spats, detachable collars, and a three-piece suit; was happily married; and took in threadbare relatives.

With my load of magazines I headed toward Belleville Avenue. That's where the people were. There were two filling stations at the intersection with Union Avenue, as well as an A&P, a fruit stand, a bakery, a barber shop, Zuccarelli's drugstore, and a diner shaped like a railroad car. For several hours I made myself highly visible, shifting position now and then from corner to corner, from shop window to shop window, to make sure everyone could see the heavy black lettering on the canvas bag that said *The Saturday Evening Post.* When the angle of the light indicated it was suppertime, I walked back to the house.

"How many did you sell, Buddy?" my mother asked.

"None."

"Where did you go?"

"The corner of Belleville and Union Avenues."

"What did you do?"

"Stood on the corner waiting for somebody to buy a *Saturday Evening Post.*"

"You just stood there?"

"Didn't sell a single one."

"For God's sake, Russell!"

Uncle Allen intervened. "I've been thinking about it for some time," he said, "and I've about decided to take the *Post* regularly. Put me down as a regular customer." I handed him a magazine and he paid me a nickel. It was the first nickel I earned.

Afterwards my mother instructed me in salesmanship. I would have to ring doorbells, address adults with charming self-confidence, and break down resistance with a sales talk pointing out that no one, no matter how poor, could afford to be without the *Saturday Evening Post* in the home.

I told my mother I'd changed my mind about wanting to succeed in the magazine business.

"If you think I'm going to raise a good-for-nothing," she replied, "you've got another think coming." She told me to hit the streets with the canvas bag and start ringing doorbells the instant school was out next day. When I objected that I didn't feel any aptitude for salesmanship, she asked how I'd like to lend her my leather belt so she could whack some sense into me. I bowed to superior will and entered journalism with a heavy heart.

My mother and I had fought this battle almost as long as I could remember. It probably started even before memory began, when I was a country child in northern Virginia and my mother, dissatisfied with my father's plain workman's life, determined that I would not grow up like him and his people, with calluses on their hands, overalls on their backs, and fourth-grade educations in their heads. She had fancier ideas of life's possibilities. Introducing me to the *Saturday Evening Post,* she was trying to wean me as early as possible from my father's world where men left with their lunch pails at sunup, worked with their hands until the grime ate into the pores, and died with a few sticks of mail-order furniture as their legacy. In my mother's vision of the better life there were desks and white collars, well-pressed suits, evenings of reading and lively talk, and perhaps—if a man were very, very lucky and hit the jackpot, really made something important of himself—perhaps there might be a fantastic salary of $5,000 a year to support a big house and a Buick with a rumble seat and a vacation in Atlantic City.

And so I set forth with my sack of magazines. I was afraid of the dogs that snarled behind the doors of potential buyers. I was timid about ringing the doorbells of strangers, relieved when no one came to the door, and scared when someone did. Despite my mother's instructions, I could not deliver an engaging sales pitch. When a door opened I simply asked, "Want to buy a *Saturday Evening Post?*" In Belleville few persons did. It was a town of 30,000 people, and most weeks I rang a fair majority of its doorbells. But I rarely sold my thirty copies. Some weeks I canvassed the entire town for six days and still had four or five unsold magazines on Monday evening; then I dreaded the coming of Tuesday morning, when a batch of thirty fresh *Saturday Evening Posts* was due at the front door.

"Better get out there and sell the rest of those magazines tonight," my mother would say.

I usually posted myself then at a busy intersection where a traffic light controlled commuter flow from Newark. When the light turned red I stood on the curb and shouted my sales pitch at the motorists.

"Want to buy a *Saturday Evening Post?*"

One rainy night when car windows were sealed against me I came back soaked and with not a single sale to report. My mother beckoned to Doris.

"Go back down there with Buddy and show him how to sell these magazines," she said.

Brimming with zest, Doris, who was then seven years old, returned with me to the corner. She took a magazine from the bag, and when the light turned red, she strode to the nearest car and banged her small fist against the closed window. The driver, probably startled at what he took to be a midget assaulting his car, lowered the window to stare, and Doris thrust a *Saturday Evening Post* at him.

"You need this magazine," she piped, "and it only costs a nickel."

Her salesmanship was irresistible. Before the light changed half a dozen times she disposed of the entire batch. I didn't feel humiliated. To the contrary. I was so happy I decided to give her a treat. Leading her to the vegetable store on Belleville Avenue, I bought three apples, which cost a nickel, and gave her one.

"You shouldn't waste money," she said.

"Eat your apple." I bit into mine.

"You shouldn't eat before supper," she said. "It'll spoil your appetite."

Back at the house that evening, she dutifully reported me for wasting a nickel. Instead of a scolding, I was rewarded with a pat on the back for having the good sense to buy fruit instead of candy. My mother reached into her bottomless supply of maxims and told Doris, "An apple a day keeps the doctor away."

By the time I was ten I had learned all my mother's maxims by heart. Asking to stay up past normal bedtime, I knew that a refusal would be explained with, "Early to bed and early to rise, makes a man healthy, wealthy, and wise." If I whimpered about having to get up early in the morning, I could depend on her to say, "The early bird gets the worm."

The one I most despised was, "If at first you don't succeed, try, try again." This was the battle cry with which she constantly sent me back into the hopeless struggle whenever I moaned that I had rung every doorbell in town and knew there wasn't a single potential buyer left in Belleville that week. After listening to my explanation, she handed me the canvas bag and said, "If at first you don't succeed . . ."

Three years in that job, which I would gladly have quit after the first day except for her insistence, produced at least one valuable result. My mother finally concluded that I would never make something of myself by pursuing a life in business and started considering careers that demanded less competitive zeal.

One evening when I was eleven I brought home a short "composition" on my summer vacation which the teacher had graded with an A. Reading it with her own schoolteacher's eye, my mother agreed that it was top-drawer seventh grade prose and complimented me. Nothing more was said about it immediately, but a new idea had taken life in her mind. Halfway through supper she suddenly interrupted the conversation.

"Buddy," she said, "maybe you could be a writer."

I clasped the idea to my heart. I had never met a writer, had shown no previous urge to write, and hadn't a notion how to become a writer, but I loved stories and thought that making up stories must surely be almost as much fun as reading them. Best of all, though, and what really gladdened my heart, was the ease of the writer's life. Writers did not have to trudge through the town peddling from canvas bags, defending themselves against angry dogs, being rejected by surly strangers. Writers did not have to ring doorbells. So far as I could make out, what writers did couldn't even be classified as work.

I was enchanted. Writers didn't have to have any gumption at all. I did not dare tell anybody for fear of being laughed at in the schoolyard, but secretly I decided that what I'd like to be when I grew up was a writer.

QUESTIONS FOR "FROM *GROWING UP*" BY RUSSELL BAKER

Talking About the Text

1. How would you characterize this author's tone? How did you feel while reading the text?
2. What do you think about the following line: "Doris could have made something of herself if she hadn't been a girl." Is Baker being humorous or serious? Do you find the line humorous? Why or why not?
3. Baker tells us that "Fifty years ago parents still asked boys if they wanted to grow up to be President, and asked it not jokingly but seriously." What does Baker imply about our current expectations? Can you explain why he would imply this?

Exploring Issues

1. Baker's mother wanted him to have a better life than his father had had: "My mother, dissatisfied with my father's plain workman's life, determined that I would not grow up like him and his people, with calluses on their hands, overalls on their backs, and fourth-grade educations in their heads." Do people today expect children to have a better life than their parents had? Why or why not? What are some differences between the 1990s and the 1930s and '40s?

2. Baker felt that his temperament was not suited to being a salesperson. What kinds of personal qualities would contribute to good saleswork? What type of person would succeed in sales work? Would you be a successful salesperson? Why or why not?

Writing Assignments

1. Write a narrative essay about your first work experience. You may either (a) explain how and why you got involved with this work, what type of work it was, and what you experienced on the job, or (b) narrate one particular event that occurred while you were on your first job, or (c) combine (a) and (b).

2. Write an essay in which you explain what sort of career you would like to enter. Explain how you got interested in this kind of job or profession, any relevant experience or education you have had, what kinds of preparation you think you will need, and why you think this work would be suited to your temperament.

Reading 11

I'm Listening As Hard As I Can

Terry Galloway

Terry Galloway graduated from the University of Texas in 1972 and developed a career in theatrical productions and as a writer. She is the author of two plays, *Heart of a Dog,* which won the Villager Award in New York, and *A Hamlet in Berlin,* and she has coauthored a public television program for deaf children. Galloway has also published a book of poems, *Buncha Crocs in Surch of Snac* (1980). In the following essay,* Galloway provides a very personal account of how she entered the world of the deaf as an adolescent.

At the age of twelve I won the swimming award at the Lions Camp for Crippled Children. When my name echoed over the PA system the girl in the wheelchair next to me grabbed the box speaker of my hearing aid and shouted, "You won!" My ear quaking, I took the cue. I stood up straight—the only physically unencumbered child in a sea of braces and canes—affixed a pained but brave grin to my face, then limped all the way to the stage.

Later, after the spotlight had dimmed, I was overcome with remorse, but not because I'd played the crippled heroine. The truth was that I was ashamed of my handicap. I wanted to have something more visibly wrong with me. I wanted to be in the same league as the girl who'd lost her right leg in a car accident; her artificial leg attracted a bevy of awestruck campers. I, on the other hand, wore an unwieldy box hearing aid buckled to my body like a dog halter. It attracted no one. Deafness wasn't, in my eyes, a blue-ribbon handicap. Mixed in with my envy, though, was an overwhelming sense of guilt; at camp I was free to splash in the swimming pool, while most of the other children were stranded at the shallow end, where lifeguards floated them in lazy circles. But seventeen years of living in the "normal" world has diminished my guilt considerably, and I've learned that every handicap has its own particular hell.

I'm something of an anomaly in the deaf world. Unlike most deaf people, who were either born deaf or went deaf in infancy, I lost my hearing in chunks over a period of twelve years. Fortunately I learned to speak before my loss grew too profound, and that ability freed me from the most severe problem facing the deaf—the terrible difficulty of making themselves understood. My opinion of deafness was just as biased as that of a person who can hear. I had never met a deaf child in my life, and I didn't know how to sign. I imagined deaf people to be like creatures from beyond: animal-like because their language was so physical, threatening because they were unable to express themselves with sophistication—that is, through speech. I *could* make myself understood, and because I had a talent for lipreading it was easy for me to pass in the wider world. And for most of my life that is exactly what I did—like a black woman playing white, I passed for something other than what I was. But in doing so I was avoiding some very painful facts. And for many years I was inhibited not only by my deafness but my own idea of what it meant to be deaf.

My problems all started when my mother, seven months pregnant with me, developed a serious kidney infection. Her doctors pumped her full of antibiotics.

Two months later I was born, with nothing to suggest that I was anything more or less than a normal child. For years nobody knew that the antibiotics had played havoc with my fetal nervous system. I grew up bright, happy, and energetic.

But by the time I was ten I knew, if nobody else did, that something somewhere had gone wrong. The people around me had gradually developed fuzzy profiles, and their speech had taken on a blurred and foreign character. But I was such a secure and happy child that it didn't enter my mind to question my new perspective or mention the changes to anyone else. Finally, my behavior became noticeably erratic—I would make nonsensical replies to ordinary questions or simply fail to reply at all. My teachers, deciding that I was neither a particularly creative child nor an especially troublesome one, looked for a physical cause. They found two: I wasn't quite as blind as a bat, but I was almost as deaf as a doornail.

My parents took me to Wilford Hall Air Force Hospital in San Antonio, where I was examined from ear to ear. My tonsils were removed and studied, ice water was injected into my inner ear, and I underwent a series of inexplicable and at times painful exploratory tests. I would forever after associate deafness with kind attention and unusual punishment. Finally a verdict was delivered: "Congenital interference has resulted in a neural disorder for which there is no known medical or surgical treatment." My hearing loss was severe and would grow progressively worse.

I was fitted with my first hearing aid and sent back home to resume my childhood. I never did. I had just turned twelve, and my body was undergoing enormous changes. I had baby fat, baby breasts, hairy legs, and thick pink cat-eye glasses. My hearing aid was about the size of a small transistor radio and rode in a white linen pouch that hit exactly at breast level. It was not a welcome addition to my pubescent woe.

As a vain child trapped in a monster's body, I was frantic for a way to survive the next few years. Glimpsing my reflection in mirrors became such agony that I acquired a habit of brushing my teeth and hair with my eyes closed. Everything I did was geared to making my body more inhabitable, but I only succeeded in making it less so. I kept my glasses in my pocket and developed an unbecoming squint; I devised a smile that hid two broken front teeth, but it looked disturbingly like the grin of a piranha; I kept my arms folded over my would-be breasts. But the hearing aid was a different story. There was no way to disguise it. I could tuck it under my blouse, but then all I could hear was the static of cotton. Besides, whenever I took a step the box bounced around like a third breast. So I resigned myself: A monster I was, a monster I would be.

I became more withdrawn, more suspicious of other people's intentions. I imagined that I was being deliberately excluded from schoolyard talk because the other children didn't make much of an effort to involve me—they simply didn't have the time or patience to repeat snatches of gossip ten times and slowly. Conversation always reached the point of ridiculousness before I could understand something as simple as "The movie starts at five." (The groovy shark's alive? The moving stars that thrive?) I didn't make it to many movies. I cultivated a lofty sense of superiority, and I was often brutal with people who offered the "wrong" kind of help at the "wrong" time. Right after my thirteenth birthday some well-meaning neighbors took me to a revivalist faith healing. I already had doubts about exuberant religions, and the knee-deep hysteria of the preacher simply confirmed them. He bounded to my side and put his hands on my head. "O Lord," he cried, "heal this poor little lamb!"

I leaped up as if transported and shouted, "I can walk!"

For the first few years my parents were as bewildered as I was. Nothing had prepared them for a handicapped child on the brink of adolescence. They sensed a whole other world of problems, but in those early stages I still seemed so normal that they just couldn't see me in a school for the deaf. They felt that although such schools were there to help, they also served to isolate. I have always been grateful for their decision. Because of it, I had to contend with public schools, and in doing so I developed two methods of survival: I learned to read not just lips but the whole person, and I learned the habit of clear speech by taking every speech and drama course I could.

That is not to say my adolescent years were easy going—they were misery. The lack of sound cast a pall on everything. Life seemed less fun than it had been before. I didn't associate that lack of fun with the lack of sound. I didn't begin to make the connection between the failings of my body and the failings of the world until I was well out of college. I simply did not admit to myself that deafness caused certain problems—or even that I was deaf.

From the time I was twelve until I was twenty-four, the loss of my hearing was erratic. I would lose a decibel or two of sound and then my hearing would stabilize. A week or a year later there would be another slip and then I'd have to adjust all over again. I never knew when I would hit bottom. I remember going to bed one night still being able to make out the reassuring purr of the refrigerator and the late-night conversation of my parents, then waking the next morning to nothing—even my own voice was gone. These fits and starts continued until my hearing finally dropped to the last rung of amplifiable sound. I was a college student at the time, and whenever anyone asked about my hearing aid, I admitted to being only slightly hard of hearing.

My professors were frequently alarmed by my almost maniacal intensity in class. I was petrified that I'd have to ask for special privileges just to achieve marginal understanding. My pride was in flames. I became increasingly bitter and isolated. I was terrified of being marked a deaf woman, a label that made me sound dumb and cowlike, enveloped in a protective silence that denied me my complexity. I did everything I could to hide my handicap. I wore my hair long and never wore earrings, thus keeping attention away from my ears and their riders. I monopolized conversations so that I wouldn't slip up and reveal what I was or wasn't hearing; I took on a disdainful air at large parties, hoping that no one would ask me something I couldn't instantly reply to. I lied about the extent of my deafness so I could avoid the stigma of being thought "different" in a pathetic way.

It was not surprising that in my senior year I suffered a nervous collapse and spent three days in the hospital crying like a baby. When I stopped crying I knew it was time to face a few things—I had to start asking for help when I needed it because I couldn't handle my deafness alone, and I had to quit being ashamed of my handicap so I could begin to live with its consequences and discover what (if any) were its rewards.

When I began telling people that I was *really* deaf, I did so with grim determination. Some were afraid to talk to me at any length, fearing perhaps that they were talking into a void; others assumed that I was somehow an unsullied innocent and always inquired in carefully enunciated sentences; "Doooooooo youuuuuuuu driiinnk liquor?" But most people were surprisingly sympathetic—they wanted to know the best way to be understood, they took great pains to talk directly to my face, and they didn't insult me by using only words of one syllable.

It was, in part, that gentle acceptance that made me more curious about my own deafness. Always before it had been an affliction to wrestle with as one would with angels, but when I finally accepted it as an inevitable part of my life, I relaxed enough to do some exploring. I would take off my hearing aid and go through a day, a night, an hour or two—as long as I could take it—in absolute silence. I felt as if I were indulging in a secret vice because I was perceiving the world in a new way—stripped of sound.

Of course I had always known that sound is vibration, but I didn't know, until I stopped straining to hear, how truly sound is a refinement of feeling. Conversations at parties might elude me, but I seldom fail to pick up on moods. I enjoy watching people talk. When I am too far away to read lips I try reading postures and imagining conversations. Sometimes, to everyone's horror, I respond to things better left unsaid when I'm trying to find out what's going on around me. I want to see, touch, taste, and smell everything within reach; I especially have to curb a tendency to judge things by their smell—not just potato salad but people as well—a habit that seems to some people entirely too barbaric for comfort. I am not claiming that my other senses stepped up their work to compensate for the loss, but the absence of one does allow me to concentrate on the others. Deafness has left me acutely aware of both the duplicity that language is capable of and the many expressions the body cannot hide.

Nine years ago I spent the summer at the University of Texas's experimental Shakespeare workshop at Winedale, and I went back each year for eight years, first as a student and then as a staff associate. Off and on for the last four years I have written and performed for Esther's Follies, a cabaret theater group in Austin. Some people think it's odd that, as deaf as I am, I've spent so much of my life working in the theater, but I find it to be a natural consequence of my particular circumstance. The loss of sound has enhanced my fascination with language and the way meaning is conveyed. I love to perform. Exactly the same processes occur onstage as off—except that onstage, once I've memorized the script, I know what everybody is saying as they say it. I am delighted to be so immediately in the know. It has provided a direct way to keep in touch with the rest of the world despite the imposed isolation.

Silence is not empty; it is simply more sobering than sound. At times I prefer the sobriety. I can still "hear" with a hearing aid—that is, I can discern noise, but I can't tell you where it's coming from or if it is laughter or a faulty drain. When there are many people talking together I hear a strange music, a distant rumbling in my consciousness. But when I take off my hearing aid at night and lie in bed surrounded by my fate, I wonder, "What is this—a foul subtraction or a blessing in disguise?" For despite my fears there is a kind of peace in the silence—albeit an uneasy one. There is, after all, less to distract me from my thoughts.

But I know what I've lost. The process of becoming deaf has at times been frightening, akin perhaps to dying, and early in life it took away my happy confidence in the image of a world where things always work right. When I first came back from the Lions Camp that summer I cursed heaven and earth for doing such terrible wrong to me and to my friends. My grandmother tried to comfort me by promising, "Honey, God's got something special planned for you."

But I thought, "Yes. He plans to make me deaf."

QUESTIONS FOR "I'M LISTENING AS HARD AS I CAN" BY TERRY GALLOWAY

Talking About the Text

1. What do you think Terry Galloway's purpose was in writing this essay? Whom do you think she was writing the essay for? Herself? Other readers? Readers who are deaf? Readers in the hearing world? How can you make this judgment?

2. How did Terry Galloway's attitude toward her hearing loss change as she grew older? What may have caused these changes?

3. Terry Galloway alludes to her problems as an adolescent. What specific problems do you think she had as a result of her hearing loss?

4. Terry Galloway writes, "It was not surprising that in my senior year [of college] I suffered a nervous collapse." What were the primary reasons for Galloway's nervous collapse? What is the importance of this nervous collapse?

Exploring Issues

1. Terry Galloway tells us that her parents had to choose between sending her to a school with other deaf children or sending her to school with hearing children. What would be the rationale for sending a child like Terry to a school for the deaf? What would be the rationale for sending a child like Terry to a school for hearing children? What would be the advantages and the disadvantages for each choice?

2. Terry Galloway does not mention spending time with other people who are deaf. Do you think she would have been better off if she had? How might this have been helpful?

Writing Assignments

1. Although ours may be less extreme and less obvious, we all have some sort of handicap—visible or invisible. It may involve interpersonal relations, talent or mental ability, or it may be a physical impairment (poor vision, lack of athletic ability, asthma, allergies, etc.) Write an essay about a handicap that you have. Describe the handicap and explain how it has affected your life. If you have learned to compensate for it, explain how you have done this.

2. View the film "Children of a Lesser God," and compare the experience of the deaf woman in that film with the experience of Terry Galloway. Write an essay in which you contrast the experiences of these two deaf women, taking into account their schooling, their families, their relationships with others, and their attitudes toward people in the deaf world and in the hearing world.

Reading 12

The Two Worlds of Edmund Perry

Robert Sam Anson

Robert Sam Anson is a free-lance journalist whose work has appeared in such publications as *Life, Time* and *New Times* magazines. He has also authored many books, including *"They've Killed the President!": The Search for the Murderers of John F. Kennedy* and *Exile: The Unquiet Oblivion of Richard M. Nixon*. The following essay first appeared in *Life* (October 1985) and has been developed into a book, *Best Intentions: The Education and Killing of Edmund Perry* (published in 1987). In this essay, Robert Anson provides an account of the life of Edmund Perry, a young black man from Harlem who is placed in a predominantly white preparatory school and finds that he is not completely at home in either world. Perry's story achieved national attention when he was shot and killed by a policeman during the course of an attempted robbery.

When the call came in, the senior staff of Phillips Exeter Academy was at principal Steve Kurtz's country house in Maine, talking over plans for the next school year. Kurtz, who was in the middle of discussing curriculum changes, got up to take it. When he came back, his face was ashen. "You won't believe it," he said. "Eddie Perry is dead. In Harlem. They say he was shot by a police officer." The people in the room looked at each other. For a long moment, no one said anything. No one believed it.

At first, no one who knew Eddie Perry believed the story they heard about him that sunny morning [in June 1985]. Not Malcolm Stephens, who had been his senior roommate, or Dave Smith, who had played on the football team with him, or Stephanie Neal, who had embraced him at graduation. None could believe it, none wanted to believe it. But it was true: Edmund Evans Perry, seventeen, honors graduate of the Exeter class of '85, about to enter Stanford University on a full scholarship, was dead, shot down on a Harlem street by a plainclothes police officer, whom, the authorities said, he had tried to mug.

It was a senseless story—"tragic," the network newscasters called it—and the details that unfolded in the days that followed, including the arrest of Eddie's nineteen-year-old brother, Jonah, as an accomplice in the aborted mugging, did little to give it meaning. How could it be, everyone wondered, that a boy with such talent and potential—this "prized symbol of hope," as an editorial in *The New York Times* called him—could come to such an end? Dr. Sidney Weinberg, a nationally known pathologist brought in by the Perrys to observe the autopsy, thought there might be a physiological explanation, meningitis perhaps, or a brain tumor. But there was evidence of none. Nor did police files contain any previous record of criminal behavior.

At Exeter, where the flag was lowered to half staff in mourning, Eddie was termed "a solid citizen" whose only trouble in four years was missing two classes. "He was too smart to get involved in something like this," said Rick Mahoney, the mystified dean of students. Schoolmates reporters talked to were similarly baffled. "Eddie never steals from anyone, no way, no way," one of his white friends told an interviewer. "He's a very moral and religious guy." Lamont O'Neil, a black classmate from Brooklyn, was even more emphatic. Eddie, he remembered, had told other blacks never to murder or rob "because it was morally wrong and a disgrace to the black community."

In the Harlem neighborhood where Eddie had grown up, and where a thousand people marched to protest his death, he was remembered, in one neighbor's words, as a model for the kids on the block, the boy who, his grade school principal said, was expected to become the first black president of the United States. "My son carried no gun or knife, because he walked with God," his grieving mother, Veronica, told a reporter. "He always said, 'Jesus fights my battles.'"

Against all this stood the word of one police officer—a word, law enforcement authorities said, that had been backed up by no fewer than twenty-three witnesses, among them two of Eddie's relatives.

"I would never have believed this would have happened to a boy like Eddie," said one of his Exeter teachers. "He had so much going for him. But then, I thought, 'Did I really know this boy?' Maybe there was another Eddie. Maybe I didn't know him as well as I wish I had."

It would be recorded in the obituaries and memories of his friends that Eddie Perry was of Harlem, and, so far as there was an emotional center to his life, it was true: Harlem was his home. Actually, though, he was born in Brooklyn, the second of three children of Veronica and Jonah Perry, an occasional laborer and handyman. Life in Brooklyn was hard for the Perrys, largely because of Jonah Sr.'s problems with alcohol, and in 1974 Veronica moved the children to Harlem, where her family had lived for four generations.

They settled in a cramped third-floor walkup on West 114th Street between Frederick Douglass and Adam Clayton Powell Jr. boulevards. Located down from the heights of Columbia University and Morningside Park, "The Valley," as the neighborhood was known, was a tough place, filled with burned-out, boarded-up tenements and drug dealers who hawked heroin openly on the streets. Once the Perrys' block had been no different. But in the late 1970s an urban renewal program renovated the buildings, lined the sidewalks with green zelkova trees and transformed it into a striver's row, where on summer nights neighbors chatted on the stoops and kept an eye on each other's kids. It was here, surrounded by aunts and uncles, grandparents and cousins, that Eddie Perry grew up.

He was a good boy, the people in the neighborhood said: well-mannered, disciplined, ambitious, and smart, a churchgoing boy who could, without embarrassment, list as his greatest strength his "faith in the Lord—the faith that tells me that no matter what happens, He will provide a way." There weren't many boys in the neighborhood who would say that, nor were there many with Eddie's sensitivity and reserve. "He had to warm up to you . . . before he would tell you the real deal," remembered the Rev. Preston Washington, pastor of Memorial Baptist Church, where Eddie was active in the youth fellowship and served as an usher. "In Sunday school, he was one of the kids who asked very direct questions like 'How do we know God exists?' He was very bright, but he didn't buy any experience lock, stock, and barrel."

The credit for all of this invariably went to his mother. With Jonah Sr. finding it hard to hold a job, it was Veronica who was the true head of the Perry household, and it was Veronica who filled Eddie with a sense of his own specialness, who, as Eddie himself once said, "put ideas into my head that there was something else." Many of those ideas had to do with politics, which, in Harlem, was frequently synonymous with opposition and race. A proud, dignified woman who had studied to be a nurse, Veronica herself was intensely involved in local political affairs, first as an outspoken leader of the PTA, later as the upset victor in an election to the community school board. She was "a tough chick," said Bill Perkins, the leader of the local Democratic club, a woman who "hustled over obstacles" for her kids, especially for Eddie. He was Veronica's prize, "our shining star," as one of his cousins put it, the person who "was going to change things for us."

Such predictions were seldom made about Eddie's older brother. Strapping and muscular, Jonah, who had been left swaybacked by a childhood injury, was neither as good-looking as Eddie, nor as favored, nor as bright. Where Eddie was thin-skinned and quick-witted, sometimes to the point of being acerbic, Jonah was more casual and easygoing. "Eddie smart," as a friend put it, "and Jonah cool." Though the boys were close, the differences produced a rivalry, a competition where Jonah usually came out the loser. "I'll settle for something," he remarked once. "Eddie always goes for the best."

But Jonah had his strengths. He was, for one thing, a far better athlete, and his prowess helped make him popular among his classmates. At Wadleigh Junior High, just down the block from the Perry apartment, he was president of his class and that, in turn, helped bring him to the attention of Edouard Plummer, the school's coordinator for A Better Chance, a Boston-based minority education organization that placed promising ghetto youths in prep schools. Terming Jonah "a willing worker who struggles hard to overcome obstacles," Plummer recommended him to ABC, and in the fall of 1980 Jonah enrolled at the Westminster School on full scholarship.

Located in Simsbury, Connecticut, a countrified suburb of Hartford, Westminster was a wholly different world from Harlem, but Jonah seemed to thrive. He played on the basketball and track teams, acted in the school's dramatic productions, and eventually racked up a number of distinctions, including a trophy in his senior year for sportsmanship and effort. Adults liked him— "There wasn't a nicer kid," said his track coach—and so did his schoolmates. "He was never bitter," one of them would say after his arrest. "He was always laughing about stuff. One day he got all this mail from Yale and Princeton, and I joked with him. I said, 'Hey, Jonah, I didn't know you were smart.' He said, laughing, 'No, I'm just black.' "

Eddie, in the meantime, was doing less well. In Jonah's absence he had been getting into trouble in school, including, he later told an Exeter classmate, striking a teacher. Had it not been for the intervention of his mother, the recommendations of friendly teachers ("meticulous, serious, and hardworking," they called him), and his own undeniable intelligence (testing in the seventh grade assessed his math and reading skills at well above the twelfth-grade level), the outcome might have been different. Instead, Plummer recommended him to ABC. Calling him "a future leader," for whom Jonah "serves as an inspiration," Plummer wrote, "This young man has a great sense of responsibility; he is well-mannered . . . alert, active, and honest . . . [and] has a great respect for authority. . . . His character is of the highest nature."

Jack Herney, the Exeter director of admissions who interviewed Eddie in Harlem, came to the same conclusion. He was especially taken with Eddie's seeming maturity. When Herney asked him what he expected to be doing twenty-five years from then, Eddie, who had a talent for impressing adults, didn't miss a beat. He was going to be a doctor and come back to help his community, he answered. "That's the kind of ambition we look for in kids," Herney said later, "someone who wants to succeed but not just for himself."

With Herney's enthusiastic endorsement, Eddie was admitted as a first-year "prep" in September 1981.

Founded in 1781 "for the purpose of promoting piety and virtue, and for the education of Youth," Phillips Exeter Academy in New Hampshire is one of the nation's oldest secondary private schools and perhaps its most prestigious. Daniel Webster went to Exeter (class of 1796), and down through the years so have Harvard- and Yale-bound men with names like Rockefeller, Getty, and Saltonstall. In more recent times, there have been increasing numbers of students with names like Washington, Rios, and Chiou, and today 40 percent of the total enrollment is female. In its traditions and commitment to "link goodness with knowledge," though, Exeter remains unchanged. It is an exacting place, one that demands the most of its students. School rules are strict, the academic regimen even stricter. "You come to Exeter to work," says one of its deans. "And we work you like hell."

To all appearances, Eddie, who was one of about 50 blacks in a student body of 980, managed the transition flawlessly. "He was eager as a prep," says Bill Bolden, an English instructor and one of three blacks on Exeter's faculty. "Many kids, black and white, are intimidated by Exeter. Eddie wasn't intimidated at all. He wanted to succeed."

Succeed Eddie did, slowly at first, but with growing confidence. After an academically so-so freshman year, his grades began to pick up, eventually reaching an average of B minus, sufficient at Exeter to qualify him as an honors student. He was particularly good in the sciences and best of all in the free-form class discussion and argument Exeter's seminar-style instruction encourages. One teacher described him as "intellectually voracious . . . bright, interested, sparkling, wanting to get as much as he could." "He was the kind of kid," says David Weber, who taught him humanities, "who brings a real energy to class, because he really cares about what is being said. It was never just an exercise to him. With Eddie, his life and his schoolwork were the same thing."

Eddie's outspokenness had its darker side. He could be sarcastic in class, boastful and abrasive. "It seemed like he was always trying to prove something," says a white student who shared several classes with him during sophomore year. "At Exeter, you don't have to prove anything to anybody. Everybody is smart. That's a given. But Eddie didn't get it. He was always trying to show you he was just as good as you."

His teachers judged him more sympathetically. It was not easy, they said, for a boy from Harlem to come to a place like Exeter, an overwhelmingly white institution set down in a small New England town, "remote," as the academy catalogue put it, "from urban influences." "Blacks don't feel fully a part of this school," an Exeter administrator said of students like Eddie, "and yet they are different from the kids back home. They have one foot in each camp and both feet in neither."

For Eddie, a scholarship student continually having to scrape, the situation was made all the more difficult by the affluence of his classmates. Many of them, noted one teacher, "had money to burn." There were stereos in their rooms, personal computers, the best from L. L. Bean. When they broke from school, it was not to Harlem that they returned but Palm Beach, Greenwich, the slopes of Gstaad. "He was a have-not sown in with a lot of haves," said one of his teachers. "He had the feeling that because he was black, the cards were stacked against him."

There were students at Exeter with Eddie's background, some from neighborhoods as mean, if not meaner, than Harlem. Few, however, seemed so acutely attuned to race. Eddie, said Lamont O'Neil, "didn't trust" whites. "If you were white," added Lamont, "he'd really watch you." The white students noted his wariness too. "He wasn't totally antiwhite," said a white classmate who worked hard at being his friend, "but he made such a huge point about being black. It crept into conversations frequently. He was so proud of his race that he expected you to dislike him for it, to look down on him because of it."

With black classmates Eddie was more at ease. Even then, his "New York attitude," as one described it, made him a difficult person to know. At first, says Stephanie Neal, who entered Exeter the same year as Eddie, he could seem "pushy and obnoxious," a forceful personality "who wouldn't let things ride." But those, like Stephanie, who did get to know him concluded in time that Eddie's seeming cockiness was really a protective shell and that underneath it was someone who was actually quite vulnerable and not at all as certain of himself as he proclaimed. "The truth of it," says one of his friends, "is that Eddie was really homesick."

On his visits home, Eddie was always greeted as the conquering hero. There were celebratory dinners to mark his return on vacation, gatherings of relatives, prayers of thanksgiving offered in the Baptist church. According to friends, he relished the attention, the status going to Exeter gave him. "He needed to be envied in a certain way," says a black adult Eddie regularly confided in. "He felt that need, to be regarded as special."

Occasionally that need caused him difficulties. He could be arrogant at home—"big on himself," as they said in the neighborhood—and his friends sometimes teased him about going "preppy" and, even worse in Harlem, losing his basketball skills.

For Eddie, an especially impressionable boy, the taunts stung, particularly because they were so correct. A part of him *was* preppy, complete with Izod shirt, but he was also Harlem black, and maintaining the two identities was proving an increasing strain. At Exeter there was a faculty-student "minority support group" that was supposed to ease such problems, but in fact the group did very little. It was not for lack of good intentions—Exeter fairly brimmed with good intentions—but for fear of singling out black students, of somehow disturbing, as one dean put it, "the integrity of the black experience." ABC, too, was intent on maintaining racial identity and tried to keep tabs on how its students were adjusting. But in the end it was largely left to the students themselves. Most made it; others dropped out. A few, like Eddie Perry, who seldom revealed himself to anyone, simply agonized.

He still had not resolved his dilemma when, in his junior year, he was offered the chance to avoid it.

The program was called School Year Abroad, and for a group of selected students, it offered the chance to spend a year of study in Barcelona. Eddie, who spoke good Spanish, leapt at it.

Spain was everything that Exeter was not: warm, foreign, and, best of all from Eddie's point of view, virtually rule-free. The year he spent there, he would later tell his classmates back at Exeter, was the happiest of his life.

Like all the forty-odd students in the program, Eddie was housed with a Spanish family. He had problems with the first household to which he was assigned, a group of conservative women who frowned on his propensity for partying, and he soon moved in with a young mother and her three-year-old daughter, where, Eddie told friends, the atmosphere was much warmer. Adjusting to the classroom routine, however, proved difficult. "He was very arrogant and very nonchalant," one of his classmates remembers. "He would sit completely spread out in class, looking bored, like everyone was wasting his time." According to his classmates, Eddie was particularly resentful of Edward Sainati, the program's resident director, who, Eddie claimed, "was trying to do something" to his brain, apparently by insisting he stick to his studies. Sainati in turn concluded that Eddie had a "chip on his shoulder," particularly over race. "I felt," Sainati said, "that he was blind to the fact that his underlying hostility toward whites was of his own making." Reporting all this to Exeter, Sainati passed along a piece of advice: "If you speak with him firmly and show him that you care, he will respect you in any situation."

Outside the classroom, life was sweet. By day Eddie played with a Spanish basketball team, wandered Barcelona, swam and sunned on the beaches of Sitges. By night he did the bars, and when the bars closed, did the discos. He was loving Spain, he told his friends. The Spanish were more open than American whites, less prejudiced, more willing to accept him for what he was. In Spain, as Eddie put it, he could be free.

In Spain, too, he found a special girl; her name was Ariel. A year ahead of Eddie in school, and from suburban Los Angeles, Ariel Nattelson was pretty, artistic, intelligent, wide-eyed and curly-haired. As it happened, she was also white.

The racial difference never seemed to matter to Ariel or to Eddie, who seemed to relax with her as with no one else. That they were friends rather than lovers did not seem to trouble him either. He doted on her and she on him. If Ariel had a problem, he would solve it; if she was upset, he would calm her, sometimes by singing her lyrics from a Bob Marley song. "Don't worry 'bout a thing," it went, "Cause every little thing's gonna be all right." They were close, Ariel and Eddie; if right now he had to choose a woman with whom he would spend the rest of his life, Eddie told a friend, it would be the white girl, Ariel.

In September Eddie returned to Exeter for the beginning of his senior year. Friends were surprised by his appearance. During the year in Spain, he had grown up, become a mature young man of six foot one. The extra height was not enough to win him a place on the basketball team, however, and he had only slightly better luck on the gridiron. He made the team, just barely, as a secondary defensive halfback, not as the starting recevier he wanted to be. The problem was not a lack of effort—"Eddie," said his football coach, "was always willing to stick his nose in"—but a shortage of skills. Eddie, his coaches said, just wasn't a physical kid.

Among a certain crowd at McConnell Hall, where Eddie took a ground-floor double, athletic ability wasn't required—only accesss to drugs. And with them Eddie was a most popular young man, indeed. As one of the McConnell druggies put it: "Eddie Perry had a lot of drugs, so Eddie Perry was cool."

Eddie Perry did have drugs, and, according to a number of his classmates, he both used and sold them. By the standards of the McConnell druggies, a tight clique of a few upperclassmen, he was not a particularly heavy user; the common reckoning was that he smoked marijuana no more than several times a week. His dealing, too, was limited: a few ounce-at-a-time marijuana and "Thai-stick" transactions spread out over the course of the first semester. It was enough, though, to gain him entrance to the club.

He was, according to those who smoked dope and drank with him, much easier to be with when he was high: more open, more easygoing, less sensitive to perceived racial slights. Harlem, however, was never far from his mind. He talked about his neighborhood incessantly, especially its seamier side. He told of the drug dealers he knew, the fights he had gotten into, his three friends who, he said, had been murdered in Central Park. Over and over again, the talk was of violence, of how, according to Eddie, it was "cool" and "fun."

"Sometimes I thought he was making things up," one of Eddie's drug friends recalls. "I mean, you had to wonder: how could a super street kid from Harlem be at Exeter? But he definitely tried to portray himself as a street kid. He used to say that we wouldn't last five minutes in the street. What he was sort of saying was that I can last a hundred years in the street. I am super streetwise."

The truth, as anyone on Eddie's block could have testified, was that Eddie was anything but streetwise. Instead of getting into fights in Harlem, he was going to the movies; instead of dealing, he was dancing. The boy who talked so knowingly of violence was, in fact, an usher in the Baptist church, who liked to write his mother poetry. "All these 'Tarzan and the Jungle' stories he told about himself were press release stuff," says a black adult Eddie confided in at home. "He wanted to come across to people as being as bad as bad can be. He became the stereotype that was projected onto him. That was his ticket into the life at Exeter. They had money, they had status. He had their image of him."

As the weeks went on, the perception of Eddie's "badness" deepened, aided and abetted by Eddie himself. He was known, for instance, to entertain women in his room Wednesday and Saturday afternoons. Out of this circumstance, not unheard of at Exeter, grew the story that Eddie was conducting "orgies" with still other women and was a member of a "sex club" where white girls passed initiation by making love on a seminar table in one of the Latin classrooms. Whether the story was true or not was almost beside the point. Around campus it gave Eddie the reputation of the stereotypical stud.

The druggies snickered about Eddie's exploits, but they were impressed by them too. By the midpoint of the first semester, they concluded that "this dangerous, seedy" person, as one called him, was capable of anything including getting them PCP.

Until then, no one at McConnell had ever tried PCP, and for good reason: Of all the hallucinogenic drugs, PCP, also known as angel dust, was far and away the most dangerous. According to an article in *Rolling Stone* that circulated through the dorm that fall semester, PCP was responsible for numerous deaths, some from overdose and suicide, others from the temporary states of psychotic violence that are one of the drug's principal effects. Much of the violence, the article went on to note, occurred in ghetto areas, where "dust" was widely available. Intrigued, the McConnell heads asked their ghetto friend Eddie to get them some.

Initially, Eddie was reluctant. PCP, he warned his friends, was an evil brew; he said he knew a lot of people who had "bugged out" on it. The druggies, however, were insistent, and after Thanksgiving break, Eddie came back to Exeter with a small plastic bag filled with what appeared to be, in the words of one student, "minced-up mint leaves in this black, real foul-smelling chemical."

Eddie said he had gotten the drug from a dealer friend. They were free to try it, he added, but he was not interested in doing it himself. "This stuff," he warned again, "will really screw you up." A half dozen of the druggies took a small sample; they discovered that Eddie was telling the truth. "We didn't do very much," one recalls. "Only three bong hits apiece. But we got pretty weirded out. Kept thinking of violence and suicide." Unsettling though the experience was, the druggies wanted more and offered to pay Eddie $25 a joint. This time Eddie said no. "He said we were crazy," one of the PCP experimenters recalls. "If we wanted to be crazy, that was up to us. But he didn't want to have any part of it."

The PCP incident enhanced Eddie's reputation with the druggies, but beneath the friendly facade there was growing friction, much of it due to race. "All of us are white and a lot of us are pretty racist, when it comes down to it," one of the druggies admitted. "There were a few black kids we really liked, but when you have a black who is really self-conscious about his blackness, it just doesn't make other people feel comfortable. That was Eddie's whole M.O.[1] at Exeter: making a big deal about race. People were getting tired of the racial rap." After a series of increasing irritants, the tension boiled over one night just before the Christmas break.

As usual, the heads were gathered in an upstairs room, tripping and listening to '60s music. Eddie walked in, asking whether there was any dope. There was none, but a member of the group invited him to try a hit of acid. After a moment's hesitation, Eddie, who had not experienced LSD until then, gulped the drug down. As the hallucinogen began to take effect, Eddie started chatting with one of the leading druggies. At first the talk, a typical acid conversation about the meaning of the universe, seemed to go well. Then, just as the student finished saying that nothing in life was finite, there were no absolutes, moral or otherwise, Eddie suddenly sprang from his chair and hurled himself across the room. Landing on his knees at the student's feet, Eddie reached up and punched him in the throat, knocking the boy backward. "Stop!" he yelled, as he punched a second, then a third time. "Stop! Stop! Stop!" Too stunned by what

---

[1]Slang abbreviation meaning "mode of operation."

was happening to do anything, the other students in the room looked on in silence. Finally, Eddie rose to his feet and without saying another word, walked out of the room.

After that, most of the white students in McConnell gave Eddie a wide berth. The few times he appeared in the drug-partying room, his former friends greeted him with silence. There were "some pretty awkward scenes," one of the druggies recalls. "We just didn't have anything to say to him. It was weird." Eddie in turn, became increasingly hostile. "He wouldn't talk to you or have any dealings with you," remembers one McConnell student who had been his friend. "I was afraid to say hello without getting jumped on. If you would say hello, he would comment to one of his black friends about how insincere it was."

Later, there were more serious incidents. On one occasion Eddie threw a punch at a white student for making what he took to be a racial remark. On several others, he was involved in shoving incidents with another white student for no apparent reason. Still later, he was suspected of stealing the second student's stereo "box." There was no evidence to support the charge, and none of the white students asked Eddie about it. By then they didn't dare to. "He was completely isolated after the first semester," says one of the McConnell white students. "No one would have anything to do with him."

Cut off from his former friends, Eddie spent nearly all of his free time now with other blacks. In his good moods, he would talk about home, the mother whom he "loved," the older brother, Jonah, now an engineering student at Cornell, whom he admired, the little sister, Nicol, about whom he worried so much. Nicol was thirteen, Eddie would say, extracting her picture from his wallet and passing it around, and the boys were beginning to call. He said he wanted to be around to watch those boys, to ensure that Nicol grew up safe and well. But when the topic turned to Exeter or whites, Eddie's tone grew bitter. Repeatedly, he railed about the racism of Exeter's "pink and green personality" and, in two cases, helped persuade unhappy underclassmen to withdraw. One of them was Lori Crozier, a sophomore from Gary, Indiana. "I was thinking about staying to get into this or that college," she says. "But Eddie kind of changed my mind about that. He said that you go to Exeter, and you get presented with a whole lot of ideas that aren't your own. . . . You gradually begin to believe them and then accept them. [Eddie said] you have to take a break and go home and talk to the brothers and the sisters. . . . He said that Exeter wasn't the place for us."

A number of the black upperclassmen shared Eddie's sentiments. What startled them was the vehemence with which he expressed them. "I was used to white people," says one of his friends. "I had been with them. I knew there were these super-rich people, and it didn't bother me the way it bothered Eddie. . . . He wouldn't let things ride. He was very, very angry."

His teachers noticed the difference in him too. Though still capable of doing excellent work, Eddie mainly coasted through the second semester, doing only what was required to get by. Some wrote it off to "the senior slide"; the more liberal, to a legitimate expression of black rage. A few, however, were troubled. Something had happened to Eddie, they said to themselves, something beyond the ordinary. None of them ever asked what it was, and Eddie never told them. By then he was not inviting concern. One teacher who called out to him on the quad to ask how he was doing got only a cynical laugh.

The full depth of Eddie's feelings was revealed to the entire Exeter community during an assembly in February. Part of a two-month-long, Exeter-sponsored symposium on racism, the assembly drew a packed house, and Eddie was the featured speaker. He used for his text a letter that had been written by another black Exeter student seven years before. Coming from Eddie Perry, the message was not dated; it was angry and defiant. He didn't care what white people thought of him, he told his classmates. Didn't care whether they helped him, didn't care whether they liked him. He wanted one thing, and one thing only from whites, he said. And that was respect.

It was a tough speech and it unsettled many of the whites who heard it. There was only one explanation, they said: Eddie Perry was a racist.

Kennett Marshall thought otherwise, and Kennett Marshall was white. A transfer "postgraduate" student from Washington, D.C., Kennett had been Eddie's best friend that year, and race had never intruded on their relationship, in part, perhaps, because Kennett's stepmother was black. That Christmas, Kennett went to Harlem, and during spring break there was a reciprocal visit to Washington, where Eddie talked politics with Kennett's stepfather, former Iowa Senator Dick Clark. Like so many white adults, Clark had been impressed by Eddie, as had Kennett's father, Pitkin Marshall, a Manhattan attorney. The boys had shown up in the midst of a dinner party at Marshall's apartment, and a high-powered group had been assembled at the table. Eddie, however, had more than held his own, particularly when the discussion turned to the effect of the Reagan budget cuts on minorities. Indeed, he had been so well-spoken that Kennett's father had assumed that he was probably from somewhere like Scarsdale. When Marshall asked how a person of his upbringing could have acquired such intimate knowledge of Harlem, Eddie merely smiled.

Come the summer, both boys would be in New York, and, as the days ticked down to graduation, they were planning their adventures. Eddie had already made one important decision; he was going to Stanford in the fall. He had had no trouble getting into Stanford, which had awarded him a full scholarship, any more than he had with the other schools to which he had applied: Penn, Berkeley, and Yale. He was looking forward to going to Stanford, he told friends. He thought California would be a lot like Spain. It was also far away.

In some conversations with friends, Eddie still talked about returning to Harlem one day, about helping, as he put it in a letter to ABC [that] April, "educate and economically advance my race." But, in other moments, he confessed that what he really wanted to do was escape, not only from Exeter and Harlem, but from the country entirely. Maybe, he told a friend, he would go overseas, take up a career in business, perhaps manage a string of hotels. He was tired of having so much expected of him. He wanted to be normal, to make money and take it easy. That was the important thing, he said to a friend: taking it easy.

Graduation at Exeter was June 2, and the week leading up to it was a social whirl. Ariel flew in from California for the prom, and Eddie was in a buoyant mood. The only hint of hard feelings was the inscription he had chosen for his yearbook picture. "Goodbye Exeter," it went. "You taught and showed me many things. . . . Some things I saw I did not like, and some things I learned I'd rather not know. It's a pity we part on less than a friendly basis, but we do. . . . Work to adjust yourself in a changing world, as will I."

After graduation, Ariel returned with Eddie to Harlem, and with Kennett they spent several days together exploring the city, taking in all the tourist spots. When it came time to go, Ariel began to cry. "Don't be sad," Eddie told her. "I'll see you in California."

Five days later, on June 12, Eddie reported for his first day of work at Kidder, Peabody & Co., a Wall Street brokerage house, where he had secured a summer job as a messenger. That evening, after dinner, while their mother attended a local school board meeting, Eddie and Jonah went to the playground at Wadleigh Junior High for a pickup game of basketball, according to the police. They played two-on-two, the brothers against a pair of neighborhood boys, with the agreement that the losers would take the winners to the movies. The Perrys lost; they also had no money. Returning home, Eddie and Jonah played cards on the stoop for a few minutes, then went inside and downed a wine cooler. Eddie may also have smoked a joint; traces of marijuana were later found in his system. Shortly after nine, they went back into the street.

A few blocks away, Officer Lee Van Houten of the 26th Police Precinct was preparing to go out on plainclothes duty. Lately there had been a rash of radio thefts from automobiles owned by the doctors at nearby St. Luke's—Roosevelt Hospital, and Van Houten's assignment was to stroll through the area on the lookout for a thief. He was a young officer, just twenty-four, with only two years on the force, and his tousled hair and baby face made him appear even younger. As he walked through the shadows at the edge of Morningside Park, togged out in sneakers, sweatshirt, and chinos, he looked anything but a cop.

At approximately 9:30, Van Houten, clutching a paper bag containing a radio linking him with three backup officers cruising in a station wagon two blocks away, neared the corner of West 113th Street and Morningside Drive. The lights of St. Luke's were less than a half block away. Suddenly, according to police, he was yoked from behind around the neck and pulled to the sidewalk by two young black men. As the youths began punching him in the face and the back of the head, Van Houten let out a muffled yell that he was a police officer. Either not hearing or ignoring him, the youths shouted, "Give it up!" and continued pounding away at him. Van Houten thought he was about to pass out. He reached down to his ankle holster and drew out a .38-caliber revolver. Three shots barked into the night. One of them caught Eddie Perry in the stomach from less than a foot away.

As Eddie toppled backward, the other assailant fled. A few minutes later, police allege, Jonah arrived at the stoop in front of his apartment, where a half dozen people were gathered, including some members of his own family. "We picked on the wrong guy," police quote him as saying. "We got a DT"—street slang for detective.

On the sidewalk where Eddie lay unconscious in a widening pool of his own blood, a bruised and bleeding Van Houten retrieved his radio and called for assistance. By 10:05, Eddie was in the St. Luke's operating room, one of the best-equipped trauma centers in the city. According to a hospital spokesman, everything that could be done was done. It was not enough. He died at 12:50 A.M.

Fifteen hundred people attended the memorial service for Edmund Evans Perry, more than the Memorial Baptist Church could accommodate. Scores stood in the aisles; hundreds more milled silently in the streets. Among them were a number of Eddie's Exeter classmates, who had flown in from around the country to attend. Many were weeping as they listened to the tributes to him. Afterward Steve Kurtz, the Exeter principal, and Michael Forrestal, the president of the board of trustees, approached some of Eddie's black classmates to offer their condolences. The students refused to shake their hands.

Two weeks later, after interviewing what were termed "dozens of witnesses," the police arrested Jonah Perry on charges of assault and attempted robbery. On the drive to jail, Jonah, according to the accompanying officers, seemed cool. One of them recalled that he talked about Cornell. Pending legal motions, his trial is expected this winter. Jonah, who has told reporters he was at his grandmother's house at the time of Eddie's shooting, has branded the charges against him "lies."

Eddie's mother, Veronica, remains active in local political affairs and was recently elected chairman of her community school board. Friends describe her as bearing up well and looking to the Bible to find strength. As for the facts of the incident that took her son's life, Mrs. Perry, who originally accused "trigger-happy" police of conducting a cover-up, now says only "God knows the truth."

Edmund Perry lies in a section of Fair Lawn Memorial Cemetery in suburban New Jersey. In the home where he grew up, his belongings have been gathered together and placed in a kind of shrine. Among the pictures and mementos is an apparently autobiographical short story Eddie wrote a few months before his death. In it, Eddie describes coming back from Exeter and meeting a grade school classmate turned drug dealer and thief. The old friend has been doing well at his trade. He has a wife, children, a big Oldsmobile, all the accoutrements of neighborhood status. A part of Eddie envies him; a part, too, is appalled by him. At the climax of the story, the drug dealer, a bag of loot under his arm, is being pursued by the police. He bumps into Eddie on the street and asks him to help by holding the bag. For a long monent, Eddie hesitates—torn between what he has learned at Exeter and the ethics of the street. Finally, he takes the bag.

"He was a sensitive boy," said a black man Eddie frequently talked to, and one of the few people he seemed to trust, "a lot more tender and vulnerable than he let on." He was a bright boy, too, the man added, though not nearly as bright as he was now being portrayed. That, said the man, who had survived many of the same experiences as Eddie and gone on to take a prominent position in the white world, was both Eddie's blessing and his curse. People were always taking him for something other than he was. ABC, Exeter, the people in Harlem, they all wanted him to be something more. "He was a symbol," as the man put it, "a slot filler. No one took the time to treat him as an individual. He didn't have the freedom to be an individual." The man paused. "Eddie wanted to be that myth. He wanted to be the way he was perceived. He talked about 'getting over' on people. He was running a game on them." And, finally, the man said, the game caught up with him.

At Phillips Exeter Academy, where the fall term is now beginning, there is a new orientation program for students with Eddie's background. It is informally called Help for People from Distant Places. They say it has nothing to do with the death of Edmund Perry.

QUESTIONS FOR "THE TWO WORLDS OF EDMUND PERRY" BY ROBERT SAM ANSON

Talking About the Text

1. Anson begins this essay with some journalistic accounts of Edmund Perry and his death, which was described as "tragic" in many news reports. Edmund Perry is described as a "prized symbol of hope," "a solid citizen," and as "a very moral and religious guy." Later in this essay we discover some of the difficulties that Edmund Perry was having as a student at Phillips Exeter Academy. What are the rhetorical effects of sequencing information in this way? Can you think of alternative organizational strategies? What is an alternative to beginning the essay with news accounts of Edmund Perry's death? What does Anson gain by beginning his essay in this way?

2. Robert Anson reports many factual incidents in his essay on Edmund Perry. Because of the details and the author's tone, we may well decide to take all the information given at face value. However, information may be organized in various ways and specific aspects of a case may be emphasized in order to give a certain slant to a story. Do you think Anson has infused this story with any of his own opinions or beliefs? If so, what are Anson's opinions or beliefs, and how does he integrate them with reported facts?

Exploring Issues

1. What are some of the difficulties that Edmund Perry faced as a working-class black student in a predominantly upper-class, "white" school? What did he gain by attending this school? What did he lose? Do you feel that the gains justified the losses in this case?

2. The facts indicate that Edmund Perry and his brother Jonah did attempt

to rob an undercover police officer. Considering all that he had to lose, why would Edmund Perry involve himself in this robbery? What do you think his motives were?

3. Robert Anson tells us that a friend of Edmund's thought "he was a symbol." If he was a symbol, what did Edmund Perry symbolize? For his friends in Harlem? For teachers and students at Exeter? For the media in initial accounts of his death?

Writing Assignments

1. Imagine that you are in the same situation as Edmund Perry, a working-class black student who has an opportunity to attend a predominantly white, upper-class school. Knowing what you do about Edmund Perry, would you choose to attend this school, or would you choose to attend a public school in your own neighborhood? Write an essay in which you explain the two alternatives as you see them and your choice.

2. Read "The Library Card" by Richard Wright. Write an essay in which you contrast the case of Richard Wright with that of Edmund Perry. Consider their opportunities, their expectations, and their difficulties. What are the important differences between these two cases? What are the similarities?

Reading 13

The New Middleground

Ellen Goodman

Ellen Goodman is a syndicated columnist whose work appears in newspapers across the United States. A winner of the Pulitzer prize for distinguished commentary, Goodman describes herself as "one of those [journalists] who chronicle change." Having participated in the media coverage of the civil rights movement, the peace movement, and the women's movement, Goodman became interested in the dynamics of people's lives in the face of a rapidly changing society. She interviewed over 150 men and women between 1975 and 1978 to learn about changes resulting from new perspectives on sex roles. The result of her research is her book entitled *Turning Points,* from which the following selection is drawn. In this passage, Goodman examines some of the attitudes that women have toward the women's movement and its effects on their lives.

"You know, it's kind of hard. Men like me, we just didn't grow up expecting our wives to be, well, like Rose . . .
"Answer this, what would a woman with a master's degree or a Ph.D. want with a guy who isn't going to go much higher up? Will my wife still be my wife if she has a Ph.D? Answer me that."

Most of us are neither radical change innovators nor hard-core resisters. We are card-carrying members of neither the vanguard nor the rearguard. We don't live in the ends of the Shuttle Zone but rather in that vast territory called the middleground.

But in a time of transition even the middleground is not necessarily a place where people can be protected from buffeting. In many ways the people in the middleground have the most ambivalent feelings about change and are the most harried commuters in the Shuttle Zone.

The people I interviewed for this chapter all identified themselves as "moderates" or middle Americans, although they ranged all the way between the two border lines of the end zones. They were all, however, typical middlegrounders in this sense: they realized that they couldn't and didn't want to avoid change but they did want to control its speed. In one way or another they chose to evolve—rather than revolt—in tune with their own internal conflicts.

What I found in the middleground was both the pull of traditions and the universality of change. I remember a clipping I'd saved from a *Ladies' Home Journal* in 1976 where the editor had, I think instinctively, described the new Middleground Woman. Lenore Hershey had written then:

> Our Woman is a "new traditionalist" seeking the best of all worlds, old and new. To her, many of our institutions represent stability and coherence. But standards and values seem to mean more now than ritual and forms. The past is valuable, nostalgic. But the present is dynamic and adventuresome, full of the promise of excitement and growth . . . along with its unhinging perils. . . . Our Woman. Yes, she is a new traditionalist, facing today's dilemmas with her head on straight and her chin held high. The women's movement? She may not call herself part of it, but she respects it for upgrading women and equality on many fronts. . . . She's newly independent and self-reliant but she can use the help of life partners, good friends, and authoritative guides.

This was a description of ambivalence, of the hope and fear which permeates the majority of people. The new traditionalists are a contradiction in terms—they seek the best of both worlds. They identify the best of the past with stablity and security and identify the best of the changes in roles with excitement and growth. They are afraid of the "unhinging perils" which many read in the early messages of the change innovators, but they too want the goodies that come from moving out into the world. In short, they want the excitement of independence and the "sameness" of dependence. They want change without risk, growth without loss. They want it all.

In that sense, the ambivalence I saw in miniature at the ends of the Shuttle Zone are magnified in the middle. The chief fear among the radical innovators was that they might lose the roots of nurturing and the security of family roles and relationships. The chief fear among the resisters was that they might miss out on the self-esteem and vitality that come from change. In the middleground men and women both try to work out a compromise course.

"I'M NOT A FEMINIST, BUT . . ."

The new female traditionalists I met often described themselves in a single code phrase, "I'm not a feminist, but . . ." I couldn't travel anywhere without hearing someone, a movie star, or a waitress, prefacing her remarks with the defusing phrase, "I'm not a feminist, but . . ."

"I'm not a feminist, but I believe in Equal Pay for Equal Work."

"I'm not a feminist, but I don't think it's fair that housewives whose husbands divorce them don't get any social security."

"I'm not a feminist, but I don't think it's fair that a woman has to pay an estate tax on the farm after her husband dies, when her husband wouldn't have to pay a nickel if she died first."

This phrase became so common in the '70s that an editorial writer in the New York *Times*, fantasizing about the first woman President, wrote that her inaugural address would probably begin with a denunciation of uppity women.

It seems to me that this is almost a motto for the middleground. I know that to some degree each of us resists labeling, the kind inherent in saying, "I Am a Feminist." We resist being pigeonholed and having our individuality denied, our complexity reduced to a bumper sticker. But this phrase is more than a reaction against being labeled. I think it is an expression of the central ambivalence of the middlegrounder going through this Shuttle Zone. To understand how they are evolving, I wanted to understand this code phrase.

Both halves of this expression—"I'm Not a Feminist" and "But"—are important. One woman explained it to me this way, "Well, first I say I'm not a feminist. That part means, 'I don't hate men and burn my bra, I'm a real gal.' Then I also say what is bugging me, which may be very women's libby, you know. It's, well, I like what women like Bella Abzug and everyone say, but I don't want to be like them. A lot of things they say are right, but not the way they say them."

BECKY: I'M NOT A FEMINIST, BUT . . .

When Becky said, "I'm not a feminist, but . . ." to me it was her way of saying, I want change without a loss of love.

In some ways Becky seemed like many of the change innovators. I first saw her, after all, when I was a passenger on the bus she was driving through her adopted city. She was five feet ten inches tall and 160 firm pounds and she grasped the wheel with an unself-conscious authority. As the passengers at my stop got on the bus, the black woman, dressed in one of those unflattering uniforms that are meant to last long rather than fit well, barked them up the stairs. She was both cheerful and noisy, handing out change and directions, with one eye on her rear-view mirror and another eye on some boisterous young boys at the back of the bus. "I won't have none of that on my bus," she yelled at them and, with one look at her, they instantly stopped fooling around.

We met again after work to discuss her life and her childhood in a town in North Carolina.

"Growing up, my daddy taught me to be independent. He used to say, 'Becky, don't take nothing off of nobody.' Now my parents always made me feel I could accomplish anything I wanted, and that, I think, put us in good stead. Now I remember in school when they'd let the boys be book monitors and the girls water the plants. All that dumb stuff. Me? I dissected my first frog when I was in the first grade. The other girls were scared. Not me. I was driving around my daddy's truck when I was thirteen, and now here I am, driving a bus."

Becky leaned over the restaurant table holding her coffee mug in both hands and told me conspiratorially: "I took this job on a dare. I saw an ad in the newspaper. I was working in an office at the time not making the bucks. My brother-in-law told me, you won't make it. But I can do it. I came out number one in seniority on the tests. And I'm liking it fine. I like to drive that bus. Now of course I want to be the first woman instructor. The next time you talk to me, I'm going to be Becky, the first woman instructor. That's my goal."

Then, more quizzically, she added: "I just don't understand why some woman would be in an office making $150 a week when she could be down here making $880 a month for starters. How do you figure them? Just too silly, I guess."

From all appearances, I would have thought of Becky as avant-garde. Her status as one of twelve women in a twelve-thousand-man system qualifies her as that. Yet, she sees herself quite differently. "Noooo. I'm not one of them women's lib types. I don't take any of that shit. When I got this job, a lot of the other girls were already hollering about it. I'm not a feminist," she says flatly and then adds her explanation like a punchline. "I still like to be treated delicatelike."

As a bus driver she wants only to be efficient and upwardly mobile. The nail polish she wears with her uniform is the only evidence on the job of what she prizes, "my old-fashioned femininity." As for the rest, she wants only to be treated equally with the men, and to be promoted on a "fair and square basis."

Moreover, she is aware that without the women's movement she wouldn't have her job. "Well, now you could not have done it because they would not have let you. Now you have an opportunity. For instance, I always wanted to be an airline stewardess back in 1959 when I graduated from high school. But there were no black stewardesses. I could not fight it. Now there are hundreds. Well, it's the same with the bus."

But, in her private life, Becky wants to be, as she puts it, "regarded as a gentlewoman, if you know what I mean." A feminist, according to Becky, would say that men are for the birds, and the men would say that she was for the birds. "Now, I don't feel that way. And I don't want men to think about me that way neither."

As we sat over coffee I could see how her father's message of independence conflicted with society's view of women. Her mother used to clean houses for the white people in her town in North Carolina and she observed them. She also observed her parents' relationship: "My dad was always the boss man." And when she was still quite little, "I knew that to find a man I'd have to cool my act." For a time she learned to cover her independence with a kind of fluttering girlishness.

She was married at twenty-three and a mother at twenty-four, twenty-five, twenty-six, twenty-seven. For those years she stayed at home taking care of her children, but she was never happy there. Her relationship with her husband became a stormy one as she began to act more in tune with her own sense of self. Now she says, "My marriage was a struggle. My husband says that if he had known what kind of a woman I really was, that I wasn't going to be bossed by him, he never would have married me. Well, now maybe I wasn't fair to him, but I didn't know it then."

Still, she stayed married for twelve years, alternating between trying to adjust to what he wanted and trying to be herself. "He would say, 'You're not doing what I want!' That's what he would say. Well, I wasn't about to do anything anybody told me if I didn't want to. I felt like it was a prison. I was in prison because I was married, I felt like obligated to him, and it made it hard for both of us. Now he's with someone who just says, 'Oh yes, Jesse, yessir, right away, sir.' Can you beat that?"

Her own ambition took off when she got divorced. "Well, now when you're on your own and you got kids to support, you just got to go for the bucks." In that sense, her experience was typical of so many other women. The economic fait accompli simply dominated any other fears or internal conflicts.

But from her new seat, it seemed that the qualities of independence, or ambition, the strengths that qualified her for her job, might always disqualify her in a relationship. So there was a piece of her that still believed that to be successful as a woman, she must be feminine. "I like to go out with a man and have him treat me and take me here and there and act like the lady."

NEW DOUBLE STANDARD

In a sense, Becky's assurance that she was not a feminist, but . . . was indicative of the new double standard of the middleground. She believed that the benefits of a personal life—love, a stable family relationship—probably depended on filling a traditional feminine role. On the other hand, the benefits of an independent life demanded a nontraditional role. That is, it seems to me, the conflict at the core of the new middle. Again and again, the middleground women I met sought the safety of traditional relationships and the excitement of new roles in the world. In this Shuttle Zone, they zigzagged between the past and the future, often playing one role at home and another in the world, or one role with men and another with women. They held up a new double standard of behavior.

Because she was single, Becky didn't have to deal every day with this double standard and, in fact, her sense of self was strong and sure. Still, it was interesting to see how reluctant that woman was to give up her psychological link to the traditional stance of women, to hear the sudden sound of reticence in the words of a gutsy bus driver.

But, I was at least as surprised to see the number of more conservative women in the middleground also become, not feminists exactly, *but* . . .

HARRIET: ONE SMALL STEP

When Harriet said, "I'm not a feminist, but . . ." it was the beginning of a limited but important fight for herself.

Harriet was not the sort of person you would expect to make a fuss. The forty-six-year-old woman was on the opposite edge of the middleground from Becky. Yet it is part of the story that she too ended up fighting in public for her "rights."

For the first time in decades, as she herself said, "I'm making waves and it feels terrific." The mother of three had decided to sue a veterans' organization that refused to accept her as a member.

Harriet found it rather odd, but exciting, to be in the spotlight and in the newspaper, especially when she considered herself a conservative woman. "I'm not a radical. I'm feminine, I would say," the graying, curly-haired woman with black rhinestone eyeglasses and a plain white shirt over her blue bermudas told me. "I want to have my cigarette lit by the fellows and the doors opened and all that jazz. That is part of being a lady, I think."

Harriet, it said happily in the newspaper, was no "libber." She liked "Mrs." better than "Ms." and was proud to be a married woman. She just wanted to join the veterans' organization and they wouldn't let her for no reason at all, except that she was a woman.

The Southwest woman talked not about women's rights, but about "fairness." "What's fair is fair," she said. What wasn't fair was that despite her tour of duty during World War II, she couldn't join the group. She wanted her rights, but didn't want to be seen as a women's rightist.

Harriet had become a change agent only when it was safer. A union leader in Michigan described safe-change agents as the kind who only make waves in a bathtub. Harriet was hardly a stormtrooper. But she was one of the hundreds of second- and third-level change agents. She wouldn't have been in this fight if she thought it would cost her what she calls her "feminity."

"I'm not about to say, okay, mister, I'm taking over. I mean there are some women who are antagonistic like that. They really get nasty. If they are trying to push something in that atmosphere, they are not going to get anywhere. Kindness kills. That's what I do and it works."

Down at the local organization where she first got the idea of applying for national membership, she insisted on being treated well. "They all treat me like a lady. If they started cussing me and didn't have any respect for what I was doing, I'd drop it."

There had always been something of a tug-of-war between the side that was traditional and the side that was willing to take on something new, something tough. Harriet was one of the few women in her high school class to ever leave the small eastern town where she grew up, the daughter of a fisherman. She was one of the very few to join the Army during World War II. She always had a fighting streak in her.

For five years the curly-haired energetic mother of three worked as a volunteer with the veterans, and then she decided to take on another fight. She had applied to the national organization with the twenty-dollar bill that her husband had given her, and she had been rejected. Harriet knew it was "discrimination" and, never mind that she didn't like to hear other women fighting for their rights, she decided to fight it.

"Five years ago I wouldn't have done this. No. Not until this whole thing has come about where everything is even-Steven. I still wouldn't have known about the national group unless they were involved in our local hall. They were doing the same thing we were doing, having the same meetings. When I get through with things here at the local, I would like to join them. So my husband says, 'here is twenty dollars, go and join them.' I said, 'it's all men.' He said to try it anyway."

"You see, I am entitled to this. It is an honor to me to have gone into the service. Anybody who served in a wartime period is eligible. But if you are female you are not, and this irritates me. How do you tell someone they are narrow-minded? They just don't see the forest for the trees. One of the guys said, what was I putting up this big hassle for? Well, they can't see the forest for the trees.

"With the women's thing the way it is today, it is equal opportunity. It has brought it all out," she said. In the areas that are safe, accepted, that don't threaten her major decisions of life, she is all for it.

"I remember during the convention in 1972, when I think it was Bella Abzug. Anyway she was saying that it was just equal opportunity for women to run for President. That's where all this started, wasn't it? I started taking notice then. I don't know anybody who thinks this way though. I guess I just heard about it on television. I haven't read about it. My husband brings home *Playgirl* for me—I wouldn't buy it—but that's about all."

"Anyway, the thing I am for is like my mother. She was a widow, the five of us were out of the house. My dad dies and she has nothing. No social security, no benefits at all. She got one fisherman's fund, twelve dollars a month. She had to go out and learn something. She tried for practical nursing and they wouldn't take her because she was too old. No matter what she tried to do, she was too old. Now, she is not the type to sit back and let the world fall over, but she was cleaning houses and things like this. I mean, what has she got? Nothing. Now she has made it okay. Bless her. She went out and scrubbed and worked to try and keep herself above water. But I agree with the women's lib thing in the social security for people like my mother. If my husband died when I was fifty-seven or something and my kids were gone, I wouldn't get anything. This is one thing I would work towards."

"But as far as being a construction worker, going into the man's world, men have always worked in construction or as plumbers. But women, how many women qualify? They are going to tear their insides out."

She thought some of the other things were okay for younger women, but not for her. "My husband," she said as an explanation, "is a very conservative, straight man. No flashy clothes. He still wants the navy blue pants and black shoes. Everything is neat as a pin. But he encouraged me in this. Whatever I want to do, I get a lot of backing from him. He helps by running errands, going to the store, fixing the doors at the Legion Hall, painting."

But they have a very separate, very traditional role-structured marriage. "He is a man and I am a woman. He has his place and I have mine. For twenty-two years we have done a good job at it. We are still together. The kids are very healthy-minded. This is the way my husband is, and this is the way our marriage is. I can see a difference in my daughter, the oldest one. She has a hard-working husband. He will pitch in and do anything. This is a difference. And it's good. I would be a fool not to like that, but this is my marriage."

For Harriet the line was drawn. She had enough. The independent young girl who joined the Army grew into the woman who wanted to join the national veterans' group. But the twenty-two-year-old who didn't hear anything else except, "You grow up, you fall in love, you get married, you have children—you know, the regular," wasn't going to question that. She bought the changes that would help her mother or win her a slot in the organization, but not the part that could upset her marriage, or withdraw the support that comes from her husband. She went only so far into the new middle.

Many women like Harriet take a small step for womankind while ferociously protecting the sanctity of their marriage or their investment in their relationships.

I sat with a woman for hours in a New York restaurant. She pulled out a file folder full of information about her sex discrimination suit, paper after paper, citing case and book on her suit. She was talking in the kind of feminist lingo—movement shorthand—that would turn off most listeners. Words like "capitalist oppression," "male chauvinism," "sex role stereotyping," piled on top of each other.

Suddenly at five-thirty she looked at her watch and her face changed its pallor as if it were the shifting fluid of a kaleroscope. "My God, I have to run," she said, cramming the papers back into her briefcase. "My husband is home at six and I have to be there."

She seemed literally panicked. For a moment it was so incongruous that I was taken aback and laughed. Then she turned and with great hostility said, "Don't judge me. This is my husband. He needs me to be his wife and that's all there is to it."

QUESTIONS FOR "THE NEW MIDDLE GROUND" BY ELLEN GOODMAN

Talking About the Text

1. In your own words, describe the ambivalence that Ellen Goodman reports that many women feel about the women's movement.
2. Goodman tells us that the "conflict at the core of the new middle" involves a constant changing of roles—from traditional feminine roles to more nontraditional independent roles. How do the cases of Becky and Harriet illustrate this conflict. In what ways are each shifting roles?
3. Ellen Goodman relies primarily on interviews to support her claim that most women are in a "middleground" between traditional feminine roles and more independent roles associated with being a "feminist" or a part of the women's movement. Do you find Goodman's interviews to be a persuasive form of evidence? Why or why not? What other forms of evidence *might* Goodman have used?

Exploring Issues

1. How do you feel about the women's movement? Do you consider your-self a "feminist"? Why or why not? What does this mean for you?
2. To what extent are men also in a "new middleground" regarding mascu-line roles? Are men's current expectations of women any different from their expectations of 20 years ago? Are men's expectations of themselves at all different from what they were 20 years ago? For example, are men today always expected to pay for dates, to provide primary support for the family, and to handle traditionally male tasks such as car repairs, plumbing, carpentry, and lawn mowing? To what extent do the men of today accept responsibility for child care, household cleaning, and for meal planning and preparation? How do you feel about changes in men's roles?

Writing Assignments

1. After reading this essay by Ellen Goodman, write a list of questions that you would like to ask women about their expectations of themselves and of the men in their lives. Then, use these questions to interview a woman. If several of your classmates are doing this assignment, try to interview women of different ages. If possible, tape record your inter-view; if that is not possible, take careful notes. Finally, write a report of your interview and share your findings with your classmates.
2. Formulate a list of questions that you would like to ask a man about changes in men's roles. Then, use these questions to interview a man about changes in men's roles. Follow the suggestions made in No. 1 above for your interview.

3. Read Deborah Tannen's essay entitled "Talk in the Intimate Relationship: His and Hers," and compare Tannen's analysis of communication styles with Goodman's analysis of the changing social roles of men and women. Then, write an essay in which you explore the implications of Goodman's findings for Tannen's theory of how men and women communicate.

Reading 14

Along the Tortilla Curtain

Pete Hamill

Pete Hamill writes a monthly column for *Esquire* magazine and is the author of a book entitled *Loving Women*. In the following essay, reprinted from *Esquire* (February 1990), Hamill examines the experiences and attitudes of people who come through the "tortilla curtain" dividing Mexico and the United States. Often dangerous and expensive, this trip across the border symbolizes hope and opportunity for young men like Jeronimo Vasquez, who has already crossed the border three times to come and work in the fields. More important, Hamill addresses the concerns of those who fear the "browning of America" and the importation of Hispanic cultures to the United States.

You move through the hot, polluted Tijuana morning, past shops and gas stations and cantinas, past the tourist traps of the Avenida Revolución, past the egg-shaped Cultural Center and the new shopping malls and the government housing with bright patches of laundry hanging on balconies; then it's through streets of painted adobe peeling in the sun, ball fields where kids play without gloves, and you see ahead and above you ten-thousand-odd shacks perched uneasily upon the Tijuana hills, and you glimpse the green road signs for the beaches as the immense luminous light of the Pacific brightens the sky. You turn, and along-side the road there's a chain link fence. It's ten feet high.

On the other side of the fence is the United States.

There are wide gashes in the fence, which was once called the Tortilla

Curtain. You could drive three wide loads, side by side, through the tears in this pathetic curtain. On this morning, on both sides of the fence (more often called *la línea* by the locals), there are small groups of young Mexican men dressed in polyester shirts and worn shoes and faded jeans, and holding small bags. These are a few of the people who are changing the United States, members of a huge army of irregulars engaged in the largest, most successful invasion ever made of North America.

On this day, they smoke cigarettes. They make small jokes. They munch on tacos prepared by a flat-faced, pig-tailed Indian woman whose stand is parked by the roadside. They sip soda. And some of them gaze across the arid scrub and sandy chaparral at the blurred white buildings of the U.S. town of San Ysidro. They wait patiently and do not hide. And if you pull over, and buy a soda from the woman, and speak some Spanish, they will talk.

"I tried last night," says the young man named Jeronimo Vasquez, who wears a Chicago Bears T-shirt under a denim jacket. "But it was too dangerous, too many helicopters last night, too much light. . . ." He looks out at the open stretch of gnarled land, past the light towers, at the distant white buildings. "Maybe tonight we will go to Zapata Canyon. . . ." He is from Oaxaca, he says, deep in the hungry Mexican south. He has been to the United States three times, working in the fields; it is now Tuesday, and he starts a job near Stockton on the following Monday, picker's work arranged by his cousin. "I have much time. . . ."

Abruptly, he turns away to watch some action. Two young men are running across the dried scrub on the U.S. side, kicking up little clouds of white dust, while a Border Patrol car goes after them. The young men dodge, circle, running the broken field, and suddenly stand very still as the car draws close. They are immediately added to the cold statistics of border apprehensions. But they are really mere sacrifices; over on the left, three other men run low and hunched, like infantrymen in a fire fight. "*Corre, corre,*" Jeronimo Vasquez whispers. "Run, run. . . ." They do. And when they vanish into some distant scrub, he clenches a fist like a triumphant fan. He is not alone. All the others cheer, as does the woman selling tacos, and on the steep hill above the road, a man stands before a tar-paper shack, waves a Mexican flag, and shouts: "*Gol!*" And everyone laughs.

We've all read articles about the 1,950-mile-long border between the United States and Mexico, seen documentaries, heard the bellowing rhetoric of the C-Span politicians enraged at the border's weakness; but until you stand beside it, the border is an abstraction. Up close, you see immediately that the border is at once a concrete place with holes in the fence, and a game, a joke, an affront, a wish, a mere line etched by a draftsman on a map. No wonder George Bush gave up on interdiction as a tactic in the War on Drugs; there are literally hundreds of Ho Chi Minh trails heading into the United States from the south (and others from Canada, of course, and the sea). On some parts of the Mexican border there is one border patrolman for every twenty-six miles; it doesn't require a smuggling genius to figure out how to get twenty tons of cocaine to a Los Angeles warehouse. To fill in the gaps, to guard all the other U.S. borders, would require millions of armed guards, many billions of dollars. And somehow, Jeronimo Vasquez would still appear on a Monday morning in Stockton.

Those young men beside the ruined fence—not the *narcotraficantes*—are the most typical members of the peaceful invasion. Nobody knows how many come across each year, although in 1988 920,000 were stopped, arrested, and sent back to Mexico by the border wardens. Thousands more make it. Some are described by the outnumbered and overwhelmed immigration police as OTMs (Other Than Mexican, which is to say, Salvadorans, Guatemalans, Nicaraguans, Costa Ricans fleeing the war zones, and South Americans and Asians fleeing poverty). Some, like Jeronimo Vasquez, come for a few months, earn money, and return to families in Mexico; others come to stay.

"When you see a woman crossing," says Jeronimo Vasquez, "you know she's going to stay. It means she has a husband on the other side, maybe even children. She's not going back. Most of the women are from Salvador, not so many Mexicans. . . ."

Tijuana is one of their major staging grounds. In 1940 it was a town of seventeen thousand citizens, many of whom were employed in providing pleasure for visiting Americans. The clenched, blue-nosed forces of American puritanism gave the town its function. In 1915 California banned horse racing; dance halls and prostitution were made illegal in 1917; and in 1920 Prohibition became the law of the land. So thousands of Americans began crossing the border to do what they could not do at home: shoot crap, bet on horses, get drunk, and get laid.

Movie stars came down from Hollywood with people to whom they weren't married. Gangsters traveled from as far away as Chicago and New York. Women with money had abortions at the Paris Clinic. Sailors arrived from San Diego to lose their virgin status, get their first doses of the clap, and too often to spend nights in the Tijuana jail. The Casino of Agua Caliente was erected in 1928, a glorious architectural mixture of the Alhambra and a Florentine villa, complete with gambling, drinking, a nightclub, big bands, tennis, golf, a swimming pool, and fancy restaurants. Babe Ruth and Jack Dempsey were among the clients, and a young dancer named Margarita Cansino did a nightclub act with her father before changing her name to Rita Hayworth. The casino was closed in 1935 by the Mexican president, and only one of its old towers still remains. But sin did not depart with the gamblers or the end of Prohibition. The town boomed during the war, and thousands of Americans still remember the bizarre sex shows and rampant prostitution of the era and the availability of something called marijuana. Today the run-down cantinas and whorehouses of the Zona Norte are like a living museum of Tijuana's gaudy past.

"It's very dangerous here for women," Jeronimo Vasquez said. "The coyotes tell them they will take them across, for money. If they don't have enough money, they talk them into becoming *putas* for a week or a month. And they never get out. . . ."

Although commercial sex and good marijuana are still available in Tijuana, sin, alas, is no longer the city's major industry. Today the population is more than one million. City and suburbs are crowded with *maquiladora* plants, assembling foreign goods for export to the United States. These factories pay the highest wages in Mexico (although still quite low by U.S. standards) and attract workers from all over the republic. Among permanent residents, unemployment is very low.

But it's said that at any given time, one third of the people in Tijuana are transients, waiting to cross to *el otro lado*. A whole subculture that feeds off this traffic can be seen around the Tijuana bus station: coyotes (guides) who for a fee will bring them across; *enganchadores* (labor contractors) who promise jobs; rooming-house operators; hustlers; crooked cops prepared to extort money from the non-Mexicans. The prospective migrants are not simply field hands, making the hazardous passage to the valleys of California to do work that even the most poverty-ravaged Americans will not do. Mexico is also experiencing a "skill drain." As soon as a young Mexican acquires a skill or craft—carpentry, wood finishing, auto repair—he has the option of departing for the north. The bags held by some of the young men with Jeronimo Vasquez contained tools. And since the economic collapse of 1982 hammered every citizen of Mexico, millions have exercised the option. The destinations of these young skilled Mexicans aren't limited to the sweatshops of Los Angeles or the broiling fields of the Imperial Valley; increasingly the migrants settle in the cities of the North and East. In New York, I've met Mexicans from as far away as Chiapas, the impoverished state that borders Guatemala.

Such men are more likely to stay permanently in the United States than are the migrant agricultural laborers like Jeronimo Vasquez. The skilled workers and craftsmen buy documents that make them seem legal. They establish families. They learn English. They pay taxes and use services. Many of them applied for amnesty under the terms of the Simpson-Rodino Act; the new arrivals are not eligible, but they are still coming.

I'm one of those who believe this is a good thing. The energy of the Mexican immigrant, his capacity for work, has become essential to this country. While Mexicans, legal and illegal, work in fields, wash dishes, grind away in sweatshops, clean bedpans, and mow lawns (and fix transmissions, polish wood, build bookcases), millions of American citizens would rather sit on stoops and wait for welfare checks. If every Mexican in this country went home next week, Americans would starve. The lettuce on your plate in that restaurant got there because a Mexican bent low in the sun and pulled it from the earth. Nothing, in fact, is more bizarre than the stereotype of the "lazy" Mexican, leaning against the wall with his sombrero pulled over his face. I've been traveling to Mexico for more than thirty years; the only such Mexicans I've ever seen turned out to be suffering from malnutrition.

But the great migration from Mexico is certainly altering the United States, just as the migration of Eastern European Jews and southern Italians changed the nation at the beginning of the century and the arrival of Irish Catholics changed it a half century earlier. Every immigrant brings with him an entire culture, a dense mixture of beliefs, assumptions, and nostalgias about family, manhood, sex, laughter, music, food, religion. His myths are not American myths. In this respect, the Mexican immigrant is no different from the Irish, Germans, Italians, and Jews.

The ideological descendants of the Know-Nothings and other "nativist" types are, of course, alarmed. They worry about the Browning of America. They talk about the high birthrate of the Latino arrivals, their supposed refusal to learn English, their divided loyalties.

Much of this is racist nonsense, based on the assumption that Mexicans are inherently "inferior" to people who look like Michael J. Fox. But it also ignores the wider context. The Mexican migration to the United States is another part of the vast demographic tide that has swept most of the world in this century: the journey from the countryside to the city, from field to factory, from south to north—and from illiteracy to the book. But there is one huge irony attached to the Mexican migration. These people are moving in the largest numbers into precisely those states that the United States took at gunpoint in the Mexican War of 1846–48: California, Arizona, New Mexico, Texas, Nevada, and Utah, along with parts of Wyoming, Colorado, and Oklahoma. In a way, those young men crossing into San Ysidro and Chula Vista each night are entering the lost provinces of Old Mexico, and some Mexican intellectuals even refer sardoni- cally to this great movement as *La Reconquista*—the Reconquest. It certainly is a wonderful turn on the old doctrine of manifest destiny, which John L. O'Sullivan, the New York journalist who coined the phrase in 1845, said was our right "to overspread the continent allotted by Providence for the free develop- ment of our yearly multiplying millions."

The yearly multiplying millions of Mexico will continue moving north unless one of two things happens: the U.S. economy totally collapses, or the Mexican economy expands dramatically. Since neither is likely to happen, the United States of the twenty-first century is certain to be browner, and speak more Spanish, and continue to see its own culture transformed. The Know-Nothings are, of course, enraged at this great demographic shift and are demanding that Washington seal the borders. As always with fanatics and paranoids, they have no sense of irony. They were probably among those flag-waving patriots who were filled with a sense of triumph when free men danced on the moral ruins of the Berlin Wall last November; they see no inconsistency in the demand for a new Great Wall, between us and Mexico.

The addled talk goes on, and in the hills of Tijuana, young men like Jeronimo Vasquez continue to wait for the chance to sprint across the midnight scrub in pursuit of the golden promise of the other side. *Corre*, hombre, *corre*. . . .

QUESTIONS: FOR "ALONG THE TORTILLA CURTAIN" BY PETE HAMILL

Talking About the Text

1. Although he begins his essay with descriptions of people and places, Pete Hamill uses these descriptions to advance an argument. What is that argument? Do you find this argument persuasive? Why or why not?

2. How does Pete Hamill feel toward illegal immigrants like Jeronimo Vasquez? What clues do you have in the text?
3. Hamill believes that there is virtually no way to secure U.S. borders from illegal entries. Do you agree with Hamill? What are some of the reasons that Hamill gives for this? Can you think of any other reasons? Would you like for the borders to be more secure than they are now? Why or why not?
4. What might Tijuana symbolize for North Americans? For Central and South Americans?

Exploring Issues

1. Hamill tells us that some Americans are concerned about the "Browning of America," that is, about a perceived loss of Anglo culture and an increase in Hispanic populations in the United States. Do you feel than an increasing Hispanic population poses any significant problems for the United States? If so, what are these problems? If not, why not? Does it matter whether the U.S. population is primarily white or brown? Why or why not?
2. How do you feel about the presence of illegal immigrants in the United States? Does it bother you that some immigrants are receiving benefits from public services but are not paying taxes? Or do you sympathize with people who come to the United States for economic or political reasons? Do you feel that Americans have any responsibility for people from countries that the U.S. government has helped to destabilize economically or politically? Why or why not?

Writing Assignments

1. Imagine that you are in Tijuana and are preparing to cross the border illegally. Write an essay in which you explain who you are, why you are attempting to cross the border, and what you expect to find in the United States. Include in your essay descriptions of your feelings, attitudes, and expectations.
2. Read the Hamill essay just preceding and the essay by Mario Cuomo in Chapter 1. Notice that both Pete Hamill and Mario Cuomo are essentially sympathetic toward all immigrants, illegal and legal. Write a response to Mario Cuomo and Pete Hamill explaining some of your concerns about having many undocumented residents in the United States. What sorts of problems does this pose? What are some issues that these authors may not have mentioned in their essays?

Reading 15

Where Do You Sleep?

Frank X. Gaspar

Originally from Provincetown, Massachusetts, Frank X. Gaspar teaches writing
at Long Beach (California) City College and writes poetry. His volume of poetry,
The Holyoke, won the 1988 Morse Prize for Poetry, and he has been a Bread
Loaf Scholar. Gaspar's poems have been published in many journals, including
Kenyon Review, Georgia Review, and *The Nation.* In the following poem
Gaspar writes of the illegal border crossings that occur on a regular basis in our
southwestern and western states. Rather than addressing these crossings as
a social or a political issue, Gaspar focuses on the human dramas involved.

I warn my son against eating the red berries
on the chaparral hillside—coyote food lumping
the odd scats we see on the clay road
that edges the long pasture
where the wild geese come down at twilight
to gabble like the crowds at the town fair,
strangers' voices winnowed through the limbs
of the bordering oaks. Once we saw
a bobcat, like a pistol-shot on the haunches
of a jackrabbit diving into the expedient dusk,
and then darkness came, and my wife's mother
walked out from the screened porch,
her breath a mist in cold starlight,
her eyes on the deepening hills.
"No fires tonight," is all she said
and nipped her bourbon, and it was true
we saw no lights then under the black
angle of ridge where the big cat had vanished,
no suspected camps of the *illegals* who make
their way up this secluded valley, pushing north,
who walk up to our sagging, whitewashed house
to barter work for sandwiches, dollars,
a chance to wash their children
in the spray of the black hose
coiled on the side of the cow-barn.

And on our rummage sometimes
through the oak knees and barbed wire, along
the steep rills of the dung-lined creek,
I look for *tramp-signs*—the cross of sticks
or diamond of stones that mark a house simply, *yes* or *no*.
We are far enough from the border
to only hear of its drama, the *other* coyotes,
their craft of promise, the government dogs
rooting spoor in the waste of the dry arroyos,
but we may be marked by some emblem here,
for they come, the men and boys mostly, lean as rails,
and I squat in the dirt of the dooryard with them,
my once-good Spanish rusting like the fence wire
or the rabbit cages stacked in the tall weeds and bamboo:
Here is some money for food. The Señora wants
the weeds knocked down in the old pasture
and will pay you the rest when you finish.
She doesn't need the work done. When the family
comes on weekends, her sisters chide, *It's dangerous.*
You don't know what they might do.
She never argues, but she never stops hiring them,
learns their names, speaks to them in signs
and single words, tries to learn
where they sleep, where they come from,
and where they think they are going.

Our valley within the valley: I have
never felt the wind here, but nights
the cold air flows down the cleft
like a slow river, invisible
under the lip of the low ridges, touching to life
each leaf and branch, brimming up to glaze the moon
and even the stars as they wheel their long track
around the pole. An owl flies, bats rise
like scraps from a fire, and something sets
our own dogs barking in the brush behind the sheds.
I rise too and softly walk inside to where my son
breathes heavily in his sleeping bag
adorned with bright monsters. He shudders
at my footfall, tosses in some deep dream,
and I lay a hand to his forehead, brush back
his hair and spend a minute in his clean boy-smell
before I go back outdoors. The dogs
have run off, and the sky
has become its own river of light.
I sit perfectly still. I cannot

tell if the owl has settled
somewhere beyond the pasture and I hear
the long night-rhythms of its call,
or if I hear the slow, persistent lilt
of a single human voice
sifting down, out of the hills.

Reading 16

One Holy Night

Sandra Cisneros

Sandra Cisneros is a Chicago-born Texan who has taught in three California colleges during the past few years. Her collection of short stories, *The House on Mango Street,* won the Before Columbus Book Award in 1985, and she will soon publish a second collection in which the following story appears. In "One Holy Night," Cisneros portrays a young Mexican girl who discovers her own sexuality and then approaches motherhood and adult responsibilities. As this young girl narrates her own story, we can make inferences about her expectations and perceptions in the context of a Mexican-American community.

About the truth, if you give it to a person, then he has power over you. And if someone gives it to you, then they have made themselves your slave. It is a strong magic. You can never take it back.
—CHAQ UXMAL PALOQUÍN

He said his name was Chaq. Chaq Uxmal Paloquín. That's what he told me. He was of an ancient line of Mayan kings. Here, he said, making a map with the heel of his boot, this is where I come from, the Yucatán, the ancient cities. This is what Boy Baby said.

It's been eighteen weeks since Abuelita chased him away with the broom, and what I'm telling you I never told nobody, except Rachel and Lourdes, who know everything. He said he would love me like a revolution, like a religion. Abuelita burned the pushcart and sent me here, miles from home, in this town of dust, with one wrinkled witch woman who rubs my belly with jade, and sixteen nosy cousins.

I don't know how many girls have gone bad from selling cucumbers. I know I'm not the first. My mother took the crooked walk too, I'm told, and I'm sure my Abuelita has her own story, but it's not my place to ask.

Abuelita says it's Uncle Lalo's fault because he's the man of the family and if he had come home on time like he was supposed to and worked the pushcart on the days he was told to and watched over his goddaughter, who is too foolish to look after herself, nothing would've happened, and I wouldn't have to be sent to Mexico. But Uncle Lalo says if they had never left Mexico in the first place, shame enough would have kept a girl from doing devil things.

I'm not saying I'm not bad. I'm not saying I'm special. But I'm not like the Allport Street girls, who stand in doorways and go with men into alleys.

All I know is I didn't want it like that. Not against the bricks or hunkering in somebody's car. I wanted it come undone like gold thread, like a tent full of birds. The way it's supposed to be, the way I knew it would be when I met Boy Baby.

But you must know, I was no girl back then. And Boy Baby was no boy. Chaq Uxmal Paloquín. Boy Baby was a man. When I asked him how old he was he said he didn't know. The past and the future are the same thing. So he seemed boy and baby and man all at once, and the way he looked at me, how do I explain?

I'd park the pushcart in front of the Jewel food store Saturdays. He bought a mango on a stick the first time. Paid for it with a new twenty. Next Saturday he was back. Two mangoes, lime juice, and chili powder, keep the change. The third Saturday he asked for a cucumber spear and ate it slow. I didn't see him after that till the day he brought me Kool-Aid in a plastic cup. Then I knew what I felt for him.

Maybe you wouldn't like him. To you he might be a bum. Maybe he looked it. Maybe. He had broken thumbs and burnt fingers. He had thick greasy fingernails he never cut and dusty hair. And all his bones were strong ones like a man's. I waited every Saturday in my same blue dress. I sold all the mango and cucumber, and then Boy Baby would come finally.

What I knew of Chaq was only what he told me, because nobody seemed to know where he came from. Only that he could speak a strange language that no one could understand, said his name translated into boy, or boy-child, and so it was the street people nicknamed him Boy Baby.

I never asked about his past. He said it was all the same and didn't matter, past and the future all the same to his people. But the truth has a strange way of following you, of coming up to you and making you listen to what it has to say.

Night time. Boy Baby brushes my hair and talks to me in his strange language because I like to hear it. What I like to hear him tell is how he is Chaq, Chaq of the people of the sun, Chaq of the temples, and what he says sounds sometimes like broken clay, and at other times like hollow sticks, or like the swish of old feathers crumbling into dust.

He lived behind Esparza & Sons Auto Repair in a little room that used to be a closet—pink plastic curtains on a narrow window, a dirty cot covered with newspapers, and a cardboard box filled with socks and rusty tools. It was there, under one bald bulb, in the back room of the Esparza garage, in the single room with pink curtains, that he showed me the guns—twenty-four in all. Rifles and pistols, one rusty musket, a machine gun, and several tiny weapons with mother-of-pearl handles that looked like toys. So you'll see who I am, he said, laying them all out on the bed of newspapers. So you'll understand. But I didn't want to know.

The stars foretell everything, he said. My birth. My son's. The boy-child who will bring back the grandeur of my people from those who have broken the arrows, from those who have pushed the ancient stones off their pedestals.

Then he told how he had prayed in the Temple of the Magician years ago as a child when his father had made him promise to bring back the ancient ways. Boy Baby had cried in the temple dark that only the bats made holy. Boy Baby who was man and child among the great and dusty guns lay down on the newspaper bed and wept for a thousand years. When I touched him, he looked at me with the sadness of stone.

You must not tell anyone what I am going to do, he said. And what I remember next is how the moon, the pale moon with its one yellow eye, the moon of Tikal, and Tulum, and Chichén, stared through the pink plastic curtains. Then something inside bit me, and I gave out a cry as if the other, the one I wouldn't be anymore, leapt out.

So I was initiated beneath an ancient sky by a great and mighty heir—Chaq Uxmal Paloquín. I, Ixchel, his queen.

The truth is, it wasn't a big deal. It wasn't any deal at all. I put my bloody panties inside my T-shirt and ran home hugging myself. I thought about a lot of things on the way home. I thought about all the world and how suddenly I became a part of history and wondered if everyone on the street, the sewing machine lady and the *panadería* saleswomen and the woman with two kids sitting on the bus bench didn't all know. *Did I look any different? Could they tell?* We were all the same somehow, laughing behind our hands, waiting the way all women wait, and when we find out, we wonder why the world and a million years made such a big deal over nothing.

I know I was supposed to feel ashamed, but I wasn't ashamed. I wanted to stand on top of the highest building, the top-top floor, and yell, I *know*.

Then I understood why Abuelita didn't let me sleep over at Lourdes's house full of too many brothers, and why the Roman girl in the movies always runs away from the soldier, and what happens when the scenes in love stories begin to fade, and why brides blush, and how it is that sex isn't simply a box you check *M* or *F* on in the test we get at school.

I was wise. The corner girls were still jumping into their stupid little hopscotch squares. I laughed inside and climbed the wooden stairs two by two to the second floor rear where me and Abuelita and Uncle Lalo live. I was still laughing when I opened the door and Abuelita asked, Where's the pushcart?

And then I didn't know what to do.

It's a good thing we live in a bad neighborhood. There are always plenty of bums to blame for your sins. If it didn't happen the way I told it, it really could've. We looked and looked all over for the kids who stole my pushcart. The story wasn't the best, but since I had to make it up right then and there with Abuelita staring a hole through my heart, it wasn't too bad.

For two weeks I had to stay home. Abuelita was afraid the street kids who had stolen the cart would be after me again. Then I thought I might go over to the Esparza garage and take the pushcart out and leave it in some alley for the police to find, but I was never allowed to leave the house alone. Bit by bit the truth started to seep out like a dangerous gasoline.

First the nosy woman who lives upstairs from the laundromat told my Abuelita she thought something was fishy, the pushcart wheeled into Esparza & Sons every Saturday after dark, how a man, the same dark Indian one, the one who never talks to anybody, walked with me when the sun went down and pushed the cart into the garage, that one there, and yes we went inside, there where the fat lady named Concha, whose hair is dyed a hard black, pointed a fat finger.

I prayed that we would not meet Boy Baby, and since the gods listen and are mostly good, Esparza said yes, a man like that had lived there but was gone, had packed a few things and left the pushcart in a corner to pay for his last week's rent.

We had to pay $20 before he would give us our pushcart back. Then Abuelita made me tell the real story of how the cart had disappeared, all of which I told this time, except for that one night, which I would have to tell anyway, weeks later, when I prayed for the moon of my cycle to come back, but it would not.

When Abuelita found out I was going to *das a luz*, she cried until her eyes were little, and blamed Uncle Lalo, and Uncle Lalo blamed this country, and Abuelita blamed the infamy of men. That is when she burned the cucumber pushcart and called me a *sixvergüenza* because I *am* without shame.

Then I cried too—Boy Baby was lost from me—until my head was hot with headaches and I fell asleep. When I woke up, the cucumber pushcart was dust and Abuelita was sprinkling holy water on my head.

Abuelita woke up early every day and went to the Esparza garage to see if news about that *demonio* had been found, had Chaq Uxmal Paloquín sent any letters, any, and when the other mechanics heard that name they laughed, and asked if we had made it up, that we could have some letters that had come for Boy Baby, no forwarding address, since he had gone in such a hurry.

There were three. The first, addressed "Occupant," demanded immediate payment for a four-month-old electric bill. The second was one I recognized right away—a brown envelope fat with cakemix coupons and fabric-softener samples—because we'd gotten one just like it. The third was addressed in a spidery Spanish to a Señor C. Cruz, on paper so thin you could read it unopened by the light of the sky. The return address a convent in Tampico.

This was to whom my Abuelita wrote in hopes of finding the man who could correct my ruined life, to ask if the good nuns might know the whereabouts of a certain Boy Baby—and if they were hiding him it would be of no use because God's eyes see through all souls.

We heard nothing for a long time. Abuelita took me out of school when my uniform got tight around the belly and said it was a shame I wouldn't be able to graduate with the other eighth graders.

Except for Lourdes and Rachel, my grandma and Uncle Lalo, nobody knew about my past. I would sleep in the big bed I share with Abuelita same as always. I could hear Abuelita and Uncle Lalo talking in low voices in the kitchen as if they were praying the rosary, how they were going to send me to Mexico, to San Dionisio de Tlaltepango, where I have cousins and where I was conceived and would've been born had my grandma not thought it wise to send my mother here to the United States so that neighbors in San Dionisio de Tlaltepango wouldn't ask why her belly was suddenly big.

I was happy. I liked staying home. Abuelita was teaching me to crochet the way she had learned in Mexico. And just when I had mastered the tricky rosette stitch, the letter came from the convent which gave the truth about Boy Baby—however much we didn't want to hear.

He was born on a street with no name in a town called Miseria. His father, Eusebio, is a knife sharpener. His mother, Refugia, stacks apricots into pyramids and sells them on a cloth in the market. There are brothers. Sisters too of which I know little. The youngest, a Carmelite, writes me all this and prays for my soul, which is why I know it's all true.

Boy Baby is thirty-seven years old. His name is Chato which means fatface. There is no Mayan blood.

I don't think they understand how it is to be a girl. I don't think they know how it is to have to wait your whole life. I count the months for the baby to be born, and it's like a ring of water inside me reaching out and out until one day it will tear from me with its own teeth.

Already I can feel the animal inside me stirring in his own uneven sleep. The witch woman says it's the dreams of weasels that make my child sleep the way he sleeps. She makes me eat white bread blessed by the priest, but I know it's the ghost of him inside me that circles and circles, and will not let me rest.

Abuelita said they sent me here just in time, because a little later Boy Baby came back to our house looking for me, and she had to chase him away with the broom. The next thing we hear, he's in the newspaper clippings his sister sends. A picture of him looking very much like stone, police hooked on either arm . . . *on the road to* Las Grutas de Xtacumbilxuna, *the Caves of the Hidden Girl* . . . *eleven female bodies . . . the last seven years . . .*

Then I couldn't read but only stare at the little black-and-white dots that make up the face I am in love with.

All my girl cousins here either don't talk to me, or those who do, ask questions they're too young to know *not* to ask. What they want to know really is how it is to have a man, because they're too ashamed to ask their married sisters.

They don't know what it is to lay so still until his sleep breathing is heavy, for the eyes in the dim dark to look and look without worry at the man-bones and the neck, the man-wrist and man-jaw thick and strong, all the salty dips and hollows, the stiff hair of the brow and sour swirl of sideburns, to lick the fat earlobes that taste of smoke, and stare at how perfect is a man.

I tell them, "It's a bad joke. When you find out you'll be sorry."

I'm going to have five children. Five. Two girls. Two boys. And one baby.

The girls will be called Lisette and Maritza. The boys I'll name Pablo and Sandro.

And my baby. My baby will be named Alegre, because life will always be hard.

Rachel says that love is like a big black piano being pushed off the top of a three-story building and you're waiting on the bottom to catch it. But Lourdes says it's not that way at all. It's like a top, like all the colors in the world are spinning so fast they're not colors anymore and all that's left is a white hum.

There was a man, a crazy who lived upstairs from us when we lived on South Loomis. He couldn't talk, just walked around all day with this harmonica in his mouth. Didn't play it. Just sort of breathed through it, all day long, wheezing, in and out, in and out.

This is how it is with me. Love I mean.

QUESTIONS FOR "ONE HOLY NIGHT" BY SANDRA CISNEROS

Talking About the Text

1. Read the opening few lines of this story and consider the author's use of language. Doesn't it sound as if the narrator is speaking rather than writing her story? In what ways does this language resemble spoken language?

2. At the end of this story, the narrator contrasts three views of love. The narrator says that for her, love is like the crazy man "who couldn't talk, just walked around all day with this harmonica in his mouth. Didn't play it. Just sort of breathed through it, all day long, wheezing, in and out, in and out." What do you think the narrator is saying about love in this passage?

3. Why do you think Cisneros titled her story "One Holy Night"?

Exploring Issues

1. Contrast the writing style of Cisneros with that of Hijuelos ("Mambo Kings"). How do these authors' styles differ? Which style seems more personal? Which style seems more complex? Does one author's style

seem more feminine and the other more masculine? Which author's style do you prefer? Why?

2. From reading this essay, what can you infer about women and women's roles in the culture portrayed by Cisneros? That is, what do women expect of themselves and what do others expect of women? How do these expectations compare with your expectations or with those of people you know?

3. On one level, this is a story about the transition from childhood to adulthood. Why might we read the story in this way? How might this interpretation of the story be problematic?

Writing Assignments

1. Examine this author's writing style closely. Notice her use of simple sentences and her use of the first person ("I") throughout the story. Notice too that she uses no quotation marks for a direct quote. Now, write a story of your own in which you imitate Cisneros's style. Use a deliberately conversational style and use "I" and "you" in the same ways that Cisneros does.

2. Write an essay in which you describe and name the narrator of this story. Provide as much detail as you can in your description, e.g., age, height, weight, facial features, physical appearance, personality traits, and personal history. Try to create a word-portrait that will allow us to "see" this character through your eyes. Draw on the story for information and fill in the gaps with your imagination.

Reading 17

The Mambo Kings

Oscar Hijuelos

Oscar Hijuelos was born of Cuban parents in New York and has published two novels, Our House in the Last World (1985) and The Mambo Kings Play Songs of Love (1989), which won the Pulitzer prize in 1990. For this novel, Hijuelos did extensive research on Cuban communities in New York and

created a fictional account of two immigrants from Havana. As mambo
musicians playing in the dance halls of New York, these two brothers
aspired to the commercial success of such stars as Desi Arnaz and Cesar
Romero. In the following passage,* we learn about their experiences as
newly arrived immigrants in 1949.

Visas in hand and sponsored by their cousin Pablo, they had turned up in New
York as part of the wave of musicians who had been pouring out of Havana since
the 1920s, when the tango and rumba crazes swept the United States and
Europe. That boom had started because so many musicians lost their jobs in pit
orchestras when talkies came in and silent movies went out. It was stay in Cuba
and starve to death or head north to find a place in a rumba band. Even in
Havana, with so many hotels, dance halls, and nightclubs, the scene was overcrowded. When Cesar had gone there in 1945, with the naïve idea of making it
big, he became just one of a thousand bolero singers struggling to earn a living.
Havana was jammed with first-rate underpaid singers and musicians like himself and Nestor, island musicians who played arrangements that sounded
quaintly archaic next to the big brass American jazz bands like those of Artie
Shaw, Fletcher Henderson, and Benny Goodman, who were much in vogue at
the time. A musician's life in Havana was poor, sociable. Pretty-boy singers,
trumpet players, and *congueros* gathered everywhere—in the arcades, plazas,
and bars. With the Paul Whiteman Orchestra playing in the casino, the more
authentic Cuban music was relegated to the alleys. Even musicians who were in
the popular tropical orchestras of Enric Madriguera and René Touzet used to
complain how badly they were being treated by the mobsters who ran the
casinos and paid the Cuban musicians shit. Ten dollars a night, with cleaning
charges for uniforms, black skins and mulattoes in one door, white musicians in
another, no drinks on the house, no overtime, and Christmas bonuses of
watered-down resealed bottles of whiskey. This at clubs like the Tropicana and
the Sans Souci.

The best—Olga Chorens, Alberto Beltrán, Nelson Piñedo, Manny
Jiménez—worked in clubs with names like the Night and Day, the New
Capri, Lucky Seven. The fabulous Ernesto Lecuona at the Montmartre, Beny
More at the Sierra.

The brothers had mainly worked in Havana as strolling troubadours and in
a cheap social band called the Havana Melody Boys. They'd played in the
lounge of a gambling casino, entertaining audiences of soaked-with-alcohol gamblers and spinster tourists from the American Midwest; shaking cocktail mixers
filled with shot, strumming guitars and blowing horns. They wore frilly-sleeved
mambo shirts and orange toreador pants so tight their paterfamilias gnarled up
like big tree knots. (Another version of the Havana Melody Boys picture tucked

*From *The Mambo Kings Play Songs of Love,* © 1989 by Oscar Hijuelos, Harper and Row,
Publishers

inside the soft cloth pocket in the Mambo King's cane suitcase that he'd brought with him into the Hotel Splendour, in a clump of old photographs, letters, and song ideas: a row of frilly-sleeved mambo musicians in white-striped blue *pantalones*, seated on a bamboo stage that is made up to look like a hut. There are nine musicians. A window opens behind them to a fake view of Havana Harbor, the sky thick with stars and a half-moon.) They had even made a record back then featuring the Fabulous Cesar Castillo, something called "*El Campesino*" (he'd make a later version of this with the Mambo Kings in 1952). Printing about a thousand copies of this 78 as a demonstration record, they sent them around to local radio stations, even got a few into the jukeboxes of Havana Amusement Park and up at La Playa de Maríanao. It was not a hit and got lost in the sea of boleros and ballads coming out of Havana at that time. A thousand crooners and female torch singers, and for each one a black plastic disc, a record for each foam-curled wave in the rippling mambo sea.

Tired of singing with the Havana Melody Boys, Cesar Castillo wanted to put together an orchestra of his own. Coming from a small town in Oriente, he had been inspired by the stories he'd heard about Cubans who'd left for the States. A woman from Holguín had become an actress and gone to Hollywood, where she had gotten rich making films with George Raft and Cesar Romero. (Raft appeared as an Argentine gaucho in a jingle-bell-rimmed gaucho's hat, performing the tango with this woman in a film called *Passion on the Pampas*.) She made enough money to live in a radiant pink mansion in a place called Beverly Hills; and there was another fellow, a rumba dancer named Ernesto Precioso, whom Cesar had known from the dance halls of Santiago de Cuba and who had been discovered by Xavier Cugat, for whom he'd starred as a featured dancer in a Hollywood short with Cugat called *The Lady in Red* and with the pianist Noro Morales the *The Latin from Staten Island*.

Others who'd done well? Alberto Socarrás playing in a nightclub called the Kubanacan in Harlem, Miguelito Valdez (the Magnificent) crooning away for Xavier Cugat at the McAlpin Hotel, Machito with his widespread New York popularity and his European tours. Tito Rodríguez at the Palm Nightclub, and the Pozo Brothers.

But the most famous success story would be that of a fellow crooner whom the brothers knew from Santiago de Cuba, where they sometimes performed in dance halls and in the *placitas*, sitting out under the moonlight, strumming guitars. Desi Arnaz. He had turned up in the States in the thirties and established himself in the clubs and dance halls of New York as a nice, decent fellow and had parlayed his conga drum, singing voice, and quaint Cuban accent into fame. And there were others: Cesar Romero and Gilbert Roland, Cuban chaps who'd made it in the movies playing nightclub gigolos and gun-toting, sombrero-pated, spur-booted *vaqueros*. Cesar was impressed by Arnaz's success and sometimes daydreamed of achieving that fame (he laughs now). That Cesar was white like Arnaz (though to some Americans he would be "a Spic") and had a good quivering baritone and blunt pretty-boy looks all seemed destined to work to his advantage.

In any case, the scene might be better in New York. Musician friends from

Havana traveled north and found work in the orchestras of people like Cugat, Machito, Morales, and Arnaz. Cesar heard rumors and received letters about money, dance halls, recording contracts, good weekly salaries, women, and friendly Cubans everywhere. He figured that if he went up there he could stay with Cousin Pablito, hook up with an orchestra, get away from trouble, make some money. And who could say what else might happen for them.

The day the brothers arrived in New York, fresh from Havana, in January of 1949, the city was covered in two feet of snow. Flying out of Havana on a Pan Am Clipper to Miami for $39.18, they then took the Florida Special north. In Baltimore they began to encounter snow, and while passing through a station in northern Maryland, they came across a water tower that had burst and blossomed into an orchid-shaped, many-petaled cascade of ice. Pablo met them at Pennsylvania Station, and, *hombre*, the brothers in their thin-soled shoes and cheap Sears, Roebuck overcoats were chilled to the bone. On the streets, people and cars seemed to disappear in the snowy winds like shredding phantoms. (They dissolved in a snow that wasn't anything like the snow they'd seen in the movies in Havana, nothing like Bing Crosby's angelic "I'm Dreaming of a White Christmas" snow, or the snow they'd imagined in dreams, lukewarm like the fake frost on a movie house *Air-Conditioned* sign.) Their thin-soled Cuban shoes soaked through, and when they stomped their feet in Pablo's lobby, they could smell the fumes of gas and electric heaters in the halls.

Pablo and his family lived at 500 La Salle, west of 124th Street and Broadway, in uptown Manhattan. It was a six-story tenement, constructed around the turn of the century to house the servant class, and it had a simple stoop with black curlicue railings, a narrow doorway framed in a crenellated brick archway. Above this rose six floors of black wrought-iron fire escapes and lamplit Venetian-blinded windows. It was two minutes from the 125th Street El, an overnight train ride and forty-five-minute flight from Havana, and five minutes from Harlem, the heartland of syncopating rhythm, as they used to say in those days. From its roof you could see the Hudson River and the domed and pillared mausoleum that was Grant's Tomb toward the northern edge of Riverside Park at 122nd Street and all the way over to the docks, and the lines of commuters and cars waiting to board the ferryboats for New Jersey.

That same night, Pablo's wife cooked them a great feast, and because it had been snowing and their feet were cold, she washed their numb toes in a pan of hot water. She was a practical and kindhearted women from Oriente, for whom marriage and child-bearing were the great events in her life. She lived to take care of the men in that house, slaved washing their clothes, cleaning the house, cooking, and attending to the children. Those first cold days, the future Mambo King spent most of his time in the kitchen drinking beer and watching her prepare big pots of stew and rice and beans and fried *plátanos*. Frying up steaks and pork chops and long strings of sausages that Pablito would bring home from his foreman's job at the meat plant. The smoke would escape out the windows, and neighbors, like their landlady, Mrs. Shannon, would shake their heads. Pablo's wife would cook breakfast, fried *chorizos* and eggs, and then iron their clothes. She sighed a lot, but immediately after sighing, she smiled, a statement of fortitude; her plump, dimpled face highlighted by long, long eyelashes whose shadows were like the hands of a clock. That was what she was like, a clock, marking her day with her chores, her sighs punctuating the hours.

"A family and love," he heard again. "That's what makes a man happy, not just playing the mambo."

And in those days Pablo would drive them around in his Oldsmobile to see the sights, or the brothers would ride the subway all over the four boroughs, faces pressed against the windows, as if counting the pillars and flashing lights for fun. Cesar favored amusement parks, circuses, movie houses, burlesques, and baseball games, while Nestor, a more quiet, docile, and tormented man, enjoyed nature and liked going to the places that Pablo's children loved the most. He liked to take the children to the Museum of Natural History, where he would revel in walking among the remains of so many reptiles, mammals, birds, fish, insects which had once vibrated, shimmered, crawled, flown, swum through the world and which were now preserved in row after row of glass cases. On one of those days, he, Cesar, Pablo, and the kids posed proudly for a photograph before the looming skeleton of Tyrannosaurus Rex. Afterwards they walked over to Central Park, the brothers strolling together as they used to down in Havana. Back then it was tranquil and clean. Old ladies sunned themselves everywhere and young men snuggled in the grass with their girls. Picnicking on the green, they ate thick steak heroes and drank Coca-Colas, enjoying the sunshine as they watched boats float across the lake. Best was the Bronx Zoo in springtime, with its lions prowling in their dens, the buffalo with their great horns and downy fur foaming like whitewater beneath their chins, long-necked giraffes whose heads curiously peeked high into the skirts of trees. Beautiful days, beyond all pain, all suffering.

At this time in New York there was a bit of malevolent prejudice in the air, postwar xenophobia, and budding juvenile delinquency on the streets. (And now? Years later? A few of the Irish old-timers stubbornly hanging on can't believe what happened on their street, the sidewalks jammed now with dominoes, shell games, card players, and radios and fruit-ice wagons, those old fellows wandering about furtively like ghosts.) Cesar would remember being shushed on the street for speaking to Nestor in Spanish, having eggs thrown at him from a rooftop as he marched up the hill to Pablito's in a flamingo-pink suit. They learned which streets to avoid, and not to go walking along the docks at night. And while they found this part of life in New York depressing at first, they took solace in the warmth of Pablo's household: the music of Pablo's record player, the aroma of cooking plantains, the affection and kisses from Pablo's wife and his three children made them happier.

That was the way it happened with most Cubans coming to the States then, when every Cuban knew every Cuban. Apartments filled with travelers or cousins or friends from Cuba—just the way it always happened on the *I Love Lucy* show when Cubans came to visit Ricky in New York, *de visita*, turning up at the door, hat in hand, heads bowed demurely, with expressions of gratitude and friendliness. Cubans who played the castanets, shook the maracas, danced the flamenco, juggled bones, who trained animals and sang, the men of moderate height with wide-open expressions, the women buxom and small, so quiet, so grateful for the hospitality.

Sleeping on cots in the living room, the brothers were chilled on some nights by the Hudson River wind seeping in through the loose windowpanes, alarmed by the clang, clang of the fire trucks down the street, startled (at first) when the ground shook and the building rattled with the arrivals and departures of the 125th Street El trains. In the winter they shivered, but in the spring they were serenaded by a band of strolling Italian minstrels—mandolin, violin, guitar, and singer. On Sunday afternoons, they searched the radio dials for nice music and listened to Machito's "Live from the El Flamingo Nightclub" broadcasts on WHN, the brothers happy whenever the percussionist bandleader would say a few words of Spanish between numbers: "And this is a little number for my *compadres* out there . . ." Leaning out the window, they watched the scissors man in his heavy black coat, bent back and grizzled face, limping up the street with a grindstone slung over his shoulders and ringing a bell. They bought buckets of ice for their drinks from the ice man, who drove a small black truck. They watched the junk man in his horse-drawn wagon. They were warmed by the coal that came rushing down a chute into the basement, barked at by wild herds of street hounds, and blessed by the priest of the red-doored Catholic church.

When they weren't out sightseeing or visiting friends, the two brothers wore sleeveless T-shirts and sat in the kitchen studying to improve their English. They read something called *A Better English Grammar for Foreign Speakers*, Captain Marvel and Tiger Boy comics, the *Daily News*, the Brooklyn *Herald*, the racetrack "blue" sheets, and the golden-spined storybooks about enchanted swans and whorl-eyed trees in the Black Forest that Pablo's kids would bring home from the parochial school. Even though the brothers already knew how to speak a polite if rudimentary English that they'd learned while working as busboys and waiters in the Havana chapter of the Explorers' Club on old Neptuno Street ("Yes sir, no sir. Please don't call me Pancho, sir"), the twisted hard consonants and terse vowels of the English language never fell on their ears like music. At dinner, the table piled high with platters of steaks and chops, *plátanos* and *yuca*, Cesar would talk about walking on the street and hearing a constant *ruido*—a noise—the whirling, garbled English language, spoken in Jewish, Irish, German, Polish, Italian, Spanish accents, complicated and unmelodic to his ear. He had a thick accent, rolled his rrrrrrs, said "jo-jo" instead of "yo-yo" and "tink," not "think"—just like Ricky Ricardo—but got along well enough to charm the American women he met here and there, and to sit out on the fire escape in the good weather, strumming a guitar, crooning out in English "In the Still of the Night." And he could walk down the street to the liquor store and say, "One Bacardi's dark, please . . ." And then, after a time, with bravado, saying to the proprietor, "How the hell are you, my friend?"

He was proud of himself, as in those days it was a mark of sophistication among the Cubans of New York to speak English. At the parties they attended, given by Cubans all over the city, the better one's English, the higher his status. Conversing rapidly in Spanish, Cesar would offer proof of his linguistic facility by throwing in a phrase like "hep cats at a jam session." Now and then he fell in with a Greewich Village crowd—American girls with bohemian spirits who would turn up at the Palladium or the Palm Nightclub; wild va-va-voom types who did not wear brassieres underneath their zebra-patterned party dresses. Meeting them on the dance floor, the Mambo King impressed them with his moves and Latin-lover mystique, and retired with them to their Village pads (with bathtubs in the kitchen) where they smoked reefers (he would feel a sugarcane field sprouting in his head), listened to bebop, and made out on dog-haired carpets and atop spring-worn couches. He picked up the words "jive" and "crazy!" (as in "Crazy, man, give me some skin!"), and with avuncular sexist tenderness lent them money and took them out to eat. In the period when he briefly went to work at the Tidy Print lithography plant on Chambers Street, to earn some extra money to buy a car, he would spend his lunch hours with this Jewish kid from Brooklyn, Bernardito Mandelbaum, teaching him Spanish. In the course of this he learned a few Yiddishisms. They'd trade words: *schlep* (dope), *schmuck* (fool), *schnook* (ignoramus), *schlemiel* (wastrel, fool), for *bobo* (dope), *vago* (lazy lout), *maricón* (fairy), and *pendejo* (ball-busting predatory louse). At some of these parties, where only English was spoken, he was famous for impressing even the driest Cuban professors with the exuberant variety of his speech. And he was a good listener, too, passing entire evenings with his hand on his chin, nodding and repeating, "Ah, yes?" and later, on his way home with Nestor, reciting the new words he had learned like a poem.

QUESTIONS FOR "THE MAMBO KINGS" BY OSCAR HIJUELOS

Talking About the Text

1. What do you notice about this writer's style? Consider, for example, the sentences: length, complexity, complete sentences versus fragments, and so on. Consider also the author's use of words. Contrast Hijuelos's style with that of Sandra Cisneros in "One Holy Night."
2. Notice that Oscar Hijuelos blends fact with fiction. Which parts of this text do you assume to be fact and which parts fiction? What purpose is served by this author's blending of fact and fiction?

Exploring Issues

1. Do you have the feeling that the Cuban immigrants described by Hijuelos felt oppressed after they arrived in the United States? Why or why not? Would you say that they are more or less fortunate than Cleófilas in "Woman Hollering Creek"? How can you account for any differences?

2. In this text, we learn that the Cuban immigrants received impressions of the United States from films and TV. They had impressions of snow from Bing Crosby's song "I'm Dreaming of a White Christmas," and they had impressions of opportunity and success from watching Desi Arnaz in "I Love Lucy" and Cesar Romero in various films. We also see that Cleófilas ("Woman Hollering Creek") received impressions about Americans leading the good life from American TV. Think about some currently popular TV programs and films: If they were exported to other countries, what impressions would they give to others about life in the United States and about Americans? Could these TV programs and films send any false impressions? If so, what are some of these false impressions? Does it matter if American TV and films present false impressions to people in other countries? Why or why not?

Writing assignments

1. Write a narrative essay about an imaginary immigrant who has just arrived in your community. Describe this character (identifying a native country) as he or she goes through the process of learing and adapting to your community. What problems is this person likely to encounter? Where would this person be likely to live? To work? To go for recreation? Who would be likely to befriend this person? Include factual representations of public places and events in your essay, just as Oscar Hijuelos does in "The Mambo Kings."

2. Write the essay just described from the point of view of the immigrant. Write your essay as if you are the immigrant. Describe your feelings, your fears, and your expectations, as well as what you do and where you go during your first few days in the United States. Include specific references to public places and events in your community.

CHAPTER 2 EXTENDED WRITING ASSIGNMENTS

2-1. For this assignment, you will temporarily experience being part of a new culture. First, find a situation in which you can observe members of a culture that is new to you. This could be a small grocery or pharmacy, a church, a social organization, or even a social club for students from a particular nation in your school. Request permission to sit and observe while taking notes for several hours on the ways people communicate (greetings, requests, commands) and on the ways different types of people communicate—men and women, older and younger people, and so on. Include in these notes on communication your observations on gestures and body movements, dress and appearance, and the use of public and private space. You will discover important aspects to note during the course of your observations.

You may decide to interview some people as part of this research. Wait until after you have started your observations to conduct the interviews, because your questions will arise from your observations. Prepare before the interview: Write out a list of questions, make sure that you have enough writing materials and, if you are going to use a tape recorder, make sure that it is in good working order before the interview.

After taking notes on your observations and interviews, read through your notes and highlight those items that you want to include in your report. It may help to organize your notes into categories such as people, places, special events, form of communication, interviews, and others.

Finally, write a report based on your notes and your analysis of these notes. In the report, clearly document the way you went about conducting your research: when and where you observed, how many hours you observed, how you took notes, whom you interviewed, and how you interviewed them. You may wish to make the latter a separate section of your report, labeled "research methods." You also may wish to use some of your categories (people, places, special events observed, etc.) as subheadings in your paper. At the end of your report, include your own comments on what you learned from doing this research and what more you would like to learn about the culture of people you observed.

2-2. Read one of the following books:

The Mambo Kings Play Songs of Love by Oscar Hijuelos

Best Intentions: The Education and Killing of Edmund Perry by Robert Sam Anson

Then, write an essay in which you report on this book for others who might wish to read it. Explain the author's purpose and as much about the book as you think readers need to know in order to become interested in reading it. Comment on the author's writing style and the book's structure (historically, by chapter, by characters, etc.). Finally, provide your own evaluation of the book, whether you would recommend the book and why or why not, and who you think might be most interested in reading this book.

Chapter
3

Community Life

*I*n 1624 the English poet John Donne wrote: "No man is an island. . . . Any man's death diminishes me because I am involved in Mankind." Over three centuries have passed since those lines were written. Yet they still ring true, for although we all have unique personalities and our own set of emotional and physical needs, none of us exists in complete isolation. We live, work, study, play—to name only a few human activities—in various types of communities. We are born into communities; at other times we may choose to belong to certain communities such as religious, political, or professional groups; and sometimes our membership in a particular community may simply be accidental, as in the case of work taking a person to a new location. The extent of our involvement in any given community is dictated by variables such as children, work, politics, survival, and emotions. Quite often these relationships with different communities have a direct impact on our self-identity and self-worth.

But how exactly do communities affect our lives? If we are to understand more fully their nature, we need to ask what the potential meanings of this word *community* might be. What qualities and characteristics constitute a community? In "The Meanings of Community," Thomas Bender offers a possible definition. He suggests that "a community involves a limited number of people in a somewhat restricted social space or network held together by shared understanding and a sense of obligation." We may often think of the community as merely the neighborhood or a section of town made up of people having similar concerns and interests; however, a community is often the creation of people who come together because of a common cause or a desire to live an alternative lifestyle. This phenomenon is illustrated in "Liberty Baptist," an excerpt from

Frances Fitzgerald's *Cities on a Hill,* which explores the religious Moral Majority in Lynchburg, Virginia, a community united by its leader, Jerry Falwell, and a commitment to a way of life defined by the church.

Yet the solidarity we would normally associate with community life does not necessarily mean that all communities are always without discord or disagreement. For example, Shirley Brice Heath, in an ethnographic study entitled "Gettin' on in Roadville," gives an account of how younger and older generations in a small mill-town community have very different perspectives about their relationship to that community and its destiny. Although most of the older generation still maintain a nostalgic respect for the simple life in Roadville, many of the younger generation want to get ahead and leave the old ways behind. We also find clashing values in a community with "A Loaf of Bread," by James Alan McPherson. In this short story, McPherson writes about a conflict between a grocer of the white business community and his customers from a black neighborhood; in doing so, McPherson looks at the ethical considerations of the various community members and the impending changes they are facing. In a similar vein, V. S. Naipaul offers a vivid portrait of a Southern black community on the verge of a metamorphosis as a result of the civil rights movement. The changes that communities often confront as a result of a higher authority's demands or actions is also the topic of J. Anthony Lukas's "Community and Equality in Conflict." Whereas Naipaul shows us subtle indicators of change in a small Southern community, Lukas examines the hard choices Boston's community neighborhoods had to make when confronted with federal legislation requiring desegregation and busing.

Thus far we have only discussed communities composed of people living in close proximity to one another. However, "A Working Community," by Ellen Goodman, offers a new slant on community life. Goodman suggests that the work environment and one's professional associates have become the neighborhood community of contemporary society. Whereas we once shared our daily tribulations and traumas with our neighbors over the back fence and at the PTA meeting, today that kind of community bonding occurs during coffee breaks and in the parking lot.

We conclude this chapter with two essays that ask us to consider the extent to which personal commitment to community can have a positive effect on the quality of our lives. In "The Futility of Global Thinking," renowned essayist and spokesperson for conservation Wendell Berry urges us all to take responsibility at the community level for the preservation of our natural resources. Similarly, Richard D. Lamm's "The Ten Commandments of a Quality Community" offers precepts for the building and maintenance of communities committed to better lives for present and future members. At the conclusion of his essay, Lamm writes that "we can no longer take 'community' for granted in the United States. We have too much evidence that we are unraveling. . . . It is dangerous and we must attempt to salvage that elusive concept of *community*." It is with this concern for salvaging "that elusive concept of community" that we invite you to contemplate the readings in this chapter.

Reading 18

The Meanings of Community

Thomas Bender

Thomas Bender is a professor of history and Samuel Rudin Professor of the Humanities at New York University. He edited a 1981 edition of Alexis de Toqueville's *Democracy in America* and coauthored *The Making of American Society*. He is the author of *Toward an Urban Vision* and *Community and Social Change in America,* from which the following selection, "The Meanings of Community," has been excerpted. In this essay, Bender offers a working definition for the concept of "community," and in doing so, provides a framework for the other selections in this chapter.

Community, which has taken many structural forms in the past, is best defined as a network of social relations marked by mutuality and emotional bonds.[1] This network, or what Kai T. Erikson refers to as the "human surround," is the essence of community, and it may or may not be coterminous with a specific, contiguous territory.[2] The New England town was a community, but it was not a

1. In the following preliminary definition, only direct quotations have specific citations. The position outlined in the next few paragraphs owes most to the following works: Ferdinand Tönnies, *Community and Society,* trans. Charles P. Loomis (New York: Harper, 1963); Max Weber, *The Theory of Social and Economic Organization,* trans. Talcott Parsons (New York: Free Press, 1964); Robert M. MacIver, *Community: A Sociological Study* (New York: Macmillan, 1936); Robert Redfield, *The Little Community* (Chicago: University of Chicago, 1955); Talcott Parsons, *The Social System* (New York: Free Press, 1951); idem, *Structure and Process in Modern Societies;* Roland Warren, ed., *Perspectives on the American Community* (Chicago: Rand McNally, 1966); Rene König, *The Community* (London: Routledge & Kegan Paul, 1968); Charles Tilly, *An Urban World* (Boston: Little, Brown, 1974); Robert Nisbet, *The Quest for Community* (New York: Oxford University Press, 1969); idem, *The Social Bond* (New York: Random House, 1970); idem, *The Sociological Tradition;* Wilson Carey McWilliams, *The Idea of Fraternity in America* (Berkeley and Los Angeles: University of California, 1973); and Martin Buber, *Paths in Utopia* (London: Routledge & Kegan Paul, 1949).

2. See Kai T. Erikson, *Everything in Its Path: Destruction of Community in the Buffalo Creek Flood* (New York: Simon & Schuster, 1976), esp. Introduction and pt. III.

definition of community. Similarly, a family, a neighborhood, a group of friends, or a class can be a community without providing a definition of the concept. One must keep an open stance toward the various structural forms that might contain community. A definition of community must, therefore, be independent of particular structures.

A community involves a limited number of people in a somewhat restricted social space or network held together by shared understandings and a sense of obligation. Relationships are close, often intimate, and usually face to face. Individuals are bound together by affective or emotional ties rather than by a perception of individual self-interest. There is a "we-ness" in a community; one is a member. Sense of self and of community may be difficult to distinguish. In its deepest sense, a community is a communion. Martin Buber captured this quality when he wrote: "A real community need not consist of people who are perpetually together; but it must consist of people who, precisely because they are comrades, have mutual access to one another and are ready for one another."[3]

Men and women in a community share a fairly wide spectrum of their lives, though not necessarily everything. A community is people who, in the words of Robert MacIver, "share, not this or that particular interest, but a whole set of interests wide enough and complete enough to include their lives."[4] Hence communal relationships are diffuse in their concerns. They are not segmental relationships, and they are not oriented to narrow or specific ends. While a community is part of broader social aggregates, it remains a distinct social grouping. Far from being a microcosm of the whole society, it has a special quality that may result in tension with larger social aggregates. One's network of community, although it may not supply all the warmth and emotional support one needs, is an elemental fact of one's emotional life.

The solidarity that characterizes communities does not mean, however, that all is unity and harmony within. Many commentators err, I think, by insisting that absence of conflict be a part of the definition of community. Communal conflict, like the family conflict we all know, is real, though it differs from, say, market competition, in being mediated by emotional bonds.[5]

A community is an end in itself: It may offer aid or advantage to its members, but its value is basically intrinsic to its own existence. It does not exist to serve external or instrumental purposes. This characteristic of community is related to a particular kind of social behavior identified by Max Weber as distinctively communal. He labeled a social relationship "communal" if its "orientation of social action . . . is based on a subjective feeling of the parties,

---

3. Buber, *Paths in Utopia*, p. 145.

4. Robert M. MacIver, *Society: Its Structure and Changes* (London: Long and Smith, 1932), pp. 9–10.

5. Weber saw community as the "antithesis of conflict" (Weber, *Theory of Social and Economic Organization*, p. 137). Charles H. Cooley, however, admitted that conflict existed in what he called "primary groups" and that the competition, passions, and conflicts that emerged in these groups were "socialized by sympathy" (Charles H. Cooley, *Social Organization: A Study of the Larger Mind* [New York: Scribner's 1909], p. 23).

whether affectual or traditional, that they belong together." He contrasted this with "associative" relationships, characteristic of modern political and economic institutions, that are based upon rational calculation of self-interest.[6]

No contemporary sociologist has written more frequently or more perceptively on community than Robert Nisbet. Perhaps it is therefore appropriate to conclude this preliminary definition with a quotation from him.

> Community is founded on man conceived in his wholeness rather than in one or another of the roles, taken separately, that he may hold in a social order. It draws its psychological strength from levels of motivation deeper than those of mere volition or interest. . . . Community is a fusion of feeling and thought, of tradition and commitment, of membership and volition. . . . Its archetype, both historically and symbolically, is the family, and in almost every type of genuine community the nomenclature of family is prominent.[7]

QUESTIONS FOR "THE MEANINGS OF COMMUNITY" BY THOMAS BENDER

Talking About the Text

1. Bender states that "in its deepest sense, a community is a communion." Why do you think Bender makes this claim? What do you see as the connection, if any, between "community" and "communion"? In what ways are these two words related?

2. Bender draws on a number of sources in an attempt to define community. What effect does this technique have on his writing?

Exploring Issues

1. Bender contrasts "communal" relationships with those that are "associative" (e.g., political and economic institutions), stating that the former is based on "a subjective feeling" of belonging together, and the latter is a "rational calculation of self-interest." To what extent do you agree with this opinion? Can you think of any economic or political institutions that might be characterized as communities? Can you think of times when these "communal" and "associative" relationships might overlap?

2. Bender asserts that "one's network of community, although it may not supply all the warmth and emotional support one needs, is an elemental fact of one's emotional life." In what ways do you think a community can provide emotional support to its individual members? Be specific.

3. Bender quotes Robert Nisbet as asserting that the community's "archetype, both historically and symbolically, is the family, and in almost

---

6. Weber, *Theory of Social and Economic Organization*, p. 136.

7. Nisbet, *Sociological Tradition*, pp. 47–48.

every type of genuine commuity the nomenclature of family is prominent." Do you agree or disagree with this assertion? Why?

Writing Assignment

With this essay Bender offers us a definition of community. Write your own
definition of "community." In developing your definition draw on your own
personal knowledge of communities. To which communities do you belong?
Why do you think of yourself as a member of these communities? What do
these communities have in common? How are they different? Use these questions and others to brainstorm. Then apply your insights to a working definition
of community.

Reading 19

Liberty Baptist

Frances FitzGerald

Frances FitzGerald received the Pulitzer prize, the Bancroft Prize for History,
and the National Book Award for her highly acclaimed book *Fires in the
Lake.* She is also the author of *America Revised* and contributes regularly to
The New Yorker, The New York Review of Books, and *Harper's.* The
following selection has been taken from her most recent book-length work,
Cities on a Hill, in which she reports on four very different communities: the
gay community of the Castro in San Francisco; the Liberty Baptist Church
community located in Lynchburg, Virginia; the retirement community of Sun
City, Florida; and the Rajneeshee community founded in Oregon by the East
Indian guru. In this piece FitzGerald explores the cultural enclave of Jerry
Falwell's Moral Majority community in Lynchburg, Virginia. Her insightful
description of this religious community illustrates how people with common
values and goals can build their entire lives around one community.

By comparison with the other evangelists (who were his competitors in what
became a fierce and expensive competition for Sunday-morning airtime),

Falwell was the most sober and conventional of preachers. His program, "The Old-Time Gospel Hour," was simply a videotape recording of the eleven o'clock service in the Thomas Road Baptist Church. (The tape was edited, and extra footage was occasionally added.) The choir behind him sang traditional Baptist hymns, and he, strong-jawed and portly of figure, wearing a thick three-piece black suit, looked every inch the Baptist preacher of the pretelevision era. True, there was a good deal of showmanship in his services. The female members of one of his singing groups, the Sounds of Liberty, wore Charlie's Angels hairdos and seemed to snuggle up against their virile-looking male counterparts. Don Norman, one of the resident soloists and a pastor of the church, had a distinctly television-era pouf to his silver-gray hair. Another resident soloist, a cherub-faced young man called Robbie Hiner, provided comic relief by joking with Falwell and by wearing, on occasion, a bright-green suit, which contrasted strikingly with the baby-blue carpeting of the church. The "inspirational" singing involved a good deal of heavy breathing and a good many references to heavenly riches. Falwell did not, however, actually say that financial rewards would accrue to those who sent him money. And, unlike many of the evangelists, he quite often mentioned the problems of leading a Christian life in a sinful world.

In a sense, it was not surprising that Falwell decided to go into politics. No otherworldly type of Baptist, he was most characteristically an organizer and a promoter. In 1956, he founded the Thomas Road Baptist Church with thirty-five people in an old factory building. Twenty-five years later, he had by far the biggest church in Lynchburg. It held four thousand people and was jammed for every service on Sundays. He had a school, Lynchburg Christian Academy, from kindergarten through the twelfth grade, for the children of his parishioners; he had a home for alcoholics, a summer camp for children, a Bible institute and correspondence course, a seminary, and Liberty Baptist College, which was accredited and for which he was engaged in building a campus. He had a few wealthy backers, but most of his funds came from small contributors in Lynchburg and around the country. Businessmen in Lynchburg said he was a born leader and the best salesman they had even seen.

But theologically Falwell had called himself "a separatist, premillennialist, pretribulationist sort of fellow." He believed, as he said, that "this is the terminal generation before Jesus comes," and in 1965 he very eloquently argued the fundamentalist doctrine of separation from the world in a sermon called "Ministers and Marchers":

> As far as the relationship of the church to the world, it can be expressed as simply as the three words which Paul gave to Timothy—"Preach the Word." We have a message of redeeming grace through a crucified and risen Lord. This message is designed to go right to the heart of man and there meet his deep spiritual need. Nowhere are we commissioned to reform the externals. We are not told to wage wars against bootleggers, liquor stores, gamblers, murderers, prostitutes, racketeers, prejudiced persons or institutions, or any other existing evil as such. Our ministry is not reformation but transformation. The gospel does not clean up the outside but rather regenerates the inside. . . .

While we are told to "render unto Caesar the things that are Caesar's," in the true interpretation, we have very few ties on this earth. We pay our taxes, cast our votes as a responsibility of citizenship, obey the laws of the land, and other things demanded of us by the society in which we live. But, at the same time, we are cognizant that our only purpose on this earth is to know Christ and to make Him known. Believing the Bible as I do, I would find it impossible to stop preaching the pure saving gospel of Jesus Christ, and begin doing anything else—including fighting Communism, or participating in civil-rights reforms.

At his press conference at the broadcasters' convention in 1980, Falwell repudiated this sermon as "false prophecy." He had moved 180 degress from his former position by vowing to undertake civil disobedience if Congress voted to draft women into the armed forces.

Why Falwell changed his mind is an interesting question, and, in view of the fact that great numbers of fundamentalist pastors and lay people around the country went through the same transformation in the seventies, it is also an important one. In the sixties, fundamentalists had been one of the least politicized groups in the country; as Falwell discovered, very few of them were even registered to vote. Whether or not their numbers were on the increase, by the mid-seventies they had begun to make their voices heard. In 1974, for instance, fundamentalist pastors and parents in Kanawha County, West Virginia, had closed the schools down in protest against the introduction of schoolbooks that they said were un-Christian, unpatriotic, and destructive of the family and constituted an incitement to racial violence. A committee of the National Education Association investigated what became a prolonged series of demonstrations and concluded that the trouble resulted in part from the cultural gap between the school board and the isolated mountain communities it served. The Kanawha County incident itself, however, turned out to be far from isolated. In the mid-seventies, groups of "concerned citizens" in many parts of the country, including the Northeast and the Midwest, attempted to purge their schools of similar books, protested against sex education, lobbied for the teaching of "scientific creationism" in biology courses, and called for the return of the old pedagogy of rote work. In hundreds of other communities—principally but not exclusively in the South—parents pulled their children out of the public schools and helped their pastors to build "Christian academies." According to Falwell, there were fourteen hundred "Christian" schools in the early sixties and sixteen thousand in October of 1980, with new ones going into construction at the rate of one every seven hours. The same period saw the growth of statewide, then nationwide, campaigns against abortion, gay rights, and the ERA. Supported by fundamentalist pastors—such as Falwell—these campaigns had considerable success in state referenda and in state legislatures. Fundamentalists were not the only constituency for these movements (Anita Bryant is a fundamentalist, while Phyllis Schlafly is a Catholic), but they were an important one, and their pastors had influence with other conservative evangelicals. By 1978, a Washington-based group of political organizers on the right—a group that included Richard Viguerie, the direct-mail specialist; Howard Phillips, the director of the Conservative Caucus; Terry Dolan, of the National Conservative

Political Action Committee; and Paul Weyrich, of the Heritage Foundation and the Committee for the Survival of a Free Congress—had identified the fundamentalist pastors as a strategic element in the building of a new coalition, which they called the New Right.

There was something extraordinary about all this. At the time of the Scopes trial, in 1925, most educated people had considered fundamentalism outmoded and irrelevant—a mere reaction to the advances in science and to modernity in general. Since then, American historians have tended to neglect the fundamentalist constituency or to see it as vestigial—the last cry of the still backwaters of the South against the modern world. But now fundamentalism was the religion of television and a part of the evangelical revival of the seventies and the eighties. The oldest Right in America had become the New Right of 1980. Instead of being typified by a businessman on the golf links, the Republican party leadership was now looking more and more like William Jennings Bryan in a double knit and television makeup. Pastors who once counseled withdrawal from the world of sin—and specifically the evils of politics—now bargained with politicians in the back rooms of Congress and gave sermons on defense policy.

Falwell's own explanation for these things had, as one might imagine, to do with the increasingly parlous state of the nation and the sense of crisis he and other Americans began to feel in the mid-seventies. That crisis, he said, now extended across the board, from the 40 percent divorce rate to the growth of the pornography industry to the feminist movement, the widespread use of drugs, social-worker intervention in the family, sex education, abortion on demand, the "abandonment" of Taiwan and the "loss" of the Panama Canal, Internal Revenue Service interference with "Christian" schools, rampant homosexuality, the notion of children's rights, and the spread of "secular humanism." In his view, all these things had corrupted the moral fiber of the country and destroyed its will to resist Communism. In his view, the country was in far worse shape than it was thirty, or even ten, years ago. In his view, moral Americans— Catholics, Protestants, Mormons, and Jews—finally woke up to this fact and realized that they must do something about it.

Public opinion polls and electoral statistics would, of course, suggest that many Americans had turned against some of the liberal reforms of the sixties and that they were worried about the divorce rate, crime in the streets, and other disorders. They would also suggest that many Americans thought the antiwar demonstrations and the "loss" of the Vietnam War weakened the country's military strength and its will to fight Communism. These sentiments might (and in fact did) lead to the election of conservative candidates. But they were not necessarily sufficient reasons for people to flock to fundamentalist churches—or to convince fundamentalist pastors to change their position 180 degrees from "separation" to a holy war. Falwell was leading a radical movement. (One of the questionnaires he sent out to his supporters asked, "Do you approve of the American flags being burned in liberal and radical anti-American demonstrations?" and "Do you approve of the ratification of the ERA, which could well lead to homosexual marriages, unisexual bathrooms, and, of course, the mandatory drafting of women for military combat?") Could the genesis of it be located uniquely in the list of issues—or abominations—he drew up? That, certainly, was Falwell's explanation, and perhaps it was the correct one. But the explanation seemed singularly farfetched in the context of Lynchburg, Virginia, for a more stable, tranquil, and family-oriented city it would be hard to find. Yet Lynchburg was the city where Falwell grew up and where he founded his first congregation.

Lynchburg lies on the James River, in a country of small farms and wooded, rolling hills at the foot of the Blue Ridge Mountains. A hundred and sixty miles southwest of Washington, it is beyond the gentleman-farming, horse-breeding country and more than halfway to Appalachia. It's a small city—only sixty-seven thousand people—far from any major urban center. All the same, it is enterprising and not wholly provincial. Several large American corporations have plants in Lynchburg, and its nearly two hundred small factories turn out a great variety of goods, including paper products, medical supplies, children's clothing, and shoes. Because of the diversity of its manufacturers, business journals sometimes use it for a Middletown or a model of the national economy as a whole. It is an old manufacturing city—one of the oldest in the South, according to its chamber of commerce—but it does not look it, for there are few belching smokestacks. The visita from the top of its one twenty-story building is mainly of trees and a bend in the river. It does not rival Charlottesville—sixty miles to the north—as a cultural center, yet it is perhaps the best known in the South for two women's colleges, Randolph-Macon and Sweet Briar.

Lynchburg was founded—fairly recently, for Virginia—in the late eighteenth century, by John Lynch, an Irish-American tobacco farmer. During the Revolutionary War, John's brother Colonel Charles Lynch set up an informal military court on his property and sentenced Tories to hanging by their thumbs—thus the origin of the word "lynching." Lynchburg began as a tobacco-trading center and an agricultural market town. In the nineteenth century, new settlers—many of them Scotch-Irish Methodists, and Presbyterians—moved in to build grain mills, an iron foundry, and small manufacturing enterprises. During the Civil War, it served as a staging area and hospital center for the Confederate Army of northern Virginia. After the war, its small tobacco farms grew less profitable, but its manufacturers prospered. When the industrial revolution came along, the Lynchburg merchants had the capital to build new foundries, cotton mills, and textile mills and a shoe factory. They used white labor almost exclusively; the blacks remained on small, poor farms in the countryside.

In 1950, Lynchburg was still a mill town, most of its factories old-fashioned and its society hidebound, stratified, and segregated. But in the mid-fifties the town underwent the kind of transformation that was taking place in communities all across the South. A number of major national corporations began to arrive in town, attracted by low property taxes, nonunion labor, and relatively low pay scales. Among them were Babcock & Wilcox, the manufacturer of nuclear reactors; General Electric, which built a radio-assembly plant; and Meredith/Burda, a printing enterprise. The national corporations stimulated local industry and attracted other large manufacturers from the North and from West Germany. Lynchburg businessmen now point with pride to the healthy diversity of the economy and to high levels of employment, even in recession times. In fact, the unemployment rate is usually lower than the national average; still, the median family income in Lynchburg is below that of Virginia as a whole. But the town has changed in other ways since 1950, for the big industries brought new money into town and new faces into the boardrooms and the country clubs. The colleges flourished. And in the mid-sixties, when the black ministers and their congregations conducted a series of sit-ins and demonstrations, they found that the white community was not immovable. Under pressure, the companies hired black workers, and the city's segregation ordinances were stricken from the books.

Lynchburg calls itself a city, but it is really a collection of suburbs, its population spread out over fifty square miles. In the fifties, its old downtown was supplanted by a series of shopping plazas, leaving it with no real center. There's a good deal of variety to its neighborhoods. Along the James River, in a section called Rivermont, stately nineteenth-century mansions look out over wooded parks and lawns. Behind them are streets of white-shingled Victorian houses and, behind *them*, tracts of comfortable post-World War II developer-built Capes and Colonials. At the edges of town, the developers are still at work, and streets with such names as Crestview and Forest Park run through sections of half-acre lots before dead-ending in the woods. There are poor neighborhoods in Lynchburg—neighborhoods where cocks crow in the backyards of trembling wooden houses—and a part of the old downtown is a depressed area of abandoned factories and boarded-up shops. But there are no real slums. The city has used federal funds to build low-cost housing, and it is now having some success in revitalizing the old downtown.

Lynchburg is not a graceful city. The automobile has cut too many swaths across it, leaving gasoline stations and fast-food places to spring up in parking-lot wastelands. But it is a clean city, full of quiet streets and shade trees. Even the factories are clean; the new ones are windowless buildings with landscaped lawns. It's a safe city and a comfortable place to live. There's not much crime or juvenile delinquency. The medical services are good. The public schools are handsome, well equipped, and good enough to send 63 percent of their students on to college. They are also racially integrated and free of racial tension. As for the things Falwell spends so much time denouncing—pornography, drugs, "the homosexual life-style"—Lynchburg harbors these things quietly if it harbors them at all. You can find *Playboy* in a few magazine racks, but the movie theaters rarely play even an R-rated film. There are a number of bar-restaurants and discos. But the hottest band in town is probably the combo that plays nightly in the lounge of the Sheraton Inn. At night, young people can go to the skating rink or to night games of the New York Mets farm team, held at the Lynchburg Municipal Stadium. If there is a single public nuisance for the young in this town, it is surely boredom.

Lynchburg is a city of churches—it has over a hundred of them—and the first question people ask of new acquaintances is not what they do but what church they attend. At church time on Sunday, the streets are empty and quiet, with almost all the cars in town parked near the churches. Dominated by its churches and by its business community, it is a conservative place in most respects. Traditionally a Byrd Democrat town, it has turned Republican in recent years, voting for Gerald Ford in 1976—while remaining faithful to Harry Byrd. Still, it has its liberal element. The population is 25 percent black, and the civil rights movement left a well-organized black community. And, besides Liberty Baptist College, Randolph-Macon, and Sweet Briar, it has another liberal-arts college: Lynchburg College, which is coeducational. These colleges do not generate much intellectual ferment or political radicalism, but they and their graduates do provide the city with other voices and a useful degree of political flexibility. The seven-member city council includes at least four moderate liberals, among them a woman and a black man. These liberals now belong. They participate in the humane and amicable consensus that runs the city. When they speak to outsiders, it is in the complacent tone of the chamber of commerce.

Falwell's church, on Thomas Road, is a block or two away from Lynchburg College, in one of the older middle-class sections. From the outside, it is not much to look at: a large, octagonal brick building fronting the street, with a three-story brick school behind it. The parking lot beside it is, however, supermarket-size, and on Sunday the cars jam up the street for blocks trying to fit into it beside the school buses. In summer, many of the cars come from out of state, for families from all over the country like to visit the church they watch on television. In winter, the cars and school buses bring Liberty Baptist College students and visitors from small rural churches in the area as well as the regular church members.

Winter and summer the congregation consists mainly of couples with two or three children, but there are a number of young adults and a number of elderly people. There is something distinctive about its looks, but at first glance that something is difficult to pin down. The men wear double-knit suits and sport gold wedding bands or heavy brass rings stamped with mottoes; the women, their hair neatly coiffed and lacquered, wear demure print dresses and single-diamond engagement rings. The young women and the high-school girls are far more fashionable. Their flowered print dresses fall to midcalf but are cut low on the bodice and worn with ankle-strap high heels. They wear their hair long, loose, and—almost uniformly—flipped and curled in Charlie's Angels style. Like the boys with their white shirts, narrow-fitted pants, and close-cropped hair, they look fresh-faced and extraordinarily clean. The members of the congregation look, in other words, much like Robbie Hiner, Don Norman, and the other singers who appear on "The Old-Time Gospel Hour." There are proportionately about the same number of blacks in the congregation as there are in the choir—which is to say, very few. (The television cameras tend to pan in on the two black choir members, thus making them more conspicuous to the television audience than they are to the congregation in the church.) What is startling about the congregation—and this is its distinctiveness—is the amount of effort people have put into creating this uniform appearance.

As it turns out, a number of the Thomas Road Church members live in the new, developer-built houses on the edges of town: comfortable suburban-style houses set on half-acre lawns, with central air-conditioning and kitchens like the ones that appear in detergent advertisements on television—and just as clean. To these houses, the Thomas Road families have added shag rugs and wallpaper or chintz curtains. A woman I visited, Nancy James, had just bought a living-room suite, and another, Jackie Gould, had ordered a new set of kitchen cabinets and had them installed without—she said, giggling—consulting her husband. One family had not only a living room but a family room, with a Naugahyde pouf, a twenty-four-inch television set, and a sliding glass door looking out over a stone-paved terrace. On a Sunday evening while I was there, this couple gave a potluck supper for twenty neighbors and fellow church members. The man of the house—resplendent in a fitted white shirt, cream-colored trousers, and white shoes—watched a boxing match on television with the other men while his wife organized the dishes of ham, baked beans, candied squash, and potato salad the other women had brought with them. At dinner, around a lace-covered table, the guests joked, and made small talk about their gardens, the water system in Lynchburg, the problems of giving a Tupperware party, and the advantages of building one's own house. After dinner, the men and women separated, the men going into the living room and the women upstairs for an hour or so of Bible reading and prayers.

In such circumstances, it was difficult to see how Falwell could complain so much about moral decay, sex, drink, drugs, the decline of the family, and so on. Conversely, it was difficult to imagine why such people would be drawn to a preacher who spent so much time denouncing drink and pornography. On the face of it, these people would seem far better suited to a tolerant, easygoing church whose pastor would not make a point—as Falwell once did—of forbidding his congregants to watch "Charlie's Angels." Of course, not all Thomas Road Church members live in such order and comfort. To go with its pastors on their rounds is to see that the Sunday-morning impression of the congregation is to some degree misleading—or in the nature of a Platonic ideal. A number of its members live in government-sponsored housing projects or in neighborhoods of old wooden houses. In one thin-walled apartment, I saw a woman sitting with her head in her hands gazing dejectedly at four squalling children under the age of nine—the baby crawling naked across the lineolum floor. (The pastor prissily told the older girl to put some underpants on the baby.) At a church-sponsored flea market, I found a number of women with worn faces buying and selling children's used clothing while their husbands squatted in a circle under a nearby tree and talked about boot camp and "Nam." According to one pastor, many of the elderly people in the church are single women who live on Social Security allowances of four or five thousand dollars a year. And most of them, according to the pastor, have never traveled outside the state of Virginia.

What is more, to talk to the people who live in the comfortable suburban-style houses is to discover that many of them did not grow up in such middle-class circumstances. William Sheehan, chairman of the church's Division of Prayer, became a lawyer late in life. He ran away from home and a drunken father at the age of eighteen and lived for a year with his grandfather in the boiler room of a school in Montana. He held various jobs, married at the age of twenty-one, and had nine children. His family responsibilities kept him hard at work at manual or clerical jobs. Only when he was in his forties did he have the time to study. He then took night courses in law, passed the state bar exam, apprenticed himself to an older lawyer, and eventually inherited a practice in a small Montana town. In conversation, Sheehan thanks God in every other sentence and gives the Lord credit for everything that he has ever done or that has ever happened to him. He never drank, he said, but he was able to stop cursing when he accepted Jesus Christ as his Saviour, at the age of nineteen.

Most of Falwell's parishioners came from closer to home, but a lot of them came from the countryside and the small towns of southern Virginia and West Virginia. One guest at the potluck supper talked about his childhood in a narrow coal-mining valley at Appalachia, where the preachers handled poisonous snakes and spoke in tongues. He has never got used to the Lynchburg traffic, he said, for where he had lived the sound of a car on the road meant that you picked up your shotgun and left by the back door.

To talk to Falwell's parishioners is to see that the geography of Lynchburg is symbolic in terms of their lives. As the city stands between Appalachia and Washington, D.C., so the arrival of new industry over the past twenty-five years made it the transfer point between the Old and the New South, between the technologically backward and the technologically modern parts of the society. Many current Lynchburg residents, including many Thomas Road members, literally made the journey between the underdeveloped countryside and the city. Many others, however, made a similar journey without moving at all. In the early fifties, Lynchburg had a relatively unskilled work force and a very small middle class; today, it was a highly skilled work force and a much larger middle class. Falwell's parishioners stand, as it were, on the cusp of this new middle class. They are clerical workers, technicians, and small businessmen, and skilled and semiskilled workers in the new factories.

Among the church members and the students at Liberty Baptist are many who grew up in fundamentalist Christian families and have never known any other way of life. Those who came from the small towns of Virginia or West Virginia think of Lynchburg as a sophisticated city; and those who came from big cities like Philadelphia think of it as a refuge from the anarchy of modern America. Among those who do not have a fundamentalist background, a high proportion seem to have had difficult, disorganized childhoods—family histories of alcoholism, physical violence, or trouble with the law. They had—or so they say—to struggle out of their families and then to struggle with themselves. They credit the Lord with their success, and they date their success from the moment they were, as they say, "saved."

Falwell's parishioners do not give the Thomas Road Baptist Church—or any other church—credit for the changes in their lives, because in their theology it is an error (specifically, a Catholic error) to suppose that institutions stand between man and God. There is some irony in this belief, for the Thomas Road Church is a great deal more than a house for prayers. It is a vast and mighty institution, with some sixty pastors and about a thousand volunteer helpers and trainees. It has Lynchburg Christian Academy, the summer camp, and Liberty

Baptist College, whose students worship and work in the church. In addition, it has separate ministries for children, young people, adults, elderly people, the deaf, the retarded, and the imprisoned. Last year, it added a ministry for divorced people and another one for unmarried young adults. On Sundays, the church holds three general services and has Sunday-school classes for children of every age group, from the nursery on up. But it is a center of activity every day of the week. There is a general prayer meeting every Wednesday night. Then, every week each ministry offers a program of activities for its age group, including Bible-study classes, lectures, trips, sports outings, and picnics. The ministries also organize groups of volunteers to visit hospitals, nursing homes, and prisons and to proselytize in the community. The organization is so comprehensive that any Thomas Road member, old or young, could spend all his or her time in church or in church-related activities. In fact, many church members do just that.

QUESTIONS FOR "LIBERTY BAPTIST" BY FRANCES FITZGERALD

Talking About the Text

1. In what ways are the writing styles of Frances FitzGerald and Shirley Brice Heath similar and different? What techniques does FitzGerald use to give us a more complete picture of the Liberty Baptist community?
2. What effect does the use of people's real names and names of companies and institutions have on the overall force of this piece? How do you think the essay would read if these details were left out?

Exploring Issues

1. FitzGerald writes that "the ministries also organize groups of volunteers to visit hospitals, nursing homes, and prisons and to proselytize in the community. The organization is so comprehensive that any Thomas Road member, old or young, could spend all his or her time in church or church-related activities. In fact, many church members do just that." To what extent do you think the church *is* the community to many residents of Lynchburg? How does the church bring people together?
2. FitzGerald writes that "many current Lynchburg residents, including Thomas Road members, literally made the journey between the under-developed countryside and the city. Many others, however, made a similar journey without moving at all." What do you think FitzGerald means by "made a similar journey without moving at all"? What effect do you think these journeys may have had on the development of the community? What kinds of journeys does Heath describe in her depiction of Roadville? How do these journeys affect that community?
3. Speculate about what you think is "the glue" that keeps Falwell's church

together. In other words, what are the qualities and characteristics of this group of people that make them a community and not simply "a group of people"?

4. To what extent is Falwell's church community a political force? Do political and social issues help bond this group into a tighter community?

Writing Assignments

Contact a member of the clergy at either a campus or local house of worship. Then, interview this person using the following question as a guideline: "To what extent do you consider your congregation a community?" Before starting the interview you should prepare a guide to help you during the interview process. The guide might include questions such as:

Who are the congregation members? What are their backgrounds? What do members have in common? Do members come from diverse or similar backgrounds?

What are the goals and aims of the congregation? What activities do congregation members participate in to fulfill these aims?

What are the guiding values and principles of members?

With the information gathered from your interview, write a report in which you assess the ways in which the congregation forms a community. Describe some members of this community and the activities they engage in as a group. Explain this community's most obvious common values and customs.

Reading 20

"Gettin' on" in Roadville

Shirley Brice Heath

Shirley Brice Heath is a professor of education at Stanford University and has published extensively on language and literacy issues. She is probably best known for her ethnographic work, *Ways with Words: Language, Life and Work in Communities and Classrooms.* In the following selection from

Ways with Words, Heath contrasts two perspectives on life in a small mill town, that of the "oldtimers" and that of "young folks," and invites us to consider relationships between these perspectives and the development of a community.

The neighborhood community of Roadville is located in Laurenceville, a town of about 10,000, which had its beginnings as a mill village in the 1930s. Though no longer indicated on any map as Roadville, the community is known to oldtimers as the early heart of the mill village. A deep gully overgrown with underbrush forms one border of Roadville. On the hill above one side of the gully sits Laurence Mill, its chimneys visible from Mull Road on the hill across the gully. One must turn off Mull Road to go down to the neighborhood community of Roadville. Here and up the hill toward Mull Road, mill houses form three short uneven rows. Though from the crest of Mull Road several streets appear to head down to the gully, only Dura Street goes all the way down to Roadville. It meanders down the hill and parallels the gully before it peters out into a dirt road which eventually connects a couple of miles out of town with the main road to the nearby town of Gateway, a sleepy mill village in the early 1920s now grown to a population of more than 50,000.

Along Dura Street are nine look-alike houses, some set back off the road a bit and others nearer the road. All are frame, painted white, with asbestos roofs; they are set in symmetrically square front yards edged by tired and thin hedgerows with a narrow driveway on one side. A double outline of flowers edges the porches: a row of pots on the porch and marigolds set in the ground across the entire length of the front. In unevenly shaped backyards are gardens, grape arbors, chicken pens, rabbit hutches, and an occasional camper van or boat. An American flag flutters from a high flagpole in the yard of the house nearest the top of the hill.

The screen door on the front porch of this first house on the street opens into a living room filled with showroom-like matching furniture: a suite of sofa and chairs, two end tables, and a coffee table fill the small room as they once did the display window of the furniture store. There have been a few additions: starched stand-up doilies encircle the bases of end table lamps, ashtrays, and vases. Flat crocheted doilies cover the arms of the chairs and sofa and the headrest position of the chairs. A hand-crocheted afghan in the suite's colors is thrown over the back of the sofa. A huge doily of four layers, and a large vase of plastic flowers top the television set. The wooden floor is covered with a large twist rug, and several small matching scatter rugs mark the path to the hall which leads to the bedrooms and kitchen. Off the hall are two bedrooms, a small kitchen and dining area combination, and to the side of the hall is the bathroom. In the bedrooms, floor space is minimal, since dressers and wardrobes take up all available wall space; a double bed fills the center of one room, and twin beds straddle the available floor space in the other bedroom. The double bed is covered by a chenille spread, but a patchwork quilt hangs be-

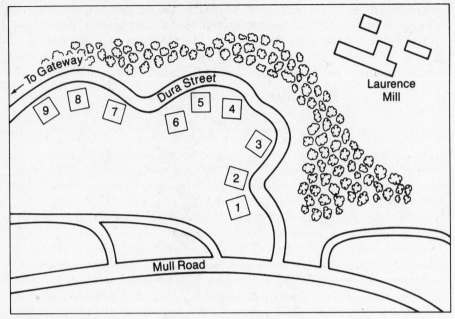

Map of Roadville

1. Mrs. Dee and daughter
2. Sue Dobbs and children
3. Mrs. Dee's son and his wife
4. Smith family
5. Macken family

6. Mrs. Dee's daughter and her husband
7. Brown family
8. Mrs. Dee's granddaughter and family
9. Turner family

neath its edges on one side. In the center of the bed is a doll with a wide skirt made of facial tissues and tied with green yarn. The family Bible on the bedside table is topped by Sunday School lesson books, and crocheted bookmarks mark places in each.

In the kitchen-dining room combination, the table is covered with a red and white checkered cloth, and the sideboard contains salt and pepper shakers in the shape of a dog and a cat, and a catsup-bottle holder which carries the name of a resort knick-knack shop just south of a neighboring state's border. The top of the sideboard is loaded with home-canned goods: jars of peaches, tomatoes, pickles, and beans. On the back porch, the freezer is full of similar products, and in the corner, stand buckets, mops, brooms, a kitchen stool, and a utility cart holding a turkey roaster, pressure cooker, and boxes of canning jars.

The widow Mrs. Dee, a plump softly wrinkled woman with fair skin and pale rose-pink fine hair pulled back in a bun, lives in this house with an unmarried daughter. In her eighties, Mrs. Dee works in her flowerbeds, keeps part of the vegetable garden, crochets, and pieces quilts. Her retirement check and her husband's Social Security provide her income. Her son and his wife live two houses down, a daughter and her husband live near the end of Dura Street, and granddaughter Martha and her young family live just before the dirt road leading toward the highway. They all help out in the big garden when they are not working at the mill, and the garden helps feed all four families. Born "away back in the mountains of North Carolina," Mrs. Dee grew up on a farm surrounded by grandparents, aunts, and uncles. Waves of hard living during her upbringing in the mountains had prepared Mrs. Dee to "work all my life."

> My daddy was a Baptist preacher and a farmer, and they was seven of us chil'rn— five girls and two boys. And we worked, you know, in the fields in the summertime, just like boys—they wasn't any boys—the boys was the youngest, so the girls had to do the work.

The children walked three miles to school and attended only four months out of the year. She finished grammar school, met her husband who was a farmer and handyman living near her father's farm, and they married in 1904. They settled in on the rented land they were to farm, and their ten children were born there. But "it was hard to make a livin' and we had so many chil'rn, and he [Mr. Dee] thought if we come to where they could get jobs in the mill . . . they could help, you know, when they wasn't at school." The family moved down to the Piedmont, and lived there for twenty years before the mill shut down during the Depression; none of the nine children who survived to adulthood finished high school. When the mill shut down in the early 1930s, the family moved further south to Roadville, so the children could get jobs in the Laurence Mill, which had opened there a decade ealier. Mrs. Dee, her husband, and three of their children found work in the mill. Seven grandchildren followed them into mill work in either Laurenceville or other towns of the region.

Roadville's community still holds the three children and one of the grandchildren. Mrs. Dee's unmarried daughter worked the same machine her mother used to work, and is now near retirement. She remembers the mountains, living near grandparents, aunts, and uncles there, moving down from the mountains because of "hard times," and facing the changes in the mill in the last twenty years. She no longer works her old machine; she is "too slow now, they say," and she looks forward to retirement. Her younger sister met her husband, a fellow millworker, in the old mill before they moved to Roadville, and she and her husband remember how all six of their children started out in the mill, but soon "got tired of it, and went lookin' for better. They moved away from here." Mrs. Dee's son also met his wife in the mill, and both continue there. One of their three children, Martha, and her husband, are the only third-generation members of the Dee family who continue in the mill, and they're "thinkin' of givin' it up." They talk of this idea with others who live in Roadville.

Of the five other families who live in Roadville, one or more members of each either now works in the mill or has worked in the mill. They all occupy mill houses either they or their parents bought. All these families have children. Adult voices in these households are divided on the place of the mill in their children's future. Between Mrs. Dee and her son lives Sue Dobbs, a widow with three children—teenager Jed, ten-year-old Lisa, and preschooler Sally. Sue vows the mill killed her husband: "hard work and that brown lung stuff they talk about," and she intends to raise her children up with a "fittin' education" so they can "do better." Sue, a wiry, jolly-spirited woman with short curly hair, works in the school lunchroom, and Jed, who quit school at sixteen, works in a local garage. He intends to marry Patsy, a fifteen-year-old who lives in Gateway, soon, and Sue hopes he will go back to night school when he "settles down and has a family."

A new family near Sue Dobbs is that of Betty and Doug Smith, who moved into the smallest of the Roadville houses when their first child was expected. They are young; they married when Betty was seventeen and Doug nineteen. Both Betty and Doug have worked in the mill, but Betty did not return to the mill after her child was born, because Doug wanted her to be with the baby. Betty's older sister Peggy and her husband Lee Brown live near the end of the street with their two boys, Martin and Danny. Their baby, Danny, was born just three months before Betty's first baby, and the families share child-care respon- sibilities. Peggy and Lee both work in the mill, so Betty helps out with Danny. Between Betty and Peggy live Mrs. Dee's daughter and her husband, and Mrs. Macken, a school teacher, and her husband Rob. Everyone always speaks of the two Mackens by naming "Mrs. Macken, the schoolteacher," first. Mrs. Macken is a tall woman with a blonde bouffant hairdo who wears all store-bought clothes. She dislikes the "backwardness" of the mill life and continually tries to pull her husband away from the mill and interest him in other occupations. But he is a loom fixer, has been for fifteen years, and wants no other job. He says he makes good money, "more'n my wife does," and he sees no reason to quit. They have two grown children and one preschooler, Kim, who is looked after by her maternal grandmother in Gateway while Mrs. Macken teaches in a Gateway school.

In the last house is the Turner family, Alice and Jay, and their three teenage children, all of whom are still in school. Both of the Turners work in the mill, but they moved to Roadville only in the late 1960s when the mill in which they worked in another part of the state closed. Mrs. Turner's mother lived in Laurenceville and encouraged them to return. Their three children have had problems in school; their boy wants to quit, and one of their girls is "going steady," and everyone expects her to get married when she "turns sixteen." The boy, however, stays on in high school, because he is a star of the baseball team, and he manages to keep "pretty good grades in math and history." He says he will go to college, maybe "even on a scholarship for baseball," but he hates school now. His sisters expect to go to business college or to nursing school "someday," but they are anxious to get out of Roadville. The town they lived in before was more the size of Alberta—the regional metropolitan center—and Laurenceville is a "hick town" in their view.

When the Turners voice aspirations for their children and distaste for Lau- renceville, other Roadville residents, with the exception of Rob Macken, do not argue with them. When Roadville parents talk of their children going on to technical school or college to become secretaries, electricians, doctors, nurses, pilots, and to own their own businesses, Rob scoffs and reminds them "that's further than any of you got." Parents tolerate Rob's general gruff nature and explain they want "better" for their children, and "it's easier now to get ahead."

Mrs. Macken urges parents to get books for their children, to read to them when they are "li'l," and when they start school to make certain they attend regularly. She holds herself up as an example of a "millhand's daughter who wanted to be a school teacher and did it through sheer hard work."

Two ways of looking at life cut across Roadville families, and each family has some members who support each perspective. The "oldtimers," who include Mrs. Dee and her children in Roadville, Rob Macken, and the Turners, remember the "hard times" and believe children in those days learned "a lot of lessons school can't teach." They take pride in their years in the mill, and they speak of past days of mill life fondly. A favorite pastime is exchanging stories about the years when the mill was "more like a family." They uphold the mill as a place which gave them work when their large families needed support and the mountains and the farm could not keep their children fed and clothed. Central to their valuing of the mill is the mill's demand for hard work, and the close links which used to exist between the mill and the community in support of work, recreation, and family life. As they watch their children and grandchildren drift away from mill life and Roadville, and newcomers move into Laurenceville, they note the difference in people and the resultant change in life. Mrs. Turner's mother explains:

> I don't know the people here now, I might not know four people on Main Street [in Laurenceville] nowadays. The place ain't kep' up the way it was either, but, of course, the young folks don't stay 'round here. Those that live here think they gotta go to Alberta. They just wanna get out on a highway and go. Back in my day, we stayed home, and the mill tried to make ways for us to do things with our chil'rn. But nowadays, that's all gone. Everybody went to church then too. Dinners there'd last all day. Most young folks met at church.

But the oldtimers do not want the young folks to deny themselves the benefits of the modern times. In fact, they themselves have incorporated into their daily living facets of the new times: a liking for travel in campers, a preference for store-bought clothes, and an avid interest in the secular and biracial activities of the Senior Citizens Center. They like to talk about old times but do not spend their days lamenting their passing. Instead they keep busy using the talents and enthusiasm for hard work and family recreation those days fostered in them.

The second perspective on life in Roadville is that identified with the "young folks," meaning, in general, any family who still has young children in school. These families, for example, Martha Dee and her husband, Sue Dobbs, and the Smiths and Browns, seem not to think of the mill as a permanent part of their own life, and they leave it entirely out of consideration for their children's future. They emphasize the success in education they expect their children to have and their assumption that education will carry their children away from the mill. These families talk about leaving the mill and Roadville, and find many of their models for dress, recreation, and aspirations in relatives in the metropolitan center and in key figures of the public media. They themselves had little more than a high school education, if that; yet the women, especially, want more schooling and find ways to mix with those who do have more education, primarily through serving as room mothers or as officers in parent-teacher organizations. The men have less interest in exposing themselves to either the content of schooling or to its personnel. But they follow with keen interest new trends in do-it-yourself projects, camping gear, and hunting and fishing equipment.

The young folks also respect and maintain a need for church life and an independence in providing for oneself. Though they do not talk as freely and as openly about religion as their parents and grandparents, they give the church and religious activities a prominent place in their lives. They also link the ability to do for oneself—to garden, sew, can, do woodworking, and maintain their homes—to moral qualities: thriftiness, industry, independence, and a proper use of God-given talents.

Many of the young folks look to a third group, "those who moved away," as models and sources of information for some aspects of their life in Roadville. Those who moved away have usually tried mill work but have now found other jobs which have taken them to Alberta or other parts of the South. Young folks in Roadville try to incorporate some of what they can learn about life in these places into their aspirations for the future, their home decorations, and preferred toys and activities for their children.

Within both perspectives is an appreciation of what the mill has done for the family. Moreover, the young folks recognize that rural-oriented Roadville offers numerous possibilities of recreation—hunting, fishing, and enjoying a slower pace of life. They all extoll the values of their neighborhood community in Laurenceville, and the way folks there are closer to each other and to the church than people are elsewhere. Yet there is an ambivalence, for Roadville's very restrictions which give privacy, a slow pace, and relative freedom from crime and dirt also keep out some of the ways of living and knowing which might help in getting ahead.

QUESTIONS FOR " 'GETTIN' ON' IN ROADVILLE" BY SHIRLEY BRICE HEATH

Talking About the Text

1. Heath spends much effort describing in detail the town of Roadville as well as its inhabitants and their homes. She even includes a map of Roadville in her essay. What do you think is Heath's purpose in giving the reader so much detail about this community?

2. Can you think of other forms of detail about which you would have liked information but that were not included? Why might these other details be useful to Heath's purpose?

3. When describing one couple, Heath says, "Everyone always speaks of the two Mackens by naming 'Mrs. Macken, the schoolteacher' first." Why do you think Heath bothers to mention this detail? Why do you think people in a mill town like Roadville might use this turn of phrase?

Exploring Issues

1. Read Ellen Goodman's essay, "A Working Community." In what sense might we think of Roadville as "a working community"? In what ways is it perhaps more than "a working community"?
2. What conflict(s) do you see being represented by the different perspectives of community life offered by members of the older and younger generations? How typical do you think this conflict is?
3. Heath states that "within both perspectives is an appreciation of what the mill has done for the family." What is the nature of this appreciation? Do you think it is the same for both the older and younger generations?
4. Heath writes that "Roadville's very restrictions which give privacy, a slow pace, and relative freedom from crime and dirt also keep out some of the ways of living and knowing which might help in getting ahead." Speculate about "the ways of living and knowing which might help in getting ahead." To what do you think Heath is referring?

Writing Assignment

Shirley Brice Heath is an ethnographer. In other words, she explores the lives of other people by becoming a participant-observer in their communities and then writes about her observations. Choose a community with which you are familiar—it need not be a neighborhood community like the one Heath has described. You might look at a school community or a work community, for example. Then write an ethnographic description of the community, using Heath's piece as a model. Be sure to focus on details that will tell us something about the community you are observing. Your overall aim should be discovery.

Reading 21

A Loaf of Bread

James Alan McPherson

James Alan McPherson was born and raised in Georgia where he attended segregated schools. He went to Morris Brown College in Atlanta and then on to Harvard Law School. McPherson has been a journalist and has taught literature at several universities. He has two collections of short stories, *Hue and City* (1969) and *Elbow Room* (1977). "A Loaf of Bread," taken from the latter collection, dramatizes a conflict in values held by a white grocer and a black deacon. This conflict has placed the entire community in turmoil, including the personal lives of the grocer, the deacon, and their wives and children.

It was one of those obscene situations, pedestrian to most people, but invested with meaning for a few poor folk whose lives are usually spent outside the imaginations of their fellow citizens. A grocer named Harold Green was caught red-handed selling to one group of people the very same goods he sold at lower prices at similar outlets in better neighborhoods. He had been doing this for many years, and at first he could not understand the outrage heaped upon him. He acted only from habit, he insisted, and had nothing personal against the people whom he served. They were his neighbors. Many of them he had carried on the cuff during hard times. Yet, through some mysterious access to a television station, the poor folk were now empowered to make grand denunciations of the grocer. Green's children now saw their father's business being picketed on the Monday evening news.

No one could question the fact that the grocer had been overcharging the people. On the news even the reporter grimaced distastefully while reading the statistics. His expression said, "It is my job to report the news, but sometimes even I must disassociate myself from it to protect my honor." This, at least, was the impression the grocer's children seemed to bring away from the television. Their father's name had not been mentioned, but there was a close-up of his store with angry black people, and a few outraged whites, marching in groups of three in front of it. There was also a close-up of his name. After seeing this, they were in no mood to watch cartoons. At the dinner table, disturbed by his children's silence, Harold Green felt compelled to say, "I am not a dishonest man." Then he felt ashamed. The children, a boy and his older sister, immediately left the table, leaving Green alone with his wife. "Ruth, I am not dishonest," he repeated to her.

Ruth Green did not say anything. She knew, and her husband did not, that the outraged people had also picketed the school attended by their children. They had threatened to return each day until Green lowered his prices. When they called her at home to report this, she had promised she would talk with him. Since she could not tell him this, she waited for an opening. She looked at her husband across the table.

"I did not make the world," Green began, recognizing at once the seriousness in her stare. "My father came to this country with nothing but his shirt. He was exploited for as long as he couldn't help himself. He did not protest or picket. He put himself in a position to play by the rules he had learned." He waited for his wife to answer, and when she did not, he tried again. "I did not make this world," he repeated. "I only make my way in it. Such people as these, they do not know enough to not be exploited. If not me, there would be a Greek, a Chinaman, maybe an Arab or a smart one of their own kind. Believe me, I deal with them. There is something in their style that lacks the patience to run a concern such as mine. If I closed down, take my word on it, someone else would do what has to be done."

But Ruth Green was not thinking of his leaving. Her mind was on other matters. Her children had cried when they came home early from school. She had no special feeling for the people who picketed, but she did not like to see her children cry. She had kissed them generously, then sworn them to silence. "One day this week," she told her husband, "you will give free, for eight hours, anything your customers come in to buy. There will be no publicity, except what they spread by word of mouth. No matter what they say to you, no matter what they take, you will remain silent." She stared deeply into him for what she knew was there. "If you refuse, you have seen the last of your children and myself."

Her husband grunted. Then he leaned toward her. "I will not knuckle under," he said. "I will *not* give!"

"We shall see," his wife told him.

The black pickets, for the most part, had at first been frightened by the audacity of their undertaking. They were peasants whose minds had long before become resigned to their fate as victims. None of them, before now, had thought to challenge this. But now, when they watched themselves on television, they hardly recognized the faces they saw beneath the hoisted banners and placards. Instead of reflecting the meekness they all felt, the faces looked angry. The close-ups looked especially intimidating. Several of the first pickets, maids who worked in the suburbs, reported that their employers, seeing the activity on the afternoon news, had begun treating them with new respect. One woman, midway through the weather report, called around the neighborhood to disclose that her employer had that very day given her a new china plate for her meals. The paper plates, on which all previous meals had been served, had been thrown into the wastebasket. One recipient of this call, a middle-aged woman known for her bashfulness and humility, rejoined that her husband, a sheet-metal worker, had only a few hours before been called "Mister" by his supervisor, a white man with a passionate hatred of color. She added the tale of a neighbor down the street, a widow-woman named Murphy, who had at first been reluctant to join the picket; this woman now was insisting it should be made a daily event. Such talk as this circulated among the people who had been instrumental in raising the issue. As news of their victory leaked into the ears of others who had not participated, they received all through the night calls from strangers requesting verification, offering advice, and vowing support. Such strangers listened, and then volunteered stories about indignities inflicted on them by city officials, policemen, other grocers. In this way, over a period of hours, the community became even more incensed and restless than it had been at the time of the initial picket.

Soon, the man who had set events in motion found himself a hero. His name was Nelson Reed, and all his adult life he had been employed as an assembly-line worker. He was a steady husband, the father three children, and a deacon in the Baptist church. All his life he had trusted in God and gotten along. But now something in him capitulated to the reality that came suddenly into focus. "I was wrong," he told people who called him. "The onliest thing that matters in this world is *money.* And when was the last time you seen a picture of Jesus on a dollar bill?" This line, which he repeated over and over, caused a few callers to laugh nervously, but not without some affirmation that this was indeed the way things were. Many said they had known it all along. Others argued that although it was certainly true, it was one thing to live without money and quite another to live without faith. But still most callers laughed and said, "You right. You *know* I know you right. Ain't it the truth, though?" Only a few people, among them Nelson Reed's wife, said nothing and looked very sad.

Why they looked sad, however, they would not communicate. And anyone observing their troubled faces would have to trust his own intuition. It is known that Reed's wife, Betty, measured all events against the fullness of her own experience. She was skeptical of everything. Brought to the church after a number of years of living openly with a jazz musician, she had embraced religion when she married Nelson Reed. But though she no longer believed completely in the world, she nonetheless had not fully embraced God. There was something in the nature of Christ's swift rise that had always bothered her, and something in the blood and vengeance of the Old Testament that was mellowing and refreshing. But she had never communicated these thoughts to anyone, especially her husband. Instead, she smiled vacantly while others professed leaps of faith, remained silent when friends spoke fiercely of their convictions. The presence of this vacuum in her contributed to her personal mystery; people said she was beautiful, although she was not outwardly so. Perhaps it was because she wished to protect this inner beauty that she did not smile now, and looked extremely sad, listening to her husband on the telephone.

Nelson Reed had no reason to be sad. He seemed to grow more energized and talkative as the days passed. He was invited by an alderman, on the Tuesday after the initial picket, to tell his story on a local television talk show. He sweated heavily under the hot white lights and attempted to be philosophical. "I notice," the host said to him, "that you are not angry at this exploitative treatment. What, Mr. Reed, is the source of your calm?" The assembly-line worker looked unabashedly into the camera and said, "I have always believed in *Justice* with a capital *J.* I was raised up from a baby believin' that God ain't gonna let nobody go *too* far. See, in *my* mind God is in charge of *all* the capital letters in the alphabet of this world. It say in the Scripture He is Alpha and Omega, the first and the last. He is just about the *onliest* capitalizer they is." Both Reed and the alderman laughed. "Now, when *men* start to capitalize, they gets *greedy.* They put a little *j* in *joy* and a littler one in *justice.* They raise up a big *G* in *Greed* and a big *E* in *Evil.* Well, soon as they commence to put a little *g* in *God,* you can expect some kind of reaction. The Savior will just raise up the *H* in *Hell* and go on from there. And that's just what I'm doin', giving these sharpies *HELL* with a big *H.*" The talk show host laughed along with Nelson Reed and the alderman. After the taping they drank coffee in the back room of the studio and talked about the sad shape of the world.

Three days before he was to comply with his wife's request, Green, the grocer, saw this talk show on television while at home. The words of Nelson Reed sent a chill through him. Though Reed had attempted to be philosophical, Green did not perceive the statement in this light. Instead, he saw a vindictive-looking black man seated between an ambitious alderman and a smug talk-show host. He saw them chatting comfortably about the nature of evil. The camera-man had shot mostly close-ups, and Green could see the set in Nelson Reed's jaw. The color of Reed's face was maddening. When his children came into the den, the grocer was in a sweat. Before he could think, he had shouted at them and struck the button turning off the set. The two children rushed from the room screaming. Ruth Green ran in from the kitchen. She knew why he was upset because she had received a call about the show; but she said nothing and pretended ignorance. Her children's school had been picketed that day, as it had the day before. But both children were still forbidden to speak of this to their father.

"Where do they get so much power?" Green said to his wife. "Two days ago, nobody would have cared. Now, everywhere, even in my home, I am con-demned as a rascal. And what do I own? An airline? A multinational? Half of South America? *No!* I own three stores, one of which happens to be in a certain neighborhood inhabited by people who cost me money to run it." He sighed and sat upright on the sofa, his chubby legs spread wide." A cab driver has a meter that clicks as he goes along. I pay extra for insurance, iron bars, pilfering by customers and employees. Nothing clicks. But when I add a little overhead to my prices, suddenly everything clicks. But for someone else. When was there last such a world?" He pressed the palms of both hands to his temples, suggesting a bombardment of brain-stinging sounds.

This gesture evoked no response from Ruth Green. She remained standing by the door, looking steadily at him. She said, "To protect yourself, I would not stock any more fresh cuts of meat in the store until after the giveaway on Saturday. Also, I would not tell it to the employees until after the first customer of the day has begun to check out. But I would urge you to hire several security guards to close the door promptly at seven-thirty, as is usual." She wanted to say much more than this, but did not. Instead, she watched him. He was looking at the blank gray television screen, his palms still pressed against his ears. "In case you need to hear again," she continued in a weighty tone of voice, "I said two days ago, and I say again now, that if you fail to do this you will not see your children again for many years."

He twisted his head and looked up at her. "What is the color of these people?" he asked.

"Black," his wife said.

"And what is the name of my children?"

"Green."

The grocer smiled. "There is your answer," he told his wife. "Green is the only color I am interested in."

His wife did not smile. "Insufficient," she said.

"The world is mad!" he moaned. "But it is a point of sanity with me to not bend. I will not bend." He crossed his legs and press one hand firmly atop his knee. "*I will not bend*," he said.

"We will see," his wife said.

Nelson Reed, after the television interview, became the acknowledged leader of the disgruntled neighbors. At first a number of them met in the kitchen at his house; then, as space was lacking for curious newcomers, a mass meeting was held on Thursday in an abandoned theater. His wife and three children sat in the front row. Behind them sat the widow Murphy, Lloyd Dukes, Tyrone Brown, Les Jones—those who had joined him on the first picket line. Behind these sat people who bought occasionally at the store, people who lived on the fringes of the neighborhood, people from other neighborhoods come to investigate the problem, and the merely curious. The middle rows were occupied by a few people from the suburbs, those who had seen the talk show and whose outrage at the grocer proved much more powerful than their fear of black people. In the rear of the theater crowded aging, old-style leftists, somber students, cynical young black men with angry grudges to explain with inarticulate gestures. Leaning against the walls, and huddled near the doors at the rear, tape-recorder-bearing social scientists looked as detached and serene as bookies at the track. Here and there, in this diverse crowd, a politician stationed himself, pumping hands vigorously and pressing his palms gently against the shoulders of elderly people. Other visitors passed out leaflets, buttons, glossy color prints of men who promoted causes, the familiar and obscure. There was a hubbub of voices, a blend of the strident and the playful, the outraged and the reverent, lending an undercurrent of ominous energy to the assembly.

Nelson Reed spoke from a platform on the stage, standing before a yellowed, shredded screen that had once reflected the images of matinee idols. "I don't mind sayin' that I have always been a sucker," he told the crowd. "All my life I have been a sucker for the words of Jesus. Being a natural-born fool, I just ain't never had the *sense* to learn no better. Even right today, while the whole world is sayin' wrong is right and up is down, I'm so dumb I'm *still* steady believin' what is wrote in the Good Book. . . ."

From the audience, especially the front rows, came a chorus singing, "Preach!"

"I have no doubt," he continued in a low baritone, "that it's true what is writ in the Good Book: 'The last shall be first and the first shall be last.' I don't know about y'all, but I have *always* been the last. I never wanted to be the first, but sometimes it look like the world get so bad that them that's holdin' onto the tree of life is the onliest ones left when God commence to blowin' dead leafs off the branches."

"Now you preaching," someone said.

In the rear of the theater a white student shouted an awkward "Amen."

Nelson Reed began walking across the stage to occupy the major part of his nervous energy. But to those in the audience, who now hung on his every word, it looked as though he strutted. "All my life," he said, "I have claimed to be a man without earnin' the right to call myself that. You know, the *average* man ain't really a man. The average man is a *boot-licker*. In fact, the *average* man would *run away* if he found hisself standing alone facin' down a adversary. I have done that *too many a time* in my life! But *not no more*. Better to be *once* was than *never* was a man. I will tell you tonight, there is somethin' *wrong* in being average. *I intend to stand up!* Now, if your average man that ain't really a man stand up, two things gonna happen: *One*, he g'on bust through all the weights that been place on his head, and *two*, he g'on feel a lot of pain. But that same hurt is what make things fall in place. That, and gettin' your hands on one of these slick four-flushers tight enough so's you can squeeze him and say, 'No more!' You do that, you g'on hurt some, but *you won't be average no more* . . ."

"No *more!*" a few people in the front rows repeated.

"I say *no more!*" Nelson Reed shouted.

"*No more! No more! No more!*" The chant rustled through the crowd like the rhythm of an autumn wind against a shedding tree.

Then people laughed and chattered in celebration.

As for the grocer, from the evening of the television interview he had begun to make plans. Unknown to his wife, he cloistered himself several times with his brother-in-law, an insurance salesman, and plotted a course. He had no intention of tossing steaks to the crowd. "And why should I, Tommy?" he asked his wife's brother, a lean, bald-headed man named Thomas. "I don't cheat anyone. I have never cheated anyone. The businesses I run are always on the up-and-up. So why should I pay?"

"Quite so," the brother-in-law said, chewing an unlit cigarillo. "The world has gone crazy. Next they will say that people in my business are responsible for prolonging life. I have found that people who refuse to believe in death refuse also to believe in the harshness of life. I sell well by saying that death is a long happiness. I show people the realities of life and compare this to a funeral with dignity, *and* the promise of a bundle for every loved one salted away. When they look around hard at life, they usually buy."

"So?" asked Green. Thomas was a college graduate with a penchant for philosophy.

"So," Thomas answered. "You must fight to show these people the reality of both your situation and theirs. How would it be if you visited one of their meetings and chalked out, on a blackboard, the dollars and cents of your operation? Explain your overhead, your security fees, all the additional expenses. If you treat them with respect, they might understand."

Green frowned. "That I would never do," he said. "It would be admission of a certain guilt."

The brother-in-law smiled, but only with one corner of his mouth. "Then you have something to feel guilty about?" he asked.

The grocer frowned at him. "*Nothing!*" he said with great emphasis.

"So?" Thomas said.

This first meeting between the grocer and his brother-in-law took place on Thursday, in a crowded barroom.

At the second meeting, in a luncheonette, it was agreed that the grocer should speak privately with the leader of the group, Nelson Reed. The meeting at which this was agreed took place on Friday afternoon. After accepting this advice from Thomas, the grocer resigned himself to explain to Reed, in as finite detail as possible, the economic structure of his operation. He vowed to suppress no information. He would explain everything: inventories, markups, sale items, inflation, balance sheets, specialty items, overhead, and that mysterious item called profit. This last item, promising to be the most difficult to explain, Green and his brother-in-law debated over for several hours. They agreed first of all that a man should not work for free, then they agreed that it was unethical to ruthlessly exploit. From these parameters, they staked out an area between fifteen and forty percent, and agreed that someplace between these two borders lay an amount of return that could be called fair. This was easy, but then Thomas introduced the factor of circumstance. He questioned whether the fact that one serviced a risky area justified the earning of profits closer to the forty-percent edge of the scale. Green was unsure. Thomas smiled. "Here is a case that will point out an analogy," he said, licking a cigarillo. "I read in the papers that a family wants to sell an electric stove. I call the home and the man says fifty dollars. I ask to come out and inspect the merchandise. When I arrive I see they are poor, have already bought a new stove that is connected, and are selling the old one for fifty dollars because they want it out of the place. The electric stove is in good condition, worth much more than fifty. But because I see what I see I offer forty-five."

Green, for some reason, wrote down this figure on the back of the sales slip for the coffee they were drinking.

The brother-in-law smiled. He chewed his cigarillo. "The man agrees to take forty-five dollars, saying he has had no other calls. I look at the stove again and see a spot of rust. I say I will give him forty dollars. He agrees to this, on condition that I myself haul it away. I say I will haul it away if he comes down to thirty. You, of course, see where I am going."

The grocer nodded. "The circumstances of his situation, his need to get rid of the stove quickly, placed him in a position where he has little room to bargain?"

"Yes," Thomas answered. "So? Is it ethical, Harry?"

Harold Green frowned. He had never liked his brother-in-law, and now he thought the insurance agent was being crafty. "But," he answered, "this man does not *have* to sell! It is his choice whether to wait for other calls. It is not the fault of the buyer that the seller is in a hurry. It is the right of the buyer to get what he wants at the lowest price possible. That is the rule. That has *always* been the rule. And the reverse of it applies to the seller as well."

"Yes," Thomas said, sipping coffee from the Styrofoam cup. "But suppose that in addition to his hurry to sell, the owner was also of a weak soul. There are, after all, many such people." He smiled. "Suppose he placed no value on the money?"

"Then," Green answered, "your example is academic. Here we are not talking about real life. One man lives by the code, one man does not. Who is there free enough to make a judgment?" He laughed. "Now you see," he told his brother-in-law. "Much more than a few dollars are at stake. If this one buyer is to be condemned, then so are most people in the history of the world. An examination of history provides the only answer to your question. This code will be here tomorrow, long after the ones who do not honor it are not."

They argued fiercely late into the afternoon, the brother-in-law leaning heavily on his readings. When they parted, a little before 5:00 P.M., nothing had been resolved.

Neither was much resolved during the meeting between Green and Nelson Reed. Reached at home by the grocer in the early evening, the leader of the group spoke coldly at first, but consented finally to meet his adversary at a nearby drugstore for coffee and a talk. They met at the lunch counter, shook hands awkwardly, and sat for a few minutes discussing the weather. Then the grocer pulled two gray ledgers from his briefcase. "You have for years come into my place," he told the man. "In my memory I have always treated you well. Now our relationship has come to this." He slid the books along the counter until they touched Nelson Reed's arm.

Reed opened the top book and flipped the thick green pages with his thumb. He did not examine the figures. "All I know," he said, "is over at your place a can of soup cost me fifty-five cents, and two miles away at your other store for white folks you chargin' thirty-nine cents." He said this with the calm authority of an outraged soul. A quality of condescension tinged with pity crept into his gaze.

The grocer drummed his fingers on the counter top. He twisted his head and looked away, toward shelves containing cosmetics, laxatives, toothpaste. His eyes lingered on a poster of a woman's apple red lips and milk white teeth. The rest of the face was missing.

"Ain't no use to hide," Nelson Reed said, as to a child. "*I* know you wrong, *you* know you wrong, and before I finish, *everybody in this city* g'on know you wrong. God don't *like* ugly." He closed his eyes and gripped the cup of coffee. Then he swung his head suddenly and faced the grocer again. "Man, why you want to *do* people that way?" he asked. "We human, same as you."

"Before *God!*" Green exclaimed, looking squarely into the face of Nelson Reed. "Before God!" he said again. "*I am not an evil man!*" These last words sounded more like a moan as he tightened the muscles in his throat to lower the sound of his voice. He tossed his left shoulder as if adjusting the sleeve of his coat, or as if throwing off some unwanted weight. Then he peered along the countertop. No one was watching. At the end of the counter the waitress was scrubbing the coffee urn. "Look at these figures, please," he said to Reed.

The man did not drop his gaze. His eyes remained fixed on the grocer's face.

"All right," Green said. "Don't look. I'll tell you what is in these books, believe me if you want. I work twelve hours a day, one day off per week, running my business in three stores. I am not a wealthy person. In one place, in the area you call white, I get by barely by smiling lustily at old ladies, stocking gourmet stuff on the chance I will build a reputation as a quality store. The two clerks there cheat me; there is nothing I can do. In this business you must be friendly with everybody. The second place is on the other side of town, in a neighborhood as poor as this one. I get out there seldom. The profits are not worth the gas. I use the loss there as a write-off against some other properties." He paused. "Do you understand write-off?" he asked Nelson Reed.

"Naw," the man said.

Harold Green laughed. "What does it matter?" he said in a tone of voice intended for himself alone. "In this area I will admit I make a profit, but it is not so much as you think. But I do not make a profit here because the people are black. I make a profit because a profit is here to be made. I invest more here in window bars, theft losses, insurance, spoilage; I deserve to make more here than at the other places." He looked, almost imploringly, at the man seated next to him. "You don't accept this as the right of a man in business?"

Reed grunted. "Did the bear shit in the woods?" he said.

Again Green laughed. He gulped his coffee awkwardly, as if eager to go. Yet his motions slowed once he had set the coffee cup down on the blue plastic saucer. "Place yourself in *my* situation," he said, his voice high and tentative. "If *you* were running my store in this neighborhood, what would be *your* position? Say on a profit scale of fifteen to forty percent, at what point in between would you draw the line?"

Nelson Reed thought. He sipped his coffee and seemed to chew the liquid. "Fifteen to forty?" he repeated.

"Yes."

"I'm a churchgoin' man," he said. "Closer to fifteen than to forty."

"How close?"

Nelson Reed thought. "In church you tithe ten percent."

"In restaurants you tip fifteen," the grocer said quickly.

"All right," Reed said, "Over fifteen."

"How much over?"

Nelson Reed thought.

"Twenty, thirty, thirty-five?" Green chanted, leaning closer to Reed. Still the man thought.

"Forty? Maybe even forty-five or fifty?" the grocer breathed in Reed's ear. "In the supermarkets, you know, they have more subtle ways of accomplishing such feats."

Reed slapped his coffee cup with the back of his right hand. The brown liquid swirled across the counter top, wetting the books. "*Damn this!*" he shouted.

Startled, Green rose from his stool.

Nelson Reed was trembling. "I ain't *you*," he said in a deep baritone. "I ain't the *supermarket* neither. All I is is a poor man that works *too* hard to see his pay slip through his fingers like rainwater. All I know is you done *cheat* me, you done *cheat* everybody in the neighborhood, and we organized now to get some of it *back!*" Then he stood and faced the grocer. "My daddy sharecropped down in Mississippi and bought in the company store. He owed them twenty-three years when he died. I paid off five of them years and then run away to up here. Now, I'm a deacon in the Baptist church. I raised my kids the way my daddy raise me and don't bother nobody. Now come to find out, after all my runnin', they done lift that *same company store* up out of Mississippi and slip it down on us here! Well, my daddy was a *fighter*, and if he hadn't owed all them years he would of raise him some hell. Me, I'm steady my daddy's child, plus I got seniority in my union. I'm a free man. Buddy, don't you know *I'm gonna raise me some hell!*"

Harold Green reached for a paper napkin to sop the coffee soaking into his books.

Nelson Reed threw a dollar on top of the books and walked away.

"I *will not* do it!" Harold Green said to his wife that same evening. They were in the bathroom of their home. Bending over the face bowl, she was washing her hair with a towel draped around her neck. The grocer stood by the door, looking in at her. "I will not bankrupt myself tomorrow," he said.

"I've been thinking about it, too," Ruth Green said, shaking her wet hair. "You'll do it, Harry."

"Why should I?" he asked. "You won't leave. You know it was a bluff. I've waited this long for you to calm down. Tomorrow is Saturday. This week has been a hard one. Tonight let's be realistic."

"Of course you'll do it," Ruth Green said. She said it the way she would say "Have some toast." She said, "You'll do it because you want to see your children grow up."

"And for what other reason?" he asked.

She pulled the towel tighter around her neck. "Because you are at heart a moral man."

He grinned painfully. "If I am, why should I have to prove it to *them?*"

"Not them," Ruth Green said, freezing her movements and looking in the mirror. "Certainly not them. By no means them. They have absolutely nothing to do with this."

"Who, then?" he asked, moving from the door into the room. "Who else should I prove something to?"

His wife was crying. But her entire face was wet. The tears moved secretly down her face.

"Who else?" Harold Green asked.

It was almost 11:00 P.M. and the children were in bed. They had also cried when they came home from school. Ruth Green said, "For yourself, Harry. For the love that lives inside your heart."

All night the grocer though about this.

Nelson Reed also slept little that Friday night. When he returned home from the drugstore, he reported to his wife as much of the conversation as he could remember. At first he had joked about the exchange between himself and the grocer, but as more details returned to his conscious mind he grew solemn and then bitter. "He ask me to put myself in *his* place," Reed told his wife. "Can you imagine that kind of gumption? I never cheated nobody in my life. All my life I have lived on Bible principles. I am a deacon in the church. I have work all my life for other folks and I don't even own the house I live in." He paced up and down the kitchen, his big arms flapping loosely at his sides. Betty Reed sat at the table, watching. "This here's a low-down, ass-kicking world," he said. "I swear to God it is! All my life I have lived on principle and I ain't got a dime in the bank. Betty," he turned suddenly toward her, "don't you think I'm a fool?"

"Mr. Reed," she said. "Let's go on to bed."

But he would not go to bed. Instead, he took the fifth of bourbon from the cabinet under the sink and poured himself a shot. His wife refused to join him. Reed drained the glass of whiskey, and then another, while he resumed pacing the kitchen floor. He slapped his hands against his sides. "I think I'm a fool," he said. "Ain't got a dime in the bank, ain't got a pot to *pee* in or a wall to pitch it over, and that there *cheat* ask me to put myself inside *his* shoes. Hell, I can't even *afford* the kind of shoes he wears." He stopped pacing and looked at his wife.

"Mr. Reed," she whispered, "tomorrow ain't a work day. Let's go to bed."

Nelson Reed laughed, the bitterness in his voice rattling his wife. "The *hell* I will!" he said.

He strode to the yellow telephone on the wall beside the sink and began to dial. The first call was to Lloyd Dukes, a neighbor two blocks away and a lieutenant in the organization. Dukes was not at home. The second call was to McElroy's Bar on the corner of 65th and Carroll, where Stanley Harper, another of the lieutenants, worked as a bartender. It was Harper who spread the word, among those men at the bar, that the organization would picket the grocer's store the following morning. And all through the night, in the bedroom of their house, Betty Reed was awakened by telephone calls coming from Lester Jones, Nat Lucas, Mrs. Tyrone Brown, the widow-woman named Murphy, all coordinating the time when they would march in a group against the store owned by Harold Green. Betty Reed's heart beat loudly beneath the covers as she listened to the bitterness and rage in her husband's voice. On several occasions, hearing him declare himself a fool, she pressed the pillow against her eyes and cried.

The grocer opened later than usual this Saturday morning, but still it was early enough to make him one of the first walkers in the neighborhood. He parked his car one block from the store and strolled to work. There were no birds singing. The sky in this area was not blue. It was smog-smutted and gray, seeming on the verge of a light rain. The street, as always, was littered with cans, papers, bits of broken glass. As always the garbage cans overflowed. The morning breeze plastered a sheet of newspaper playfully around the sides of a rusted garbage can. For some reason, using his right foot, he loosened the paper and stood watching it slide into the street and down the block. The movement made him feel good. He whistled while unlocking the bars shielding the windows and door of his store. When he had unlocked the main door he stepped in quickly and threw a switch to the right of the jamb, before the shrill sound of the alarm could shatter his mood. Then he switched on the lights. Everything was as it had been the night before. He had already telephoned his two employees and given them the day off. He busied himself doing the usual things— hauling milk and vegetables from the cooler, putting cash in the till—not thinking about the silence of his wife, or the look in her eyes, only an hour before when he left home. He had determined, at some point while driving through the city, that today it would be business as usual. But he expected very few customers.

The first customer of the day was Mrs. Nelson Reed. She came in around 9:00 A.M. and wandered about the store. He watched her from the checkout counter. She seemed uncertain of what she wanted to buy. She kept glancing at him down the center aisle. His suspicions aroused, he said finally, "Yes, may I help you, Mrs. Reed?" His words caused her to jerk, as if some devious thought had been perceived going through her mind. She reached over quickly and lifted a loaf of whole wheat bread from the rack and walked with it to the counter. She looked at him and smiled. The smile was a broad, shy one, that rare kind of smile one sees on virgin girls when they first confess love to themselves. Betty Reed was a woman of about forty-five. For some reason he could not comprehend, this gesture touched him. When she pulled a dollar from her purse and laid it on the counter, an impulse, from no place he could locate with his mind, seized control of his tongue. "Free," he told Betty Reed. She paused, then pushed the dollar toward him with a firm and determined thrust of her arm. "Free," he heard himself saying strongly, his right palm spread and meeting her thrust with absolute force. She clutched the loaf of bread and walked out of his store.

The next customer, a little girl, arriving well after 10:30 A.M., selected a candy bar from the rack beside the counter. "Free," Green said cheerfully. The little girl left the candy on the counter and ran out of the store.

At 11:15 A.M. a wino came in looking desperate enough to sell his soul. The grocer watched him only for an instant. Then he went to the wine counter and selected a half-gallon of medium-grade red wine. He shoved the jug into the belly of the wino, the man's sour breath bathing his face. "Free," the grocer said. "But you must not drink it in here."

He felt good about the entire world, watching the wino through the window gulping the wine and looking guiltily around.

At 11:25 A.M. the pickets arrived.

Two dozen people, men and women, young and old, crowded the pavement in front of his store. Their signs, placards, and voices denounced him as a parasite. The grocer laughed inside himself. He felt lighthearted and wild, like a man drugged. He rushed to the meat counter and pulled a long roll of brown wrapping paper from the rack, tearing it neatly with a quick shift of his body resembling a dance step practiced fervently in his youth. He laid the paper on the chopping block and with the black-inked, felt-tipped marker scrawled, in giant letters, the word Free. This he took to the window and pasted in place with many strands of Scotch tape. He was laughing wildly. "Free!" he shouted from behind the brown paper. "Free! Free! Free! Free! Free! Free!" He rushed to the door, pushed his head out, and screamed to the confused crowd, "*Free!*" Then he ran back to the counter and stood behind it, like a soldier at attention.

They came in slowly.

Nelson Reed entered first, working his right foot across the dirty tile as if tracking a squiggling worm. The others followed: Lloyd Dukes dragging a placard, Mr. and Mrs. Tyrone Brown, Stanley Harper walking with his fists clenched, Lester Jones with three of his children, Nat Lucas looking sheepish and detached, a clutch of winos, several bashful nuns, ironic-smiling teenagers and a few students. Bringing up the rear was a bearded social scientist holding a tape recorder to his chest. "Free!" the grocer screamed. He threw up his arms in a gesture that embraced, or dismissed, the entire store. *"All free!"* he shouted. He was grinning with the grace of a madman.

The winos began grabbing first. They stripped the shelf of wine in a matter of seconds. Then they fled, dropping bottles on the tile in their wake. The others, stepping quickly through this liquid, soon congealed it into a sticky, blood-like consistency. The young men went for the cigarettes and luncheon meats and beer. One of them had the prescience to grab a sack from the counter, while the others loaded their arms swiftly, hugging cartons and packages of cold cuts like long-lost friends. The students joined them, less for greed than for the thrill of the experience. The two nuns backed toward the door. As for the older people, men and women, they stood at first as if stuck to the wine-smeared floor. Then Stanley Harper, the bartender, shouted, "The man said *free*, y'all heard him." He paused. "Didn't you say *free* now?" he called to the grocer.

"I said free," Harold Green answered, his temples pounding.

A cheer went up. The older people began grabbing, as if the secret lusts of a lifetime had suddenly seized command of their arms and eyes. They grabbed toilet tissue, cold cuts, pickes, sardines, boxes of raisins, boxes of starch, cans of soup, tins of tuna fish and salmon, bottles of spices, cans of boned chicken, slippery cans of olive oil. Here a man, Lester Jones, burdened himself with several heads of lettuce, while his wife, in another aisle, shouted for him to drop those small items and concentrate on the gourmet section. She herself took imported sardines, wheat crackers, bottles of candied pickles, herring, anchovies, imported olives, French wafers, an ancient, half-rusted can of paté, stocked, by mistake, from the inventory of another store. Others packed their arms with detergents, hams, chocolate-coated cereal, whole chickens with hanging asses, wedges of bologna and salami like squashed footballs, chunks of cheeses, yellow and white, shriveled onions, and green peppers. Mrs. Tyrone Brown hung a curve of pepperoni around her neck and seemed to take on instant dignity, much like a person of noble birth in possession now of a long sought-after gem. Another woman, the widow Murphy, stuffed tomatoes into her bosom, holding a half-chewed lemon in her mouth. The more enterprising fought desperately over the three rusted shopping carts, and the victors wheeled these along the narrow aisles, sweeping into them bulk items—beer in six-packs, sacks of sugar, flour, glass bottles of syrup, toilet cleanser, sugar cookies, prune, apple and tomato juices—while others endeavored to snatch the carts from them. There were several fistfights and much cursing. The grocer, standing behind the counter, hummed and rang his cash register like a madman.

Nelson Reed, the first into the store, followed the nuns out, empty-handed.

In less than half an hour the others had stripped the store and vanished in many directions up and down the block. But still more people came, those late in hearing the news. And when they saw the shelves were bare, they cursed soberly and chased those few stragglers still bearing away goods. Soon only the grocer and the social scientist remained, the latter stationed at the door with his tape recorder sucking in leftover sounds. Then he too slipped away up the block.

By 12:10 P.M. the grocer was leaning against the counter, trying to make his mind slow down. Not a man given to drink during work hours, he nonetheless took a swallow from a bottle of wine, a dusty bottle from beneath the wine shelf, somehow overlooked by the winos. Somewhat recovered, he was preparing to remember what he should do next when he glanced toward a figure at the door. Nelson Reed was standing there, watching him.

"All gone," Harold Green said. "My friend, Mr. Reed, there is no more." Still the man stood in the doorway, peering into the store.

The grocer waved his arms about the empty room. Not a display case had a single item standing. "All gone," he said again, as if addressing a stupid child. "There is nothing left to get. You, my friend, have come back too late for a second load. I am cleaned out."

Nelson Reed stepped into the store and strode toward the counter. He moved through wine-stained flour, lettuce leaves, red, green, and blue labels, bits and pieces of broken glass. He walked toward the counter.

"All day," the grocer laughed, not quite hysterically now, "all day long I have not made a single cent of profit. The entire day was a loss. This store, like the others, is *bleeding* me." He waved his arms about the room in a magnificent gesture of uncaring loss. "Now do you understand?" he said. "Now will you put yourself in my shoes? I have nothing here. Come, now, Mr. Reed, would it not be so bad a thing to walk in my shoes?"

"Mr. Green," Nelson Reed said coldly. "My wife bought a loaf of bread in here this mornin'. She forgot to pay you. I, myself, have come here to pay you your money."

"Oh," the grocer said.

"I think it was brown bread. Don't that cost more than white?"

The two men looked away from each other, but not at anything in the store.

"In my store, yes," Harold Green said. He rang the register with the most casual movement of his finger. The register read fifty-five cents.

Nelson Reed held out a dollar.

"And two cents tax," the grocer said.

The man held out the dollar.

"After all," Harold Green said. "We are all, after all, Mr. Reed, in debt to the government."

He rang the register again. It read fifty-seven cents.

Nelson Reed held out a dollar.

QUESTIONS FOR "A LOAF OF BREAD" BY JAMES ALAN McPHERSON

Talking About the Text

1. Re-read the opening paragraph. Describe the narrator's tone. How does the tone affect how you respond emotionally to the characters and their actions?
2. Green says, "I did not make this world. . . . I only make my way in it. Such people as these, they do not know enough to not be exploited. If not me, there would a Greek, a Chinaman, maybe an Arab or a smart one of their own kind." Why does Green make this statement? In what sense might he be right? In what sense wrong?
3. What roles do Mrs. Green and Mrs. Reed play in this conflict? How would you interpret their actions?
4. How would you characterize the community values represented by the deacon? By the grocer? By their wives?

Exploring Issues

1. Bread and wine are Christian symbols of community sacrifice. How might this religious dimension contribute to your understanding of this story?
2. There seem to be two codes in conflict here: the code of business and a moral code. Describe these two codes and show how each of the main characters deals with both of them.

Writing Assignments

1. In an analytic essay, offer your interpretation of the ending. What do the actions of Green and Reed signify? How is the conflict resolved? In your interpretation draw on evidence from the text to support your claims. You will probably also have to account for the actions of other characters, particularly the wives' actions, as you interpret the events leading up to the final scene.
2. Reexamine the passage in which Green begins telling everyone that his groceries are free. He keeps repeating this word. Write a response in which you explore the various meanings this word might have for the characters in the story. Consider what individuals might be freed "from" as well as what they might be free to do.
3. Take the scene from the drugstore in which Green meets Reed and rewrite it substituting for the two men their respective wives. You might try to write this scene as the narrator would, including the dialogue of the two women as they discuss the growing turmoil and what might be done about it.

Reading 22

Down Home: A Landscape of Small Ruins

V. S. Naipaul

V. S. Naipaul is originally from Trinidad and was educated at Oxford. After completing his studies at Oxford in 1954, Naipaul began a writing career. He has published 20 books of both fiction and nonfiction, including *Finding the Center, Among the Believers, The Enigma of Arrival,* and *A Bend in the River.* "Down Home: A Landscape of Small Ruins" is the prologue to Naipaul's first book about life in the American South, *A Turn in the South.* In this selection Naipaul shares with us a poignant account of his visit to Bowen, a small black community located outside of Greensboro, North Carolina, undergoing change as a result of the civil rights movement.

Jimmy worked in New York as a designer and lettering artist. Howard was his assistant. Jimmy, who could become depressed at times, said to Howard one day, "Howard, if I had to give up, and you couldn't get another job, what would you do?" Howard, who was from the South, said, "I would go home to my mama."

Jimmy was as struck by this as I was when Jimmy told me: that Howard had something neither Jimmy nor I had, a patch of the earth he thought of as home, absolutely his. And that was where—many months after I had heard this story—I thought I should begin this book about the South: with the home that Howard had.

Howard arranged the visit. Jimmy decided to come with us. We went on the Easter weekend; the timing was pure chance.

It was raining, had been raining in New York for two days.

At La Guardia Howard said, "I hated the place when I was young, for the continuity."

I thought he meant historical continuity, the past living on. But from other things he then said, I felt he meant only that it was a country place where little changed and little happened. I had this trouble with Howard's words sometimes; I was too ready to find in them meanings he didn't intend.

Howard was six feet tall, but slender and light of movement. He was in his late twenties or early thirties. He was very much his own man. He lived alone, and he preferred not to live in Harlem. He was a serious reader of newspapers and magazines, and he had a special interest in foreign affairs. He liked to cook; and he kept himself fit by playing paddle ball on weekends. He was easy to be with, not spiky; and I put this down in part to the home he was so sure of and still close to.

Howard said, "You see how the South begins. More black people here, on the plane."

Most of the passengers were black, and they were not like an African or West Indian crowd. They were almost subdued, going home from the big city for Easter.

We landed at Greensboro. It was a big airport; and then, just a few minutes away, proof of the scale of things here, there was another airport, just as big. We got off there. There were military people in the waiting areas. It was warmer than in New York; I changed into a lighter jacket.

Soon we were on the highway.

Howard said, "Look, the dogwood and the pines. It is what you see a lot of in the South."

The dogwood was a small tree, and it was now in single-petaled white blossom. Not the dogwood of England, the water-loving red-stemmed shrub or small tree that made a bright autumn and winter show. And there were—Howard identified them for me—oaks and maples, in the freshest spring-green.

The land was flat, like the pampas of Argentina or the llanos of Venezuela. But trees bordered the fields and gave a human scale to things. We passed tobacco barns, tallish, squarish, corrugated-iron structures, where in the old days tobacco was cured. They were in decay, the corrugated iron rusted dark red, the wood weathered gray. Against the green this corrugated-iron rust was a lovely color; it gave an extra beauty to the land.

The highway looked like highways everywhere else in the United States: boards for motels and restaurants and gas stations.

Tobacco was still a crop. We saw the seedlings being mechanically planted: one black man on the tractor, two men on the trolley behind dropping earth-rooted seedlings down a shafted dibble. All this used to be done by hand, Howard said. He picked tobacco in the school holidays. The resin from the green leaf stained his hands black and was hard to clean off. I never knew about this black-staining resin from the green leaf, but it was immediately comprehensible. It was for that resin, that tar, that people smoked the cured leaf.

We had driven so fast on the highway that we were in Howard's area almost before I was ready for it. There was a small town center, a small rich white suburb attached to that town, and then outside that a black area. The differences were noticeable. But Howard, near his home now, appeared to claim both the white area and the black area.

He had been excited all morning; he was more excited now. And then, entering another little town, we were seeing the places he had known as a boy. He had cut the grass and cleaned the swimming pool and mopped the porch of that house, the Bowen house, the house of the people who still more or less owned the little town that was called Bowen. And he had done the same job for people in that other house.

That little green wooden house, now closed up, just beside the highway, had been his mother's house. He had grown up there. His mother lived in another house now; another house—bigger and newer—was home. We saw it from the highway. It was a concrete-block house set back from the road, behind some other houses: not the old, tree-embowered house I had had in my imagination. We didn't stop; we were going first to the motel, which was some way outside the town.

The main building of the motel was a loghouse. In the sandy yard there were subsidiary little barracklike room-rows below trees and behind shrubs. A black boy was hosing down the veranda floor of the loghouse. He looked timid—for the first time that morning I had a feeling of racial constraint—and he said the office was inside.

There was no apparent office. Only an empty low-ceilinged room with two or three close-set rows of little tables with red- or blue-checked tablecloths. The air conditioning had been turned off a long time before, and the air was dead and smelly.

Howard called out, and after some time a young white man in shorts, with a yellow plastic apron and a large kitchen knife, came in from the back, through two doors. He was sallow, open-mouthed, and his movements were uncoordinated. A little while later a fat old white woman with a twisted face came in through the same two doors. I felt we had been wrong to disturb them, the old woman and the young man who was really a boy.

Two rooms? Would we want two double rooms or two single rooms? I couldn't understand the old woman's questions. But then, putting down his knife, the boy with the shorts and the yellow plastic apron half beckoned to us, and we followed him—he walked with stamping, awkward steps—out of the dining room to the sandy yard below the pine trees, and then to a low building at the edge of the yard. The ground there was damp; and the small rooms that the boy opened up, one after the other, had the dampness of the ground, with a shut-in, old smell, and with stained cheap carpets.

Better judgment was at work, however. And even while Jimmy and I were looking at the rooms with the silent boy in the yellow apron, Howard—who had not followed us—had heard from somebody in the motel (perhaps the old woman with the twisted face) that there was a more up-to-date motel in the next town, Peters. (Bowen, Peters: American places, big and small, are often named after people; and the ordinariness of the names can make some itineraries read like the muster of an army squad or a sports team.)

To Peters, then, we went, through the highway landscape. And the Peters motel was an altogether bigger affair, with a number of two-story buildings in red brick. It even advertised a swimming pool (though something had happened to the filter, and the pool was green with algae).

Howard, going up the steps ahead of us and entering the office through the two doors, turned to me and said mysteriously, with a touch of humor, "This is something for you."

And what he meant by that was that the lady in the office was Indian, unmistakably, Indian from India, though she was not in a sari, and though there was an un-Indian confidence in her voice and manner. Her speech was American—to me. It let her down only once, when she said, in her brisk, undeferential way, that coffee and things like that were not available on the "pre-mises," making the word rhyme with "vices." That was Indian; that had a flavor of India.

I heard later from Howard that in the last six years or so Indians from India had been buying the motels in the South from white people. (And this perhaps explained the big neon sign, AMERICAN OWNED, that I saw some time later on a motel in northwestern Georgia.)

So there, in the place that was home to Howard: the white folk, who might have come out of a novel; and, not far away, people from the other side of the world who were already making themselves American, according to the special idea they would have had of the word.

The motel lady's husband came into the office. He too was Indian. He wore a short-sleeved fawn-colored velour shirt, and he had a Texas accent—or so it seemed to me. His wife had said (and he now confirmed) that he had been in the oil business, as a petroleum engineer, in Houston. He had left oil and Houston six years before; and he thought (as his wife had said earlier, though admitting that Peters, North Carolina, was a very quiet place) he had made a good decision.

Hetty's house, Howard's new home, had been built in parts by Hetty herself, with her own hands. It was set back from the road, behind other houses in the settlement, and a drive led to it from the highway. The site had been well chosen. The house had a front portico with steps on either side, and a porch-garage at the end of the drive from the highway. At the back of the house was woodland.

The fluffy, carpeted, upholstered sitting room was welcoming. In one corner was the kitchen, with a dining or serving counter. The bedrooms and general rooms were on either side of a central corridor that ran off from the sitting room.

Hetty was a big but shapely woman. She was sixty, but her skin was still good. She wore glasses. She made a great deal of friendly noise welcoming Jimmy, whom she knew; and Howard acted out the role of the son returning home. He sat on a high stool in front of the kitchen counter, relaxed, his limbs elegantly arranged, one leg folded, one leg straight: in this house a son and now, in addition, half our host. On the wall beside the door that led to the porch-garage there were family photographs, including one of Howard in a graduation gown.

We had lunch: fried fish, collard greens, sweet potatoes with the color of boiled carrots. Four of us sat at the dining table in the dining part of the front reception room.

While we were sitting—I with my back to the front door, which opened out onto the portico with the steps on either side—there were great shouts. A party had arrived: Hetty's sister from Augusta, Dee-Anna (as I heard the name), and Dee-Anna's husband and son. Dee-Anna didn't look like Hetty. She was much bigger and more full of bulges than Hetty, and darker (Hetty was brown). She was more vivacious—acting up a little to her figure—but she had more searching eyes. She didn't have Hetty's serenity.

Dee-Anna's son seemed sloppily dressed at first, but then I saw that his outfit had been assembled with care and was absolutely for show: a slate-blue jacket in the contemporary shapeless style, a shining, textured white shirt, tapered trousers with patches and exposed labels, and new shows (new from the near-white appearance of the instep). Easter visitors; holiday dressing up.

They talked for a while about a recent big boxing match. They all liked the winner. Howard said he was like a modern black man, smooth and educated; the other fellow was big and strong, but rougher.

The young man with the contemporary clothes asked what I was doing in North Carolina.

When I told him, he said, "What sort of book? Historical?"

And when Howard and I explained, Dee-Anna said, with a knitting of her brows, "I hope you are not going to give us the gloom."

Her son—his seriousness now seeming quite separate from his clothes—said, "We've had too much of the past." They were not interested in the past; they were interested in the present.

It had not occurred to me to ask whether Hetty did a job. Howard hadn't told me; and it was only after we had got to the house that I gathered that she worked part-time in the café side of a convenience store that was owned by the present head of the Bowen family. She took Jimmy and me to meet him after lunch. She said he was a good man.

The convenience store was only one of Mr. Bowen's interests. We went to see him in his furniture factory. He said that he wasn't really a Bowen. He had only married into the family, but people spoke of him as a Bowen, and he had grown to accept the name. The first record of the name in the town of Bowen was a few years before the Declaration of Independence, but at that time the name of the town was Lawrence (which suggested some kind of dispossession during or after the War of Independence).

History, though, wasn't what Mr. Bowen wanted to talk about. He was a big man in his early sixties, and he wanted Jimmy and me to see the furniture he made; he wanted to talk about business in Bowen; he wanted us to know that the little town was a go-ahead place, that, though it had only a few thousand people, there were very many millions deposited in the local banks. He was a Bowen man through and through; and while he gave us all the figures, walking Jimmy and me round the furniture factory, showing us the things he or his machines did with veneers, Hetty stood aside, in her full denim skirt, with something of Howard's elegance in her posture.

Bowen—I had never heard of the name of the place until Howard had told me. And here it was everywhere, attached to every kind of local business, farm equipment and agricultural supplies, general store, video rentals, gas station, furniture, convenience store.

He was a good man, Hetty said again, after we had left Mr. Bowen and the furniture factory. She had gone to him when she wanted $5,000 for her house.

He had spoken that same day to the bank, and a loan had been arranged, and all that the bank had required as security was Hetty's car and some other small thing. And Mr. Bowen was a religious man, Hetty said. He had given land for the black cemetery. She had a family plot there, with carved headstones.

We drove through suburban woodland to the cemetery. We drove up almost to the headstones. Hetty wanted us to see them, but she didn't encourage us to get out of the car. We stayed in the car and looked for a while. It was a small cemetery, not set apart by a fence or any kind of planting. Now, with all the spring growth, it was like part of the woodland.

One of the headstones was of Hetty's father. When we were back in the house she told us something about him. He was a smart man; there had always been a lot of food in the house because of him. He worked on a farm for a white man—and I was beginning to understand how necessary it was for Hetty to define people in the way she did. The white man took no interest in his farm. Hetty's father did it all for him, the selling of the produce and everything. Now the farmhouse—where Hetty's father had lived and died—had deteriorated. It was still owned by the white family, but they didn't want to sell; they wanted to keep it for the memory.

Where did this father of Hetty's come from? He had died in 1961. Had he perhaps been born around 1900? In 1894, Howard said. That was the year on the headstone in the black cemetery, on the land given by Mr. Bowen. And the story of the father was vague. He had been orphaned; he had run away from a difficult uncle and had found a job on the railroad and had then fetched up here, sharecropping for Mr. Smith, the white man, and ending successfully, being one of the first black men in the area to own a car. It was not possible to get more about this father, to push back further into time. Beyond that was vagueness, and the gloom Hetty's sister and the sister's son, and perhaps all black people, had had too much of.

Later, after a nap—Jimmy in one of the bedrooms of Hetty's house, I in another—and after tea, we went out for a drive. Hetty knew the land well; she knew who owned what. It was like a chant from her, as we drove.

"Black people there, black people there, white people there. Black people, black people, white people, black people. All this side black people, all this side white people. White people, white people, black people, white people."

Sometimes she said, "Black people used to own this land." She didn't like that—that black people had lost land because they had been slack or because of family disputes. But blacks and whites appeared here to live quite close to one another, and Hetty herself had no racial complaints. White people had been good to her, she said. But then she said that that might have been only because she liked people.

It was a landscape of small ruins. Houses and farmhouses and tobacco barns had simply been abandoned. The decay of each was individual, and they were all beautiful in the afternoon light. Some farmhouses had very wide eaves, going down low, the corrugated iron that once provided shelter now like a too-heavy weight, the corrugated-iron sheets sagging, fanning out in places.

We went to see the house, now abandoned, where Hetty's father had lived when he had sharecropped for Mr. Smith. Bush grew right up against the open house. The pecan trees, still almost bare, just a few leaves now, were tall above the house and the tobacco barns. The colors were gray (tree trunks and weathered timber) and red (rusted corrugated iron) and green and the straw-gold of reeds. As we stood there Hetty told us of the death of her father in that house; the event was still vivid to her.

Another house, even more beautiful, was where Hetty and her husband had lived for ten years. It was a farmhouse with a big green field, with forest trees bounding the distance on every side.

Home was not for Howard just his mother's house, the little green house that was now closed up, or the new concrete-block house she had moved to. Home was what we had seen. And we had seen only a part: all about these country roads, within a few miles, were houses and fields connected with various members of Howard's family. It was a richer and more complicated past than I had imagined; and physically much more beautiful. The houses I was taken to were bigger than the houses many people in Trinidad or England might have lived in.

But, still, in the past there was that point where darkness fell, the historical darkness, even here, which was home.

We went to dinner at the Seafood Bar-B-Q. It was really the only place possible. It was a roadhouse, a big dimly lit room with a silent jukebox and a few dressed-up white family groups. Beer couldn't be served. So we had the iced tea, which Howard said was very Southern. It was syrupy, the taste no doubt of the waitresses, who were white and young and friendly. One of them was very young, perhaps about twelve, and delighted to be dressed like a waitress, helping out a sister or a parent during the holiday weekend, serving goodies.

I asked Hetty what she wanted for herself and her family. Her reply was strange and moving. For her family, she said, she wished that one of her sons had been cured of his drinking. And this was strange because it was a look backwards: the son she spoke of was dead.

For herself, she said she would like, if it were possible, to get married. She didn't want to get married for the sake of getting married. She was old—she knew that—but that was why she would like to get married. She spent too much time alone; she wanted the companionship. Howard understood. But both he and Hetty didn't think it would be easy for her to find someone.

Hetty said: "Men are scarce here. There are very few men here. Go to church and count the men. The good ones have gone away. And the ones who have stayed are no good. There may be a couple of good ones on the quiet, but . . ."

What of the past, though? Had it been a reasonable sort of life? She said she had no regret for the past. Hadn't things got better for her? Hadn't things got better in the 1950s?

She said, "I hardly think even about my own past."

And Howard said, "I can hardly remember the past."

The words were like the words spoken at lunchtime by Hetty's sister.

But then Hetty said: "I didn't like the tobacco. It would make me sick at the end of one row, smell and all. When I was married we would get up early in the morning, when the dew was still on the tobacco leaves, and it didn't smell then. Even now tobacco makes me sick. When I was young I would be in a field and after two hours I would cry. That was when I was working with my father."

And behind that was the unmentionable past.

On Saturday Hetty had talked with holiday excitement of the Easter Sunday sunrise service at five in the morning. She had said she might go to that. But when Jimmy and I checked out of the Peters Indian motel in the morning and went to the house for breakfast, we found Hetty there. The driving around the previous afternoon had tired her; she hadn't been able to make the sunrise service. She thought now she would go to the eleven o'clock service.

Jimmy and I thought that we would go at eleven-thirty to hear the singing and at least the beginning of the sermon, which Hetty said would start at twelve. The problem about that was Jimmy's clothes. In New York Howard had said that Bowen was a very country sort of place and that casual clothes and sneakers would be enough for whatever we might have to do. The only warm-weather clothes Jimmy had was a Banana Republic safari outfit. Hetty said it would be all right; but she would at a certain stage have to stand up in church and ask the congregation's forgiveness for his clothes.

On the television set in Hetty's sitting room there was constant religious excitement, with services from black churches and white churches, pastor and choir always stylishly dressed, each church having its own colors in clerical gowns, almost its own livery.

One preacher, with a serious, hectoring manner, broke off from the matter in hand to give a puff for a new book about the Bible and the afterlife. The book answered the questions people asked, he said. "Will we be merry in heaven?" And before I could fully savor that "merry"—merry with wine, Merry Christmas, Old King Cole was a merry old soul—the other question the book answered was spoken: "Will there be progress in heaven?" This American heaven clearly being a replication of American earth, with black and white, and North and South, and Republicans and Democrats.

Hetty, going into her room in her denim skirt, came out dressed for church in a bright-pink dress, quite overwhelming; and then she put on her flat dark-blue hat. The hat, and her glasses, gave her an executive appearance.

She drove to church. Howard had allowed his driver's license to lapse; he couldn't drive Hetty and then come back for us. We walked. The church was about a mile away. Jimmy was in his Banana Republic clothes. Howard was casually dressed and in sneakers; he wasn't going to the service. He said he didn't like going to church; it was something he had had to do too often when he was a child.

The road was wide. Cars went by one or two at a time. The grass was full of purple spring flowers; and from time to time, unexpectedly, there was black swamp (making one think of the primeval land, before the settlers came, and of the desolation the settlers must have felt sometimes).

We walked past Mr. Alexander's house. He was an old black man, formally dressed for Sunday, with a jacket and tie and hat; and he was in the bare patch of ground at the side of his house, practicing putts, or at any rate holding a golf club. The area in front of his small house was choked with ornamental garden statuary and anything that could be put in a yard as an ornament. He said his grandfather had started the collection; and then, with his own quicksilver sense of time, he said, "Two hundred years." Some of the pieces came from Jamaica in the West Indies; Mr. Alexander pronounced it "Jee-maica."

Howard said, as we walked on, "You can tell he's an oddball. Not only because of the golf club. But because he's not at church."

A car stopped on the road beside us. There were three white men inside—the race and color of people being now what was very noticeable about them. They wanted to know where the country club golf course was. Howard said he couldn't help them; he was a visitor himself. And they drove on.

The church was small and neat, in red brick, with a white spire and with the pediment of its portico resting on slender wooden columns. There were many cars in the yard at the side of the church. I said the cars made the town look rich. Howard said everybody had a car; cars meant nothing.

As we went up the steps to the portico Howard said, "They're singing." He didn't go in with us. He said—very boyish now, very much the licensed son—that he would wait outside.

A slender young brown woman welcomed Jimmy and me at the door and gave us an order of service. We sat at the back. And I remembered what Hetty had said: "Go to the church. Count the men." The men were fewer than the women. Some children were at the back, with their mothers. And everyone—as Hetty had hinted—was in his Sunday best.

The church inside was as plain and neat as it was outside. It had newish blond hardwood pews and a fawn-colored carpet. At the end of the hall, on a dais, was the choir, with a pianist on either side. The men of the choir, in the back row, were in suits; the women and girls, in the three front rows, were in gold gowns. So that it was like a local and smaller version of what we had been seeing on the television in Hetty's sitting room.

At the back of the choir, at the back of the girls in gold and the men in dark suits, was a large, oddly transparent-looking painting of the baptism of Christ: the water blue, the riverbanks green. The whiteness of Christ and the Baptist was a surprise. (As much a surprise as, the previous night, in the house of the old retired black teacher, the picture of Jesus Christ had been: a bearded figure, looking like General Custer in *Little Big Man.*) But perhaps the surprise or incongruity lay only in my eyes, the whiteness of Jesus being as much an iconographical element as the blueness of the gods in the Hindu pantheon, or the Indianness of the first Buddhist missionary, Daruma, in Japanese art.

The singing ended. It was time for "Reports, Announcements, and Recognition of Visitors." The short black man in a dark suit who announced this—not the pastor—spoke the last word in an extraordinary way, breaking the word up into syllables and then, as though to extract the last bit of flavor from the word, giving a mighty stress to the final syllable, saying something like "vee-zee-TORRS."

He spoke, and waited for declarations. One man got up and said he had come from Philadelphia; he had come back to see some of his family. Then Hetty stood up, in her flat blue hat and pink dress. She looked at us and then addressed the man in the dark suit. We were friends of her son, she said. He was outside somewhere. She explained Jimmy's tieless and jacketless appearance, and asked forgiveness for it.

We got up then, I first, Jimmy after me, and announced ourselves as the man from Philadelphia had done. A pale woman in one of the front rows turned around and said to us that she too was from New York; she welcomed us as people from New York. It was like a binding together, I thought. And when, afterwards, the man in the dark suit spoke of brothers and sisters, the words seemed to have a more than formal meaning.

The brass basin for the collection was passed up and down the pews. (The figure for the previous week's collection, a little over $350, was given in the order of service.) The pastor, a young man with a clear, educated voice, asked us to meditate on the miracle of Easter. To help us, he called on the choir.

The leader of the choir, a big woman, adjusted the microphone. And after this small, delicate gesture, there was passion. The hymn was "What About Me?" There was hand-clapping from the choir, and swaying. One man stood up in the congregation—he was in a brown suit—and he clapped and sang. A woman in white, with a white hat, got up and sang. So I began to feel the pleasures of the religious meeting: the pleasures of brotherhood, union, formality, ritual, clothes, music, all combining to create a possibility of ecstasy.

It was the formality—derived by these black people from so many sources—that was the surprise; and the idea of community.

Someone else in a suit got up and spoke to the congregation after the black man in the dark suit had spoken. "This *is* a great day," the new speaker said. "This is the day the Lord *rose*. He rose for everybody." There were constant subdued cries of "Amen!" from the congregation. The speaker said, "A lot of people better off than we are didn't have this privilege."

Finally the educated young pastor in his elegant gown with two red crosses spoke. "Jesus had to pray. *We* have to pray. Jesus had to cry. *We* have to cry. . . . God has been so good to us. He has given us a second chance."

Torture and tears, luck and grief: these were the motifs of this religion, this binding, this consoling union—union the unexpected, moving idea to me. And, as in Muslim countries, I understood the power a preacher might have.

As Howard said afterwards, as he and Jimmy and I were walking back to the house, "*Everything* happens in the church."

We came upon another local oddball, to use the word Howard had used on the way out: this was the drinker of the black community. We were some way from the man's house when Howard spotted him looking out of a window. And Howard said, "Look down. Don't talk to him. Don't see him." It was one of the ways Howard had learned, both here and in New York, of avoiding trouble: avoiding "eye contact," which, he said, provoked the mugger, the beggar, the racial fanatic, the madman, the alcoholic.

The drinking man, framed in his window, considered us as we walked towards his house. When we passed the house I glanced at him out of the corner of my eye. Standing at his window in his undershirt, isolated in his house, he was red-eyed, spiritually and mentally far away.

I told Howard that the idea I had been given that morning of a black community with its own strict code was surprising to me.

He said, "This community, or what you see, is going to disappear in twenty or twenty-five years." Segregation had preserved the black community. But now blacks and whites, especially of the younger generation, were doing more things together. This gave point to what Hetty (grieving for a son) had said the day before about black and white boys now "drinking together." And I wasn't sure whether Howard or Hetty wholly liked the new mixing and what it foreshadowed. I didn't think that Hetty could be as serene as she was, without her community.

At lunch, when Hetty had come back from church, we talked for a little about the position of black people. We hadn't touched that subject the day before.

Black people had lived through the bad times. Now, when things should have been easier for them, there were new racial elements in the country: Mexicans and Cubans and the other foreigners. The Mexicans were soon going to be politically powerful in the country. The Asians were not just buying motels; they were going into other kinds of business as well; and they had been here only a few years. In a hospital not far away, Hetty said, there were only two *American* doctors.

And soon Howard and Hetty were reminding each other of the way things were changing. In the old days trucks would come around to pick up blacks for the fruit-picking. The trucks didn't come now: the Mexicans did the fruit-picking. And Howard said the blacks had eased themselves out of Miami. The blacks hadn't wanted the hotel jobs; they thought those jobs demeaning. So the Cubans had taken over those jobs, and the blacks wouldn't be allowed to get in there again. In ways like that the blacks had allowed the Cubans to get control of the city. Spanish was now the language of Miami.

Later, when we were going back to the airport, we saw a white congregation coming out of the other Baptist church in Bowen. It wasn't far from the black church where we had been. And it was only then that I realized that what I had been seeing was a segregated small town, with old segregated institutions.

It gave a fuller meaning to Hetty's words, her chant, as we had driven through the countryside: "All this side white people, all that side black people. Black people, black people, white people, black people. Black people, white people."

Reading the familiar land in her own way—where I saw only the colors of the spring, the purple flowers on the roadside, the sour weed, the pines and dogwood and oaks and maples, and the gray and green and dark-red colors of abandoned farmhouses and tobacco barns. Going back to the airport now, I saw the past a little more clearly. I saw a little more clearly what I had seen the day before.

And I began to see how Howard, leaving his home and going to New York, could hold himself separate both from the past and from the rage of Harlem.

I asked him why he didn't live in Harlem.

"My rhythm is different. And they pick up on that. Rhythm? It's like your energy level. How shall I put it? I'm not angry. Most people in Harlem are angry." And, trying to explain more about himself, he said, "I'm different. I felt different at the high school. It's what you think and what you feel that makes you different. I always felt different. Which leads me to believe I was born in the wrong town. Like many people."

Two days later, in New York (and just before I began my true Southern journey), I talked again with Howard, to make sure I had got certain things right.

About the presence of Asians and Cubans and Mexicans he said, "I get very pro-American when I think about that." And that pro-American attitude extended to foreign affairs, which were his special interest. So, starting from the small Southern black community of Bowen, Howard had become a conservative. He said, "I think that when you come out of a Southern Baptist background that is the groundwork of being a conservative."

I asked him about what he had said about the black community as we had walked back from the church. He had said that the community was going to disappear in twenty to twenty-five years; and he had seemed to talk neutrally about that. Was he really neutral?

He didn't commit himself. He said that there would be less unity in the community, but that good would come of the change. Making a mystical leap, he said, "Change is like death. Good things can come out of it. It's like the Civil War, when a whole way of life ended."

So at the end it turned out that his early comment, about the continuity of his home town, had had to do with history, as I had thought at the beginning. I had changed my mind because the word had then appeared to contain the idea of sameness and dullness: the same buildings, the ruins left standing in the fields, the dullness of the small-town life. He had meant that; but he had also meant the past living on. It was as though, talking to me, a stranger, he had had to find a way of talking about the unmentionable past.

QUESTIONS FOR "DOWN HOME: A LANDSCAPE OF SMALL RUINS" BY V. S. NAIPAUL

Talking About the Text

1. What do you think might be the significance of the title "Down Home: A Landscape of Small Ruins"? In what sense do you think the community of Bowen might be "a landscape of small ruins"?

2. What rhetorical and literary techniques does Naipaul use when describing his trip to Bowen? At times he seems to draw us into his experience. How does he show and not merely tell about his visit to Bowen?

Exploring Issues

1. Naipaul writes, "I told Howard that the idea I had been given that morning of a black community with its own strict code was surprising to me." Specifically, what institutions and codes do you think helped to create the black community of Bowen? Can you see these kinds of institutions and codes at work in other communities with which you are familiar?
2. Naipaul writes that "segregation had preserved the black community. But now blacks and whites, especially of the younger generation, were doing more things together. . . . And I wasn't sure whether Howard or Hetty wholly liked the new mixing and what it foreshadowed. I didn't think Hetty could be as serene as she was, without her community." What do you think this new mixing foreshadowed? What would end when desegregation started to erode the community lines?
3. Speaking of his friend Howard, Naipaul writes: "He said there would be less unity in the community, but that good would come of the change. Making a mystical leap, he said, 'Change is like death. Good things can come out of it. It's like the Civil War, when a whole way of life ended.' " To what "good things" do you think Howard was referring? Can you think of any examples in which some changes, initially perceived as negative, had positive outcomes?
4. Naipaul writes: "So at the end it turned out that his early comment, about the continuity of his home town, had had to do with history, as I had thought at the beginning." Speculate on the relationship between "continuity" and "community." Is "continuity" necessary for "community"? What is your experience? What is the relationship of the past to a community?

Writing Assignment

Naipaul has written a "going home" account, not of his own home, but of a friend's. Write a narrative about a time you went back "home" to a place you had left. You need not write about your family's home. You might choose to write about another community you left but occasionally visit, such as a school, a group of friends, a sports team, a work environment. Alternatively, go "back home" with a friend to the friend's community. In either case, your aim should be twofold: give us a sense of the institutions and codes that bind the community together, and describe any changes in the community that have occurred during the interim between your earliest experience of the community and your latest experience of it.

Reading 23

Community and Equality in Conflict

J. Anthony Lukas

After receiving his BA from Harvard in 1955, J. Anthony Lukas went on to pursue a career in journalism. In 1958, Lukas worked for the *Balitmore Sun* and later spent nine years on the staff of the *New York Times*. His assignments at the *Times* included those of foreign correspondent and roving national correspondent. In 1968 his journalistic talent was rewarded with a Pulitzer prize for local reporting. Lukas is also the author of *The Barnyard Epithet and Other Obscenities: Notes on the Chicago Conspiracy Trial* (1970) and *Don't Shoot—We Are Your Children!* (1971). He won a second Pulitzer for his book, *Common Ground: A Turbulent Decade in the Lives of Three American Families* (1985), in which he recounts the story of three Boston families dealing with the changes brought about by a court decision mandating the busing of Boston public school children. The following selection was originally published in the September 8, 1985 issue of the *New York Times* and deals with one of the issues raised in *Common Ground*—the needs of the neighborhood community versus those of the larger society.

One dusky evening not so long ago, I sat at the beer-stained bar of a tavern in Charlestown, a predominantly Irish-Catholic Boston neighborhood, known as the site of the Battle of Bunker Hill and other more recent struggles. Above the click of billiard balls and the clink of ice, I overheard two regulars in conversation:

First Drinker: "So I told him I'm an American, you know, and I got as much rights as anybody."

Second Drinker: "Yea, but you're a Townie first. The Townies don't take flapdoodle off any man."

It was an idle exchange after a day of drudgery. But somehow it struck me as emblematic of Boston's recent travail—and indeed of the nation's continuing debate over issues of race, class and ethnicity. For the drinkers were invoking one of the deepest divisions in American life—between the demands of equality and the call of community.

I have recently completed a book about three Boston families: an Irish-

Catholic widow and her seven children in Charlestown; a black welfare mother and her six children; a Yankee lawyer and his wife. As these three strands of American life converged, I found their struggle all too frequently rooted in the conflict between community and equality.

On one hand is arrayed the majesty of the Constitution, the Bill of Rights, the Supreme Court and that whole body of law and precedent that embodies much of what it means to be an American; on the other is the warmth, intimacy and comfort of family, church, tavern and neighborhood that lies at the heart of what many Americans mean by "home." The tension between these two constellations is reflected today in a whole skein of national issues from school desegregation and affirmative action to urban redevelopment and gentrification.

It is a conflict as old as the nation itself—between the notion of community expressed by John Winthrop when he set out to found a "city upon a hill" in the Massachusetts Bay Colony, and the idea of equality enshrined in the Declaration of Independence.

The communal intensity of Winthrop's Massachusetts was rooted in the "covenant," the sacred compact that each cluster of settlers made with God and with each other. By the very act of joining the congregation, the Puritan accepted not only one God and one religion, but one polity, one law, one allegiance. The towns they formed could not tolerate diversity: Sudbury enacted resolutions to bar "such whose dispositions do not suit us." Dedham banned "the contrarye minded."

Clearly Boston during that period was not the Athens of America that has lived so long in legend—the open, generous, diverse, big-spirited seat of American democracy. If anything, it was the national Sparta—narrow, closed, intolerant, a community in quest not of democracy but self-perfection. Yet the notion that communities ought to control their own destinies—even at the expense of outsiders—was a deeply held American value with an ancient and honorable pedigree.

Eventually, a mercantile economy eroded Winthrop's dream of the self-sustaining community. The tight little 17th- and 18th-century towns gradually had to recognize the entitlements of American citizenship, among them the equality of free men.

But the recognition of such universal principles did not destroy the counterclaims of what James Madison called "the spirit of locality." This older communalism survived side by side with the abstract ideals of American constitutionalism. Tocqueville recognized that Americans had not one but two political systems: "The one fulfilling the ordinary duties and responding to the daily and infinite calls of a community; the other circumscribed within certain limits and exercising an exceptional authority over the general interests of the country." For 70 years, this delicate balance prevailed, reassuring Americans that the demands of nationalism were compatible with the intimacies of community.

In the mid-19th century, of course, this revolutionary settlement broke down, the centralizing impulse dashing on the hard rock of particularism. The battle was joined in the Lincoln-Douglas debates, in which Lincoln argued that the essence of democratic government was "the equality of all men" derived from natural law, while Douglas insisted it was the "principle of popular sovereignty," the right of American communities to decide fundamental issues, like slavery, for themselves. Ultimately, force of arms held the nation together and emancipated the slaves, but the tug of war between community and equality was by no means resolved.

In the flowering of 1960's idealism, Americans persuaded themselves that community and equality were not only compatible but mutually reinforcing principles. In 1964, as the educator Diane Ravitch has pointed out, the Johnson Administration secured passage of both the Civil Rights Act, which curbed racial discrimination in Southern schools, and the Economic Opportunity Act, which gave poor people a chance to control their own communities. They were twin expressions of the nation's conscience at mid-decade.

But soon the tensions between community and equality reasserted themselves. After all, civil rights legislation sought to override local law or custom—often equated with bigotry—in the name of human rights. The poverty program, on the other hand, encouraged "community control" as an antidote to bureaucratic centralization—and white ethnics soon invoked that very doctrine, first designed to aid blacks, in a vigorous defense of their own prerogatives.

By 1974 in Boston the two ideals that had seemed to run parallel for much of the 60's had turned at right angles and confronted each other head-on. A Federal district judge, determined to enforce constitutional guarantees of equality, confronted a pack of aggrieved neighborhoods intent on preserving their own sense of community.

In recent years, Boston and other American cities have learned that they have to make some hard choices: between racial justice and self-determination, between equality of educational opportunity and neighborhood schools, between a black child's right to a desegregated education and a white mother's right to control her own child's upbringing. What makes this experience rise to the level of genuine tragedy is precisely that these are not choices between right and wrong, or between judicial dictatorship and sound social policy, but between competing values, between right and right.

QUESTIONS FOR "COMMUNITY AND EQUALITY IN CONFLICT" BY J. ANTHONY LUKAS

Talking About the Text

1. Lukas makes reference to John Winthrop's "city upon a hill." To what is he referring, and how does this reference relate to Lukas's essay as a whole?
2. Read Frances Fitzgerald's "Liberty Baptist." What connections can you make between her observations and those of Lukas?
3. What rhetorical purpose do you think the opening conversation between the two drinkers serves?

Exploring the Issues

1. To what extent do you think the demands of nationalism and the U.S. Constitution can today coexist with the "intimacies of community"? What specific examples come to mind that could illustrate this conflict?
2. Lukas writes that "eventually, a mercantile economy eroded Winthrop's dream of the self-sustaining community. The tight little 17th- and 18th-century towns gradually had to recognize the entitlements of American citizenship, among them the equality of free men." How do you think the ideal of equality hindered the preservation of a small, self-sustaining community?
3. Besides equality of education, what other ideals of American constitutionalism might create conflict for members of smaller, more intimate communities?
4. What current or recent news issues point to the conflict between the ideals of the State and those of smaller communities?
5. When addressing various communities' reactions to desegregation and equal educational opportunity, Lukas states: "What makes this experience rise to the level of genuine tragedy is precisely that these are not choices between right and wrong, or between judicial dictatorship and sound social policy, but between competing values, between right and right." What do you think Lukas means by "choices between right and right"? Do you agree with this assessment?

Writing Assignment

Choose a controversy in which a community came into conflict with a larger government body, either state or national. The issue may be current or historical. Research this controversy, and then write an essay that examines the causes and/or effects of the controversy.

Reading 24

A Working Community

Ellen Goodman

Ellen Goodman was educated at Radcliffe and worked as a reporter for *Newsweek* and the *Detroit Free Press* before coming to the *Boston Globe* in 1967. Since 1972 Goodman has written a now-nationally syndicated feature column for the *Globe* on subjects such as family, work, gender, and other topics concerning American manners and values. She is the recipient of the 1980 Pulitzer prize for journalism as well as other honors. Her columns have been collected into three volumes: *Close to Home* (1979), *At Large* (1981), and *Keeping in Touch* (1985), from which "A Working Community" has been taken. In this selection, Goodman makes the observation that the traditional neighborhood community of the fifties has been replaced by a community of peers and colleagues from our daily environments and professional worlds.

Boston—I have a friend who is a member of the medical community. It does not say that, of course, on the stationery that bears her home address. This membership comes from her hospital work.

I have another friend who is a member of the computer community. This is a fairly new subdivision of our economy, and yet he finds his sense of place in it.

Other friends and acquaintances of mine are members of the academic community, or the business community, or the journalistic community. Though you cannot find these on any map, we know where we belong.

None of us, mind you, was born into these communities. Nor did we move into them, U-Hauling our possessions along with us. None has papers to prove we are card-carrying members of one such group or another. Yet it seems that more and more of us are identified by work these days, rather than by street.

In the past, most Americans lived in neighborhoods. We were members of precincts or parishes or school districts. My dictionary still defines community, first of all in geographic terms, as "a body of people who live in one place."

But today fewer of us do our living in that one place; more of us just use it for sleeping. Now we call our towns "bedroom suburbs," and many of us, without small children as icebreakers, would have trouble naming all the people on our street.

It's not that we are more isolated today. It's that many of us have transferred a chunk of our friendships, a major portion of our everyday social lives, from home to office. As more of our neighbors work away from home, the workplace becomes our neighborhood.

The kaffeeklatsch of the fifties is the coffee break of the eighties. The water cooler, the hall, the elevator, and the parking lot are the back fences of these neighborhoods. The people we have lunch with day after day are those who know the running saga of our mother's operations, our child's math grades, our frozen pipes, and faulty transmissions.

We may be strangers at the supermarket that replaced the corner grocer, but we are known at the coffee shop in the lobby. We share with each other a cast of characters from the boss in the corner office to the crazy lady in Shipping, to the lovers in Marketing. It's not surprising that when researchers ask Americans what they like best about work, they say it is "the shmoose [chatter] factor." When they ask young mothers at home what they miss most about work, it is the people.

Not all the neighborhoods are empty, nor is every workplace a friendly playground. Most of us have had mixed experiences in these environments. Yet as one woman told me recently, she knows more about the people she passes on the way to her desk than on her way around the block.

Our new sense of community hasn't just moved from house to office build-ing. The labels that we wear connect us with members from distant companies, cities, and states. We assume that we have something "in common" with other teachers, nurses, city planners.

It's not unlike the experience of our immigrant grandparents. Many who came to this country still identified themselves as members of the Italian com-munity, the Irish community, the Polish community. They sought out and assumed connections with people from the old country. Many of us have up-dated that experience. We have replaced ethnic identity with professional iden-tity, the way we replaced neighborhoods with the workplace.

This whole realignment of community is surely most obvious among the mobile professions. People who move from city to city seem to put roots down into their professions. In an age of specialists, they may have to search harder to find people who speak the same language.

I don't think that there is anything massively disruptive about this shifting sense of community. The continuing search for connection and shared enter-prise is very human. But I do feel uncomfortable with our shifting identity. The balance has tipped and we seem increasingly dependent on work for our sense of self.

If our offices are our new neighborhoods, if our professional titles are our new ethnic tags, then how do we separate our selves from our jobs? Self-worth isn't just something to measure in the marketplace. But in these new communities, it becomes harder and harder to tell who we are without saying what we do.

QUESTIONS FOR "A WORKING COMMUNITY" BY ELLEN GOODMAN

Talking About the Text

1. Goodman uses a very personal, anecdotal tone to make her point. What is the effect of this technique on you as the reader?
2. Goodman has titled her essay "A Working Commuity." In one sense she is referring to the idea of a workplace or a profession as being a commu-nity. In another sense she might mean a community that works—one which functions well and has purpose. Do you think all working environ-ments can "work well" as communities? What qualities do you think need to be present before a work environment can become "a working community"?

Exploring Issues

1. Goodman asks the question: "If our offices are our new neighborhoods, if our professional titles are our new ethnic tags, then how do we sepa-

rate ourselves from the job?" What do you think are the potential implications and/or consequences of a self that merges too closely with a job
or career?

2. Speculate about the relationship between personal identity and community. What are Goodman's opinions of this relationship?

3. To what extent do you think professional communities interact with each
other to form larger communities? What benefits and/or disadvantages
might there be from this sort of interaction?

4. Goodman writes that "the kaffeeklatsch of the fifties is the coffee break
of the eighties. The water cooler, the hall, the elevator, and the parking
lot are the back fences of these neighborhoods. The people we have
lunch with day after day are those who know the running saga of our
mother's operations, our child's math grades, our frozen pipes, and
faulty transmissions." In this passage Goodman demonstrates how the
functions of community have shifted from the neighborhood to the
workplace. Do you think there are certain functions of the neighborhood community that cannot be replaced by those of the work community? What are they and why can't the work community replace them?

Writing Assignment

Other than a neighborhood community, think of the various kinds of communities to which you belong. Then write an analytical essay about the nature of your
relationship to one of these communities. When starting your essay, you might
consider the following questions: What function(s) does this community serve?
To what extent does membership to this community help form your identity?

Reading 25

The Futility of
Global Thinking

Wendell Berry

Wendell Berry is a farmer and has written extensively about conservation
issues as they relate to communities. He is the author of *The Unsettling of
America* and *Standing by Words: Essays*. "The Futility of Global Thinking"

is the second selection by Wendell Berry we have included in this text.
"Seven Amish Farms," which appears in Chapter 4: "Our Environments,"
explores the alternative lifestyle of the Amish farming community. "The
Futility of Global Thinking" has been adapted from "Word and Flesh," a
commencement address given by Berry at the College of the Atlantic in Bar
Harbor, Maine, in June 1989.

Toward the end of *As You Like It*, Orlando says: "I can live no longer by
thinking." He is ready to marry Rosalind. It is time for incarnation. Having
thought too much, he is at one of the limits of human experience, or of human
sanity. If his love does put on flesh, we know he must sooner or later arrive at
the opposite limit, at which he will say, "I can live no longer without thinking."
Thought—even consciousness—seems to live between these limits: the abstract and the particular, the word and the flesh.

All public movements of thought quickly produce a language that works as a
code, useless to the extent that it is abstract. It is readily evident, for example,
that you can't conduct a relationship with another person in terms of the rhetoric of the civil rights movement or the women's movement—as useful as those
rhetorics may initially have been to personal relationships.

The same is true of the environment movement. The favorite adjective of
this movement now seems to be *planetary.* This word is used, properly enough,
to refer to the interdependence of places, and to the recognition, which is
desirable and growing, that no place on the earth can be completely healthy
until all places are.

But the word *planetary* also refers to an abstract anxiety or an abstract
passion that is desperate and useless exactly to the extent that it is abstract.
How, after all, can anybody—any particular body—do anything to heal a
planet? Nobody can do anything to heal a planet. The suggestion that anybody
could do so is preposterous. The heroes of abstraction keep galloping in on
their white horses to save the planet—and they keep falling off in front of the
grandstand.

What we need, obviously, is a more intelligent—which is to say, a more
accurate—description of the problem. The description of a problem as planetary arouses a motivation for which, of necessity, there is no employment. The
adjective *planetary* describes a problem in such a way that it cannot be
solved. In fact, though we now have serious problems nearly everywhere on
the planet, we have no problem that can accurately be described as planetary.
And, short of the total annihilation of the human race, there is no planetary
solution.

There are also no national, state, or county problems, and no national, state, or county solutions. That will-o'-the-wisp, the large-scale solution to the large-scale problem, which is so dear to governments, universities, and corporations, serves mostly to distract people from the small, private problems that they may, in fact, have the power to solve.

The problems, if we describe them accurately, are all private and small. Or they are so initially.

The problems are our lives. In the "developed" countries, at least, the large problems occur because all of us are living either partly wrong or almost entirely wrong. It was not just the greed of corporate shareholders and the hubris of corporate executives that put the fate of Prince William Sound into one ship; it was also our demand that energy be cheap and plentiful.

The economies of our communities and households are wrong. The answers to the human problems of ecology are to be found in economy. And the answers to the problems of economy are to be found in culture and in character. To fail to see this is to go on dividing the world falsely between guilty producers and innocent consumers.

The planetary versions—the heroic versions—of our problems have attracted great intelligence. Our problems, as they are caused and suffered in our lives, our households, and our communities, have attracted very little intelligence.

There are some notable exceptions. A few people have learned to do a few things better. But it is discouraging to reflect that, though we have been talking about most of our problems for decades, we are still mainly *talking* about them. The civil rights movement has not given us better communities. The women's movement has not given us better marriages or better households. The environment movement has not changed our parasitic relationship to nature.

We have failed to produce new examples of good home and community economies, and we have nearly completed the destruction of the examples we once had. Without examples, we are left with theory and the bureaucracy and the meddling that come with theory. We change our principles, our thoughts, and our words, but these are changes made in the air. Our lives go on unchanged.

For the most part, the subcultures, the countercultures, the dissenters, and the opponents continue mindlessly—or perhaps just helplessly—to follow the pattern of the dominant society in its extravagance, its wastefulness, its dependencies, and its addictions. The old problem remains: How do you get intelligence *out* of an institution or an organization?

My small community in Kentucky has lived and dwindled for a century at least under the influence of four kinds of organizations: governments, corporations, schools, and churches—all of which are distant (either actually or in interest), centralized, and consequently abstract in their concerns.

Governments and corporations (except for employees) have no presence in our community at all, which is perhaps fortunate for us, but we nevertheless feel the indifference or the contempt of governments and corporations for communities such as ours.

We have had no school of our own for nearly thirty years. The school system takes our young people, prepares them for "the world of tomorrow," which it does not expect to take place in any rural area, and gives back expert (that is, extremely generalized) ideas.

The church is present in the town. We have two churches. But both have been used by their denominations, for almost a century, to provide training and income for student ministers, who do not stay long enough even to become disillusioned.

For a long time, then, the minds that have most influenced our town have not been *of* the town and so have not tried even to perceive, much less to honor, the good possibilities that are there. They have not wondered on what terms a good and conserving life might be lived there. In this, my community is not unique but is like almost every other neighborhood in our country and in the "developed" world.

The question that *must* be addressed, therefore, is not how to care for the planet but how to care for each of the planet's millions of human and natural neighborhoods, each of its millions of small pieces and parcels of land, each one of which is in some precious way different from all the others. Our understandable wish to preserve the planet must somehow be reduced to the scale of our competence—that is, to the wish to preserve all of its humble households and neighborhoods.

What can accomplish this reduction? I will say again, without overweening hope but with certainty nonetheless, that only love can do it. Only love can bring intelligence out of the institutions and organizations, where it aggrandizes itself, into the presence of the work that must be done.

Love is never abstract. It does not adhere to the universe or the planet or the nation or the institution or the profession but to the singular sparrows of the street, the lilies of the field, "the least of these my brethren." Love is not, by its own desire, heroic. It is heroic only when compelled to be. It exists by its willingness to be anonymous, humble, and unrewarded.

The older love becomes, the more clearly it understands its involvement in partiality, imperfection, suffering, and mortality. Even so, it longs for incarnation. It can live no longer by thinking.

And yet to put on flesh and do the flesh's work, it must think.

In his essay on Kipling, George Orwell wrote: "All left-wing parties in the highly industrialized countries are at bottom a sham, because they make it their business to fight against something which they do not really wish to destroy. They have internationalist aims, and at the same time they struggle to keep up a standard of life with which those aims are incompatible. We all live by robbing Asiatic coolies, and those of us who are 'enlightened' all maintain that those coolies ought to be set free; but our standard of living, and hence our 'enlightenment,' demands that the robbery shall continue."

This statement of Orwell's is clearly applicable to our situation now; all we need to do is change a few nouns. The religion and the environmentalism of the highly industrialized countries are at bottom a sham, because they make it their business to fight against something that they do not really wish to destroy. We all live by robbing nature, but our standard of living demands that the robbery shall continue.

We must achieve the character and acquire the skills to live much poorer than we do. We must waste less. We must do more for ourselves and each other. It is either that or continue merely to think and talk about changes that we are inviting catastrophe to make.

The great obstacle is simply this: the conviction that we cannot change because we are dependent upon what is wrong. But that is the addict's excuse, and we know that it will not do.

How dependent, in fact, are we? How dependent are our neighborhoods and communities? How might our dependencies be reduced? To answer these questions will require better thoughts and better deeds than we have been capable of so far.

We must have the sense and the courage, for example, to see that the ability to transport food for hundreds or thousands of miles does not necessarily mean that we are well off. It means that the food supply is more vulnerable and more costly than a local food supply would be. It means that consumers do not control or influence the healthfulness of their food supply and that they are at the mercy of the people who have the control and influence. It means that, in eating, people are using large quantities of petroleum that other people in another time are almost certain to need.

I am trying not to mislead you, or myself, about our situation. I think that we have hardly begun to realize the gravity of the mess we are in.

Our most serious problem, perhaps, is that we have become a nation of fantasists. We believe, apparently, in the infinite availability of finite resources. We persist in land-use methods that reduce the potentially infinite power of soil fertility to a finite quantity, which we then proceed to waste as if it were an infinite quantity. We have an economy that depends not upon the quality and quantity of necessary goods and services but on the behavior of a few stockbrokers. We believe that democratic freedom can be preserved by people ignorant of the history of democracy and indifferent to the responsibilities of freedom.

Our leaders have been for many years as oblivious to the realities and dangers of their time as were George III and Lord North. They believe that the difference between war and peace is still the overriding political difference—when, in fact, the difference has diminished to the point of insignificance. How would you describe the difference between modern war and modern history—between, say, bombing and strip mining, or between chemical warfare and chemical manufacturing? The difference seems to be only that in war the victimization of humans is directly intentional and in industry it is "accepted" as a "trade-off."

Were the catastrophes of Love Canal, Bhopal, Chernobyl, and the *Exxon Valdez* episodes of war or of peace? They were, in fact, peacetime acts of aggression, intentional to the extent that the risks were known and ignored.

We are involved unremittingly in a war not against "foreign enemies" but against the world, against our freedom, and indeed against our existence. Our so-called industrial accidents should be looked upon as revenges of Nature. We forget that Nature is necessarily party to all our enterprises and that she imposes conditions of her own.

Now she is plainly saying to us: "If you put the fates of whole communities or cities or regions or ecosystems at risk in single ships or factories or power plants, then I will furnish the drunk or the fool or the imbecile who will make the necessary small mistake."

And so, graduates, my advice to you is simply my hope for us all:

Beware the justice of Nature.

Understand that there can be no successful human economy apart from Nature or in defiance of Nature.

Understand that no amount of education can overcome the innate limits of human intelligence and responsibility. We are not smart enough or conscious enough or alert-enough to work responsibly on a gigantic scale.

In making things always bigger and more centralized, we make them both more vulnerable in themselves and more dangerous to everything else. Learn, therefore, to prefer small-scale elegance and generosity to large-scale greed, crudity, and glamour.

Make a home. Help to make a community. Be loyal to what you have made.

Put the interest of the community first.

Love your neighbors—not the neighbors you pick out, but the ones you have.

Love this miraculous world that we did not make, that is a gift to us.

As far as you are able make your lives dependent upon your local place, neighborhood, and household—which thrive by care and generosity—and independent of the industrial economy, which thrives by damage.

Find work, if you can, that does no damage. Enjoy your work. Work well.

QUESTIONS FOR "THE FUTILITY OF GLOBAL THINKING" BY WENDELL BERRY

Talking About the Text

1. Berry is arguing for a way of life in this essay. What do you see as the central points to his argument, and how successful do you think the argument is? Why?

2. This essay is an adaptation of a commencement address given by Berry to the College of the Atlantic Class of 1989. If you were a member of that graduating class, what response might you have to the advice Berry gives to graduates at the end of his address? Do you think his advice is appropriate or unrealistic given the events of today's political and social scene?

Exploring Issues

1. Speculate about the nature of the conflict Berry sees between large organizations (such as, governments, churches, schools, and corporations) and his small Kentucky community. What tensions does he perceive? Have you ever experienced a similar conflict?

2. Berry asserts that

> . . . the minds that have most influenced our town have not been *of* the town and so have not tried even to perceive, much less to honor, the good possibilities that are there. They have not wondered on what terms a good and conserving life might be lived there. In this, my community is not unique but is like almost every other neighborhood in our country and in the "developed" world.

   To what extent do you agree with Berry's statement? What has been your personal experience in your own communities?

3. What connections can you make between the inherent ideas in the foregoing quotation and those of J. Anthony Lukas in "Community and Equality in Conflict"?

4. In discussing the environmental excesses of a highly industrialized nation such as the United States, Berry asks, "How dependent, in fact, are we? How dependent are our neighborhoods and communitites? How might our dependencies be reduced?" What is your response to this question?

5. Berry suggests that difficult issues such as the gradual demise of the environment and our natural resources cannot be dealt with on "planetary" terms; rather, these problems must be the concern of small-scale communities and neighborhoods. Why do you think Berry makes this judgment? What do you think?

Writing Assignment

Berry gives the advice: "Put the interest of the community first." Write an argumentative essay in which you either defend or refute this statement. In developing support for your argument, you should probably consider some of the following questions:

What is a community? What elements make up a community?

Who benefits or loses by putting the community first?

What are some of the short-term and long-term consequences of always putting the community first?

What specific issues might make us have to choose between considering or not considering the community first?

One way you might approach this writing assignment is by looking at one specific issue or controversy in relationship to Berry's assertion.

Reading 26

The Ten Commandments of a Quality Community

Richard D. Lamm

Richard D. Lamm is a former governor of Colorado and presently the director of the Center for Public Policy and Contemporary Issues at the University of Denver. "The Ten Commandments of a Quality Community" appeared in the February 15, 1990 issue of *Vital Speeches of the Day* and was delivered originally as a speech to the San Mateo 2000 (County Forum, San Mateo, California) on January 24, 1990. In his speech Lamm shares his growing concern over the declining quality of life in the United States and suggests that more care and consideration be given to the community and its members if any positive changes are to be made for the future.

There is a story that John Stuart Mill woke up one morning and had this overwhelming feeling that the "answer to the question of the ages" had come to him in the middle of the night. But he forgot what it was. He then placed a quill and paper next to his bed, and a few mornings later he awoke with a similar feeling, yet this time he found on the paper in his own handwriting "Think in different terms."

We are sailing into a new world of public policy; a world as strange and new as Columbus discovered. It is a world where infinite government demands have run straight into finite resources. It is an America made up increasingly of diverse people. It is an aging society. Most of our institutional memories and political culture come out of the 1960s and 1970s when America was largely European and had the industrial world's highest rate of productivity growth and was doubling its wealth every 30 or 40 years. Government had a substantial yearly growth dividend it could spend. Now a much more diverse America has the lowest rate of productivity growth in the industrial world and it now takes approximately 130 years to double our national wealth. We go into debt to maintain current levels of government. Being in government today is like sleeping with a blanket that is too short: we do not have the resources to cover all our needs.

A multi-racial nation that is the world's largest debtor nation with a massive federal debt cannot merely duplicate the solutions that worked when it was a creditor nation with little federal debt. The health care of a society which dies in old age of a chronic illness is vastly different from that of a society which died at an average of 47 after a short episode of infectious disease. Geometric demand for public services cannot be met by arithmetically growing tax resources.

It is my belief that an old world of public policy is dying and a new world of public policy is being born. The essence of this new world is that the economy of 1990s cannot support the dreams of the 1960s. The next major challenge of government will be the "revolution of lower expectations" as we find our dreams exceed our resources.

We already live in a time of unprecedented tension between the races, sexes, even generations. Compounding this, public policy cannot count on historic revenue growth and thus cannot chase geometric curves of public spending. It will require us to much better understand what a "community" is and how it is formed and reinforced. I suggest that this world of ever-growing public needs and shrinking resources will require us to reconceptualize much of *what* government does and *how* it does it. It will cause us to define what is absolutely fundamental in many of our basic institutions.

A community is much more than a place on a map. It is a state of mind, a shared vision, a common fate. A community is not a state of nature. A "herd" is a state of nature, a "flock," a "covey," a "gaggle," is a state of nature but alas—not a community. A community of different religions, races and nationalities is against most of the lessons of history, as we are seeing daily on our TV sets. Humans bond to families, but not necessarily with their neighbors. A community requires social architecture: bridge builders, structural engineers who build bonds, bridges, who remove barriers.

We have not recently tested community. It is easy to keep a community when we are dividing up the spoils of a rich continent and a growing economy. It is adversity, not success, that tests community. Do we cooperate during times of adversity—to solve, soothe and mitigate, or do we form tribes and, like ravenous dogs, fight over a static pie. Community—like friendship—is never really tested until it *jointly* faces adversity. A rising tide not only raises all ships—it keeps them from bumping into each other.

In light of these new economic and social realities we must ask—how do we build a quality community?

I believe this to be an immensely important question. We see daily the results of *not* building a community—in Lebanon, in Sri Lanka, in Eastern Europe, in the Soviet Union.

What is going on today in Azerbaijan and Yugoslavia is not a failure of communism. It is failure of community. The Armenians and Azerbaijans, the Serbs and the Slovenians were killing each other before Marx was born. The people in Lebanon are no more diverse than in the United States—the secret is that we formed a community (E. Pluribus Unum) and Lebanon didn't.

People that share a geographic area must become a *community*—or they become balkanized, fragmented, factionalized. We all bond not only to our families but to our geographic location.

"If you don't know where you are you don't know who you are," says Wendell Berry.

But we don't bond easily to our *neighbors*. We seem to instinctively view them as competitors.

A community needs a shared stake in the future. It needs a shared language, shared culture, shared norms and values. It needs, in short, a social glue that is the essence of community. It must understand their shared fate. To say my fate is not tied to your fate is like saying "your end of the boat is sinking."

Emanuel Kant said, "Religion and language are the world's great dividers."

Not totally true, as we see in the religious diversity of the United States—but sobering to our Baskin-Robbins 31 Flavor society.

We must give more thought to those things that build community—that hold us together as a community—and how to minimize those factors that separate us—like race, religion and ethnicity. Melting pots that don't melt become pressure cookers. Diversity carried too far is divisiveness.

Building communities becomes highly important public policy and imperative to our public and private futures. I should thus like to give you my TEN COMMANDMENTS OF A QUALITY COMMUNITY; ten building blocks that are imperative as we try to renew and expand our sense of quality communities.

COMMANDMENT I: God is not an American

Too many Americans believe that God is an American and will watch over us no matter how hedonistic, selfish, myopic or inefficient we become.

This is a dangerous hubris. No great nation in history has ever withstood the ravages of time. Toynbee warns us that all great nations rise and all fall, and that the "autopsy of history is that all great nations commit suicide."

Every once-great nation in history thought God was on their side but, to date, God has never allowed any great civilizations to exist for very long. Greatness in nations is not a geopolitical status, but an ephemeral stage. Nations rise and inevitably fall. God may save you personally, but not as a nation. We talk about "American exceptionalism," but we are merely whistling past history's graveyard—in which lies buried every other once-great civilization.

COMMANDMENT II relates to that—and it is: The future isn't something we inherit—it is something we create.

We can't rely on past success to insure future success, and we can't take the future for granted.

Successful communities—successful countries—are built by dedication and hard work.

COMMANDMENT III: A great community needs great leaders and great citizens

Leadership is important. We all know that. Churchill said, "An army of lions led by sheep will always lose to an army of sheep led by a lion." But *citizens* are equally important.

America in many respects faces more of a "followership" problem than a leadership problem. One wise historian observed:

> "To make a nation truly great a handful of heroes capable of great deeds at supreme moment is not enough. Heroes are not always available and one can often do without them! But it *is* essential to have thousands of reliable people—honest

citizens—who steadfastly place the public interest before their own." (Pasquale Villani)

John Gardner, former Secretary of the Department of Health and Human Services, similarly warns:

> "Our society cannot achieve greatness unless individuals at many levels of ability accept the need for high standards of performance and strive to achieve those standards within the limits possible for them. We want the highest conceivable excellence, of course, in the activities crucial to our effectiveness and creativity as a society; but that isn't enough. If the man in the street says, 'Those fellows at the top have to be good, but I'm just a slob and can act like one'—then our days of greatness are behind us. We must foster a conception of excellence which may be applied to every degree of ability and to every socially acceptable activity. A missile may blow up on its launching pad because the designer was incompetent or because the mechanic who adjusted the last valve was incompetent. The same is true of eveything else in our society. We need excellent physicists and excellent mechanics. We need excellent cabinet members and excellent first-grade teachers. The tone and fiber of our society depend upon a pervasive and almost universal striving for good performance."

A quality community can only be built on the bedrock of quality citizens. *COMMANDMENT IV: Woe unto the community that lays house upon house and field upon field, until there be no place that they can be alone—or recreate—or relax*

A valued community is one that works; that offers amenities, recreation and beauty to its citizens. I believe a quality community is one which has anticipated its future through planning.

We know that every urban area has land use problems relating to leap frog development, urban sprawl and costly extension of public utilities. We have the study "The Costs of Sprawl" which shows that different settlement patterns generate vastly different public costs and revenues. We know that low density urban sprawl is not only unsightly, it is inefficient and consumptive of those assets a community has the least of: clean air, tax monies, vacant land.

A quality community has a comprehensive plan that is the midwife of a livable future. Communities need open space, parks, recreation. We must be able to lift our eyes to the hills, from whence comes our strength, and see something besides billboards.

COMMANDMENT V: A quality community is one that honors thy mother and father, but also honors thy children

The German thinker Dietrich Bonhoeffer observed during his fight against Hitler that "the ultimate question for a responsible man is . . . how the coming generation will live." My generation has not been good trustees for America. We have not met the most basic of history's tests: we have not left our children a sustainable society. We have and are improving our standard of living at the expense of our children. We have inserted into their future a large number of fiscal time bombs. We have not maintained strong, vigorous and sustainable institutions. Let me give you the evidence:

I graduated from high school in 1953. I inherited the world's largest creditor nation yet I leave to my children the world's largest debtor nation. I inherited an economy that was supreme in everything yet I leave an economy that is supreme in practically nothing. When I graduated from high school almost all of the world's largest corporations were American—now a small percentage of them are American. I inherited a world where the world's largest financial institutions were American; now they are Japanese. The world I inherited had its epicenter of finance in Wall Street—today it is in Tokyo. History has few examples of a profligate people losing wealth and national prestige as fast as my generation of Americans.

I have hung an albatross of debt around the necks of my children. Not only the $2.9 trillion federal debt (which is equivalent to a $40,000 mortgage on each of us), but a wide range of unfunded and contingent liabilities which the current S&L crisis shows often comes due. When we pierce all the "creative accounting" of the federal government I suggest that our children will have to pay off between 10 and 14 trillion dollars of *our* federal debt. Plus interest. Under the most optimistic scenario our children will have to take approximately $.25 out of every tax dollar they spend just to pay the interest on *our* federal debt. My generation of politicians has run deficits for 28 of the last 30 years. Rather than pay for the governmental programs we wanted, we put them on our children's credit card. One Congressman called it "fiscal child abuse."

But that is by no means all the debt I have accumulated. The feeding frenzy of L.B.O.s has run up corporate debt to a recent all-time high and today consumes almost half of corporate income. Total U.S. debt, public and private, is approximately 230 percent of GNP, a level the nation experienced only well into the Great Depression.

We have used our political power to pick our children's pockets. Social Security, Medicare, military pensions, federal civil service pensions, state and local pensions; all these (and more) are chain letters to the future. Medicare is one recession away from bankruptcy. The average person retiring today will receive back in Social Security five or six times what they paid in, while our children will be lucky to even get their own money back. Programs that worked and were good social policy when we had a growing economy, many children, and died at 70 don't make economic sense to a society with far fewer children, a less productive economy, and which lives to 80.

The elderly are 12 percent of America yet they get 57 percent of federal social spending—despite the fact that the elderly are no longer disproportionately poor. It is political power, not social justice, that sets our priorities, and money desperately needed to prepare the next generation is being transferred to the last generation whether they need it or not. Money desperately needed by poor children in St. Paul is transferred instead to wealth retirees in St. Petersburg.

The sad list goes on. Virtually everyone in my generation could purchase a home—today few young couples (even with two incomes) can afford to purchase a home. We have not maintained our infrastructure. It would take at least another trillion dollars in repairs and reconstruction just to put our roads, bridges, ports, subways, etc. back into the shape they were in in the early 1970s. Our children will pay all their lives (and perhaps with their lives) for toxic, hazardous and nuclear waste we inadequately disposed of. E.P.A. estimates there are at least 10,000 toxic and hazardous waste sites that have to be redone.

We have presided over a shattering deterioration in our education system. Practically every year of my adulthood we have seen a drop in our education levels and a corresponding rise in illiteracy. By not maintaining our educational standards we have locked in further decline. A nation with a second rate educational system will soon have a second rate economy.

Like the spendthrift children of wealth, we received a rich inheritance and, first, we mortgaged our inheritance, then we started to sell it to maintain our excesses. The percentage of our assets owned by foreign investors has grown geometrically and America is in danger of losing its economic sovereignty. As a friend lamented to me the other day, "the most important thing to teach our children is how to say 'yes, sir' in Japanese." Extreme? Perhaps, but one has to go back to 17th century Spain to find a historical example of a country that has lost as much wealth as fast as we have in the last twenty years.

In all cultures, in all nations and in all religions there is a universal theme against profligacy and urging justice for future generations. A community cares about posterity. An old Middle East proverb observes, "the beginning of wisdom comes when a person plants a tree, the shade under which he knows he will never sit." Alas, my generation has cut down the shade trees we inherited.

COMMANDMENT VI: *A community that works has institutions that work. Thou shall not worship golden images of the status quo*

A quality community has institutions that work.

I'm not sure that America does.

The economist Schumpeter says all human institutions become *inefficient, bureaucratic, incestuous.* I fear that America and its problem solving machinery has become inefficient, bureaucratic and incestuous.

No one spends as much money on health care, and yet we don't keep our children as healthy as Europe, Canada or Japan. We have five percent of the world's population and two-thirds of its lawyers. We have an inefficient and ineffective educational system. No country has as many units of government. We have in the United States 41 units of government for every 100,000. No one spends as much money electing its politicians to office.

A working community must have institutions that deliver basic services. We cannot continue to allow our institutions to impose such large transactional costs on American goods and services. We are in the midst of a new world of international competition. To use an Olympic metaphor, I suggest that all the world's nations are lined up at the starting line in a race for the world's wealth. The race is to see who will win the economic gold medal and have the world's strongest economy. One runner has a Japanese flag on his back, one a German flag, and one of the runners has an American flag on his back. On the back of the American runner we are heaping among the highest wages in the industrialized world, the highest health care costs in the industrialized world, the highest insurance rates in the industrialized world, the highest litigation costs in the industrialized world, the highest rate of alcohol and drug abuse among its workers, and the highest number of functional illiterates. This cannot continue. We must look to increasing the efficiency and effectiveness of all our institutions.

COMMANDMENT VII: *A community needs a shared cultue and shared language*

John Gardner says:

> "If the community is lucky, and fewer and fewer are, it will have a shared history and tradition. It will have its 'story,' its legends and heroes, and will retell that story often. It will have symbols of group identity—a name, a flag, a location, songs and stories . . . which it will use to heighten its members' sense of belonging."

He goes on to say:

> "To maintain the sense of belonging and the dedication and commitment so essential to community life, members need inspiring reminders of shared goals and values."

I am convinced that one of the "shared values" we must have is a shared language. One scholar, Seymour Martin Lipset, put it this way:

> "The history of bilingual and bicultural societies that do not assimilate are histories of turmoil, tension, and tragedy. Canada, Belgium, Malaysia, Lebanon— all face crises of national existence in which minorities press for autonomy, if not independence. Pakistan and Cyprus have divided. Nigeria suppressed an ethnic rebellion. France faces difficulties with its Basques, Bretons, and Corsicans. In Spain, Basques and Catalans demand linguistic rights and greater autonomy."

The United States, in my opinion, is at a crossroads. It must move toward either greater integration or toward more fragmentation. It will either have to assimilate much better all of the peoples within its boundaries, or it will see an increasing alienation and fragmentation. Bilingual and bicultural nations are inherently unstable. We found in the '50s that "separate was inherently unequal." But we must also find that separate is also inherently divisive.

America *can* accept additional immigrants, but we must be sure that they become American. We can be a Joseph's coat of many nations, but we must be unified. We must have English as one of the common glues that hold us together. We should be color blind, but not linguistically deaf. We should be a rainbow, but not a cacophony. We should welcome different people, but not adopt different languages. We can teach English via bilingual education, but we should take great care not to become a bilingual society because they don't work—anywhere.

COMMANDMENT VIII: *A great community is one that has developed a great community culture*

I think more and more about *culture* these days. Why do certain people succeed in disproportionate numbers and others fail in disproportionate numbers? We are all God's children but we form different cultures.

The most economically successful people in America are minorities who have been discriminated against. When you look at family income, you see the top earners in America are: Japanese, Chinese, Jews, Koreans.

Why?

I believe because they came from cultures that promote education and delayed gratification, ambition and hard work, and other traits that are most often equated with success. Daniel Patrick Moynihan states,

> "The central conservative truth is that it is culture, not politics, that determines the success of a society. The central liberal truth is that politics can change a culture and save it from itself."

Likewise, successful communities have a successful corporate culture. James Fallows puts it this way: "In the long run, a society's strength depends on the way that ordinary people voluntarily behave." A successful community culture encourages certain traits: citizen participation, community leadership, volunteerism and philanthropy, civic education, community pride, justice.

They build an institutional capacity for cooperation and consensus building. To have a community you must have justice. People must feel that they have been dealt with fairly. Successful communities have successful corporate/community cultures.

Fallows goes on to say that

> "Successful societies—those which progress economically and politically and can control the terms on which they deal with the outside world—succeed because they have found ways to match individual self-interest to the collective good."

But some cultures are more supportive of appropriate and useful "voluntary behaviors" than others. Lawrence Harrison, author of the provocative book *Underdevelopment Is A State of Mind*, who spent many years as an official in Latin America attached to the Agency for International Development, has summarized the seven ingredients of what he calls a "useful" culture. These, according to Harrison, are the "conditions that encourage the expression of human creative capacity."

—The expectation of fair play.
—Availability of educational opportunities.
—Availability of health services.
—Encouragement of experimentation and criticism.
—Matching of skills and jobs.
—Rewards for merit and achievement.
—Stability and continuity.

COMMANDMENT IX: Thou shall not ask what your community can do for you. Thou shall ask what you can do for your community

Lastly, I believe a quality community is one which balances rights and privileges with duties and responsibilities. No society can live on rights and privileges alone and we have tried too long. Our community and our nation—which nurtured us—now needs something in return.

Admiral Nelson, off of Trafalgar, hoisted these words: "England expects every man to do his duty."

Adam Smith's theory of an ecomomy where every man seeking his own self interest created a prosperous economy but the "invisible hand" model—if it works in economics—does not build a community. It leaves us a collection of disparate, autonomous, unconnected individuals. We may have made ourselves rich but we have *not* made ourselves a community. Communities must expect something in return from all men and women who make them up.

I shall not give you a Tenth Commandment. You must give it to me during the dialogue. What else is needed for commuity? I do know that it is an increasingly important question that needs all of our thinking.

An old Presbyterian hymn out of my youth says:

"New occasions teach new duties. Time makes ancient good uncouth."

"Time makes ancient good uncouth." We can no longer take "community" for granted in the United States. We have too much evidence that we are unraveling. There is too much tension, too much misunderstanding.

Too many separate tribes yelling at each other.

It is a "dialogue" between the blind and the deaf. It is dangerous and we must attempt to salvage that elusive concept of *community.*

QUESTIONS FOR "THE TEN COMMANDMENTS OF A QUALITY COMMUNITY" BY RICHARD D. LAMM

Talking About the Text

1. What rhetorical effect do you think using the *Ten Commandments* as a model for structuring this essay has on the reader? Why do you think Lamm chose this device?

2. At the start of his essay, Lamm relates an anecdote about John Stuart Mill, the outcome of which is the phrase "Think in different terms." Why do you think Lamm chose to begin his essay with this story? To what "terms" is he referring?

Exploring Issues

1. How would you say Lamm conceives of "community"? What qualities keep a community together for Lamm? For you?

2. At one point in his essay Lamm quotes Wendell Berry as saying "If you don't know where you are you don't know who you are." What connections can you make between Lamm's views on community and those of Berry in "The Futility of Global Thinking"?

3. Commandment VII states: "A community needs a shared culture and a shared language." Read through this commandment. To what extent do you think Lamm's advice is valid? What are the potential positive and/or negative ramifications of this suggestion?

4. In Commandment II Lamm says, "The future isn't something we inherit—it is something we create." What do you think is necessary for the creation of a successful future?

Writing Assignment

At the end of his essay, Lamm writes, "I shall not give you a Tenth Commandment. You must give it to me during the dialogue. What else is needed for community? I do know that it is an increasingly important question that needs all of our thinking." In an exploratory essay, respond to Lamm's request.

CHAPTER 3: EXTENDED WRITING ASSIGNMENTS

3-1. Research the origins and growth of the community in which you either presently reside or a community where you formerly lived. The size of the community you choose to explore does not matter, but you should define the boundaries of this community before you start. Some guiding questions might include:

What brought people to this particular area?

What made people stay?

Were there geographic qualities about the area that helped build and maintain the community?

Where did and do the peole come from who form the community?

How old is the community?

Where do people work?

Do younger generations tend to stay in the community or move away?

What makes this particular community a "community"?

What changes has this community gone through over the years?

You should consider this project an act of discovery and exploration. Your scources might include interviews with senior members of the community as well as historical archives from the local library, schools, churches, newspapers, and industries, to mention a few. When you have collected all of your data, write up your findings and conclusions in the form of an informative essay. You might consider submitting your essay to a local newspaper or magazine for publication.

3-2. Choose a current controversial issue that is affecting or has already affected a particular community (for example, regentrification of urban communities, development of nuclear power plants, preservation of historic landmarks, use of natural resources by industries, unemployment caused by factory and mill closings, etc.). Then write an essay that takes a position on the controversy. In developing your essay, you will need to give enough background on the complexities of the issue so that your audience can understand your position.

3-3. Write a personal narrative that explores the roles you play in one of the communities to which you belong. In developing your response, consider the following questions:

Why do you consider yourself a member of this community?

What do you consider your functions in this community?

What benefits do you derive from belonging to this community?

What constraints does your belonging to this community place upon you?

What are your responsibilities to this community?

Chapter
4

Our Environments

*I*f we are to understand the various cultural and sociologic groupings of Americans, it is important to recognize certain scenic considerations. One aspect of scene is regional affiliation: where we live or have lived often helps us define our sense of who we are and what we value. Another important aspect of scene is a more general sense of land, property, and environment. Although our rural populations are slowly dying out as our culture becomes increasingly urbanized, we can still recall the symbolic significance of "living on the land," and we all have good reason to care about the environment we live in. Certainly, there is increasing public awareness of the effects of pollution, pesticides, and other chemicals on our health; in fact, environmental issues are becoming more and more prevalent in political platforms and may well play a major role in upcoming presidential elections.

In a democratic society such as ours, any arena will offer a divergence of public opinion and philosophical perspective. So it is with our environments, as we have aimed to indicate in our selection of texts for this section. Where some see in nature a living organism deserving of care and even reverence, others perceive a material object to be conquered and controlled. And while some worry about the effects of chemicals and new technologies on the environment, others value the products made possible by these chemicals and technologies. Developing our collective awareness of these differences can help us to understand various cultural and philosophical perspectives as well as related controversies and consequences.

You may well discover something about your own attitudes and values as you confront the issues raised in this chapter. As you read through these selections, we hope you will question old assumptions and begin to articulate your own philosophy of the land and of your environments.

A good place to begin is with your own sense of regional identity. In "Where Is the Midwest?" Susan Wintsch asks us to consider the problem of territorially mapping out a certain region and then explaining the particular character of that region's people. Here, we begin to see that American pluralism extends beyond the boundaries of ethnicity to include regional identity as well. In his poem, "Nebraska," William Wallis elaborates on this theme with suggestive images and impressionistic recollections of life in an agricultural community.

In a shift of focus from the rural to the urban, we include in this section Edward Hoagland's "Too Much, Too Blindly, Too Fast," an essay on the changing nature of life in New York, a city of stark contrasts and fast-paced lifestyles. Edward Field balances Hoagland's view with a response to all those whose primary associations with New York City are "junkies, muggings, dirt, and noise." In his poem "New York," Field celebrates his city as a "people paradise," as a place where people silently embrace with a look or a gesture as they pass one another on busy streets. Yet another aspect of New York is revealed by Langston Hughes in his poem entitled "Harlem." We encourage you to read the Hoagland essay and the poems by Field and Hughes together and to compare these three different perspectives on life in New York City.

As we shift our collective gaze from urban dwelling to the "frontier," we foreground attitudes toward the land and our environments. The issue of land ownership is addressed directly by William Kittredge, who explores the "mythology of the West" in "Owning It All." Rather than owning and controlling nature, Kittredge suggests, we should respect the integrity of natural environments and recognize the paradox in any notion of human "ownership" of nature. Peter MacDonald extends this theme in "Navajo Natural Resources," explaining the Native American view of land as "holy" and "sacred," as something that is "not for sale."

These two general perspectives on nature came into conflict when biologists predicted the extinction of the spotted owl resulting from the loss of old-growth forests in the Pacific Northwest. Environmentalists who wish to preserve these forests clashed with the loggers—who wish to preserve a way of life—and, of course, with the timber industry. The complexities of this controversy are laid out for us by Ted Gup in his essay, "Owl vs. Man."

Along another dimension of environmental concerns is the issue of pollution by pesticides and other chemicals. To what degree are we changing the ecology of our environment by injecting manufactured chemicals into the air, soil, and water? What are the long-term consequences of these practices, and how will they affect human health? This issue was addressed long ago by Rachel Carson, and her message is as relevant today as it was in 1962 when she published *Silent Spring*. However, not all reactions to her message were positive, as we can see in Jamie L. Whitten's "Silent Spring: The Committee Staff Report." Whitten's critique of Carson offers us an alternative perspective on the dangers of pesticides, a perspective that underscores the importance of increased production at lower costs made possible by pesticide use.

Rounding off this chapter's topic is a description of Amish farming practices and the underlying values and way of life that support these practices. This approach nears the new "Western mythology" that William Kittredge proposes in "Owning It All" and offers us an opportunity to explore the complex interrelationships among personal values and possible consequences in the worlds we inhabit.

Reading 27

Where Is the Midwest?

Susan Wintsch

Susan Wintsch has published as a free-lance writer in such publications as *Geology Today, Geographical Magazine,* and the *Christian Science Monitor.* She has also served as an editor for the U.S. Office of Technology Assessment, for UNESCO, and for an Indiana newspaper, the *Bloomington Herald.* As a resident of Bloomington, Indiana, Wintsch might be classified a Midwesterner, but *who* and *what* is a Midwesterner? This is the subject addressed by Wintsch in the essay below, originally published in the *TWA Ambassador* (March 1988).

A sizable chunk of the North American continent belongs to the fabled Midwest. Just how sizable depends on whom you talk to. Twenty-two years ago Roy Meyer, in a study of American farm novels, defined the American Midwest as "that great central area of the nation including the 12 states of Ohio, Indiana, Illinois, Michigan, Wisconsin, Minnesota, Iowa, Missouri, Kansas, Nebraska, South Dakota, and North Dakota." This view of the Midwest as everything from Ohio westward through Kansas and northward to the Canadian border may be convenient for some purposes—like writing textbooks—but is not without its challengers. Today, as in the past, the Midwest is a term loosely used and rarely defined with precision.

In fact, Americans have grappled with the question of the Midwest's regional boundaries since before the turn of the century, when popular writers began to use the term "Middle West" without really agreeing on what it was they were describing.

The situation had not much changed by 1973, prompting one scholar to complain, "Everyone within or outside the Middle West knows of its existence, but no one seems sure where it begins or ends." Going even further in his 1981 book *The Nine Nations of North America, Washington Post* writer Joel Garreau suggested that those who would lump Ohio with Nebraska, and Cleveland with Omaha don't understand how America really works. Garreau called the "midwest" a myth, an outmoded geographical concept.

Nevertheless, when University of Kansas geographer James Shortridge recently surveyed some 2,000 university students across the nation, he found the concept of a Midwest alive and well. Shortridge was intrigued that the Midwest the students defined was centered somewhat west of the classic 12-state "textbook" model. And he has some interesting ideas about why this is so.

As a geographer, Shortridge had already begun thinking about how regional terms like "Appalachia," the "Great Plains," and the "Corn Belt" evolve. He found himself dwelling more and more on the problem of the Midwest, to his mind the vaguest and most profound of American regional concepts.

The name "Middle West" (later shortened to Midwest) seems to have come into use about 100 years ago. In 1898, Kansas journalist Charles Moreau Harger used the term casually, as if it had at least some precedence in the popular literature. His Middle West described the plains area of Kansas and Nebraska as distinct from the newer states of Minnesota and the Dakotas to the north, and from Texas and the Indian territories to the south. He used "Middle West" in a latitudinal sense.

Not until about 1912, according to Shortridge, did "Middle West" come into its own as a major regional term, one denoting an east–west rather than a north–south division. Yet as the term gained familiarity, its exact meaning remained elusive. During the first decade of this century two conflicting schools of thought emerged. Harger and several other authors continued using "Middle West" to describe the central plains areas of Kansas and Nebraska, a gradually maturing agricultural society still occasionally referred to as part of the West. Other commentators used "Midwest" in a much broader sense to include Minnesota and the Dakotas, Ohio, and Indiana as well. Harger himself vacillated, at one point putting the term "Middle West" in quotes and admitting it could be only vaguely defined.

In 1916, Rollin Lynde Hartt, writing in *The Century* magazine, playfully illustrated just how shaky the geographical identity of this hugely sprawling Midwest actually remained:

> Although the prairies begin at Batavia, New York, Buffalonians resent being termed Middle-Westerners. Omaha, I should describe as unquestionably Middle-Western, yet there are Middle-Westerners who repudiate Nebraska, and only tepidly accept Kansas. . . . A dear soul in Montana remarked to me: "How jolly to hear that you came from the East! I'm an Easterner myself. I lived in Iowa."
>
> Where then is the Middle West? In the words of the immortal Artemus, I answer, "Nowheres—nor anywheres else."

Although a broader definition of the Midwest gradually became the preferred one, 20th-century geographers have been as inconsistent as turn-of-the-century writers in their use of the term "Midwest"—so complained scholar Joseph W. Brownell in 1960 when he made what was apparently the first attempt to define the "vernacular" Midwest—the Midwest as the American population, not just professional geographers, was then defining it. Brownell surveyed 536 postmasters within a several-hundred-mile radius of Chicago with a single question: "In your opinion, does your community lie in the Midwest?"

Almost 90 percent of the individuals surveyed responded, and nearly 55 percent answered yes. They described a core region spread across all or almost all of Ohio, Indiana, Illinois, Wisconsin, Minnesota, Iowa, Missouri, the Dakotas, Kansas, and Nebraska. More than half of Michigan and the western half of Oklahoma also defined the core which, all told, covered 20 percent of the continental United States and accounted for 28 percent of the nation's population.

The boundaries of this region were sharp in the northwest along the western borders of the Dakotas and in the southeast along the southern borders of Illinois and Missouri. Peripheral zones, where neighboring communities disagreed about their designation, spilled across broad areas of Oklahoma and Colorado.

Many of the postmasters west of the Mississippi considered that river to be the eastern border of the region. As one explained, "We resent persons from Ohio and Indiana referring to themselves as 'midwesterners' as actually they are mideasterners.'"

Shortridge thinks that a great deal more lies behind the term "Midwest" in the minds of Americans than any fixed set of boundaries, and he believes he has evidence of this in his survey results. In his survey, students were given a map of the United States and asked to draw a line around the Midwest. They were also asked to list the characteristics they associated with the Midwest and its peoples.

The resulting summary map contained some surprises. Over 50 percent of the students excluded Chicago—traditionally hailed as the "capital" of the Midwest. Wyoming was midwestern to as many students as was Ohio, and, in general, the Midwest that emerged from the survey was more westerly than the 12-state "textbook" Midwest. Students from the Northeast, Southwest, and West centered the Midwest in Kansas and Nebraska, as did students from those two states, creating the dominant pattern on the composite map. Students from Illinois, Iowa, Missouri, North Dakota, South Dakota, and Wisconsin tended to put their own states at the core of the Midwest, a tendency that was not widely shared outside their state borders. Students from Michigan, Indiana, and Ohio included themselves as marginally midwestern, placing the region's core far to the west. These three states were not included in the Midwest by the majority of students living outside their borders.

Shortridge proposes that as urbanization and industrialization profoundly changed the Great Lakes and Ohio Valley states in this century, two choices emerged: "modify the rural image of the Middle West to conform to the new reality in these states . . . or shift the regional core westward to the Great Plains where rural society still prevailed." His survey indicates that Americans may have elected the latter course.

What intrigued Shortridge most were not the differing geographic definitions revealed in the survey, but the overwhelmingly similar responses to the question about midwestern characteristics. These strongly parallel images of rural independence and pastoral democracy that first emerged in the popular literature about the Midwest in the early years of this century. Shortridge wonders whether the Midwest isn't as much an actual place as an idea—an idea that is now more compatible with life on the plains than the modern reality of the more industrialized and urban "midwestern" states like Indiana and Ohio.

As early as 1910 the vision of the Midwest as rural America, as the most American and friendliest part of America, held a firm place in the national psyche. As one traveler from "back East" exclaimed, "There are Midwesterners who slap you on the back after an hour's acquaintance." Shortridge has found in many turn-of-the-century descriptions of the Midwest (wherever authors located the region geographically) a life-cycle analogy—one still employed, though somewhat differently, in the 1980s. In contrast with the older, more aristocratic and tradition-bound eastern states (where, one Iowan observed in 1912, the children are so listless "they have to be incited to play"); and unlike the very young, energetic, and somewhat raw West, the Midwest was seen as the region of balance and maturity, the seat of a near-perfect democracy.

An economic depression affecting the central plains in the 1880s and 1890s, Shortridge believes, was a watershed event. According to commentators of the time, the region emerged from hard times confident and optimistic, having "outgrown the undesirable traits of youth such as thriftlessness, impatience, radicalism, and boomer philosophy." The first generation of midwesterners had already buried their parents, and in cases, children, in midwestern sod, establishing roots that gradually replaced those tugging at them from the east.

As the 20th century opened, the Midwest began to be extolled as a "fat land" of rural abundance. A professor of economics at Harvard University, traveling through Kansas in the early 1900s, dubbed the corn belt "the most considerable area in the world where agriculture is uniformly prosperous." As for the corn growers, they were "an independent progressive class, drawing their sustenance from the soil and not from other people."

It was not until about 1915 that hints of excessive conservatism, of "fished out" communities north of the Ohio valley, of industrial squalor here and there, contradicted some of the overwhelmingly flattering portrayals in turn-of-the-century reports. Almost invariably, criticisms were overshadowed by new and stronger praise for the region.

Shortridge's survey illustrates that much of the positive imagery that persists in association with the Midwest is rural in emphasis. Only students from Indiana and Ohio associated industry with the Midwest, and even they saw the Midwest primarily as a place of fields and farms.

Many students used terms related to a life cycle in describing the region, but the images that emerged were more those of increasing age than young maturity. Terms like "traditional" overshadowed "progressive" and "liberal." Synonyms for intolerance were offered about five times more frequently than phrases from the past like "open-mindedness." On the other hand, Shortridge notes, no respondent described the Midwest as smug or self-satisfied, nor were adjectives such as corrupt or nonegalitarian used to describe this region of the country.

If geographers follow Shortridge's lead, the Midwest—long synonymous with the American self-image—will come to be viewed more in terms of this symbolism than as any fixed place.

Where, then, is the Middle West? It may indeed be "nowheres—nor any-wheres else." But, in concept, at least, it seems to be "somewheres" deeply rooted in American experience and thought.

QUESTIONS FOR "WHERE IS THE MIDWEST?" BY SUSAN WINTSCH

Talking About the Text

1. Why might it be important to answer the question expressed in the title? In addition to the geographical problem of identifying a certain territory, what other problems are posed by Susan Wintsch when she asks "where is the Midwest?"

2. What are some of the values and characteristics that the author associates with midwestern people? Do your own views correspond closely to those of the author or do you have some other ideas about the nature of midwest-erners? Can you think of any negative stereotypes about midwesterners?

3. In his survey of university students, James Shortridge found that "the Midwest was seen as the region of balance and maturity, the seat of a near-perfect democracy." This characterization could lead us to believe that the Midwest serves as a symbol for the entire nation. Do you consider the Midwest, or another region such as New England or the West, to be most representative of the United States as a whole? Which region? Why?

Exploring Issues

1. How would you carve up the United States into geographical regions? How many do you identify? Does this number agree with that of your classmates?

2. Of the regions you have identified, which ones do you find most pres-tigious and/or influential nationally? Why? Which ones are least prestigious and/or influential nationally? Why? In which regions would you prefer to live? How do you arrive at this decision?

3. Do you have a strong sense of belonging to or of coming from a particu-lar region? How do you make this judgment? How important is this to your own sense of personal identity?

4. Has anyone ever indicated a prejudice against you because of your regional identity? In what way? Do you have any prejudice against people from other regions? What is the nature of this prejudice?

Writing Assignments

1. In a personal essay, write about the region in which you grew up and the influence that this has had, if any, on your values, customs, personal qualities, and temperament, education, religion, attitudes towards others and so on.

2. Write a narrative essay about a trip you have made to another region of the United States. Use your narrative essay to point out some of the impressions you had as an outsider observing the people, the institutions, and the environment of this region.

Reading 28

Nebraska

William Wallis

William Wallis teaches composition and literature at Los Angeles Valley College and has published two volumes of poetry: *Poems* (Blue Stem Press, 1972) and *Biographer's Notes* (Yellow Barn Press, 1984). The following poem is taken from a collection entitled *Four Valley Poets,* edited by John Zounes. In this poem, we can discern impressions and images of Nebraska, a state best known for its agriculture. We suggest that you read this poem in tandem with "Harlem" by Langston Hughes and consider the reference to a dream in each poem.

Those years mowing dry yards in west Lincoln
Left crabgrass memories, a clutching hatred
Of sharp white fences and shrill narrow gates,
Of thrifty chats hinting at sandy mouths.
Flat land spreads guilt thin, as summer's sluggish
Thigh drifts listless on the soil's loose sheets.
Intensity and glow fade from the pale child's
Dusty piping for a sense of place.
Nebraskaland is bruised with fields of sand,

Its culture worn cropless by dull lust.
A nation's oldest dream fades in the hands of
Fourth generation mechanics of the earth's crust.
  Still, the child can see the horizon rear,
  Crust with cloud jewels, rain blood and fear.

Reading 29

Too Much, Too Blindly, Too Fast: The Hunger in Manhattan Life

Edward Hoagland

A well-known essayist and prose stylist, Edward Hoagland has been widely published in magazines such as *Harper's,* from which this essay is taken (June 1989). His best essays written over the past 20 years have recently been published in a book entitled *Heart's Desire.* In "Too Much, Too Blindly, Too Fast," Hoagland describes the changing nature of New Yorkers as they attempt to cope with the stark inequalities that confront them daily on their city streets. While still valuing New York as "a fine hotbed in which to be young," Hoagland nevertheless recognizes a certain hardening of heart that he attributes, in part, to technological innovations in communication and transportation and to "velocities too fast to stay abreast of."

Most of us realized early on that we are not our "brother's keeper." Yet perhaps we also came to recognize that "there but for the grace of God go I." If the jitters we experience on a particularly awful afternoon were extended and became prolonged until we couldn't shake them off, after a few drastic months we might end up sleeping on the sidewalk too. Character is fate, we like to say: hard work and fidelity (or call it regularity) will carry the day. And this is just true enough to believe. But chemistry is also fate: the chemistry of our tissues and the chemistry of our brains. We know that just as some people among us get cancer at a pitiably young age, others go haywire through no fault of their ethics, pluck, or upbringing.

Still, what do most of us do when we notice a hungry, disoriented person slumped on the street in obvious despair? Why, we pass quickly by, averting our eyes toward an advertisement, the stream of taxis, the window dressing in a shop. Part of the excitement of a great metropolis is how it juxtaposes: starvelings blowing on their fingers in front of Bergdorf Goodman, Saks, and Lord & Taylor; urchins shilling for a three-card monte pitchman alongside a string of smoked-glass limousines; old people coughing, freezing next to a restaurant where young professionals are licking sherbet from their spoons to clear their palates.

Already in the eighteenth century Tom Paine wrote that in New York City "the contrast of affluence and wretchedness is like dead and living bodies chained together." Or as is said nowadays: Takes all kinds.

Those hungry people foraging in garbage cans apparently didn't start a Keogh plan or get themselves enrolled in some corporation's pension program thirty years ago and stick to the job. They didn't "get a degree" when they were young; they were uncertain in direction, indecisive about money; they plotted their course badly or slipped out of gear somewhere along the line. Or they may simply be "defective" in Hitler's sense of the word—a bit retarded, a trifle nuts. So they are not being maintained at the requisite room temperature society provides for the rest of us year-round; they are standing in the cold wind, hat in hand, as the saying goes, or lined up forlornly in front of a convent for a baloney sandwich at 11 A.M.

It's not as if we had the leisure or quietude to worry overmuch about the souls we are well acquainted with who, in reasonably comfortable, well-stocked apartments, may nonetheless be drinking themselves to death. Yet what might we do about those on the street? Empty our wallets and rush to a money machine for more cash to give out? Run for office on a philanthropic platform? Become social workers? Move to the country and forget it all? "New York is getting unlivable," people say. An adage among the privileged is that "you can't live in New York on less than $150,000" (a year). But if this isn't swinishness talking, the real meaning is that it costs that much *not* to be in the city—to be elevated above the fracases, grief, and dolor of the streets, with sufficient "doorman" protection to shield you from the dangers there, to exclude anyone with a lesser income, and to conceal from you the fact that a city is its streets. A city is its museums too, but here in New York Goya is in the streets more than in the museums.

Our ancestral wish as predators is that somebody be worse off than we are— that we see subordinates, surplus prey, or rivals hungering. This assures us we're prospering. Rather in the same way that we dash sauces on our meat (Worcestershire, horseradish, A.1., or béarnaise) to restore a tartness approximating the taint of spoilage that wild meat attains, we want a city with a certain soupçon of visible misfortune, some people garishly on the skids, scouting in the gutter for a butt and needing to be "moved on" (the policeman's billy club for banging on their shoes if they fall asleep on a park bench). In a major city, in other words, there should be store detectives collaring shoplifters while we finger our credit cards, white-haired men being bullied by mid-level executives younger than they are or being forced to hustle around the subway system as messengers, occasional young women selling themselves and suffering exhibitionists publicly going mad. That quick-footed, old-eyed gentleman with the wife in a lynx coat, grabbing a cab on Sixth Avenue to go uptown after a gala evening, leaves behind an old Purple Heart soldier with his broken leg in a cast, scrambling for a tip, who may sleep on a grating tonight in the icy cold. *You're sick? You have no co-op to go to? No CDs, T-bills, mutual funds? Where've you been?*

A city is supposed to be a little bit cruel. What's the point of "making it" at all if the servants in hotels and restaurants aren't required to act like automatons, and if plenty of people at your own place of business don't have to bootlick and brownnose? A city with its honking traffic jams, stifling air, and brutal cliffs of glass and stone is supposed to watch you enigmatically, whether you are living on veal *médaillons* and poached salmon or begged coins and hot dogs. But stumble badly and it will masticate you. Sing a song and exhibit your sores on the subway and it will nickel-and-dime you as you gradually starve.

All this Dickensian tough stuff, however, has often verged on the playful in American myth, because in the past it has been tied in with rags-to-riches stories. The ragamuffin enshrouded in burlap, sleeping underneath a bush at the edge of the park, might be a new immigrant who in another seven years would grab his first million in the garment trade. He has links to the Statue of Liberty, to put it bluntly, so don't be a fool and dismiss him glibly. Ben Franklin entered Philadelphia that first time to make his name with one "Dutch dollar" to live on.

Or he might be a hobo, riding the rods for freedom and fun, a hero of folk songs and such, whose worst sin was stealing Mom's apple pie as it cooled on the kitchen porch and a chicken from the dooryard for his "jungle" stew. He might be a labor organizer traveling on the q.t. Or if the figure asleep in the park was female, she might be Little Orphan Annie, soon to charm Daddy Warbucks and be spruced up by him.

And in hard, bad times like the Depression, the Arkie and Okie families hitting the open road for a chance at a better life—one of the most hallowed American rites—were, let's be frank about this, white. For many urbanites, what makes the heart pound at being surrounded by street people is that a preponderance of them are black. Also, when those disheartened farmers from the Dust Bowl indulged in what is lately called "substance abuse," hey, they were just winos, drunks. We all knew what getting three sheets to the wind (and the hangover) was like. There was nothing arcanely, explosively mind-blitzing about liquor anyhow, even during Prohibition. Hillbillies (or "Legs" Diamond) smuggled it into town, not "Colombian drug lords." Besides, during the Depression we were all in a mess together.

Then we pulled together to fight World War II. And the veterans came back, as from previous wars, and had to start over. Even ten years after 1945 it was easy for a white man to hitchhike anywhere—just stick out your thumb. And you probably remember how "the best things in life are free"? This happy slogan was sometimes said tongue in cheek but seldom cynically. Religious faith, for example, surely was free, sunlight and open spaces were free, children were free, falling in love was the next thing to free, and friendship wasn't necessarily "networking." Movie idols played happy-go-lucky roles, with the good guys the poor guys a lot. Every middle-class person in the city wasn't stitched into the disciplines of a telephone answering machine, exercise club, and psychotherapy. People let the phone ring, let a call slip by once in a while, and walked between business appointments when they could. They weren't keyed nearly to computer tempo, fax speed.

What has also happened in New York is that we no longer assume we like most people—that strangers are not a cause for alarm, may be worth a second glance or tarrying over. In the old neighborhoods of mixed incomes, one's tribal affiliation was not just mercenary. All kinds of factors operated to populate the place, and the people living in it didn't all appear as if they could raise (or not raise) a loan of a certain sum. The stores too, when rents weren't skyhigh, could be handed down from father to son, acquiring a "mystery" or no-cash-flow look. The almighty dollar, where spoken of irreverently, was not.

But now when we take note of people on the sidewalk, we flee on past them, dodging by as if the human shape had become adversarial. And along with the dusty shops and greasy spoons and rent-stabilized buildings with a quirky variety of tenants has gone the idea that the smattering of bums one used to see were familiar characters. There on the corner by the subway steps each morning stood "Buffalo Bill," "Grover Cleveland," "V. I. Lenin," or "Yogi Berra" to contribute to—not an encampment of war-zone refugees fighting for space on a steam grating, under a scrap of carpeting, or in a sofa carton. Statistically, New York was more crowded when it was less violent. People merely had homes.

The discovery that you could build dwellings taller and taller or sell air rights above a building was like when the Indians discovered that they could sell land: and then it was gone. Sunlight, like falling in love and raising children conscientiously, has become expensive, and with the money pressure unrelenting ("We have no *downtime*," as a friend who is doing okay expressed it), the flippant malevolence of racism increases, as well as a general sense of malaise and deterioration or imminent menace. A man with his head bandaged says at a party, "I was on my way to work and half the world seemed to be standing around on the platform, including a Guardian Angel, while those creeps were beating me, but for a minute I had this ludicrous feeling that I was about to die."

Some days the ills of the city seem miasmal and mental, a delirium of drugs and dysfunctions, a souring in the gut like dysentery. The creeds or the oratory that ought to invigorate us seem exhausted, whether derived from Marx, Freud, or capitalism (newly perverse). Nationalism as idealism reached its nadir with the collapse of the Axis powers, and has not carried our own country far since Korea. Judaism has bent itself awry in the conflicted Middle East; Christianity hasn't been tried in years (maybe since Gandhi). "Tell it to the Marines!" one of the elder statesmen of finance hurrying to lunch might want to tell the sad-sack young blacks wanting a coin on Fifty-first Street, but some of them have already *been* in the Marines. The fact that the city's former economic base of muscular industries like transport and manufacturing has been supplanted by an employment pattern of money-processing and "information" jobs—electronic paper-pushing—has made it a city of myriad keypunchers, legal assistants, and market researchers: the suddenly rich, the high-flying strivers who live by their wits and their countless clerks, and a piggishness to suit. The leavening of physical work that was present before brought more good humor, loosened the effect of so many people whose bread and butter is their nerves.

I remember trolley cars, and business deals clinched with a handshake, New Yorkers who knew the night sky's constellations, and how easy it was to raise a thumb, catch a ride, and reach Arizona on ten bucks, I can't claim this made it a golden age or even that the city's faces were much happier then. Needless to say, I see lovers now too, and businesspeople alive to their work, and immigrants thick in speech but alight with hopes. High is handsome and fast is fun, not just brutal. No other world city has such a bounce; is dreamed about from so very far off. A "mecca," we say, still almost a religion, and a fine hotbed in which to be young. And that it has curdled doesn't mean it's not still so rich that you could choke.

"But they're so ruthless," several of my middle-aged friends suggest, speaking of the new professionals sprinting as they start. I don't know. Planes are more ruthless than cars, but more gleeful as well, as long as they don't burn up travel itself. I love planes, arriving out of the heavens at strange locations and picking up instant friendships, easy come, easy go. Or call them battlefield alliances, if you prefer. Anyway, that's the style of the day. Look at your watch, pat your passport, and expand upon conversations you had last evening in a different city, a different time zone, with somebody these people won't ever know.

We New Yorkers, rushing to keep up with our calendars, pausing to open a fast-food package and finding the plastic wrapper resists our fingers, immediately, unthinkingly, move it up to our teeth. Wild we still are, but possessed by velocities too fast to stay abreast of ourselves, strewing empathy and social responsibility behind us as we go.

QUESTIONS FOR "TOO MUCH, TOO BLINDLY, TOO FAST: THE HUNGER IN MANHATTAN LIFE" BY EDWARD HOAGLAND

Talking About the Text

1. After reading this essay, consider the implications of Hoagland's title. What is it that has, for New Yorkers, been "too much"? Who has acted "too blindly"? And what or who has come "too fast"? Consider as well the meaning of Hoagland's subtitle, "The Hunger in Manhattan Life."

2. Hoagland makes many references to other authors and texts as well as to concrete things and places, particularly places in New York City. How do these references to authors, texts, things, and places affect your

reading of this text? If you do not know some of these references, do you skip right past them or are they a distraction? How about the references you do know? How do they affect your reading?

3. Hoagland includes himself among New Yorkers by using the pronouns "we" and "us" consistently throughout his essay. Imagine that, instead, Hoagland had written about New Yorkers as "you" or "they." What would be some differences in the effects of these two approaches? Why do you think Hoagland chose the approach he did?

Exploring Issues

1. Hoagland points out that many of us "quickly pass by, averting our eyes" when we notice the hungry and homeless on our city streets. What might motivate many of us to avert our glance rather than looking directly into the eyes of these people? Why do we pass by quickly rather than slowing down and enquiring about these people's welfare?

2. Hoagland seems to deplore the common middle-class experience of being "stitched into the disciplines of a telephone answering machine, exercise club, and psychotherapy." Hoagland also appears to regret the association of friendship with "networking" and the generally fast pace that has replaced a more leisurely attitude toward time and work. What is Hoagland implying about the values of people living in such a society? Do you sympathize with Hoagland's sense of loss? Why or why not?

3. Although Hoagland is describing New Yorkers, his description might be of Americans in general. What aspect(s) of the American character is Hoagland attempting to capture? How do Hoagland's observations complement or contrast with Susan Wintsch's observations about mid-westerners?

Writing Assignments

1. No matter what city or state we live in, we have all come into contact with homeless people (if only through the media). Consider your own feelings about those who live in the city streets. How do you or might you feel as you pass by them on your way to work or during a visit to the city for a special occasion? Write an essay in which you explore and articulate your own feelings about your encounters with homeless people in the United States today. You may wish to describe some actual encounters you have had in order to lay the groundwork for your discussion.

2. Read Susan Wintsch's essay entitled "Where Is the Midwest?" in this chapter. Then, write a list of the characteristics of midwesterners, as described by Wintsch. Do the same for Hoagland's characterization of New Yorkers. Finally, write an essay in which you compare these two characterizations and discuss the potential value of each in explaining something about Americans' character generally.

Reading 30

New York

Edward Field

Edward Field has published several volumes of his own poetry and edited a collection entitled *A Geography of Poets* (1979). In the last chapter of this book, we have included a second poem of Field's, entitled "Both My Grandmothers." After reading "New York," we suggest that you discuss your impressions of New York City, both negative and positive, and then compare Field's representation of this metropolis with your own impressions.

I live in a beautiful place, a city
people claim to be astonished
when you say you live there.
They talk of junkies, muggings, dirt, and noise,
missing the point completely.

I tell them where they live it is hell,
a land of frozen people.
They never think of people.

Home, I am astonished by this environment
that is also a form of nature
like those paradises of trees and grass

but this is a people paradise
where we are the creatures mostly
though thank God for dogs, cats, sparrows, and roaches.

This vertical place is no more an accident
than the Himalayas are.
The city needs all those tall buildings
to contain the tremendous energy here.
The landscape is in a state of balance.
We do God's will whether we know it or not:
Where I live the streets end in a river of sunlight.

Nowhere else in the country do people
show just what they feel—
we don't put on any act.
Look at the way New Yorkers
walk down the street. It says,
I don't care. What nerve,
to dare to live their dreams, or nightmares,
and no one bothers to look.

True, you have to be an expert to live here.
Part of the trick is not to go anywhere, lounge about,
go slowly in the midst of the rush for novelty.
Anyway, beside the eats the big event here
is the streets which are full of love—
we hug and kiss a lot. You can't say that
for anywhere else around. For some
it is the sex part they care about and get—
there's all the opportunity in the world if you want it.
For me it is different:
Out walking, my soul seeks its food.
It knows what it wants.
Instantly it recognizes its mate, our eyes meet,
and our beings exchange a vital energy,
the universe goes on Charge
and we pass by without holding.

Reading 31

Harlem

Langston Hughes

Langston Hughes, widely recognized for his association with the Harlem
Renaissance, has long been known for his representations of African
American culture in verse. His first volume of poetry, *The Weary Blues,* was
published in 1926, and a collection of his best work appears in *The Selected*

Poems of Langston Hughes (1959, 1965). After reading this poem, consider the "dream deferred" that Hughes refers to and then contrast it with "a nation's oldest dream [that] fades" in William Wallis's "Nebraska."

What happens to a dream deferred?

　　Does it dry up
　　like a raisin in the sun?
　　Or fester like a sore—
　　And then run?
　　Does it stink like rotten meat?
　　Or crust and sugar over—
　　like a syrupy sweet?

　　Maybe it just sags
　　like a heavy load.

　　Or does it explode?

Reading 32

Owning It All

William Kittredge

William Kittredge grew up on a ranch in southeastern Oregon, where he farmed until he was 35. Kittredge then went on to teach creative writing at the University of Montana and to publish stories and essays in such magazines as *Atlantic, Harper's, TriQuarterly, Outside,* and *The Paris Review.* He has also participated in the *Cord* series of western novels and the script for the film *Heartland.* The following essay appears as a chapter in *Owning It All* (Saint Paul, MN: Greywolf Press, 1987), a book that examines Western mythologies in the broader context of contemporary American culture. In this essay Kittredge focuses on the desire to own and control property and the consequences of that desire for the land and its people.

Imagine the slow history of our country in the far reaches of southeastern Oregon, a backlands enclave even in the American West, the first settlers not arriving until a decade after the end of the Civil War. I've learned to think of myself as having had the luck to grow up at the tail end of a way of existing in which people lived in everyday proximity to animals on territory they knew more precisely than the patterns in the palms of their hands.

In Warner Valley we understood our property as others know their cities, a landscape of neighborhoods, some sacred, some demonic, some habitable, some not, which is as the sea, they tell me, is understood by fishermen. It was only later, in college, that I learned it was possible to understand Warner as a fertile oasis in a vast featureless sagebrush desert.

Over in that other world on the edge of rain-forests which is the Willamette Valley of Oregon, I'd gone to school in General Agriculture, absorbed in a double-bind sort of learning, studying to center myself in the County Agent/ Corps of Engineers mentality they taught and at the same time taking classes from Bernard Malamud and wondering with great romantic fervor if it was in me to write the true history of the place where I had always lived.

Straight from college I went to Photo Intelligence work in the Air Force. The last couple of those years were spent deep in jungle on the island of Guam, where we lived in a little compound of cleared land, in a quonset hut.

The years on Guam were basically happy and bookish: we were newly married, with children. A hundred or so yards north of our quonset hut, along a trail through the luxuriant undergrowth between coconut palms and banana trees, a ragged cliff of red porous volcanic rock fell directly to the ocean. When the Pacific typhoons came roaring in, our hut was washed with blowing spray from the great breakers. On calm days we would stand on the cliff at that absolute edge of our jungle and island, and gaze out across to the island of Rota, and to the endlessness of ocean beyond, and I would marvel at my life, so far from southeastern Oregon.

And then in the late fall of 1958, after I had been gone from Warner Valley for eight years, I came back to participate in our agriculture. The road in had been paved, we had Bonneville Power on lines from the Columbia River, and high atop the western rim of the valley there was a TV translator, which beamed fluttering pictures from New York and Los Angeles direct to us.

And I had changed, or thought I had, for a while. No more daydreams about writing the true history. Try to understand my excitement as I climbed to the rim behind our house and stood there by our community TV translator. The valley where I had always seen myself living was open before me like another map and playground, and this time I was an adult, and high up in the War Department. Looking down maybe 3,000 feet into Warner, and across to the high basin and range desert where we summered our cattle, I saw the beginnings of my real life as an agricultural manager. The flow of watercourses in the valley was spread before me like a map, and I saw it as a surgeon might see the flow of blood across a chart of anatomy, and saw myself helping to turn the fertile homeplace of my childhood into a machine for agriculture whose features could be delineated with the same surgeon's precision in my mind.

It was work which can be thought of as craftsmanlike, both artistic and mechanical, creating order according to an ideal of beauty based on efficiency, manipulating the forces of water and soil, season and seed, manpower and equipment, laying out functional patterns for irrigation and cultivation on the surface of our valley. We drained and leveled, ditched and pumped, and for a long while our crops were all any of us could have asked. There were over 5,000 water control devices. We constructed a perfect agricultural place, and it was sacred, so it seemed.

• • •

Agriculture is often envisioned as an art, and it can be. Of course there is always survival, and bank notes, and all that. But your basic bottom line on the farm is again and again some notion of how life should be lived. The majority of agricultural people, if you press them hard enough, even though most of them despise sentimental abstractions, will admit they are trying to create a good place, and to live as part of that goodness, in the kind of connection which with fine reason we call *rootedness*. It's just that there is good art and bad art.

These are thoughts which come back when I visit eastern Oregon. I park and stand looking down into the lava-rock and juniper-tree canyon where Deep Creek cuts its way out of the Warner Mountains, and the great turkey buzzard soars high in the yellow-orange light above the evening. The fishing water is low, as it always is in late August, unfurling itself around dark and broken boulders. The trout, I know, are hanging where the currents swirl across themselves, waiting for the one entirely precise and lucky cast, the Renegade fly bobbing toward them.

Even now I can see it, each turn of water along miles of that creek. Walk some stretch enough times with a fly rod and its configurations will imprint themselves on your being with Newtonian exactitude. Which is beyond doubt one of the attractions of such fishing—the hours of learning, and then the intimacy with a living system that carries you beyond the sadness of mere gaming for sport.

What I liked to do, back in the old days, was pack in some spuds and an onion and corn flour and spices mixed up in a plastic bag, a small cast-iron frying pan in my wicker creel and, in the late twilight on a gravel bar by the water, cook up a couple of rainbows over a fire of snapping dead willow and sage, eating alone while the birds flitted through the last hatch, wiping my greasy fingers on my pants while the heavy trout began rolling at the lower ends of the pools.

The canyon would be shadowed under the moon when I walked out to show up home empty-handed, to sit with my wife over a drink of whiskey at the kitchen table. Those nights I would go to bed and sleep without dreams, a grown-up man secure in the house and the western valley where he had been a child, enclosed in a topography of spirit he assumed he knew more closely than his own features in the shaving mirror.

So, I ask myself, if it was such a pretty life, why didn't I stay? The peat soil in Warner Valley was deep and rich, we ran good cattle, and my most sacred memories are centered there. What could run me off?

Well, for openers, it got harder and harder to get out of bed in the mornings and face the days, for reasons I didn't understand. More and more I sought the comfort of fishing that knowable creek. Or in winter the blindness of television.

My father grew up on a homestead place on the sagebrush flats outside Silver Lake, Oregon. He tells of hiding under the bed with his sisters when strangers came to the gate. He grew up, as we all did in that country and era, believing that the one sure defense against the world was property. I was born in 1932, and recall a life before the end of World War II in which it was possible for a child to imagine that his family owned the world.

Warner Valley was largely swampland when my grandfather bought the MC Ranch with no downpayment in 1936, right at the heart of the Great Depression. The outside work was done mostly by men and horses and mules, and our ranch valley was filled with life. In 1937 my father bought his first track-layer, a secondhand RD6 Caterpillar he used to build a 17-mile diversion canal to carry the spring floodwater around the east side of the valley, and we were on our way to draining all swamps. The next year he bought an RD7 and a John Deere 36 combine which cut an 18-foot swath, and we were deeper into the dream of power over nature and men, which I had begun to inhabit while playing those long-ago games of war.

The peat ground left by the decaying remnants of ancient tule beds was diked into huge undulating grainfields—Houston Swamp with 750 irrigated acres, Dodson Lake with 800—a final total of almost 8,000 acres under cultivation, and for reasons of what seemed like common sense and efficiency, the work became industrialized. Our artistry worked toward a model whose central image was the machine.

The natural patterns of drainage were squared into dragline ditches, the tules and the aftermath of the oat and barley crops were burned—along with a little more of the combustible peat soil every year. We flood-irrigated when the water came in spring, drained in late March, and planted in a 24-hour-a-day frenzy which began around April 25 and ended—with luck—by the 10th of May, just as leaves on the Lombardy poplar were breaking from their buds. We summered out cattle on more than a million acres of Taylor Grazing Land across the high lava rock and sagebrush desert out east of the valley, miles of territory where we owned most of what water there was, and it was ours. We owned it all, or so we felt. The government was as distant as news on the radio.

The most intricate part of my job was called "balancing water," a night and day process of opening and closing pipes and redwood headgates and running the 18-inch drainage pumps. That system was the finest plaything I ever had.

And despite the mud and endless hours, the work remained play for a long time, the making of a thing both functional and elegant. We were doing God's labor and creating a good place on earth, living the pastoral yeoman dream— that's how our mythology defined it, although nobody would ever have thought to talk about work in that way.

And then it all went dead, over years, but swiftly.

You can imagine our surprise and despair, our sense of having been profoundly cheated. It took us a long while to realize some unnamable thing was wrong, and then we blamed it on ourselves, our inability to manage enough. But the fault wasn't ours, beyond the fact that we had all been educated to believe in a grand bad factory-land notion as our prime model of excellence.

We felt enormously betrayed. For so many years, through endless efforts, we had proceeded in good faith, and it turned out we had wrecked all we had not left untouched. The beloved migratory rafts of waterbirds, the green-headed mallards and the redheads and canvasbacks, the cinnamon teal and the great Canadian honkers, were mostly gone along with their swampland habitat. The hunting, in so many ways, was no longer what it had been.

We wanted to build a reservoir, and litigation started. Our laws were being used against us, by people who wanted a share of what we thought of as our water. We could not endure the boredom of our mechanical work, and couldn't hire anyone who cared enough to do it right. We baited the coyotes with 1080, and rodents destroyed our alfalfa; we sprayed weeds and insects with 2-4-D Ethyl and Malathion, and Parathion for clover mite, and we shortened our own lives.

In quite an actual way we had come to victory in the artistry of our play-ground warfare against all that was naturally alive in our native home. We had reinvented our valley according to the most persuasive ideal given us by our culture, and we ended with a landscape organized like a machine for growing crops and fattening cattle, a machine that creaked a little louder each year, a dreamland gone wrong.

One of my strongest memories comes from a morning when I was maybe 10 years old, out on the lawn before our country home in spring, beneath a bluebird sky. I was watching the waterbirds coming off the valley swamps and grain-fields where they had been feeding overnight. They were going north to nesting grounds on the Canadian tundra, and that piece of morning, inhabited by the sounds of their wings and their calling in the clean air, was wonder-filled and magical. I was enclosed in a living place.

No doubt that memory has persisted because it was a sight of possibility which I will always cherish—an image of the great good place rubbed smooth over the years like a river stone, which I touch again as I consider why life in Warner Valley went so seriously haywire. But never again in my lifetime will it be possible for a child to stand out on a bright spring morning in Warner Valley and watch the waterbirds come through in enormous, rafting vee-shaped flocks of thousands—and I grieve.

My father is a very old man. A while back we were driving up the Bitterroot Valley of Montana, and he was gazing away to the mountains. "They'll never see it the way we did," he said, and I wonder what he saw.

We shaped our piece of the West according to the model provided by our mythology, and instead of a great good place such order had given us enormous power over nature, and a blank perfection of fields.

· · ·

A mythology can be understood as a story that contains a set of implicit instructions from a society to its members, telling them what is valuable and how to conduct themselves if they are to preserve the things they value.

The teaching mythology we grew up with in the American West is a pastoral story of agricultural ownership. The story begins with a vast innocent continent, natural and almost magically alive, capable of inspiring us to reverence and awe, and yet savage, a wilderness. A good rural people come from the East, and they take the land from its native inhabitants, and tame it for agricultural purposes, bringing civilization: a notion of how to live embodied in law. The story is as old as invading armies, and at heart it is a racist, sexist, imperialist mythology of conquest; a rationale for violence—against other people and against nature.

At the same time, that mythology is a lens through which we continue to see ourselves. Many of us like to imagine ourselves as honest yeomen who sweat and work in the woods or the mines or the fields for a living. And many of us are. We live in a place where some vestige of the natural world still exists in working order. Many of us hold that natural world as sacred to some degree, just as it is in our myth. Lately, more and more of us are coming to understand our society in the American West as an exploited colony, threatened by greedy outsiders who want to take our sacred place away from us, or at least to strip and degrade it.

In short, we see ourselves as a society of mostly decent people who live with some connection to a holy wilderness, threatened by those who lust for power and property. We look for Shane to come riding out of the Tetons, and instead we see Exxon and the Sierra Club. One looks virtually as alien as the other.

And our mythology tells us we own the West, absolutely and morally—we own it because of our history. Our people brought law to this difficult place, they suffered and they shed blood and they survived, and they earned this land for us. Our efforts have surely earned us the right to absolute control over the thing we created. The myth tells us this place is ours, and will always be ours, to do with as we see fit.

That's a most troubling and enduring message, because we want to believe it, and we do believe it, so many of us, despite its implicit ironies and wrongheadedness, despite the fact that we took the land from someone else. We try to ignore a genocidal history of violence against the Native Americans.

In the American west we are struggling to revise our dominant mythology, and to find a new story to inhabit. Laws control our lives, and they are designed to preserve a model of society based on values learned from mythology. Only after re-imagining our myths can we coherently remodel our laws, and hope to keep our society in a realistic relationship to what is actual.

In Warner Valley we thought we were living the right lives, creating a great precise perfection of fields, and we found the mythology had been telling us an enormous lie. The world had proven too complex, or the myth too simple-minded. And we were mortally angered.

The truth is, we never owned all the land and water. We don't even own very much of them, privately. And we don't own anything absolutely or forever. As our society grows more and more complex and interwoven, our entitlement becomes less and less absolute, more and more likely to be legally diminished. Our rights to property will never take precedence over the needs of society. Nor should they, we all must agree in our grudging hearts. Ownership of property has always been a privilege granted by society, and revokable.

• • •

Down by the slaughterhouse my grandfather used to keep a chicken-wire cage for trapping magpies. The cage was as high as a man's head, and mounted on a sled so it could be towed off and cleaned. It worked on the same principle as a lobster trap. Those iridescent black-and-white birds could get in to feed on the intestines of butchered cows—we never butchered a fat heifer or steer for our own consumption, only aged dry cows culled from the breeding herd—but they couldn't get out.

Trapped under the noontime sun, the magpies would flutter around in futile exploration for a while, and then would give in to a great sullen presentiment of their fate, just hopping around picking at leftovers and waiting.

My grandfather was Scots-English, and a very old man by then, but his blue eyes never turned watery and lost. He was one of those cowmen we don't see so often anymore, heedless of most everthing outside his playground, which was livestock and seasons and property, and, as the seasons turned, more livestock and more property, a game which could be called accumulation.

All the notes were paid off, and you would have thought my grandfather would have been secure, and released to ease back in wisdom.

But no such luck. It seemed he had to keep proving his ownership. This took various forms, like endless litigation, which I have heard described as the sport of kings, but the manifestation I recall most vividly was that of killing magpies.

In the summer the ranch hands would butcher in the after-supper cool of an evening a couple of times a week. About once a week, when a number of magpies had gathered in the trap, maybe 10 or 15, my grandfather would get out his life-time 12-gauge shotgun and have someone drive him down to the slaughterhouse in his dusty, ancient gray Cadillac, so he could look over his catch and get down to the business at hand. Once there, the ritual was slow and dignified, and always inevitable as one shoe after another.

The old man would sit there a while in his Cadillac and gaze at the magpies with his merciless blue eyes, and the birds would stare back with their hard black eyes. The summer dust would settle around the Cadillac, and the silent confrontation would continue. It would last several minutes.

Then my grandfather would sigh, and swing open the door on his side of the Cadillac, and climb out, dragging his shotgun behind him, the pockets of his gray gabardine suit-coat like a frayed uniform bulging with shells. The stock of the shotgun had been broken sometime deep in the past, and it was wrapped with fine brass wire, which shone golden in the sunlight while the old man thumbed shells into the magazine. All this without saying a word.

In the ear of my mind I try to imagine the radio playing softly in the Cadillac, something like "Room Full of Roses" or "Candy Kisses," but there was no radio. There was just the ongoing hum of insects and the clacking of the mechanism as the old man pumped a shell into the firing chamber.

He would lift the shotgun, and from no more than 12 feet sighting down that barrel where the bluing was mostly worn off, through the chicken wire into the eyes of those trapped magpies, he would kill them one by one, taking his time, maybe so as to prove that this was no accident.

He would fire and there would be a minor explosion of blood and feathers, the huge booming of the shotgun echoing through the flattening light of early afternoon, off the sage-covered hills and down across the hay meadows and the sloughs lined with dagger-leafed willow, frightening great flights of blackbirds from the fence lines nearby, to rise in flocks and wheel and be gone.

"Bastards," my grandfather would mutter, and then he would take his time about killing another, and finally he would be finished and turn without looking back, and climb into his side of the Cadillac, where the door still stood open. Whoever it was whose turn it was that day would drive him back up the willow-lined lane through the meadows to the ranch house beneath the Lombardy poplar, to the cool shaded living room with its faded linoleum where the old man would finish out his day playing pinochle with my grandmother and anyone else he could gather, sometimes taking a break to retune a favorite program on the Zenith Trans-Oceanic radio.

No one in our family, so far as I ever heard, knew any reason why the old man had come to hate magpies with such specific intensity in his old age. The blackbirds were endlessly worse, the way they would mass together in flocks of literally thousands, to strip and thrash in his oat and barley field, and then feed all fall in the bins of grain stockpiled to fatten his cattle.

"Where is the difference?" I asked him once, about the magpies.

"Because they're mine," he said. I never did know exactly what he was talking about, the remnants of entrails left over from the butchering of culled stocker cows, or the magpies. But it became clear he was asserting his absolute lordship over both, and over me, too, so long as I was living on his property. For all his life and most of mine the notion of property as absolute seemed like law, even when it never was.

Most of us who grew up owning land in the West believed that any impairment or our right to absolute control of that property was a taking, forbidden by the so-called "taking clause" of the Constitution. We believed regulation of our property rights could never legally reduce the value of our property. After all, what was the point of ownership if it was not profitable? Any infringement on the control of private property was a communist perversion.

But all over the West, as in all of America, the old folkway of property as an absolute right is dying. Our mythology doesn't work anymore.

We find ouselves weathering a rough winter of discontent, snared in the uncertainties of a transitional time and urgently yearning to inhabit a story that might bring sensible order to our lives—even as we know such a story can only evolve through an almost literally infinite series of recognitions of what, individually, we hold sacred. The liberties our people came seeking are more and more constrained, and here in the West, as everywhere, we hate it.

Simple as that. And we have to live with it. There is no more running away to territory. This is it, for most of us. We have no choice but to live in community. If we're lucky we may discover a story that teaches us to abhor our old romance with conquest and possession.

My grandfather died in 1958, toppling out of his chair at the pinochle table, soon after I came back to Warner, but his vision dominated our lives until we sold the ranch in 1967. An ideal of absolute ownership that defines family as property is the perfect device for driving people away from one another. There was a rule in our family. "What's good for the property is good for you."

"Every time there was more money we bought land," my grandmother proclaimed after learning my grandfather had been elected to the Cowboy Hall of Fame. I don't know if she spoke with pride or bitterness, but I do know that, having learned to understand love as property, we were all absolutely divided at the end; relieved to escape amid a litany of divorce and settlements, our family broken in the getaway.

I cannot grieve for my grandfather. It is hard to imagine, these days, that any man could ever again think he owns the birds.

• • •

Thank the Lord there were other old men involved in my upbringing. My grandfather on my mother's side ran away from a Germanic farmstead in Wisconsin the year he was fourteen, around 1900, and made his way to Butte. "I was lucky," he would say. "I was too young to go down in the mines, so they put me to sharpening steel."

Seems to me such a boy must have been lucky to find work at all, wandering the teeming difficult streets of the most urban city in the American West. "Well no," he said. "They put you to work. It wasn't like that. They were good to me in Butte. They taught me a trade. That's all I did was work. But it didn't hurt me any."

After most of ten years on the hill—broke and on strike, still a very young man—he rode the rails south to the silver mines in what he called "Old Mexico," and then worked his way back north through the mining country of Nevada in time for the glory days in Goldfield and Rhyolite and Tonopah. At least those are the stories he would tell. "This Las Vegas," he would say. "When I was there you could have bought it all for a hundred and fifty dollars. Cost you ten cents for a drink of water."

To my everlasting sadness, I never really quizzed him on the facts. Now I look at old photographs of those mining camps, and wonder. It's difficult for me to imagine the good gentle man I knew walking those tough dusty streets. He belonged, at least in those Butte days, to the International Brotherhood of Blacksmiths and Helpers. I still have his first dues card. He was initiated July 11, 1904, and most of the months of 1904 and 1905 are stamped, DUES PAID.

• • •

Al died in an old folks' home in Eugene, Oregon. During the days of his last summer, when he knew the jig was up, a fact he seemed to regard with infallible good humor, we would sit in his room and listen to the aged bemused woman across the hall chant her litany of childhood, telling herself that she was somebody and still real.

It was always precisely the same story, word by particular word. I wondered then how much of it was actual, lifting from some deep archive in her memory, and now I wonder how much of it was pure sweet invention, occasioned by the act of storytelling and by the generative, associative power of language. I cannot help but think of ancient fires, light flickering on the faces of children and storytellers detailing the history of their place in the scheme of earth.

The story itself started with a screen-door slamming and her mother yelling at her when she was a child coming out from the back porch of a white house, and rotting apples on the ground under the trees in the orchard, and a dog which snapped at the flies. "Mother," she would exclaim in exasperation, "I'm fine."

The telling took about three minutes, and she told it like a story for grandchildren. "That's nice," she would say to her dog. "That's nice."

Then she would lapse into quiet, rewinding herself, seeing an old time when the world contained solace enough to seem complete, and she would start over again, going on until she had lulled herself back into sleep. I would wonder if she was dreaming about that dog amid the fallen apples, snapping at flies and yellowjackets.

At the end she would call the name of that dog over and over in a quavering, beseeching voice—and my grandfather would look to me from his bed and his eyes would be gleaming with laughter, such an old man laughing painfully, his shoulders shaking, and wheezing.

"Son of a bitch," he would whisper, when she was done calling the dog again, and he would wipe the tears from his face with the sleeve of his hospital gown. *Son of a bitch.* He would look to me again, and other than aimless grinning acknowledgment that some mysterious thing was truly funny, I wouldn't know what to do, and then he would look away to the open window, beyond which a far-off lawn mower droned, like this time he was the one who was embarrassed. Not long after that he was dead, and so was the old woman across the hall.

"Son of a bitch," I thought, when we were burying Al one bright afternoon in Eugene, and I found myself suppressing laughter. Maybe it was just a way of ditching my grief for myself, who did not know him well enough to really understand what he thought was funny. I have Al's picture framed on my wall, and I can still look to him and find relief from the old insistent force of my desire to own things. His laughter is like a gift.

QUESTIONS FOR "OWNING IT ALL" BY WILLIAM KITTREDGE

Talking About the Text

1. Notice that the author of this text begins several times before he finally ends his essay. Each new narrative provides another opportunity for him to probe his subject, the mythologies of the West. Why do you

think Kittredge wrote his essay in this manner? What sorts of effects does this essay's structure have on you as a reader? Are there any advantages to this method of essay organization? Any disadvantages?

2. In this essay, Kittredge focuses on the traditional mythology of the West, a mythology that Kittredge explains as follows:

> Our mythology tells us we own the West, absolutely and morally—we own it because of our history. Our people brought law to this difficult place, they suffered and they shed blood and they survived, and they earned this land for us. Our efforts have surely earned us the right to absolute control over the things we created. This myth tells us this place is ours, and will always be ours, to do with as we see fit.

How is Kittredge using the term *mythology* in this essay? Why is this mythology of the West important enough for Kittredge to devote his time to it? What are some of the concerns that Kittredge has about this traditional mythology of the West?

3. Kittredge tells a story of his grandfather's shooting magpies after they have been trapped. What is the significance of this story? What is the difference between the magpies before they are trapped and after they are trapped?

4. Kittredge contrasts one of his grandfathers with the other. What point is Kittredge trying to make by making this contrast?

Exploring Issues

1. William Kittredge, who describes himself as an "agricultural manager," says, "[I] saw myself helping to turn the fertile homeplace of my childhood into a machine for agriculture." What are some of the implications of viewing agriculture (or the land) as a "machine"? How does this view of agriculture differ from that of Amish farmers, as described by Wendell Berry in "Seven Amish Farms"? How does this attitude toward nature (as object) differ from that of the Navajo, as described by Peter MacDonald in "Navajo Natural Resources"?

2. Kittredge suggests that a new mythology of the West is needed. What form do you think this new mythology would take if Kittredge could create it? Is it likely that a new mythology will develop or is already developing? What changes in values are needed for a new mythology to emerge?

Writing Assignments

1. Consider the three views of nature presented by Peter MacDonald ("Navajo Natural Resources"), Wendell Berry ("Seven Amish Farms") and William Kittredge. Write an essay in which you contrast these three views of nature. Note both similarities and differences in your contrastive analysis.

2. Write an essay in which you trace the development of Kittredge's thinking about nature. Use paraphrase, summary, and quotations to support
your analysis. Describe Kittredge's earlier views of nature, and then
explain how and why his ideas change.

Reading 33

Navajo Natural Resources

Peter MacDonald

Peter MacDonald is a past chairperson of the Navajo Tribal Council of the
Navajo nation. In his essay below, MacDonald addresses the subject of
Native American land and resources in the context of the Navajo, who have
managed to maintain a large land base with abundant energy resources. This
essay was originally published in a volume of essays, edited by Christopher
Vecsey and Roberta W. Venabla, entitled *American Indian Environments:
Ecological Issues in Native American History.*

As I prepared this chapter, I received word from the tribal lawyer that the state
of Arizona just passed a law that would put all water litigation into state courts
rather than federal courts. The Navajo position is that we have a better chance
fighting for our water rights in federal courts than state courts because states
really have their own self-interest in mind when you go into state court. State
people being what they are, they decided to pass a law. But the governor has
not yet signed it, so what we want to do is file our suit for water rights in
Colorado before the governor signs it and file it in federal court so that at least
we may beat them to the punch before their act becomes law. It's that sort of a
battle all the time.

There is a story about an easterner who went down west and got to Muskogee, Oklahoma, which always likes to pride itself as the Indian capital of the
world. The man got to the train station and got out of the train, looking around
wanting to see Indians and saw a big giant of a man standing right there. A
fellow tourist nudged him in the side and said, "Say, where are the Indians?"

And this big man standing there dressed in a three-piece suit looked down at the tourist and said "I'm an Indian," The tourist looked up and said, "You're an Indian? Where's your feathers?" And the Indian said, "It's molting season."

So it is, I guess, molting season for some of us.

I went to school in Muskogee—Bacome Junior College. And from there I went to the University of Oklahoma, not because it's a great institution of higher learning but because the years I went there Bud Wilkinson was the football coach, and they had the number one football team in the nation. I just love football, and I thought that would be a good way to see football for at least three or four years. I graduated there as an electrical engineer and went to work for Howard Hughes in Culver City, California. I worked for him for six and a half years and then returned to the Navajo reservation and eventually became chairman of the nation.

I am an engineer by trade—an electrical engineer. Now I'm a human engineer. When I first took office in 1971 on the Navajo nation, I received a call from NASA from Houston, and they asked if they could bring their astronauts to the reservation to practice the moon mission that was scheduled for them the next month. It was an Apollo 15 mission, Jim Urwin and David Scott. The reason they wanted to do this is that the southwestern portion of the Navajo reservation resembled very much the terrain and the location where the astronauts were going to land. So I said yes; they came up, the invited, myself, and a few of the tribal leaders, and we watched them.

They actually set up a mock space capsule, a landing craft, right on the reservation. They had full communication equipment, communicating with Houston all the time, and the two astronauts had their space suits and helmets on. They actually went through the motions as they would on the moon, getting off the landing craft down on the ground and getting on the moon buggy and riding around. And while they were doing this, an old Navajo medicine man showed up, and he asked me, "What are these two funny looking fellows doing here on the reservation?" They had the space suits on, and I said these two fellows are going to the moon next month and the medicine man said, "Is that right?" I said yes.

He said, "You know in our legend, Navajo legend, the Navajos were on the moon once on their way to the sun." He said, if these two guys are going to the moon mext month, he'd like to send a message, maybe there are some Navajos still there on the moon. So I didn't say very much until the astronauts came back, and they were very pleased to see the medicine man, and then I told the astronauts what the medicine man wanted to do. And, of course, Jim Urwin said, yes, have him write it on a piece of paper and if we run into some Navajos we'll deliver the message. I said Navajo is not a written language. "Well," he said, "that's all right, here's a tape recorder, have him put it on tape, and if we run into some Navajos on the moon we'll play the tape for them." So I told this to the medicine man and he said OK. So the astronauts went back out to do some more work, and I turned the tape recorder on and the medicine man taped his message and stuck around a little bit and then went home.

Later on in the day the astronauts came in, and we had some refreshments and Jim Urwin said, "Did the medicine man tape a message?" I said yes, well let's listen to it. So I turned it on, but of course the message was in Navajo. Urwin asked, "What is he saying?" And I said, "He says, beware of these two fellows, they will want to make a treaty with you."

The Navajo nation represents about 160,000 individuals, and we are growing at 2 percent net each year. The Navajo reservation is in three states, New Mexico, Arizona, and Utah. It's a large land area representing about 18 million acres, or twenty-four thousand square miles. It's about the size of the state of West Virginia or the size of Connecticut, Massachusetts, Rhode Island, Delaware, and Vermont all put together. That's the size of the Navajo nation. We have a treaty with the United States. The treaty was executed back in 1868 after Colonel Kit Carson was successful in rounding up the Navajos. We were marched 300 miles east into New Mexico, to Bosque Redondo and Fort Sumner where we were imprisoned for four and a half years after they couldn't handle the Navajos in terms of civilizing us or making us farmers or whatever they wanted to do with us. They decided to make a treaty with us. So the treaty of 1868 is the treaty between the Navajo nation and the United States government, and to date that is the basis of our relationship with the federal government.

Often easterners, sociologists, and politicians have a great deal of difficulty in understanding what the United States' or a state's relationship is with the Indians. A lot of them feel that the United States' relationship with Indians is more like the United States' relationship with the blacks, Chicanos, or other minorities. This is not so. Sovereignty no doubt is something that really no one agrees upon as to what it means or how it should be applied with respect to the government's relationship with the Indian tribes. We the Indians feel that sovereignty implies dealings with other nations. We fought the Germans, the Japanese. We conquered them, but we left them their sovereignty. By treaty we only took away what we thought would be appropriate for their existence and survival. The same applies with Indians who have treaties with the United States. We maintain that we had sovereignty; we were nations before we were conquered, and treaty provisions took away a certain degree of our sovereignty but not all of our sovereignty. And some of the provisions of the treaty state that in return for giving up the land, the United States would do this, this, this, and this forever. So in that sense, the United States' obligation, and the obligation of future generations is not based upon the fact that Indians are poor. Yes, indeed, we are poor. As a matter of fact we share in everything that the United States has—we have our share of poverty. But the thing that I want to come to is the issue of all the assistance going to the Indians. I'd like to make it as simple as possible. It probably isn't that simple. But suppose your grandmother had something that was very valuable and I wanted it. By whatever method I made an agreement with your grandmother and I want that something that she had. And I say, if you would give me that thing that you have I'll agree that I'll take care of you, your children and their children forever regarding their educational needs, their health needs, and their economic needs. And your grandma and grandpa got rid of whatever they had that I wanted. They gave it to me, and I put my thumb print on and they signed it. And now my obligation to your father and your grandfather and to you and your children, their children from here on out would be that I'll always provide them with adequate education and see to their health needs and their economic well-being. It doesn't matter whether everyone of you have become millionaires or not. A deal is a deal. That's the way you would look at. Well, treaties with Indians are the same way.

The treaties exist. For instance, the Navajo had more than 50 million acres of land that they ceded in exchange for a small portion. In return there were certain guarantees that were made forever. That's what the treaty says, not ninety days, but forever. So on that basis, we have this relationship with the federal government.

Now, regarding the natural resources that the Indian tribes have and how we look at these resources and also the impact they have on our environment: let me talk about the Navajo first. The Navajo nation has more than 5 billion tons of coal on the reservation, and we produce on an annual basis more than 13 million tons a year and most of it is being strip mined. We also produce 12 million barrels of oil per year. We produce 30 million cubic feet of natural gas a year and about a million pounds of uranium ore per year now, and that's projected to go as high as 15 million pounds of uranium ore. That's not johnny cake. We have about 500 thousand acres of timber on the Navajo reservation, and we have now in production about 50 million board feet of lumber each year. We have rights to the Colorado River and Little Colorado River, San Juan River. I already told you that our land base has shrunk from 50 million to 18 million acres.

There are other tribes who have these energy resources. In 1975 I formed an organization called Council of Energy Resource Tribes, CERT. There are twenty-five tribes represented in this organization. Most all of them are west of Mississippi. They all have one thing in common. They all have energy resources in production on their reservations, coal, uranium, oil, and gas. These twenty-five tribes together have on their reservations better than 50 percent of all known uranium reserves in the United States, more than 30 percent of the self-strippable coal west of the Mississippi, 10 percent of all coal reserves in America, and 3 percent of oil and gas production in the United States. These are substantial holdings. Since there was a national energy crunch, since the United States wants to become energy independent, and since we have a substantial amount of the energy reserves, we wanted to become a part of their nation's goal to become energy independent. I have written to the federal agencies and the president. I said that we, the twenty-five tribes who have these energy resources, want to be involved at the highest level with respect to energy policy making, regulations, and programs on the short and long-range basis that will affect America and certainly will affect those of us who have these energy resources.

Since I was not getting any response at all, I then approached whomever I felt would give us some assistance, because with all these resources in our hands we did not have the necessary technical expertise to program what we would do with these resources. Certainly we don't want to repeat what has happened in the past when our trustee, the federal government, through the Department of

Interior and Bureau of Indian Affairs negotiated for many of these mineral resources on our behalf at such ridiculous and unconscionable prices in returns to the Navajo nation.

To give an example, on the Black Mesa Peabody Coal mining operation, the Bureau of Indian Affairs of the federal government negotiated back in the early 1960s on the Navajo nation's behalf. For the exploration and mining of that coal which belonged to the Navajo, the Navajo would get fifteen cents per ton for the coal mined on the Navajo reservation forever as long as the coal shall last. At the same time, the United Mine Workers negotiated a union contract with Peabody for the operation on Black Mesa and received in their contract sixty cents per ton for the coal mined on the Navajo reservation on an escalating basis depending on the cost of living. Yet the Navajo, the owners, were receiving 15 cents a ton forever no matter what the inflation rate was. Those were the kinds of contracts that we had in our hands, and we didn't want it repeated. There were hardly any reclamation provisions. There were hardly any provisions for people who would be relocated because of the project. There was absolutely nothing regarding air pollution and water pollution, depletion of water. So the twenty-five tribes that I have organized decided to go out somewhere and get some help.

The first thing that came to my mind was the OPEC nations because they and the Indian tribes have similar situations. They were dealing with the same companies that we were dealing with: Exxon, Texaco, Philips Petroleum, Standard Oil. So I made contact with the OPEC nations to see what they knew about the companies and to see if we could exchange some ideas as to how together we might deal with these same outfits that were seemingly exploiting us. The OPEC nations were in similar positions some years back, and now they are appreciating their depleting resources, and we want to do the same thing. The minute I did that, news went across the nation that the Indians are going to join the OPEC nations and how terrible for Indians to do that; here we were nice to them and being gracious to them in every way, how ungrateful of them to go to the OPEC nations, our enemies. That's what the editorial pages across the country were saying. The Indians are unpatriotic, MacDonald is unpatriotic. Well, that's not the case. As I said, the reason we want some help with our resources is to make sure that we do not make the same mistake that was made on our behalf by our trustee.

What are some of the mistakes? One of the mistakes was this. The Navajo nation has had oil and gas in production for the last thirty years. Those early contracts were made on our behalf by the federal government, as I said. For example, last year we had to shut down several oil fields, simply because the oil companies were constantly going across our land as though they owned it. We had many women and children herding sheep and cattle out in those areas. Well, the oil companies disregarded this. Oil workers shot at the sheep and cattle. In some cases they just drove by, caught a goat, and butchered it right in front of the Navajo owners. They let oil they were pumping run down into our water. They ran after young Navajo women. The companies were Conoco, Texaco, Superior Oil, and Philips Petroleum. We stopped twenty-three thousand barrels a day until a new agreement could be reached to protect the people, the environment, and the land.

Another problem is two power plants which are on Navajo land and expel sulphur dioxide into the air: 120 million pounds of sulphur dioxide per year. The Navajo nation decided to require that the pollution be reduced to one million pounds per year. The utility company filed lawsuits in Arizona, New Mexico, and Utah saying the Navajo have no right to make such laws. They also said that it would bankrupt them to pay the fines we Navajo intended to impose if the pollution continued: ten cents per pound the first year, to seventy-five cents per pound at the end of five years. We wanted the company to put in scrubbers which have already been invented and already exist. We also have problems with the reclamation of lands that have been strip mined for their coal. Many of these issues are still in litigation.

Today radiation has been found in the tailings of the uranium mines on Navajo land. Several deaths have been attributed to this because the workers and local people were not protected. The mines let wash-off of yellowcake into the water of our people and our livestock. So this has brought in CERT for a better deal. Ten uranium producers will soon meet with me to resolve this problem.

I would like to explain a major problem regarding the economic development of the Navajo nation, for all Indian people. We have land and other resources. But we have never been given a fair market value for these resources. By fair market value I mean the highest price possible arrived at within a reasonable time, willingly agreed to by both buyer and seller. There has never been a fair market price set for Indians' resources. Your government says "sale." We say "condemnation." Condemnation is the alternative to a fair market value. I would like to make three propositions:

1. Indians have never received a fair market value for their resources.
2. Indians are not receiving fair market values now.
3. Indians *cannot*—ever—receive fair market value.

The reasons for these circumstances are many. First, the United States government has no understanding of Navajo values, values which to us would be part of determining what would be a fair market value. Furthermore, our resources are never put on the open market. We must deal with the supervision of the United States government. Indian resources can never be offered to all bidders, like the United Nations, or the Organization of American States, or the World Bank. American industries making airplanes are not in an open market either, but they get a better deal than Indians.

There is also the fact that in Indian dealings there is no absence of compulsion or duress. These are exerted upon us by the government and others. Finally, because Indians must deal through the United States government, Indians never know the buyers' needs. We don't have economic or social projections. We have one lawyer, the companies have thirty lawyers. That's not the white people's fault, though. These are facts of life, so we Indians must learn to understand this. We have done this in the past. In the early 1920s United States government officials came to one of our council meetings. After some time, an elder got up and spoke to the visitors: "You will forgive me if I tell you that we are not afraid of our trails."

To put the issue of fair market value in perspective, take my word, we are loyal Americans who care—in the past, however, we know that we had lax immigration laws and shaky border patrols! Now, all we want is to hold on to what was left to us. My people must go beyond subsistence and survival through economic development. In the future we must have self-sufficiency based on using our resources to serve future generations. This means we must be conservationists and find a balance of all life. This we will do because of our religious concepts, our traditions—our nation's relationship to our land. It is holy land. Non-Indians do not understand our view of our sacred land. But you understand Jerusalem. Would you put a price on Israel? No. Our sacred land is watched over by our Sky Father and our Earth Mother. It is not subject to partition. Some things are not for sale.

While we ask you to respect our beliefs, we appreciate the American dream you have, and we are patriotic to the United States. During the wars of the twentieth century, including the recent Vietnam War, our youth served—and during Vietnam only non-Indian youth, not our youth, protested.

For better or worse, we are bound up in the same future. The United States can't win respect around the globe if it is not respected internally.

We Navajo understand your needs for energy resources. You should understand our needs. We should have a reciprocal agreement that national need is not biased. Our Navajo land is not the most expendable. Our land can provide solar and wind energy. But we also have a culture on that land which we want to preserve. We ask you to seek your own alternatives.

We are vulnerable. We may win a scrimmage with your government now and then, and some non-Indians panic. But we know what the stakes are. In 1864 after destroying our homes and crops, United States troops drove us off our lands—rounded us up and marched us from the Canyon de Chelly in Arizona, to the desolate Bosque Redondo of New Mexico—the Long Walk of the Navajo. In 1868 we were finally allowed to return. Exile and expropriation has been our fate in the past. We know we can be rounded up again.

QUESTIONS FOR "NAVAJO NATURAL RESOURCES" BY PETER MACDONALD

Talking About the Text

1. Whom does Peter MacDonald address this essay to? Which issues and/or people is he responding to? How can you make this judgement? How would you describe MacDonald's stance toward his readers?

2. At the beginning of this essay, MacDonald tells two humorous stories—one about Indian feathers and another about the old medicine man. Why do you think that MacDonald does this? What does he gain rhetorically by using humor?

3. At several points in this essay, MacDonald uses the pronouns *you* and *your;* for example, "But suppose your grandmother had something valuable. . . ." and "I have already told you that our land base has shrunk from 50 million to 18 million acres." What rhetorical purpose is served by this author's use of *you* and *your?* How do you feel when you read these words in this text?

Exploring Issues

1. If a treaty was made with an Indian nation before a natural resource such as coal or oil is found on reservation land, should the Indian nation have full ownership and control of the natural resource or does the U.S. government have a right to partial or total control of that resource? How did you arrive at your decision?
2. What is the Indian perspective on land, and how does that differ from the views of other cultures, such as the Western mythology discussed by William Kittredge? How could these different views lead to misunderstanding and conflict?

Writing Assignments

1. Write a personal essay in which you explore what you know already about Native Americans and how you came to this knowledge. Consider the possibility that you may hold some stereotypical ideas about this group of people, and consider the source of those stereotypes.
2. Read Ted Gup's "Owl vs. Man" and compare the philosophical perspective of some environmentalists with the Indian perspective on the land. Consider both the similarities and the differences between these two groups' attitudes toward nature and the land.

Reading 34

Owl vs. Man

Ted Gup

Ted Gup is a professional writer whose work has appeared in such publications as the *Washington Post* and *Time* magazine. He has won several awards for journalism, including the George Polk award for national reporting, the Worth Bingham award for investigative reporting, and the Gerald Loeb award for business and financial reporting. Gup has also been a finalist for the Pulitzer prize. The following essay is one of several on the environment by Gup that *Time* has published—Gup's "The Ivory Trail" was the cover story for *Time*'s October 16, 1989, issue, and the following essay appeared as the cover story for the June 25, 1990, issue. In it, Gup addresses the conflict between the loggers and the timber industry on the one hand and the environmentalists on the other. Although Gup's essay has the appearance of a fairly neutral analysis, Gup actually embeds his own point of view in his discussion of the issues.

What would the world
  be, once bereft
Of wet and of
  wildness? Let
  them be left,
O let them be left,
  wildness and wet;
Long live the weeds
  and the wilderness yet.

   —"Inversnaid," by Gerard Manley Hopkins; *Poems* (1876–89)

In Oregon's Umpqua National Forest, a lumberjack presses his snarling chain saw into the flesh of a Douglas fir that has held its place against wind and fire, rockslide and flood, for 200 years. The white pulpy fiber scatters in a plume beside him, and in 90 seconds, 4 ft. of searing steel have ripped through the thick bark, the thin film of living tissue and the growth rings spanning ages. With an excruciating groan, all 190 ft. of trunk and green spire crash to earth. When the cloud of detritus and needles settles, the ancient forest of the Pacific Northwest has retreated one more step. Tree by tree, acre by acre, it falls, and with it vanishes the habitat of innumerable creatures. None among these creatures is more vulnerable than the northern spotted owl, a bird so docile it will descend from the safety of its lofty bough to take a mouse from the hand of a man.

The futures of the owl and the ancient forest it inhabits have become entwined in a common struggle for survival. Man's appetite for timber threatens to consume much of the Pacific Northwest's remaining wilderness, an ecological frontier whose deep shadows and jagged profile are all that remain of the land as it was before the impact of man. But rescuing the owl and the timeless forest may mean barring the logging industry from many tracts of virgin timberland, and that would deliver a jarring economic blow to scores of timber-dependent communities across Washington, Oregon and Northern California. For generations, lumberjacks and millworkers there have relied on the seemingly endless bounty of the woodlands to sustain them and a way of life that is as rich a part of the American landscape as the forest itself. For many, all that may be coming to an end.

This week the U.S. Fish and Wildlife Service is expected to announce whether it will list the northern spotted owl as a threatened species. If the owl is listed, as many predict, the Government will be required by the Endangered Species Act to protect the bird. And if a preservation plan advocated by biologists is put into effect, it could be one of the most sweeping environmental actions ever undertaken. Federal and state agencies say the plan, fully carried out, would set aside an additional 3 million acres of forests. That would slash by more than one-third timber production on federal lands, which accounts for nearly 40% of the region's total harvest. The possible result: mill closings and cutbacks costing 30,000 jobs over the next decade. Real estate prices would tumble, and states and counties that depend on shares of the revenue from timber sales on federal land could see those funds plummet. Oregon would be hardest hit, losing hundreds of millions of dollars in revenue, wages and salaries, say state officials. By decade's end the plan could cost the U.S. Treasury $229 million in lost timber money each year.

All this to protect an owl that stands barely 2 ft. tall and weighs 22 oz. Granted, it is one of the most regal birds of the forest, with its chocolate-color plumage, dappled with white spots, and its enormous eyes, like onyx cabochons, scouring the forest for prey. A fine bird, yes, but it was never really the root cause of this great conflict.

More than a contest for survival between a species and an industry, the owl battle is an epic confrontation between fundamentally different philosophies about the place of man in nature. At issue: Are the forests—and by extension, nature itself—there for man to use and exploit, or are they to be revered and preserved? How much wilderness does America need? How much human discomfort can be justified in the name of conservation? In the Pacific Northwest the nation's reinvigorated environmental movement is about to collide head on with economic reality. What happens here will shape the outcome of similar conflicts between ecological and economic concerns for years to come. It will also enhance or diminish U.S. credibility overseas, as America tries to influence other nations to husband their natural resources and protect their endangered species. From Brazil to Japan, the decision will be carefully observed. The stakes are that high.

Environmentalists claim that talk of an economic doomsday is wildly exaggerated and is intended to whip up popular opposition to conservation efforts that threaten industry profits. The skeptics question figures coming from those federal agencies—the U.S. Forest Service and Bureau of Land Management— that lease timber rights on public lands and have long been seen as being cozy with the logging industry. Privately, some agency officials concede that the dire economic forecasts were rushed and based on shaky assumptions. Still, they have bolstered industry's attack on the owl-preservation plan and fueled community fears. Already there are signs that those agencies, under directions from the White House, may try to scale down the plan urged by biologists. A joint Forest Service-BLM study indicates that the very fabric holding some communities together would unravel if the biologists' plan were fully implemented. "In severe cases of community dysfunction," says the report, "increased rates of domestic disputes, divorce, acts of violence, delinquency, vandalism, suicide, alcoholism and other social problems are to be expected."

In many ways, however, the owl dispute merely hastened an inevitable crisis facing the Pacific Northwest. For decades, the timber industry, driven by the nation's voracious housing needs, leveled private and public land for timber with little regard for long-term consequences. "We've been running an ecological deficit, and the bill has come in," says Jerry Franklin, a research scientist with the Forest Service. "There's going to be pain for owls, for people and for trees." The industry's reforestation practices have markedly improved over the past decade, but the reinvestment is too little too late.

The life cycle of the Pacific Northwest's primeval woodlands is measured not in decades but in centuries. No amount of saplings and science can make up for years of wanton harvesting, or replace a thousand-year-old fir. Only time can do that—and time may be short for those mills that are specially designed to devour the old firs. The owners eye the forests hungrily, knowing they cannot wait for the millions of seedlings and young trees to mature. If the industry is allowed to keep cutting, some forestry experts say, the last ancient forests outside wilderness areas could fall within 30 years. Thus many mills may be forced to close no matter what. Owl or no owl, the timber industry faces a painful conversion from its dependence on giant old-growth trunks to smaller trees in reforested stands.

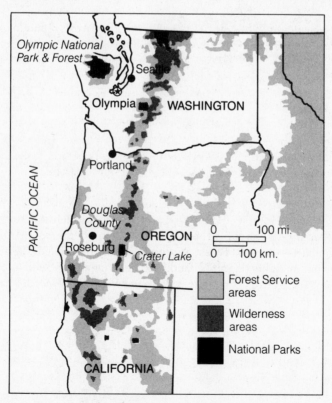

Already the old growth has all but vanished from private lands. Most of the remaining great trees are in areas under federal control, administered primarily by the Forest Service. Many Americans believe these lands are all included in the national parks, and that the U.S. Forest Service is a gentle custodian of the woodlands. Except in certain protected wilderness areas, that is not so. The Forest Service and BLM, which oversee the public lands, are empowered to sell timber rights to the highest bidder, and sell they have—a staggering 5 billion board feet a year, sweeping away 70,000 acres of old-growth forest annually. What is grown in its stead is not forest but "fiber," as the timber industry refers to wood.

One can grasp the distinction by looking out from any one of a thousand promontories in the Northwest. Clear-cutting—the indiscriminate leveling of every tree in an area—has left the wilderness fragmented and scarred. Long after the last truck has pulled out, heavy with logs, and the debris has been torched, what remains is a blackened earth, pockmarked and studded with tombstone-like stumps. "Its looks like Alamogordo, as if it's been nuked, concedes Dan Schindler, a Forest Service district ranger.

Though the timber industry has zealously replanted over the past two decades, the hallmark of old growth, biodiversity, has been lost. Gone are the broken-topped dead trees or "snags" favored by owl, osprey and pileated woodpecker. Gone the multilayered canopies and rich understory, the scattering of hemlock, incense cedar and sugar pine. Gone the centuries-old firs in their noble dotage. Increasingly, the forests have been transmogrified into tree farms of numbing uniformity, countless ankle-high seedlings and spindly saplings germinated from seeds selected for their productive capacity. The logging operations have tattered the seamless fabric of old growth that once covered the land. "There are more holes in the blanket than there is blanket," laments BLM biologist Frank Oliver. According to the National Audubon Society, each year enough old-growth trees are taken from the Pacific Northwest to fill a convoy of trucks 20,000 miles long.

"The landscape has been so transformed by ignorance, arrogance and greed that those who must prove their case are not those who call for forest protection, but those who call for business as usual," says Richard Brown of the National Wildlife Federation. Less than 10% of the ancient forest that once covered the Northwest remains. From Alaska to British Columbia to Oregon, forests that predate the 13 Colonies are being sacrificed for plywood, planks and pulp. The rapidity with which these primeval stands are being cut down has driven a handful of environmental extremists to sabotage timber-industry equipment, tie themselves to trees slated for harvesting and booby-trap trees with buried spikes that can mangle saws or injure unwary cutters.

All this bewilders timber-industry leaders, who say there are plenty of owls, plus abundant old-growth stands set aside in wilderness areas, that are safe from the saw. In Oregon about half the state's estimated 3 million acres of old growth cannot be logged because it is unsuitable or designated as wilderness. But that leaves 1.5 million acres of old growth that can be cut. Some of these areas contain no owls and are not likely to be protected.

How much ancient forest is enough? The question is not just one of aesthetics or recreational adequacy. No one knows how much forest is needed to sustain an intricate and little understood ecosystem upon which animals and plants, and, yes, man too, depend. What is known is that the old growth plays an integral role in regulating water levels and quality, cleaning the air, enhancing the productivity of fisheries and enriching the stability and character of the soil. "We're probably just on the edge in terms of our understanding," says Eric Forsman, a biologist with the Forest Service. "If we continue pell-mell down the path of eliminating these old forests, we'll never have the opportunity to learn because they won't be there to study." He and others have come to believe that where science ends, the mystery that is the ancient forest begins.

To understand what is at stake in human terms, it helps to visit a community that depends on timber for its existence. Take Oregon's Douglas County, which, like the fir, is named for the Scottish botanist David Douglas. Oregon produces more lumber than any other state, and Douglas County boasts that it is the timber capital of the world. It stretches from the Cascades in the east to the Pacific Ocean on the west. There one can tune in to Timber Radio KTBR, feel the roads tremble beneath logging trucks and watch children use Lego sets to haul sticks out of imaginary forests. In the current struggle, Douglas County is ground zero, likely to take as direct an economic hit as any site in the region. "Something is going to happen in the next few months that will rip the rug right out from under us," says Lonnie Burson, who works in a sawmill and presides over the union, Local 2949, that represents 3,400 lumber- and millworkers.

The controversy is on everyone's mind there, and the owl gets much of the blame. A banner headline in the local paper declared: SAVING SPOTTED OWL SEEN AS THREAT TO SCHOOLS. Douglas County may lose more than $13 million a year in timber revenue that the Federal Government returns to the county to help pay for public administration, roads and schools. At the local Ford dealership, the only owls that are welcomed are those made out of ceramic, which stand on the roofline warding off swallows intent on building nests under the eaves. Cars and trucks are not selling. Too much uncertainty. Says salesman Bruce Goetsch: "We survived without the dinosaur. What's the big deal about the owl?"

At Bud's Pub in Roseburg, a spotted owl hangs in effigy over the bar. Shops offer T shirts saying I LOVE SPOTTED OWLS . . . FRIED. And in the cabin of logger Bill Haire's truck, beneath the mirror, swings a tiny owl with an arrow through its head. "I can still maintain some sense of humor," says Haire. His father Tom, 65, works with him in the forest, and his son Brian, 12, hopes one day to join them there. "If it comes down to my family or that bird," says Haire, "that bird's going to suffer. Where would we be right now if everything that lived on this earth still survived—the saber-toothed tiger, the woolly mammoth? Things adapt or they become extinct." That applies to his industry as well, says Haire. "If we don't adapt, we'll become extinct."

The crisis has forced many in Douglas County to reappraise a life-style more precious now that it is endangered. Those who work in the woods can make $35,000 to $45,000 a year. Millworkers generally make less. But the issue is more than money. They have also been forced to re-examine themselves and the ecological legacy they have been left. Douglas County has always been dependent on natural resources, though it has not always used them prudently. In the 19th century, furriers killed off many of the furbearing animals and, in so doing, their trade as well. Later, prospectors emptied the rivers of gold, and the mining camps were reclaimed by the forest. Millworkers and their families often ask union leader Burson what will become of them. "What do I tell them, 'It's going to be O.K.'?" asks Burson. "I can't. Who do I blame? Do I blame the industry for raping the lands in the East and raping the lands in the West 50 years ago and not replanting? Do I blame my father? Do I blame my grandfather? Do I blame myself for not reading the paper every single night and being critically involved in these issues? How do I answer these people?"

Mill town after mill town is buried beneath an avalanche of contradictory statistics tossed out by timber-industry officials and environmentalists. "To put it bluntly, we don't know what the hell is going on," says Burson. "We're being blackmailed and threatened from both sides. Industry is saying 'Support our side, or you'll lose your jobs.' Environmentalists are saying 'Support our side, or you won't have clean air to breathe.' People are scared to death."

Many who draw their living from timber concede that the owl is not their only problem. Jobs have been lost to automation too. A Forest Service study predicts that technological changes will displace 13% of the work force during the next 15 years. The recession of 1980–82 also took its toll. Export of logs overseas, particularly to Japan and China, has reduced the work available for local mills. And high production costs for lumber and plywood make the region vulnerable to competition from the South and Canada.

Burson knows the little owl draws attention away from these complex problems, some of which the industry brought upon itself. And he suspects industry is exploiting community fears for its own ends. "It's part of the corporate strategy to scare the hell out of us so we write letters and communicate with other people," says Burson. In a popular timber publication, industry lawyer Mark Rutzick wrote an article titled "You Have Enemies Who Want to Destroy You." The Enemies: the National Audubon Society and the National Wildlife Federation.

The mill owners, self-made men of considerable influence in their communities, are stunned that their livelihoods are threatened because of a nocturnal bird so unobtrusive that few have ever seen it. "We came out here in the 1850s," says Milton Herbert, the owner of Herbert Lumber in Riddle, Ore. "We spend our lives trying to understand trees, to live with the environment, not against it. I hunt and fish. This is my home. I get real uptight when I think they gave my ancestors 160 acres for homesteading, and they're giving the owl 2,200 acres." He is perplexed by calls to preserve the ancient forest. "They're trying to stop time, and that's one thing we can't do," say Herbert. "Bugs, fire or man are going to harvest the trees; they don't live forever." That's the industry's view. Timber is a crop, simple as that. Rod Greene, logging manager with Sun Studs Inc. in Roseburg speaks of the old growth as "overripe," "wasteful" and "inefficient." Behind him, as far as the eye can see, in 55-ft.-stacks, rises the mill's inventory of tree trunks, more than 13,000 trees that once covered 300 acres or more. Gobbling up some 320 trees a day, the mill will consume the inventory in less than six weeks. Inside, computers align the logs by laser, then blades unwrap them like rolls of paper towel, spinning out a ribbon of veneer 8 ft. wide and four miles long every hour. Other machines carve out 3,000 "studs," or construction posts, every hour, 20 hours a day, seven days a week. In town after town, the scene is repeated. Nature cannot keep pace.

Fred Sohn, owner of Sun Studs, sees no difference between the reforested stands and the ancient forest they replace. "I believe I as an individual can replicate the forest, redo it like a farmer growing a crop and do it better than nature," he says. "I can remake the old forest the same way nature did, only quicker." Talk like that riles environmentalists, who see the forest as more than just another fungible asset. Steve Erickson, whose father was in the timber industry and whose brother works in a mill, is writing a book about hiking trails. But Erickson finds it hard to share his vision of the forest. "It's like being in an artery in God's body," he says. Biologists and botanists speak in more scientific terms. They say the ancient forest is more than an aggregation of trees. To them the ancient forest's rotting trunks, decrepit firs and deep debris represent not waste, but vital nutrients in a vastly complex ecosystem.

Those who cut down the great firs may not see the forest that way, but many have no less reverence for it. The lumberjacks of Douglas County are not boisterous back-slapping rubes but pensive men who feel as much a part of this rugged landscape as the black-tailed deer and elk that retreat from the sound of their saws. A popular bumper sticker here declares, FOR A FORESTER, EVERY DAY IS EARTH DAY. Rather than surrender the name "environmentalist" to their foes, they have labeled the opposition "preservationists." Many loggers never finished high school but followed their fathers and grandfathers into the woods. They rise in the dark at 3 or 4 in the morning, pull up their suspenders and adust rough hide pads on their left shoulders. The pads cradle the saws and, like trivets, shield the men from the hot blades that would burn their flesh through their flannel shirts. Their pants legs are tattered so that if they are suddenly snagged, the material will tear rather than hold. They do not wear steel-tipped shoes for fear that if a massive limb falls on their feet, it may turn the metal down and sever their toes. Better that their toes be crushed than pinched off.

Few loggers or environmentalists have ever seen the elusive spotted owl. They know it as either a costly subject of litigation or a rare distillation of the forest spirit. But on the summit of a steep ravine in Douglas County, a pair of spotted owls assert themselves, as if to prove they are more than a mere abstraction. Nesting in the cavity of a broken-topped fir, they scan for prey and ponder the rare two-legged observer far below. Their gentle mewing gives way to a distinctive four-note hoot: "who-who, who-who." The male drops down for a closer look and settles on a limb 15 ft. from BLM biologist Oliver. "They have no fear of man," he says. In his hand, Oliver hides a mouse. The moment he exposes it, dangling it by its tail, the mouse disappears in a blur of wings and razor-sharp talons. The owl has carried it off and up to its mate, who snips off the mouse's head and ferries it skyward to the nest, where two snowy hatchlings devour it.

Oliver is enchanted by the owls' trusting ways, their grace and their attention to their young. He worries about their future, seemingly dependent as they are for both prey and nesting sites on old-growth forests. But Oliver and others have observed that it is not the age of the forest that appears to be critical to the habitat of the owl, but rather the structure and character of the forest. He and other biologists hope that one day they will be able to identify those key components and, by preserving them in reforested tracts, both widen the owls' habitat and open the way for a resumption of timbering on a selective basis. But the owl is not alone in the forest. As an "indicator species," its well-being is a measure of how other creatures and the ecosystem as a whole are faring. "The spotted owl is almost certainly just the tip of the iceberg," says the Forest Service's Franklin. "There are probably dozens of other species just as threatened as the owl."

The dispute over the owl has festered more than 15 years, a period in which the ancient forests receded ever farther and the timbering continued largely unabated. Efforts to find a solution were thwarted by the power of the timber industry, the bungling and inertia of the federal bureaucracy and the stridency of an environmental movement as quick to alienate as to persuade. But the conflict should never have reached the current crisis point. Forest ranger Schindler believes the coming economic turmoil might have been averted if the Government had weaned industry from its dependence on old growth by gradually reducing the level of harvesting. Instead the industry has been allowed to enjoy record harvests in recent years.

U.S. Forest Service biologist Eric Forsman, who has studied the owl since 1968, believes it was the strategy of the federal agencies to stall for time by continually asking for more studies on the owl. "I've seen how the games are played," says Forsman. BLM in particular ignored repeated alarms. As early as 1976, BLM biologist Mayo Call warned his superiors that unless swift action was taken to protect the owl, it might one day have to be put on the endangered-species list, curtailing timber harvests on federal lands.

And the U.S. Fish and Wildlife Service, which is charged with protecting species, refused to call for the owl to be listed as endangered until a federal court in 1988 judged that refusal to be "arbitrary and capricious." Later the General Accounting Office discovered that Fish and Wildlife officials had rewritten portions of a major study, expunging critical references suggesting the owl was endangered. One biologist said he felt pressured to "sanitize the report." For years, economics and politics, not biology, have controlled the decisions of BLM, the Forest Service and Fish and Wildlife.

The controversy offers the U.S. an opportunity to reassess the cost of past profligacy and salvage what remains of a treasured legacy of wildlife and ancient forest. Neither the owl nor the timbermen are served by further governmental inaction or sham solutions. What is gained by waiting until the last fir topples, the owl slips closer to extinction, or the mills finally retool or shut down because there are no more old-growth trees available? The lesson of the owl is not that environmental and economic concerns are incompatible, but that the longer society lacks the political courage to act, the harder it is to find a solution. After years of industry obstructionism and governmental acquiescence, the Forest Service is finally experimenting with requiring more selective harvesting of trees, rather than clear-cutting. But many environmentalists fear that such half measures will not preserve the forest ecosystem.

In a sense, everyone is to blame for the current dilemma. Says Jolene Unsoeld, a Congresswoman from Washington State: "It is the accumulated actions of all of us—those of us who admire a beautiful wood-paneled wall, environmentalists who want their grandchildren to know the ancient forests, and those of us who come from generations of hard-working, hard-living loggers. We are all at fault, because all of us wanted the days of abundance to go on forever, but we didn't plan, and we didn't manage for that end."

Since most old-growth forests are on federal land, they belong not to an industry or a region but to the nation. The federal bureaucracies that manage them have too often operated under antiquated guidelines, framed when the forests seemed inexhaustible and man was oblivious to all but his own needs. Those agencies must reappraise their roles as custodians of the land and recognize the widest interests of the nation, not merely the most deeply vested. To place timber production above every other concern in this era of expanding environmental awareness is an abrogation of the public trust.

These are times of shifting societal values, from an appetite for natural resources to a concern for environmental quality, from the need for a strong defense to the reality of eased world tensions. Each shift brings dislocation and hardship. When revisions to the Clean Air Act pass Congress, the use of high-sulfur coal will be curbed, and thousands of West Virginia miners will lose their careers. And the scaling back of the defense budget could put thousands more on the unemployment line.

What is the Government's obligation to those workers and to the loggers of the Northwest? It would be impossibly costly for Congress to insure every citizen against the winds of change. But when scores of communities are imperiled, relief measures are necessary. In the case of the Northwest, the Federal Government should help retrain loggers and millworkers and provide towns with grants to spur economic diversification. Congress could also help sustain the Northwest's processing mills by passing legislation aimed at reducing raw-log exports.

There is no way to avoid hard choices. The U.S. will have to recognize that no society can have it all at all times—unfettered harvesting of natural resources, full employment and a healthy and rich environment. The soft hoot of the owl, an ancient symbol of wisdom and foresight, beckons us to resolve both its future and our own.

QUESTIONS FOR "OWL VS. MAN" BY TED GUP

Takling About the Text

1. The author of this essay, Ted Gup, identifies an essential philosophical issue as follows: "Are the forests—and by extension, nature itself— there for man to use and exploit, or are they to be revered and preserved?" How could a person justify the view that nature is to be used and exploited? What are some good reasons for preserving wilderness areas?

2. Logger Bill Haire says, "If it comes down to my family or that bird [the spotted owl] . . . that bird's going to suffer. . . . Things adapt or they become extinct." How would you respond to this statement if you could talk to Mr. Haire? Is it important to prevent a species such as the owl from dying out? Why or why not?

3. In this essay, the writer does take a stand. What is it? Do you agree with the writer's position?

Exploring Issues

1. Who would be likely to support the loggers in their quest to preserve their way of life? Why would these people be inclined to support the loggers? How do you feel about the loggers' concerns?

2. Are wilderness areas important for a culture such as that of the United States of America? Why or why not? What do people gain and what do they lose when certain territories are designated as wilderness areas? How would these gains and losses be perceived by environmentalists? By loggers?

3. One member of the logging community makes the following comment: "I believe I as an individual can replicate the forest, redo it like a farmer growing a crop and do it better than nature. . . . I can remake the old forest the same way nature did, only quicker." Compare this statement with some of William Kittredge's views as he expresses them in the first part of "Owning It All." What do you think about this logger's attitude toward nature?

Writing Assignments

1. Pretend that your family depends on the timber industry for its livelihood and that the environmentalists' concern for preserving forests is threatening your parents' present or your own future employment. Write an essay in which you describe how you feel about the forest (nature as wilderness), about your dependence on the forest for employment and as a way of life, and about the points of view of those biologists, social activists, and politicians who want to preserve old-growth forests.

2. Write an essay in which you explain and defend some of the reasons for preserving the spotted owl. Take into consideration the forests, the general philosophical perspective of preserving and revering nature, and the concerns of the loggers and the timber industry.

Reading 35

From *Silent Spring*

Rachel Carson

As a marine biologist with the U.S. Fish and Wildlife Service, Rachel Carson became alarmed by the increasing use of DDT and other chemicals in agriculture. After trying unsuccessfully to interest a magazine in the subject (publishers feared the withdrawal of advertising), Carson decided to write the book *Silent Spring,* which was published in 1966. This book attained national prominence in its effort to alert the public to the potential hazards of pesticides and other chemicals. A well-know author, Carson has published several influential books. *The Sea Around Us, Under the Sea Wind, The Edge of the Sea.* The following excerpt, however, is perhaps the most widely known of her writings.

1. A FABLE FOR TOMORROW

There was once a town in the heart of America where all life seemed to live in harmony with its surroundings. The town lay in the midst of a checkerboard of prosperous farms, with fields of grain and hillsides of orchards where, in spring, white clouds of bloom drifted above the green fields. In autumn, oak and maple and birch set up a blaze of color that flamed and flickered across a backdrop of pines. Then foxes barked in the hills and deer silently crossed the fields, half hidden in the mists of the fall mornings.

Along the roads, laurel, viburnum and alder, great ferns and wildflowers delighted the traveler's eye through much of the year. Even in winter the roadsides were places of beauty, where countless birds came to feed on the berries and on the seed heads of the dried weeds rising above the snow. The countryside was, in fact, famous for the abundance and variety of its bird life, and when the flood of migrants was pouring through in spring and fall people traveled from great distances to observe them. Others came to fish the streams, which flowed clear and cold out of the hills and contained shady pools where trout lay. So it had been from the days many years ago when the first settlers raised their houses, sank their wells, and built their barns.

Then a strange blight crept over the area and everything began to change. Some evil spell had settled on the community: mysterious maladies swept the flocks of chickens; the cattle and sheep sickened and died. Everywhere was a shadow of death. The farmers spoke of much illness among their families. In the town the doctors had become more and more puzzled by new kinds of sickness appearing among their patients. There had been several sudden and unexplained deaths, not only among adults but even among children, who would be stricken suddenly while at play and die within a few hours.

There was a strange stillness. The birds, for example—where had they gone? Many people spoke of them, puzzled and disturbed. The feeding stations in the backyard were deserted. The few birds seen anywhere were moribund; they trembled violently and could not fly. It was a spring without voices. On the mornings that had once throbbed with the dawn chorus of robins, catbirds, doves, jays, wrens, and scores of other bird voices there was now no sound; only silence lay over the fields and woods and marsh.

On the farms the hens brooded, but no chicks hatched. The farmers complained that they were unable to raise any pigs—the litters were small and the young survived only a few days. The apple trees were coming into bloom but no bees droned among the blossoms, so there was no pollination and there would be no fruit.

The roadsides, once so attractive, were now lined with browned and withered vegetation as though swept by fire. These, too, were silent, deserted by all living things. Even the streams were now lifeless. Anglers no longer visited them, for all the fish had died.

In the gutters under the eaves and between the shingles of the roofs, a white granular powder still showed a few patches; some weeks before it had fallen like snow upon the roofs and the lawns, the fields and streams.

No witchcraft, no enemy action had silenced the rebirth of new life in this stricken world. The people had done it themselves.

This town does not actually exist, but it might easily have a thousand counterparts in America or elsewhere in the world. I know of no community that has experienced all the misfortunes I describe. Yet every one of these disasters has actually happened somewhere, and many real communities have already suffered a substantial number of them. A grim specter has crept upon us almost unnoticed, and this imagined tragedy may easily become a stark reality we all shall know.

What has already silenced the voices of spring in countless towns in America? This book is an attempt to explain.

2. THE OBLIGATION TO ENDURE

The history of life on earth has been a history of interaction between living things and their surroundings. To a large extent, the physical form and the habits of the earth's vegetation and its animal life have been molded by the environment. Considering the whole span of earthly time, the opposite effect, in which life actually modifies its surroundings, has been relatively slight. Only within the moment of time represented by the present century has one species—man—acquired significant power to alter the nature of his world.

During the past quarter century this power has not only increased to one of disturbing magnitude but it has changed in character. The most alarming of all man's assaults upon the environment is the contamination of air, earth, rivers, and sea with dangerous and even lethal materials. This pollution is for the most part irrecoverable; the chain of evil it initiates not only in the world that must support life but in living tissues is for the most part irreversible. In this now universal contamination of the environment, chemicals are the sinister and little-recognized partners of radiation in changing the very nature of the world—the very nature of its life. Strontium 90, released through nuclear explosions into the air, comes to earth in rain or drifts down as fallout, lodges in soil, enters into the grass or corn or wheat grown there, and in time takes up its abode in the bones of a human being, there to remain until his death. Similarly, chemicals sprayed on croplands or forests or gardens lie long in soil, entering into living organisms, passing from one to another in a chain of poisoning and death. Or they pass mysteriously by underground streams until they emerge and, through the alchemy of air and sunlight, combine into new forms that kill vegetation, sicken cattle, and work unknown harm on those who drink from once pure wells. As Albert Schweitzer has said, "Man can hardly even recognize the devils of his own creation."

It took hundreds of millions of years to produce the life that now inhabits the earth—eons of time in which that developing and evolving and diversifying life reached a state of adjustment and balance with its surroundings. The environment, rigorously shaping and directing the life it supported, contained elements that were hostile as well as supporting. Certain rocks gave out dangerous radiation; even within the light of the sun, from which all life draws its energy, there were short-wave radiations with power to injure. Given time—time not in years but in millennia—life adjusts, and a balance has been reached. For time is the essential ingredient; but in the modern world there is no time.

The rapidity of change and the speed with which new situations are created follow the impetuous and heedless pace of man rather than the deliberate pace of nature. Radiation is no longer merely the background radiation of rocks, the bombardment of cosmic rays, the ultraviolet of the sun that have existed before there was any life on earth; radiation is now the unnatural creation of man's tampering with the atom. The chemicals to which life is asked to make its adjustment are no longer merely the calcium and silica and copper and all the rest of the minerals washed out of the rocks and carried in rivers to the sea; they are the synthetic creations of man's inventive mind, brewed in his laboratories, and having no counterparts in nature.

To adjust to these chemicals would require time on the scale that is nature's; it would require not merely the years of a man's life but the life of generations. And even this, were it by some miracle possible, would be futile, for the new chemicals come from our laboratories in an endless stream; almost five hundred annually find their way into actual use in the United States alone. The figure is staggering and its implications are not easily grasped—500 new chemicals to which the bodies of men and animals are required somehow to adapt each year, chemicals totally outside the limits of biologic experience.

Among them are many that are used in man's war against nature. Since the mid-1940's over 200 basic chemicals have been created for use in killing insects, weeds, rodents, and other organisms described in the modern vernacular as "pests"; and they are sold under several thousand different brand names.

These sprays, dusts, and aerosols are now applied almost universally to farms, gardens, forests, and homes—nonselective chemicals that have the power to kill every insect, the "good" and the "bad," to still the song of birds and the leaping of fish in the streams, to coat the leaves with a deadly film, and to linger on in soil—all this though the intended target may be only a few weeds or insects. Can anyone believe it is possible to lay down such a barrage of poisons on the surface of the earth without making it unfit for all life? They should not be called "insecticides," but "biocides."

The whole process of spraying seems caught up in an endless spiral. Since DDT was released for civilian use, a process of escalation has been going on in which ever more toxic materials must be found. This has happened because insects, in a triumphant vindication of Darwin's principle of the survival of the fittest, have evolved super races immune to the particular insecticide used, hence a deadlier one has always to be developed—and then a deadlier one than that. It has happened also because, for reasons to be described later, destructive insects often undergo a "flareback," or resurgence, after spraying, in numbers greater than before. Thus the chemical war is never won, and all life is caught in its violent crossfire.

Along with the possibility of the extinction of mankind by nuclear war, the central problem of our age has therefore become the contamination of man's total environment with such substances of incredible potential for harm—substances that accumulate in the tissues of plants and animals and even penetrate the germ cells to shatter or alter the very material of heredity upon which the shape of the future depends.

Some would-be architects of our future look toward a time when it will be possible to alter the human germ plasm by design. But we may easily be doing so now by inadvertence, for many chemicals, like radiation, bring about gene mutations. It is ironic to think that man might determine his own future by something so seemingly trivial as the choice of an insect spray.

All this has been risked—for what? Future historians may well be amazed by our distorted sense of proportion. How could intelligent beings seek to control a few unwanted species by a method that contaminated the entire environment and brought the threat of disease and death even to their own kind? Yet this is precisely what we have done. We have done it, moreover, for reasons that collapse the moment we examine them. We are told that the enormous and expanding use of pesticides is necessary to maintain farm production. Yet is our real problem not one of *overproduction?* Our farms, despite measures to remove acreages from production and to pay farmers *not* to produce, have yielded such a staggering excess of crops that the American taxpayer in 1962 is paying out more than one billion dollars a year as the total carrying cost of the surplus-food storage program. And is the situation helped when one branch of the Agriculture Department tries to reduce production while another states, as it did in 1958, "It is believed generally that reduction of crop acreages under provisions of the Soil Bank will stimulate interest in use of chemicals to obtain maximum production on the land retained in crops."

All this is not to say there is no insect problem and no need of control. I am saying, rather, that control must be geared to realities, not to mythical situations, and that the methods employed must be such that they do not destroy us along with the insects.

The problem whose attempted solution has brought such a train of disaster in its wake is an accompaniment of our modern way of life. Long before the age of man, insects inhabited the earth—a group of extraordinarily varied and adaptable beings. Over the course of time since man's advent, a small percentage of the more than half a million species of insects have come into conflict with human welfare in two principal ways: as competitors for the food supply and as carriers of human disease.

Disease-carrying insects become important where human beings are crowded together, especially under conditions where sanitation is poor, as in time of natural disaster or war or in situations of extreme poverty and deprivation. Then control of some sort becomes necessary. It is a sobering fact, however, as we shall presently see, that the method of massive chemical control has had only limited success, and also threatens to worsen the very conditions it is intended to curb.

Under primitive agricultural conditions the farmer had few insect problems. These arose with the intensification of agriculture—the devotion of immense acreages to a single crop. Such a system set the stage for explosive increases in specific insect populations. Single-crop farming does not take advantage of the principles by which nature works; it is agriculture as an engineer might conceive it to be. Nature has introduced great variety into the landscape, but man has displayed a passion for simplifying it. Thus he undoes the built-in checks and balances by which nature holds the species within bounds. One important natural check is a limit on the amount of suitable habitat for each species. Obviously then, an insect that lives on wheat can build up its population to much higher levels on a farm devoted to wheat than on one in which wheat is intermingled with other crops to which the insect is not adapted.

The same thing happens in other situations. A generation or more ago, the towns of large areas of the United States lined their streets with the noble elm tree. Now the beauty they hopefully created is threatened with complete destruction as disease sweeps through the elms, carried by a beetle that would have only limited chance to build up large populations and to spread from tree to tree if the elms were only occasional trees in a richly diversified planting.

Another factor in the modern insect problem is one that must be viewed against a background of geologic and human history: the spreading of thousands of different kinds of organisms from their native homes to invade new territories. This worldwide migration has been studied and graphically described by the British ecologist Charles Elton in his recent book *The Ecology of Invasions*. During the Cretaceous Period, some hundred million years ago, flooding seas cut many land bridges between continents and living things found themselves confined in what Elton calls "colossal separate nature reserves." There, isolated from others of their kind, they developed many new species. When some of the land masses were joined again, about 15 million years ago, these species began to move out into new territories—a movement that is not only still in progress but is now receiving considerable assistance from man.

The importation of plants is the primary agent in the modern spread of species, for animals have almost invariably gone along with the plants, quarantine being a comparatively recent and not completely effective innovation. The United States Office of Plant Introduction alone has introduced almost 200,000 species and varieties of plants from all over the world. Nearly half of the 180 or so major insect enemies of plants in the United States are accidental imports from abroad, and most of them have come as hitchhikers on plants.

In new territory, out of reach of the restraining hand of the natural enemies that kept down its numbers in its native land, an invading plant or animal is able to become enormously abundant. Thus it is no accident that our most troublesome insects are introduced species.

These invasions, both the naturally occurring and those dependent on human assistance, are likely to continue indefinitely. Quarantine and massive chemical campaigns are only extremely expensive ways of buying time. We are faced, according to Dr. Elton, "with a life-and-death need not just to find new technological means of suppressing this plant or that animal"; instead we need the basic knowledge of animal populations and their relations to their surroundings that will "promote an even balance and damp down the explosive power of outbreaks and new invasions."

Much of the necessary knowledge is now available but we do not use it. We train ecologists in our universities and even employ them in our governmental agencies but we seldom take their advice. We allow the chemical death rain to fall as though there were no alternative, whereas in fact there are many, and our ingenuity could soon discover many more if given opportunity.

Have we fallen into a mesmerized state that makes us accept as inevitable that which is inferior or detrimental, as though having lost the will or the vision to demand that which is good? Such thinking, in the words of the ecologist Paul Shepard, "idealizes life with only its head out of water, inches above the limits of toleration of the corruption of its own environment. . . . Why should we tolerate a diet of weak poisons, a home in insipid surroundings, a circle of acquaintances who are not quite our enemies, the noise of motors with just enough relief to prevent insanity? Who would want to live in a world which is just not quite fatal?"

Yet such a world is pressed upon us. The crusade to create a chemically sterile, insect-free world seems to have engendered a fanatic zeal on the part of many specialists and most of the so-called control agencies. On every hand there is evidence that those engaged in spraying operations exercise a ruthless power. "The regulatory entomologists . . . function as prosecutor, judge and jury, tax assessor and collector and sheriff to enforce their own orders," said Connecticut entomologist Neely Turner. The most flagrant abuses go unchecked in both state and federal agencies.

It is not my contention that chemical insecticides must never be used. I do contend that we have put poisonous and biologically potent chemicals indiscriminately into the hands of persons largely or wholly ignorant of their potentials for harm. We have subjected enormous numbers of people to contact with these poisons, without their consent and often without their knowledge. If the Bill of Rights contains no guarantee that a citizen shall be secure against lethal poisons distributed either by private individuals or by public officials, it is surely only because our forefathers, despite their considerable wisdom and foresight, could conceive of no such problem.

I contend, furthermore, that we have allowed these chemicals to be used with little or no advance investigation of their effect on soil, water, wildlife, and man himself. Future generations are unlikely to condone our lack of prudent concern for the integrity of the natural world that supports all life.

There is still very limited awareness of the nature of the threat. This is an era of specialists, each of whom sees his own problem and is unaware of or intolerant of the larger frame into which it fits. It is also an era dominated by industry, in which the right to make a dollar at whatever cost is seldom challenged. When the public protests, confronted with some obvious evidence of damaging results of pesticide applications, it is fed little tranquilizing pills of half truth. We urgently need an end to these false assurances, to the sugar coating of unpalatable facts. It is the public that is being asked to assume the risks that the insect controllers calculate. The public must decide whether it wishes to continue on the present road, and it can do so only when in full possession of the facts. In the words of Jean Rostand, "The obligation to endure gives us the right to know."

QUESTIONS FOR "FROM *SILENT SPRING*" BY RACHEL CARSON

Talking About the Text

1. We have included the first two chapters of Carson's *Silent Spring* in this reading selection. In her first chapter, entitled "A Fable for Tomorrow," Carson presents a scenario of what *could* happen to our environment. Why do you think Carson began her book in this way? Can you think of

other possible introductions to a book on the dangers of pollution? What are the advantages *and* the disadvantages of beginning a book of this sort with a short fable?

2. Carson presents an argument in her second chapter, "The Obligation to Endure." What is this argument? What is the thesis, and what forms of support or evidence are offered?

3. Notice that about halfway through her essay, Carson begins to use the pronoun *we* and continues to do so repeatedly throughout her essay in Chapter 2. (For example, "We train ecologists in our universities and even employ them in our governmental agencies but we seldom take their advice.") What rhetorical effect does Carson achieve by her continual use of *we* and *our?*

Exploring Issues

1. Are you concerned about pollution in your environment? What kinds of pollution concern you the most? How did you come to be aware of this issue?

2. What are some concrete steps we can take to address the problems posed by certain specific types of pollution (such as waste disposal or air pollution)? Are there community programs for recycling in your neighborhood or city? Are there laws regulating emission-control devices on cars? Can you imagine programs that could be implemented in the future?

3. Are you concerned about the effects of chemicals on the fruits and vegetables you consume? Would you buy organically grown products if they were available to you? Would you buy organically grown foods if they cost more than others? Would you eat them even if they looked less attractive (in terms of color, blemishes, or size)?

Writing Assignments

1. Write a personal essay in which you respond to Carson's text. You may wish to identify a particular issue, problem, or source of confusion as a starting point for your writing, or you may wish to respond to several aspects of this text. It may be the case that your essay will *not* have such features as a thesis statement or an argument: your essay may be a loosely connected set of ideas, all part of your general response to Carson's text.

2. In a personal essay, explain your general attitude toward the safety of your food and water. How concerned are you about chemical pollutants in your food and water? Why are *you* or are *you* not concerned? How did you come to be concerned? What action do you take, if any, to ensure that your food and water are relatively free of contaminants?

Reading 36

Silent Spring and the Committee Staff Report

Jamie L. Whitten

Jamie L. Whitten of Mississippi, a Member of Congress, chairs the House Committee on Appropriations and the Subcommittee on Rural Development and Agriculture. As a result of Rachel Carson's *Silent Spring,* Whitten and the subcommittee were asked to authorize millions of dollars for research on pesticides and pest control. After a close study of Rachel Carson's work, they eventually did authorize $27 million for this research. The following essay, taken from Whitten's *That We May Live,* presents some of the findings of Whitten's subcommittee.

Few responsible people with knowledge of the subject defend all the conclusions of Miss Rachel Carson's *Silent Spring.* Even those who hail the work for awakening the American people to the perils they see in pesticides concede that some conclusions are overdrawn or are based on inadequate evidence.

For instance, Dexter W. Masters, director of Consumers Union, which thought enough of *Silent Spring* to bring out an edition of it, said in the foreword to that edition:

> Consumers Union cannot and does not endorse every point Miss Carson makes. . . . [F]rom the wide range of her factual material she has proceeded to some conclusions with respect to dangers to human health which seem to CU's medical advisers extreme.[1]

Even when conceding the point, the typical advocate of *Silent Spring* shrugs and says Miss Carson's methods were necessary to counter the threat to our environment. Representative is this passage from an editorial in the Washington *Evening Star:*

> We do not doubt that some of the points made by Miss Carson in her book are debatable, largely because no one really knows all the facts. And the value of

---

[1]Reported in Consumer Reports, XXVIII (1963), p. 37.

pesticides, properly used, should be obvious to anyone. It seems, however, that Miss Carson's detractors have missed the point of her book. What she wanted to do—and did do—was to jolt Americans out of their apathy toward the dangers of the indiscriminate use of pesticides. If she overdrew her conclusions, this was incidental to a message to her fellow countrymen that came through loud and clear. What will be remembered is that her book warned human beings of the dangers of becoming victims, if not directly then indirectly, of their own ingenuity.[2]

In other words, the end justifies the means. It would seem preferable to examine the issue dispassionately, correct any abuses that might be observed, and carefully balance any criticism of excess with the evidence easily obtainable on the benefits to man from the use of pesticides.

Perhaps the most impressive assessment of Miss Carson's work is provided by the report on pesticides of the Surveys and Investigations Staff of the House of Representatives' Committee on Appropriations. At the request of the Subcommittee on the Department of Agriculture, of which the author has the honor to be chairman, the staff undertook an objective and comprehensive study of the effects of the use of agricultural pesticides on public health. The staff of the Committee is headed by an experienced investigator. Once the purpose of the study was stated, the members of the committee had no voice in the staff's investigating procedures or in the choice of the experts it interviewed. The intention was for the staff to present the committee with a judicious summary of it findings, though the mass of raw data is filed with the committee.

By a directive dated June 18, 1964, an inquiry was requested into the following subjects:

(1) The extent to which the Departments of Agriculture, Interior, and Health, Education and Welfare cooperate, collaborate, and coordinate their activities so as to protect the public health while minimizing any adverse effect on agricultural producers and processors and protecting the food supply for all Americans with particular reference to—

(a) Regulations, procedures, and practices used in approving and registering agricultural pesticides and other control materials.

(b) Regulations, procedures, and practices followed in formulating, reviewing, and agreeing upon changes in standards or tolerances previously used as basis for approval.

(c) Extent to which changes are reviewed and approved by all appropriate Federal agencies prior to announcement to the public.

(d) Extent to which such announced changes are based on claims and documented evidence that the public health is endangered.

(2) Regulations, if any, to control irresponsible actions, statements, and criticisms of agricultural pesticides and the instances of the effect on producers, processors, and consumers during the past 10 years of such actions, statements, and criticisms, including information on:

(a) A chronological record of all instances similar to the cranberry incident

---

[2]Quoted in *Conservation News*, XXX, No. 14 (July 1, 1965), p. 8.

in 1959, the more recent condemnation of milk in Maryland, and claims as to fishkills in the lower Mississippi and Missouri Rivers.

(b) The basis for expressed or implied claims and charges made public in each instance and the Federal agency concerned.

(c) Efforts made to coordinate the actions of all Federal agencies concerned with the problem.

(d) The ultimate costs to the producers, processors, consumers, and the Federal Government in each instance.

(e) The extent to which initial claims and charges were borne out by subsequent developments and findings.

(3) Information on current and long-range implications of programs and activities of the Department of Agriculture to minimize effects of the use of pesticides and to find alternative methods and practices of insect and disease control. The following areas of research were to be reviewed:

(a) Use of insect parasites, predators, attractants, and sterile insects.

(b) Use of electrical and physical control devices.

(c) Development of crops resistant to insects and diseases.

(d) Development of safe pesticides and more efficient and less hazardous methods of application.

(e) Better methods of control of diseases and parasites of livestock and poultry.

(4) The degree of coordination between Federal and State agencies in connection with entomology and pest control research and in the approval and use of pesticides, including efforts made to strengthen the well-established and effective Federal-State cooperative relationship in this area.[3]

The completed report was placed on public record in hearings on Department of Agriculture appropriations for 1966, held March 19, 1965.

In conducting the study, the staff interviewed about 185 outstanding scientists and 23 physicians. These experts included biochemists, biologists, chemists, entomologists, nutritionists, pharmacologists, plant pathologists, toxicologists, zoologists, a geneticist, officials of the American Medical Association, members of medical-school faculties, and experts in agriculture, conservation, and public health.[4]

The report's record of the federal, state, and local agencies, the laboratories and universities, the business and conservation groups represented in its interviews leaves little doubt as to the thoroughness and integrity of the staff's work. After the report was made public, those who had been interviewed were asked for permission to have their names made known. Of the more than two hundred persons interviewed, only eight, most of whom are identified with organizations known for their antipesticide stand, and two because of official positions, declined to grant permission (two others unfortunately had died in the meantime). The names of those who had no objection to having their names released to the

---

[3]*Department of Agriculture Appropriations for 1966,* hearings before a subcommittee of the Committee on Appropriations, House of Representatives, 89th Congress, 1st Session (Washington: Government Printing Office, 1965), Part I, pp. 165–166.

[4]*Ibid.*, pp. 166–167.

public are listed in the Appendix. Significantly, many of them offered words of high praise for the report. Here are just a few of them.

> I would like to compliment the staff on the general excellence of this report. It was objective, comprehensive, forthright, and fair and I believe has gone a long way toward setting the record straight on this important and complex subject.

> I have read your report and would like to congratulate you on a job well done. Other governmental agencies would do well to operate on such objective principles rather than the crusader's urge which erodes the rights and privileges of the people.

> I have read this meticulously detailed and objective report and assure you I will be proud to have my name listed among those interviewed.

> I recall the very pleasant but searching interview with your two staff members last August. They indicated a wide knowledge but no bias and at the close of the interview we wondered what direction the report would go. I would wish to commend them both as highly talented interrogators.

What did the investigative staff discover about the experts' opinion of *Silent Spring?* Here is its conclusion.

> The staff was advised, by scientists and by physicians, that the book is superficially scientific in that it marshals a number of accepted scientific facts. However, it is unscientific in (a) drawing incorrect conclusions from unrelated facts, and (b) making implications that are based on possibilities as yet unproved to be actual facts.[5]

The staff cited several specific examples of misleading statements or incorrect implications. These included:

The allegations that persistent pesticides initiate a "chain of evil."

The charge that chemicals are "little-recognized partners of radiation in changing the very nature of the world."

The implication that because some pesticides have "no counterparts in nature" they must be harmful to man.

The unsubstantiated statement, "To adjust to these chemicals would require . . . not merely the years of man's life but the life of generations."

An exaggeration of the number of new pesticidal chemicals introduced each year and the implication that they somehow require the human body to adapt to them, when in fact "only a few of these chemicals reached man's body, and then only in minute traces, except by accident, suicide, and murder."[6]

The analysis continued:

---

[5] *Ibid.*, p. 168.

[6] *Ibid.*

According to Miss Carson, man has now upset a supposedly ideal state of adjustment and balance of life on earth by using chemical pesticides which are staggering in number and "have the power to kill every insect . . . to still the song of birds and the leaping of fish in the streams . . . and to linger on in soil," but of the 394 chemical pesticides registered for agricultural use as of January 1, 1965, the majority, properly applied, do not produce such effects. It was pointed out to the staff by various scientists that the defoliation of many thousands of acres of forests by insects is a conspicuous example of nature out of balance, and that an insect-control program is an effort to restore the balance. Similarly, the housefly with its disease organisms and the Anopheles mosquito with its malarial parasites are just as much a part of the balance of nature as are brook trout, robins, and deer.

The author stated that vast acreages have been treated with chemical pesticides. USDA [United States Department of Agriculture] has reported that less than 5 per cent of the total acreage in the 50 States has had any pesticide treatment, 15 per cent of the acreage planted to crops and 5 per cent of the forests has been so treated, only 0.4 per cent of the acreage available to wildlife has been treated, and less than 10 per cent of the areas producing mosquitoes has been treated with pesticides.

The author stated that chemical pesticides were being used with "little or no advance investigation of their effect on soil, water, wildlife, and man himself," which statement ignored the numerous studies being conducted on such effects. Without proof, the author indicated that pesticides will produce cancer, sterility, and cellular mutations in man, and supposed that pesticides will eventually extinguish plant life, wildlife, aquatic life, domestic animals, and man. Thus, the book created an atmosphere of panic, foretold an impending disaster, and barely mentioned the immensely useful role played by pesticides in the U.S. economy.[7]

The staff summarized its findings on several topics, such as the effects on wildlife, that are taken up in other sections of this book. It is worthwhile quoting here its report on what the American Medical Association and others had to say about Miss Carson's apprehension over the effect of pesticides on man.

[T]he staff was informed by the association and by numerous outstanding scientists that, in order to support Miss Carson's thesis that chemical pesticides have harmful chronic effects on humans, she repeatedly drew faulty conclusions from unrelated facts. For example, she correctly pointed out that (a) there has been a gradual rise in deaths from leukemia and (b) there has been an increase in the use of chemical pesticides; she then implied that the pesticides were responsible for the rise in deaths from leukemia. Although there is no evidence that pesticides cause leukemia in humans, there is an excellent correlation between the increase in the number of leukemia patients and the increased use of X-rays and other radiation.

The author also correctly stated that certain pesticides can cause cancer and sterility in animals, and then implied that chemical pesticides cause cancer and sterility in man. However, the American Medical Association and other authorities

---

[7]*Ibid.*, p. 169.

advised the staff that there is no proof that traces of chemical pesticides cause either cancer or sterility in humans.[8]

The report's conclusion on the effects of *Silent Spring* points out that the book performed a service in alerting the public to the dangers of improper use of pesticides. It also notes that much has been done to pursue the goals the author stressed—the development of more selective pesticides that will kill only one particular pest, the search for physical and biological control methods, and greater study of acute and chronic effects of pesticides in man and animals. "Greater effort has, indeed, been devoted to such problems since the publication of *Silent Spring*," the report notes.[9]

In a review of *Silent Spring*, Cynthia Westcott, plant pathologist widely known as the "plant doctor," answered the point this way:

> This reviewer, who has worked with entomologists and plant pathologists all her life and who has had a fair amount of contact with manufacturing chemists, cannot concur in this biased viewpoint. . . .
> Miss Carson says, "When the public protests, confronted with some obvious evidence of damaging results of pesticide applications, it is fed little tranquilizing pills of half truth. The public must decide whether it wishes to continue on the present road and it can do so only when in full possession of the facts."[10] I say that throughout *Silent Spring* we are given pills of half truth, definitely not tranquilizing, and the facts are carefully selected to tell only one side of the story.[11]

A few paragraphs later, Dr. Westcott noted:

> I hope that *Silent Spring* will make the average home gardener aware that his package of pesticide has a label with vital information for his safety, but this may be too much to expect. Miss Carson quotes the survey of an industrial firm indicating that fewer than 15 people out of 100 are even aware of the warnings on the containers. My own experience bears this out. I agree with Miss Carson's implication that the juxtaposition of pesticides and groceries in the supermarket makes the average citizen unaware that he is dealing with toxic chemicals. I also agree that we are too apt to use weed-killers as a "bright new toy." All too often I have been called in to diagnose a plant disease that turned out to be 2, 4-D injury. I go along with Miss Carson in abhorring the brown sprayed strips along our roadsides.
> However, I am not sure that eliminating the trees and keeping the rest of the natural growth is sufficient for safety. I attended a garden club meeting that had been called to protest roadside spraying. A day or so before the meeting a child was killed bicycling out of a driveway because neither he nor the motorist could see each

---

[8]*Ibid.*, p. 170.

[9]*Ibid.*

[10]Rachel Carson, *Silent Spring*, (Boston: Houghton Mifflin Co., 1962), pp. 258–259.

[11]Cynthia Westcott, *Half-Truths or Whole Story? A Review of "Silent Spring"* (n.p., n.d.), brochure distributed by Manufacturing Chemists' Association, Inc.

other through the tangle. There was no further protest, a child was more important than wild flowers.[12]

What is there about Miss Carson's message that evoked such a response that her book remained on the best-seller list for many months and is everywhere quoted with love and reverence? The chord she strikes about nature in her almost unmatchable prose and the resonance this arouses in one's own spirit are doubtless the main reasons. Such a theme, after all, was a great factor in the success of her other works. But some of the most interesting speculation on other aspects of this phenomenon have been furnished by Edwin Diamond, a senior editor of *Newsweek* and the magazine's former science editor, who for a time assisted Miss Carson as she began preparing *Silent Spring*.

Mr. Diamond reminds us that popular distrust of scientists is not a new thing in America. He recalls that years ago a best-seller titled *100,000,000 Guinea Pigs* depicted the perils the nation faced from "an unholy trinity of government bureaucrats, avaricious businessmen, and mad scientists" who "had turned American consumers into laboratory test animals. I recall most vividly the danger ascribed to a certain toothpaste, which, if used in sufficient quantity, could cause a horrible death."[13]

He also points out that *Silent Spring* followed close on the thalidomide tragedy, when use of a drug resulted in the birth of children with physical defects. He quotes a newspaper interview of Miss Carson in which she said: "It is all of a piece, thalidomide and pesticides. They represent our willingness to rush ahead and use something new without knowing what the results will be." A third point Diamond makes is that any exaggeration tends to attract attention.[14]

Diamond also offers the provocative suggestion that *Silent Spring* played on a latent public paranoia, the common distrust of others that sometimes takes the form of a belief that all one's neighbors hate one and that sometimes centers on vague fears that "some wicked 'they' were out to get 'us.'" He shares the opinion of many others that Miss Carson's conclusions were exaggerated and were based on the use of half-facts and the omission of full facts.[15]

The opinions of many other people in a position to evaluate the methods and conclusions of *Silent Spring* are included in sections of this work dealing with the issues raised—effects on man, wildlife, and so on. Now, though one dislikes to take issue with a woman of impressive accomplishments and possessed of such a gift for words, it seems appropriate to look at the forces which may have moved her. She evidently had a deep rooted love for nature. For years, she worked for the Fish and Wildlife Service. Her deep feeling is apparent in these words from her earlier book, *The Sea Around Us*.

---

[12]*Ibid.*

[13]Edwin Diamond, "The Myth of the 'Pesticide Menace,'" *Saturday Evening Post*, CCXXXVI, No. 33 (Sept. 28, 1963), p. 16.

[14]*Ibid.*

[15]*Ibid.*

I am deeply interested in the preservation of the few remaining areas of unde-
veloped sea shore, where plants and animals are preserved in their original relations, in the delicate balance of nature. In such places we may answer some of the
eternal "whys" of the riddle of life.

More of her love of nature appears in the following passage from *Under the
Sea Wind.*

To stand at the edge of the sea, to sense the ebb and flow of the tides, to feel the
breath of a mist over a great salt marsh, to watch the flight of shore birds that have
swept up and down the surf lines of the continents for untold thousands of years, to
see the running of the old eels and the young shad to the sea, is to have knowledge
of things that are as near eternal as any earthly life can be.

Perhaps Miss Carson's mainspring was the age-old desire we all share in
varying degrees to recapture the days of one's youth—to be young again with all
things as they were, when the sound of birds in springtime brought the keenest
pleasure. Miss Carson pictures wonderfully the "good old days" when man was
more in tune with other living things, when nature did not need to be controlled to the extent it does today to meet the needs of population growth and
world leadership. In this practical world in which we live, however, we must be
careful not to let sentiment and nostalgia blind us to the realistic requirements
of modern society.

• • •

QUESTIONS FOR "*SILENT SPRING* AND THE COMMITTEE STAFF REPORT" BY JAMIE L. WHITTEN

Talking About the Text

1. Do you find Jamie Whitten's argument persuasive? What sorts of evidence does he provide? What is his line of reasoning?
2. Jamie Whitten refers to Rachel Carson as "Miss Carson" and to her
argument about pesticides as one based on "sentiment and nostalgia."
He also says, "One dislikes to take issue with a woman of impressive
accomplishments and possessed of such a gift for words." How do these
two aspects of Whitten's text affect your perception of Rachel Carson?
Of Jamie Whitten?
3. Do you feel that Whitten makes some legitimate criticisms of Carson's
text? If so, what are they and why do you find them to be fair criticisms?
4. What is the difference between the authority behind Whitten's voice
and the authority behind Carson's voice? Do you find one author more
authoritative and/or persuasive than the other?

Exploring Issues

1. Jamie Whitten, in trying to account for the popularity of Carson's *Silent
Spring,* mentions the "popular distrust of scientists." Do you agree that
there is a popular distrust of scientists? If so, how can you account for

this distrust? Do you agree that *Silent Spring*'s popularity may be partly attributable to a distrust of scientists?

2. One of the most obvious criticisms of Carson's *Silent Spring* is that it is nonscientific. What does this mean? Is this a valid criticism of Carson's work? Why or why not? What does this criticism imply about knowledge?

3. Jamie Whitten believes that the risks of pesticide use must be taken in order to assure that we produce enough food at reasonable costs. This food production affects not only the United States but all countries to which we export food. How do you feel about this issue? Are the risks of pesticides worth the production of more food at lower costs?

Writing Assignments

1. Compare the two texts by Carson and Whitten. Think about which one you find more persuasive. Consider your own initial knowledge and attitudes toward pesticides and other chemicals in our environment. Consider also each author's tone, language use, sources of evidence, and line of reasoning. Write an essay in which you explain which author you found more persuasive and why you found his or her point of view more convincing.

2. Jamie Whitten's argument (throughout his book, *That We May Live*) is that pesticides allow us to grow more food more efficiently and therefore to feed greater numbers of people at lower costs. Whitten also argues that low levels of chemicals are not toxic in humans and that we must not exaggerate the possibility of harmful effects. Write an essay in which you respond to Whitten's arguments. Explain which parts of his text you agree with and which parts you disagree with. Bring into your discussion any other readings or personal experiences you deem important. You may also discuss Whitten's rhetoric if you think it is important.

Reading 37

Seven Amish Farms

Wendell Berry

Wendell Berry, poet, essayist, and novelist, has published widely on conservation and sustainable agriculture. A recipient of Guggenheim and

Rockefeller fellowships, Berry has become an eloquent spokesperson for conservation and sustainable agriculture, topics he has addressed in *The Unsettling of America* and in *Meeting the Expectations of the Land* (coedited with Wes Jackson and Bruce Colman). The following essay, written in 1981, is taken from *The Gift of Good Land: Further Essays Cultural and Agricultural,* a collection of opinion pieces that examine agricultural practices against the cultural landscape of contemporary issues.

In typical Midwestern farming country the distances between inhabited houses are stretching out as bigger farmers buy out their smaller neighbors in order to "stay in." The signs of this "movement" and its consequent specialization are everywhere: good houses standing empty, going to ruin; good stock barns going to ruin; pasture fences fallen down or gone; machines too large for available doorways left in the weather; windbreaks and woodlots gone down before the bulldozers; small schoolhouses and churches deserted or filled with grain.

In the latter part of March this country shows little life. Field after field lies under the dead stalks of last year's corn and soybeans, or lies broken for the next crop; one may drive many miles between fields that are either sodded or planted in winter grain. If the weather is wet, the country will seem virtually deserted. If the ground is dry enough to support their wheels, there will be tractors at work, huge machines with glassed cabs, rolling into the distances of fields larger than whole farms used to be, as solitary as seaborne ships.

The difference between such country and the Amish farmlands in northeast Indiana seems almost as great as that between a desert and an oasis. And it is the *same* difference. In the Amish country there is a great deal more life: more natural life, more agricultural life, more human life. Because the farms are small—most of them containing well under a hundred acres—the Amish neighborhoods are more thickly populated than most rural areas, and you see more people at work. And because the Amish are diversified farmers, their plowed croplands are interspersed with pastures and hayfields and often with woodlots. It is a varied, interesting, healthy looking farm country, pleasant to drive through. When we were there, on the twentieth and twenty-first of last March, the spring plowing had just started, and so you could still see everywhere the annual covering of stable manure on the fields, and the teams of Belgians or Percherons still coming out from the barns with loaded spreaders.

Our host, those days, was William J. Yoder, a widely respected breeder of Belgian horses, an able farmer and carpenter, and a most generous and enjoyable companion. He is a vigorous man, strenuously involved in the work of his farm and in the life of his family and community. From the look of him and the look of his place, you know that he has not just done a lot of work in his time, but has done it well, learned from it, mastered the necessary disciplines. He speaks with heavy stress on certain words—the emphasis of conviction, but also of pleasure, for he enjoys the talk that goes on among people interested in horses and in farming. But unlike many people who enjoy talking, he speaks with care. Bill was born in this community, has lived there all his life, and he has grandchildren who will probably live there all their lives. He belongs there, then, root and branch, and he knows the history and the quality of many of the farms. On the two days, we visited farms belonging to Bill himself, four of his sons, and two of his sons-in-law.

The Amish farms tend to divide up between established ones, which are prosperous looking and well maintained, and run-down, abused, or neglected ones, on which young farmers are getting started. Young Amish farmers *are* still getting started, in spite of inflation, speculators' prices, and usurious interest rates. My impression is that the proportion of young farmers buying farms is significantly greater among the Amish than among conventional farmers.

Bill Yoder's own eighty-acre farm is among the established ones. I had been there in the fall of 1975 and had not forgotten its aspect of cleanness and good order, its well-kept white buildings, neat lawns, and garden plots. Bill has owned the place for twenty-six years. Before he bought it, it had been rented and row cropped, with the usual result: it was nearly played out. "The buildings," he says, "were nothing," and there were no fences. The first year, the place produced five loads (maybe five tons) of hay, "and that was mostly sorrel." The only healthy plants on it were the spurts of grass and clover that grew out of the previous year's manure piles. The corn crop that first year "might have been thirty bushels an acre," all nubbins. The sandy soil blew in every strong wind, and when he plowed the fields his horses' feet sank into "quicksand potholes" that the share uncovered.

The remedy has been a set of farming practices traditional among the Amish since the seventeenth century: diversification, rotation of crops, use of manure, seeding of legumes. These practices began when the Anabaptist sects were disfranchised in their European homelands and forced to the use of poor soil. We saw them still working to restore farmed-out soils in Indiana. One thing these practices do is build humus in the soil, and humus does several things: increases fertility, improves soil structure, improves both water-holding capacity and drainage. "No humus, you're in trouble," Bill says.

After his rotations were established and the land had begun to be properly manured, the potholes disappeared, and the soil quit blowing. "There's something in it now—there's some substance there." Now the farm produces abundant crops of corn, oats, wheat, and alfalfa. Oats now yield 90–100 bushels per acre. The corn averages 100–125 bushels per acre, and the ears are long, thick, and well filled.

Bill's rotation begins and ends with alfalfa. Every fall he puts in a new seeding of alfalfa with his wheat; every spring he plows down an old stand of alfalfa, "no matter how good it is." From alfalfa he goes to corn for two years, planting thirty acres, twenty-five for ear corn and five for silage. After the second year of corn, he sows oats in the spring, wheat and alfalfa in the fall. In the fourth year the wheat is harvested; the alfalfa then comes on and remains through the fifth and sixth years. Two cuttings of alfalfa are taken each year. After curing in the field, the hay is hauled to the barn, chopped, and blown into the loft. The third cutting is pastured.

Unlike cow manure, which is heavy and chunky, horse manure is light and breaks up well coming out of the spreader; it interferes less with the growth of small seedlings and is less likely to be picked up by a hay rake. On Bill's place, horse manure is used on the fall seedings of wheat and alfalfa, on the young alfalfa after the wheat harvest, and both years on the established alfalfa stands. The cow manure goes on the corn ground both years. He usually has about 350 eighty-bushel spreader loads of manure, and each year he covers the whole farm—cropland, hayland, and pasture.

With such an abundance of manure there obviously is no *dependence* on chemical fertilizers, but Bill uses some as a "starter" on his corn and oats. On corn he applies 125 pounds of nitrogen in the row. On oats he uses 200–250 pounds of 16-16-16, 20-20-20, or 24-24-24. He routinely spreads two tons of lime to the acre on the ground being prepared for wheat.

His out-of-pocket costs per acre of corn last year were as follows:

Seed (planted at a rate of seven acres per bushel) .. $ 7.00
Fertilizer 7.75
Herbicide (custom applied, first year only) 16.40

That comes to a total of $31.15 per acre—or, if the corn makes only a hundred bushels per acre, a little over $0.31 per bushel. In the second year his per acre cost is $14.75, less than $0.15 per bushel, bringing the two-year average to $22.95 per acre or about $0.23 per bushel.

The herbicide is used because, extra horses being on the farm during the winter, Bill has to buy eighty to a hundred tons of hay, and in that way brings in weed seed. He had no weed problem until he started buying hay. Even though he uses the herbicide, he still cultivates his corn three times.

His cost per acre of oats came to $33.00 ($12.00 for seed and $21.00 for fertilizer)—or, at ninety bushels per acre, about $0.37 per bushel.

Of Bill's eighty acres, sixty-two are tillable. He has ten acres of permanent pasture, and seven or eight of woodland, which produced the lumber for all the building he has done on the place. In addition, for $500 a year he rents an adjoining eighty acres of "hill and woods pasture" which provides summer grazing for twenty heifers; and on another neighboring farm he rents varying amounts of cropland.

All the field work is done with horses, and this, of course, comes virtually free—a by-product of the horse-breeding enterprise. Bill has an ancient Model D John Deere tractor that he uses for belt power.

At the time of our visit, there were twenty-two head of horses on the place. But that number was unusually low, for Bill aims to keep "around thirty head." He has a band of excellent brood mares and three stallions, plus young stock of assorted ages. Since October 1 of last year, he had sold eighteen head of registered Belgian horses. In the winters he operates a "urine line," collecting "pregnant mare urine," which is sold to a pharmaceutical company for the extraction of various hormones. For this purpose he boards a good many mares belonging to neighbors; that is why he must buy the extra hay that causes his weed problem. (Horses are so numerous on this farm because they are one of its money-making enterprises. If horses were used only for work on this farm, four good geldings would be enough.)

One bad result of the dramatic rise in draft horse prices over the last eight or ten years is that it has tended to focus attention on such characteristics as size and color to the neglect of less obvious qualities such as good feet. To me, foot quality seems a critical issue. A good horse with bad feet is good for nothing but decoration, and at sales and shows there are far too many flawed feet disguised by plastic wood and black shoe polish. And so I was pleased to see that every horse on Bill Yoder's place had sound, strong-walled, correctly shaped feet. They were good horses all around, but their other qualities were well founded; they stood on good feet, and this speaks of the thoroughness of his judgment and also of his honesty.

Though he is a master horseman, and the draft horse business is more lucrative now than ever in its history, Bill does not specialize in horses, and that is perhaps the clearest indication of his integrity as a farmer. Whatever may be the dependability of the horse economy, on this farm it rests upon a diversified agricultural economy that is sound.

He was milking five Holstein cows; he had fifteen Holstein heifers that he had raised to sell; and he had just marketed thirty finished hogs, which is the number that he usually has on fence. All the animals had been well wintered—Bill quotes his father approvingly: "Well wintered is half summered"—and were in excellent condition. Another saying of his father's that Bill likes to quote—"Keep the horses on the side of the fence the feed is on"—has obviously been obeyed here. The feeding is careful, the feed is good, and it is abundant. Though it was almost spring, there were ample surpluses in the hayloft and in the corn cribs.

Other signs of the farm's good health were three sizable garden plots, and newly pruned grapevines and raspberry canes. The gardener of the family is Mrs. Yoder. Though most of the children are now gone from home, Bill says that she still grows as much garden stuff as she ever did.

All seven of the Yoders' sons live in the community. Floyd, the youngest, is still at home. Harley has a house on nearly three acres, works in town, and returns in the afternoons to his own shop where he works as a farrier. Henry, who also works in town, lives with Harley and his wife. The other four sons are now settled on farms that they are in the process of paying for. Richard has eighty acres, Orla eighty, Mel fifty-seven, and Wilbur eighty. Two sons-in-law also living in the community are Perry Bontrager, who owns ninety-five acres, and Ervin Mast, who owns sixty-five. Counting Bill's eighty acres, the seven families are living on 537 acres. Of the seven farms, only Mel's is entirely tillable, the acreages in woods or permanent pasture varying from five to twenty-six.

These young men have all taken over run-down farms, on which they are establishing rotations and soil husbandry practices that, being traditional, more or less resemble Bill's. It seemed generally agreed that after three years of this treatment the land would grow corn, as Perry Bontrager said, "like anywhere else."

These are good farmers, capable of the intelligent planning, sound judgment, and hard work that good farming requires. Abused land heals and flourishes in their care. None of them expressed a wish to own more land; all, I believe, feel that what they have will be enough—when it is paid for. The big problems are high land prices and high interest rates, the latter apparently being the worst.

The answer, for Bill's sons so far, has been town work. All of them, after leaving home, have worked for Redman Industries, a manufacturer of mobile homes in Topeka. They do piecework, starting at seven in the morning and quitting at two in the afternoon, using the rest of the day for farming or other work. This, Bill thinks, is now "the only way" to get started farming. Even so, there is "a lot of debt" in the community—"more than ever."

With a start in factory work, with family help, with government and bank loans, with extraordinary industry and perseverance, with highly developed farming skills, it is still possible for young Amish families to own a small farm that will eventually support them. But there is more strain in that effort now than there used to be, and more than there should be. When the burden of usurious interest becomes too great, these young men are finding it necessary to make temporary returns to their town jobs.

The only one who spoke of his income was Mel, who owns fifty-seven acres, which, he says, *will be* enough. He and his family milk six Holsteins. He had nine mares on the urine line last winter, seven of which belonged to him. And he had twelve brood sows. Last year his gross income was $43,000. Of this, $12,000 came from hogs, $7,000 from his milk cows, the rest from his horses and the sale of his wheat. After his production costs, but *before* payment of interest, he netted $22,000. In order to cope with the interest payments, Mel was preparing to return to work in town.

These little Amish farms thus become the measure both of "conventional" American agriculture and of the cultural meaning of the national industrial economy.

To begin with, these farms give the lie direct to that false god of "agribusiness": the so-called economy of scale. The small farm is not an anachronism, is not unproductive, is not unprofitable. Among the Amish, it is still thriving, and is still the economic foundation of what John A. Hostetler (in *Amish Society,* third edition) rightly calls "a healthy culture." Though they do not produce the "record-breaking yields" so touted by the "agribusiness" establishment, these farms are nevertheless highly productive. And if they are not likely to make their owners rich (never an Amish goal), they can certainly be said to be sufficiently profitable. The economy of scale has helped corporations and banks, not farmers and farm communities. It has been an economy of dispossession and waste—plutocratic, if not in aim, then certainly in result.

What these Amish farms suggest, on the contrary, is that in farming there is inevitably a scale that is suitable both to the productive capacity of the land and to the abilities of the farmer; and that agricultural problems are to be properly solved, not in expansion, but in management, diversity, balance, order, responsible maintenance, good character, and in the sensible limitation of investment and overhead. (Bill makes a careful distinction between "healthy" and "unhealthy" debt, a "healthy debt" being "one you can hope to pay off in a reasonable way.")

Most significant, perhaps, is that while conventional agriculture, blindly following the tendency of any industry to exhaust its sources, has made soil erosion a national catastrophe, these Amish farms conserve the land and improve it in use.

And what is one to think of a national economy that drives such obviously able and valuable farmers to factory work? What value does such an economy impose upon thrift, effort, skill, good husbandry, family and community health?

In spite of the unrelenting destructiveness of the larger economy, the Amish— as Hostetler points out with acknowledged surprise and respect—have almost doubled in population in the last twenty years. The doubling of a population is, of course, no significant achievement. What is significant is that these agricultural communities have doubled their population *and yet remained agricultural communities* during a time when conventional farmers have failed by the millions. This alone would seem to call for a careful look at Amish ways of farming. That those ways have, during the same time, been ignored by the colleges and the agencies of agriculture must rank as a prime intellectual wonder.

Amish farming has been so ignored, I think, because it involves a complicated structure that is at once biological and cultural, rather than industrial or economic. I suspect that anyone who might attempt an accounting of the economy of an Amish farm would soon find himslf dealing with virtually unaccountable values, expenses, and benefits. He would be dealing with biological forces and processes not always measurable, with spiritual and community values not quantifiable; at certain points he would be dealing with mysteries—and he would be finding that these unaccountables and inscrutables have results, among others, that are economic. Hardly an appropriate study for the "science" of agricultural economics.

The economy of conventional agriculture or "agribusiness" is remarkable for the simplicity of its arithmetic. It involves a manipulation of quantities that are all entirely accountable. List your costs (land, equipment, fuel, fertilizer, pesticides, herbicides, wages), add them up, subtract them from your earnings, or subtract your earnings from them, and you have the result.

Suppose, on the other hand, that you have an eighty-acre farm that is not a "food factory" but your home, your given portion of Creation which you are morally and spiritually obliged "to dress and to keep." Suppose you farm, not for wealth, but to maintain the integrity and the practical supports of your family and community. Suppose that, the farm being small enough, you farm it with family work and work exchanged with neighbors. Suppose you have six Belgian brood mares that you use for field work. Suppose that you also have milk cows and hogs, and that you raise a variety of grain and hay crops in rotation. What happens to your accounting then?

To start with, several of the costs of conventional farming are greatly diminished or done away with. Equipment, fertilizer, chemicals all cost much less. Fuel becomes feed, but you have the mares and are feeding them anyway; the work ration for a brood mare is not a lot more costly than a maintenance ration. And the horses, like the rest of the livestock, are making manure. Figure that in, and figure, if you can, the value of the difference between manure and chemical fertilizer. You can probably get an estimate of the value of the nitrogen fixed by your alfalfa, but how will you quantify the value to the soil of its residues and deep roots? Try to compute the value of humus in the soil—in improved drainage, improved drought resistance, improved tilth, improved health. Wages, if you pay your children, will still be among your costs. But compute the difference between paying your children and paying "labor." Work exchanged with neighbors can be reduced to "man-hours" and assigned a dollar value. But compute the difference between a neighbor and "labor." Compute the value of a family or a community to any one of its members. We may, as we must, grant that among the values of family and community there is economic value—but what is it?

In the Louisville *Courier-Journal* of April 5, 1981, the Mobil Oil Corporation ran an advertisement which was yet another celebration of "scientific agriculture." American farming, the Mobil people are of course happy to say, "requires *more petroleum products than almost any other industry.* A gallon of gasoline to produce a single bushel of corn, for example. . . ." This, they say, enables "each American farmer to feed sixty-seven people." And they say that this is "a-maizing."

Well, it certainly is! And the chances are good that an agriculture totally dependent on the petroleum industry is not yet as amazing as it is going to be. But one thing that is already sufficiently amazing is that a bushel of corn produced by the burning of one gallon of gasoline has already cost more than *six times* as much as a bushel of corn grown by Bill Yoder. How does Bill Yoder escape what may justly be called the petroleum tax on agriculture? He does so by a series of substitutions: of horses for tractors, of feed for fuel, of manure for fertilizer, of sound agricultural methods and patterns for the exploitive methods and patterns of industry. But he has done more than that— or, rather, he and his people and their tradition have done more. They have substituted themselves, their families, and their communities for petroleum. The Amish use little petroleum—and need little—because they have those other things.

I do not think that we can make sense of Amish farming until we see it, until we become willing to see it, as belonging essentially to the Amish practice of Christianity, which instructs that one's neighbors are to be loved as oneself. To farmers who give priority to the maintenance of their community, the economy of scale (that is, the economy of *large* scale, of "growth") can make no sense, for it requires the ruination and displacement of neighbors. A farm cannot be increased except by the decrease of a neighborhood. What the interest of the community proposes is invariably an economy of *proper* scale. A whole set of agricultural proprieties must be observed: of farm size, of methods, of tools, of energy sources, of plant and animal species. Community interest also requires charity, neighborliness, the care and instruction of the young, respect for the old; thus it assures its integrity and survival. Above all, it requires good stewardship of the land, for the community, as the Amish have always understood, is no better than its land. "If treated violently or exploited selfishly," John Hostetler writes, the land "will yield poorly." There could be no better statement of the meaning of the *practice* and the practicality of charity. Except to the insane narrow-mindedness of industrial economics, selfishness does not pay.

The Amish have steadfastly subordinated economic value to the values of religion and community. What is too readily overlooked by a secular, exploitive society is that their ways of doing this are not "empty gestures" and are not "backward." In the first place, these ways have kept the communities intact through many varieties of hard times. In the second place, they conserve the land. In the third place, they yield economic benefits. The community, the religious fellowship, has many kinds of value, and among them is economic value. It is the result of the practice of neighborliness, and of the practice of stewardship. What moved me most, what I liked best, in those days we spent with Bill Yoder was the sense of the continuity of the community in his dealings with his children and in their dealings with their children.

Bill has helped his sons financially so far as he has been able. He has helped them with his work. He has helped them by sharing what he has—lending a stallion, say, at breeding time, or lending a team. And he helps them by buying good pieces of equipment that come up for sale. "If he ever gets any money," he says of one of the boys, for whom he has bought an implement, "he'll pay me for it. If he don't, he'll just use it." He has been their teacher, and he remains their advisor. But he does not stand before them as a domineering patriarch or "authority figure." He seems to speak, rather, as a representative of family and community experience. In their respect for him, his sons respect their tradition. They are glad for his help, advice, and example, but there is nothing servile in this. It seems to be given and taken in a kind of familial friendship, respect going both ways.

Everywhere we went, when school was not in session, the children were at the barns, helping with the work, watching, listening, learning to farm in the way it is best learned. Wilbur told us that his eleven-year-old son had cultivated twenty-three acres of corn last year with a team and a riding cultivator. That reminded Bill of the way he taught Wilbur to do the same job.

Wilbur was little then, and he loved to sit in his father's lap and drive the team while Bill worked the cultivator. If Wilbur could drive, Bill thought, he could do the rest of it. So he got off and shortened the stirrups so the boy could reach them with his feet. Wilbur started the team, and within a few steps began plowing up the corn.

"Whoa!" he said.

And Bill, who was walking behind him, said, "Come up!"

And it went that way for a little bit:

"Whoa!"

"Come up!"

And then Wilbur started to cry, and Bill said:

"Don't cry! Go ahead!"

QUESTIONS FOR "SEVEN AMISH FARMS" BY WENDELL BERRY

Talking About the Text

1. In this essay, Wendell Berry describes some of the Amish methods of farming and then attempts to explain why the Amish farmers have been so successful. Why do you think Berry wrote this essay? What is his purpose? Which readers might Berry be most likely to convince and which readers might he irritate?
2. What values underlie (a) the "agribusiness" perspective and (b) the Amish perspective on agriculture?
3 In what ways does the Amish approach toward farming differ from that of other family-owned farms? Why do the Amish appear to be more successful?

Exploring Issues

1. Why should the general urban population care what approach to agriculture is used? Consider the following: food quality, food prices, the effect of pesticides on the environment, the American tradition of the family farm, agriculture as an industry, profits, and the "bottom line."
2. Would it be possible for other communities to learn from the Amish tradition of agriculture? Which aspects of this tradition could be replicated by non-Amish farmers? Which aspects would be difficult to replicate?
3. If you have some knowledge of farming, can you find any problems with the Amish way of farming? Do you have any criticisms of their methods or of their general philosophy, as described by Wendell Berry?

Writing Assignments

1. In an expository essay, describe the Amish approach to farming and explain some of the most valuable lessons to be learned from that approach. Explain how these individual "lessons" are related to each other and to a more general philosophy of living.
2. Wendell Berry describes a people who actually live according to their principles (as articulated in the Amish practice of Christianity). Have you ever known a person or a group of people who live in deliberate accordance with certain principles (religious, moral, philosophical)? If so, describe this person (or group of people), the principles, and the ways in which these principles are followed. Use concrete descriptions to illustrate your general explanations. You may also wish to include your general attitude(s) toward this person or group.

CHAPTER 4: EXTENDED WRITING ASSIGNMENTS

4-1. Write an essay in which you fully describe one particular approach to land (living on the land, land ownership) and illustrate this approach with a character portrait drawn from one of the following films: *Heartland, Country,* or *Places of the Heart.*

Before you begin writing, read a few or all four of the essays by William Kittredge, Ted Gup, Peter MacDonald, and Wendell Berry. Consider the various reasons people can have for living on the land, away from large urban areas, and consider, as well, responses people have to nature, to the land, and to the idea of land ownership.

Then, view one or more of the films just mentioned and select a character that you would like to write about. Describe the character's appearance, personality, work and recreational habits, family and friends, values, and any other attributes that you deem important.

Use your character portrayal to illustrate a particular approach to land and to living on the land. Discuss this approach explicitly, drawing from your reading selections for explanation and support. Use descriptions of scenes and dialogue from the film to support your character portrayal.

4-2. Write an essay about an environmental issue within your own community or state.

To discover such an issue, read local periodicals and listen to radio or TV news reports over a period of three to four weeks, or read back issues of newspapers at your local library. Develop a file of your own notes and of newspaper articles about the issue you have chosen.

After you have developed some understanding of the issue, find at least two people you can interview to find out more about the problem. Make up a list of questions before each interview and ask the person you interview if you may audiotape the session. If you do not record the interview, take careful notes that you may refer back to later.

Use your reading research and your interview reports to write a documented essay about an environmental issue in your community. Explain what the problem is and what sorts of solutions are being proposed or put into effect. Describe any conflicts that may exist about which solutions people favor.

Chapter
5

Family Life and
Personal Growth

What is a "family"? The usually accepted definition is that a family consists of a mother and father and children, but are there variations on this form that we should still find viable and accept within our definition? Further, what is the function of the family, and what are the roles individual members should or might perform? And last, what is the future of the family faced with adapting to the revolutionary social and economic changes of the present time? You may not have consciously thought about these questions, yet they directly concern you and those you love and are questions that, as your own life unfolds, you will continue to confront.

The multigenerational family is an extremely important entity, playing a crucial role in a child's physical, intellectual, moral, and spiritual development. The family, however, does not exist solely for children: mothers and fathers can and should draw sustenance from family life as well. Although a parent's development unfolds in ways and at levels much different from the child's, mothers and fathers can mature in all of those significant areas so crucial to the child's growth.

Yet merely accepting a family as consisting of Mom, Dad, and the kids does not seem realistic today, nor does this general definition call for some of the vital ingredients necessary for a child's and a parent's development. One of the things you will discover in this chapter is that in American society the traditional family as so defined really applies only to a limited population during specific historical periods. Currently, in the 1990s, the "family" is a kaleidoscopic pattern encompassing great variety, to the point that it may be impossible to pin down exactly.

We would hope that while you read, think, talk, and compose your views you keep trying to define for yourselves what might be some essential elements for strong, viable families. We know that the integrity of today's family is threatened by powerful cultural, social, economic, and political forces. But if we are to safeguard an intimate and secure environment in which humans— both young and adult—can grow and realize their potential as individuals, then it is also our responsibility not only to recognize what a family is, but to understand how to create and preserve what is vital to it.

In our opening selection, Garrison Keillor narrates through a boy's eyes the family ritual of slaughtering chickens. In Keillor's casual and humorous tale, attempt to discover what very important things he might be saying about families and their importance for initiating children into some of the mysteries of life.

Following Keillor, *Los Angeles Times* staff writer David Haldane reports on serious conflicts between Asian daughters and their parents. Here you might pause and consider the inevitability of conflicts in the family. Are conflicts always the occasion for disruption, or can they be viewed as necessary to personal growth? Serving as counterpoint to Haldane's article, Cathy Song's poem captures the emotional pain of separation when a sister, who has left her family behind in China, faces the reality of her rebellion. To some degree, the next selection, from Amy Tan's bestseller *The Joy Luck Club*, reinforces but also diverges from Haldane's report. Tan's story will probably remind you of a time when one of your parents insisted that you do something you hated and rebelled against.

Next, an article from a special edition of *Newsweek* looks at what has happened to the family over the decades. Here we catch a glimpse of where the family has been and where it might be going in the uncertain future. In "True Blue," Lynn Darling tells us about the Patera family, whose father has recently lost his job when a Pittsburgh steel mill shut down. Confronting this catastrophe in midlife, Patera must now confront self-doubts about his own and his family's future welfare. Following "True Blue," Maxine Hong Kingston offers us in *China Men* a revealing portrait of "The American Father." He is not a stereotypical father; indeed, after reading this selection, you may consider whether there is such a thing as a typical American father.

Our chapter then turns darker, as Itabari Njeri narrates and comments on life in Harlem, focusing on her cousin and aunt and the tragedy that eventually befalls them. Finally, we move to the West Coast to a series of unsettling portrayals of mothers and their sons and the gangs in central and suburban Los Angeles, where gangs have become a subculture so far resistant to remedies for the rising violence of gang warfare. In one sense, gangs may serve as substitute families; as you read this selection, think about how this may be a possibility and what gangs might implicitly be saying about the health of today's families. Then, do not stop there: Consider what families might do to protect themselves from disintegrating and how family members might respond to the lure of life on the streets.

Reading 38

Chicken

Garrison Keillor

This following selection is taken from *Leaving Home* (1987). Garrison Keillor has also previously published *Happy to Be Here* (1982), *Lake Wobegon Days* (1985), and most recently, *We Are Still Married* (1990). He has also performed some of his humorous tales on national public radio, and tapes, both video and audio, of his monologues are available in libraries. This tale is about a boy trying to change his role as he participates in his family's ritual of slaughtering chickens.

It has been a quiet week in Lake Wobegon. It was cool and rainy, no good for farmers to pick corn, so some of them came and sat in the Chatterbox Cafe for a while and tried to be a comfort to each other by telling a few familiar jokes. Roger and Rollie and Harold and Virgil Berge, sitting in the back booth, began with a few clean ones about animals walking into a bar and asking for a drink, and a cannibal joke, and the pig-in-the-apple-tree joke, and the ventriloquist who spends the night at the sheep farmer's, and the one about the Norwegian trying to get into heaven. Then Harold started one about a seed salesman who was traveling through. His voice dropped as he came to the part where the lady tiptoes out to the privy in the moonlight and her dog follows her, and everyone leaned in close, and Mr. Lundberg and Bud and Russell came and huddled over the booth, waiting to be killed by this beloved old classic, and he said, "So Clarissa seen a petunia growing near the path and bent down to pick it up . . . and the dog he . . . " and Harold, who has been under a lot of pressure lately, began to slowly explode. He leaked air out of his nose and ears. He gasped and whinnied, tears running down his face, he grabbed on to the table, out of control, he stood up and motioned to be let out, but they were starting to leak too and couldn't move. He attempted to climb over them but was too weak. He tried to say the punchline, but it wouldn't come out. So he fell down on the floor and crawled out under the table.

Uncle Al was there, having a bite of meat loaf. He told me later, "You know, some people only know how to tell a joke, but Harold knows how to make people laugh."

Strange for my uncle Al to eat in a commercial establishment, seeing as he is married to Aunt Flo, whose cooking can make the lame walk, but this was a cool fall day when we were butchering chickens in her backyard, and Uncle Al is a gentle man who has no stomach for killing. He loves to eat fried chicken but not one whom he knew personally, so he killed a couple hours uptown as the rest of us executed forty-seven chickens that Dad brought in from Uncle Larry's farm the night before. There had been forty-eight chickens but one got loose when we emptied them out of the gunny sacks into Al's garage to spend their last night. She flew up in my face, a burst of feathers that made me let go, and took off like a bat out of hell. Dad went after her but he is seventy years old. The chicken tore around the trash barrel and down the alley. The others milled in the garage all night, mumbling to themselves—that it wasn't fair that *she* got to go when *they* had to stay, that if *anyone* got to go, then *everyone* should go— and finally the sun came up and a young rooster sang and about nine o'clock we arrived and sat down to have coffee. My mother had been up since four and had drunk three cups of coffee already, on account of a dream in which someone was chasing her. "I always have bad dreams when we butcher chickens," she said.

"Your problem is, you drink too much coffee," said my dad. "Coffee makes you sleep light, so a bad dream wakes you up. Me, I sleep right through my bad dreams, they don't bother me at all, not even the worst nightmares."

But it isn't that. My mother feels bad about butchering and so do I. Dad and Aunt Flo are country people, and in the country you do as you like, but Mother and I grew up in town, so we worry more about what people think, and when you have forty-seven chickens in the garage, you know the neighbors are talking. People in Lake Wobegon don't slaughter chickens anymore, not in their backyards; it's not considered decent. Oh, you might do one or two, in the evening, but forty-seven in broad daylight, a chicken massacre—people would think you're common. People buy chickens at Ralph's; they come in plastic bags, big white cold oblong things.

For our sake, to accommodate squeamishness, Aunt Flo tried to give up butchering and be content with store-bought chicken, but it was against her principles. She cooks to bring happiness, it is part of her ministry, so to put tasteless chicken on the table is to preach false doctrine. She believes in the goodness and worth and beauty of chicken. Any fool can cook a hunk of cow, whack off a slab, slap it on a platter, and call it dinner, but chicken is delicate and has got to be done right. The chickens in the store were pumped full of feed and kept drugged and in the dark and you could taste the misery of the bird in its meat. Aunt Flo's philosophy is to let them run free, to feed them table scraps and delicacies and talk to them while you feed them, to keep them in chicken bliss right up to the moment their heads hit the block.

Once, on a trip to Minneapolis to visit relatives, she was dragged by them to a swank restaurant where she sat dazzled by crystal and silver and white linen, and ordered . . . chicken—or La Poulet Alla Cacciatore de Jardinera à la Estragon con Piña Colonna—and it was borne to the table in a golden dish and served with a flourish, but underneath the hoopla and publicity was a pitiful corpse of an unhappy creature, which to her represented the wretched dishonesty of these times, and she pushed it aside and decided it would either be vegetarianism or butchering. And there we were on a fall morning about to do business in the backyard.

"Well," Aunt Flo said, standing up to rinse out her coffee cup, "I don't think those chickens are going to butcher each other."

My mother already had two big pots of water on to boil, my dad had sharpened the ax blade, and out we went, into the wet cold yard. The chickens fell silent in the garage when the back door slammed. I looked in the alley for the forty-eighth chicken. "Well," we said, "we might as well get started."

My parents and Aunt Flo have been butchering chickens since long before I was around to help, so they don't really need me. My dad kills them, my mother plucks them, and Aunt Flo cleans them. When he's done killing, my dad helps with the plucking, and then they all help clean. My job hasn't changed since I was a child: I help out here and there doing this and that, but mainly my job is to select the chicken and catch its legs with a long wire hook and grab its ankles and carry it to my dad, who takes care of the rest.

When I opened the side door of the garage, a volunteer chicken flew up and I grabbed it and there was the first one. I turned and walked back to the garage and put my hand on the knob and heard the *whack* and went in for the next one.

All the chickens had to die, so it wasn't like I had any real power; I was only a lower-level bureaucrat trying to keep things going smoothly. I didn't have the power of clemency, so why did they look at me that way—why did I feel cheap? I closed the door behind me and stood in the dim light with my hook and work gloves, the chickens milling away from me, and I took a deep breath and snagged one and it cried out, "Oh no, gosh no, please no, don't do this," and I took it to my dad and handed it over and turned my back, not wanting to watch as this creature, who had been alive in my hands just a moment before, now—*whack*—was gone. I didn't want to see the blood or watch my mother at the big boiler on the back step or smell the hot wet feathers when she dipped the carcass in boiling water, the hiss, the ripping of feathers. Didn't want to look and didn't want the neighbors to see me, so I strolled back and forth from the garage to the block, as if I was taking them to the doctor, as the crowd in the garage got smaller and smaller, and then I thought: You really ought to kill one yourself before they're all gone. This is something you should know how to do if you eat meat, otherwise you better stick to celery. You're dishonest, I said to myself: you come from an honest family that faces life and death, but you live like it's a story and you made it up—it's time you become an adult and kill a chicken. Eight chickens left, and then six, and the fifth one, I watched my dad do it.

He's a one-handed butcher. Holds it by the legs in one hand, flops it down, and the ax in the right hand is already up high on the backswing and down *whack* and the head drops like a cut flower and the blood runs out in the dirt. My uncle Larry paints a line on the chopping block and places the chicken gently down on its belly with its beak on the line, and that line hypnotizes the chicken—it lies very quietly, staring cross-eyed at the yellow line, thinking about infinity, and then suddenly it stops thinking. Uncle Larry likes to swing the ax with two hands. My dad uses one.

We were down to two chickens unless No. 48 walked in, so when I took out the next-to-last one, I said, "Maybe I'll do the next one." Okay, he said. I caught the last chicken. I was glad to be getting rid of it, the last witness to the massacre. My dad said, "Want me to hold it for you?" I shook my head. My mother said, "You be careful, now." Imagine going to bat against your first chicken, you cut your own foot off, and walk funny the rest of your life, a stiff walk, like a chicken.

I got a grip on the chicken's legs and swung it up on the block and hauled off with the ax and hit down hard and missed by two inches. I had to pry the ax out of the wood and now I was mad. I swung again and down it came dead center *whack* and at the same time I let go and the chicken took off running. It had no head. It dashed across the yard and out in the street and was gone— I never saw a chicken move so fast. I guess without the extra weight they can really go.

My dad explained afterward that when I missed the first time and planted the blade in the block, the blade got hot. So when I cut the chicken's head off, the blade cauterized the wound and stopped the flow of blood, and you had a running chicken in pretty good shape except with no brain.

We took off after it down the street and around the corner and up and across the neighbor's yard. A high-speed chicken. It raced through flower beds and bounced off fences, pure energy, no thought, kept going—fast. Ran over two little kids in a sandbox. Ran past a couple of dogs, who looked up and decided not to get involved with it. My dad and me trotting along far behind. We heard the squeal of brakes when two cars stopped and the headless chicken tore across Main Street by Bunsen Motors, just as Harold came tottering out of the Chatterbox Cafe, weak from his privy joke. It sped past him and he vowed to give up coffee from now on. It went up behind the cafe toward Our Lady Church, losing speed. Mrs. Mueller was standing by her garbage can and she has a face that would stop a clock. It slowed down the chicken to where she was able to trip it and grab it. She took it in and rebutchered it and plucked and cleaned it and put it in her fridge, but my dad and I didn't know that until hours later. So when we came wheezing along the alley and saw a chicken walking toward us with its head on its shoulders, we were momentarily confused.

It was the forty-eighth chicken, of course, and we chased it in behind the church and cornered it against the fence and snatched it and took it home. Then Mrs. Mueller called. We said, "You can keep it." We put on a pot of water to boil and drove out to a cornfield my dad knows about where it's shady and the corn has matured more slowly. We picked three dozen ears of sweet corn and raced home to the boiling water and put in the ears and had a wonderful vegetable dinner along with potatoes and beets and some squash. It was delicious. That was Thursday. I imagine that tomorrow we may try some fresh chicken.

QUESTIONS FOR "CHICKEN" BY GARRISON KEILLOR

Talking About the Text

1. What are the contrasts being developed in this narrative? What do these contrasts illustrate?
2. "Chicken" is also a story about a family ritual. What can you make of the significant differences Keillor sets up betwen the ritual joke-telling scene opening the story and the chicken-killing ritual?
3. Each person in Keillor's family plays a special role during the chicken slaughtering. Yet the narrator is the only one who attempts to change his role. What is important about this attempt?
4. "Chicken" plays on differences concerning attitudes toward killing, preparing, and eating food. What are some other cultural beliefs, attitudes, and activities surrounding food?

Exploring Issues

1. At the end of this chapter you will be asked to compose your own definition of the family by citing examples from the various selections that you have read. As a way of beginning this research, respond to the following: a) define what you believe a family to be; b) describe possible variations of this form that still fit your definition; and finally, c) specify what variations of "family" would not fit your definition.
2. Now list all possible functions that you believe a family should carry out. As you analyze these functions, describe what roles family members might play. Then, consider the variations you would permit regarding the kinds of roles each family member could possibly play.
3. In what ways might today's family differ from past versions of "family?" How may "family" change in the future? How might the "family" vary across cultures?

Writing Assignments

1. Describe in detail a special family ritual and explain its significance. Assume your readers know nothing about your family ritual, so you must provide lots of information and explanation. Use some of the events in "Chicken" to help you get into recounting one of your family rituals. Note the roles that a mother, a father, a brother, a sister, or other relatives might play. This does not necessarily have to be a ritual you like: the ritual could certainly be one you despise or find silly or meaningless.
2. After generating a list of responses for Question 1 in the "Exploring Issues" section, begin a draft—either on your own or in collaboration with others—in which you tentatively put forth your definition of the family, your understanding of its functions, your conception of the roles

individual members play, and your estimation of to what degree the form may vary before you would no longer consider it to be a "family."

3. In class discuss a family event in which you had to "grow up" in some meaningful way. Then write a draft explaining the situation, the factors involved, what happened, and what significance it all had for you. After completing a draft, share it with your classmates and invite comments. Use your judgment in revising your draft, and work on it until you are satisfied.

Reading 39

Asian Girls: A Cultural Tug of War

David Haldane

David Haldane is a journalist presently working for the *Los Angeles Times*. This investigative report first appeared on the front page of the *Los Angeles Times* on September 24, 1988. He has also written for several newspapers in Southern California and has contributed work to *Penthouse* magazine. Haldane received a BA in Creative Writing from Goddard College in Vermont in 1972. Here Haldane reports on the sometimes serious consequences resulting when young Asian women struggle to adjust to American culture while their parents expect them to follow traditional Asian customs.

In many respects Crystal Hul, 16, is more American than Cambodian.

The daughter of a well-known leader in Southern California's Cambodian refugee community, she has been in the United States since the age of 4. She speaks fluent English, gets good grades, was recently nominated for sophomore princess by her classmates and hopes to pursue a career in political science.

Yet when Crystal walks through the front door of her Long Beach home, she enters a different world. Here she must never allow her head to rise above that of her father's. She must continually refill his rice bowl until he finishes dinner and signals that she may eat. She must never leave the house alone. She is not allowed to date, drive a car, enter a movie theater or attend any party not also attended by her brothers. And she fully expects her parents to eventually choose a husband for her—with whom she is unlikely to even speak before the wedding.

PARENTS ARE 'GODS'

"The rules are different at home than at school," she said. "We respect our father and mother as gods. I could never find the heart to disobey them."

Meet an unusual group of immigrant Americans. They are young Asians deeply rooted in ancient cultures that consider women subservient. And for the girls especially, life in America can be one of stark contrasts, even two clashing existences: life at home and life outside.

"I trust my parents to make the right decisions for me," Crystal said. "I feel loved. But sometimes it's hard."

So hard, according to psychologists and social workers, that increasing numbers are breaking under the strain.

The story of these young women's struggle to balance two worlds has its beginnings in ancient history. Five hundred years before the birth of Christ, the Chinese philosopher Confucius, whose teachings form the basis for much of Asian society, preached the subservient of women and the suppression of individual needs in favor of those of the group.

'MINIMIZE CONFLICTS'

"It's the sense that the family is more important than the individual," said Lucie Cheng, a professor of sociology at UCLA who is a Chinese-American and director of the university's Center for Pacific Rim Studies. "The idea that it's not individuals expressing their individualism that is important, but how everyone can preserve the harmony within the family to keep it going and minimize conflicts."

While similar values prevailed to some extent in early Western societies, experts say, the rapid technological development of the West tended to mitigate them while the lingering agricultural life styles of the East allowed them to flourish. Thus for generations, especially in East and Southeast Asian countries, women were taught to serve their husbands without question, a role they began preparing for almost from birth.

And while their male siblings were also under pressure to respect and obey their elders, the girls in particular were raised as revered and protected beings who learned their proper roles at their mothers' apron strings.

Recent years have seen some disruptions in that tradition.

In mainland China, for instance, where the Communist government has long discouraged traditional views of femininity, young people have discovered the sexual revolution with the result that as many as 30% have experienced premarital sex, according to one recent estimate.

JAPAN LIBERALIZING

Japan, strongly influenced by the West through economic and cultural ties, has also undergone some liberalization of its values regarding women.

And during the 1960s and '70s Southeast Asian countries such as Vietnam, Cambodia and Laos came under Communist rule, with the result that traditional family ties and gender roles there were severely challenged.

It is refugees from these Southeast Asian countries—about 340,000 of whom have settled in California since 1975—who tend to cling to their traditional values most strongly.

"They feel guilty about leaving their countries," said Florentius Chan, a psychologist and director of the Asian Pacific Mental Health Center in Long Beach. Buffeted by media portrayals of what they perceive as an alien and dangerous American culture and wracked by uncertainties regarding their own future in it, the refugees in many cases are interpreting their own traditions more rigidly than they ever did at home. "The only thing they can control," said Chan, who was born in Taiwan, "is their value system."

For some families, the effort seems to be working.

Crystal, for instance, says that despite occasional teasing from her friends, she is comfortable with the way she is being brought up, including the eventual selection of a mate by her parents, and intends to raise her own daughters the same way.

"My husband will love me as a daughter, a little sister and a wife," the teenager says. "I know that my mom and dad will make a good decision. It's one less thing I have to worry about."

For others, though, the attempt to live Asian lives in a Western culture can prove devastating.

One 18-year-old Cambodian student, who did not want her name used, said she became so upset at her mother's attempts at controlling her life that she ran away from home, spent several nights in a seedy hotel, got drunk and attempted suicide.

"She tried to bring me up in the Cambodian way," the young woman said, "but I just didn't know how to act. I was young when we left Cambodia; it's too difficult to act like that."

Eventually, the youngster received counseling and returned to her Long Beach home, where she says her mother is now somewhat less restrictive.

Another girl, age 16, said she rebelled by moving into a Cambodian Buddhist Temple. Later she moved to a shelter, then to a foster home. "I didn't like that way I was being treated," said the girl, who continues to live in the foster home, where she says she is freer to pursue her own interests.

These problems are often aggravated, experts say, because many immigrant parents expect their daughters to get good educations and pursue careers as well as behave in traditionally feminine ways. Thus, added to the pressures on Asian-American students of both genders to excel in their academic and professional pursuits is the demand that young women do so without sacrificing their traditional feminine passivity. The resulting tension has been well chronicled in the art and literature of Asian-Americans.

In 1976, Maxine Hong Kingston, a Chinese-American woman born and raised in Stockton, won the National Book Critics Circle Award for "Woman Warrior," a memoir of her girlhood based on stories her mother told her while working in the family laundry.

In the book, Kingston, who now lives in Studio City, told of purposely acting stupid and clumsy in the presence of young Chinese men chosen by her parents as potential mates. The idea, she said, was to make herself undesirable enough to be left alone.

"I refused to cook," Kingston wrote. "When I had to wash the dishes, I would crack one or two. 'Bad girl!' my mother yelled, and sometimes that made me gloat rather than cry. Isn't a bad girl almost a boy?"

Jude Narita, a young Japanese-American, presented a one-woman play last year called "Coming Into Passion/Song for a Sansei." Working through a series of vignettes, the show, which recently closed at the Fountain Theater in Hollywood, explored the lives of several Asian-American women, including an American teen-ager of Japanese descent, a Filipina mail-order bride, a Vietnamese prostitute and a grown-up who had been detained at a World War II camp for Japanese-Americans.

"Education changes everything," Narita said. "The benefit of coming to America is unlimited opportunity, but one of the side effects is that you lose total control of your children. That's the natural progression; the older generation tries to hold it back, but it's like trying to hold back the wind." Experts say they have no overall statistics on how many Asian girls are running away, becoming involved with drugs and prostitution or attempting suicide as a result of these cultural pressures. Most, however, say such cases are on the rise.

Chan's experience in Long Beach, where his agency deals primarily with Cambodians, may be instructive. Of his 30 current cases, the psychologist said, two-thirds involve girls who are having serious problems adjusting to the expectations of two cultures. Based on his experience, Chan said, he estimates that as many as half of the area's Cambodian families are encountering similar difficulties, with the number of cases requiring professional help increasing by about 20% per year. Chan attributes the increase to the continuing influx of refugees, combined with the fact that more and more girls who were very young when they arrived in the United States are reaching the rebellious teen-age years.

PARENTS WORRIED

"It's getting worse and worse," Chan said. "We have parents calling us crying—they just don't know what to do." Joselyn Yap, director of the child and youth division of the Asian Pacific Counseling and Treatment Center in Los Angeles, reports an alarming increase in child-abuse cases—the majority involving girls—among clients from the Philippines, Vietnam and China, where some segments of the population consider corporal punishment acceptable. Of the 100 cases her agency sees each month, Yap said, about 20%—a twenty-fold increase since 1985—involve abused children.

Yap attributes the increase in reported incidents of abuse to the rising level of stress felt by immigrants dealing with the changing cultural values of their children, as well as enhanced professional awareness of the problem. One teacher was very surprised that when she said she had to discipline a child, the parents said that that was OK as long as she didn't break any of the child's bones," recalled Ben Marte, a behavioral science consultant with the agency.

And Johng Song, intervention program coordinator for Los Angeles' Korean Youth Center, said that about 40% of his agency's estimated 450 clients each year are girls having trouble adapting to their dual roles.

A smattering of academic studies have touched on various aspects of the problem.

A 1980 paper done at Columbia University focused on Chinese women who had immigrated to the United States. Among its conclusions: that the earlier in their lives they emigrated, the less likely they were to suffer from serious emotional maladjustments. In 1984 a psychologist at UCLA published a paper documenting impaired motivation, increased conflict with children and a growing divorce rate among female Southeast Asian refugees.

One result of this attention has been a proliferation of special programs aimed at helping Asian parents and children. Yap's agency, for instance, offers classes for parents designed to improve their child-rearing skills, as well as individual and group therapy sessions for teen-age boys and girls. At Song's center, teen-agers are encouraged to discuss their culture's double standard for males and females at special workshops. The Asian Pacific Family Center in Rosemead offers therapy designed to help ease the acculturation process.

"Our goal is to change the conflict model into more of an integration adjustment model," said George Choi, the center's clinical director. "One can adapt by recognizing the boundaries in either world, working comfortably within those boundaries and still being comfortable with one's self. A lot of the time, [the girls] are not trying to abdicate either role as much as trying to integrate both."

Indeed, many young Asian women seem to be doing so.

Shung Kim, a 19-year-old Korean who has been in the country since age 3 and studies psychology at UCLA, said she has learned to accept the fact that her parents expect her home by 11:30 p.m., while her 17-year-old brother is permitted to stay out until 2 a.m.

'IN THE MIDDLE'

"For a while I challenged them," she said, "but it's pretty much instilled in me now. I'm like a combination of Korean and American; right in the middle."

Thuly Nguyen, 16, a Vietnamese high school student who lives in Wilmington, says she understands why her parents won't let her date. "They've been over there longer than they've been over here," she said. "I can't expect them to change that much."

And at 23, Vuthy Chek, a Cambodian refugee, has finally worked out an arrangement that she believes she can live with. A student at Cal State Long Beach with a full-time job, she still resides with her parents, is allowed to date only in groups and must be home by 11 p.m.

But when it comes time to marry, she said, her family will make a slight departure from tradition. "They would love to have an arranged marriage," Chek said, "but they have compromised. I have the right to say no."

QUESTIONS FOR "ASIAN GIRLS: A CULTURAL TUG OF WAR" BY DAVID HALDANE

Talking About the Text

1. Because this is a newspaper article, we get neither details nor in-depth analyses of the conflicts between parents and their daughters. Use your reading of this article and your experience to look at these conflicts from the parents' and the daughters' perspectives. What do both sides want and what do both fear?
2. Why do you think that some of these daughters manage to work out a compromise with their parents while others do not?

Exploring Issues

1. Discuss other conflicts between parents and their sons and daughters in which family cultural values conflict with social expectations. For instance, consider various ethnic groups and their respective philosophies concerning the role of a woman in the home and her role in the larger society. What behaviors in the home are not acceptable outside the home that might possibly create conflicts for the children? What outside behaviors are not acceptable in the home?
2. Identify some important decisions young people might have to make that they know will conflict with their parent's wishes. How might you deal with these problems? In your responses, present the problems from the viewpoints of all parties involved.

Writing Assignments

1. Follow up Question 2 in the previous section by interviewing your parents or someone else's parents concerning their views on possible conflicts with their teen-agers. Isolate problems that parents worry about. If possible, work with a partner, ideally one from a different ethnic background than your own. Then report your findings, reflecting as fairly as possible, all views of the conflicts.

2. Identify a problem that seems to occur frequently between parents and their sons and daughters. Then examine possible ways of dealing with the problem through further research that includes some experts' views. In a report, demonstrate the probable results of their proposed solution(s).

Reading 40

Lost Sister

Cathy Song

Cathy Song grew up in Hawaii and attended Wellesley College, where she earned her BA, and later went on to Boston University, where she received her MA in creative writing. She has taught creative writing at various universities. This poem is from *Picture Bride* (1983), a book that in manuscript form was selected by Richard Hugo as the winner in the Yale Younger Poet series. In "Lost Sister," the speaker reflects upon the gains and losses of leaving China and coming to America, losses that threaten one's identity yet are the result of the speaker's rebellion in relinquishing her family name.

1

In China,
even the peasants
named their first daughters
Jade—
the stone that in the far fields

could moisten the dry season,
could make men move mountains
for the healing green of the inner hills
glistening like slices of winter melon.

And the daughters were grateful:
They never left home.
To move freely was a luxury
stolen from them at birth.
Instead, they gathered patience,
learning to walk in shoes
the size of teacups,
without breaking—
the arc of their movements
as dormant as the rooted willow,
as redundant as the farmyard hens.
But they traveled far
in surviving,
learning to stretch the family rice,
to quiet the demons,
the noisy stomachs.

2

There is a sister
across the ocean,
who relinquished her name,
diluting jade green
with the blue of the Pacific.
Rising with a tide of locusts,
she swarmed with others
to inundate another shore.
In America,
there are many roads
and women can stride along with men.

But in another wilderness,
the possibilities,
the loneliness,
can strangulate like jungle vines.
The meager provisions and sentiments
of once belonging—
fermented roots, Mah-Jong tiles and firecrackers—set but
a flimsy household
in a forest of nightless cities.
A giant snake rattles above,
spewing black clouds into your kitchen.
Dough-faced landlords

slip in and out of your keyholes,
making claims you don't understand,
tapping into your communication systems
of laundry lines and restaurant chains.

You find you need China:
your one fragile identification,
a jade link
handcuffed to your wrist.
You remember your mother
who walked for centuries,
footless—
and like her,
you have left no footprints,
but only because
there is an ocean in between,
the unremitting space of your rebellion.

Reading 41

Jing-Mei Woo: Two Kinds

Amy Tan

"Two Kinds" is excerpted from *The Joy Luck Club,* Amy Tan's first novel, which quickly became a national bestseller. Tan was born in Oakland, California, in 1952, just two and one-half years after her parents immigrated to the United States. Although her parents wanted her to become a neurosurgeon and a concert pianist, Tan decided to become a consultant to programs for disabled children and later to become a free lance writer.

My mother believed you could be anything you wanted to be in America. You could open a restaurant. You could work for the government and get good retirement. You could buy a house with almost no money down. You could become rich. You could become instantly famous.

"Of course you can be prodigy, too," my mother told me when I was nine. "You can be best anything. What does Auntie Lindo know? Her daughter, she is only best tricky."

America was where all my mother's hopes lay. She had come here in 1949 after losing everything in China: her mother and father, her family home, her first husband, and two daughters, twin baby girls. But she never looked back with regret. There were so many ways for things to get better.

We didn't immediately pick the right kind of prodigy. At first my mother thought I could be a Chinese Shirley Temple. We'd watch Shirley's old movies on TV as though they were training films. My mother would poke my arm and say, "Ni kan"—You watch. And I would see Shirley tapping her feet, or singing a sailor song, or pursing her lips into a very round O while saying, "Oh my goodness."

"Ni kan," said my mother as Shirley's eyes flooded with tears. "You already know how. Don't need talent for crying!"

Soon after my mother got this idea about Shirley Temple, she took me to a beauty training school in the Mission district and put me in the hands of a student who could barely hold the scissors without shaking. Instead of getting big fat curls, I emerged with an uneven mass of crinkly black fuzz. My mother dragged me off to the bathroom and tried to wet down my hair.

"You look like Negro Chinese," she lamented, as if I had done this on purpose.

The instructor of the beauty training school had to lop off these soggy clumps to make my hair even again. "Peter Pan is very popular these days," the instructor assured my mother. I now had hair the length of a boy's, with straight-across bangs that hung at a slant two inches above my eyebrows. I liked the haircut and it made me actually look forward to my future fame.

In fact, in the beginning, I was just as excited as my mother, maybe even more so. I pictured this prodigy part of me as many different images, trying each one on for size. I was a dainty ballerina girl standing by the curtains, waiting to hear the right music that would send me floating on my tiptoes. I was like the Christ child lifted out of the straw manger, crying with holy indignity. I was Cinderella stepping from her pumpkin carriage with sparkly cartoon music filling the air.

In all of my imaginings, I was filled with a sense that I would soon become *perfect.* My mother and father would adore me. I would be beyond reproach. I would never feel the need to sulk for anything.

But sometimes the prodigy in me became impatient. "If you don't hurry up and get me out of here, I'm disappearing for good," it warned. "And then you'll always be nothing."

Every night after dinner, my mother and I would sit at the Formica kitchen table. She would present new tests, taking her examples from stories of amazing children she had read in *Ripley's Believe It or Not,* or *Good Housekeeping, Reader's Digest,* and a dozen other magazines she kept in a pile in our bathroom. My mother got these magazines from people whose houses she cleaned.

And since she cleaned many houses each week, we had a great assortment. She would look through them all, searching for stories about remarkable children.

The first night she brought out a story about a three-year-old boy who knew the capitals of all the states and even most of the European countries. A teacher was quoted as saying the little boy could also pronounce the names of the foreign cities correctly.

"What's the capital of Finland?" my mother asked me, looking at the magazine story.

All I knew was the capital of California, because Sacramento was the name of the street we lived on in Chinatown. "Nairobi!" I guessed, saying the most foreign word I could think of. She checked to see if that was possibly one way to pronounce "Helsinki" before showing me the answer.

The tests got harder—multiplying numbers in my head, finding the queen of hearts in a deck of cards, trying to stand on my head without using my hands, predicting the daily temperatures in Los Angeles, New York, and London.

One night I had to look at a page from the Bible for three minutes and then report everything I could remember. "No Jehoshaphat had riches and honor in abundance and . . . that's all I remember, Ma," I said.

And after seeing my mother's disappointed face once again, something inside of me began to die. I hated the tests, the raised hopes and failed expectations. Before going to bed that night, I looked in the mirror above the bathroom sink and when I saw only my face staring back—and that it would always be this ordinary face—I began to cry. Such a sad, ugly girl! I made high-pitched noises like a crazed animal, trying to scratch out the face in the mirror.

And then I saw what seemed to be the prodigy side of me—because I had never seen that face before. I looked at my reflection, blinking so I could see more clearly. The girl staring back at me was angry, powerful. This girl and I were the same. I had new thoughts, willful thoughts, or rather thoughts filled with lots of won'ts. I won't let her change me, I promised myself. I won't be what I'm not.

So now on nights when my mother presented her tests, I performed listlessly, my head propped on one arm. I pretended to be bored. And I was. I got so bored I started counting the bellows of the foghorns out on the bay while my mother drilled me in other areas. The sound was comforting and reminded me of the cow jumping over the moon. And the next day, I played a game with myself, seeing if my mother would give up on me before eight bellows. After a while I usually counted only one, maybe two bellows at most. At last she was beginning to give up hope.

• • •

Two or three months had gone by without any mention of my being a prodigy again. And then one day my mother was watching *The Ed Sullivan Show* on TV. The TV was old and the sound kept shorting out. Every time my mother got halfway up from the sofa to adjust the set, the sound would go back on and Ed would be talking. As soon as she sat down, Ed would go silent again. She got up, the TV broke into loud piano music. She sat down. Silence. Up and down, back and forth, quiet and loud. It was like a stiff embraceless dance between her and the TV set. Finally she stood by the set with her hand on the sound dial.

She seemed entranced by the music, a little frenzied piano piece with this mesmerizing quality, sort of quick passages and then teasing lilting ones before it returned to the quick playful parts.

"*Ni kan,*" my mother said, calling me over with hurried hand gestures. "Look here."

I could see why my mother was fascinated by the music. It was being pounded out by a little Chinese girl, about nine years old, with a Peter Pan haircut. The girl had the sauciness of a Shirley Temple. She was proudly modest like a proper Chinese child. And she also did this fancy sweep of a curtsy, so that the fluffy skirt of her white dress cascaded slowly to the floor like the petals of a large carnation.

In spite of these warning signs, I wasn't worried. Our family had no piano and we couldn't afford to buy one, let alone reams of sheet music and piano lessons. So I could be generous in my comments when my mother bad-mouthed the little girl on TV.

"Play note right, but doesn't sound good! No singing sound," complained my mother.

"What are you picking on her for?" I said carelessly. "She's pretty good. Maybe she's not the best, but she's trying hard." I knew almost immediately I would be sorry I said that.

"Just like you," she said. "Not the best. Because you not trying." She gave a little huff as she let go of the sound dial and sat down on the sofa.

The little Chinese girl sat down also to play an encore of "Anitra's Dance" by Grieg. I remember the song, because later on I had to learn how to play it.

Three days after watching *The Ed Sullivan Show,* my mother told me what my schedule would be for piano lessons and piano practice. She had talked to Mr. Chong, who lived on the first floor of our apartment building. Mr. Chong was a retired piano teacher and my mother had traded housecleaning services for weekly lessons and a piano for me to practice on every day, two hours a day, from four until six.

When my mother told me this, I felt as though I had been sent to hell. I whined and then kicked my foot a little when I couldn't stand it anymore.

"Why don't you like the way I am? I'm *not* a genius! I can't play the piano. And even if I could, I wouldn't go on TV if you paid me a million dollars!" I cried.

My mother slapped me. "Who ask you be genius?" she shouted. "Only ask you be your best. For you sake. You think I want you be genius? Hnnh! What for! Who ask you!"

"So ungrateful," I heard her mutter in Chinese. "If she had as much talent as she has temper, she would be famous now."

Mr. Chong, whom I secretly nicknamed Old Chong, was very strange, always tapping his fingers to the silent music of an invisible orchestra. He looked ancient in my eyes. He had lost most of the hair on top of his head and he wore thick glasses and had eyes that always looked tired and sleepy. But he must have been younger than I thought, since he lived with his mother and was not yet married.

I met Old Lady Chong once and that was enough. She had this peculiar smell like a baby that had done something in its pants. And her fingers felt like a dead person's, like an old peach I once found in the back of the refrigerator; the skin just slid off the meat when I picked it up.

I soon found out why Old Chong had retired from teaching piano. He was deaf. "Like Beethoven!" he shouted to me. "We're both listening only in our head!" And he would start to conduct his frantic silent sonatas.

Our lessons went like this. He would open the book and point to different things, explaining their purpose: "Key! Treble! Bass! No sharps or flats! So this is C major! Listen now and play after me!"

And then he would play the C scale a few times, a simple chord, and then, as if inspired by an old, unreachable itch, he gradually added more notes and running trills and a pounding bass until the music was really something quite grand.

I would play after him, the simple scale, the simple chord, and then I just played some nonsense that sounded like a cat running up and down on top of garbage cans. Old Chong smiled and applauded and then said, "Very good! But now you must learn to keep time!"

So that's how I discovered that Old Chong's eyes were too slow to keep up with the wrong notes I was playing. He went through the motions in half-time. To help me keep rhythm, he stood behind me, pushing down on my right shoulder for every beat. He balanced pennies on top of my wrists so I would keep them still as I slowly played scales and arpeggios. He had me curve my hand around an apple and keep that shape when playing chords. He marched stiffly to show me how to make each finger dance up and down, staccato like an obedient little soldier.

He taught me all these things, and that was how I also learned I could be lazy and get away with mistakes, lots of mistakes. If I hit the wrong notes because I hadn't practiced enough, I never corrected myself. I just kept playing in rhythm. And Old Chong kept conducting his own private reverie.

So maybe I never really gave myself a fair chance. I did pick up the basics pretty quickly, and I might have become a good pianist at that young age. But I was so determined not to try, not to be anybody different that I learned to play only the most ear-splitting preludes, the most discordant hymns.

Over the next year, I practiced like this, dutifully in my own way. And then one day I heard my mother and her friend Lindo Jong both talking in a loud bragging tone of voice so others could hear. It was after church, and I was leaning against the brick wall wearing a dress with stiff white petticoats. Auntie Lindo's daughter, Waverly, who was about my age, was standing farther down the wall about five feet away. We had grown up together and shared all the closeness of two sisters squabbling over crayons and dolls. In other words, for the most part, we hated each other. I thought she was snotty. Waverly Jong had gained a certain amount of fame as "Chinatown's Littlest Chinese Chess Champion."

"She bring home too many trophy," lamented Auntie Lindo that Sunday. "All day she play chess. All day I have no time do nothing but dust off her winnings." She threw a scolding look at Waverly, who pretended not to see her.

"You lucky you don't have this problem," said Auntie Lindo with a sigh to my mother.

And my mother squared her shoulders and bragged: "Our problem worser than yours. If we ask Jing-mei wash dish, she hear nothing but music. It's like you can't stop this natural talent."

And right then, I was determined to put a stop to her foolish pride.

A few weeks later, Old Chong and my mother conspired to have me play in a talent show which would be held in the church hall. By then, my parents had saved up enough to buy me a secondhand piano, a black Wurlitzer spinet with a scarred bench. It was the showpiece of our living room.

For the talent show, I was to play a piece called "Pleading Child" from Schumann's *Scenes from Childhood*. It was a simple, moody piece that sounded more difficult than it was. I was supposed to memorize the whole thing, playing the repeat parts twice to make the piece sound longer. But I dawdled over it, playing a few bars and then cheating, looking up to see what notes followed. I never really listened to what I was playing. I daydreamed about being somewhere else, about being someone else.

The part I liked to practice best was the fancy curtsy: right foot out, touch the rose on the carpet with a pointed foot, sweep to the side, left leg bends, look up and smile.

My parents invited all the couples from the Joy Luck Club to witness my debut. Auntie Lindo and Uncle Tin were there. Waverly and her two older brothers had also come. The first two rows were filled with children both younger and older than I was. The littlest ones got to go first. They recited simple nursery rhymes, squawked out tunes on miniature violins, twirled Hula Hoops, pranced in pink ballet tutus, and when they bowed or curtsied, the audience would sigh in unison, "Awww," and then clap enthusiastically.

When my turn came, I was very confident. I remember my childish excitement. It was as if I knew, without a doubt, that the prodigy side of me really did exist. I had no fear whatsoever, no nervousness. I remember thinking to myself, This is it! This is it! I looked out over the audience, at my mother's blank face, my father's yawn, Auntie Lindo's stiff-lipped smile, Waverly's sulky expression. I had on a white dress layered with sheets of lace, and a pink bow in my Peter Pan haircut. As I sat down I envisioned people jumping to their feet and Ed Sullivan rushing up to introduce me to everyone on TV.

And I started to play. It was so beautiful. I was so caught up in how lovely I looked that at first I didn't worry how I would sound. So it was a surprise to me when I hit the first wrong note and I realized something didn't sound quite right. And then I hit another and another followed that. A chill started at the top of my head and began to trickle down. Yet I couldn't stop playing, as though my hands were bewitched. I kept thinking my fingers would adjust themselves back, like a train switching to the right track. I played this strange jumble through two repeats, the sour notes staying with me all the way to the end.

When I stood up, I discovered my legs were shaking. Maybe I had just been nervous and the audience, like Old Chong, had seen me go through the right motions and had not heard anything wrong at all. I swept my right foot out, went down on my knee, looked up and smiled. The room was quiet, except for Old Chong, who was beaming and shouting, "Bravo! Bravo! Well done!" But then I saw my mother's face, her stricken face. The audience clapped weakly, and as I walked back to my chair, with my whole face quivering as I tried not to cry, I heard a little boy whisper loudly to his mother, "That was awful," and the mother whispered back, "Well, she certainly tried."

And now I realized how many people were in the audience, the whole world it seemed. I was aware of eyes burning into my back. I felt the shame of my mother and father as they sat stiffly throughout the rest of the show.

We could have escaped during intermission. Pride and some strange sense of honor must have anchored my parents to their chairs. And so we watched it all: the eighteen-year-old boy with a fake mustache who did a magic show and juggled flaming hoops while riding a unicycle. The breasted girl with white makeup who sang from *Madama Butterfly* and got honorable mention. And the eleven-year-old boy who won first prize playing a tricky violin song that sounded like a busy bee.

After the show, the Hsus, the Jongs, and the St. Clairs from the Joy Luck Club came up to my mother and father.

"Lots of talented kids," Auntie Lindo said vaguely, smiling broadly.

"That was somethin' else," said my father, and I wondered if he was referring to me in a humorous way, or whether he even remembered what I had done.

Waverly looked at me and shrugged her shoulders. "You aren't a genius like me," she said matter-of-factly. And if I hadn't felt so bad, I would have pulled her braids and punched her stomach.

But my mother's expression was what devastated me: a quiet, blank look that said she had lost everything. I felt the same way, and it seemed as if everybody were now coming up, like gawkers at the scene of an accident, to see what parts were actually missing. When we got on the bus to go home, my father was humming the busy-bee tune and my mother was silent. I kept thinking she wanted to wait until we got home before shouting at me. But when my father unlocked the door to our apartment, my mother walked in and then went to the back, into the bedroom. No accusations. No blame. And in a way, I felt disappointed. I had been waiting for her to start shouting, so I could shout back and cry and blame her for all my misery.

I assumed my talent-show fiasco meant I never had to play the piano again. But two days later, after school, my mother came out of the kitchen and saw me watching TV.

"Four clock," she reminded me as if it were any other day. I was stunned, as though she were asking me to go through the talent-show torture again. I wedged myself more tightly in front of the TV.

"Turn off TV," she called from the kitchen five minutes later.

I didn't budge. And then I decided. I didn't have to do what my mother said anymore. I wasn't her slave. This wasn't China. I had listened to her before and look what happened. She was the stupid one.

She came out from the kitchen and stood in the arched entryway of the living room. "Four clock," she said once again, louder.

"I'm not going to play anymore," I said nonchalantly. "Why should I? I'm not a genius."

She walked over and stood in front of the TV. I saw her chest was heaving up and down in an angry way.

"No!" I said, and now I felt stronger, as if my true self had finally emerged. So this was what had been inside me all along.

"No! I won't!" I screamed.

She yanked me by the arm, pulled me off the floor, snapped off the TV. She was frighteningly strong, half pulling, half carrying me toward the piano as I kicked the throw rugs under my feet. She lifted me up and onto the hard bench. I was sobbing by now, looking at her bitterly. Her chest was heaving even more and her mouth was open, smiling crazily as if she were pleased I was crying.

"You want me to be someone that I'm not!" I sobbed. "I'll never be the kind of daughter you want me to be!"

"Only two kinds of daughters," she shouted in Chinese. "Those who are obedient and those who follow their own mind! Only one kind of daughter can live in this house. Obedient daughter!"

"Then I wish I wasn't your daughter. I wish you weren't my mother," I shouted. As I said these things I got scared. I felt like worms and toads and slimy things were crawling out of my chest, but it also felt good, as if this awful side of me had surfaced, at last.

"Too late change this," said my mother shrilly.

And I could sense her anger rising to its breaking point. I wanted to see it spill over. And that's when I remembered the babies she had lost in China, the ones we never talked about. "Then I wish I'd never been born!" I shouted. "I wish I were dead! Like them."

It was as if I had said the magic words. Alakazam!—and her face went blank, her mouth closed, her arms went slack, and she backed out of the room, stunned, as if she were blowing away like a small brown leaf, thin, brittle, lifeless.

It was not the only disappointment my mother felt in me. In the years that followed, I failed her so many times, each time asserting my own will, my right to fall short of expectations. I didn't get straight As. I didn't become class president. I didn't get into Stanford. I dropped out of college.

For unlike my mother, I did not believe I could be anything I wanted to be. I could only be me.

And for all those years, we never talked about the disaster at the recital or my terrible accusations afterward at the piano bench. All that remained unchecked, like a betrayal that was now unspeakable. So I never found a way to ask her why she had hoped for something so large that failure was inevitable.

And even worse, I never asked her what frightened me the most: Why had she given up hope?

For after our struggle at the piano, she never mentioned my playing again. The lessons stopped. The lid to the piano was closed, shutting out the dust, my misery, and her dreams.

So she surprised me. A few years ago, she offered to give me the piano, for my thirtieth birthday. I had not played in all those years. I saw the offer as a sign of forgiveness, a tremendous burden removed.

"Are you sure?" I asked shyly. "I mean, won't you and Dad miss it?"

"No, this your piano," she said firmly. "Always your piano. You only one can play."

"Well, I probably can't play anymore," I said. "It's been years."

"You pick up fast," said my mother, as if she knew this was certain. "You have natural talent. You could been genius if you want to."

"No I couldn't."

"You just not trying," said my mother. And she was neither angry nor sad. She said it as if to announce a fact that could never be disproved. "Take it," she said.

But I didn't at first. It was enough that she had offered it to me. And after that, every time I saw it in my parents' living room, standing in front of the bay windows, it made me feel proud, as if it were a shiny trophy I had won back.

Last week I sent a tuner over to my parents' apartment and had the piano reconditioned, for purely sentimental reasons. My mother had died a few months before and I had been getting things in order for my father, a little bit at a time. I put the jewelry in special silk pouches. The sweaters she had knitted in yellow, pink, bright orange—all the colors I hated—I put those in moth-proof boxes. I found some old Chinese silk dresses, the kind with little slits up the sides. I rubbed the old silk against my skin, then wrapped them in tissue and decided to take them home with me.

After I had the piano tuned, I opened the lid and touched the keys. It sounded even richer than I remembered. Really, it was a very good piano. Inside the bench were the same exercise notes with handwritten scales, the same second-hand music books with their covers held together with yellow tape.

I opened up the Schumann book to the dark little piece I had played at the recital. It was on the left-hand side of the page, "Pleading Child." It looked more difficult than I remembered. I played a few bars, surprised at how easily the notes came back to me.

And for the first time, or so it seemed, I noticed the piece on the right-hand side. It was called "Perfectly Contented." I tried to play this one as well. It had a lighter melody but the same flowing rhythm and turned out to be quite easy. "Pleading Child" was shorter but slower; "Perfectly Contented" was longer but faster. And after I played them both a few times, I realized they were two halves of the same song.

QUESTIONS FOR "JING-MEI WOO: TWO KINDS" BY AMY TAN

Talking About the Text

1. Amy Tan begins her account with a cultural myth. Identify this myth and explain how it influences Jing-Mei Woo, her mother, and her friends.
2. Many can relate to Jing-Mei Woo's experience of having to take piano lessons or of enduring similar parent-inspired self-improvement projects. How does Jing-Mei handle this situation? What does Jing-Mei think she is accomplishing by this strategy? Evaluate Jing-Mei's and her parents' initial reactions to her piano recital performance. How would you react if you were Jing-Mei? Her parents?
3. Re-read with attention the bitter argument scene between Jing-Mei and her mother. What do you think is really at stake in their battle? Is this conflict resolved at the end? Use evidence from the story to support your view.

Exploring Issues

1. Identify a possible cultural conflict in Amy Tan's account. Compare this conflict with that experienced by other Asian girls from the selection by David Haldane.
2. Television helps to influence the images we form about who we are and who we want to be. Survey a few current television shows. How do they depict the "successful" person? The "failure"?

Writing Assignments

1. Write a narrative about a time in your life when your mother or father wanted you to do something you really resented. How did you handle the situation? Explain in your account what you believe both you and your parents expected of one another. If you can, go even further in this assignment and try to explain what was motivating you and your parents' actions and expectations.
2. Write a dialogue between a parent and son or daughter focusing on a single conflict. In your dialogue you may choose to try to resolve the conflict, or you may leave it unresolved.
3. Imagine that you are the counselor trying to help resolve a parent-teen-ager conflict. Assume that you are talking to both of the parties and first identify what you think each perceives the conflict to be. Next, present as fairly as you can what you think each side feels about the situation. Then go on to offer your advice about how the parent and teen-ager might work out their dilemma.
4. Write an argument in which you take a position regarding a conflict

between a son or daughter and his or her parents. Try to focus on specific issues related to the rights of the parents versus those of their offspring. You might, for example, single out dating practices and cur-few regulations, career conflicts, finances, one's choice of friends, or drug and/or alcohol use. In developing your argument, articulate a specific opinion you wish to defend and support your argument with reasons, examples, and possibly with references (either through quota-tion, paraphrase, or summary) from relevant texts.

Reading 42

What Happened to the Family?

Jerrold Footlick, with Elizabeth Leonard

The following essay was the lead article in *Newsweek*'s special edition (Winter/Spring 1990) entitled "The 21st Century Family." Jerrold Footlick, the primary writer of this article, is a senior editor of *Newsweek* and has received numerous journalism honors for his work, particularly for his writing on legal affairs and recently for his work as editor of *Newsweek* on Campus from 1986 to 1988. The writers provide us with an overview of the family, explaining where it has been as an institution and where it is now. They describe some disturbing trends which, if these trends hold steady, may spell far-reaching social, economic, and political consequences.

The American family does not exist. Rather, we are creating many American families of diverse styles and shapes. In unprecedented numbers, our families are unalike: We have fathers working while mothers keep house; fathers and mothers both working away from home; single parents; second marriages bring-ing children together from unrelated backgrounds; childless couples; unmar-ried couples, with and without children; gay and lesbian parents. We are living through a period of historic change in American family life.

The upheaval is evident everywhere in our culture. Babies have babies, kids refuse to grow up and leave home, affluent Yuppies prize their BMWs more than children, rich and poor children alike blot their minds with drugs, people casually move in with each other and out again. The divorce rate has doubled since 1965, and demographers project that half of all first marriages made today will end in divorce. Six out of 10 second marriages will probably collapse. One third of all children born in the past decade will probably live in a stepfamily before they are 18. One out of every four children today is being raised by a single parent. About 22 percent of children today were born out of wedlock; of those, about a third were born to a teenage mother. One out of every five children lives in poverty; the rate is twice as high among blacks and Hispanics.

Most of us are still reeling from the shock of such turmoil. Americans—in their living rooms, in their boardrooms and in the halls of Congress—are struggling to understand what has gone wrong. We find family life worse than it was a decade ago, according to a NEWSWEEK Poll, and we are not sanguine about the next decade. For instance, two thirds of those polled think a family should be prepared to make "financial sacrifices so that one parent can stay home to raise the children." But that isn't likely to happen. An astonishing two thirds of all mothers are in the labor force, roughly double the rate in 1955, and more than half of all mothers of infants are in the work force.

Parents feel torn between work and family obligations. Marriage is a fragile institution—not something anyone can count on. Children seem to be paying the price for their elders' confusion. "There is an increasing understanding of the emotional cost of having children," says Larry L. Bumpass, a University of Wisconsin demographer. "People once thought parenting ended when their children were 18. Now they know it stretches into the 20s and beyond." Divorce has left a devastated generation in its wake, and for many youngsters, the pain is compounded by poverty and neglect. While politicians and psychologists debate cause and solution, everyone suffers. Even the most traditional of families feel an uneasy sense of emotional dislocation. Three decades ago the mother who kept the house spotless and cooked dinner for her husband and children each evening could be confident and secure in her role. Today, although her numbers are still strong—a third of mothers whose children are under 18 stay home—the woman who opts out of a paycheck may well feel defensive, undervalued, as though she were too incompetent to get "a real job." And yet the traditional family retains a profound hold on the American imagination.

The historical irony here is that the traditional family is something of an anomaly. From Colonial days to the mid-19th century, most fathers and mothers worked side by side, in or near their homes, farming or plying trades. Each contributed to family income, and—within carefully delineated roles—they shared the responsibility of child rearing. Only with the advent of the Industrial Revolution did men go off to work in a distant place like a factory or an office. Men alone began producing the family income; by being away from home much of the time, however, they also surrendered much of their influence on their children.. Mothers, who by social custom weren't supposed to work for pay outside the home, minded the hearth, nurtured the children and placed their economic well-being totally in the hands of their husbands.

Most scholars now consider the "bread-winner-homemaker" model unusual, applicable in limited circumstances for a limited time. It was a distinctly white middle-class phenomenon, for example; it never applied widely among blacks or new immigrants, who could rarely afford to have only a single earner in the family. This model thrived roughly from 1860 to 1920, peaking, as far as demographers can measure, about 1890. Demographers and historians see no dramatic turning point just then, but rather a confluence of social and economic circumstances. Husbands' absolute control of family finances and their independent lives away from home shook the family structure. A long recession beginning in 1893 strained family finances. At the same time, new attention was being paid to women's education. Around this period, the Census Bureau captured a slow, steady, parallel climb in the rates of working women and divorce—a climb that has shown few signs of slowing down throughout this century.

The years immediately after World War II, however, seemed to mark a reaffirmation of the traditional family. The return of the soldiers led directly to high fertility rates and the famous baby boom. The median age of first marriage, which had been climbing for decades, fell in 1956 to a historic low, 22.5 years for men and 20.1 for women. The divorce rate slumped slightly. Women, suddenly more likely to be married and to have children, were also satisfied to give up the paid jobs they had held in record numbers during the war. A general prosperity made it possible for men alone to support their families. Then, by the early '60s, all those developments, caused by aberrational postwar conditions, reverted to the patterns they had followed throughout the century. The fertility rate went down, and the age of first marriage went back up. Prosperity cycled to recession, and the divorce rate again rose and women plunged back heartily into the job market. In 1960, 19 percent of mothers with children under 6 were in the work force, along with 39 percent of those with children between 6 and 17. Thus, while the Cleaver family and Ozzie and Harriet were still planting the idealized family deeper into the national subconscious, it was struggling.

Now the tradition survives, in a way, precisely because of Ozzie and Harriet. The television programs of the '50s and '60s validated a family style during a period in which today's leaders—congressmen, corporate executives, university professors, magazine editors—were growing up or beginning to establish their own families. (The impact of the idealized family was further magnified by the very size of the postwar generation.) "The traditional model reaches back as far as personal memory goes for most of those who [currently] teach and write and philosophize," says Yale University historian John Demos. "And in a time when parents seem to feel a great deal of change in family experience, that image is comfortingly solid and secure, a counterpoint to what we think is threatening for the future."

We *do* feel uneasy about the future. We have just begun to admit that exchanging old-fashioned family values for independence and self-expression may exact a price. "This is an incendiary issue," says Arlie Hochschild, a sociologist at the University of California, Berkeley, and author of the controversial book "The Second Shift." "Husbands, wives, children are not getting enough family life. Nobody is. People are hurting." A mother may go to work because her family needs the money, or to afford luxuries, or because she is educated for a career or because she wants to; she will be more independent but she will probably see less of her children. And her husband, if she has a husband, is not likely to make up the difference with the children. We want it both ways. We're glad we live in a society that is more comfortable living with gay couples, working women, divorced men and stepparents and single mothers—people who are reaching in some fashion for self-fulfillment. But we also understand the value of a family life that will provide a stable and nurturing environment in which to raise children—in other words, an environment in which personal goals have to be sacrificed. How do we reconcile the two?

The answer lies in some hard thinking about what a family is for. What do we talk about when we talk about family? Many of us have an emotional reaction to that question. Thinking about family reminds us of the way we were, and the way we dreamed we might be. We remember trips in the car, eager to find out whose side of the road would have more cows and horses to count. We remember raking leaves and the sound of a marching band at the high-school football game. We remember doing homework and wondering what college might be like. It was not all fun and games, of course. There were angry words spoken, and parents and grandparents who somehow were no longer around, and for some of us not enough to eat or clothes not warm enough or nice enough. Then we grow up and marvel at what we can accomplish, and the human beings we can produce, and we sometimes doubt our ability to do the things we want to do—have to do—for our children. And live our own lives besides.

Practical considerations require us to pin down what the family is all about. Tax bills, welfare and insurance payments, adoption rights and other real-life events can turn on what constitutes a family. Our expectations of what a family ought to be will also shape the kinds of social policies we want. Webster's offers 22 definitions. The Census Bureau has settled on "two or more persons related by birth, marriage or adoption who reside in the same household." New York state's highest court stretched the definition last summer: it held that the survivor of a gay couple retained the legal rights to an apartment they had long shared, just as a surviving husband or wife could. Looking to the "totality of the relationship," the court set four standards for a family: (1) the "exclusivity and longevity of a relationship"; (2) the "level of emotional and financial commitment"; (3) how the couple "conducted their everyday lives and held themselves out to society"; (4) the "reliance placed upon one another for daily services." That approach incenses social critic Midge Decter. "You can call homosexual households 'families,' and you can define 'family' any way you want to, but you can't fool Mother Nature," says Decter. "A family is a mommy and a daddy and their children."

A State of California task force on the future of the family came up with still another conclusion. It decided a family could be measured by the things it should do for its members, which it called "functions": maintain the physical health and safety of its members; help shape a belief system of goals and values; teach social skills, and create a place for recuperation from external stresses. In a recent "family values" survey conducted for the Massachusetts Mutual Insurance Co., respondents were given several choices of family definitions; three quarters of them chose "a group who love and care for each other." Ultimately, to appropriate U.S. Supreme Court Justice Potter Stewart's memorable dictum, we may not be able to define a family, but we know one when we see it.

We enter the 21st century with a heightened sensitivity to family issues. Helping parents and children is a bottom-line concern, no longer a matter of debate. Economists say the smaller labor force of the future means that every skilled employee will be an increasingly valuable asset; we won't be able to afford to waste human resources. Even now companies cannot ignore the needs of working parents. Support systems like day care are becoming a necessity. High rates of child poverty and child abuse are everybody's problem, as is declining school performance and anything else that threatens our global competitiveness. "By the end of the century," says Columbia University sociologist Shelia B. Kamerman, "it will be conventional wisdom to invest in our children."

Those are the familiar demographic forces. But there are other potential tremors just below the surface. By 2020, one in three children will come from a minority group—Hispanic-Americans, African-Americans, Asian-Americans and others. Their parents will command unprecedented political clout. Minorities and women together will make up the majority of new entrants into the work force. Minority children are usually the neediest among us, and they will want government support, especially in the schools. At about the same time, many baby boomers will be retired, and they will want help from Washington as well. Billions of dollars are at stake, and the country's priorities in handing out those dollars are not yet clear. After all, children and the elderly are both part of our families. How should the government spend taxpayers' dollars—on long-term nursing care or better day care?

So far, the political debate on family issues has split largely along predictable ideological lines. Conservatives want to preserve the family of the '50s; they say there has been too much governmental intrusion already, with disastrous results. Their evidence: the underclass, a veritable caste of untouchables in the inner cities where the cycle of welfare dependency and teenage pregnancy thwarts attempts at reform. Liberals say government can and should help. We can measure which programs work, they say; we just don't put our money and support in the right places. Enrichment programs like Head Start, better prenatal care, quality day care—no one questions the effectiveness of these efforts. And liberals see even more to be done. "We have a rare opportunity to make changes now that could be meaningful into the next century," says Marian Wright Edelman, president of the Children's Defense Fund. But many elements that liberals would like to see on a children's agenda are certain to generate bitter political controversy. Among some of the things that could be included in a national family policy:

- Child and family allowances with payments scaled to the number of children in each family;
- Guarantees to mothers of full job protection, seniority and benefits upon their return to work after maternity leave;
- Pay equity for working women;
- Cash payments to mothers for wages lost during maternity leave;
- Full health-care programs for all children;
- National standards for day care.

Our legacy to the future must be a program of action that transcends ideology. And there are indications that we are watching the birth of a liberal/conservative coalition on family issues. "Family issues ring true for people across the political spectrum," says David Blankenhorn, president of the Institute for American Values, a New York think tank on family policy issues. "The well-being of families is both politically and culturally resonant; it is something that touches people's everyday lives." The government is already responding to the challenge in some ways. For example, President George Bush agreed at the recent Education Summit to support increased funding for Head Start, which is by common consent the most successful federal program for preschoolers, yet now reaches only 18 percent of the eligible children.

These issues will occupy us on a national level well into the next century. Yet in our everyday lives, we have begun to find solutions. Some mothers, torn between a desire to stay home with their children and to move ahead in their careers, are adopting a style known as sequencing. After establishing themselves in their career or earning an advanced degree, they step off the career ladder for a few years to focus on children and home. When children reach school age, they return to full-time jobs. Others take a less drastic approach, temporarily switching to part-time work or lower-pressure jobs to carve out more time with their young children. But renewing careers that have been on hiatus is not easy, and women will always suffer vocationally if it is they who must take off to nurture children. There is, obviously, another way: fathers can accept more home and family responsibilities, even to the point of interrupting their own careers. "I expect a significant change by 2020," says sociologist Hochschild. "A majority of men married to working wives will share equally in the responsibilities of home." Perhaps tradition will keep us from ever truly equalizing either child rearing or ironing—in fact, surveys on chore sharing don't hold much promise for the harried working mother. But we have moved a long way since the 1950s. And just because we haven't tried family equality yet doesn't mean we won't ever try it.

That's the magic for American families in the 21st century: we can try many things. As certainly as anything can be estimated, women are not going to turn their backs on education and careers, are not going to leave the work force for adult lives as full-time homemakers and mothers. And the nation's businesses will encourage their efforts, if only because they will need the skilled labor. Yet Americans will not turn their backs completely on the idealized family we remember fondly. Thus, we must create accommodations that are new, but reflect our heritage. Our families will continue to be different in the 21st century except in one way. They will give us sustenance and love as they always have.

QUESTIONS FOR "WHAT HAPPENED TO THE FAMILY?" BY JERROLD K. FOOTLICK WITH ELIZABETH LEONARD

Talking About the Text

1. Why do you think this *Newsweek* article begins with this sentence: "The American family does not exist"?
2. What is the "ideal" family image? How, according to Footlick, has this image been perpetuated? Why do you think this ideal image has persisted in the imaginations of some segments of our society?
3. According to these *Newsweek* writers, what are some of the disruptive forces pulling families apart?
4. Re-read the discussion about various attempts to define the family. What is gained and lost in terms of our understanding of the family by some of these proposed definitions?
5. U.S. Supreme Court Justice Potter Stewart is paraphrased as saying that "we may not be able to define a family, but we know one when we see it." What do you think he means by this? In what ways might he be wrong?

Exploring Issues

1. How realistic is the traditional family? Describe some alternatives and debate their viability as effective "families."
2. Do you agree that such things as divorce and teenage pregnancy are serious threats to the well-being of the family? Why do you agree or disagree?
3. What do you see as some very real dangers to the family? What do you propose can be done about minimizing these dangers?

Writing Assignments

1. Attempt a revision of your earlier definition paper on the family. Try to include what you have learned since your last draft and rewrite another draft citing examples from later selections you have read as well as from opinions generated by class discussions.
2. As head of a government agency responsible for recommending types of assistance for low-income families, you have been asked to write recommendations and justify them. Do some research to find out what is currently available for these families. Gather and evaluate a variety of possibilities before you decide on your recommendations.

3. Write a letter to a mother- or father-to-be telling him or her what insights you have obtained about effective parenting. Discuss some of the typical problems the parent will encounter and what could be effective ways of dealing with such conflicts.

Reading 43

True Blue

Lynn Darling

The essay that follows is from *Esquire* magazine's book *Portrait of America* (1985). Lynn Darling, a frequent contributor to *Esquire,* was born in Pittsburgh and knows well the life surrounding work in the steel mills. Here she tells us about Falco Paterra and the severe problems he faces subsequent to the mill's closing down for good. Paterra reflects on his past achievements, considers his future prospects, and hopes his children can avoid his fate.

In a softly falling snow Falco Paterra drives down to the gates of the National Works steel mill, the place that for thirty-four years defined his life. The mill is nearly closed now. There is nothing much to see except the maze of long, low buildings and rust-reddened smokestacks, no noise except the gossip and laughter of the security guards, but it remains an enormous presence, flanking the town of McKeesport for two miles along the Monongahela River.

It is still a little strange for him to see the mill this way, cold and quiet, strange to see the town this way. Downtown McKeesport is almost empty. The display windows of the big department stores are covered, giving the city a blind, groping quality. Deserted watchtowers look over the center of the town, where the railroad once ran, where the long trains of coal cars sometimes took half an hour to pass by. CLOSED UN   THER NOTICE says the sign over the last movie theater.

Falco among the ruins: he is a working man, the son and the grandson of steelworkers, blue-collar all of his life. He is fifty-four years old, the father of three children, a square-built man with deep-set, dark-circled eyes and a voice that is perpetually hoarse, as if it had been worn away by the constant crash and roar of the mill. He wears a soft cloth cap over his head, partly because it is cold outside and partly because he is a little self-conscious about growing bald. Beneath his shirt he wears two medals: one of Saint Christopher, who protects the traveler, and the other of Saint Peter, "who was like me," he says, "weak and strong at the same time."

He is an ordinary man, leading an ordinary life, of the kind that usually become visible only when they crack, when anger or violence forces them open and the headlines examine the fragments for whatever meaning they can find. But Falco didn't crack. All his life he has done what has been expected of him and drawn his strength and his pride from the fact that he is the author of his family's fate. Doing right was the way he gained control of his life, in a world dominated by the arbitrary power of the mill.

But now there is nothing to do.

Now Falco's family is grown and the mill is closed and he has discovered that unemployment is a kind of exile from the rock on which he anchored himself. And yet he seems untouched by the bitterness and sense of betrayal that hang over much of McKeesport. "We're down, but we're not out," he likes to say to the wraithlike old men who were the local football heroes of his youth. The old men smile and nod their heads.

The mill was supposed to go on forever. That was part of the deal in the Monongahela Valley. And since the turn of the century, things stayed pretty much the same there as long as the steel was being made. It is a place of taverns and churches, of neat small homes on steep twisting streets that curve precipitously past the geography of rock and river. It is a place of hard work, saving grace, and cherished rituals, the kind of place where the commercials on late-night local television advertise sales on communion dresses.

But now the valley is dying, and the little towns that held the mills in their dependent embrace are dying, too. It was always a place of good times and bad times, but now the good times seem to be permanently gone. Now it's the hour for holding on to whatever's left, and what is left is family. It was the way the immigrants survived when they arrived here, and it is the way their descendants survive now. Family: it's what they preached in this valley. You've got nothing but your family.

Falco remembers so clearly what it was like when he was young, as if memory were a lighthouse calling him home. Years ago his world was round and whole, as smoothly perfect as an egg. He grew up in the Third Ward, hard by the river and the railroad tracks, where a train rushing by at night could shake a boy loose from his dreams. Everyone had pretty much the same then, which is to say, not much of anything, except the urge to have something better.

Like almost everyone in the valley, his neighbors came from someplace else. Falco's people, a family of black-haired, handsome men, came from Palena, Italy. The Paterra brothers all worked in the hot mill, and they all played football. Even Uncle Herb, who lost all his fingers in the mill, still found a way to catch the ball, to keep on playing. On Moran Field there was always the possibility of one clean moment—the bright arc of a ball, the anticipated play—that brought with it a giddy peace. Sports kept the community together; when you had nothing else, you could always play ball.

In the summer the old Third Ward gang, Flizzie and Clang and Bo and the rest, played street hockey and baseball and cooled off the in the public pool. It was the season of national-day picnics and weddings. Every summer the Holy Family Polish Church held a carnival, and every summer Falco won a basket of fruit.

In winter the days were given over to the discipline of the nuns of St. Mary's German Catholic School, who kept the peace with wooden paddles and bamboo rattans. The priests were like God then: one of them called the boy Tony because, he said, there had never been a saint named Falco.

When Falco was in ninth grade, his father got a better job in the mill and was working more steadily. They moved away from Railroad Street, up the hill to a dark-gray house on Jenny Lind Street. Falco's grandparents lived next door. There he danced with his aunts on the hard wood floor of the sun parlor and watched his grandfather make dark, sweet wine from the grapes he planted on the arbors in the back, and he grew up safe in a world that pointed him like an arrow to the mill.

"You wish it could be like that again," Falco says. "Things were a lot simpler then. You knew you could get a job. If you were willing to put up with the heat and the dirt, you could get a job anywhere."

He drives slowly through the old neighborhood, past empty lots and faded frame houses. He knows just about everyone he meets, the cop on the beat and the number baron's nephew, the pensioner heading home from 12:30 Mass. He still attends St. Mary's Church, but the stern-eyed nuns are gone now, and in their place is Father Tom Smith, who calls himself the Singing and Dancing Priest and forages for souls in the local supper clubs, wearing top hat and tails. Life is a gas, he sings, it's a ring-a-ding-ding.

There is talk that they'll tear the mills down and put up an industrial park, and then maybe the valley will live again. The politicians and the developers like to say that the area is changing its image, that a service-oriented high-tech economy will bring a new prosperity. The mill workers know what that means—they'll be flipping hamburgers instead of making steel. You can't stake a future on the minimum wage: the means to make it on their own will have gone for good.

Falco started in the mill when he was nineteen. He remembers the date: May 26, 1950. He was scared that first day, all that hot metal flying around and these guys getting so close to it he wondered how they didn't get burned. He began to see that working in a mill was like living in a foxhole. The pride came from knowing what to do in ridiculous, often dangerous situations. Once in a while, on the open hearth, there would be a wild heat, somebody was going to get burned up. You never knew.

It takes a man ten years to just learn his way around a steel mill. Falco started in the labor gang, digging ditches. He kept his mouth shut, did his job, lent a hand when he could. He worked the soaking pits, where a man walked knee-deep in water. He scaled away the crust that formed when the ingots were soaked, while the ash fell and the heat blazed. He stamped the steel and cut and hauled it. He learned the hot mill, from the catwalks to the pouring floor, the blast furnace, the open hearth, and learned how it all came together, the complicated alchemy that turned the red-orange of molten iron into cold, blue-gray steel.

Three years after he started in the mill, he married. Falco met Edna at a Sunday-afternoon football game when she was still in high school. She was standing on the sidelines, and he practically plowed into her on one play, covered with mud. The next time he saw her was at the Friday-night dance at St. Stephen's, where you could dance all evening for a dime. They danced to Sinatra singing "Five Minutes More," and after that no one else asked her to dance. He walked her home that night, but he waited two months before he kissed her.

Young men grow up fast in the valley. They marry girls they've known all their lives and have their children quickly. The talk, even when it is overheard in restaurants and shopping centers, is intensely intimate and interconnected, hungering for the latest dispatch on Jenny's other son, Karen's younger sister. So they raise their children and fly them like flags, a salute to their ability to make good.

Now some of the younger unemployed steelworkers are punch-drunk on their anger, having watched wives and children slip away like dust motes on the air. "Love goes out with the paycheck," they say between clenched teeth. But it was different for Falco and Edna.

They started out with nothing—rented rooms and borrowed furniture. A month after they were married, Falco was laid off. In the beginning that threat was always over their heads. He never knew how much he was going to work.

Edna was nineteen when she left her father's house for her husband's house. Two days after they were married, Falco went to work. It was a night shift, she remembers, because she had never in her life been alone at night.

"You're so stupid then," Edna says. "You don't think about being laid off, about not working. That was all I wanted out of life. Times were tough, but times are tougher now. We always figured things would keep getting better. We wanted to see our kids do better than we did, and if you have that to shoot at, you can make it."

There were years that ate all their savings, when they had to cash in an insurance policy in order to live, years when Falco's parents helped keep him afloat, but, he says, "She never made me feel bad about it."

"I always felt," Edna says, "that we were in it together." She is still a pretty woman, with dark eyes easily moved to laughter and to tears. There was a temper in her, too, in her younger days, she says; her husband's not so sure the past tense is appropriate.

"I have to give Edna 95 percent of the credit," he says.

"I knew how to save you money, didn't I?" she replies. "I knew how to stretch a penny. If I only had a dollar, I could still make supper on a dollar."

They had three children, two girls and then a boy, who grew up in the narrow two-story house with white aluminum siding they bought four years after they married, the house they live in still. They had wanted a brick home— there was more status to a brick home—but there was always something more important they needed the money for: the girls' weddings and their son's college education.

Falco didn't have much time with his children. He worked around the clock. Day shift followed night shift followed afternoon shift, a week of each. There was just enough time to get adjusted to one before it was time for the next. There was so much that he missed. Falco rarely saw his kids opening their presents on Christmas morning, and he never saw the way his daughters looked coming down the stairs in their prom dresses. His gift was the money he could bring them and the fierce watchfulness he cast over them.

Falco made the rules that kept them out of traffic when they were young and the harsher rules that protected them from even faster moves later on. His vigilance drove his daughters crazy.

That was how he kept them safe. Safe from the ways in which the world in the late seventies was changing—the drugs and the defiance and the fights between black and white. There in the little white house on the sloping hill, he surrounded them with his sense of right.

Janet and Linda followed their mother's lead and married young, to men who worked in the mill. For both of them, marriage wasn't a psychological sandbar on which to strand a life—it was a way to live. "I think my mom and dad are the reason why when I was nineteen I was ready to marry Mark," Linda says, "because they made it look so easy to run a family. I know they never had a lot of money to work with, the hard years that they had to put in, but we always ate, and when we needed clothes it was always, 'We'll get it.' They managed to make the money go."

Falco and Edna had made a promise to themselves: their children would not go through the uncertainty they had survived. But it didn't work out that way. Linda and Mark made a fast start, a baby and a two-story brick house within a year; but when Mark was laid off from the mill, the only work he could get was his current job, as a night watchman for the county.

It's been a little easier for Janet and Dan. Dan went back to college while he was still in the mill. Afterward, during one of the layoffs, he took a job with Equitable Life Assurance at less than half the pay. When the mill came back up for a while, Dan was tempted to return. It was Falco who told him to stay where he was.

Dan had a promotion recently, and the couple is looking for a bigger house. Edna teases them about leading the good life now. But Janet is still angry for her father.

"I'm bitter because he went to work every day and he didn't call in sick because it was Christmas. He gave it all. He sweated for the money to buy our dresses, he sweated for it all, and it wasn't a sacrifice, it was the right thing to do. He deserved more. It wasn't just a job to him, it was everything."

The last job Falco had in the mill was the one he liked the best. It was an office job, scheduler-expediter. He tracked the steel from beginning to end, saw it through its phases, scrounged and connived to get the heat up on time. In time he was talking to the bosses, telling them what to do when things weren't going right. Sometimes they'd even call him at home. It was a good job, it had prestige. He took pride when he heard the men say, "Falco's working tonight; we're gonna make money tonight."

It was steady work, and it paid well. By the time Jeff went to high school, Edna says, the other kids thought he was a rich man's son. They started saving for his college education when he was still in grade school. He finished first in his class at McKeesport High School.

Last summer Jeff graduated from Carnegie-Mellon University and went to work in North Carolina for IBM, making nearly as much money at the beginning of his career as his father did at the end of his. Are things different for his son? "Yes," says his father softly. Will they change him? "I hope not," he says, but in the end Falco must know it's a gamble.

Each generation is stepping up and stepping away. Falco Paterra wanted his son to go to college. Paul Pattera, Falco's father, wanted his sons to stay on the right side of God and the law. "They stayed out of trouble, that was the main thing," he says.

Paul Paterra is old now, pale and bent by recent heart attacks, and his gaunt frame bears only mute testimony to the power and strength that still fire the imagination of his son. He started in the mill when he was fourteen and retired ten years ago, when he was sixty-five. The old man still remembers how his childhood ended, how he finished the eighth grade in the morning and went to work that afternoon, walking past the pool and into the hot mill, where grown men fainted from the heat. "You learn to live tough," he says of that time.

It's hard now for the father to see his son tossed out of work at such an early age. "He don't let on how he's doing. So many times, we try to give him something, and he says, 'No, Mama, I don't need it.' Oh, he's proud, I told her, he's too proud. I try to give him money or something, we pretend it's a gift, but he's too proud to take anything from us. He's smart though, he keeps himself occupied."

Falco carried his responsibilities in the mill with pride, but he had no illusions about his importance. The mill had a way of reminding him just where he fit in. One day he found a dead man there. It was the man who always gave him the hot-metal tonnage reports. He found him slumped over his desk.

He ran out to call someone, but the only one around was Yuno, the dwarf from the janitorial crew, who said, "What's the matter, what's the matter with Tom?"

"Don't go in there, Yuno," Falco said. He told him Tom was dead.

Yuno went running by Falco, screaming like a banshee. Falco called the guards, and when they came he helped them to carry Tom out and put him in an ambulance.

As he was walking back through the mill, one of the observers, Ross Azzarello, walked by and said, "Hey, Falco, what are you doing there?" and Falco said, "Keep quiet, Ross, I think old Tom is dead." And just then, as they were standing there, the whistle blew loud and long and sharp, and that meant "Give us an ingot now, we're ready to roll it."

Falco said, "Look at that, Ross, here's this guy dead here, and we ain't even shut the mill down, we're still rolling ingots, nobody even cares that he's dead. They hauled that guy out and they never lost a minute. To them he's nothing."

"When me and you go, Falco, it's going to be the same," Ross said. "They ain't gonna care about us."

But it wasn't quite the same when Falco went. The end came slowly, with a series of signs that something was wrong. Work that was normally done in their end was taken someplace else. A machine would break down, and instead of repairing it, they'd steal a part from another place in the mill, cannibalizing the machinery.

Falco started running in the hours after his shift was finished—it was a way to release the dread. He didn't want the family to know, didn't want his wife to worry; Jeff was still in school.

But it came finally, the last day the rolling mills ran. It was in March 1982. Falco was the last man out. Before he left he had to tally everything up, do the inventory, finalize all the records. He stayed a couple of hours, had a last look around, then walked out of the mill alone. He took the bag that held his clothes and work shoes, but he left his helmet inside. He figured he was still coming back.

"In the back of my mind, I always had hopes that the fact that we were so skillful down there would convince the company to keep the work here," he says. "I couldn't see them being dumb enough to let the work go elsewhere, where it wouldn't be handled the right way, like we could handle it in this plant. I didn't know that there wasn't going to be the orders to bring here. Or anywhere."

He went to the unemployment office to collect the benefits that were due him, but he couldn't stand it, the way the men standing in line tried to hide from one another. He found out that with his seniority he could go back into the mill if he were willing to work on the janitorial crew. It was the bottom rung of the ladder, but it was work. He called his daughters to make sure they wouldn't be embarrassed; they told him they would be proud.

It was torture going in there in the mornings, he remembers. He'd walk into the offices of the managers who used to consult him, and they'd look up and smile and say, "Well, if it isn't the expert from the lower end," just as they always had, only this time all he had to say in return was, "Where's your toilet at?"

They wouldn't believe it at first, the smiling young men who had come to him for help. But he showed them his bucket and his mop, and they showed him where the washroom was.

Even that job came to an end after a few months. Last year Falco got the letter telling him to come in and sign up for his pension, and whatever lingering hope there was finally had to be put to rest.

It was over. He had watched his world slide slowly away, but through it all he kept to his code. He worked hard, he provided for his family, and against forces larger than himself he made them safe. In the end he forged a kind of heroism in the promises that he kept.

But now that Falco is retired, the days stretch long and empty at times, and he and Edna are careful to stay out of each other's way. In the spring and summer he coaches high school baseball, in the fall he referees high school football, and in the long winter months he runs. Every Tuesday Edna volunteers down at the Allegheny County home for senior citizens; on Fridays she brings them Holy Communion.

The future now is narrow. The modest expectations of a trip to Italy, a newer house, have been replaced by the fear that the new brick senior-citizens' apartment building will be their final home. But the deepest regret is for their grandchildren. "I would have liked to have been around so that if they needed money for college, I could have helped them," Falco says. "I'm still hoping I can do it somehow." He is still a young man, too young to have nothing to do, but too old to be hired for a new job, he has discovered. Yet he still goes through the classifieds, looking for something to fill up the days. "I'm still not used to it," he says. "Every day, you have to think about what you're going to do."

Jeffrey Paterra drives down the broad boulevards of Charlotte, North Carolina, in a brand-new car, dark-haired, intently serious, and very young. His voice is already swept clean of a Pittsburgh accent, meeting the discreet demands of his corporate culture. Still, there are echoes of his father in the large, dark eyes, in the quiet guard he has set on his privacy.

He lives alone in an apartment overlooking the tennis courts in a stucco townhouse complex with other young singles he rarely sees. At night he watches MTV or listens to Bruce Springsteen or the Who, cooks his dinner, and goes to bed on time, for it does neither him nor IBM any good if he doesn't get his rest.

He works on flextime in an office building of white stone and smoked glass, and he talks proudly of how well Big Blue takes care of its employees. He is a mechanical engineer, but his work is confidential, something to do with the development of a new printer.

He chose IBM after interviews with thirty other companies. He flirted with the automakers, but the environment reminded him too much of the steel industry: the sheet-metal siding on the big plants, the union influence, the history of layoffs.

He talks about the mobility he will have, the places he wants to go. No, there is nothing about McKeesport he will miss, except for his family. He had known almost from the beginning that his life was going to be different from Falco's. He knew he would get a job that was more secure than his father's, a decent, respectable job. "I don't think that working in the mill was not respectable," he says. "I think it is, but I think a lot of people have a misconception about the kinds of people that work there."

He remembers watching a football game last year, the Bears against the 49ers. The announcers were talking about Mike Ditka. They talked about how, as a player, he'd been nicknamed Iron Mike, how he came from the valley, that his father was a steelworker. And, they said, he played like it.

"And I wanted to say, 'How does the son of a lawyer play football?' " he remembers. " 'Does he go for his books and say *whereas* and *therefore?*' I don't know. So what were they trying to imply, that he would bite, scratch, and kick? . . . I didn't like that at all, really. Because it meant that he had different values, would approach anything in life differently than the son of a lawyer or a doctor or anything else."

He talks to his parents every week. "A lot of things happened to our family," he says, "and a lot of people may consider them harsh, but they never seemed bad, because we knew that the family was there, and that held everything together. There was nothing to worry about, because we always had each other. That sounds like something out of one of those TV shows, but it's really true."

One summer, between semesters at Carnegie-Mellon, Jeff worked in the steel mill. He learned some lessons there. "Your father is your father," he says, "and you may not analyze him the way you might someone else, maybe because you don't feel like you're entitled to. When I was in the mill I could see that a lot of people there may have been wishing they were doing something else, but that wasn't the way their life worked out. But they knew they couldn't just quit and go to college and get a degree, that was not realistic, so they just . . . put up with it. They were doing it because they had responsibilities, they had a family and they had to provide for them. I thought that was really admirable. You could see it in their faces almost, that some of them didn't want to be there and yet they were, every day, they were there."

At the end of the summer the company offered the college boys permanent jobs. Jeff asked his father what he thought of his going into the mill.

Falco said he'd shoot him first.

QUESTIONS FOR "TRUE BLUE" BY LYNN DARLING

Talking About the Text

1. Do you like Falco Paterra? Why or why not?
2. How do you think Falco defines himself and his life? What does he value?
3. How close does Falco's family approach the traditional ideal family? In what ways might it differ?
4. Re-read this selection and note places in the text where economic conditions influence Falco's family. Draw some preliminary conclusions about the relationship between jobs and income and family unity.

5. How does the writer, Lynn Darling, create a reader's image of Falco and his family?
6. Is Falco's advice to his son an admission of defeat? Explain.

Exploring Issues

1. Consider some or all of the selections you have read before. Can you identify any elements in Falco's family similar to those in other families you have encountered? How might the Paterra family differ from others?
2. Later in this chapter you will read about external forces threatening to tear families apart. Make a list now of those factors seriously affecting the well-being of the family. As you read further in this chapter, return to your list and expand and modify it as you deem appropriate.

Writing Assignments

1. Interview your mother and father and find out a little of their history. What roles did each play? How were decisions made? Who worked? Where? How did economic conditions affect their lives, particularly regarding their planning a family and decisions about where to live?
2. Compare your family to the Paterra family. Use a representative example of a family conflict and show how it was handled by the family as a way of explaining how roles, functions, and family activities are carried out.
3. Write a character sketch of one of your family members using dialogue and action to bring out and illustrate that person's strengths and weaknesses.

Reading 44

The American Father

Maxine Hong Kingston

Maxine Hong Kingston is probably best known for *A Woman Warrior,* (1976) her autobiographical account of her early experiences living in America. Many anthologies have excerpted sections from that work; however, we

have selected "The American Father" from a later work, *China Men* (1980).
In the following narrative revealed by a Chinese immigrant's daughter, we
can glimpse some of the cultural, social, and economic problems that these
immigrants encountered earlier in this century. But we also gain a
memorable portrait of an eccentric "American" father—BaBa—and his
unique manner of dealing with these conflicts.

In 1903 my father was born in San Francisco, where my grandmother had come
disguised as a man. Or, Chinese women once magical, she gave birth at a
distance, she in China, my grandfather and father in San Francisco. She was
good at sending. Or the men of those days had the power to have babies. If my
grandparents did no such wonders, my father nevertheless turned up in San
Francisco an American citizen.

He was also married at a distance. My mother and a few farm women went
out into the chicken yard, and said words over a rooster, a fierce rooster, red of
comb and feathers; then she went back inside, married, a wife. She laughs
telling this wedding story; he doesn't say one way or the other.

When I asked MaMa why she speaks different from BaBa, she says their
parents lived across the river from one another. Maybe his village was America,
the river an ocean, his accent American.

My father's magic was also different from my mother's. He pulled the two
ends of a chalk stub or a cigarette butt, and between his fingers a new stick of
chalk or a fresh cigarette grew long and white. Coins appeared around his
knuckles, and number cards turned into face cards. He did not have a patter but
was a silent magician. I would learn these tricks when I became a grown-up and
never need for cigarettes, money, face cards, or chalk.

He also had the power of going places where nobody else went, and making
places belong to him. I could smell his presence. He owned special places the
way he owned special things like his copper ashtray from the 1939 World's Fair
and his Parker 51. When I explored his closet and desk, I thought, this is a
father place; a father belongs here.

• • •

Another father place was the attic of our next house. Once I had seen his
foot break through the ceiling. He was in the attic, and suddenly his foot broke
through the plaster overhead.

I watched for the day when he left a ladder under the open trap door. I
climbed the ladder through the kitchen ceiling. The attic air was hot, too thick,
smelling of pigeons, their hot feathers. Rafters and floor beams extended in
parallels to a faraway wall, where slats of light slanted from shutters. I did not
know we owned such an extravagance of empty space. I raised myself up on my
forearms like a prairie dog, then balanced sure-footed on the beams, careful not
to step between them and fall through. I climbed down before he returned.

The best of the father places I did not have to win by cunning; he showed me it himself. I had been young enough to hold his hand, which felt splintery with calluses "caused by physical labor," according to MaMa. As we walked, he pointed out sights; he named the plants, told time on the clocks, explained a neon sign in the shape of an owl, which shut one eye in daylight. "It will wink at night," he said. He read signs, and I learned the recurring words: *Company, Association, Hui, Tong.* He greeted the old men with a finger to the hat. At the candy-and-tobacco store, BaBa bought Lucky Strikes and beef jerky, and the old men gave me plum wafers. The tobacconist gave me a cigar box and a candy box. The secret place was not on the busiest Chinatown street but the street across from the park. A pedestrian would look into the barrels and cans in front of the store next door, then walk on to the herbalist's with the school supplies and saucers of herbs in the window, examine the dead flies and larvae, and overlook the secret place completely. (The herbs inside the hundred drawers did not have flies.) BaBa stepped between the grocery store and the herb shop into the kind of sheltered doorway where skid-row men pee and sleep and leave liquor bottles. The place seemed out of business; no one would rent it because it was not eyecatching. It might have been a family association office. On the window were dull gold Chinese words and the number the same as our house number. And delightful, delightful, a big old orange cat sat dozing in the window; it had pushed the shut venetian blinds aside, and its fur was flat against the glass. An iron grillwork with many hinges protected the glass. I tapped on it to see whether the cat was asleep or dead; it blinked.

BaBa found the keys on his chain and unlocked the grating, then the door. Inside was an immense room like a bank or a post office. Suddenly no city street, no noise, no people, no sun. Here was horizontal and vertical order, counters and tables in cool gray twilight. It was safe in here. The cat ran across the cement floor. The place smelled like cat piss or eucalyptus berries. Brass and porcelain spittoons squatted in corners. Another cat, a gray one, walked into the open, and I tried following it, but it ran off. I walked under the tables, which had thick legs.

BaBa filled a bucket with sawdust and water. He and I scattered handfuls of the mixture on the floors, and the place smelled like a carnival. With our pushbrooms leaving wet streaks, we swept the sawdust together, which turned gray as it picked up the dirt. BaBa threw his cigarette butts in it. The cat shit got picked up too. He scooped everything into the dustpan he had made out of an oil can.

We put away our brooms, and I followed him to the wall where sheaves of paper hung by their corners, diamond shaped. "Pigeon lottery," he called them. "Pigeon lottery tickets." Yes, in the wind of the paddle fan the soft thick sheaves ruffled like feathers and wings. He gave me some used sheets. Gamblers had circled green and blue words in pink ink. They had bet on those words. You had to be a poet to win, finding lucky ways words go together. My father showed me the winning words from last night's games: "white jade that grows in water," "red jade that grows in earth," or—not so many words in Chinese—"white waterjade," "redearthjade," "firedragon," "waterdragon." He gave me pen and ink, and I linked words of my own: "rivercloud," "riverfire," the many combinations with *horse, cloud,* and *bird.* The lines and loops connecting the words, which were in squares, a word to a square, made designs too. So this was where my father worked and what he did for a living, keeping track of the gamblers' schemes of words.

We were getting the gambling house ready. Tonight the gamblers would come here from the towns and the fields; they would sail from San Francisco all the way up the river through the Delta to Stockton, which had more gambling than any city on the coast. It would be a party tonight. The gamblers would eat free food and drink free whiskey, and if times were bad, only tea. They'd laugh and exclaim over the poems they made, which were plain and very beautiful: "Shiny water, bright moon." They'd cheer when they won. BaBa let me crank the drum that spun words. It had a little door on top to reach in for the winning words and looked like the cradle that the Forty-niner ancestors had used to sift for gold, and like the drum for the lottery at the Stockton Chinese Community Fourth of July Picnic.

He also let me play with the hole puncher, which was a heavy instrument with a wrought-iron handle that took some strength to raise. I played gambler punching words to win—"cloudswallow," "riverswallow," "river forking," "swallow forking." I also punched perfect round holes in the corners so that I could hang the papers like diamonds and like pigeons. I collected round and crescent confetti in my cigar box.

While I worked on the floor under the tables, BaBa sat behind a counter on his tall stool. With black elastic armbands around his shirtsleeves and an eyeshade on his forehead, he clicked the abacus fast and steadily, stopping to write the numbers down in ledgers. He melted red wax in candle flame and made seals. He checked the pigeon papers, and set out fresh stacks of them. Then we twirled the dials of the safe, wound the grandfather clock, which had a long brass pendulum, meowed at the cats, and locked up. We bought crackly pork on the way home.

According to MaMa, the gambling house belonged to the most powerful Chinese American in Stockton. He paid my father to manage it and to pretend to be the owner. BaBa took the blame for the real owner. When the cop on the beat walked in, BaBa gave him a plate of food, a carton of cigarettes, and a bottle of whiskey. Once a month, the police raided with a paddy wagon, and it was also part of my father's job to be arrested. He never got a record, however, because he thought up a new name for himself every time. Sometimes it came to him while the city sped past the barred windows; sometimes just when the white demon at the desk asked him for it, a name came to him, a new name befitting the situation. They never found out his real names or that he had an American name at all. "I got away with aliases," he said, "because the white demons can't tell one Chinese name from another or one face from another." He had the power of naming. He had a hundred dollars ready in an envelope with which he bribed the demon in charge. It may have been a fine, not a bribe, but BaBa saw him pocket the hundred dollars. After that, the police let him walk out the door. He either walked home or back to the empty gambling house to straighten out the books.

. . .

Sometimes we waited up until BaBa came home from work. In addition to a table and crates, we had for furniture an ironing board and an army cot, which MaMa unfolded next to the gas stove in the wintertime. While she ironed our clothes, she sang and talked story, and I sat on the cot holding one or two of the babies. When BaBa came home, he and MaMa got into the cot and pretended they were refugees under a blanket tent. He brought out his hardbound brown book with the gray and white photographs of white men standing before a flag, sitting in rows of chairs, shaking hands in the street, hand-signaling from car windows. A teacher with a suit stood at a blackboard and pointed out things with a stick. There were no children or women or animals in this book. "Before you came to New York," he told my mother, "I went to school to study English. The classroom looked like this, and every student came from another country." He read words to my mother and told her what they meant. He also wrote them on the blackboard, it and the daruma, the doll which always rights itself when knocked down, the only toys we owned at that time. The little *h*'s looked like chairs, the *e*'s like lidded eyes, but those words were not *chair* and *eye*. " 'Do you speak English?' " He read and translated. " 'Yes, I am learning to speak English better.' 'I speak English a little.' " " 'How are you?' 'I am fine, and you?' " My mother forgot what she learned from one reading to the next. The words had no crags, windows, or hooks to grasp. No pictures. The same *a*, *b*, *c*'s for everything. She couldn't make out ducks, cats, and mice in American cartoons either.

During World War II, a gang of police demons charged into the gambling house with drawn guns. They handcuffed the gamblers and assigned them to paddy wagons and patrol cars, which lined the street. The wagons were so full, people had to stand with their hands up on the ceiling to keep their balance. My father was not jailed or deported, but neither he nor the owner worked in gambling again. They went straight. Stockton became a clean town. From the outside the gambling house looks the same closed down as when it flourished.

My father brought his abacus, the hole punch, and extra tickets home, but those were the last presents for a while. A dismal time began for him.

He became a disheartened man. He was always home. He sat in his chair and stared, or he sat on the floor and stared. He stopped showing the boys the few kung fu moves he knew. He suddenly turned angry and quiet. For a few days he walked up and down on the sidewalk in front of businesses and did not bring himself to enter. He walked right past them in his beautiful clothes and acted very busy, as if having an important other place to go for a job interview. "You're nothing but a gambler," MaMa scolded. "You're spoiled and won't go looking for a job." "The only thing you're trained for is writing poems," she said. "I know you," she said. (I hated her sentences that started with "I know you.") "You poet. You scholar. You gambler. What use is any of that?" "It's a wife's job to scold her husband into working," she explained to us.

My father sat. "You're scared," MaMa accused. "You're shy. You're lazy." "Do something. You never do anything." "You let your so-called friends steal your laundry. You let your brothers and the Communists take your land. You have no head for business." She nagged him and pampered him. MaMa and we kids scraped his back with a porcelain spoon. We did not know whether it was the spoon or the porcelain or the message that was supposed to be efficacious. "Quit being so shy," she advised. "Take a walk through Chinatown and see if any of the uncles has heard of a job. Just ask. You don't even need to apply. Go find out the gossip." "He's shy," she explained him to us, but she was not one to understand shyness, being entirely bold herself. "Why are you so shy? People invite you and go out of their way for you, and you act like a snob or a king. It's only human to reciprocate." "You act like a piece of liver. Who do you think you are? A piece of liver?" She did not understand how some of us run down and stop. Some of us use up all our life force getting out of bed in the morning, and it's a wonder we can get to a chair and sit in it. "You piece of liver. You poet. You scholar. What's the use of a poet and a scholar on the Gold Mountain? You're so skinny. You're not supposed to be so skinny in this country. You have to be tough. You lost the New York laundry. You lost the house with the upstairs. You lost the house with the back porch." She summarized, "No loyal friends or brothers. Savings draining away like time. Can't speak English. Now you've lost the gambling job and the land in China."

Somebody—a Chinese, it had to be a Chinese—dug up our loquat tree, which BaBa had planted in front of the house. He or she had come in the middle of the night and left a big hole. MaMa blamed BaBa for that too, that he didn't go track down the tree and bring it back. In fact, a new loquat tree had appeared in the yard of a house around the corner. He ignored her, stopped shaving, and sat in his T-shirt from morning to night.

He seemed to have lost his feelings. His own mother wrote him asking for money, and he asked for proof that she was still alive before he would send it. He did not say, "I miss her." Maybe she was dead, and the Communists maintained a bureau of grandmother letter writers in order to get our money. That we kids no longer received the sweet taste of invisible candy was no proof that she had stopped sending it; we had outgrown it. For proof, the aunts sent a new photograph of Ah Po. She looked like the same woman, all right, like the pictures we already had but aged. She was ninety-nine years old. She was lying on her side on a lounge chair, alone, her head pillowed on her arm, the other arm along her side, no green tints at her earlobes, fingers, and wrists. She still had little feet and a curved-down mouth. "Maybe she's dead and propped up," we kids conjectured.

BaBa sat drinking whiskey. He no longer bought new clothes. Nor did he go to the dentist and come back telling us the compliments on his perfect teeth, how the dentist said that only one person in a thousand had teeth with no fillings. He no longer advised us that to have perfect teeth, it's good to clamp them together, especially when have a bowel movement.

MaMa assured us that what he was looking forward to was when each child came home with gold. Then he or she (the pronoun is neutral in the spoken language) was to ask the father, "BaBa, what kind of a suit do you want? A silk gown? Or a suit from the West? An Eastern suit or a Western suit? What kind of a Western suit do you want?" She suggested that we ask him right now. Go-out-on-the-road. Make our fortunes. Buy a Western suit for Father.

I went to his closet and studied his suits. He owned gray suits, dark blue ones, and a light pinstripe, expensive, successful suits to wear on the best occasions. Power suits. Money suits. Two-hundred-dollars-apiece New York suits. Businessmen-in-the-movies suits. Boss suits. Suits from before we were born. At the foot of the closet arranged in order, order his habit, were his leather shoes blocked on shoe trees. How could I make money like that? I looked in stores at suits and at the prices. I could never learn to sew this evenly, each suit perfect and similar to the next.

MaMa worked in the fields and the canneries. She showed us how to use her new tools, the pitters and curved knives. We tried on her cap pinned with union buttons and her rubber gloves that smelled like rubber tomatoes. She emptied her buckets, thermoses, shopping bags, lunch pail, apron, and scarf; she brought home every kind of vegetable and fruit grown in San Joaquin County. She said she was tired after work but kept moving, busy, banged doors, drawers, pots and cleaver, turned faucets off and on with *kachunk's* in the pipes. Her cleaver banged on the chopping block for an hour straight as she minced pork and steak into patties. Her energy slammed BaBa back into his chair. She took care of everything; he did not have a reason to get up. He stared at his toes and fingers. "You've lost your sense of emergency," she said; she kept up her sense of emergency every moment.

He dozed and woke with a jerk or a scream. MaMa medicated him with a pill that came in a purple cube lined with red silk quilting, which cushioned a tiny black jar; inside the jar was a black dot made out of ground pearls, ox horn, and ox blood. She dropped this pill in a bantam broth that had steamed all day in a little porcelain crock on metal legs. He drank this soup, also a thick beef broth with gold coins in the bottom, beef teas, squab soup, and still he sat. He sat on. It seemed to me that he was getting skinnier.

"You're getting skinny again," MaMa kept saying. "Eat. Eat. You're less than a hundred pounds."

I cut a Charles Atlas coupon out of a comic book. I read all the small print. Charles Atlas promised to send some free information. "Ninety-seven-pound weakling," the cartoon man called himself. "I'll gamble a stamp," he said. Charles Atlas did not say anything about building fat, which was what my father needed. He already had muscles. But he was ninety-seven pounds like the weakling, maybe ninety pounds. Also he kicked over chairs like in the middle panel. I filled in the coupon and forged his signature. I did not dare ask him how old he was, so I guessed maybe he was half as old as his weight: age forty-five, weight ninety. If Charles Atlas saw that he was even skinnier than the weakling, maybe he would hurry up answering. I took the envelope and stamp from BaBa's desk.

Charles Atlas sent pamphlets with more coupons. From the hints of information, I gathered that my father needed lessons, which cost money. The lessons had to be done vigorously, not just read. There seemed to be no preliminary lesson on how to get up.

The one event of the day that made him get up out of his easy chair was the newspaper. He looked forward to it. He opened the front door and looked for it hours before the mailman was due. *The Gold Mountain News* (or *The Chinese Times*, according to the English logo) came from San Francisco in a paper sleeve on which his name and address were neatly typed. He put on his gold-rimmed glasses and readied his smoking equipment: the 1939 World's Fair ashtray, Lucky Strikes, matches, coffee. He killed several hours reading the paper, scrupulously reading everything, the date on each page, the page numbers, the want ads. Events went on; the world kept moving. The hands on the clocks kept moving. This sitting ought to have felt as good as sitting in his chair on a day off. He was not sick. He checked his limbs, the crooks of his arms. Everything was normal, quite comfortable, his easy chair fitting under him, the room temperature right.

MaMa said a man can be like a rat and bite through wood, bite through glass and rock. "What's wrong?" she asked.

"I'm tired," he said, and she gave him the cure for tiredness, which is to hit the inside joints of elbows and knees until red and black dots—the tiredness—appear on the skin.

He screamed in his sleep. "Night sweats," MaMa diagnosed. "Fear sweats." What he dreamed must have been ax murders. The family man kills his entire family. He throws slain bodies in heaps out the front door. He leaves no family member alive; he or she would suffer too much being the last one. About to swing the ax, screaming in horror of killing, he is also the last little child who runs into the night and hides behind a fence. Someone chops at the bushes beside him. He covers his ears and shuts his mouth tight, but the scream comes out.

I invented a plan to test my theory that males feel no pain; males don't feel. At school, I stood under the trees where the girls played house and watched a strip of cement near the gate. There were two places where boys and girls mixed; one was the kindergarten playground, where we didn't go any more, and the other was this bit of sidewalk. I had a list of boys to kick: the boy who burned spiders, the boy who had grabbed me by my coat lapels like in a gangster movie, the boy who told dirty pregnancy jokes. I would get them one at a time with my heavy shoes, on which I had nailed toe taps and horseshoe taps. I saw my boy, a friendly one for a start. I ran fast, crunching gravel. He was kneeling; I grabbed him by the arm and kicked him sprawling into the circle of marbles. I ran through the girls' playground and playroom to our lavatory, where I looked out the window. Sure enough, he was not crying. "See?" I told the girls. "Boys have no feelings. It's some kind of immunity." It was the same with Chinese boys, black boys, white boys, and Mexican and Filipino boys. Girls and women of all races cried and had feelings. We had to toughen up. We had to be as tough as boys, tougher because we only pretended not to feel pain.

One of my girl friends had a brother who cried, but he had been raised as a girl. Their mother was a German American and their father a Chinese American. This family didn't belong to our Benevolent Association nor did they go to our parties. The youngest boy wore girls' dresses with ruffles and bows, and brown-blondish ringlets grew long to his waist. When this thin, pale boy was about seven, he had to go to school; it was already two years past the time when most people started school. "Come and see something strange," his sister said on Labor Day. I stood in their yard and watched their mother cut off his hair. The hair lay like tails around his feet. Mother cried, and son cried. He was so delicate, he had feelings in his hair; it hurt him to have his hair cut. I did not pick on him.

There was a war between the boys and the girls; we sisters and brothers were evenly matched three against three. The sister next to me, who was like my twin, pushed our oldest brother off the porch railing. He landed on his face and broke two front teeth on the sidewalk. They fought with knives, the cleaver and a boning knife; they circled the dining room table and sliced one another's arms. I did try to stop that fight—they were cutting bloody slits, an earnest fight to the death. The telephone rang. Thinking it was MaMa, I shouted, "Help. Help. We're having a knife fight. They'll kill each other." "Well, do try to stop them." It was the owner's wife; she'd gossip to everybody that our parents had lost control of us, such bad parents who couldn't get respectable jobs, mother gone all day, and kids turned into killers. "That was Big Aunt on the phone," I said, "and she's going to tell the whole town about us," and they quit after a while. Our youngest sister snuck up on our middle brother, who was digging in the ground. She was about to drop a boulder on his head when somebody shouted, "Look out." She only hit his shoulder. I told my girl friends at school that I had a stepfather and three wicked stepbrothers. Among my stepfather's many aliases was the name of my real father, who was gone.

The white girls at school said, "I got a spanking." I said we never got spanked. "My parents don't believe in it," I said, which was true. They didn't know about spanking, which is orderly. My mother swung wooden hangers, the thick kind, and brooms. We got trapped behind a door or under a bed and got hit anywhere (except the head). When the other kids said, "They kissed me good night," I also felt left out; not that I cared about kissing but to be normal.

We children became so wild that we broke BaBa loose from his chair. We goaded him, irked him—*gikked* him—and the gravity suddenly let him go. He chased my sister, who locked herself in a bedroom. "Come out," he shouted. But, of course, she wouldn't, he having a coat hanger in hand and angry. I watched him kick the door; the round mirror fell off the wall and crashed. The door broke open, and he beat her. Only, my sister remembers that it was she who watched my father's shoe against the door and the mirror outside fall, and I who was beaten. But I know I saw the mirror in crazy pieces; I was standing by the table with the blue linoleum top, which was outside the door. I saw his brown shoe against the door and his knee flex and the other brothers and sisters watching from the outside of the door, and heard MaMa saying, "Seven years bad luck." My sister claims that same memory. Neither of us has the recollection of curling up inside that room, whether behind the pounding door or under the bed or in the closet.

A white girl friend, whose jobless and drunk father picked up a sofa and dropped it on her, said, "My mother saw him pushing *me* down the stairs, and *she* was watching from the landing. And I remember him pushing *her,* and *I* was at the landing. Both of us remember looking up and seeing the other rolling down the stairs."

He did not return to sitting. He shaved, put on some good clothes, and went out. He found a friend who had opened a new laundry on El Dorado Street. He went inside and chatted, asked if he could help out. The friend said he had changed his mind about owning the laundry, which he had named New Port Laundry. My father bought it and had a Grand Opening. We were proud and quiet as he wrote in gold and black on big red ribbons. The Chinese community brought flowers, mirrors, and pictures of flowers and one of Guan Goong. BaBa's liveliness returned. It came from nowhere, like my new idea that males have feelings. I had no proof for this idea but took my brothers' word for it.

BaBa made a new special place. There was a trap door on the floor inside the laundry, and BaBa looked like a trap-door spider when he pulled it over his head or lifted it, emerging. The basement light shone through the door's cracks. Stored on the steps, which were also shelves, were some rolled-up flags that belonged to a previous owner; gold eagles gleamed on the pole tips.

We children waited until we were left in charge of the laundry. Then some of us kept a lookout while the rest, hanging on to the edge of the hole, stepped down between the supplies. The stairs were steep against the backs of our legs.

The floor under the building was gray soil, a fine powder. Nothing had ever grown in it; it was sunless, rainless city soil. Beyond the light from one bulb the blackness began, the inside of the earth, the insides of the city. We had our flashlights ready. We chose a tunnel and walked side by side into the dark. There are breezes inside the earth. They blow cool and dry. Blackness absorbed our lights. The people who lived and worked in the four stories above us didn't know how incomplete civilization is, the street only a crust. Down here under the sidewalks and the streets and the cars, the builders had left mounds of loose dirt, piles of dumped cement, rough patches of concrete tamping down and holding back some of the dirt. The posts were unpainted and not square on their pilings. We followed the tunnels to places that had no man-made materials, wild areas, then turned around and headed for the lighted section under the laundry. We never found the ends of some tunnels. We did not find elevators or ramps or the undersides of the buckling metal doors one sees on sidewalks. "Now we know the secret of cities," we told one another. On the shelves built against the dirt walls, BaBa had stacked boxes of notebooks and laundry tickets, rubber stamps, pencils, new brushes, blue bands for the shirts, rolls of wrapping paper, cones of new string, bottles of ink, bottles of distilled water in case of air raids. Here was where we would hide when war came and we went underground for gorilla warfare. We stepped carefully; he had set copper and wood rat traps. I opened boxes until it was time to come up and give someone else a chance to explore.

So my father at last owned his house and his business in America. He bought chicks and squabs, built a chicken run, a pigeon coop, and a turkey pen; he dug a duck pond, set the baby bathtub inside for the lining, and won ducklings and goldfish and turtles at carnivals and county fairs. He bought rabbits and bantams and did not refuse dogs, puppies, cats, and kittens. He told a funny story about a friend of his who kept his sweater on while visiting another friend on a hot day; when the visitor was walking out the gate, the host said, "Well, Uncle, and what are those chicken feet wiggling out of your sweater?" One morning we found a stack of new coloring books and follow-the-dot books on the floor next to our beds. "BaBa left them," we said. He buried wine bottles upside down in the garden; their bottoms made a path of sea-color circles. He gave me a picture from the newspaper of redwoods in Yosemite, and said, "This is beautiful." He talked about a Los Angeles Massacre, but I wished that he had not, and pretended he had not. He told an ancient story about two feuding poets: one killed the other's plant by watering it with hot water. He sang "The Song of the Man of the Green Hill," the end of which goes like this: "The disheveled poet beheads the great whale. He shoots an arrow and hits a suspended flea. He sees well through rhinoceros-horn lenses." This was a song by Kao Chi, who had been executed for his politics; he is famous for poems to his wife and daughter written upon leaving for the capital; he owned a small piece of land where he grew enough to eat without working too hard so he could write poems. BaBa's luffa and grapevines climbed up ropes to the roof of the house. He planted many kinds of gourds, peas, beans, melons, and cabbages—and perennials—tangerines, oranges, grapefruit, almonds, pomegrantes, apples, black figs, and white figs—and from seed pits, another loquat, peaches, apricots, plums of many varieties—trees that take years to fruit.

QUESTIONS FOR "THE AMERICAN FATHER" BY MAXINE HONG KINGSTON

Talking About the Text

1. Why does Maxine Hong Kingston begin her story with this weird anecdote about her father's many possible origins?
2. This story focuses on BaBa, yet MaMa also plays a major role. What are the differences between BaBa and MaMa? What does each value?
3. Through whose eyes is this story told? What effect does this have on your reading?
4. The narrator associates BaBa with special places. In what sense does this searching out and maintaining of special places contribute to a reader's understanding of BaBa's depression and inaction after losing his job? What connections can you make between BaBa's love of poetry and love of special places?

5. Where does the narrator get her theory that "males feel no pain" and that "males don't feel"?
6. What do you think of MaMa's treatment of BaBa during the period of his unemployment and depression?
7. What cures BaBa? Is it important that the narrator presents conflicting versions of who did what to whom? Why?

Exploring Issues

1. Speculate on the kinds of jobs BaBa might consider acceptable. Why does he seem to be so reluctant to go out and look for work? What does this suggest to you about the relationship between work and one's sense of self worth?
2. Compare Falco Paterra from "True Blue" with BaBa. What kinds of cultural, ethnic, or personal values seem to shape their attitudes concerning the importance of work and the role each character plays in his respective family? How do Falco's and BaBa's actions reveal differences in understanding masculinity?
3. The narrator says that when she learned that other kids were kissed good night, she felt "left out." Yet she did not feel left out because she cared about kissing but because she wanted "to be normal." Identify some of the actions by various family members in this story that make them seem "abnormal." Then try to define the standards by which you are judging these actions to deviate from the norm. How much of a role do cultural or ethnic influences play in determining normal behavior?

Writing Assignments

1. In an expository essay, analyze the psychology MaMa uses on BaBa in attempting to cure him of his depression and in coercing him into getting a job. Then go on to present alternative approaches that you think might be more effective in helping BaBa. Would you talk to BaBa differently? Would you encourage him to explore a kind of work that might be more suited to his talents? What else might you try?
2. Write a brief version of "The American Father" told from either MaMa's or BaBa's point of view. Compare versions including both points of view and discuss what MaMa's and BaBa's strengths and weaknesses were in response to the conflicts each had to confront.

Reading 45

Who's Bad?

Itabari Njeri

Itabari Njeri, who previously was a writer, arts critic, and essayist for the
Miami Herald, is currently a writer on the staff of the *Los Angeles Times.*
She has also performed as an actress and singer. *Every Good-Bye Ain't
Gone: Family Portraits and Personal Escapades* is Njeri's first book. "Who's
Bad?" a chapter from that book, recounts her cousin Jeffrey's tragic life in
Harlem, revealing the often insurmountable odds an African American male
faces growing up in an urban ghetto.

My cousin Jeffrey looked like Ricky Nelson and always wanted to be the baddest
nigger on the block.

"Little girl, come here. What you doin' with that white man?" the black
supermarket clerk asked, eyeing me with concern.

"He's not white, that's my cousin," I told him, then ran to catch up with Jeff
several aisles away in the Safeway.

"That man wanted to know if I was white, didn't he?" Jeff asked.

"No he didn't," I said, my face as fixed as granite. Jeff looked me straight in
the eyes but I didn't blink. I knew nothing made him feel worse than people
calling him a white man.

We paid for our groceries—the candy we lifted was in our pockets—then
walked up the hill from Amsterdam Avenue to my parents' apartment on Convent and 129th Street.

"You make a really good sandwich," he said, seated at the dining table. I
glowed. Jeff didn't often hang out with me. He and my cousin Karen were the
oldest grandchildren. I was only number five, and there were a lot of cousins
after me, most of them Jeffrey's brothers and sisters. His mother, my aunt Glo,
had six kids. It was hard to get any attention in that house when I visited.

An old white man, Mr. Javitz, lived there, too. His family couldn't figure why
he chose to spend his last years rooming with my aunt in the heart of Harlem,
116th Street and Seventh Avenue. But I guess Mr. Javitz had the same attitude as
my grandmother, who lived there most of the time, as well: "I'm a Harlemite,"
she boasted, though she'd yet to give up her Jamaican citizenship after more than
forty years in America. She loved the neighborhood's insomnia—sirens in the

night suggesting a death, a fight, a fire. The constant bustle of humanity hustling to earn a cent below her bedroom window from daylight to dark.

Brooklyn, where I lived most of my life, was just too quiet, my grandmother said. Jeff felt the same way. The lure of the neighborhood streets and the incessant household traffic at my aunt's kept me an afterthought in Jeffrey's world—not to mention my age. But he was in my living room now, eating my hero. I stared at him mutely, watching his jaws move. I was eleven and half, counting the days till twelve, and he was almost seventeen.

"Where you goin'?" I asked. He stood up and smoothed his puckered shirt.

"I got to go back downtown."

"I can go with you," I told him, rushing to clear his plate from the table.

"I'm not going straight downtown," he said, following me into the kitchen. He washed his hands in the sink, dried them on a paper towel, then quickly inspected his nails. "I got to make a couple of stops first."

"Oh," I said simply. Some girl, I thought. I followed him down the long hallway in our apartment to the front door. He bent down and kissed me softly on the cheek.

"Thanks for the sandwich. See ya later," he said, and ran down the six flights instead of taking the elevator.

It was the usual chaos the next time I saw him at Aunt Glo's.

"Hey man *stoooop*," Jeff screamed as he fell back in the kitchen chair, laughing and yelling at Karen, our oldest cousin. She was pouring a pitcher of grape Kool-Aid over his head. He had put ice down her back.

Aunt Glo, a useless disciplinarian dressed in a muumuu, marched into the kitchen waving a big yellow spoon dangerously close to Jeffrey's head. "What are you guys doing," she yelled, then burst out laughing.

Ducking, Jeff yelled, "Don't hit me. Karen's the one."

Karen—all the younger cousins called her Kay-Kay—was pretty, twenty, and had her arms folded across her infinitesimal bosom. Her smile was villainous. Her nostrils flared and I started giggling uncontrollably.

"What are you laughing at, Linkatara head?" she demanded. Kay-Kay had all sorts of pet names for me.

"Your face," I said weakly, doubled over from laughing.

"You better stop," she warned, "or you know what's gonna happen, you'll be peeing on the floor."

"Oh no she won't, you uncouth children." Aunt Glo giggled. "My niece only urinates. She was the only four-year-old I ever met who said 'urinate' instead of 'pee.'"

Not only that, in my house one didn't have a belly button, or even a navel: "Make sure your umbilicus is clean," my mother instructed at bathtime. She was the oldest of four children. Aunt Glo was the youngest, and a fast-and-high-liver by profession.

She looked down at me knotted on the kitchen linoleum, holding my stomach. "Girl, go to the bathroom."

"Not before me," Karen yelled—also the inheritor of a weak bladder—and dashed past me.

The ruckus didn't seem to faze Mr. Javitz, who was in bed, in the room-with-bath, right off the kitchen. He never complained about the noise. He either slept right through it or was too removed from reality to care. On these visits to Aunt Glo, I'd occasionally see him shuffle out of his room to dish up dinner from the always present pots on the stove. He'd eat in silence then return to his room. He was never unfriendly, just a bent, yellowing man with liver spots and nothing left to say.

How he and Aunt Glo found each other, I don't know. From my mother's perspective, everything about Aunt Glo is best kept hermetically sealed. When it came to her sister, my mother would just shake her head and say, "Going to hell in a chariot."

Like her son, Aunt Glo never wanted people to think she was white. When she shopped in fancy department stores in the 1950s with my brown-skinned mother, white people would approach her *tsk, tsk, tsking,* at their intimate chatter. "You shouldn't be with that colored woman," they'd take my aunt aside and say.

"That's my sister," she'd spit at them.

Aunt Glo had many personas before her expanding figure was relegated to the capacious muumuu she wore in the kitchen that afternoon, waving the big yellow spoon.

St. Patrick's Day, circa 1950, she stepped off a jet wrapped in a white ermine coat, her dyed-green hair framing her naturally alabaster face. My mother looked for a place to hide as this portent of punk approached her in the airport terminal.

I was born too late to hang with Aunt Glo in her salad days. Back then, she'd take Kay-Kay to the Harlem hot spots and let her sip Shirley Temples at the bar. After a night out, she'd get to sleep in Aunt Glo's bed with a mink coat as a quilt.

Aunt Glo had theatrical aspirations. Burl Ives—Burl Ives? right, that's what Kay-Kay told me—was supposed to have thought her very talented. He planned to help her break into show business, Kay-Kay said. Promises, promises. She missed out on stage fame, but her connections with Harlem's underworld in the 1940s and 1950s did generate some notice—a few inches in one of the New York tabloids, family legend has it.

The ignominious publicity compelled my mother to leave Harlem after college and escape to the more genteel borough of Brooklyn.

But we were living in Harlem now, as well, and would for another few years. Living in Harlem kept me straight, kept me balanced, kept me from being culturally denuded. And Aunt Glo was a counterweight—if an extreme one—to my mother's sometimes sterile primness.

My mother's healthier bourgeois values, however, could not be undermined merely by contact with school friends who were thugs-in-the-making, whose mothers hooked, whose fathers ran numbers and worse, or by the general hustling into which certain members of my own family delved. Instead, their influence kept me in touch with the complex realities of a race constantly under seige and endlessly adapting to survive. Between my mother and my extended family of relatives and friends, I had the opportunity to experience, synthesize or discard—very early—the variegated elements of black urban culture.

But Jeffrey never had the consistent guidance I had. He was raised, initially, not by his mother, but by a childless couple old enough to be his grandparents. When his foster mother died, Aunt Glo married his foster father—dead a few years by the time Kay-Kay poured Kool-Aid over Jeffrey's jet black hair.

Jeff jiggled when he laughed, I remember now. He was tall but tended to be pudgy in his teens. The extra flesh added to the altar boy innocence of his face. He was a good Catholic kid who attended parochial school for years. He could take apart and put together anything electrical. He could have been an engineer. But he was a black male surrounded by the hustling life without a counterweight, without a sense of options—and since it was the early sixties, without the reality of many options. He bought into the street life, but because of his looks, the price of admission was made exceedingly high. He looked too much like the enemy, and always had to prove how bad he was.

Jeff was about nineteen, I think, and just out of jail, the last time we had friendly dealings. He was living with Karen's mother in that shattered urban zone called the South Bronx. I lived there, too, off and on for a year because it was closer to the junior high school I was attending—one of the best in the city but far from my Harlem neighborhood.

I was walking from Willis Avenue up 147th Street, past vast, junk-heaped lots, past five-story walk-ups with broken-down front stoops, their iron railings supporting the tight asses of fine, lean Borinquen young men posturing—legs spread open, hands on their balls—and pimple-faced, fatter ones spreading their cheeks on the iron to less effect.

"Pssst pssst, pssst pssst." One called me. I was thirteen now and my flat-chested cousin, Kay-Kay, didn't call me Linkatara anymore. She called me Milk Maid Bessie. The block was full of Borinquen gang members at war with neighboring black gangs. Black people lived on the block, most of them middle-aged and older, but few my age. I ignored them and kept walking. My aunt's building was still a half block away. I passed another occupied stoop.

"Somebody back there wants you," a Borinquen said. "How come you not talking to my friends?" he asked, moving down the steps toward me. Jeffrey suddenly appeared behind him on the stoop.

"Hey Jill," he called to me. He told the men on the steps, "That's my cousin."

"For real?" one of them asked, looking him up and down.

"Yeah," he said.

No one on the street bothered me after that. If someone even tried, another Borinquen would warn him off. "No man, that's Jeff's cousin."

It had gotten to the point where Jeffrey was tired of denying he was white to black people, especially in the joint. Borinquens, as Jeff explained it, assumed he was a spic born in the States who never learned Spanish. They never thought he was a nigger. Out of jail, on the street, bloods told him he was so white why deal with the hassle of being black? Just go on and pass.

I realize Jeffrey didn't look like a redbone, a high yellow or anything else in the nomenclature of color African-Americans use to distinguish our varied complexions. He looked like one of Ozzie and Harriet's kids. But African-Americans are the product of a New World culture: it's been estimated that 80 percent of us are of mixed-race backgrounds. And while U.S. social custom and law have denied that miscegenated reality to perpetuate their own system of apartheid, it wouldn't be the first trick bag black people got hip to and out of.

But more than twenty years after I walked down that South Bronx block, a whole new generation of African-Americans are either hyping or putting down each other based on skin complexion, still perpetuating what Alice Walker calls colorism and what Spike Lee scratched the surface of in his film about color and class conflict among African-Americans, *School Daze.*

And as I write this, Jeffrey's sister—fair-skinned, golden-haired and living in a tenement above crack-infested Harlem—hopes her second baby looks *black, black, black,* 'cause that will validate her in the eyes of other black people, she says. In the meantime, she'd like to give her older son to somebody else to raise, like her mother, Aunt Glo, 'cause he's so *light, light, light* . . .

The judge, preparing to sentence him, put down Jeffrey's arrest record and looked at him from the bench. My cousin was into drugs now and into theft to support his habit. The judge opened his mouth to speak; Jeffrey beat him to it.

"I'd like something corrected, Your Honor. I am not white, I am black," he said, and demanded the racial classification in his records be changed.

"I'm looking right at you and you look white to me," the judge replied.

"That's my grandmother right there," Jeffrey persisted, pointing to the brown woman in the black felt hat. Physical appearance is always a matter of genetic roulette among so mixed a race of people as the descendents of Africans in the New World. Her light brown skin had grayed with age and actually looked the color of taupe now. "If she's black, I'm black," he said with increased belligerence.

The judge changed his racial designation and added a year to his sentence, too.

Jeff seemed straight for a long time after he left the penitentiary. But it didn't last. He started using heroin again. He stole from my mother. He stole from our grandmother. After that, I wouldn't have anything to do with him.

I was cold and formal the last time we spoke. He was staring out the living room window of my aunt's latest apartment when I walked in. The apartment was just a few blocks from the one on Seventh Avenue where Mr. Javitz had roomed. Mr. Javitz was long dead. The building was sprawling, half inhabited, rundown and poised for urban renewal. "Hello, Jeffrey," I said stiffly.

He looked at me sideways, said "Hi," then quickly averted his eyes, fixing his gaze on the cityscape of Harlem rooftops, crumbling crowns on stone, gray prisons.

He did not look like Ricky Nelson anymore. His face was pasty and pocked. His hair was sandy and thin. But he really had stopped using drugs. He had a daughter. Her Borinquen mother was an addict. Jeff didn't want that for his child. He put her in a Catholic school and took a job as superintendent of the tenement where he and Aunt Glo lived.

I talked with my aunt but said nothing to Jeff. When I was ready to leave, I moved toward him to say good-bye, but couldn't. I felt him shrink away from me; I felt him shrinking inside. I simply said, "Bye."

A few months later his bloated body was found on one of those crumbling Harlem rooftops. Parties to a drug deal gone sour more than a year before had tracked him down and shot him.

I came to New York for the funeral from Miami, where I was working as a journalist. My aunt wanted a big funeral. My mother said there was no money for a big funeral, but she'd do the best she could. She caught a priest on the fly in the funeral home and said, "Father, my nephew is dead and I'd like you to say a few words over him before he's buried." The priest was glad to oblige.

I waited in a vestibule with my other cousins while dozens of friends from Aunt Glo's and Jeff's neighborhood filed into the room where he lay in the alloyed equivalent of a plain pine box. There were no flowers. Thelma, my mother's first cousin, got up from her seat and placed a small bunch of violets on top of the coffin.

"This ain't the type of funeral Jeffrey should have," complained one of his brothers.

"Then you should have paid for it, motherfucker," I told him and walked away. He was peddling drugs and had gotten a younger brother, not even in his teens, busted in a deal.

They carried Aunt Glo in wailing, a person on each side supporting her obese, tented frame. For years she had rarely been seen in public. She almost never left her house.

The priest entered. It was obvious from his slightly quizzical expression and darting eyes that he was trying to figure out what the white man in the coffin had to do with all these very dark and very light and everything-between people.

My mother had told him Jeffrey's full name, and after a few stock religious phrases he began the Hail Mary. ". . . the Lord is with thee, blessed art thou amongst women, and blessed is the fruit of they womb Jesus—"

"Amen," a voice rose.

"Yes Lord," another black Protestant cried, injecting an unaccustomed emotionalism into the prayer. I spotted my mother and Thelma exchanging quick glances. I tried not to laugh when my mother turned and rolled her eyes at me.

"Holy Mary, mother of God, pray for us sinners—"

"Please Jesus, yes."

"—now, and at the hour of our death, Ah-men," the priest concluded.

"Amen," a voice echoed.

Aunt Glo stood in the kitchen of yet another apartment after the funeral. "It was nice of you to come all the way from Miami," she told me. "How come Kay-Kay wouldn't come?"

"She's angry," I said.

"Angry at what?" she snapped. "What has she got to be mad at me about?" I peered into my aunt's eyes and wondered what was behind them. "I don't know what I did wrong," she said. "Your mother is lucky, two fine kids. But my kids, I lose them to the streets."

Jeffrey's daughter, a beautiful girl of about eight, sat quietly in the living room. Her father was dead and her mother had last been seen shooting up in a hallway. Aunt Glo was going to raise her. I looked around the room. The furniture was old, worn and different from the solid pieces she'd had in previous apartments, but she still had her complete set of encyclopedias. I crossed my fingers and hoped by the time Jeff's daughter reached puberty she wouldn't be pregnant and lost to the streets, too.

When I returned to that apartment three years later, Jeffrey's youngest sister was in college and planning to become an attorney. His daughter was a very independent young lady of about eleven. We went shopping one afternoon and she spent the night with me at my mother's house. The next morning, she had already carefully made her bed and was fixing a bowl of cereal when I found her in the kitchen.

Aunt Glo asked me later how she'd behaved and I said great. "I told her how you could take care of yourself and run the house when you were just a little girl. She's got to do the same thing," said my aunt, her once-green hair now in a short, pretty, salt-and-pepper Afro, all her teeth gone, emphysema cutting her breath short. "She's got to know how to do for herself," my aunt said. "I won't always be here."

After her thirteenth birthday, almost to the day, I learned my hopes for Jeffrey's daughter were in vain. The street now owns her and she can be found on it at the midnight hour, with my aunt's consent. And my aunt, who still rarely has the energy to leave home, can work up enough steam to flail her arms and shriek profanity to anyone who tells her someone else should be raising Jeffrey's child.

QUESTIONS FOR "WHO'S BAD?" BY ITABARI NJERI

Talking About the Text

1. Consider the title to this autobiographical account: "Who's Bad?" How would you answer this question?
2. What does Njeri mean when she writes: "Between my mother and my extended family of relatives and friends, I had the opportunity to experience, synthesize or discard—very early—the variegated elements of black urban culture"?
3. We catch only glimpses of Njeri's mother and extended family. But what can you say about Njeri's relationship with her mother in contrast to Jeffrey's and Kay-Kay's relationships with Aunt Glo?
4. Ostensibly Jeffrey is killed because of a bad drug deal. Yet, reflecting on the title further, consider possible familial and social factors contributing to his death.

Exploring Issues

1. What is "colorism"? And how are Jeffery and Aunt Glo caught within this system?
2. You might have noticed the absence of any mention of fathers in this selection. Why is that? Some critics claim that such films as *The Color Purple* present a stereotypical, negative view of the black male. Based on your knowledge, what do you think would be an accurate portrayal of the black male experience in our society?
3. Compare Njeri's extended family conflicts with those of others you have read about. Note what is similar and different.

Writing Assignments

1. Write a brief character sketch of some of the people described in "Who's Bad?" Then have each of them step forward and explain why they do the things that they do. For instance, why does Jeffrey get involved with drugs, why does Kay-Kay refuse to come to the funeral, and why does Aunt Glo believe she can raise Jeffrey's daughter?
2. Assume you can turn back the clock to when Aunt Glo's children were still quite young. Writer a letter to her and gently explain what you think she might do to help her children survive the streets.

Reading 46

Mothers, Sons and the Gangs

Sue Horton

This investigative report by Sue Horton appeared in the *Los Angeles Times Magazine* of October 16, 1988. Horton is presently an assistant professor of journalism at the University of Southern California. She is the author of one book, *The Billionaire Boys Club,* and dozens of magazine and newspaper articles. In the following report Horton has focused on a mother's dilemma in trying to raise her sons while living in crowded urban areas that are overrun with gangs and saturated with drugs.

On the side of a market in East Los Angeles is a roughly done mural, painted by gang members from the Lil' Valley Barrio. The untrained artists did the wall to honor homeboys who met violent deaths on the streets. Two blocks away, the same gang painted another mural, this one depicting the mothers of slain gang members. But, when earthquake repairs were made on the small store that held the mural, the painting was covered over. The mothers are forgotten.

To many mothers of gang members, all across Southern California, the obliterated mural could be taken as an appropriate symbol of their lives. They are, they feel, almost invisible, ignored by many of the law-enforcement agencies and institutions set up to deal with their sons. These women feel isolated, frustrated and angry. "I am tired of people assuming I must be a bad person because my son is a Crip," says a mother who lives in South-Central L.A. "I love my son and have cared for him just like any other mother. Maybe I wasn't perfect, but what mother is?"

Lately, however, some of the officials most involved in dealing with local street gangs have come to realize that to blame a gang member's family and upbringing is to grossly oversimplify the problem. "There is no typical profile of a gang parent," says Jim Galipeau, a Los Angeles County probation officer who works exclusively with gang kids and their families in South-Central Los Angeles. "I have one mother who owns a 12-unit complex, and on the other end of the spectrum is a mom who's a cocaine addict and a prostitute. Mostly it's a one-parent family with the mom making the money, but there are working families with nice homes and gardeners. These parents just happen to live where the gangs are a way of life and their kids become involved."

In many parts of Southern California where street gangs flourish, drop-out rates from neighborhood high schools are as high as 35%. A significant proportion of the families in South-Central and East L.A. are living below the poverty level. Drug use and violent crime are rampant. And opportunities for jobs, education and recreation are limited. It's a setting, authorities say, that causes youths to turn to gangs regardless of their upbringing. "For a lot of these kids," says one LAPD officer, "the gang is about the only happening thing in the neighborhood."

Gangs and gang violence have become subjects of great interest and concern for all of Southern California. Law-enforcement agencies are expending enormous resources in their fight against gang-related crime. But, for the mothers of the targets of this law-enforcement effort, the problem is far more immediate than newspaper headlines and stories on TV news. The problem is family.

And now, some police departments are beginning to realize that mothers, instead of being viewed as part of the problem, should be enlisted to help search for solutions.

Capt. Jack Blair of the Pomona Police Department leads weekly gang-truce meetings attended by parents, gang members and local clergy. In the course of his yearlong involvement with the Pomona program, he has become convinced that "parents are the key to [solving] the whole problem." At his meetings, and at other meetings of parents around the county, Blair believes that parents have begun to make a difference. "Once the parents unite and form groups, talking to each other and sharing information, that is threatening to the gang members. They want anonymity. They don't want their tactics or activities talked about with parents of rival gangs. When the moms are saying, 'Hey, don't go over to this neighborhood,' or 'I know that you went over to that neighborhood,' there is a certain amount of sport removed."

"Ours is not a program to turn your kid in. We don't ask parents to be informants on their child. But the moms realize what an effect they can have on the kids," Blair says. "The kids may go out gang-banging at night, but eventually they have to go back home and eat the dinner their mom's prepared. Even though they might exhibit some of the machismo characteristics, there is still concern on how they are impacting their family."

"Just because you shoot someone," Galipeau adds, "it doesn't mean that you don't love your mother."

Still, even as outsiders begin to recognize the contributions they can make, mothers of gang members face constant fear and worry. They feel overwhelming guilt, asking themselves again and again where they've failed as parents. And they have to deal with the scorn of a society that holds them in some measure responsible for the actions of their sons.

Although these mothers of gang members live in divergent parts of the city and come from a variety of cultures, they share similar pains. These are some of their stories.

TERESA RODRIGUEZ

Fear: Her Son Lived and the Family Became the Target

Teresa Rodriguez spends her Friday nights cowering in a back bedroom of the tiny stucco house she shares with her husband and eight children in a west Pomona barrio. The living room, she knows from experience, is simply not safe.

During the past two years, most often on Fridays, Rodriguez's home has been shot up half a dozen times, and one night recently when her husband came home late from work, someone shot at him. The family's car and house still bear bullet holes.

The problems all started two years ago, when Rodriguez's youngest son was 13. Unbeknown to his mother, he had become a member of a small Pomona gang, Sur 13. One day when he and several other Sur 13 members were out walking, a car full of rival gang members passed by. "Which barrio are you from?" the other gang demanded to know. Most of the Sur 13 boys didn't answer; Rodriguez's son did. Upon hearing the hated neighborhood name spoken aloud, one of the boys in the car leaned out the window with a gun and pulled the trigger.

Rodriguez didn't know for several hours that her son had been shot. "His friends took him to the hospital and left him there. They couldn't find the courage to tell me," she said recently through an interpreter. Finally, one of the neighborhood kids came to the door and told Rodriguez what had happened. She was stunned. Having come to the United States from Mexico in 1973, she was still timid and uncertain about the culture here. "I had no idea any of my sons was in a gang until that day," she said.

The bullet had lodged near the 13-year-old's heart but hadn't damaged any internal organs. "The doctor told me we were very, very lucky," Rodriguez recalls. Her son recovered, but Rodriguez's life was irreversibly changed.

Because the boy claimed his neighborhood with so much bravado on the day he was shot, he has become a target for the rival gang, which now sees the boy as Sur 13's most visible member. "Whenever there is a problem, they come after him," his mother says. "The problem is no longer just on him; it is on the house."

Immediately after the shooting, Rodriguez was too grateful that her son was alive to reprimand him. But events soon prompted her to take action. Shortly after the boy returned to school, Rodriguez was summoned by the principal. Four members of the rival gang had been circling the campus all day waiting for her son. The school couldn't take that sort of disruption, so officials were asking the boy to leave and attend continuation school. "My older son told me that if I didn't get [his brother] away from here, he'd be killed," Rodriguez says. He is looked on as a particular enemy now."

Rodriguez says she knew she would have to talk to the boy, as her husband had always left rearing the children to her. But getting her son to listen proved difficult. "I said to him, 'You're going to get killed,' but he just said, 'I don't care.' He is very rebellious."

This year he is enrolled in a Pomona program for gang members who are at risk in other schools. He continues to dress like and act the part of a Sur 13, although he no longer hangs out on the street. "I finally told him that if he went out, I would send him to live in Mexico," Rodriguez says. "He doesn't want that, so he stays inside."

The shooting, says Rodriguez, has had some positive effects. For one thing, she acknowledged that all three of her older sons were in the gang. "Looking back now, I remember that when they were 9 years old they started wearing khakis and white T-shirts. They started coming home later and later," Rodriguez says. One son had a size 32 waist, but he had his mother buy him size 42 pants. "I didn't know these were gang clothes. Now I do.

"My 16-year-old threw away his *cholo* clothes right when he heard about his brother," she says. "He hasn't been with the gang since then. The two older boys are very repentant, but it is hard to step away from their pasts."

Rodriguez has begun attending meetings of the Pomona chapter of Concerned Parents, a group working to stop gang violence, and is hopeful for the first time that something can be done to prevent recurrences of the kind of gang activity that nearly killed her son. "Communication between parents, police and the church is very important. Together we can solve the problem. We can't do it alone."

Still, Rodriquez dreads Friday nights. On her front door, where a thick board has replaced a window shot out by a gang, she has posted a small picture of Jesus on the cross. "The only thing I can do about the shooting is put it in his hands," she says, gesturing toward the picture. "He's the only one who can take care of me."

MAGGIE GARCIA

Acceptance: Mean Streets, But the Neighborhood Is Still Everything

A few blocks from the Rodriguez house, in another Pomona barrio, Maggie Garcia doesn't really see her youngest son as a gang member. He is just, she says, very loyal to his friends and his neighborhood.

Loyalty to the Cherryville barrio in Pomona where she lives is something Garcia understands completely: "I was raised in the house next door to the one in which I raised my kids. Two of my sisters and one of my brothers live in the neighborhood, too." Maggie Garcia's whole life, she says, is wrapped up in the few blocks radiating from her house. "Here in the neighborhood, it is family."

Garcia realizes that her youngest son has taken his feelings for his barrio a little far on occasion. Last September, when the boy had just turned 14, he got into a fight at school. "He claimed his neighborhood, and the other boy claimed his neighborhood, and all of a sudden they are fighting for two gangs."

After the fight, he was expelled and sent to a local continuation school. "The principal at his old school was upset because my son said, 'I'd die for my neighborhood.' If he'd said, 'I'd die for my country,' the principal probably would have given him a medal."

Garcia worried about her son at the continuation school. Because it drew students from the whole Pomona school district, her son was in constant contact with boys from rival gangs. "One day, two boys from Twelfth Street [another Pomona gang] laid in wait for my son. He came home all bloody and with bruises," Garcia recalls. "I told him you're not going back to school. You could be killed."

Garcia knew that inter-neighborhood conflicts could be deadly in the Pomona barrios: Three nephews and three of her nieces' boyfriends had been killed by rival gang members. She told her son that if he was out late with his cousins, he wasn't to walk home on the streets but should instead cut through neighbors' back yards. When he goes out the door, Garcia blesses him in hopes that God will protect him out on the streets. But there is only so much, she feels, that she can do. "I've tried to talk to him," she says. "Some people think I should forbid him from being with his friends, but that would be like his telling me, 'Mom, I don't want you hanging out with your best friends in this neighborhood.' It's such a small neighborhood, there are only a few boys my son has here. If he didn't hang out with them, he wouldn't have any friends."

"I see it this way," she says. "Nowadays you have to protect yourself as much as possible, and the friends help protect. The Bible says when you are slapped you turn the other cheek, but you don't do that around here because they will shoot you if you're not looking. Children in any neighborhood have to be aware and have eyes in the back of their heads or they will be dead. They are streetwise. I've taught them to be that way. I feel that when a child is running with three or four of his friends it's better than being alone."

So instead of forbidding her son to associate with the gang, Garcia says, she has taken a more moderate line. "I tell him you can live in the fire, but you don't have to let yourself get burned. You've got to learn to live outside, but when you see something about to go down, you have to get out of there."

In early August, it became apparent that Garcia's youngest son hadn't absorbed the lessons his mother was trying to teach him. After coming home late one night, the boy went back out into the neighborhood. What happened next is in dispute, but in the end he was arrested and charged with an armed robbery that took place a few blocks from his house. Garcia insists that her son was simply in the wrong place at the wrong time. After being held at Los Padrinos Juvenile Hall in Downey, he was released into this mother's custody and is attending school through a Pomona program for gang members who are at risk in other schools. His case will be reviewed by a judge in December.

"My older son has gotten very angry at my younger son," Garcia says. "He tells [his brother], 'You know, if they kill you, your friends will go to your Rosary and they'll go to your funeral. Then they'll have a party and forget you.' But my younger son doesn't see it that way. He sort of says, 'Here today, gone tomorrow—so what?' "

GAYLE THOMAS KARY

Death: Just When She Thought She'd Beaten the Odds

Fifteen-year-old Jamee Kary hadn't been active in the Five Deuce Broadway Crips in recent months. But that didn't matter to a car full of the rival Blood gang members who spotted the boy crossing West 27th Street on the night of Sept. 10. The Bloods called the boy to their car. Words were exchanged. The Bloods began to drive off, but then stopped and got out of their car. Jamee tried to run, but he was shot in the face before he could reach cover. He died within minutes.

Gayle Thomas Kary had worried frantically about Jamee, her middle son, for more than two years before his death. His problems, she feels, started four years ago when tight finances forced her to move from Long Beach to a family-owned house in South-Central Los Angeles half a block from the Harbor Freeway. In the old neighborhood, there had been so much for an adolescent boy to do. There were youth centers and year-round organized sports. In the new neighborhood, there was only the gang.

Because Jamee had a slight learning disability, school had always been difficult for him, but he had always had friends. A charming boy with a quick smile and easy affability, Jamee fit right into the new neighborhood. By the time he was 13, he had fit right into the gang.

Kary could tell from her son's style of dress and friends that he had become a gang member. And she was very worried. A data-entry operator with a full-time job and a steady life style, Kary had always believed that if she set a good example and enforced limits, her sons would turn out well. Her oldest son, now 20, had always met his mother's expectations. But Jamee seemed torn. At home he was respectful and loving, but out on the streets, he seemed like a different boy. "He knew that he was loved at home," Kary says, sitting in the immaculate California bungalow she shares with her sons. "But he somehow felt the need to be out there with those boys and not be considered a wimp."

One day during the summer of 1986, when Jamee was 13, his mother found him cutting up soap to look like cocaine. Kary was horrified that the boy found the drug culture so appealing. Within weeks, she sent Jamee off to stay with his father, a Louisiana minister, hoping that a change of environment would divert Jamee from trouble. Three weeks later, his father sent him back, saying he couldn't control the boy.

Later that summer, Jamee stole his mother's car one evening. He was stopped by police for driving the wrong way on a one-way street. But the police just gave the boy a traffic citation and told him to lock up the car and go home. When Kary heard about the incident, she was outraged. She bundled Jamee into the car, drove to the police station, and asked the police there to arrest her son. "I needed help in dealing with my son, but they just said, 'There's nothing we can do,'" Kary says, a bitter sorrow apparent in her voice.

In the months that followed, Jamee was increasingly out of control. Kary had always expected her sons to abide by certain household rules if they wanted to live under her roof. Jamee was required to attend school and do his home-work, to keep his room clean, to wash his clothes, to wash dishes on alternate days and to feed the dogs. It was not too much to ask, Kary felt.

Jamee, by the fall of his 14th year, felt differently. "Jamee started seeing these guys out there who were wearing expensive clothes and they didn't have to go to school or do chores or ask their parents for money," Kary recalls. Unwilling to meet his mother's demands, Jamee began running away from home for short periods of time to live with members of the Five Deuce Broad-way Crips. By this time, his mother knew from other kids in the neighborhood, her son was also selling drugs.

During his times away from home, Kary tried to keep tabs on him. "I always knew where he was and that he was safe," Kary says. "He'd sneak over and try to get his brothers to get him a clean set of clothes." Eventually, Jamee would tire of life on the streets and return home. "He'd always promise to toe the line," Kary says. "He'd say he had changed. He knew my rules were the same."

When her son was at home, Kary tried to reason with him. "I told him that kind of life could lead to no good," Kary says with tears in her eyes. "I told him that a fast life goes fast." She warned him, she says, that he could be arrested or killed. "He would just tell me he wouldn't get busted because he could run faster than the police. He told me nobody would kill him because he didn't do any bad drug deals."

In the spring of 1987, Jamee was arrested for possession of cocaine with intent to sell. The arrest was a relief for his mother, who hoped that at last her son would be in the hands of people who could help him. But when the time came for Jamee's sentencing, Kary was once again disappointed. "They wanted to give him probation. The conditions were things like he had to be in by 10 and stop associating with gang members. I told them I'd been trying to get him to do those things and he wouldn't. There was no way he was going to do them now, either. I said I wouldn't take him," Kary recalls.

Instead, the court sentenced Jamee to juvenile hall and later to a youth camp. After five months, Jamee returned home. At first he seemed to be less involved with the gang, but he soon returned to his old ways. There was just one difference now: Jamee had been assigned to probation officer Jim Galipeau, who seemed to really care about they boy. Galipeau also listened to Kary's concerns.

"I called Mr. Galipeau and said Jamee was in trouble again. He told me to keep a record of what he was doing and when," Kary recalls. Thankful for something to do, Kary kept detailed notes on her son's transgressions, hoping to build a case for revoking Jamee's probation. But before she could do that, Galipeau had a heart-to-heart talk with her son. "Jamee told Mr. Galipeau he was tired of life on the streets," Kary says. "He got tired of the police swooping up the street and having to run and not knowing where he was going to sleep." At his probation officer's suggestion, Jamee agreed to request placement in a county-run youth facility to get away from his life in Los Angles.

By last summer, Jamee was doing beautifully. "I knew I still had to take it one day at a time," his mother says, "but he really seemed to have changed. It was like he was the child I used to know. He wouldn't even go up to Broadway [where the gang liked to hang out]. The friends he associated with were not gang members."

Jamee arrived home for his last weekend furlough on Friday, Sept. 9. On Saturday evening, he asked his mother if he could go with a friend to pick up another fellow and get something to eat. She readily agreed. An hour and a half later, a neighbor came to the door with the news that Jamee had been shot on 27th Street.

Kary raced to the scene, where she saw police had cordoned off a large area. "I saw that yellow police rope, and I knew right then my son was dead," Kary recalls. But police at the scene refused to let her see whether the victim was her son, and after pleading to no avail for information, Kary was finally persuaded to go home and wait. Several hours later, the police called and asked Kary's oldest son to go and identify photographs. Kary finally knew for sure. Her 15-year-old son was dead.

After Jamee's killing, Kary continued to learn what it was like to have a gang member for a son. She wanted to have the funeral service at her own church, but neighbors dissuaded her. "They told me there was a rival gang over there. They said, 'You can't have it there or there'll be troubles,' " Kary says. She also realized with shock that colors, particularly Crip blue, had taken on a new meaning in her life. "All those years that blue stood for boys, and I couldn't let my boy wear blue at his funeral or have the programs printed in blue," Kary says. She had originally planned to wear her nicest dress to the services, but then she realized that it, too, was blue. "A friend told me, 'You can't wear that or you'll be sitting there looking the queen Crip mother,' " Kary says.

Kary worried about how the Five Deuce Broadways would behave at her son's funeral. But that, she says, turned out to be a pleasant surprise. Several days after Jamee's death, some 20 of the gang's members came to Kary's house. While Jamee was alive, she had never allowed gang members in her house, but this once she decided to make an exception.

The young men who gathered in her living room were, she says, very respectful. "They said that even though Jamee wasn't actively involved with them at the time, he was still a member of their family, and they wanted to offer financial support," Kary recalls. The boys contributed about $400 toward funeral costs.

"After they spoke," Kary says, "I said to them, 'I don't like what you do out there on the streets, but I want to tell you something from my heart. You say Jamee was a member of your family. That makes you a member of my family, too, because Jamee was my son. I'm asking you a favor as family members. I don't want any colors at the funeral. I don't want rags, and I don't want trouble.' " To a person, Kary says, the young men honored her requests, and since the funeral they have been eager to help in any way they can.

In the aftermath of Jamee's death, Kary feels lost. Her youngest son, 11-year-old Lewis, had decided just before his brother's death to go live with his father in Louisiana. "He did not want to be involved on the streets with the gangs and the colors and the drugs. He was scared. He didn't want to go to junior high school here," Kary recalls. While Kary supports Lewis' decision, she is lonely. "I feel so empty inside," she says. "I can't remember when I last felt my heart beat inside my chest. The only thing I can feel in my whole body is my head because it hurts all the time."

In her lowest moments, Kary takes some solace in a poem Jamee wrote for her while he was incarcerated after his cocaine arrest. She included the poem, which Jamee had entitled "If You Only Knew," in the program for Jamee's funeral.

> I sit here on my bunk
> And don't know what to do
> My life just caught up in a mess
> Because I was a fool
> I sometimes wonder to myself
> With my heart just full of pain
> Boy when I get out of this place
> My life won't be the same
> I'm sorry for all the pain I caused

For you as well as them
I promise you, and I'll try my best
To not do wrong again
Every night and every day
I always think of you
I just sit here thinking but
If you only knew

Dedicated to my Mom
I love you

QUESTIONS FOR "MOTHERS, SONS AND THE GANGS" BY SUE HORTON

Talking About the Text

1. One mother is quoted as saying, "I am tired of people assuming I must be a bad person because my son is a Crip." What reasons might she have for saying this? How is this article a response to this perception?
2. Based on evidence from these mothers' stories, what kinds of familial and social conditions seem conducive to the formation and growth of gang culture?
3. Examine closely these mothers' reactions to their sons being involved with gangs. What would you do if you were the parent of a son who was hanging out with a gang?
4. Explain how parents in working together can be a potentially strong force in counteracting gang activity?

Exploring Issues

1. If reading about gangs is a remote experience for you, then you are no doubt fortunate. Nevertheless, elements such as poverty, unemployment, drugs, and racism are forces that many of you might know about to some degree. How might some of these elements contribute to the formation of gangs and to their way of life?
2. Compare Jeffrey's experience in the previous selection with that of some of the young men described by Sue Horton. What are similarities and differences? Then compare and contrast the mothers' responses to their sons in this article with the responses of Aunt Glo, Kay-Kay, and Jill (Njeri) in "Who's Bad?" Could these individuals have done anything differently to help Jeffrey before it was too late?
3. Gang members or potential gang members are often depicted as victims of an unjust system. How would you respond to such a characterization?
4. Depending on how one views such things, gangs can be seen as an epidemic plaguing society or as a symptom of larger social ills. Gangs are actually forming a culture of their own, perpetuating and enlarging themselves by including more than one generation. Explore the possibil-

ity that gangs serve as substitute families. What would this mean in terms of what you have identified as characteristic of families? Consider also how gangs may differ significantly from viable families.

Writing Assignments

1. Write a profile of what you think defines the typical gang member. Include in your profile a description of the family life as well as the street life where your subject lives.

2. Write a dialogue between a mother and her son, focused on her son's gang activities.

3. Assume that you are on a committe to analyze the gang situation and to make recommendations for effective action in dealing with this growing problem. Investigate this issue by doing some research and, if possible, interviewing people directly involved with gangs. Report your findings. Consider showing your report to the public through publication in the newspaper or through discussions with community leaders.

4. Write an analytic essay in which you compare and contrast the ways that gangs satisfy certain personal needs with the ways other, more benign groups—fraternities and sororities, clubs, athletic teams, etc.—satisfy those same needs. Or expand your focus and consider how groups such as religious cults or radical political groups compare and contrast with gang culture and the needs the latter satisfy.

CHAPTER 5: EXTENDED WRITING ASSIGNMENTS

5-1. Now that you have read through this chapter and discussed and written about various aspects of family life, rewrite a final draft of your essay defining the family. Try to develop your own definition, but be sure to make it flexible enough to include various kinds of families. Then detail some of the pressures and conflicts that threaten the family, and offer some concluding remarks concerning the future prospects of this important and necessary social entity.

5-2. Identify a family conflict and explain how various characters you've read about might deal with it. For instance, you might interpret this problem through Jing-Mei Woo's mother's eyes, through BaBa's, through Falco Patera's, through Aunt Glo's, and through one of the mother's perspectives in the last selection.

5-3. Using details from selections in this chapter, write an account with one of the following titles: "Life in the Immigrant Family," "Family Life in the City," "Family Life on the Farm," "Conflicts in Family Life," or "The Joys and Sorrows of Some Typical American Families."

Use your imaginations and come up with your own titles if you don't like ours. But because your goal in this assignment is to weave a synthesis of what you have read, your title should encompass a significant aspect or idea you have found in this chapter. Use evidence from various selections to back your claims and illustrate your assertions.

Chapter
6

Teaching and Learning

Although most of us have been in school for a long time, we sometimes fail to remember that teaching and learning are activities not merely confined to the classroom. Nor is teaching simply a matter of the instructor conveying information and students learning by giving back that information to the teacher in the form of answers on quizzes or exams. Many important elements come to mind when we consider what it means for a person to become educated. The value individuals place on education and the purposes it plays in their lives are significant factors affecting what people learn and how they might approach that learning. Moreover, when any of us learn anything, we usually are taught by a teacher—even if that "teacher" happens to be ourselves. Therefore the quality of the teaching has a tremendous influence on what is learned.

Certainly cultural, social, political, and economic factors constrain this teaching and learning relationship. Many of our schools are overcrowded or lack the necessary supplies and equipment so that they cannot compete with schools materially sufficient. The training and backgrounds of our teachers also affects the teaching-learning relationship. These affects are especially apparent—unfortunately, often negatively so—when ethnic, linguistic, and gender differences between teachers and their students help create and exacerbate misperceptions and misunderstandings.

Schools should not be thought of as the sole institutions in which young people are first introduced and guided in their learning. We begin learning from the moment we are born and can continue our intellectual growth as far as we are consciously able and willing to take it. Our family life and personal experiences obviously play crucial roles in shaping our development. Yet our education is also influenced by forces from another side, as the rapidly changing needs of our technologically complex society compel us to learn new skills in order to perform jobs that emerge in tandem with technological innovations.

Because the production, distribution, and reception of information has become paramount in our society, it follows that all citizens should achieve some measure of literacy. The ability to read and write seems essential for our personal development in this society, and even though we have heard of cases where individuals who cannot read or write have become outwardly successful, they tell us of the very real anguish they often silently endure in trying to compensate for their inadequate levels of literacy. Though we all may agree that literacy is extremely important, in the next breath we will begin debating just what we mean by being "literate." We need to know how to define literacy, how to cultivate it, and, indeed, to consider that there are multiple literacies in addition to print literacy that our college graduates might need to achieve. We need to debate what college students should know and how they should best learn these essentials.

These twin questions—perennial questions—about what one should learn and how one might optimally achieve such learning, serve to frame this chapter. Our first selection by the outspoken Jonathan Kozol dramatically portrays the plight of "illiterates," as he calls them, trapped in a condition that severely restricts and can create circumstances endangering their lives. Moreover, illiteracy contributes to unemployment, poverty, and crime as well.

In the next selection Mike Rose considers a particular kind of literacy—"academic" literacy—and the painful conflicts students from different backgrounds undergo as they struggle to achieve this seemingly elusive kind of literacy. Rose questions the experts who claim that students must know a certain body of information in order to become sufficiently literate. Following Rose, Kenneth Bechtel analyzes and illustrates the historical inequalities in education. He focuses on the history of black education in the United States, and in an engaging and convincing account argues that "educational policies toward blacks were generally designed with one goal in mind: to ensure the political, social, economic, and intellectual inferiority of blacks."

Succeeding Bechtel's argument, we offer Toni Cade Bambara's well-known short story "The Lesson." Bambara's fiction spurs us to consider further just what is most important for students to learn. But, more important, she dramatizes for us the often harsh experience involved as a particularly effective school "lesson" forces young students to step outside their limited worlds.

Our next selection is a historical piece by the little-known American essayist, Agnes Repplier. "Historical" should be qualified, however, because although Repplier is writing at around the turn of the century, the issue she discusses in her very distinct and witty voice concerns our felt need to make education "interesting," an issue that continues to raise questions about the relevance of the educational curriculum and the "how" of teaching it. Then Tom Romano provides a teacher's poetic reflection concerning the role he assumes in leading his students. Romano likens himself to being a scoutmaster leading his troops on a long hike. Following Romano, we attempt to extend our understanding of how we learn and teach by considering women's education. First Mary Belenky and others explain the unsettling situation women often find themselves in as they attempt to receive an education oriented to a characteristically masculine mode of presentation. The authors conclude by proposing an alternate pedagogy more suitable to a woman's needs.

Our chapter ends with a personal essay by Frank Conroy, who takes the question of what it means to be educated one step further. Through several intriguing examples Conroy shows us how we can continue learning throughout our lives. So, along with Conroy, we invite you to think about these ideas as you read the following selections and write about the issues and concerns that you have regarding your own education.

Reading 47

The Human Cost of an Illiterate Society

Jonathan Kozol

As teacher and social critic, Jonathan Kozol has written movingly and provocatively on topics such as the failure of American education and, most recently, on the plight of the homeless, *Rachel and Her Children,* (1988). This selection, "The Human Cost of an Illiterate Society," is chapter 4 in Kozol's book, *Illiterate America* (1985), in which he describes the sometimes desperate and always humiliating plight of those who cannot read.

PRECAUTIONS. READ BEFORE USING.
Poison: Contains sodium hydroxide (caustic soda-lye).
Corrosive: Causes severe eye and skin damage, may cause blindness.
Harmful or fatal if swallowed.
If swallowed, give large quantities of milk or water.
Do not induce vomiting.
Important: Keep water out of can at all times to
prevent contents from violently erupting . . .

—warning on a can of Drano

We are speaking here no longer of the dangers faced by passengers on Eastern Airlines or the dollar costs incurred by U.S. corporations and taxpayers. We are speaking now of human suffering and of the ethical dilemmas that are faced by a society that looks upon such suffering with qualified concern but does not take those actions which its wealth and ingenuity would seemingly demand.

Questions of literacy, in Socrates' belief, must at length be judged as matters of morality. Socrates could not have had in mind the moral compromise peculiar to a nation like our own. Some of our Founding Fathers did, however, have this question in their minds. One of the wisest of those Founding Fathers (one who may not have been most compassionate but surely was more prescient than some of his peers) recognized the special dangers that illiteracy would pose to basic equity in the political construction that he helped to shape.

"A people who mean to be their own governors," James Madison wrote, "must arm themselves with the power knowledge gives. A popular government without popular information or the means of acquiring it, is but a prologue to a farce or a tragedy, or perhaps both."

Tragedy looms larger than farce in the United States today. Illiterate citizens seldom vote. Those who do are forced to cast a vote of questionable worth. They cannot make informed decisions based on serious print information. Sometimes they can be alerted to their interests by aggressive voter education. More frequently, they vote for a face, a smile, or a style, not for a mind or character or body of beliefs.

The number of illiterate adults exceeds by 16 million the entire vote cast for the winner in the 1980 presidential contest. If even one third of all illiterates could vote, and read enough and do sufficient math to vote in their self-interest, Ronald Reagan would not likely have been chosen president. There is, of course, no way to know for sure. We do know this: Democracy is a mendacious term when used by those who are prepared to countenance the forced exclusion of one third of our electorate. So long as 60 million people are denied significant participation, the government is neither of, nor for, nor by, the people. It is a government, at best, of those two thirds whose wealth, skin color, or parental privilege allows them opportunity to profit from the provocation and instruction of the written word.

The undermining of democracy in the United States is one "expense" that sensitive Americans can easily deplore because it represents a contradiction that endangers citizens of all political positions. The human price is not so obvious at first.

Since I first immersed myself within this work I have often had the following dream: I find that I am in a railroad station or a large department store within a city that is utterly unknown to me and where I cannot understand the printed words. None of the signs or symbols is familiar. Everything looks strange: like mirror writing of some kind. Gradually I understand that I am in the Soviet Union. All the letters on the walls around me are Cyrillic. I look for my pocket dictionary but I find that it has been mislaid. Where have I left it? Then I recall that I forgot to bring it with me when I packed my bags in Boston. I struggle to remember the name of my hotel. I try to ask somebody for directions. One person stops and looks at me in a peculiar way. I lose the nerve to ask. At last I reach into my wallet for an ID card. The card is missing. Have I lost it? Then I remember that my card was confiscated for some reason, many years before. Around this point, I wake up in a panic.

This panic is not so different from the misery that millions of adult illiterates experience each day within the course of their routine existence in the U.S.A.

Illiterates cannot read the menu in a restaurant.

They cannot read the cost of items on the menu in the *window* of the restaurant before they enter.

Illiterates cannot read the letters that their children bring home from their teachers. They cannot study school department circulars that tell them of the courses that their children must be taking if they hope to pass the SAT exams. They cannot help with homework. They cannot write a letter to the teacher. They are afraid to visit in the classroom. They do not want to humiliate their child or themselves.

Illiterates cannot read instructions on a bottle of prescription medicine. They cannot find out when a medicine is past the year of safe consumption; nor can they read of allergenic risks, warnings to diabetics, or the potential sedative effect of certain kinds of nonprescription pills. They cannot observe preventive health care admonitions. They cannot read about "the seven warning signs of cancer" or the indications of blood-sugar fluctuations or the risks of eating certain foods that aggravate the likelihood of cardiac arrest.

Illiterates live, in more than literal ways, an uninsured existence. They cannot understand the written details on a health insurance form. They cannot read the waivers that they sign preceding surgical procedures. Several women I have known in Boston have entered a slum hospital with the intention of obtaining a tubal ligation and have emerged a few days later after having been subjected to a hysterectomy. Unaware of their rights, incognizant of jargon, intimidated by the unfamiliar air of fear and atmosphere of ether that so many of us find oppressive in the confines even of the most attractive and expensive medical facilities, they have signed their names to documents they could not read and which nobody, in the hectic situation that prevails so often in those overcrowded hospitals that serve the urban poor, had even bothered to explain.

Childbirth might seem to be the last inalienable right of any female citizen within a civilized society. Illiterate mothers, as we shall see, already have been cheated of the power to protect their progeny against the likelihood of demolition in deficient public schools and, as a result, against the verbal servitude within which they themselves exist. Surgical denial of the right to bear that child in the first place represents an ultimate denial, an unspeakable metaphor, a final darkness that denies even the twilight gleamings of our own humanity. What greater violation of our biological, our biblical, our spiritual humanity could possibly exist than that which takes place nightly, perhaps hourly these days, within such overburdened and benighted institutions as the Boston City Hospital? Illiteracy has many costs; few are so irreversible as this.

Even the roof above one's head, the gas or other fuel for heating that protects the residents of northern city slums against the threat of illness in the winter months become uncertain guarantees. Illiterates cannot read the lease that they must sign to live in an apartment which, too often, they cannot afford. They cannot manage check accounts and therefore seldom pay for anything by mail. Hours and entire days of difficult travel (and the cost of bus or other public transit) must be added to the real cost of whatever they consume. Loss of interest on the check accounts they do not have, and could not manage if they did, must be regarded as another of the excess costs paid by the citizen who is excluded from the common instruments of commerce in a numerate society.

"I couldn't understand the bills," a woman in Washington, D.C., reports, "and then I couldn't write the checks to pay them. We signed things we didn't know what they were."

Illiterates cannot read the notices that they receive from welfare offices or from the IRS. They must depend on word-of-mouth instruction from the welfare worker—or from other persons whom they have good reason to mistrust. They do not know what rights they have, what deadlines and requirements they face, what options they might choose to exercise. They are half-citizens. Their rights exist in print but not in fact.

Illiterates cannot look up numbers in a telephone directory. Even if they can find the names of friends, few possess the sorting skills to make use of the yellow pages; categories are bewildering and trade names are beyond decoding capabilities for millions of nonreaders. Even the emergency numbers listed on the first page of the phone book—"Ambulance," "Police," and "Fire"—are too frequently beyond the recognition of nonreaders.

Many illiterates cannot read the admonition on a pack of cigarettes. Neither the Surgeon General's warning nor its reproduction on the package can alert them to the risks. Although most people learn by word of mouth that smoking is related to a number of grave physical disorders, they do not get the chance to read the detailed stories which can document this danger with the vividness that turns concern into determination to resist. They can see the handsome cowboy or the slim Virginia lady lighting up a filter cigarette; they cannot heed the words that tell them that this product is (not "may be") dangerous to their health. Sixty million men and women are condemned to be the unalerted, high-risk candidates for cancer.

Illiterates do not buy "no-name" products in the supermarkets. They must depend on photographs or the familiar logos that are printed on the packages of brand-name groceries. The poorest people, therefore, are denied the benefits of the least costly products.

Illiterates depend almost entirely upon label recognition. Many labels, however, are not easy to distinguish. Dozens of different kinds of Campbell's soup appear identical to the nonreader. The purchaser who cannot read and does not dare to ask for help, out of the fear of being stigmatized (a fear which is unfortunately realistic), frequently comes home with something which she never wanted and her family never tasted.

Illiterates cannot read instructions on a pack of frozen food. Packages sometimes provide an illustration to explain the cooking preparations; but illustrations are of little help to someone who must "boil water, drop the food—*within* its plastic wrapper—in the boiling water, wait for it to simmer, instantly remove."

Even when labels are seemingly clear, they may be easily mistaken. A woman in Detroit brought home a gallon of Crisco for her children's dinner. She thought that she had bought the chicken that was pictured on the label. She had enough Crisco now to last a year—but no more money to go back and buy the food for dinner.

Recipes provided on the packages of certain staples sometimes tempt a semiliterate person to prepare a meal her children have not tasted. The longing to vary the uniform and often starchy content of low-budget meals provided to the family that relies on food stamps commonly leads to ruinous results. Scarce funds have been wasted and the food must be thrown out. The same applies to distribution of food-surplus produce in emergency conditions. Government inducements to poor people to "explore the ways" by which to make a tasty meal from tasteless noodles, surplus cheese, and powdered milk are useless to nonreaders. Intended as benevolent advice, such recommendations mock reality and foster deeper feelings of resentment and of inability to cope. (Those, on the other hand, who cautiously refrain from "innovative" recipes in preparation of their children's meals must suffer the opprobrium of "laziness," "lack of imagination . . .")

Illiterates cannot travel freely. When they attempt to do so, they encounter risks that few of us can dream of. They cannot read traffic signs and, while they often learn to recognize and to decipher symbols, they cannot manage street names which they haven't seen before. The same is true for bus and subway stops. While ingenuity can sometimes help a man or woman to discern directions from familiar landmarks, buildings, cemeteries, churches, and the like, most illiterates are virtually immobilized. They seldom wander past the streets and neighborhoods they know. Geographical paralysis becomes a bitter metaphor for their entire existence. They are immobilized in almost every sense we can imagine. They can't move up. They can't move out. They cannot see beyond. Illiterates may take an oral test for drivers' permits in most sections of America. It is a questionable concession. Where will they go? How will they get there? How will they get home? Could it be that some of us might like it better if they stayed where they belong?

Travel is only one of many instances of circumscribed existence. Choice, in almost all its facets, is diminished in the life of an illiterate adult. Even the printed TV schedule, which provides most people with the luxury of preselection, does not belong within the arsenal of options in illiterate existence. One consequence is that the viewer watches only what appears at moments when he happens to have time to turn the switch. Another consequence, a lot more common, is that the TV set remains in operation night and day. Whatever the program offered at the hour when he walks into the room will be the nutriment that he accepts and swallows. Thus, to passivity, is added frequency—indeed, almost uninterrupted continuity. Freedom to select is no more possible here than in the choice of home or surgery or food.

"You don't choose," said one illiterate woman. "You take your wishes from somebody else." Whether in perusal of a menu, selection of highways, purchase of groceries, or determination of affordable enjoyment, illiterate Americans must trust somebody else: a friend, a relative, a stranger on the street, a grocery clerk, a TV copywriter.

"All of our mail we get, it's hard for her to read. Settin' down and writing a letter, she can't do it. Like if we get a bill . . . we take it over to my sister-in-law . . . My sister-in-law reads it."

Billing agencies harass poor people for the payment of the bills for purchases that might have taken place six months before. Utility companies offer an agreement for a staggered payment schedule on a bill past due. "You have to trust them," one man said. Precisely for this reason, you end up by trusting no one and suspecting everyone of possible deceit. A submerged sense of distrust becomes the corollary to a constant need to trust. "They are cheating me . . . I have been tricked . . . I do not know . . ."

Not knowing: This is a familiar theme. Not knowing the right word for the right thing at the right time is one form of subjugation. Not knowing the world that lies concealed behind those words is a more terrifying feeling. The longitude and latitude of one's existence are beyond all easy apprehension. Even the hard, cold stars within the firmament above one's head begin to mock the possibilities for self-location. Where am I? Where did I come from? Where will I go?

"I've lost a lot of jobs," one man explains. "Today, even if you're a janitor, there's still reading and writing . . . They leave a note saying, 'Go to room so-and-so . . .' You can't do it. You can't read it. You don't know."

"The hardest thing about it is that I've been places where I didn't know where I was. You don't know where you are . . . You're lost."

"Like I said: I have two kids. What do I do if one of my kids starts choking? I go running to the phone . . . I can't look up the hospital phone number. That's if we're at home. Out on the street, I can't read the sign. I get to a pay phone. 'Okay, tell us where you are. We'll send an ambulance.' I look at the street sign. Right there, I can't tell you what it says. I'd have to spell it out, letter for letter. By that time, one of my kids would be dead . . . These are the kinds of fears you go with, every single day . . ."

"Reading directions, I suffer with. I work with chemicals . . . That's scary to begin with . . ."

"You sit down. They throw the menu in front of you. Where do you go from there? Nine times out of ten you say, 'Go ahead. Pick out something for the both of us.' I've eaten some weird things, let me tell you!"

Menus. Chemicals. A child choking while his mother searches for a word she does not know to find assistance that will come too late. Another mother speaks about the inability to help her kids to read: "I can't read to them. Of course that's leaving them out of something they should have. Oh, it matters. You *believe* it matters! I ordered all these books. The kids belong to a book club. Donny wanted me to read a book to him. I told Donny: 'I can't read.' He said:

'Mommy, you sit down. I'll read it to you.' I tried it one day, reading from the pictures. Donny looked at me. He said, 'Mommy, that's not right.' He's only five. He knew I couldn't read . . ."

A landlord tells a woman that her lease allows him to evict her if her baby cries and causes inconvenience to her neighbors. The consequence of challenging his words conveys a danger which appears, unlikely as it seems, even more alarming than the danger of eviction. Once she admits that she can't read, in the desire to maneuver for the time in which to call a friend, she will have defined herself in terms of an explicit impotence that she cannot endure. Capitulation in this case is preferable to self-humiliation. Resisting the definition of oneself in terms of what one cannot do, what others take for granted, represents a need so great that other imperatives (even one so urgent as the need to keep one's home in winter's cold) evaporate and fall away in face of fear. Even the loss of home and shelter, in this case, is not so terrifying as the loss of self.

"I come out of school. I was sixteen. They had their meetings. The directors meet. They said that I was wasting their school paper. I was wasting pencils . . ."

Another illiterate, looking back, believes she was not worthy of her teacher's time. She believes that it was wrong of her to take up space within her school. She believes that it was right to leave in order that somebody more deserving could receive her place.

Children choke. Their mother chokes another way: on more than chicken bones.

People eat what others order, know what others tell them, struggle not to see themselves as they believe the world perceives them. A man in California speaks about his own loss of identity, of self-location, definition:

"I stood at the bottom of the ramp. My car had broke down on the freeway. There was a phone. I asked for the police. They was nice. They said to tell them where I was. I looked up at the signs. There was one that I had seen before. I read it to them: ONE WAY STREET. They thought it was a joke. I told them I couldn't read. There was other signs above the ramp. They told me to try. I looked around for somebody to help. All the cars was going by real fast. I couldn't make them understand that I was lost. The cop was nice. He told me: "Try once more.' I did my best. I couldn't read. I only knew the sign above my head. The cop was trying to be nice. He knew that I was trapped. 'I can't send out a car to you if you can't tell me where you are.' I felt afraid. I nearly cried. I'm forty-eight years old. I only said: "I'm on a one-way street . . .' "

The legal problems and the courtroom complications that confront illiterate adults have been discussed above. The anguish that may underlie such matters was brought home to me this year while I was working on this book. I have spoken, in the introduction, of a sudden phone call from one of my former students, now in prison for a criminal offense. Stephen is not a boy today. He is twenty-eight years old. He called to ask me to assist him in his trial, which comes up next fall. He will be on trial for murder. He has just knifed and killed a man who first enticed him to his home, then cheated him, and then insulted him—as "an illiterate subhuman."

Stephen now faces twenty years to life. Stephen's mother was illiterate. His grandparents were illiterate as well. What parental curse did not destroy was killed off finally by the schools. Silent violence is repaid with interest. It will cost us $25,000 yearly to maintain this broken soul in prison. But what is the price that has been paid by Stephen's victim? What is the price that will be paid by Stephen?

Perhaps we might slow down a moment here and look at the realities described above. This is the nation that we live in. This is a society that most of us did not create but which our President and other leaders have been willing to sustain by virtue of malign neglect. Do we possess the character and courage to address a problem which so many nations, poorer than our own, have found it natural to correct?

The answers to these questions represent a reasonable test of our belief in the democracy to which we have been asked in public school to swear allegiance.

NOTES FOR "THE HUMAN COST OF AN ILLITERATE SOCIETY"

Socrates on literacy and morality: cited in "Readings on Literacy," by Tela Zasloff, in *Literacy in Historical Perspective,* cited above.

James Madison: letter to W. T. Barry, August 4, 1822, in *The Complete Madison,* edited by Paul Padover, Harper & Brothers, New York, 1953.

"I couldn't understand the bills . . ." Conversation reported to author during interviews with literacy workers, Washington, D.C., April 1984.

All quotations not taken from author's interviews are drawn from two sources:

(1) *Foresight,* vol. 1, no. 3, Southern Growth Policies Board, Research Triangle Park, North Carolina, September 1983.

(2) *The Adult Illiterate Speaks Out,* by Anne Eberle and Sandra Robinson, National Institute of Education, Washington, D.C., September 1980.

The second document, one of the most moving and insightful I have seen, derives from the experience of people who have been involved in Vermont Adult Basic Education. Despite my reservations in regard to many of the techniques employed by ABE, this remarkable paper is a tribute to the capability of some extraordinary literacy workers to listen closely to the needs of those they serve. Many of the viewpoints I have stated in this chapter were provoked by my initial reading of this data several years ago. The authors draw some of these words from interviews conducted by other authors. Passages have been condensed and edited for clarity.

QUESTIONS FOR "THE HUMAN COST OF AN ILLITERATE SOCIETY" BY JONATHAN KOZOL

Talking About the Text

1. Note how Kozol opens his essay. Do you think that the way he begins is appropriate and justifed? Or is it too extreme or overly dramatic?
2. Consider the evidence Kozol mounts to illustrate the severity of the problem of illiteracy. Are all his exmaples equal in weight? Are they relevant? Accurate? Can you imagine other problems arising from illiteracy that Kozol does not consider?
3. Kozol's essay is primarily descriptive. Yet at the end he accuses our political leaders of neglecting the situation. Is this true? Who is to blame for this serious and extensive problem?

Exploring Issues

1. Kozol's critics claim that he overinflates his figures regarding the number of illiterates in this country. Much of the problem stems from how "literacy" is defined. How would you define a "literate" person? What degrees are there in achieving literacy? Try to identify other forms of literacy besides print literacy.
2. How is it possible that in such a wealthy, technologically advanced nation with open education illiteracy could remain a problem?
3. How might we deal with this problem?
4. What role do our schools play in both contributing to and in helping to solve this problem?

Writing Assignments

1. The simple fact that you are able to understand what Kozol is talking about means that you are literate to some degree. Observe and record the myriad occasions when print literacy is used in some fashion either at home or in the workplace. Then report your findings in an essay similar to Kozol's, with your focus on how much print literacy is involved in our daily activities.
2. Write an essay in which you explore possible causes and consequences of illiteracy. Focus your essay on a particular area, such as illiteracy in the home, in the community, or at work. Revise your draft in light of what you learn from the similar essays of others.
3. Write a proposal for how families and teachers might include more reading and writing in their daily activities. In the beginning of your proposal, define literacy in order to focus your subsequent discussion. Address this proposal specifically to teachers, advising them about imaginative ways to help students become more proficient in reading and writing.

Reading 48

Crossing Boundaries

Mike Rose

Mike Rose—poet, teacher, scholar, researcher—is associate director of
UCLA Writing Programs. His general concerns are literacy and the problems
of America's underclass in our educational institutions. Rose has written and
edited *Writer's Block: The Cognitive Dimension* (1986) and coedited
Perspectives on Literacy (1989). This selection is excerpted from the last
chapter of *Lives on the Boundary* (1989), in which Rose details the individual
lives of a few of the students he has encountered, showing us the obstacles
they must overcome in struggling to receive an education. Toward the end
of this selection Rose responds to those like E. D. Hirsch, Jr., who Rose
believes want to codify knowledge in order to gauge our national
intelligence.

Pico Boulevard, named for the last Mexican governor of California, runs an
immense stretch west to east: from the wealth of the Santa Monica beaches to
blighted Central Avenue, deep in Los Angeles. Union Street is comparatively
brief, running north to south, roughly from Adams to Temple, pretty bad off all
the way. Union intersects Pico east of Vermont Avenue and too far to the
southwest to be touched by the big-money development that is turning downtown Los Angeles into a whirring postmodernist dreamscape. The Pico-Union
District is very poor, some of its housing as unsafe as that on Skid Row,
delapidated, overcrowded, rat-infested. It used to be a working-class Mexican
neighborhood, but for about ten years now it has become the concentrated
locale of those fleeing the political and economic horror in Central America.
Most come from El Salvador and Guatemala. One observer calls the area a
gigantic refugee camp.

As you move concentrically outward from Pico-Union, you'll encounter a
number of other immigrant communities: Little Tokyo and Chinatown to the
northeast, Afro-Caribbean to the southwest, Koreatown to the west. Moving
west, you'll find Thai and Vietnamese restaurants tucked here and there in
storefronts. Filipinos, Southeast Asians, Armenians, and Iranians work in the
gas stations, the shoe-repair stores, the minimarts. A lawnmower repair shop

posts its sign in Korean, Spanish, and English. A Korean church announces "Jesus Loves You" in the same three languages. "The magnitude and diversity of immigration to Los Angeles since 1960," notes a report from UCLA's Graduate School of Architecture and Urban Planning, "is comparable only to the New York-bound wave of migrants around the turn of the century." It is not at all uncommon for English composition teachers at UCLA, Cal-State L.A., Long Beach State—the big urban universities and colleges—to have, in a class of twenty-five, students representing a dozen or more linguistic backgrounds: from Spanish and Cantonese and Farsi to Hindi, Portuguese, and Tagalog. Los Angeles, the new Ellis Island.

On a drive down the Santa Monica Freeway, you exit on Vermont and pass Rick's Mexican Cuisine, Hawaii Discount Furniture, The Restaurant Ecuatoriano, Froggy's Children's Wear, Seoul Autobody, and the Bar Omaha. Turn east on Pico, and as you approach Union, taking a side street here and there, you'll start seeing the murals: The Virgin of Guadalupe, Steve McQueen, a scene resembling Siqueiros's heroic workers, the Statue of Liberty, Garfield the Cat. Graffiti are everywhere. The dreaded Eighteenth Street gang—an established Mexican gang—has marked its turf in Arabic as well as Roman numerals. Newer gangs, a Salvadoran gang among them, are emerging by the violent logic of territory and migration; they have Xed out the Eighteenth Street *placas* and written their own threatening insignias in place. Statues of the Blessed Mother rest amid potted plants in overgrown front yards. There is a rich sweep of small commerce: restaurants, markets, bakeries, legal services ("Income Tax y Amnestia"), beauty salons ("Lolita's Magic Touch—Salon de Belleza—Unisex"). A Salvadoran restaurant sells teriyaki burgers. A "Discoteca Latina" advertises "great rap hits." A clothing store has a Dick Tracy sweatshirt on a half mannequin; a boy walks out wearing a blue t-shirt that announces "Life's a Beach." Culture in a Waring blender.

There are private telegram and postal services: messages sent straight to "domicilio a CentroAmerica." A video store advertises a comedy about immigration: *Ni de Aqui/Ni de Alla,* "Neither from Here nor from There." The poster displays a Central American Indian caught on a wild freeway ride: a Mexican in a sombrero is pulling one of the Indian's pigtails, Uncle Sam pulls the other, a border guard looks on, ominously suspended in air. You see a lot of street vending, from oranges and melons to deco sunglasses: rhinestones and plastic swans and lenses shaped like a heart. Posters are slapped on posters: one has rows of faces of the disappeared. Santa Claus stands on a truck bumper and waves drivers into a ninety-nine cent outlet.

Families are out shopping, men loiter outside a cafe, a group of young girls collectively count out their change. You notice, even in the kaleidoscope you pick out his figure, you notice a dark-skinned boy, perhaps Guatemalan, walking down Pico with a cape across his shoulders. His hair is piled in a four-inch rockabilly pompadour. He passes a dingy apartment building, *a pupuseria,* a body shop with no name, and turns into a storefront social services center. There is one other person in the sparse waiting room. She is thin, her gray hair pulled back in a tight bun, her black dress buttoned to her neck. She will tell you, if you ask her in Spanish, that she is waiting for her English class to begin. She might also tell you that the people here are helping her locate her son—lost in Salvadoran resettlement camps—and she thinks that if she can learn a little English, it will help her bring him to America.

The boy is here for different reasons. He has been causing trouble in school, and arrangements are being made for him to see a bilingual counselor. His name is Mario, and he immigrated with his older sister two years ago. His English is halting, unsure; he seems simultaneously rebellious and scared. His caseworker tells me that he still has flashbacks of Guatemalan terror: his older brother taken in the night by death squads, strangled, and hacked apart on the road by his house. Then she shows me his drawings, and our conversation stops. Crayon and pen on cheap paper: blue and orange cityscapes, eyes on billboards, in the windshields of cars, a severed hand at the bus stop. There are punks, beggars, piñatas walking the streets—upright cows and donkeys—skeletal homeboys, corseted girls carrying sharpened bones. "He will talk to you about these," the caseworker tells me. "They're scary, aren't they? The school doesn't know what the hell to do with him. I don't think he really knows what to do with all that's in him either."

In another part of the state, farther to the north, also rich in immigration, a teacher in a basic reading and writing program asks his students to interview one another and write a report, a capsule of a classmate's life. Caroline, a black woman in her late forties, chooses Thuy Anh, a Vietnamese woman many years her junior. Caroline asks only five questions—Thuy Anh's English is still difficult to understand—simple questions: What is your name? Where were you born? What is your education? Thuy Anh talks about her childhood in South Vietnam and her current plans in America. She is the oldest of nine children, and she received a very limited Vietnamese education, for she had to spend much of her childhood caring for her brothers and sisters. She married a serviceman, came to America, and now spends virtually all of her time pursuing a high school equivalency, struggling with textbook descriptions of the American political process, frantically trying to improve her computational skills. She is not doing very well at this. As one of her classmates observed, she might be trying too hard.

Caroline is supposed to take notes while Thuy Anh responds to her questions, and then use the notes to write her profile, maybe something like a reporter would do. But Caroline is moved to do something different. She's taken by Thuy Anh's account of watching over the babies. "Mother's little helper," she thinks. And that stirs her, this woman who has never been a mother. Maybe, too, Thuy Anh's desire to do well in school, her driven eagerness, the desperation that occasionally flits across her face, maybe that moves Caroline as well. Over the next two days, Caroline strays from the assignment and writes a two-and-a-half-page fiction that builds to a prose poem. She recasts Thuy Anh's childhood into an American television fantasy.

Thuy Anh is "Mother's little helper." Her five younger sisters "are happy and full of laughter . . . their little faces are bright with eyes sparkling." The little girls' names are "Hellen, Ellen, Lottie, Alice, and Olie"—American names—and they "cook and sew and make pretty doll dresses for their dolls to wear." Though the family is Buddhist, they exchange gifts at Christmas and "gather in the large living room to sing Christmas carols." Thuy Anh "went to school every day she could and studied very hard." One day, Thuy Anh was "asked to wright a poem and to recite it to her classmates." And, here, Caroline embeds within her story a prose poem—which she attributes to Thuy Anh:

> My name is Thuy Anh I live near the Ocean. I see the waves boisterous and impudent bursting and splashing against the huge rocks. I see the white boats out on the blue sea. I see the fisher men rapped in heavy coats to keep their bodys warm while bringing in large fishes to sell to the merchants, Look! I see a larg white bird going on its merry way. Then I think of how great God is for he made this great sea for me to see and yet I stand on dry land and see the green and hillie side with flowers rising to the sky. How sweet and beautiful for God to have made Thuy Anh and the sea.

I interview Caroline. When she was a little girl in Arkansas, she "would get off into a room by myself and read the Scripture." The "poems in King Solomon" were her favorites. She went to a segregated school and "used to write quite a bit" at home. But she "got away from it" and some years later dropped out of high school to come west to earn a living. She's worked in a convalescent hospital for twenty years, never married, wishes she had, comes, now, back to school and is finding again her love of words. "I get lost . . . I'm right in there with my writing, and I forget all my surroundings." She is classified as a basic student—no diploma, low-level employment, poor test scores—had been taught by her grandmother that she would have to earn her living "by the sweat of my brow."

Her work in the writing course had been good up to the point of Thuy Anh's interview, better than that of many classmates, adequate, fairly free of error, pretty well organized. But the interview triggered a different level of performance. Caroline's early engagement with language reemerged in a lyrical burst: an evocation of an imagined childhood, a curious overlay of one culture's fantasy over another's harsh reality. Caroline's longing reshaped a Vietnamese girlhood, creating a life neither she nor Thuy Anh ever had, an intersection of biblical rhythms and *Father Knows Best*.

Over Chin's bent head arches a trellis packed tight with dried honeysuckle and chrysanthemum, sea moss, mushrooms, and ginseng. His elbow rests on the cash register—quiet now that the customers have left. He shifts on the stool, concentrating on the writing before him: "A young children," he scribbles, and pauses. "Young children," that doesn't sound good, he thinks. He crosses out "children" and sits back. A few seconds pass. He can't think of the right way to say it, so he writes "children" again and continues: "a young children with his grandma smail . . ." He pulls a Chinese-English dictionary from under the counter.

In front of the counter and extending down the aisle are boxes of dried fish:

shark fins, mackerel, pollock. They give off a musky smell. Behind Chin are rows of cans and jars: pickled garlic, pickled ginger, sesame paste. By the door, comic books and Chinese weeklies lean dog-eared out over the thin retaining wire of a dusty wooden display. Chin has found his word: It's not *smail*, it's *smile*. "A young children with his grandma smile . . ." He reaches in the pocket of his jeans jacket, pulls out a piece of paper, and unfolds it. There's a word copied on it he has been wanting to use. A little bell over the door jingles. An old man comes in, and Chin moves his yellow pad aside.

Chin remembers his teacher in elementary school telling him that his writing was poor, that he didn't know many words. He went to middle school for a few years but quit before completing it. Very basic English—the ABCs and simple vocabulary—was, at one point, part of his curriculum, but he lived in a little farming community, so he figured he would never use it. He did, though, pick up some letters and a few words. He immigrated to America when he was seventeen, and for the two years since has been living with his uncle in China-town. His uncle signed him up for English classes at the community center. He didn't like them. He did, however, start hanging out in the recreation room, playing pool and watching TV. The English on TV intrigued him. And it was then that he turned to writing. He would "try to learn to speak something" by writing it down. That was about six months ago. Now he's enrolled in a community college literacy program and has been making strong progress. He is especially taken with one tutor, a woman in her mid-thirties who encourages him to write. So he writes for her. He writes stories about his childhood in China. He sneaks time when no one is in the store or when customers are poking around, writing because he likes to bring her things, writing, too, because "sometime I think writing make my English better."

The old man puts on the counter a box of tea guaranteed to help you stop smoking. Chin rings it up and thanks him. The door jingles and Chin returns to his writing, copying the word from his folded piece of paper, a word he found in *People* magazine: "A young children with his grandma smile *gleefully.*"

Frank Marell, born Meraglio, my oldest uncle, learned his English as Chin is learning his. He came to America with his mother and three sisters in September 1921. They came to join my grandfather who had immigrated long before. They joined, as well, the millions of Italian peasants who had flowed through Customs with their cloth-and-paper suitcases, their strange gestural language, and their dark, empty pockets. Frank was about to turn eight when he immigrated, so he has faint memories of Calabria. They lived in a one-room stone house. In the winter, the family's scrawny milk cow was brought inside. By the door there was a small hole for a rifle barrel. Wolves came out of the hills. He remembers the frost and burrs stinging his feet as he foraged the countryside for berries and twigs and fresh grass for the cow. *Chi esce riesce,* the saying went—"he who leaves succeeds"—and so it was that my grandfather left when he did, eventually finding work amid the metal and steam of the Pennsylvania Railroad.

My uncle remembers someone giving him bread on the steamship. He remembers being very sick. Once in America, he and his family moved into the company housing projects across from the stockyard. The house was dirty and had gouges in the wood. Each morning his mother had to sweep the soot from in front of the door. He remembers rats. He slept huddled with his father and mother and sisters in the living room, for his parents had to rent out the other rooms in order to buy clothes and shoes and food. Frank never attended school in Italy. He was eight now and would enter school in America. America, where eugenicists were attesting, scientifically, to the feeblemindedness of his race, where the popular press ran articles about the immorality of these swarthy exotics. Frank would enter school here. In many ways, you could lay his life like a template over a current life in the Bronx, in Houston, in Pico-Union.

He remembers the embarrassment of not understanding the teacher, of not being able to read or write. Funny clothes, oversize shoes, his hair slicked down and parted in the middle. He would lean forward—his assigned seat, fortunately, was in the back—and ask other Italian kids, ones with some English, to tell him what for the love of God was going on. He had big, sad eyes, thick hands, skin dark enough to yield the nickname Blacky. Frank remembers other boys—Carmen Santino, a kid named Hump, Bruno Tucci—who couldn't catch on to this new language and quit coming to school. Within six months of his arrival, Frank would be going after class to the back room of Pete Mastis's Dry Cleaners and Shoeshine Parlor. He cleaned and shined shoes, learned to operate a steam press, ran deliveries. He listened to the radio, trying to mimic the harsh complexities of English. He spread Pete Mastis's racing forms out before him, copying words onto the margins of newsprint. He tried talking to the people whose shoes he was shining, exchanging tentative English with the broken English of Germans and Poles and other Italians.

Eventually, Frank taught his mother to sign her name. By the time he was in his teens, he was reading flyers and announcements of sales and legal documents to her. He was also her scribe, doing whatever writing she needed to have done. Frank found himself immersed in the circumstance of literacy.

With the lives of Mario and Caroline and Chin and Frank Marell as a backdrop, I want to consider a current, very powerful set of proposals about literacy and culture.

There is a strong impulse in American education—curious in a country with such an ornery streak of antitraditionalism—to define achievement and excellence in terms of the acquisition of a historically validated body of knowledge, an authoritative list of books and allusions, a canon. We seek a certification of our national intelligence, indeed, our national virtue, in how diligently our children can display this central corpus of information. This need for certification tends to emerge most dramatically in our educational policy debates during times of real or imagined threat: economic hard times, political crises, sudden increases in immigration. Now is such a time, and it is reflected in a number of influential books and commission reports. E. D. Hirsch argues that a core national vocabulary, one oriented toward the English literate tradition—Alice in Wonderland to zeitgeist—will build a knowledge base that will foster the literacy of all Americans. Diane Ravitch and Chester Finn call for a return to a traditional historical and literary curriculum: the valorous historical figures and the classical literature of the once-elite course of study. Allan Bloom, Secretary of Education William Bennett, Mortimer Adler and the Paideia Group, and a number of others have affirmed, each in their very different ways, the necessity of the Great Books: Plato and Aristotle and Sophocles, Dante and Shakespeare and Locke, Dickens and Mann and Faulkner. We can call this orientation to educational achievement the canonical orientation.

At times in our past, the call for a shoring up of or return to a canonical curriculum was explicitly elitist, was driven by a fear that the education of the select was being compromised. Today, though, the majority of the calls are provocatively framed in the language of democracy. They assail the mediocre and grinding curriculum frequently found in remedial and vocational education. They are disdainful of the patronizing perceptions of student ability that further restrict the already restricted academic life of disadvantaged youngsters. They point out that the canon—its language, conventions, and allusions—is central to the discourse of power, and to keep it from poor kids is to assure their disenfranchisement all the more. The books of the canon, claim the proposals, the Great Books, are a window onto a common core of experience and civic ideals. There is, then, a spiritual, civic, and cognitive heritage here, and *all* our children should receive it. If we are sincere in our desire to bring Mario, Chin, the younger versions of Caroline, current incarnations of Frank Marell, and so many others who populate this book—if we truly want to bring them into our society—then we should provide them with this stable and common core. This is a forceful call. It promises a still center in a turning world.

I see great value in being challenged to think of the curriculum of the many in the terms we have traditionally reserved for the few; it is refreshing to have common assumptions about the capacities of underprepared students so boldly challenged. Many of the people we have encountered in these pages have displayed the ability to engage books and ideas thought to be beyond their grasp. There were the veterans: Willie Oates writing, in prison, ornate sentences drawn from *The Mill on the Floss*. Sergeant Gonzalez coming to understand poetic ambiguity in "Butch Weldy." There was the parole aide Olga who no longer felt walled off from *Macbeth*. There were the EOP students at UCLA, like Lucia who unpackaged *The Myth of Mental Illness* once she had an orientation and overview. And there was Frank Marell who, later in his life, would be talking excitedly to his nephew about this guy Edgar Allan Poe. Too many people are kept from the books of the canon, the Great Books, because of misjudgments about their potential. Those books eventually proved important to me, and, as best I know how, I invite my students to engage them. But once we grant the desirability of equal curricular treatment and begin to consider what this equally distributed curriculum would contain, problems arise: If the canon itself is the answer to our educational inequities, why has it historically invited few and denied many? Would the canonical orientation provide adequate guidance as to how a democratic curriculum should be constructed and how it should be taught? Would it guide us in opening up to Olga that "fancy talk" that so alienated her?

Those who study the way literature becomes canonized, how linguistic creations are included or excluded from a tradition, claim that the canonical curriculum students would most likely receive would not, as is claimed, offer a common core of American experience. Caroline would not find her life represented in it, nor would Mario. The canon has tended to push to the margin much of the literature of our nation: from American Indian songs and chants to immigrant fiction to working-class narratives. The institutional messages that students receive in the books they're issued and the classes they take are powerful and, as I've witnessed since my Voc. Ed. days, quickly internalized. And to revise these messages and redress past wrongs would involve more than adding some new books to the existing canon—the very reasons for linguistic and cultural exclusion would have to become a focus of study in order to make the canon act as a democratizing force. Unless this happens, the democratic intent of the reformers will be undercut by the content of the curriculum they propose.

And if we move beyond content to consider basic assumptions about teaching and learning, a further problem arises, one that involves the very nature of the canonical orientation itself. The canonical orientation encourages a narrowing of focus from learning to that which must be learned: It simplifies the dynamic tension between student and text and reduces the psychological and social dimensions of instruction. The student's personal history recedes as the what of the classroom is valorized over the how. Thus it is that the encounter of student and text is often portrayed by canonists as a transmission. Information, wisdom, virtue will pass from the book to the student if the student gives the book the time it merits, carefully traces its argument or narrative or lyrical progression. Intellectual, even spiritual, growth will *necessarily* result from an encounter with Roman mythology, *Othello*, and "I heard a Fly buzz—when I died—," with biographies and historical sagas and patriotic lore. Learning is stripped of confusion and discord. It is stripped, as well, of strong human connection. My own initiators to the canon—Jack MacFarland, Dr. Carothers, and the rest—knew there was more to their work than their mastery of a tradition. What mattered most, I see now, were the relationships they established with me, the guidance they provided when I felt inadequate or threatened. This mentoring was part of my entry into that solemn library of Western thought—and even with such support, there were still times of confusion, anger, and fear. It is telling, I think, that once that rich social network slid away, once I was in graduate school in intense, solitary encounter with that tradition, I abandoned it for other sources of nurturance and knowledge.

The model of learning implicit in the canonical orientation seems, at times, more religious than cognitive or social: Truth resides in the printed texts, and if they are presented by someone who knows them well and respects them, that truth will be revealed. Of all the advocates of the canon, Mortimer Adler has given most attention to pedagogy—and his Paideia books contain valuable discussions of instruction, coaching, and questioning. But even here, and this is doubly true in the other manifestos, there is little acknowledgment that the material in the canon can be not only difficult but foreign, alienating, overwhelming.

We need an orientation to instruction that provides guidance on how to determine and honor the beliefs and stories, enthusiasms, and apprehensions that students reveal. How to build on them, and when they clash with our curriculum—as I saw so often in the Tutorial Center at UCLA—when they clash, how to encourage a discussion that will lead to reflection on what students bring and what they're currently confronting. Canonical lists imply canonical answers, but the manifestos offer little discussion of what to do when students fail. If students have been exposed to at least some elements of the canon before—as many have—why didn't it take? If they're encountering it for the first time and they're lost, how can we determine where they're located—and what do we do then?

Each member of a teacher's class, poor *or* advantaged, gives rise to endless decisions, day-to-day determinations about a child's reading and writing: decisions on how to tap strength, plumb confusion, foster growth. The richer your conception of learning and your understanding of its social and psychological dimensions, the more insightful and effective your judgments will be. Consider the sources of literacy we saw among the children in El Monte: shopkeepers' signs, song lyrics, auto manuals, the conventions of the Western, family stories and tales, and more. Consider Chin's sources—television and *People* magazine—and Caroline's oddly generative mix of the Bible and an American media illusion. Then there's the jarring confluence of personal horror and pop cultural flotsam that surfaces in Mario's drawings, drawings that would be a rich, if volatile, point of departure for language instruction. How would these myriad sources and manifestations be perceived and evaluated if viewed within the framework of a canonical tradition, and what guidance would the tradition provide on how to understand and develop them? The great books and central texts of the canon could quickly become a benchmark against which the expressions of student literacy would be negatively measured, a limiting band of excellence that, ironically, could have a dispiriting effect on the very thing the current proposals intend: the fostering of mass literacy.

To understand the nature and development of literacy we need to consider the social context in which it occurs—the political, economic, and cultural forces that encourage or inhibit it. The canonical orientation discourages deep analysis of the way these forces may be affecting performance. The canonists ask that schools transmit a coherent traditional knowledge to an ever-changing, frequently uprooted community. This discordance between message and audience is seldom examined. Although a ghetto child can rise on the lilt of a Homeric line—books *can* speak dreams—appeals to elevated texts can also divert attention from the conditions that keep a population from realizing its dreams. The literacy curriculum is being asked to do what our politics and our economics have failed to do: diminish differences in achievement, narrow our gaps, bring us together. Instead of analysis of the complex web of causes of poor performance, we are offered a faith in the unifying power of a body of knowledge, whose infusion will bring the rich and the poor, the longtime disaffected and the uprooted newcomers into cultural unanimity. If this vision is democratic, it is simplistically so, reductive, not an invitation for people truly to engage each other at the point where cultures and classes intersect.

I worry about the effects a canonical approach to education could have on cultural dialogue and transaction—on the involvement of an abandoned underclass and on the movement of immigrants like Mario and Chin into our nation. A canonical uniformity promotes rigor and quality control; it can also squelch new thinking, diffuse the generative tension between the old and the new. It is significant that the canonical orientation is voiced with most force during times of challenge and uncertainty, for it promises the authority of tradition, the seeming stability of the past. But the authority is fictive, gained from a misreading of American cultural history. No period of that history was harmoniously stable; the invocation of a golden age is a mythologizing act. Democratic culture is, by definition, vibrant and dynamic, discomforting and unpredictable. It gives rise to apprehension; freedom is not always calming. And, yes, it can yield fragmentation, though often as not the source of fragmentation is intolerant misunderstanding of diverse traditions rather than the desire of members of those traditions to remain hermetically separate. A truly democratic vision of knowledge and social structure would honor this complexity. The vision might not be soothing, but it would provide guidance as to how to live and teach in a country made up of many cultural traditions.

We are in the middle of an extraordinary social experiment: the attempt to provide education for all members of a vast pluralistic democracy. To have any prayer of success, we'll need many conceptual blessings: A philosophy of language and literacy that affirms the diverse sources of linguistic competence and deepens our understanding of the ways class and culture blind us to the richness of those sources. A perspective on failure that lays open the logic of error. An orientation toward the interaction of poverty and ability that undercuts simple polarities, that enables us to see simultaneously the constraints poverty places on the play of mind and the actual mind at play within those constraints. We'll need a pedagogy that encourages us to step back and consider the threat of the standard classroom and that shows us, having stepped back, how to step forward to invite a student across the boundaries of that powerful room. Finally, we'll need a revised store of images of educational excellence, ones closer to egalitarian ideals—ones that embody the reward and turmoil of education in a democracy, that celebrate the plural, messy human reality of it. At heart, we'll need a guiding set of principles that do not encourage us to retreat from, but move us closer to, an understanding of the rich mix of speech and ritual and story that is America.

QUESTIONS FOR "CROSSING BOUNDARIES" BY MIKE ROSE

Talking About the Text

1. What is Rose's position on those two fundamental questions concerning what is taught and how it is taught?
2. How does Rose's extensive use of examples in the first half of his essay

support his overall argument? In your response evaluate how typical and relevant his examples are.

3. An important aspect of Rose's argument rests on the kinds of "experiences" students bring to school with them. What do you consider to be important experiences students carry with them to college?

4. In the way Rose describes it, how might a canonical orientation treat those experiences?

Exploring Issues

1. Try summarizing Rose's summary of his opponent's views favoring a canonical orientation for students. Are there any books that you think students should know about? What are they?

2. How does Rose's version of literacy compare with Kozol's? What would be the purpose of each of their versions?

3. Rose says, "The literacy curriculum is being asked to do what our politics and our economics have failed to do: diminish differences in achievement, narrow our gaps, bring us together." In what sense can a literacy curriculum accomplish these goals? In which ways can it not?

4. Compare and contrast the experiences of some of the students Rose describes with the language problems encountered by "The Girl Who Wouldn't Sing" (in Chapter 1). What tentative conclusions can you draw about the difficulties students from different cultures experience in struggling to achieve school literacy?

Writing Assignments

1. Try this experiment. Read a selection in this book which has not been read or discussed previously. Then write a response to something significant found in the reading. Share these individual responses in class. Following this, analyze one of your classmate's responses in detail and write a report that tries to account for both similarities and differences in how another reads.

2. Write a literacy autobiography in which you talk about how you learned to read and write. Include the conflicts and difficulties as well as the successes you encountered in this process. Your account does not need to end with a neat conclusion.

3. Compare and contrast your autobiographical account with your classmates'. Then begin to work on your theory of what people should learn and how they should learn it. Be prepared to revise your theory as you proceed through this chapter and through this course.

4. Interview a relative or someone with a different background from yours. Find out how she acquired her present level of literacy and write a report about what you discover.

Reading 49

Education of Blacks

H. Kenneth Bechtel

This selection is from the first chapter of *Blacks, Science, and American Education* (1989), coedited by Willie Pearson, Jr., and H. Kenneth Bechtel. Bechtel developed his interest in the history of black education from three years of discussions with Willie Pearson and from his interest in Edward Bouchet, an early American black scientist. Bechtel is an associate professor at Wake Forest University in North Carolina where he pursues his teaching and research in historical sociology. In this selection Bechtel maintains that blacks have been denied an equal education and instead often encouraged to pursue vocational education.

For most of the history of the United States, educational policies toward blacks were generally designed with one goal in mind: to ensure the political, social, economic, and intellectual inferiority of blacks. The policies worked well, and even after America began to revoke them, their legacy remains the major cause of the educational deprivation and retardation of blacks.

During the first half-century of the nation's history, in New England and the mid-Atlantic states specifically, revolutionary spirit, growing abolitionist sentiment, and Christian missionary fervor favored the education of blacks. The work of various religious groups, most notably the Quakers, to establish schools for blacks is well documented. The efforts to provide instruction to blacks during this period were generally local and unconnected, reflecting the interests of the diverse groups involved. Thus, some communities provided integrated public instruction while others had separate facilities. The growing intensity of antislavery sentiments in parts of the North prompted some communities to adopt policies that would allow more blacks to attend public schools (Woodson 1915; Frazier 1949; Franklin 1973).

The results of this movement were impressive as free blacks took advantage of opportunities to get an education. Of the 2,000 blacks in Boston in 1850, almost 1,500 were in school; and in the states and territories as a whole, 32,629 blacks were in school in 1860. Blacks also began to move into higher education: in 1826 Edward Jones graduated from Amherst while John Russwurm was getting his degree from Bowdoin—the first blacks to graduate from college in America. Blacks were attending Oberlin and other institutions of higher education well before the Civil War (Franklin 1973; Pifer 1973).

Although most of these educational efforts were provided and controlled by whites, blacks also played a role. A few schools were established by blacks, and in such large cities as Philadelphia blacks began to organize literary societies as early as the 1780s (Funke 1920; Winston 1971).

The social climate in the South during the slavery era effectively precluded educating blacks. Interest in public education in general was low. Whites who wanted schooling were expected to rely on their families for financial support. There were a few isolated efforts to provide free blacks with an education, and some progressive plantation owners felt morally bound to teach their slaves to read and write. Any possibility of these practices gaining widespread support quickly vanished with the abortive revolts by Prosser (1800) and Vesey (1822), and the Turner rebellion (1831). These actions by blacks who had been educated so frightened the planters that laws were passed throughout the South making it illegal to instruct any slave or free black (Funke 1920; Franklin 1973; Low and Clift 1981).

During the decade of Reconstruction following the Civil War, blacks made temporary gains in their social and political conditions. Passage of the Thirteenth, Fourteenth, and Fifteenth amendments to the Constitution and the Civil Rights Act of 1866 gave blacks freedom and rights of citizenship and hindered restrictive legislation that attempted to reestablish antebellum social relationships (Bond 1969; Brawley 1970). Probably the most significant change came in the area of education. The emancipated slaves were eager to take advantage of their new status and felt that getting an education was of primary importance. And many individuals and organizations interested in aiding the freedmen were quick to offer their services (Woodson 1969).

Even before the war ended, missionaries began to make their way into the Southern states to establish educational programs for those blacks freed by the advancing Union troops. Immediately after the war, religious organizations, such as the American Missionary Association and the government-sponsored Freedmen's Bureau, established schools in the South. Blacks responded eagerly, and thousands were attending schools by the late 1860s (Funke 1920; Bond 1934; Cruden 1969).

White Southerners, however, were unprepared for such a radical change and opposed efforts to provide education for blacks, who were considered innately inferior—the idea of educating them was viewed as absurd. Providing educational opportunities to blacks would have meant extending a privilege that had historically been restricted to the upper classes in the South; it would elevate the former slave to a status higher than that of most former slave owners. Conservative Southerners feared that the schools taught by Northerners would instill Republican ideals of equality and further undermine their political power. The hostile reaction by Southerners to black education was a predictable part of their attempt to maintain the traditional antebellum social order in the face of massive social dislocation.

Nevertheless, some Southern whites grasped an obvious fact: the freedmen would have to be educated simply to survive and provide for their own basic needs. At the end of the Civil War, 95 percent of the black population in America was illiterate. To most enlightened observers, the presence of this large number of "ignorant black rabble was a menacing Trojan horse" (Winston 1971, 681). White Southerners faced a serious dilemma that went beyond simple questions of educational philosophy. The way this problem was addressed would have a significant impact on important issues of political and economic relationships, because once whites chose to educate blacks, they had to decide what type of education should be provided. And that decision ultimately depended upon the role that whites saw for blacks in the American social order.

From an egalitarian perspective, education is a means of raising those less fortunate up to a level on par with the rest of society. If such a goal had been paramount at the end of the Civil War, what sort of educational program could have been developed? Allen Ballard (1973, 11) describes a possible scenario.

First, there would have to be federally funded elementary schools in every village. Second, a federally funded group of highly trained teachers would have been sent to those villages. Centers of literacy would have to be established for adult education. This first thrust could have carried through for five to ten years, to be followed by the establishment of regional high schools with both vocational and academic curricula to serve as the funnel through which the most able black youth would have gone on to federally subsidized colleges. Over a period of fifty or seventy-five years the educational level of the Africans would have risen to that of white Americans.

Ballard makes clear that it was unthinkable that whites during Reconstruction would have allowed anything of the sort. If blacks had to be educated, white Southerners felt, let that education be suited to their inferior mental capacities and to their proper, subservient place in society. With the goal decided upon, the two pillars of post-Reconstruction black educational philosophy emerged: a system of separate and unequal schools for blacks, and industrial education.

During Reconstruction, the quality of education provided in the South had been generally poor for both blacks and whites, but it was administered on a fairly equal basis. After the end of Reconstruction and the reemergence of Southern conservatives in political power, the policies of black social and political disenfranchisement extended to black education as well. Through deception, blatant discrimination, and law, white schools were improved at the expense of black schools. An examination of the data on school expenditures from the mid-1870s to 1930 clearly reveals the massive disparities between the education of whites and blacks in the South.

Data (Bond 1934, 153) for the state of Alabama indicate the changes that took place over the fifty-five-year period from 1875 to 1930. During the 1875/1876 school term, Alabama spent an average of $1.30 per pupil for white teachers' salaries and $1.46 per pupil for black teachers' salaries. This difference in favor of blacks reflects the impact of the Reconstruction administration. By 1885, however, Alabama was paying black teachers 85 percent of what was paid to white teachers ($1.09 versus $1.28). And twenty-five years later, black Alabama teachers still received only $1.10 per pupil while their white counterparts got nearly six times as much ($6.42).

While the figures from Alabama show the dramatic decline over time in expenditures to black teachers, the data from Tennessee reveal no change whatsoever over the sixty-year period from 1870 to 1930. In 1870 Tennessee paid its white teachers $11.83 per pupil compared to $7.48 for black teachers— 63 percent of the white teachers' salary. By 1931 Tennessee was paying its white teachers $27.55 per pupil compared to $17.25 for black teachers—again only 63 percent of the white teachers' salary (Bond 1934, 158–159).

Harlan (1968, 38) noted that the regional differences in funding for white schools paled when compared to the economic disadvantages suffered by black schools. In 1915 the North Central states spent an average of $28.00 per white child for education compared to only $14.00 per white child in South Carolina. But at the same time, South Carolina was spending only $1.13 per black child for education.

The data presented in Table 1 reveal the degree of inferiority of funding of black education compared to that of whites in the South. Using Washington, D.C., as a point of comparison, one finds that spending by the six Southern states on school expenses, school property, and teacher salaries falls far short of anything that could be remotely called "equal" education. The breadth of the discrimination against black education is revealed in other areas as well. For example, during the 1933/1934 school year, ten Southern states spent a total of $20 million on transporting rural school children. But, only 3 percent of this money was spent on black children who constituted 34 percent of the total school population. In 1935/1936 over half (55 percent) of the 24,405 black public elementary schools in the eighteen states with separate schools were one-room schools. In terms of total property value, in ten Southern states for which data were available, for every $1.00 invested in school property for each white student, only $0.19 was invested for each black student (Frazier 1949, 434–435).

Factors other than direct discrimination in finances also undermined the ability of blacks to acquire an adequate education. Black attendance remained relatively low because black schools were often distant and so little transportation was provided. But because the number of black teachers was also small, the typical teacher in a black school would, on the average, have twice as many students as the typical teacher in a white school (see Table 1). Possibly most damaging was the practice of having shorter terms for the black schools. In the 1929/1930 school year, for example, the average length of the term for the eighteen Southern and border states, including Washington, was 164 days for whites and 144 days for blacks. However, in South Carolina the average school term was 173 days for whites compared to only 114 days for blacks (Work 1931, 205). After eight years of school, the typical black student in South Carolina would have been in class 472 days less than the typical white student—in other words, he or she would be approximately four years behind. This policy, combined with the fact that few secondary schools were established for blacks, goes far toward explaining why few blacks during this period attained more than a sixth-grade education (Rice 1971).

Table 1. PUBLIC SCHOOL EXPENDITURES

	Average exp. per pupil		Black % exp.	Black % pop.	Average value of school property per pupil		Average annual teacher salary		Pupils per teacher	
	W	B			W	B	W	B	W	B
D.C.	$112.79	$96.31	26.0	25.2	$289.33	$237.23	$2,229	$2,099	29	32
Alabama	37.00	7.16	10.1	38.4	86.36	15.40	832	354	33	48
Georgia	31.52	6.98	14.0	41.7	73.34	11.01	768	260	34	46
Louisiana	40.64	7.84	12.1	38.9	140.68	18.53	1,159	496	30	53
Mississippi	31.33	5.94	20.0	52.2	93.94	17.30	908	350	30	53
S.C.	52.89	5.20	10.3	51.4	125.00	14.10	1,047	316	28	51
Virginia	47.46	13.30	11.0	29.9	111.03	38.28	902	502	31	40

Source: Work 1931, 204–207.

Note: Selected data for six Southern states and the District of Columbia, 1930–1931.

Much of this discussion of black education has focused on the Southern states. One must not conclude that the educational experiences of blacks in the North were any better. During the eighteenth and nineteenth centuries, blacks were few in number in the North and West and did not arouse the fear and apprehension found in the South. Life was therefore different for those blacks who lived in the various Northern states. They were not subject to the whims of a master; the restrictions on their activities were less severe; they could protest against injustices; and there were more opportunities for self-expression (such as churches and newspapers) and improvement in one's political and economic position (Quarles 1969; Litwack 1961).

Popular beliefs and attitudes about blacks were not restricted to a particular region of the country, and the belief in black inferiority was shared by most white Americans. Discrimination and racial segregation were facts of life for blacks North and South. And the justification for such practices was the same everywhere: blacks constituted an inferior race suited only for the most menial of positions (Litwack 1961).

Despite having comparatively greater freedom in the North, blacks found that there was strong opposition to their receiving an education. Many Northern states were unwilling to spend money on schools for blacks, fearing that more of them would move into their states or communities seeking education. Northerners seemed no more fond of blacks than Southerners. Ohio, Illinois, and Oregon had laws forbidding the migration of free blacks into their states. Although Northern states did not pass laws prohibiting the teaching of blacks, there was an undercurrent of resentment toward educating blacks that found expression in the forcible closing of schools, the intimidation and driving away of teachers, and the destruction of school buildings (Bond 1934; Beale 1975).

While some white schools in the North admitted blacks, this occurred mostly during the early 1800s. By 1830 most Northern states had excluded blacks from white schools and required them to attend separate all-black schools. Reflecting the prevailing belief in the limited intellectual capacity of blacks, these separate schools were often as unequal as those in the South, with substandard teachers, inadequate facilities, and inferior curricula (Litwack 1961).

Frazier (1949) has remarked that the problems facing blacks in the public schools of the North were similar to those faced by the large number of immigrants who settled in the major urban centers. As with the immigrants, blacks had been forced to live in the poorest sections of the cities and their children had to attend old, inferior, and overcrowded schools. Nevertheless, blacks suffered additional problems: because of their color, they were restricted in their movement both socially and economically. Greer (1973) notes that with varying degrees of speed, foreign immigrants were able to become part of American society, while blacks remained on the margin. Both groups were vulnerable because of their low social status, but it was the individual immigrant who suffered the consequences of economic change, while for blacks the entire group was affected. Thus, caste through race added a significant dimension to the life of the lower-class black in the urban North.

Despite widespread animosity toward blacks, they did receive more education in the North, although the quality of that education was inferior. Frazier (1949, 445–446) reports figures for 1940 that show the proportion of blacks with four years of high school in the South was only 25 percent of the total, while in the North it ranged from 50 to 75 percent of the total. The reality, however, is that North or South, blacks in America received an inadequate and inferior education when compared to that available for most whites.

The content of black schooling accurately reflected white goals for blacks in the social order. Industrial training was an effective way of ensuring that blacks could not rise beyond what was seen as their natural sphere as laborers and servants.

Industrial education had its beginning at Hampton Institute under the direction of General Samuel Armstrong, a Freedmen's Bureau administrator in Hampton, Virginia. A believer in the innate inferiority of blacks, Armstrong thought that the best training for blacks was one that would instill self-control and provide a check on what he believed was the natural tendency of blacks toward rebellion. His program of education was intended to affect a change in the freedman's innately flawed character, to "civilize" the black by instilling "habits of living and labor" (Spivey 1978, 19). Armstrong believed that blacks were ultimately destined to "form the working classes" and remain at the bottom of the economic hierarchy (Spivey 1978, 22). Having no faith in blacks' intellectual capacity, Armstrong thought it was a waste of time to give them academic training, stating that courses involving "reading and elocution, geography and mathematics, history, the sciences . . . would, I think, make a curriculum that would exhaust the best powers of . . . those who would for years enter" Hampton (Spivey 1978, 26). Thus, education at Hampton under Armstrong was designed to maintain the Southern status quo. Black students would be trained in the principles of agriculture, unskilled menial labor, and domestic service—activities that would not be a threat to white skilled workers and would keep blacks in their proper place in the social and economic structure (Spivey 1978). But while Armstrong was the originator of vocational education, it took a black man to make industrial training a prominent feature of black education.

Booker T. Washington was a student at Hampton and became convinced that vocational education was the only means by which blacks would become successful in America. In 1881 Washington went to Alabama and founded Tuskegee Institute, where he put into practice his belief that the ultimate solution to the race problem was for blacks to prove themselves worthy by becoming reliable and superior laborers, eventually making themselves indispensable to the economic well-being of the country. In order to accomplish this, blacks must have the right form of education: an education that would be beneficial in an economic sense. Given his experience at Hampton, Washington felt that industrial education was superior to academic education for achieving his goal of black social improvement (Spivey 1978, 50–51). As quoted in Franklin (1973, 285), Washington believed that black education "should be so directed that the greatest proportion of the mental strength of the masses will be brought to bear upon the everyday practical things of life, upon something that is needed to be done, and something which *they will be permitted to do* in the community in which they reside" (emphasis added).

The basic philosophy of industrial education as practiced at Hampton and Tuskegee was quite simple. The training in various domestic and trade skills within an authoritarian and religiously based environment would produce a black who would fit into the lower end of the occupational structure and, more important, know his or her place among whites and come to accept that place as proper.

Such a form of education was just what white society sought. For Southerners, it would keep blacks subservient and exploitable. For Northerners, it would serve as a way of calming racial tensions and providing a well-trained laboring underclass that could be used in the effort to industrialize the South. For these reasons, wealthy philanthropists in both the North and the South were willing to give large grants to institutions that adopted this vocational model while ignoring those institutions which remained academically oriented (Quarles 1969; Winston 1971; Franklin 1973).

The results were as dramatic as they were devastating. The ideology of vocational education became the panacea for the race problem in America. Except for a few institutions of higher learning (Fisk, Atlanta, and Howard), black colleges took the financial windfalls and adopted the vocational curriculum. Educationally, vocational training was a failure: it not only failed to prepare blacks to move up in society, but it also guaranteed that they would move down. The emphasis on manual training and the trades served to destroy the educational aspirations that had been aroused during Reconstruction and wiped out the hope that education could provide a way out of poverty. By 1930 industrial education was seen as a "cynical political strategy, not a sound educational policy" and proved to be the "great detour" for blacks from which they are just beginning to return (Winston 1971, 683).

SCIENTIFIC CAREERS

The few blacks who managed to overcome educational obstacles and enter careers in science and technology still faced bigotry in other aspects of their lives. This discrimination extended to the lack of public recognition of names and accomplishments of black scientists, medical researchers, and inventors. Only recently have scholars begun to search out evidence of these blacks' contributions and discover that, although blacks are rare in the history of American science, they are by no means missing or negligible. It is worth noting that, for many of the same kinds of reasons, the presence and activities of women in science were long overlooked by historians and only recently have been reexamined (Rossiter 1974).

It is appropriate to describe briefly the work of some of these black American scientists and inventors and to examine the ways in which they surmounted the formidable barriers to intellectual achievement.

Before the Civil War, the United States was not known for its scientific accomplishments. It would not make sense to expect blacks to be the exception to this rule. For most slaves and free blacks, the main issue was gaining and keeping their freedom. Many blacks with exceptional abilities directed their talents to devising ways to gain their own freedom and to interest others in supporting such efforts. Inevitably, preachers and orators outnumbered inventors among the black community during the antebellum period (Baker 1917; Bardolph 1955).

But it is also true that black inventors, especially in the South, were unrecognized by historians. Slaves who invented mechanical devices to relieve the physical burden of labor could not protect their rights to the inventions (Baker 1917). They were not recognized as citizens and therefore could not enter into contracts. The federal government refused to grant them patents or to allow them to transfer patent rights to their owners. This did not preclude the outright theft of inventions by the slave owners, who would claim them as their own. Given this situation, it can never be known how many inventions were originated by slaves (Haber 1970). Among free blacks, inventors preferred to have their race kept secret for fear that the information would impair the commercial success of their devices (Baker 1913).

The government restriction on the granting of patents to slaves did not apply to free blacks. For example, James Forten (1766–1842), a free black Philadelphian, had no difficulty in getting a patent for his invention for handling sails or deriving a comfortable living from its manufacture. The same could be said of Norbert Rillieux. Born in New Orleans 17 March 1806, Rillieux was the son of Vincent Rillieux, a wealthy plantation owner, and his slave Constance Vivant. Because of his father's position, the young Rillieux had the advantages of both freedom and wealth. He attended Catholic schools in New Orleans and studied engineering in France. At the age of twenty-four he became the youngest instructor in applied mechanics at L'Ecole Centrale in Paris and contributed papers on steam technology to engineering journals (A. E. Klein 1971). His major accomplishment came in 1846 when he invented and patented a vacuum pan that transformed the process of refining sugar. The device yielded a superior product—granulated sugar—at a low price. The invention was a boon to the sugar industry in Louisiana and revolutionized the production of sugar worldwide (Baker 1917; Haber 1970; Toppin 1971; Ploski and Williams 1983).

A discussion of early black inventors cannot fail to mention the accomplishments of Benjamin Banneker. The son of a free black mother and a slave she had purchased, Banneker was born in Baltimore County, Maryland, in 1731. Taught to read and write at home by his grandmother, Banneker also attended an integrated public school where he obtained the equivalent of an eighth grade education. His curiosity about mechanical devices led him in 1761 to construct a wooden striking clock so accurately made that it kept perfect time for over twenty years. His knowledge of astronomy and his mathematical ability enabled him to predict the solar eclipse of 1789. And during the next ten years he published an almanac of tide tables, eclipses, and medicinal formulas. His most notable contribution came as a surveyor with the team chosen by George Washington to develop the plans for the new national capital. Although publicly recognized in France and England for his scientific accomplishments, he received little official recognition in the United States—although in 1970 Banneker Circle in Washington, D.C., was named in his honor (Haber 1970; Toppin 1971; Ploski and Williams 1983).

• • •

Most of the black scientists and inventors of the nineteenth century were very gifted, self-taught individuals who lacked academic or professional training in the physical sciences. This should not be surprising since the description would apply equally to white American scientists and inventors at the same time. In fact, it was only in 1861 that the first doctorate was granted in a science—physics—at Yale University. Probably the most noteworthy accomplishment in the history of blacks in science occurred just fifteen years later. In 1876 Edward Alexander Bouchet, a twenty-four-year-old black man, was awarded a Ph.D. in physics from Yale University for a dissertation in geometrical optics entitled *On Measuring Refracting Indices.* Bouchet was the first black to receive a doctorate from an American university and only the sixth person in the United States to be awarded a Ph.D. in physics. Yet, other than an occasional footnote in the history of black education, Bouchet and his accomplishments remain virtually unknown to the world of science and literally unheard of by the world in general. What happened to Bouchet provides a glimpse into the adversity facing educated blacks in post-Civil War America.

Edward Bouchet was born in 1852 to free parents in New Haven, Connecticut, where he attended a public "colored school." Like most of the schools for blacks in the city, it was small, ungraded, and had only one teacher. In 1868 Bouchet was the first black to be accepted into Hopkins Grammar School, a preparatory school for the classical and scientific departments at Yale College. During his two years at Hopkins he studied Latin and Greek grammar, geometry, algebra, and Greek history. He graduated in 1870 first in his class and was chosen valedictorian (Bechtel 1986).

Bouchet entered Yale in the fall of 1870 and continued to excel. When he graduated in 1874, his grade-point average was 3.22 on a 4.0-point scale, the sixth highest in a class of 124. In 1875 Bouchet returned to Yale to pursue graduate work in physics. During his two years in the graduate school, he paid special attention to chemistry, mineralogy, and experimental physics. Under the direction of Arthur Wright, he successfully completed his dissertation (Bechtel 1986).

Bouchet's graduate education was encouraged and financed by Alfred Cope, a member of the board of managers of a Friends school for blacks in Philadelphia, the Institute for Colored Youth (ICY). Firm believers in the value of liberal education and the unlimited capabilities of blacks, Cope and the other managers offered at ICY a curriculum that included ancient history, geography, Greek and Latin classics, algebra, geometry, and chemistry. In an effort to expand the school's offerings, Cope established a Scientific Fund to promote learning in the principles of applied science. It was the establishment of the Scientific Fund that led Cope to invite Bouchet to head the new science program (Perkins 1978).

Bouchet arrived in Philadelphia in the fall of 1876 and taught at the ICY for the next twenty-six years. However, as with all American blacks during the last two decades of the nineteenth century, Bouchet's life took a turn for the worse. By the mid-1890s, many Philadelphia Quakers were becoming disillusioned with the black community as they now questioned the ability of blacks to respond to the efforts being made on their behalf. In 1894 a study made of the institute's curriculum suggested that it be simplified, stating that the courses were "pitched too high." By the end of the century, the new managers had become openly hostile to classical and academic education and receptive to Booker T. Washington's educational philosophy. In their efforts to redirect the ICY along the line of industrial training at Hampton and Tuskegee, the managers proceeded to fire all the teachers, including Bouchet, and replaced them with instructors favorable to industrial education (Perkins 1978; Bechtel 1986).

No white college would have considered him seriously for a position on its faculty even with his superior qualifications. But barriers other than race had an impact on Bouchet's career. The ascendance of vocational-industrial instruction during the latter half of the nineteenth century, and the overwhelming acceptance of the Hampton-Tuskegee model for blacks in particular, served to limit Bouchet's opportunities. His academic education and his training in the natural sciences made him increasingly unattractive as a candidate at black colleges that had adopted the industrial-education philosophy. As noted by DuBois (1973, 65), the debate between academic and industrial education for blacks was a bitter one. "The disputants came to rival organizations, to severe social pressure, to anger and even to blows. . . . Employment and promotion depended often on a Negro's attitude toward industrial education. . . . Men were labeled and earmarked by the allegiance to one school of thought or to the other."

The difficulties that the industrial-education movement created for Bouchet were tragic not only for him but also for the generations of students he might have trained in science. The movement stopped students from striving for professional careers; it perpetuated stereotypes about black intellectual inferiority; and it kept blacks in economically inferior jobs. Even on its own terms, it misjudged the demand for blacks in the trades, arousing the hostility of white workers. It failed to see that the rise of the large corporation would put many tradesmen and craftsmen out of business (DuBois 1973; Franklin 1973).

Although whites enthusiastically endorsed industrial training for blacks and helped to implement it through contributions to black schools, it is noteworthy that some blacks resisted. W. E. B. DuBois led this movement against industrial education, while leaders at some black colleges refused to change their curriculum in the direction of Tuskegee and Hampton. An important change occurred at the beginning of the twentieth century as a small number of men and women began to move into the fields of science and engineering. Consider, for example, three blacks who made significant contributions to biology and medicine: E. E. Just, Percy Julian, and Charles Drew.

Born in Charleston, South Carolina, in 1883, Ernest Just received his bachelor's degree with honors from Dartmouth. In college he developed an interest in biology, especially cell structure and development. After graduating from Dartmouth, he taught biology at Howard University and began a twenty-year period of summer research at the Marine Biological Laboratories at Woods Hole, Massachusetts. In 1916 he received his Ph.D. in biology from the University of Chicago. During his career, he published two books and over sixty papers in scholarly journals. His ideas on cell-membrane activity completely changed the scientific opinion of his time as he successfully demonstrated that the cell's cytoplasm and ectoplasm are equally important as the nucleus in heredity. As with most of the black scientists of the period, Just never received proper recognition in the United States, although he was respected and honored in the scientific capitals of Europe (Haber 1970; Toppin 1971; Ploski and Williams 1983; Manning 1983).

•   •   •

The achievements of black intellectuals and scientists in white America have been largely hidden, ignored, or diminished in importance. The world of science and research was the private domain of white males. Society provided blacks with more appropriate arenas for gaining success and notoriety, arenas more fitting their place in the American social order. The roles of gladiator and jester have long been traditional among powerless people and are seen often by the dominant group as more appropriate than that of scholar or scientist (Lewis 1972). According to the stereotype, blacks were to perform, produce, or entertain, not invent, design, or create. The former activities require only simple innate abilities; the latter intelligence and creativity—characteristics not thought to be present in blacks.

From the perspective of white America at the turn of the century, educated and intellectual blacks presented a grave problem. They were not supposed to exist, and the fact that they did exist challenged the very foundation of the white belief in black intellectual and social inferiority (Winston 1971). Therefore, such individuals had to be explained away (they were called freaks), minimized (they were accused of stealing their ideas from whites), hidden (they were not acknowledged), or destroyed (they suffered discrimination and violence). The lives of the early black scientists were filled not only with the challenge and elation of scientific discovery, but with the specter of racism and discrimination as well.

During his brief tenure at St. Paul's College in Lawrenceville, Virginia, Edward Bouchet was respected and admired in the community. Nevertheless, he was assaulted by a white lawyer he accidently bumped into as they came around a corner (Bechtel 1986). Percy Julian was denied appointment as head of DePauw's chemistry department because he was black, and he would not go to Appleton, Wisconsin, for a job interview because of a city statute prohibiting blacks from staying overnight. During his tenure at Glidden, his house in Oakbrook was set afire and bombed in several acts of racial violence. Ernest Just, despite his scientific discoveries, was never offered an appointment at a major American research center or university and was urged by whites to teach at Black universities in order to help his race (Haber 1970; Logan and Winston 1982; Manning 1983).

More important than these acts of racism toward individuals are the patterns of institutional discrimination that created an almost insurmountable obstacle to the black scientist. Segregation produced isolation: black Ph.D.s in science were forced to teach in black colleges and high schools, which were often unsympathetic to the needs of a research scientist. Edward Bouchet and Charles Turner spent most of their careers in high schools with limited resources and poorly equipped labs. Those who were fortunate enough to find positions in black colleges (like Just or Julian) often taught students from the inner city or rural areas, who lacked advanced training in mathematics and English. These teachers seldom had the scientist's pleasure of training students to surpass their mentors. The black colleges had little money available for scientific equipment or libraries. In the South, where most black colleges were located, black scholars were denied use of public libraries and white university laboratories and were barred from local chapters of learned societies (Julian 1969; Winston 1971).

To this can be added Jim Crow laws designed to restrict the social and political actions of blacks, the constant threat of violence reinforced by numerous lynchings every year, and the exclusion from the community of science in general. In this type of restricted and fearful environment, the Ph.D. degree was a farce (Julian 1969). Excluded because of their race from full participation in the American scientific community, these scientists languished in obscurity.

Under such historical conditions, it is no wonder that so few blacks chose to study science. Ernest Just's motives in discouraging his students from pursuing careers in science grew out of his own bitter recognition of the reality they faced (Winston 1971; Manning 1983). For blacks at the turn of the century, education had to provide marketable skills, a point of view that continues to direct scientifically talented students into careers in education, medicine, or law rather than biology, physics, or chemistry. For any black who knew about Just, Julian, or Turner, the lesson was clear: Even those with the highest level of education and degrees from America's most prestigious universities were denied the recognition and respect befitting their qualifications and scientific accomplishments. In the fields of medicine, teaching, and law, one could find jobs and prosper, albeit while restricted to serving a black clientele. Under the rules made by whites concerning the roles blacks were to play in American society, the pragmatic black decided it was better to be an employed teacher or lawyer than an underemployed scientist.

Specific evidence supports this argument. Edwards (1959), in a survey of three hundred blacks professionals, found that half of the respondents had given serious consideration to careers other than the one they presently had. Many expressed a primary interest in becoming engineers, architects, or research scientists, but felt that blacks could not earn a decent living in these occupations. One of Edwards's respondents, a physicist now working as a teacher, had wanted to enter the field of engineering. He changed his mind when it became clear that despite his ranking near the top of the class, white classmates who were far below him could get jobs as student laboratory technicians while he could not.

The black scientist is both rare and relatively unknown: rare because of an educational philosophy that produced laborers not scholars, and unknown because white society has often refused to recognize the contributions of those able to overcome the obstacles placed before them. In part, this failure to recognize the black scientist stems from beliefs about black inferiority. To acknowledge these individuals would be to demonstrate the fallacy of those beliefs and the error of the policies that deprived blacks of equal and quality education.

Separate, unequal, and discriminatory educational policies served to keep a generation of blacks at the bottom socially, politically, and economically. And while a few (such as Bouchet, Just, and Julian) were able to break through and acquire a quality eduation, being black meant that in most instances the rewards were withheld. The rare black scientist was faced with a lack of research facilities, funds, and recognition for achievements that by any standard were of superior quality and importance. Given the historical conditions, one can understand why black scientists were treated in such a manner. But to understand is not to justify. Educational policies served to suppress and demoralize generations of blacks in America, creating discredible castes within an ostensibly open society.

History is more than description and explanation; one can often use the past to examine the present. What has the past taught with regard to current educational policies directed toward blacks? Several major themes can be identified. First are *interest* and *motivation*. Historical evidence shows that blacks in America had a strong interest in and motivation for getting an education. This desire continues as large numbers of blacks seek higher education. Second is *opportunity*. The evidence is just as clear that blacks were denied the opportunity for a quality education by legal and extralegal means. Today, blacks are able to take advantage of educational opportunities as many of the barriers of the past have been removed. And third, is the *reward* or *payoff*. Given the historical conditions, for most blacks there was no payoff for getting an education. Today, the picture appears more positive as blacks are found in all professions and at all levels of achievement.

Yet, below the surface a different image can be seen. Less than 2 percent of all doctoral scientists in America are black, and few black students take courses in the sciences or express a desire to pursue such careers. For those who complete graduate school, the door to a science career is opened. The problem, as in the past, remains at the level of basic educational opportunity and experience. America has desegregated its white schools and has renounced its past practices as counterproductive and mean-spirited. But those practices remain, in effect, in the form of tracking, curriculum reform, and teacher expectations.

Eighty years ago, vocational education served to perpetuate black social and economic inferiority, locking a generation of blacks into low-paying, low-status jobs. Today black children are bused to excellent schools in an attempt to equalize educational opportunity. Yet once off the bus and in the school, they are tracked, counseled, or intimidated away from academic courses into less rigorous curricula. At the turn of the century, the typical student at Hampton or Tuskegee learned simple trades and domestic skills, while outside American industry was going through a transformation that was making those skills obsolete. Today, the typical black student studies a watered-down curriculum devoid of higher-level math and science courses, while outside the computer is transforming the world into a more complex and scientifically sophisticated arena.

To break the hold of the past, parents, educators, and policymakers need to move forward and address the educational deficiencies that continue to derail the science careers of black students in America.

• • •

BIBLIOGRAPHY

Baker, H. E. 1913. *The Colored Inventor.* Reprint, New York: Arno Press, 1969.

———. 1917. "The Negro in the Field of Invention." *Journal of Negro History* 2:21–36.

Ballard, A. B. 1973. *The Education of Black Folk: The Afro-American Struggle for Knowledge in White America.* New York: Harper and Row.

Beale, H. K. 1975. "The Education of Negroes before the Civil War." In *The American Experience in Education,* ed. J. Barnard and D. Bruner, 85–97. New York: Franklin Watts.

Bechtel, H. K. 1986. "Edward Alexander Bouchet: America's First Black Doctorate." Paper read at the annual meeting of the Mid-South Sociological Association, Jackson, Mississippi.

Bond, H. M. 1934. *The Education of the Negro in the American Social Order.* New York: Prentice-Hall.

———. 1969. *Negro Education in Alabama: A Study in Cotton and Steel.* New York: Atheneum.

Brawley, B. 1970. *A Social History of the American Negro.* New York: Macmillan.

Cruden, R. 1969. *The Negro in Reconstruction.* Englewood Cliffs, N.J.: Prentice-Hall.

DuBois, W. E. B. 1973. *The Education of Black People: Ten Critiques, 1906–1960.* Amherst: University of Massachusetts Press.

Edwards, G. F. 1959. *The Negro Professional Class.* Glencoe, Ill.: Free Press.

Franklin, J. H. 1973. *From Slavery to Freedom: A History of Negro Americans.* New York: Knopf.

Frazier E. F. 1949. *The Negro in the United States.* New York: Macmillan.

Funke, L. 1920. "The Negro in Education." *Journal of Negro History* 5:1–21.

Greer, C. 1973. "Immigrants, Negroes, and the Public Schools." In *Education in American History,* ed. M. B. Katz, 284–290. New York: Praeger.

Haber, L. 1970. *Black Pioneers of Science and Invention.* New York: Harcourt Brace and World.

Harlan, L. R. 1968. *Separate and Unequal: Public School Campaigns and Racism in the Southern Seaboard States, 1901–1915.* Chapel Hill: Univ. of North Carolina Press.

Julian, P. L. 1969. "On Being Scientist, Humanist, and Negro." In *Many Shades of Black*, ed. S. L. Wormley and L. H. Fenderson, 147–157. New York: Morrow.

Klein, A. E. 1971. *Hidden Contributions: Black Scientists and Investors in America.* Garden City, N.Y.: Doubleday.

Litwack, L. 1961. *North of Slavery: The Negro and the Free States, 1790–1860.* Chicago: University of Chicago Press.

Low, W. A., and V. A. Clift. 1981. *Encyclopedia of Black America.* New York: McGraw-Hill.

Manning, K. R. 1983. *Black Apollo of Science: The Life of Ernest Everett Just.* New York: Oxford University Press.

Perkins, L. M. 1978. "Fanny Jackson Coppin and the Institute for Colored Youth." Ph.D. dissertation, University of Illinois at Urbana-Champaign.

Pifer, A. 1973. *The Higher Education of Blacks in the United States.* New York: Carnegie Corporation.

Ploski, H. A., and J. Williams. 1983. *The Afro-American,* 4th ed. New York: Wiley.

Quarles, B. 1969. *The Negro in the Making of America.* New York: Macmillan.

Rice, L. D. 1971. *The Negro in Texas, 1874–1900.* Baton Rouge: Louisiana State University Press.

Rossiter, M. W. 1974. "Women Scientists in America before 1920." *American Scientist* 62:312–323.

Spivey, D. 1978. *Schooling for the New Slavery: Black Industrial Education, 1868–1915.* Westport, Conn.: Greenwood.

Toppin, E. A. 1971. *A Biographical History of Blacks in America since 1528.* New York: David McKay.

Winston, M. R. 1971. "Through the Back Door: Academic Racism and the Negro Scholar in Historical Perspective." *Daedalus* 100:678–719.

Woodson, C. G. 1915. *The Education of the Negro prior to 1861.* New York: Putnam.

———. 1969. *The Negro Professional Man and the Community.* New York: Negro University Press.

Work, M. N. 1931. *Negro Year Book: An Annual Encyclopedia of the Negro, 1931–1932.* Tuskegee, Ala.: Negro Year Book Publishing Company.

QUESTIONS FOR "EDUCATION OF BLACKS" BY H. KENNETH BECHTEL

Talking About the Text

1. We considered placing this selection in the chapter on prejudice, but decided the focus of this essay is on defining and accounting for the quality of black education and the limited forms of literacies open to them. Nevertheless, that "quality" is severely influenced by forces and attitudes that can be separated from strictly educational concerns. Summarize Bechtel's explanations for why African Americans have historically been the victims of inferior schooling.

2. Distinguish between Bechtel's representation of Booker T. Washington's reasons for supporting industrial education and Bechtel's evaluation of those reasons. Can you see any justification for Washington's beliefs?
3. Why are there not more African–Americans working as professionals in the sciences?

Exploring Issues

1. The history of black education as presented in this selection raises troubling questions about the need for vocational training. What are your views regarding the need for this kind of training? Consider the kind of literacy one might acquire in pursuing this kind of education.
2. Why do you think it is necessary that blacks understand the history of their education in this country? Would it also be necessary for caucasians and various other racial and ethnic groups to understand their educational history in the nation?
3. How might we encourage blacks, particularly, and other groups to pursue careers in science?
4. How responsive should schools be to the economic needs of society in composing their curricula?

Writing Assignments

1. Interview one or two people at least one generation removed from you. Find out their educational histories, paying special attention to the kind of education they received as well as to the careers they were encouraged to pursue. Write a report based on your findings.
2. After considering Bechtel's arguments, write your own proposal for what college students of the 1990s should learn in their general education courses.
3. Debate the following statement in class, and then write an argument based on what you think is the most sensible view to take in the 1990s:

> Not everyone should be encouraged to go to college. Instead, those high school students who choose to do so should learn practical skills that would help them secure employment immediately after graduating.

Reading 50

The Lesson

Toni Cade Bambara

Toni Cade Bambara grew up in Harlem and in Bedford-Stuyvesant, New York City, where she was born in 1939. She received a BA from Queens College and an MA from City College of New York. After graduating, she worked as a welfare investigator, community organizer, and free lance writer. Some of her works are *Tales and Stories of Black Folks* (1971), *Gorilla, My Love* (1972), *The Sea Birds Are Still Alive* (1977), and *The Salt Eaters* (1980). "The Lesson," published in 1972, dramatizes the fact that learning is much more than reading and writing and classroom exercises.

Back in the days when everyone was old and stupid or young and foolish and me and Sugar were the only ones just right, this lady moved on our block with nappy hair and proper speech and no makeup. And quite naturally we laughed at her, laughed the way we did at the junk man who went about his business like he was some big-time president and his sorry-ass horse his secretary. And we kinda hated her too, hated the way we did the winos who cluttered up our parks and pissed on our handball walls and stank up our hallways and stairs so you couldn't halfway play hide-and-seek without a goddamn gas mask. Miss Moore was her name. The only woman on the block with no first name. And she was black as hell, cept for her feet, which were fish-white and spooky. And she was always planning these boring-ass things for us to do, us being my cousin, mostly, who lived on the block cause we all moved North the same time and to the same apartment then spread out gradual to breathe. And our parents would yank our heads into some kinda shape and crisp up our clothes so we'd be presentable for travel with Miss Moore, who always looked like she was going to church, though she never did. Which is just one of things the grownups talked about when they talked behind her back like a dog. But when she came calling with some sachet she'd sewed up or some gingerbread she'd made or some book, why then they'd all be too embarrassed to turn her down and we'd get handed over all spruced up. She'd been to college and said it was only right that she should take responsibility for the young ones' education, and she not even related by marriage or blood. So they'd go for it. Specially Aunt Gretchen. She was the main gofer in the family. You got some ole dumb shit foolishness you want somebody to go for, you send for Aunt Gretchen. She been screwed into the go-along for so long, it's a blood-deep natural thing with her. Which is how she got saddled with me and Sugar and Junior in the first place while our mothers were in a la-de-da apartment up the block having a good ole time.

So this one day Miss Moore rounds us all up at the mailbox and it's puredee hot and she's knockin herself out about arithmetic. And school suppose to let up in summer I heard, but she don't never let up. And the starch in my pinafore scratching the shit outta me and I'm really hating this nappy-head bitch and her goddamn college degree. I'd much rather go to the pool or to the show where it's cool. So me and Sugar leaning on the mailbox being surly, which is a Miss Moore word. And Flyboy checking out what everybody brought for lunch. And Fat Butt already wasting his peanut-butter-and-jelly sandwich like the pig he is. And Junebug punchin on Q.T.'s arm for potato chips. And Rosie Giraffe shifting from one hip to the other waiting for somebody to step on her foot or ask her if she from Georgia so she can kick ass, preferably Mercedes'. And Miss Moore asking us do we know what money is, like we a bunch of retards. I mean real money, she say, like it's only poker chips or monopoly papers we lay on the grocer. So right away I'm tired of this and say so. And would much rather snatch Sugar and go to the Sunset and terrorize the West Indian kids and take their hair ribbons and their money too. And Miss Moore files that remark away for next week's lesson on brotherhood, I can tell. And finally I say we oughta get to the subway cause it's cooler and besides we might meet some cute boys. Sugar done swiped her mama's lipstick, so we ready.

So we heading down the street and she's boring us silly about what things cost and what our parents make and how much goes for rent and how money ain't divided up right in this country. And then she gets to the part about we all poor and live in the slums, which I don't feature. And I'm ready to speak on that, but she steps out in the street and hails two cabs just like that. Then she hustles half the crew in with her and hands me a five-dollar bill and tells me to calculate 10 percent tip for the driver. And we're off. Me and Sugar and Junebug and Flyboy hangin out the window and hollering to everybody, putting lipstick on each other cause Flyboy a faggot anyway, and making farts with our sweaty armpits. But I'm mostly trying to figure how to spend this money. But they all fascinated with the meter ticking and Junebug starts laying bets as to how much it'll read when Flyboy can't hold his breath no more. Then Sugar lays bets as to how much it'll be when we get there. So I'm stuck. Don't nobody want to go for my plan, which is to jump out at the next light and run off to the first bar-b-que we can find. Then the driver tells us to get the hell out cause we there already. And the meter reads eighty-five cents. And I'm stalling to figure out the tip and Sugar say give him a dime. And I decide he don't need it bad as I do, so later for him. But then he tries to take off with Junebug foot still in the door so we talk about his mama something ferocious. Then we check out that we on Fifth Avenue and everybody dressed up in stockings. One lady in a fur coat, hot as it is. White folks crazy.

"This is the place," Miss Moore say, presenting it to us in the voice she uses at the museum. "Let's look in the windows before we go in."

"Can we steal?" Sugar asks very serious like she's getting the ground rules squared away before she plays. "I beg your pardon," say Miss Moore, and we fall out. So she leads us around the windows of the toy store and me and Sugar screamin, "This is mine, that's mine, I gotta have that, that was made for me, I was born for that," till Big Butt drowns us out.

"Hey, I'm goin to buy that there."

"That there? You don't even know what it is, stupid."

"I do so," he say punchin on Rosie Giraffe. "It's a microscope."

"Whatcha gonna do with a microscope, fool?"

"Look at things."

"Like what, Ronald?" ask Miss Moore. And Big Butt ain't got the first notion. So here go Miss Moore gabbing about the thousands of bacteria in a drop of water and the somethinorother in a speck of blood and the million and one living things in the air around us is invisible to the naked eye. And what she say that for? Junebug go to town on that "naked" and we rolling. Then Miss Moore ask what it cost. So we all jam into the window smudgin it up and the price tag say $300. So then she ask how long'd take for Big Butt and Junebug to save up their allowances. "Too long," I say. "Yeh," adds Sugar, "outgrown it by that time." And Miss Moore say no, you never outgrow learning instruments. "Why, even medical students and interns and," blah, blah, blah. And we ready to choke Big Butt for bringing it up in the first damn place.

"This here costs four hundred eighty dollars," say Rosie Giraffe. So we pile up all over her to see what she pointin out. My eyes tell me it's a chunk of glass cracked with something heavy, and different-color inks dripped into the splits, then the whole thing put into a oven or something. But for $480 it don't make sense.

"That's a paperweight made of semi-precious stones fused together under tremendous pressure," she explains slowly, with her hands doing the mining and all the factory work.

"So what's a paperweight?" asks Rosie Giraffe.

"To weigh paper with, dumbbell," say Flyboy, the wise man from the East.

"Not exactly," say Miss Moore, which is what she say when you warm or way off too. "It's to weigh paper down so it won't scatter and make your desk untidy." So right away me and Sugar curtsy to each other and then to Mercedes who is more the tidy type.

"We don't keep paper on top of the desk in my class," say Junebug, figuring Miss Moore crazy or lyin one.

"At home, then," she say. "Don't you have a calendar and a pencil case and a blotter and a letter-opener on your desk at home where you do your home-work?" And she know damn well what our homes look like cause she nosys around in them every chance she gets.

"I don't even have a desk," say Junebug. "Do we?"

"No. And I don't get no homework neither," say Big Butt.

"And I don't even have a home," say Flyboy like he do at school to keep the white folks off his back and sorry for him. Send this poor kid to camp posters, is his specialty.

"I do," says Mercedes. "I have a box of stationery on my desk and a picture of my cat. My godmother bought the stationery and the desk. There's a big rose on each sheet and the envelopes smell like roses."

"Who wants to know about your smelly-ass stationery," say Rosie Giraffe fore I can get my two cents in.

"It's important to have a work area all your own so that . . ."

"Will you look at this sailboat, please," say Flyboy, cuttin her off and pointin to the thing like it was his. So once again we tumble all over each other to gaze at this magnificent thing in the toy store which is just big enough to maybe sail two kittens across the pond if you strap them to the posts tight. We all start reciting the price tag like we in assembly. "Handcrafted sailboat of fiberglass at one thousand one hundred ninety-five dollars."

"Unbelievable," I hear myself say and am really stunned. I read it again for myself just in case the group recitation put me in a trance. Same thing. For some reason this pisses me off. We look at Miss Moore and she lookin at us, waiting for I dunno what.

"Who'd pay all that when you can buy a sailboat set for a quarter at Pop's, a tube of glue for a dime, and a ball of string for eight cents? It must have a motor and a whole lot else besides," I say. "My sailboat cost me about fifty cents."

"But will it take water?" say Mercedes with her smart ass.

"Took mine to Alley Pond Park once," say Flyboy. "String broke, Lost it. Pity."

"Sailed mine in Central Park and it keeled over and sank. Had to ask my father for another dollar."

"And you got the strap," laugh Big Butt. "The jerk didn't even have a string on it. My old man wailed on his behind."

Little Q.T. was staring hard at the sailboat and you could see he wanted it bad. But he too little and somebody'd just take it from him. So what the hell. "This boat for kids, Miss Moore?"

"Parents silly to buy something like that just to get all broke up," say Rosie Giraffe.

"That much money it should last forever," I figure.

"My father'd buy it for me if I wanted it."

"Your father, my ass," say Rosie Giraffe getting a chance to finally push Mercedes.

"Must be rich people shop here," say Q.T.

"You are a very bright boy," say Flyboy. "What was your first clue?" And he rap him on the head with the back of his knuckles, since Q.T. the only one he could get away with. Though Q.T. liable to come up behind you years later and get his licks in when you half expect it.

"What I want to know is," I says to Miss Moore though I never talk to her, I wouldn't give the bitch that satisfaction, "is how much a real boat costs? I figure a thousand'd get you a yacht any day."

"Why don't you check that out," she says, "and report back to the group?" Which really pains my ass. If you gonna mess up a perfectly good swim day least you could do is have some answers. "Let's go in," she say like she got something up her sleeve. Only she don't lead the way. So me and Sugar turn the corner to where the entrance is, but when we get there I kinda hang back. Not that I'm scared, what's there to be afraid of, just a toy store. But I feel funny, shame. But what I got to be shamed about? Got as much right to go in as anybody. But somehow I can't seem to get hold of the door, so I step away for Sugar to lead. But she hangs back too. And I look at her and she looks at me and this is ridiculous. I mean, damn, I have never ever been shy about doing nothing or going nowhere. But then Mercedes steps up and then Rosie Giraffe and Big Butt crowd in behind and shove, and next thing we all stuffed into the doorway with only Mercedes squeezing past us, smoothing out her jumper and walking right down the aisle. Then the rest of us tumble in like a glued-together jigsaw done all wrong. And people lookin at us. And it's like the time me and Sugar crashed into the Catholic church on a dare. But once we got in there and everything so hushed and holy and the candles and the bowin and the handkerchiefs on all the drooping heads, I just couldn't go through with the plan. Which was for me to run up to the altar and do a tap dance while Sugar played the nose flute and messed around in the holy water. And Sugar kept givin me the elbow. Then later teased me so bad I tied her up in the shower and turned it on and locked her in. And she'd be there till this day if Aunt Gretchen hadn't finally figured I was lyin about the boarder takin a shower.

Same thing in the store. We all walkin on tiptoe and hardly touchin the games and puzzles and things. And I watched Miss Moore who is steady watchin us like she waitin for a sign. Like Mama Drewery watches the sky and sniffs the air and takes note of just how much slant is in the bird formation. Then me and Sugar bump smack into each other, so busy gazing at the toys, 'specially the sailboat. But we don't laugh and go into our fat-lady bump-stomach routine. We just stare at that price tag. Then Sugar run a finger over the whole boat. And I'm jealous and want to hit her. Maybe not her, but I sure want to punch somebody in the mouth.

"Watcha bring us here for, Miss Moore?"

"You sound angry, Sylvia. Are you mad about something?" Givin me one of them grins like she tellin a grown-up joke that never turns out to be funny. And she's lookin very closely at me like maybe she plannin to do my portrait from memory. I'm mad, but I won't give her that satisfaction. So I slouch around the store bein very bored and say, "Let's go."

Me and Sugar at the back of the train watchin the tracks whizzin by large then small then gettin gobbled up in the dark. I'm thinkin about this tricky toy I saw in the store. A clown that somersaults on a bar then does chin-ups just cause you yank lightly as his leg. Cost $35. I could see me askin my mother for a $35 birthday clown. "You wanna who that costs what?" she'd say, cocking her head to the side to get a better view of the hole in my head. Thirty-five dollars could buy new bunk beds for Junior and Gretchen's boy. Thirty-five dollars and the whole household could go visit Granddaddy Nelson in the country. Thirty-five dollars would pay for the rent and the piano bill too. Who are these people that spend that much for performing clowns and

$1,000 for toy sailboats? What kinda work they do and how they live and how come we ain't in on it? Where we are is who we are, Miss Moore always pointin out. But it don't necessarily have to be that way, she always adds then waits for somebody to say that poor people have to wake up and demand their share of the pie and don't none of us know what kind of pie she talkin about in the first damn place. But she ain't so smart cause I still got her four dollars from the taxi and she sure ain't gettin it. Messin up my day with this shit. Sugar nudges me in my pocket and winks.

Miss Moore lines us up in front of the mailbox where we started from, seem like years ago, and I got a headache for thinkin so hard. And we lean all over each other so we can hold up under the draggy-ass lecture she always finishes us off with at the end before we thank her for borin us to tears. But she just looks at us like she readin tea leaves. Finally she say, "Well, what did you think of F.A.O. Schwartz?"

Rosie Giraffe mumbles, "White folks crazy."

"I'd like to go there again when I get my birthday money," says Mercedes, and we shove her out the pack so she has to lean on the mailbox by herself.

"I'd like a shower. Tiring day," say Flyboy.

Then Sugar surprises me by sayin, "You know, Miss Moore, I don't think all of us here put together eat in a year what that sailboat costs." And Miss Moore lights up like somebody goosed her. "And?" she say, urging Sugar on. Only I'm standin on her foot so she don't continue.

"Imagine for a minute what kind of society it is in which some people can spend on a toy what it would cost to feed a family of six or seven. What do you think?"

"I think," say Sugar pushing me off her feet like she never done before, cause I whip her ass in a minute, "that this is not much of a democracy if you ask me. Equal chance to pursue happiness means an equal crack at the dough, don't it?" Miss Moore is besides herself and I am disgusted with Sugar's treachery. So I stand on her foot one more time to see if she'll shove me. She shuts up, and Miss Moore looks at me, sorrowfully I'm thinkin. And somethin weird is going on, I can feel it in my chest.

"Anybody else learn anything today?" lookin dead at me. I walk away and Sugar has to run to catch up and don't even seem to notice when I shrug her arm off my shoulder.

"Well, we got four dollars anyway," she says.

"Uh hunh."

"We could go to Hascombs and get half a chocolate layer and then go to the Sunset and still have plenty money for potato chips and ice-cream sodas."

"Uh hunh."

"Race you to Hascombs," she say.

We start down the block and she gets ahead which is O.K. by me cause I'm going to the West End and then over to the Drive to think this day through. She can run if she want to and even run faster. But ain't nobody gonna beat me at nuthin.

QUESTIONS FOR "THE LESSON" BY TONI CADE BAMBARA

Talking About the Text

1. Re-read the opening sentence of this short story. What does it reveal about the narrator?
2. Why does Bambara tell this story through Sylvia? What would be the effect if Miss Moore were the narrator?
3. What, if anything, does Sylvia learn from her "lesson"?
4. In what way does your understanding of "The Lesson" help you to interpret Sylvia's last statement?
5. Sylvia and her classmates—with Mercedes the possible exception— speak differently from Miss Moore. How does this difference in speaking styles contribute to your understanding of the meaning of "The Lesson"?
6. Why is it important that Miss Moore is not a member of the community? Could she teach her "lesson" if she were?

Exploring Issues

1. Is Miss Moore's "lesson" a proper one to be learned in school? Would the children have learned it anyway? How might they have learned it?
2. At one point Sylvia says that Miss Moore speaks about the stores on Fifth Avenue "in the voice she uses at the museum." Later, entering the toy store for Sylvia is likened to entering "the Catholic church." How might you intepret these associations? Why might such cultural and religious institutions make these children feel so self-conscious and awkward?
3. Mike Rose writes, "To understand the nature and development of literacy we need to consider the social context in which it occurs—the political, economic, and cultural forces that encourage or inhibit it." How might Rose characterize the literacy of Sylvia and her classmates? What might he predict about their future literacy development? What kind of "curriculum" might he suggest for them?

Writing Assignments

1. Write an interpretation of this story from Miss Moore's viewpoint. How does she perceive her students? Their parents? The environment in which they live? How does she understand her role as teacher? What does she want her students to learn? Go back to the text as often as you need to in gathering evidence to support your interpretation. Compare your draft with those of your fellow classmates.
2. Make out a Christmas list for one or more of the following: Sylvia, Rosie Giraffe, Sugar, Flyboy, Junebug, Mercedes, Big Butt, Q.T.—a child who might ask for the $1,195 sailboat, Miss Moore, or one of the parents of Sylvia and her classmates. Then analyze your lists and explain what they say about the motivations and aspirations of these individuals.

Reading 51

Popular Education

Agnes Repplier

Agnes Repplier is well known in a few small circles of people who enjoy the genre of the popular essay. Repplier was an accomplished essayist and a prolific writer with over 26 different volumes to her credit. A frequent contributor to *The Atlantic Monthly,* Repplier's last essay appeared in that magazine in 1940. She died a few years later, a successful literary artist, whose life and career spanned over eight decades. "Popular Education" is taken from the volume of essays, *Counter-Currents,* published in 1916. Repplier wittily expresses her concerns over what she sees as the increasing trend toward making education entertaining and fun for students.

This is so emphatically the children's age that a good many of us are beginning to thank God we were not born in it. The little girl who said she wished she had lived in the time of Charles the Second, because then "education was much neglected," wins our sympathy and esteem. It is a doubtful privilege to have the attention of the civilized world focussed upon us both before and after birth. At the First International Eugenics Congress, held in London in the summer of 1912, an Italian delegate made the somewhat discouraging statement that the children of very young parents are more prone than others to theft; that the children of middle-aged parents are apt to be of good conduct, but of low intelligence; and that the children of elderly parents are, as a rule, intelligent, but badly behaved. It seems to be a trifle hard to bring the right kind of a child into the world. Twenty-seven is, in this eugenist's opinion, the best age for parentage; but how bend all the complicated conditions of life to meet an arbitrary date; and how remain twenty-seven long enough to insure satisfactory results? The vast majority of babies will have to put up with being born when their time comes, and make the best of it. This is the first, but by no means the worst, disadvantage of compulsory birth; and compulsory birth is the original evil which scientists and philanthropists are equally powerless to avert.

If parents do not know by this time how to bring up their children, it is not for lack of instruction. A few generations ago, Solomon was the only writer on child-study who enjoyed any vogue. Now his precepts, the acrid fruits of experience, have been superseded by more genial, but more importunate counsel.

Begirt by well-wishers, hemmed in on every side by experts who speak of "child-material" as if it were raw silk or wood-pulp, how can a little boy, born in this enlightened age, dodge the educational influences which surround him? It is hard to be dealt with as "child-material," when one is only an ordinary little boy. To be sure, "child-material" is never thrashed, as little boys were wont to be, it is not required to do what it is told, it enjoys rights and privileges of a very sacred and exalted character; but, on the other hand, it is never let alone, and to be let alone is sometimes worth all the ministrations of men and angels. The helpless, inarticulate reticence of a child is not an obstacle to be overcome, but a barrier which protects the citadel of childhood from assault.

We can break down this barrier in our zeal; and if the child will not speak, we can at least compel him to listen. He is powerless to evade any revelations we choose to make, any facts or theories we choose to elucidate. We can teach him sex-hygiene when he is still young enough to believe that rabbits lay eggs. We can turn his work into play, and his play into work, keeping well in mind the educational value of his unconscious activities, and, by careful oversight, pervert a game of tag into a preparation for the business of life. We can amuse and interest him until he is powerless to amuse and interest himself. We can experiment with him according to the dictates of hundreds of rival authorities. He is in a measure at our mercy, though nature fights hard for him, safeguarding him with ignorance of our mode of thought, and indifference to our point of view. The opinions of twelve-year-old Bobby Smith are of more moment to ten-year-old Tommy Jones than are the opinions of Dr. and Mrs. Jones, albeit Dr. Jones is a professor of psychology, and Mrs. Jones the president of a Parents' League. The supreme value of Mr. Robert Louis Stevenson's much-quoted "Lantern Bearers" lies in its incisive and sympathetic insistence upon the aloofness of the child's world,—an admittedly imperfect world which we are burning to amend, but which closed its doors upon us forever when we grew into knowledge and reason.

My own childhood lies very far away. It occurred in what I cannot help thinking a blissful period of intermission. The educational theories of the Edgeworths (evolved soberly from the educational excesses of Rousseau) had been found a trifle onerous. Parents had not the time to instruct and admonish their children all day long. As a consequence, we enjoyed a little wholesome neglect, and made the most of it. The new era of child-study and mothers' congresses lay darkling in the future. "Symbolic education," "symbolic play," were phrases all unknown. The "revolutionary discoveries" of Karl Groos had not yet overshadowed the innocent diversions of infancy. Nobody drew scientific deductions from jackstones, or balls, or gracehoops, save only when we assailed the wealth of nations by breaking a window-pane. Nobody was even aware that the impulses which sent us speeding and kicking up our heels like young colts were "vestigial organs of the soul." Dr. G. Stanley Hall had not yet invented this happy phrase to elucidate the simplicities of play. How we grasped our "objective relationship" to our mothers without the help of bird's-nest games, I do not know. Perhaps, in the general absence of experimentation, we had made time in which to solve the artless problems of our lives. Psychologists in those days were frankly indifferent to us. They had yet to discover our enormous value in the realms of conjectural thought.

The education of my childhood was embryonic. The education of to-day is exhaustive. The fact that the school-child of to-day does not seem to know any more than we knew in the dark ages, is a side issue with which I have no concern. But as I look back, I can now see plainly that the few things little girls learned were admirably adapted for one purpose,—to make us parts of a whole, which whole was the family. I do not mean that there was any expression to this effect. "Training for maternity" was not a phrase in vogue; and the short views of life, more common then than now, would have robbed it of its savour. "Training for citizenship" had, so far as we were concerned, no meaning whatsoever. A little girl was a little girl, not the future mother of the race, or the future saviour of the Republic. One thing at a time. Therefore no deep significance was attached to our possession of a doll, no concern was evinced over our future handling of a vote. If we were taught to read aloud with correctness and expression, to write notes with propriety and grace, and to play backgammon and whist as well as our intelligence permitted, it was in order that we should practise these admirable accomplishments for the benefit of the families of which we were useful, and occasionally ornamental features.

And what advantage accrued to *us* from an education so narrowed, so illiberal, so manifestly unconcerned with great social and national issues? Well, let us admit that it had at least the qualities of its defects. It was not called training for character, but it was admittedly training for behaviour, and the foundations of character are the acquired habits of youth. "Habit," said the Duke of Wellington, "is ten times nature." There was precision in the simple belief that the child was strengthened mentally by mastering its lessons, and morally by mastering its inclinations. Therefore the old-time teacher sought to spur the pupil on to keen and combative effort, rather than to beguile him into knowledge with cunning games and lantern slides. Therefore the old-time parent set a high value on self-discipline and self-control. A happy childhood did not necessarily mean a childhood free from proudly accepted responsibility. There are few things in life so dear to girl or boy as the chance to turn to good account the splendid self-confidence of youth.

If Saint Augustine, who was punished when he was a little lad because he loved to play, could see how childish pastimes are dignified in the pedagogy of the twentieth century, he would no longer say that "playing is the business of childhood." He would know that it is the supremely important business, the crushing responsibility of the pedagogue. Nothing is too profound, nothing too subtle to be evolved from a game or a toy. We are gravely told that "the doll with its immense educational power should be carefully introduced into the schools," that "Pussy-in-the-Corner" is "an Ariadne clew to the labyrinth of experience," and that a ball, tossed to the accompaniment of a song insultingly banal, will enable a child "to hold fast one high purpose amid all the vicissitudes of time and place." If we would only make organized play a part of the school curriculum, we should have no need of camps, or drills, or military training. It is the moulder of men, the upholder of nations, the character-builder of the world.

Mr. Joseph Lee, who has written a book of five hundred pages on "Play in Education," and Mr. Henry S. Curtis, who has written a book of three hundred and fifty pages on "Education through Play," have treated their theme with profound and serious enthusiasm, which, in its turn, is surpassed by the fervid exaltation of their reviewers. These counsellors have so much that is good to urge upon us, and we are so ready to listen to their words, that they could have well afforded to be more convincingly moderate. There is no real use in saying that it is play which makes the world go round, because we know it isn't. If it were, the world of the savage would go round as efficaciously as the world of the civilized man. When Mr. Lee tells us that the little boy who plays baseball "follows the ball each day further into the unexplored regions of potential character, and comes back each evening a larger moral being than he set forth," we merely catch our breath, and read on. We have known so many boys, and we are disillusioned. When Mr. Curtis points out to us that English school-boys play more and play better than any other lads, and that their teachers advocate and encourage the love of sport because it breeds "good common sense, and resourcefulness which will enable them to meet the difficulties of life," we ask ourselves doubtfully whether Englishmen do meet life's difficulties with an intelligence so keen and adjusted as to prove the potency of play. The work which is demanded of French and German school-boys would seem to English and American school-boys (to say nothing of English and American parents) cruel and excessive; yet Frenchmen and Germans are not destitute of resourcefulness, and they meet the difficulties of life with a concentration of purpose which is the wonder of the world.

Even the moderate tax which is now imposed upon the leisure and freedom of American children has been declared illegal. It is possible and praiseworthy, we are assured, to spare them all "unnatural restrictions," all uncongenial labour. There are pastimes in plenty which will impart to them information, without demanding any effort on their part. Folk-songs, and rhythmic dances, and story-telling, and observation classes, and "wholesome and helpful games," fill up a pleasant morning for little pupils; and when they grow bigger, more stirring sports await them. Listen to Judge Lindsey's enthusiastic description of the school-room of the future, where moving pictures will take the place of books and blackboards, where no free child will be "chained to a desk" (painful phrase!), and where "progressive educators" will make merry with their pupils all the happy day.

"Mr. Edison is coming to the rescue of Tony," says Judge Lindsey. (Tony is a boy who does not like school as it is at present organized.) "He will take him away from me, and put him in a school that is not a school at all, but just one big game;—just one round of joy, of play, of gladness, of knowledge, of sunshine, warming the cells in Tony's head until they all open up as the flowers do. There will be something moving, something doing at that school all the time, just as there is when Tony goes down to the tracks to see the engines.

"When I tell him about it, Tony shouts, 'Hooray for Mr. Edison!' right in front of the battery, just as he used to say, 'To hell wid de cop.'"

Now this is an interesting exposition of the purely sentimental view of education. We have been leading up to it for years, ever since Froebel uttered his famous "Come, let us live with our children!" and here it is set down in black and white by a man who has the welfare of the young deeply at heart. Judge Lindsey sympathizes with Tony's distaste for study. He points out to us that it is hard for a boy who is "the leader of a gang" to be laughed at by less enterprising children because he cannot cipher. Yet to some of us it does not seem altogether amiss that Tony should be brought to understand the existence of other standards than those of hoodlumism. Ciphering is dull work (so, at least, I have always found it), and difficult work too; but it is hardly fair to brand it as ignoble. Compared with stealing rails from a freight-car, which is Tony's alternative for school attendance, it even has a dignity of its own; and the perception of this fact may be a salutary, if mortifying lesson. Judge Lindsey's picturesque likening of our antiquated school system which compels children to sit at desks, with the antiquated Chinese custom which bound little girls' feet, lacks discernment. The underlying motives are, in these instances, measurably different, the processes are dissimilar, the results have points of variance.

Nobody doubts that all our Tonys, rich and poor, lawless and law-abiding, would much prefer a school that is not a school at all, "but just one big game"; nobody doubts that a great deal of desultory information may be acquired from films. But desultory information is not, and never can be, a substitute for education; and habits of play cannot be trusted to develop habits of work. Our efforts to protect the child from doing what he does not want to do, because he does not want to do it, are kind, but unintelligent. Life is not a vapid thing. "The world," says Emerson, "is a proud place, peopled with men of positive quality." No pleasure it can give, from the time we are seven until the time we are seventy, is comparable to the pleasure of achievement.

Dr. Münsterberg, observing with dismay the "pedagogical unrest" which pervades our communities, expresses a naïve surprise that so much sound advice, and so much sound instruction, should leave the teacher without inspiration or enthusiasm. "The pile of interesting facts which the sciences heap up for the teacher's use grows larger and larger, but the teacher seems to stare at it with growing hopelessness."

I should think so. A pile of heterogeneous facts—segments of segments of subjects—reduces any sane teacher to hopelessness, because he, at least, is well aware that his pupils cannot possibly absorb or digest a tithe of the material pressed upon their acceptance. Experience has taught him something which his counsellors never learn,—the need of limit, the "feasibility of performance." Hear what one teacher, both sane and experienced, has to say concerning the riot of facts and theories, of art and nature, of science and sentiment, which the school is expected to reduce into an orderly, consistent, and practical system of education.

"It is not enough that the child should be taught to handle skillfully the tools of all learning,—reading, writing, and arithmetic. His sense of form and his aesthetic nature must be developed by drawing; his hand must be trained by manual work; his musical nature must be awakened by song; he must be brought into harmony with his external environment by means of nature lessons and the study of science; his patriotic impulses must be roused by American history and by flag-drills; temperance must be instilled into him by lessons in physiology, with special reference to the effects of alcohol on the human system; his imagination must be cultivated by the help of Greek and Norse mythology; he must gain some knowledge of the great heroes and events of general history; he must acquire a love for and an appreciation of the best literature through the plentiful reading of masterpieces, while at the same time his mind should be stocked with choice gems of prose and verse, which will be a solace to him throughout his later life.

"It might be well if, by displacing a little arithmetic or geography, he could gain some knowledge of the elements of Latin or of a modern language; in some manner there must be roused in him a love for trees, a respect for birds, an antipathy to cigarettes, and an ambition for clean streets; and somewhere, somewhere in this mad chaos he must learn to spell! Do you wonder that teachers in progressive schools confide to us that they fear their pupils are slightly bewildered? Do you wonder that pupils do not gain the habit and the power of concentrated consecutive work?"[1]

And this irrational, irrelevant medley, this educational vaudeville, must be absorbed unconsciously, and without effort, by children roused to interest by the sustained enthusiasm of their teachers, whom may Heaven help! If the programme is not full enough, it can be varied by lectures on sex-hygiene, lessons in woodcraft (with reference to boy scouts), and pictures illustrating the domestic habits of the house-fly. These, with plenty of gymnastics, and a little barefoot dancing for girls, may bring a school measurably near the ideal proposed by Judge Lindsey,—a place where "there is something moving, something doing all the time," and which finds its closest counterpart in the rushing of engines on their tracks.

The theory that school work must appeal to a child's fluctuating tastes, must attract a child's involuntary attention, does grievous wrong to the rising generation; yet it is upheld in high places, and forms the subject-matter of many addresses vouchsafed year after year to long-suffering educators. They should bring to bear the "energizing force of interest," they should magnetize their pupils into work. Even Dr. Eliot reminds them with just a hint of reproach that, if a child is interested, he will not be disorderly; and this reiterated statement appears to be the crux of the whole difficult situation. Let us boldly suppose that a child is not interested,—and he may conceivably weary even of films,—is it then optional with him to be, or not to be, disorderly, and what is the effect of his disorder on other children whose tastes may differ from his own?

The Right Reverend Mandell Creighton, who appears to have made more addresses to the teachers of England than any other ecclesiastic of his day, repeatedly warned them that they should not attempt to teach any subject without first making clear to children why this subject should command attention. If they failed to do so, said the bishop triumphantly, the children would

---

[1]*The Existing Relations between School and College*, by Wilson Farrand.

not attend. He was of the opinion that little pupils must not only be rationally convinced that what they are asked to do is worth their doing, but that they must enjoy every step of their progress. A teacher who could not make a child feel that it is "just as agreeable" to be in school as at play, had not begun his, or her, pedagogical career.

This is a hard saying and a false one. Every normal child prefers play to work, and the precise value of work lies in its call for renunciation. Nor has any knowledge ever been acquired and retained without endeavour. What heroic pains were taken by Montaigne's father to spare his little son the harsh tasks of the schoolboy! At what trouble and cost to the household was the child taught "the pure Latin tongue" in infancy, "without bookes, rules, or grammar, without whipping or whining"! Greek was also imparted to him in kindly fashion, "by way of sporte and recreation." "We did tosse our declinations and conjugations to and fro, as they doe, who, by means of a certaine game at tables, learne both Arithmeticke and Geometrie." Assuredly the elder Montaigne was a man born out of date. In our happier age he would have been a great and honoured upholder of educational novelties, experimenting with the school-rooms of the world. In the sixteenth century he was only a country gentleman, experimenting with his son,—a son who bluntly confesses that, of the Greek thus pleasantly trifled with, he had "but small understanding," and that the Latin which had been his mother tongue was speedily "corrupted by discontinuance."

All the boy gained by the most elaborate system ever devised for the saving of labour was that he "overskipped" the lower forms in school. What he lost was the habit of mastering his "prescript lessons," which he seems to have disliked as heartily as any student of Guienne. Neither loss nor gain mattered much to a man of original parts. The principal result of his father's scheme was the lingering of certain Latin words among the simple folk of Perigord, who, having painfully acquired these strange terms in order to rescue their little master from his schoolbooks, retained and made use of them all their lives.

An emphatic note of protest against our well-meant but enfeebling educational methods was struck by Professor William James in his "Talks to Teachers," published in 1899. The phrase "Economy of Effort," so dear to the kindly hearts of Froebel's followers, had no meaning for Dr. James. The ingenious system by which the child's tasks, as well as the child's responsibilities, are shifted to the shoulders of the teacher, made no appeal to his incisive intelligence. He stoutly asserted that effort is oxygen to the lungs of youth, and that it is sheer nonsense to suppose that every step of education can possibly be made interesting. The child, like the man, must meet his difficulties, and master them. There is no lesson worth learning, no game worth playing, which does not call for exertion. Rousseau, it will be remembered, would not permit Émile to know what rivalry meant. That harassed child never even ran a race, lest the base spirit of competition should penetrate his nerveless little being. But Professor James, deaf to social sentimentalities, averred that rivalry is the spur of action, and the impelling force of civilization. "There is a noble and generous kind of rivalry as well as a spiteful and greedy kind," he wrote truthfully, "and the noble and generous form is particularly common in childhood. All games owe the zest which they bring with them to the fact that they are rooted in the emulous passion, yet they are the chief means of training in fairness and magnanimity."

I am aware that it is a dangerous thing to call kindness sentimental; but our feeling that children have a right to happiness, and our sincere effort to protect them from any approach to pain, have led imperceptibly to the elimination from their lives of many strength-giving influences. A recent volume on "Child Culture" (a phrase every whit as reprehensible as "child-material") speaks always of naughty children as "patients," implying that their unfortunate condition is involuntary, and must be cured from without, not from within. The "rights of children" include the doubtful privilege of freedom from restraint, and the doubtful boon of shelter from obligation. It seems sweet and kind to teach a child high principles and steadfastness of purpose by means of symbolic games rather than by any open exaction. Unconscious obedience, like indirect taxation, is supposed to be paid without strain. Our feverish fear lest we offend against the helplessness of childhood, our feverish concern lest it should be denied its full measure of content, drive us, burdened as we are with good intentions, past the border-line of wisdom. If we were

"Less winning soft, less amiably mild,"

we might see more clearly the value of standards.

Two years ago I had sent me several numbers of a Los Angeles newspaper. They contained a spirited and sympathetic account of a woman who had been arrested for stealing a child's outfit, and who pleaded in court that she wanted the garments for her daughter, the little girl having refused to go to school, because other children had laughed at her shabby clothes. The effect of this pathetic disclosure was instantaneous and overwhelming. The woman was released, and kind-hearted people hastened to send "nicey" frocks by the "wagon-load" to the ill-used child. A picture of the heroic mother in a large plumed hat, and another of little Ellen in curls and hair-ribbons, occupied prominent places in the paper. The public mind was set at rest concerning the quality of the goods donated. "Ellen is going to school to-day," wrote the jubilant reporter. "She is going to wear a fluffy new dress with lace, and hair-ribbons to match. And if any rude boy so far forgets himself as to tear that wondrous creation, there will be others at home to replace it. Happy, oh, so happy was the little miss, as she shook her curls over the dainty dress to-day. And the mother? Well, a faith in the inherent goodness of mankind has been rekindled in her bosom."

Now the interesting thing about this journalistic eloquence, and the public sentiment it represented, is that while shabbiness was admittedly a burden too heavy for a child to bear, theft carried with it no shadow of disgrace. Children might jeer at a little girl in a worn frock, but a little girl in "lace and hair-ribbons" was manifestly above reproach. Her mother's transgression had covered her with glory, not with shame. There seems to be some confusion of standards in such a verdict, some deviation from the paths of rectitude and honour. It is hard for a child to be more poorly dressed than her companions;

but to convince her that dishonesty is the best policy and brings its own reward, is but a dubious kindness. Nor is it impossible to so stiffen her moral fibre that her poor dress may be worn, if not with pride, at least with sturdy self-control.

On this point I know whereof I speak, for, when I was a little girl, my convent school sheltered a number of Southern children, reduced to poverty by the Civil War, and educated (though of this no one was aware) by the boundless charity of the nuns. These children were shabby, with a pathetic shabbiness which fell far below our very moderate requirements. Their dresses (in my prehistoric days, school uniforms were worn only on Thursday and Sundays) were strangely antiquated, as though cut down from the garments of mothers and grandmothers, their shoes were scuffed, their hats were hopeless. But the unquenchable pride with which they bore themselves invested such hardships with distinction. Their poverty was the honourable outcome of war; and this fact, added to their simple and sincere conviction that a girl born below the Mason and Dixon line must necessarily be better than a girl born above it, carried them unscathed through the valley of humiliation. Looking back now with an unbiassed mind, I am disposed to consider their claim to superiority unfounded; but, at the time, their single-mindedness carried conviction. The standards they imposed were preeminently false, but they were less ignoble than the standards imposed by wealth. No little American boy or girl can know to-day what it means to have the character set in childhood by history, by the vividness of early years lived under strange and violent conditions, by the sufferings, the triumphs, the high and sad emotions of war.

There is a story told by Sir Francis Doyle which illustrates, after the rude fashion of our forebears, the value of endurance as an element of education. Dr. Keate, the terrible head-master of Eton, encountered one winter morning a small boy crying miserably, and asked him what was the matter. The child replied that he was cold. "Cold!" roared Keate. "You must put up with cold, sir! You are not at a girls' school."

It is a horrid anecdote, and I am kindhearted enough to wish that Dr. Keate, who was not without his genial moods, had taken the lad to some generous fire (presuming such a thing was to be found), and had warmed his frozen hands and feet. But it so chanced that in that little snivelling boy there lurked a spark of pride and a spark of fun, and both ignited at the rough touch of the master. He probably stopped crying, and he certainly remembered the sharp appeal to manhood. Fifteen years later he charged with the Third Dragoons at the strongly entrenched Sikhs (thirty thousand of the best fighting men of the Khalsa) on the curving banks of the Sutlej. When the word was given, he turned to his superior officer, a fellow Etonian who was scanning the stout walls and the belching guns. "As old Keate would say, this is no girls' school," he chuckled; and rode to his death on the battlefield of Sobraon, which gave Lahore to England.

Contemplating which incident, and many like it, we become aware that ease is not the only good in a world consecrated to the heroic business of living and of dying.

QUESTIONS FOR "POPULAR EDUCATION" BY AGNES REPPLIER

Talking About the Text

1. Agnes Repplier speaks to her readers in a voice not previously heard by other writers in this chapter. Here, for instance, is how she opens her essay: "This is so emphatically the children's age that a good many of us are beginning to thank God we were not born in it." A little later she says, "If parents do not know by this time how to bring up their children, it is not for lack of instruction." How would you characterize her voice?

2. Although many of her references to individuals are dated (we do not recognize many of them ourselves), what is it about her views regarding "popular education" that seem just as controversial today as they might have been earlier in this century?

3. Repplier creates incongruity between the science of education and the experience of it from the child's, parents', and teacher's point of view. Try to characterize these various perspectives.

4. What kind of a teacher to you think Repplier would make? Do you think she would be effective?

Exploring Issues

1. If it has not come up in your class discussions or writing by now, it's time we face one of the toughest questions regarding schooling: What is the purpose of education? In answering this question, make some assumptions about what kind of individuals our schools should attempt to form. You'll also need to consider whether school should be entertaining or whether it is possible for school to be educational as well as interesting.

2. How might Kozol, Rose, or Bechtel respond to this challenge. Concerning the purpose of education and whether it can be simultaneously interesting and educational?

3. Do you think the general public perceives college students as serious and hardworking or as more interested in having fun and enjoying interesting experiences? Why? How do you think the public perceives college professors? Why?

Writing Assignments

1. Write a humorous description of "The Typical College Class," of "The Typical College Student/Professor," or of "Life at College."

2. Evaluate the merits as well as possible shortcomings of some of the commonplace views that you believe many people generally hold about the purpose and the method of education. Speculate about the kinds of citizens possibly produced by this type of education. Write this as a commentary that describes and responds to "popular views of education."

Reading 52

This poem by Tom Romano is taken from the *National Council of Teachers of English Post Pal Postcard* (1982). The speaker in the poem reflects on his role and duties as "the teacher."

The Teacher

Tom Romano

Why do I forget question marks.
I am notorious for it.
My students scoff at me,
"How can you teach English when
you don't punctuate proper?"

I don't teach you anyway, I think,
just lead you like a scout master
and hope you'll dip your hand
into the brook—cold like no
tap water you've ever felt,
let you marvel, a little frightened,
at a snake, mouth agape,
before it darts between rocks,
an image you'll carry for years,
spur you to anger when I won't
stop to let you rest,
even hope you catch poison ivy,
and, as we race up the hill,
urge you on when
you leave me behind,
gasping,
a seeming spear
wedged between my ribs.

Of the absent question mark, I say,
"An innocent, harmless error,"
And those of you who aren't smug

point out that I should
extend to you
the same courteous understanding.
I uncap my canteen,
drop to the grass, and,
before I take a long swig,
say, "Why not."

Reading 53

Connected Teaching

Mary Field Belenky, Blythe McVicker Clinchy, Nancy Rule Goldberger, and Jill Mattuck Tarule

Mary Field Belenky is an assistant research professor at the University of Vermont. Blythe McVicker Clinchy is a professor of psychology at Wellesley College. Nancy Rule Goldberger is a visiting scholar in psychology at New York University, and Jill Mattuck Tarule is an associate professor at Lesley College Graduate School in Cambridge, Massachusetts. This essay is from chapter 10 of their book, *Women's Ways of Knowing: The Development of Self, Voice, and Mind* (1986). These authors argue that traditional teaching methods prevent students from understanding how professors arrive at their knowledge as the students only see the finished product typically presented in lecture format.

SHARING THE PROCESS

Paulo Freire describes traditional education as "banking": The teacher's role is "to 'fill' the students by making deposits of information which the teacher considers to constitute true knowledge" (1971, p. 63). The student's job is merely to "store the deposits."

The banking concept distinguishes two stages in the action of the educator. During the first, he cognizes a cognizable object while he prepares his lessons in his study or his laboratory; during the second, he expounds to his students about the object. The students are not called upon to know, but to memorize the contents narrated by the teacher. Nor do the students practice any act of cognition, since the object towards which that act should be directed is the property of the teacher. (Pp. 67–68)

Although none of the institutions in our sample adhered closely to the banking model, our interviews contain poignant accounts of occasions on which teachers seemed trapped against their will into the banker role. The teacher who invited Faith and her classmates to "rip into" his interpretation of *The Turn of the Screw* is a case in point. It is easy to feel compassion for this beleaguered man. He has probably toiled much of the previous night over his interpretation. He is excited about it and imagines that the students, too, will get excited. He imagines hands waving, voices raised in passionate debate. Instead, he sees rows of bowed heads, hears only the scratching of twenty-five pencils. The teacher does not wish to deposit his words in the students' notebooks, but the students insist upon storing them there. They treat his words as sacrosanct. He cannot understand why they will not risk a response.

But the teacher himself takes few risks. True to the banking concept, he composes his thoughts in private. The students are permitted to see the product of his thinking, but the process of gestation is hidden from view. The lecture appears as if by magic. The teacher asks his students to take risks he is unwilling—although presumably more able—to take himself. He invites the students to find holes in his argument, but he has taken pains to make it airtight. He would regard as scandalous a suggestion that he make the argument more permeable. He has, after all, his "standards," the standards of his discipline, to uphold, and he is proud of the rigor of his interpretation. The students admire it, too. It would seem to them an act of vandalism to "rip into" an object that is, as Freire might say, so clearly the teacher's private property.

A woman needs to know, one alumna said, that her own ideas can be "very good" and "thoroughly reliable," that a theory is "something that somebody thought up, and that's all that a theory is.. It's not this mysterious thing only Einstein could figure out." Because they are in positions of power, teachers who speak in their own voices risk turning their students' voices into echoes of their own. On the other hand, the utterly objective, "disembodied" voice carries its own dangers. Rich quotes a university teacher of psychology:

It seems to me that the form of many communications in academia, both written and verbal, is such as to not only obscure the influence of the personal or subjective but also to give the impression of divine origin—a mystification composed of syballine statements—from beings supposedly emptied of the "dross" of the self. (1979, p. 144)

So long as teachers hide the imperfect processes of their thinking, allowing their students to glimpse only the polished products, students will remain convinced that only Einstein—or a professor—could think up a theory.

The problem is especially acute with respect to science. Science is usually taught by males and is regarded as the quintessentially masculine intellectual activity. And science is taught—or, at least, it is heard by students in most introductory courses—as a series of syballine statements. The professor is not indulging in conjecture; he is telling the truth. And, in one of the most shocking statements in all our hundreds of pages of transcripts, a student concluded that "science is not a creation of the human mind."

Simone, one of our most sophisticated science students, said in an interview during her first year at college that you had to "accept at face value" anything a chemistry professor said. By her senior year Simone had come to realize that the professors had been talking not about facts but about models, although they presented the information as if it were fact. "Why do they do that?" we asked. "I don't know," Simone replied. "Maybe they think you wouldn't believe them otherwise. Maybe they do tell you that it's a model, and you just say, 'Oh, well, it must be true,' because a professor is telling you. I mean, he has a Ph.D. Who am I to argue?"

Simone was wise enough to wonder if she might have misheard the professors, but her story suggests that it is especially critical that teachers of science do all that they can to avoid the appearance of omniscience. Between the scientific expert and the layman, says the feminist scholar Elizabeth Fee, there is rarely any dialogue: "The voice of the scientific authority is like the male voice-over in commercials, a disembodied knowledge that cannot be questioned, whose author is inaccessible" (1983, p. 19).

• • •

It can be argued, of course, that students need models of impeccable reasoning, that it is through imitating such models that students learn to reason. But none of the women we interviewed named this sort of learning as a powerful experience in their own lives. They did mention the deflation of authority as a powerful learning experience. Recall Faith, who learned, through catching her high school teacher in an error about Mount Everest, that teachers' words should not be accepted at "face value." Another student said she felt emancipated when she told her teacher she could not understand a book she was reading and the teacher replied, "Oh, yeah, I know the guy who wrote it. He's an asshole." The student had not realized that authors could be people, let alone assholes, and she was pleased to be disillusioned.

Women have been taught by generations of men that males have greater powers of rationality than females have. When a male professor presents only the impeccable products of his thinking, it is especially difficult for a woman student to believe that she can produce such a thought. And remember that in the groves of academe, in spite of the women's movement, most of the teachers are still male, although more than half of the students are now female. Women students need opportunities to watch women professors solve (and fail to solve) problems and male professors fail to solve (and succeed in solving) problems. They need models of thinking as a human, imperfect, and attainable activity.

CONNECTED CLASSES

In Freire's "problem-posing" method, the object of knowledge is not the private property of the teacher. Rather, it is "a medium evoking the critical reflection of both teacher and students." Instead of the teacher thinking about the object privately and talking about it publicly so that the students may store it, both teacher and students engage in the process of thinking, and they talk out what they are thinking in a public dialogue. As they think and talk together, their roles merge. "Through dialogue, the teacher-of-the-students and the students-of-the-teacher cease to exist and a new term emerges: teacher-student with students-teachers" (1971, p. 67).

Several women cherished memories of classes in which such dialogue had occurred. Bess described an English course that the teacher usually conducted in the banking mode: "He just hands you his thoughts." On one memorable occasion, however, he allowed a discussion to erupt.

> We were all raising our hands and talking about I forget what book, and some of the students brought up things that he hadn't thought about that made him see it in a whole different way, and he was really excited, and we all came to a conclusion that none of us had started out with. We came up with an answer to a question we thought was unanswerable in the beginning, and it just made you all feel really good when you walked out of class. You felt you had accomplished something and that you understood the book. And he was pleased, too.

Rushing eagerly into the classroom at the next meeting, Bess found to her dismay that the professor had returned to his podium. "I guess he doesn't like that method," she said.

At this traditional, elite institution the students had to adapt to whatever method the teacher chose. Another, older sophomore in an experimental adult program told us quite a different story about a "stern" new teacher who tried to lecture. The students soon set him straight. "We really wanted to be very involved and we wanted to talk as much as he did, and it took him a while to understand that. He kind of rebelled at that because he felt that the other way would be better. He was good after that, but it took a while."

In a connected class no one apologizes for uncertainty. It is assumed that evolving thought will be tentative. Spacks, writing about feminist criticism, argues that women can mimic a masculine authority rooted in "a universal systematic methodology" and therefore speak with certainty, but we can also try to construct a different sort of authority, based on personal individual experience and acknowledging "the uncertainties implicit in an approach which values the personal" (1981, p. 16).*

*Catherine Stimpson, a pioneer in the development of women's studies, writes, "We need to find a judicious balance between the claims of personal authority and the waste of reinventing the wheel that occurs when non-personal authority is rejected" (1978, p. 17).

The discussion that erupted in Bess's English class was not a debate between finished interpretations. It was a conversation in which teacher and
students collaborated in constructing a new interpretation. It is this sort of class
that women remember with pleasure. Marylyn Rands, who teaches at a
women's college, encourages students in her innovative social psychology
course to use a variety of formats in making their presentations. Not one student
has ever chosen the debate.[†] In a "woman-centered university," Adrienne Rich
says, more courses would be conducted in the style of community, fewer in the
"masculine adversary style of discourse," which has dominated much of Western education (1979, p. 138).

In a community, unlike a hierarchy, people get to know each other. They do
not act as representatives of positions or as occupants of roles but as individuals
with particular styles of thinking. A first-year undergraduate remarked that her
editing group composed of three classmates in a writing course was not working.

> We just talk about commas and junk like that. I had a peer editing group in
> high school, and it was terrific. But we all knew each other inside out, so
> you knew what each person was trying to do in her writing and you knew
> what kinds of criticisms helped her and what kind hurt her feelings. You
> can't really help if you don't know people.

Unless she knew the critic personally and the critic knew her personally, she
found criticism of her work "hurtful but not helpful"; and she found the concept
of "blind grading" simply incomprehensible.

Our vision of a connected class follows directly from our conception of
connected epistemology. Norman Holland, a teacher of literature who shares
our epistemological assumptions, describes the epistemological assumptions
underlying many literature courses.

> People often speak as though the literary work or, in general, some other existed in
> all its fullness, while I perceive that fullness imperfectly, subtracting out certain
> aspects. It is as though my perception of the other equaled the other *minus* some-
> thing. . . . Thinking this way leads to images like the *prison* of the self or the *limits*
> of what I can see, or the *risk,* even the *peril* of interpreting wrongly. All such
> discomfort proceeds from the debilitating assumption that each of us experiences
> something imperfectly and someone else knows just how imperfectly. (1975, pp.
> 281–82)

Given such a model, students in such a class must inevitably "measure their
words" in an attempt to avoid disgrace. The model is, as Holland says, both
"confusing and discouraging," because "we cannot suddenly know more"
(p. 282). We cannot stop being ourselves or step out of ourselves. As one
woman told us, "I live within myself. I know only through myself."

"All this confusion and sense of limitation and loss," Holland says, "comes
from positing a literary work or, in general, an other which is full and complete
and from which we subtract" (p. 282). Suppose that instead of asking what
readers fail to see (what they subtract from the text in constructing their own

[†]Personal communication, October 1984.

experience of it), we start not with the text but with the students and ask, as Holland suggests, what they are adding to themselves by the act of reading. When teachers and students learn to ask this question of each other, to respect and to enter into each other's unique perspectives, the connected class comes into being.

The connected class recognizes the core of truth in the subjectivist view that each of us has a unique perspective that is in some sense irrefutably "right" by virtue of its existence. But the connected class transforms these private truths into "objects," publicly available to the members of the class who, through "stretching and sharing," add to themselves as knowers by absorbing in their own fashion their classmates' ideas.

The connected class constructs truth not through conflict but through "consensus," whose original meaning, Holland reminds us, was "feeling or sensing together," implying not agreement, necessarily, but a "crossing of the barrier between ego and ego," bridging private and shared experience (p. 291).

OBJECTIVITY IN CONNECTED TEACHING

Connected teachers try to discern the truth inside the students. It is essential that the search be disinterested. A fifty-four-year-old mother of six in her second term at an adult program said,

> I keep discovering things inside myself. I see myself for the first time through the eyes of others. In the past, whenever I've seen myself through the eyes of others it's been another that I cared a great deal about, who had the power to destroy me, and usually did. Now I see myself through the eyes of others who matter, but not that closely. I'm not entwined with them emotionally. I feel that it's a truer thing that I'm getting back from these people.

Several women spontaneously remarked that in this adult program they were able for the first time since childhood to initiate a conversation, because they knew that they would be listened to in their own terms. "Everyone wants what's best for me," said one.

Connected teachers welcome diversity of opinion in class discussion. Many of the women we interviewed spoke with appreciation of teachers who refrained from "inflicting" (a common term) their own opinions on the students. Elizabeth remembered a Bible course as "just great."

> We had Baptists and we had Jews in there and we had atheists in there. We had people with just absolute disregard for humanity in there. And all of us could contribute and learn something and gain something because he could tolerate so many different views. I think that's a mark of excellence, the ability to accept dissent from your own opinion.

PORTRAIT OF A CONNECTED TEACHER

Candace remembered an English professor at the women's college who could serve as an ideal prototype of a connected teacher. Candace was "moved" by this woman's "rigorous" approach to teaching. "You had to assume that there was a purpose to everything the writer did. And if something seemed odd, you couldn't overlook it or ignore it or throw it out." This teacher was throughly "objective" in treating the students' responses as real and independent of her own.

> She was intensely, genuinely interested in everybody's feelings about things. She asked a question and wanted to know what your response was. She wanted to know because she wanted to see what sort of effect this writing was having. She wasn't using us as a sounding board for her own feelings about things. She really wanted to know.

She was careful not to use the students to "develop her own argument."

Candace recalled with special vividness an occasion when the teacher became embroiled in a real argument with a student and stubbornly refused to hear the student's point.

> And she came in the next day and said, "You know, my response to this student was being governed by my own biases." And she learned from that, she said, how she really did feel about something, and then she related it actually to the work we were studying. And it was just so wonderful, so amazing that somebody would really—in this theater of the classroom—that she was fully engaged in what was going on.

This teacher managed not only to present herself as a person while retaining her objectivity but to present objectivity as a personal issue. By her actions as well as her words she made it clear that to overlook or ignore or throw out a piece of data or another person's words was a violation of her own person. And the violation itself became another piece of data not to be overlooked or ignored or thrown out. Instead, it had to be acknowledged in full view of the class, understood, and even used to illuminate the material the class was studying. The personal became the professional; the professional became the personal. And subjectivity and objectivity became one. . . .

Candace's English teacher . . . did not treat her own experience of the material under study as primary, and she did not assume that her students experienced the material as she did. . . . She really wanted to know how the students were experiencing the material. As a teacher, she believed she had to trust each student's experience, although as a person or a critic she might not agree with it. To trust means not just to tolerate a variety of viewpoints, acting as an impartial referee, assuring equal air time to all. It means to try to *connect*, to enter into each student's perspective.

But, again, subjectivity is disciplined. Like the participant-observer, the connected teacher is careful not to "abandon" herself to these perspectives (Wilson 1977, p. 259). A connected teacher is not just another student; the role carries special responsibilities. It does not entail power over the students; however, it does carry authority, an authority based not on subordination but on cooperation.

REFERENCES

Fee, E. (1983). Women's nature and scientific objectivity. In M. Loew & R. Hubbard (Eds.), *Woman's nature: Rationalizations of inequality* (pp. 9–27). New York: Pergamon Press.

Freire, P. (1971). *Pedagogy of the oppressed.* New York: Seaview.

Holland N. N. (1975). *Five readers reading.* New Haven: Yale University Press.

Rich, A. (1979). *On lies, secrets, and silence: Selected prose—1966–78.* New York: Norton.

Spacks, P. (1981). The difference it makes. In E. Langland and W. Gove (Eds.), *A feminist perspective in the academy* (pp. 7–24). Chicago: University of Chicago Press.

Stimpson, C. (1978, May). Women's studies: An overview. *Ann Arbor Papers in Women's Studies* (Special Issue), pp. 14–26.

Wilson, S. (1977). The use of ethnographic techniques in educational research. *Review of Educational Research, 47,* 245–265.

QUESTIONS FOR "CONNECTED TEACHING" BY MARY BELENKY ET AL.

Talking About the Text

1. The authors begin this selection with Paulo Freire's analogy comparing traditional education to banking. Based on your understanding of what traditional education is, in what sense is this analogy appropriate? In what sense is it inappropriate?
2. Why is it that women students may be more at a disadvantage in some classrooms? What about students from ethnic backgrounds differing from the teacher's?
3. What point are these authors making when they quote the teacher who tells the student that the writer of a book the student was reading is "an asshole"? Evocative descriptions aside, is there a relationship between one's character and one's knowledge?
4. "Epistemology" is the study of what knowledge is and how we achieve and validate it. The four authors are offering us a different way of teaching, which they believe is based on their specific "epistemological assumptions." From what you have read here, what do you think these authors believe knowledge to be, and how can students best achieve it?
5. How would you describe the kind of teacher these four writers prefer?

Exploring Issues

1. This selection sympathetically illustrates the dilemma a female student might experience in learning difficult material. As a group, write a list of factors that might make it difficult for women to learn a particular subject matter. List difficulties for students of different ethnic backgrounds, and those for *any* student. In your lists try to consider differences in learning facility that might need to be accounted for in math, science, literature, and history.

2. Some people think that the way we learn something is the same as actually knowing that thing. Others think that these two are related but are not identical experiences. Consider those two fundamental questions concerning what one learns and how one learns it by first considering how Belenky et al. might address it and then by considering how Agnes Repplier might respond.

3. Although none of our writers have really analyzed to any great length the role of testing, what do you think about tests? Should there be any? If so, what kinds?

Writing Assignments

1. Write an essay in which you describe learning something important, and then explain how you learned it. Consider the anxieties and doubts you might have experienced and how you might have overcome those fears and doubts. Speculate about how you might teach someone else the same thing you learned.

2. Interview a teacher to find out his or her theory of teaching. Report your findings and compare these with what you have learned from reading Belenky et al. and Repplier.

3. Write a satirical "how to" essay in which you explain how to most effectively teach something in a way that guarantees that nobody will learn it.

Reading 54

Think About It

Frank Conroy

This essay first appeared in *Harper's Magazine* and has been reprinted in *The Best American Essays—1989,* edited by Geoffrey Wolff. Frank Conroy is the director of the Iowa Writer's Workshop. He is also the author of *Stop-Time* and *Midair.* His stories and essays have appeared in *The New Yorker, Esquire, GQ,* and *Harper's.* Conroy is also a jazz pianist and has written about American music. "Think About It" belongs to a genre called the personal essay in which Conroy shows us how we can continually learn throughout our entire lives by paying attention to those experiences that initially intrigue us.

When I was sixteen I worked selling hot dogs at a stand in the Fourteenth Street subway station in New York City, one level above the trains and one below the street, where the crowds continually flowed back and forth. I worked with three Puerto Rican men who could not speak English. I had no Spanish, and although we understood each other well with regard to the tasks at hand, sensing and adjusting to each other's body movements in the extremely confined space in which we operated, I felt isolated with no one to talk to. On my break I came out from behind the counter and passed the time with two old black men who ran a shoeshine stand in a dark corner of the corridor. It was a poor location, half hidden by columns, and they didn't have much business. I would sit with my back against the wall while they stood or moved around their ancient elevated stand, talking to each other or to me, but always staring into the distance as they did so.

As the weeks went by I realized that they never looked at anything in their immediate vicinity—not at me or their stand or anybody who might come within ten or fifteen feet. They did not look at approaching customers once they were inside the perimeter. Save for the instant it took to discern the color of the shoes, they did not even look at what they were doing while they worked, but rubbed in polish, brushed, and buffed by feel while looking over their shoulders, into the distance, as if awaiting the arrival of an important person. Of course there wasn't all that much distance in the underground station, but their behavior was so focused and consistent they seemed somehow to transcend the physical. A powerful mood was created, and I came almost to believe that these men could see through walls, through girders, and around corners to whatever hyperspace it was where whoever it was they were waiting and watching for would finally emerge. Their scattered talk was hip, elliptical, and hinted at mysteries beyond my white boy's ken, but it was the staring off, the long, steady staring off, that had me hypnotized. I left for a better job, with handshakes from both of them, without understanding what I had seen.

Perhaps ten years later, after playing jazz with black musicians in various Harlem clubs, hanging out uptown with a few young artists and intellectuals, I began to learn from them something of the extraordinarily varied and complex riffs and rituals embraced by different people to help themselves get through life in the ghetto. Fantasy of all kinds—from playful to dangerous—was in the very air of Harlem. It was the spice of uptown life.

Only then did I understand the two shoeshine men. They were trapped in a demeaning situation in a dark corner in an underground corridor in a filthy subway system. Their continuous staring off was a kind of statement, a kind of dance. Our bodies are here, went the statement, but our souls are receiving nourishment from distant sources only we can see. They were powerful magic dancers, sorcerers almost, and thirty-five years later I can still feel the pressure of their spell.

The light bulb may appear over your head, is what I'm saying, but it may be a while before it actually goes on. Early in my attempts to learn jazz piano, I used to listen to recordings of a fine player named Red Garland, whose music I admired. I couldn't quite figure out what he was doing with his left hand, however; the chords eluded me. I went uptown to an obscure club where he was playing with his trio, caught him on his break, and simply asked him. "Sixths," he said cheerfully. And then he went away.

I didn't know what to make of it. The basic jazz chord is the seventh, which comes in various configurations, but it is what it is. I was a self-taught pianist, pretty shaky on theory and harmony, and when he said sixths I kept trying to fit the information into what I already knew, and it didn't fit. But it stuck in my mind—a tantalizing mystery.

A couple of years later, when I began playing with a bass player, I discovered more or less by accident that if the bass played the root and I played a sixth based on the fifth note of the scale, a very interesting chord involving both instruments emerged. Ordinarily, I suppose I would have skipped over the matter and not paid much attention, but I remembered Garland's remark and so I stopped and spent a week or two working out the voicings, and greatly strengthened my foundations as a player. I had remembered what I hadn't understood, you might say, until my life caught up with the information and the light bulb went on.

I remember another, more complicated example from my sophomore year at the small liberal-arts college outside Philadelphia. I seemed never to be able to get up in time for breakfast in the dining hall. I would get coffee and a doughnut in the Coop instead—a basement area with about a dozen small tables where students could get something to eat at odd hours. Several mornings in a row I noticed a strange man sitting by himself with a cup of coffee. He was in his sixties, perhaps, and sat straight in his chair with very little extraneous movement. I guessed he was some sort of distinguished visitor to the college who had decided to put in some time at a student hangout. But no one ever sat with him. One morning I approached his table and asked if I could join him.

"Certainly," he said. "Please do." He had perhaps the clearest eyes I had ever seen, like blue ice, and to be held in their steady gaze was not, at first, an entirely comfortable experience. His eyes gave nothing away about himself while at the same time creating in me the eerie impression that he was looking directly into my soul. He asked a few quick questions, as if to put me at my ease, and we fell into conversation. He was William O. Douglas from the Supreme Court, and when he saw how startled I was he said, "Call me Bill. Now tell me what you're studying and why you get up so late in the morning." Thus began a series of talks that stretched over many weeks. The fact that I was an ignorant sophomore with literary pretensions who knew nothing about the law didn't seem to bother him. We talked about everything from Shakespeare to the possibility of life on other planets. One day I mentioned that I was going to have dinner with Judge Learned Hand. I explained that Hand was my girlfriend's grandfather. Douglas nodded, but I could tell he was surprised at the coincidence of my knowing the chief judge of the most important court in the country save the Supreme Court itself. After fifty years on the bench Judge Hand had become a famous man, both in and out of legal circles—a living legend, to his own dismay. "Tell him hello and give him my best regards," Douglas said.

Learned Hand, in his eighties, was a short, barrel-chested man with a large, square head, huge, thick, bristling eyebrows, and soft brown eyes. He radiated energy and would sometimes bark out remarks or questions in the living room as if he were in court. His humor was sharp, but often leavened with a touch of self-mockery. When something caught his funny bone he would burst out with explosive laughter—the laughter of a man who enjoyed laughing. He had a large repertoire of dramatic expressions involving the use of his eyebrows—very useful, he told me conspiratorially, when looking down on things from behind the bench. (The court stenographer could not record the movement of his eyebrows.) When I told him I'd been talking to William O. Douglas, they first shot up in exaggerated surprise, and then lowered and moved forward in a glower.

"*Justice* William O. Douglas, young man," he admonished. "Justice Douglas, if you please." About the Supreme Court in general, Hand insisted on a tone of profound respect. Little did I know that in private correspondence he had referred to the Court as "The Blessed Saints, Cherubim and Seraphim," "The Jolly Boys," "The Nine Tin Jesuses," "The Nine Blameless Ethiopians," and my particular favorite, "The Nine Blessed Chalices of the Sacred Effluvium."

Hand was badly stooped and had a lot of pain in his lower back. Martinis helped, but his strict Yankee wife approved of only one before dinner. It was my job to make the second and somehow slip it to him. If the pain was particularly acute he would get out of his chair and lie flat on the rug, still talking, and finish his point without missing a beat. He flattered me by asking for my impression of Justice Douglas, instructed me to convey his warmest regards, and then began talking about the Dennis case, which he described as a particularly tricky and difficult case involving the prosecution of eleven leaders of the Communist party. He had just started in on the First Amendment and free speech when we were called in to dinner.

William O. Douglas loved the outdoors with a passion, and we fell into the habit of having coffee in the Coop and then strolling under the trees down toward the duck pond. About the Dennis case, he said something to this effect: "Eleven Communists arrested by the government. Up to no good, said the government; dangerous people, violent overthrow, etc. First Amendment, said the defense, freedom of speech, etc." Douglas stopped walking. "Clear and present danger."

"What?" I asked. He often talked in a telegraphic manner, and one was expected to keep up with him. It was sometimes like listening to a man thinking out loud.

"Clear and present danger," he said. "That was the issue. Did they constitute a clear and present danger? I don't think so. I think everybody took the language pretty far in Dennis." He began walking, striding along quickly. Again, one was expected to keep up with him. "The FBI was all over them. Phones tapped, constant surveillance. How could it be clear and present danger with the FBI watching every move they made? That's a ginkgo," he said suddenly, pointing at a tree. "A beauty. You don't see those every day. Ask Hand about clear and present danger."

I was in fact reluctant to do so. Douglas's argument seemed to me to be crushing—the last word, really—and I didn't want to embarrass Judge Hand. But back in the living room, on the second martini, the old man asked about Douglas. I sort of scratched my nose and recapitulated the conversation by the ginkgo tree.

"What?" Hand shouted. "Speak up, sir, for heaven's sake."

"He said the FBI was watching them all the time so there couldn't be a clear and present danger," I blurted out, blushing as I said it.

A terrible silence filled the room. Hand's eyebrows writhed on his face like two huge caterpillars. He leaned forward in the wing chair, his face settling, finally, into a grim expression. "I am astonished," he said softly, his eyes holding mine, "at Justice Douglas's newfound faith in the Federal Bureau of Investigation." His big, granite head moved even closer to mine, until I could smell the martini. "I had understood him to consider it a politically corrupt, incompetent organization, directed by a power-crazed lunatic." I realized I had been holding my breath throughout all of this, and as I relaxed, I saw the faintest trace of a smile cross Hand's face. Things are sometimes more complicated than they first appear, his smile seemed to say. The old man leaned back. "The proximity of the danger is something to think about. Ask him about that. See what he says."

I chewed the matter over as I returned to campus. Hand had pointed out some of Douglas's language about the FBI from other sources that seemed to bear out his point. I thought about the words "clear and present danger," and the fact that if you looked at them closely they might not be as simple as they had first appeared. What degree of danger? Did the word "present" allude to the proximity of the danger, or just the fact that the danger was there at all—that it wasn't an anticipated danger? Were there other hidden factors these great men were weighing of which I was unaware?

But Douglas was gone, back to Washington. (The writer in me is tempted to create a scene here—to invent one for dramatic purposes—but of course I can't do that.) My brief time as a messenger boy was over, and I felt a certain frustration, as if, with a few more exchanges, the matter of *Dennis* v. *United States* might have been resolved to my satisfaction. They'd left me high and dry. But, of course, it is precisely because the matter did not resolve that has caused me to think about it, off and on, all these years. "The Constitution," Hand used to say to me flatly, "is a piece of paper. The Bill of Rights is a piece of paper." It was many years before I understood what he meant. Documents alone do not keep democracy alive, nor maintain the state of law. There is no particular safety in them. Living men and women, generation after generation, must continually remake democracy and the law, and that involves an ongoing state of tension between the past and the present which will never completely resolve.

Education doesn't end until life ends, because you never know when you're going to understand something you hadn't understood before. For me, the magic dance of the shoeshine men was the kind of experience in which under-standing came with a kind of click, a resolving kind of click. The same with the experience at the piano. What happened with Justice Douglas and Judge Hand was different, and makes the point that understanding does not always mean resolution. Indeed, in our intellectual lives, our creative lives, it is perhaps those problems that will never resolve that rightly claim the lion's share of our energies. The physical body exists in a constant state of tension as it maintains homeostasis, and so too does the active mind embrace the tension of never being certain, never being absolutely sure, never being done, as it engages the world. That is our special fate, our inexpressibly valuable condition.

QUESTIONS FOR "THINK ABOUT IT" BY FRANK CONROY

Talking About the Text

1. What does Conroy mean when he says, "I had remembered what I hadn't understood, you might say, until my life caught up with the information and the light bulb went on"?
2. Describe Conroy's frame of mind in each of the three instances in which he learned something valuable.
3. What is significant about the places and the characters involved in Conroy's "education"?

4. Look at the exchanges between Judge Hand and Justice Douglas. Try to fill in the gaps and explain what each was suggesting in the exchanges.

Exploring Issues

1. Conroy states that "Education doesn't end until life ends." What does he mean by this? How might formal schooling fit into this philosophy?
2. Compare Conroy's views of learning with Agnes Repplier's. What might each say about the necessity of discipline and hard work? About what students don't know but might need to know?
3. In what ways might Conroy's illustration of lifelong learning be applicable to literacy and to how individuals personally develop and extend their reading and writing skills?

Writing Assignments

1. Write a personal essay similar to Conroy's, drawing on insights you have gained through your own experiences. Consider one or several instances when you experienced something significant but did not know exactly what it meant until later. Describe those situations and then explain what you think you learned.
2. Write an essay in which you explain a time when you taught somebody something. What did you teach? How did you teach your "lesson"? What were some of the problems?

CHAPTER 6: EXTENDED WRITING ASSIGNMENTS

6-1. Revise and expand your literacy autobiography by including factors that either helped or hindered your development. Consider such things as specific teachers encountered; courses taken; experiences outside of the classroom; problems involving linguistic, cultural, and social differences; home environment; your attitude toward school and studying, reading, and writing; and your overall developing awareness of your abilities and of your degree of mastery of the skills you were learning and are continuing to develop.

6-2. Do a research paper on literacy. Find out what current statistics show regarding the number of "illiterates" (you may want to question whether this is really an acceptable term to use in the first place). Be sure to find out how these researchers are defining "literacy." Include a discussion of different kinds of literacy. Finally, by incorporating some of the selections in this chapter, conclude your research paper with your recommendations for encouraging literacy development.

6-3. Write a proposal for curricular change for the college you presently attend. Include detailed discussions of what you would change, how you would make those changes, and why those changes might be necessary. In your proposal, consider such issues as bilingual education, ethnic studies, pedagogy, exams, and the place of writing in your curriculum.

6-4. Write an essay in which you explore as many reasons as you can for why people remain in school or drop out. Conclude your essay with your tentative recommendations for how our society can increase the opportunities for all people to continue their educations throughout their lives.

6-5. Write an argumentative essay in which you rethink and expand on the following statement:

Everyone should go to college.

Chapter
7

Prejudice and Oppression

*N*ame-calling in the schoolyard, a joke at a party, a quip by a co-worker—most of us have at one time or another witnessed or been party to prejudicial or discriminatory behavior. In a multiracial and multiethnic society such as that of the United States, few of us will have escaped prejudice's omnipresent tendencies. On a more cataclysmic and global scale, the twentieth century has been witness to events rooted in prejudice so horrifying—the Holocaust of Nazi Germany and the Killing Fields of Kampuchea being only two of the more infamous—that one questions whether humanity has enough stamina to make it to the twenty-first century.

But our time has also seen the uprising of oppressed peoples in groups such as those of the civil rights movement, black power, and the women's movement. These movements, however, have not been without upheaval and violence; the race riots of the late sixties are just one example. This turbulence in part is the result of prejudice—of fearing the power or control over one's life by an "other" or by "those not like us." As John Stuart Mill wrote in "The Subjection of Women" (1869), "where liberty cannot be hoped for, and powe can, power becomes the grand object of human desire." Many of the essays selected for this chapter confront the relationship of fear and power to prejudice.

Our aim in this chapter, however, is not to focus on any one form of prejudice or discrimination but rather to look at how various manifestations of this phenomenon affect both the individual human spirit and the society as a whole. In doing so, we hope to encourage a dialogue that embraces the complexities of prejudice in an attempt to understand its potential consequences.

We begin the chapter with an excerpt from Peter Rose's book *They and We*, entitled "Prejudice." In this essay Rose explores what he sees as the roots and origins of prejudice. His use of Rudyard Kipling's poem "They and We" helps us to understand the relationship of ethnocentric thinking to prejudice and discrimination. Rose's observations are further illustrated in "We Are Outcasts," a selection from Monica Sone's autobiography, *Nisei Daughter*. This piece tells the story of a young Japanese–American girl who experiences the pain of being a "they" in a world of "we's" while growing up on the West Coast just before the start of World War II. Eventually fear forces these Nisei (American-born Japanese-Americans) into internment camps far from the West Coast. Rosemary Bray also confronts the complex relationship between fear and prejudice in "It's Ten O'Clock and I Worry About Where My Husband Is" when she explores her fear that her African-American husband will cross paths with fearful whites. This fear of innocents in the path of violence resulting from racism is voiced once more by Tracy Chapman in the lyrics of her song, "Across the Lines."

Examining the role of power in race relations, Shelby Steele, in "I'm Black, You're White, Who's Innocent?", asserts: "No power can long insist on itself without evoking an opposing power." He argues that we can achieve racial harmony only if we adopt a philosophy of moral power over racial power. This power issue is echoed in Walter Williams's essay "Campus Racism." In this selection, Williams suggests that a rise in campus racism is the result of African Americans receiving what he considers preferential treatment in admission policies, whereas other groups such as whites and Asians do not gain admission to elite universities even though they have higher grades and scores. Williams asserts that such a policy can only build resentment and bitterness. From a different vantage point, Richard Wright confronts racism's connection to education. In "The Library Card," taken from Wright's autobiography, *Black Boy*, we are told the compelling story of the discrimination Wright encountered when attempting to obtain a library card. His eventual manipulation of the racist library system opened to him a world of literacy and new ideas.

Turning to a more subtle form of discrimination, Gloria Steinem addresses the subject of prejudice against women. Arguing that women tend to grow more liberal with age, Steinem explores the reasons for this surprising pattern. Primary among these reasons is the fact that direct confrontations with discrimination come later in life for women, at the workplace, in marriage, and in the process of aging.

In the final essay in this section, "John Woolman" discusses the hazards of homophobia in "A Conservative Speaks Out for Gay Rights." In this piece, which originally appeared as a letter to William F. Buckley, Jr. in the September 12, 1986 issue of the *National Review*, "Woolman" airs his concern for the growing prejudice against homosexuals by members of the conservative movement. We suggest that you contrast this form of prejudice with some of the other forms addressed in this chapter and consider reasons for these various prejudicial attitudes and their consequences.

Reading 55

Prejudice

Peter Rose

Peter I. Rose is a professor of sociology and anthropology at Smith College and has been a Fulbright Professor in England, Japan, and Australia. He has published numerous works on racial and ethnic issues, including *The Subject Is Race* (1968), *Strangers in Their Midst* (1977), and *They and We* (1981), from which the following selection on prejudice is taken. In this essay, Rose explores the nature of prejudice and some of the various forms it can take.

ON BEING CULTURE-BOUND

All good people agree,
  And all good people say,
All nice people like Us, are We
  And everyone else is They.

In a few short lines, Rudyard Kipling captured the essence of what sociologists and anthropologists call *ethnocentric thinking*. Members of all societies tend to believe that "All nice people like Us, are We . . ." They find comfort in the familiar and often denigrate or distrust others. Of course, with training and experience in other climes, they may learn to transcend their provincialism, placing themselves in others' shoes. Or, as Kipling put it,

. . . if you cross over the sea,
  Instead of over the way,
You may end by (think of it!) looking on We
  As only a sort of They.

In a real sense, a main lesson of the sociology of intergroup relations is to begin to "cross over the sea," to learn to understand why other people think and act as they do and to be able to empathize with their perspectives even if one still does not accept them. But this is no easy task. Many barriers—political, economic, social, and personal—stand in the way of such international (and intergroup) understanding. According to William Graham Sumner, ethnocentrism "leads a people to exaggerate and intensify everything in their own folkways which is peculiar and which differentiates them from others." Intensive socialization to particular points of view and notions of what is right and wrong and good and bad has a long-lasting effect.

Sometimes the teaching is very explicit regarding the superior quality of one's own culture; sometimes it is more subtle. Consider the following poem written by Robert Louis Stevenson and taught to many English and American children.

> Little Indian, Sioux or Crow,
> Little frosty Eskimo,
> Little Turk or Japanese,
> O! don't you wish that you were me?
>
> You have seen the scarlet trees
> And the lions over seas;
> You have eaten ostrich eggs,
> And turned the turtles off their legs.
>
> Such a life is very fine,
> But it's not so nice as mine;
> You must often, as you trod,
> Have wearied, not to be abroad.
>
> You have curious things to eat,
> I am fed on proper meat;
> You must dwell beyond the foam
> But I am safe to live at home.
>
> Little Indian, Sioux or Crow,
> Little frosty Eskimo,
> Little Turk or Japanese,
> O! don't you wish that you were me?

Raised on such literary fare it should not be surprising that children develop negative ideas about the ways of others. Undoubtedly many young people in this society still find it hard to understand how those in other lands can become vegetarians, worship ancestors, practice infanticide, or engage in polygamy. They are confused by the fact that many Moslem women wear the *chador* (the veil to cover their faces), that Balinese women go bare-breasted, and that some people wear no clothes at all. They are troubled when they learn that many nations emerging from colonial status favor one-party states and communism over our political system.

American ethnocentricity, while manifest in general attitudes toward others is, of course, tempered somewhat by the very heterogeneity of the population that we have been examining. Thus, while there are the broad standards—expressed in the ways most Americans set goals for their children, organize their political lives, and think about their society in contrast to others—living in our racial and ethnic mosaic makes us more inclined to think in terms of layers or circles of familiarity. A black from Chicago feels and thinks very "American" in Lagos or Nairobi as does an Italian from Brooklyn when visiting relatives in Calabria or Sicily. But when they get home, they will generally revert to feeling "black" in contrast to "white" and Italian in comparison to other Americans in their own communities.

Ethnocentrism is found in political as well as in ethnic contexts. Much of the discussion of patriotism and loyalty is couched in language that reflects rather narrow culture-bound thinking. At various periods in our history this phenomenon has been particularly marked—we remind ourselves of the nativistic movements of the pre-Civil War period, of the anti-foreign organizations during the time of greatest immigration, and the McCarthyism of the early 1950s. During the McCarthy era there was a widespread attempt to impose the notion that anyone who had ever joined a Marxist study group, supported the Loyalists in the Spanish Civil War, or belonged to any one of a number of liberal organizations was "un-American."

It is clear that not only those "over the sea" are viewed (and view others) ethnocentrically. These distinctions between "they" and "we" exist within societies as well. In modern industrial societies most individuals belong to a wide array of social groups that differentiate them from others—familial, religious, occupational, recreational, and so on. Individuals are frequently caught in a web of conflicting allegiances. This situation is often surmounted by a hierarchical ranking of groups as referents for behavior. In most societies, including our own, the family is the primary reference group. As we have seen in the United States, ethnic or racial identity and religious affiliation are also relevant referents. Members of other ethnic, racial, and religious groups are often judged on the basis of how closely they conform to the standards of the group passing judgment.

Thus, several studies have shown that in American society many whites holding Christian beliefs, who constitute both the statistical majority and the dominant group, rank minorities along a continuum of social acceptability. They rate members of minority groups in descending order in terms of how closely the latter approximate their image of "real Americans." Early studies of "social distance" indicated that most ranked groups in the following manner: Protestants from Europe at the top, then, Irish Catholics, Iberians, Italians, Jews, Spanish–Americans, American-born Chinese and Japanese, blacks, and foreign-born Asians. A 1966 study suggested the following rank order: English, French, Swedes, Italians, Scots, Germans, Spaniards, Jews, Chinese, Russians, and blacks. (In late 1979 Iranian–Americans became scapegoats for many other Americans frustrated by the takeover of the United States Embassy in Teheran by supporters of the Ayatollah Khomeini. Were a social distance scale constructed at the time Iranians—and Muslims in general—probably would have ranked very low.) While, over the years, most Americans generally have considered those of English or Canadian ancestry to be acceptable citizens, good neighbors, social equals, and desirable marriage partners, relatively few feel the same way about those who rank low in scales of social distance.

There is an interesting correlate to this finding. Investigators have found that minority-group members themselves tend to accept the dominant group's ranking system—with one exception: each tends to put his or her own group at the top of the scale.

Ranking is one characteristic of ethnocentric thinking; generalizing is another. The more another group differs from one's own, the more one is likely to generalize about its social characteristics and to hold oversimplified attitudes toward its members. When asked to describe our close friends, we are able to cite their idiosyncratic traits: we may distinguish among subtle differences of physiognomy, demeanor, intelligence, and interests. It becomes increasingly difficult to make the same careful evaluation of casual neighbors; it is almost impossible when we think of people we do not know at first-hand. Understandably, the general tendency is to assign strangers to available group categories that seem to be appropriate. Such labeling is evident in generalized images of "lazy" Indians, "furtive" Japanese, "passionate" Latins, and "penny-pinching" Scots.

Ranking others according to one's own standards and categorizing them into generalized stereotypes together serve to widen the gap between "they" and "we." Freud has written that "in the undisguised antipathies and aversions which people feel toward strangers with whom they have to do we may recognize the expression of self-love—of narcissim." In sociological terms, a function of ethnocentric thinking is the enhancement of group cohesion. There is a close relationship between a high degree of ethnocentrism on the part of one group and an increase of antipathy toward others. This relationship tends to hold for ethnocentrism of both dominant and minority groups.

QUESTIONS FOR "PREJUDICE" BY PETER ROSE

Talking About the Text

1. What effect does Rose's use of the poems by Kipling and Stevenson have on our understanding of prejudice? Why do you think Rose chose those poems to begin his essay? How easy or difficult do you think it might be "looking on We / As only a sort of They"?
2. Explain what Rose means by *ethnocentric thinking*. Can you point to any examples of it in history and politics? In contemporary American society? In your own experience?
3. What role do you think emotion plays in the forming of group prejudices? What emotions or feelings do you think might be most prevalent in the forming of these prejudices? Can you think of examples in which emotions may have helped to create and perpetuate prejudice? What other factors do you think are involved in the creation of prejudices?
4. What does Rose mean when he asserts "living in our racial and ethnic mosaic makes us more inclined to think in terms of "layers or circles of familiarity"? Have you experienced these "layers or circles of familiarity"?

Exploring Issues

1. As you read through some of the other essays in this chapter, consider various ways in which group prejudice and discrimination manifest themselves. Where do we find prejudice and discrimination today? Have the indicators of discrimination changed at all over the years?

2. Do you think prejudice is more or less prevalent today than it was 50 years ago? Have the indicators or forms of prejudice and discrimination changed at all over time? Given laws such as the Civil Rights Act, do you think prejudice and discrimination have merely become more subtle?
3. What long-term effects do you think continual prejudicial and discriminatory behavior might have on American society as a whole if it goes unchecked?
4. Do you think it is possible to eliminate prejudice and discrimination in American society? Why or why not?

Writing Assignments

1. Identify some prejudicial attitude or discriminatory behavior that you feel is particularly unjust. Then write an essay in which you define and explore the nature of the prejudice: its origins, its complexities, and its future.
2. Write an essay in which you identify and explore the nature of your own prejudices (cultural, regional, professional, etc.). Describe actual experiences you have had, and discuss the ways in which your prejudices affected your actions.

Reading 56

We Are Outcasts

Monica Sone

Monica Sone first published *Nisei Daughter* in 1953. In that book-length autobiographical narrative, Sone recounts her experience as a young Nisei (American-born child of Japanese-American parents) growing up on the West Coast just prior to the bombing of Pearl Harbor and of her eventual relocation to an internment camp after the United States entered into war with Japan. In the following excerpt from *Nisei Daughter,* "We Are Outcasts," Sone recalls her first realization that she and her family were victims of racial discrimination when they are denied summer housing at a local beach resort.

A gray gloom settled down over our family. Sumiko was ill. Always during the winter she had asthmatic attacks, but this particular winter was the worst. The little black kitten, Asthma, which Mrs. Matsui had given her because, she said, black cats could cure asthma, mewed all day long and rubbed its back against the bed. Almost every day Dr. Moon climbed the long flight of stairs and walked through the hotel without a glance at our rough-looking hotel guests who stared rudely at him. His large, clean, pink-scrubbed hands were strong and tender as he turned Sumiko over and thumped on her thin shoulder blades. Sumiko, wheezing heavily, submitted to the doctor's examination. Her eyes were black and alert as she tried not to look frightened. Dr. Moon told Father he was concerned about Sumiko's cough and the drop of blood she had spit out. He would send a specialist to see her.

Soon a short, burly man with sandy hair, growing wreathlike on his bald head bustled into the hotel. He was Dr. Stimson, director of the King County Tuberculosis Department. Father stuttered as he thanked him for taking time to come and see Sumiko, but Dr. Stimson waved Father's stumbling words aside, "No trouble, no trouble. It's my job. Well, how's the young lady feeling this morning?"

His bright blue eyes peered intently at Sumiko through thick glasses as he examined her. Dr. Stimson said Sumiko must have an X ray taken of her chest. He gave us a pamphlet describing the North Pines Sanitarium and how it took care of sick children. There were bright appealing photographs of children in sun suits and floppy white hats playing in a beautiful garden. A shuddering chill seized me. Did Sumiko have to go away? She was just six. She would be so unhappy away from all of us.

One morning Mother carefully dressed Sumiko and took her to the city clinic for an X ray. Then we waited for the fatal news with a sense of heavy foreboding. Mother moved about as if she were walking in a dream. As I sat by Sumiko's bedside, sewing dresses for our dolls, Sumiko asked me suddenly, "Do I have to go away?"

"Maybe . . ." I tried to find the right words. "It's not definite yet, Sumiko, but if you do have to, you will go to a wonderful place. It'll be just like going on a real vacation, Sumiko." I tried to be enthusiastic. "There're lots of beautiful trees and flowers and you'll go on walks and picnics with other boys and girls, all dressed in white shorts and sun hats. And you'll eat lots of ice cream, and when you come back you'll be so tanned and husky, we won't recognize you at all."

"Really?" Sumiko's enormous eyes sparkled. "How do you know?"

"I read all about it. You'll just play all day, sleep a lot and eat plenty of good food. Golly, I wouldn't mind going!"

As I talked, I thought I heard a door close but no one was in the parlor. Much later, I learned that it had been Father. He had overheard our conversation about the wonderful sanitarium and had started to laugh, but a sob came out instead. He quickly left and locked himself in the kitchen where he could cry undisturbed.

That evening Dr. Stimson came. We stood, gray-lipped, quietly waiting to hear the verdict. Dr. Stimson's eyes twinkled as he told us that Sumiko did not have tuberculosis. We cried with relief as we hugged Sumiko, swathed in a heavy flannel nightgown and smelling of camphor oil. Like a thin little sparrow burrowed deep in its nest, Sumiko cocked her Dutch-bobbed head at us and spoke carefully so as not to wheeze or cough. "I'm glad I don't have to go on that vacation!"

Dr. Stimson said Sumiko must have plenty of milk, rest, and sunshine. So Father and Mother decided to rent a cottage by the sea for the summer. Father said, "Yes, we must do it this summer. We'll start looking right away for a suitable place near Alki Beach."

I leaped into the air and did ten cartwheels in a row. Sumiko, sitting hunched over in Mother's bed, rasped out a gurgling chuckle, but Henry said, "Aw, who cares about Alki. That's sissy stuff."

Henry would be going to the farm in Auburn, as he did every summer, to pick berries. It was customary for Japanese parents to send their sons to rural areas to work on farms where they could harden their muscles and their self-reliance under the vigilant eyes of a Japanese farmer. Henry was proud that he was going off to work to earn his own living, something that girls could never do.

But Sumiko and I dreamed about a little white cottage by the beach, planning in detail how we would spend our days. We would wake with the sun no matter how sleepy we might be, put on our bathing suits and dash out for an early morning dip. We would race back to our cottage, rout Mother and Father out of bed and have a wonderful big breakfast together. We would see Father off to work, help Mother with the house chores and prepare a lunch basket to spend the rest of the day on the beach. Every evening Father would join us at the beach and he would build a roaring bonfire for us. We would watch the evening sun melt the sky into a fiery mass of purple and magenta and wait until the last streak of wine had faded into the blackness behind Vashon Island. Then we would walk slowly back to the cottage, deeply tired and content. A brisk shower to rinse off the sand, the seaweed and salt water, then to bed. And all night we would listen to the muffled rhythmic beat of the ocean waves on the black sands.

Early one day, Mother and I set out to Alki to find a cottage near the beach where we always picnicked. We found a gray house with a FOR RENT sign on its window, just a block from the beach. One side of the house was quilted with wild rambler roses and the sprawling green lawn was trim behind a white-painted picket fence. When I pressed the doorbell, musical chimes rang softly through the house. A middle-aged woman wearing a stiffly starched apron opened the door. "Yes, what can I do for you?" she asked, looking us over.

Mother smiled and said in her halting English, "You have nice house. We like to rent this summer." Mother paused, but the woman said nothing. Mother went on, "How much do you want for month?"

The woman wiped her hands deliberately on her white apron before she spoke, "Well, I'm asking fifty dollars, but I'm afraid you're a little too late. I just promised this place to another party."

"Oh," Mother said, disappointed. "That's too bad. I'm sorry. We like it so much."

I swallowed hard and pointed to the sign on the window. "You still have the sign up. We thought the house was still open."

"I just rented it this morning. I forgot to remove it. Sorry, I can't do anything for you," she said sharply.

Mother smiled at her, "Thank you just the same. Good-by." As we walked away, Mother said comfortingly to me, "Maybe we'll find something even nicer, Ka-chan. We have a lot of looking to do yet."

But we scoured the neighborhood with no success. Every time it was the same story. Either the rent was too much or the house was already taken. We had even inquired at a beautiful new brick apartment facing the beach boulevard, where several VACANCY signs had been propped against empty windows, but the caretaker told us unsmilingly that these apartments were all taken.

That night I went to bed with burning feet. From my darkened bedroom, I heard Mother talking to Father in the living room. "Yes, there were some nice places, but I don't think they wanted to rent to Japanese."

I sat bolt upright. That had not occurred to me. Surely Mother was mistaken. Why would it make any difference? I knew that Father and Mother were not Americans, as we were, because they were not born here, and that there was a law which said they could not become naturalized American citizens because they were Orientals. But being Oriental had never been an urgent problem to us, living in Skidrow.

A few days later, we went to Alki again. This time I carried in my purse a list of houses and apartments for rent which I had cut out from the newspaper. My hands trembled with a nervousness which had nothing to do with the pure excitement of house-hunting. I wished that I had not overheard Mother's remark to Father.

We walked briskly up to a quaint, white Cape Cod house. The door had a shiny brass knocker in the shape of a leaping dolphin. A carefully marcelled, blue-eyed woman, wearing a pince-nez on her sharp nose, hurried out. The woman blinked nervously and tapped her finger on the wall as she listened to Mother's words. She said dryly, "I'm sorry, but we don't want Japs around here," and closed the door. My face stiffened. It was like a sharp, stinging slap. Blunt as it was, I had wanted to hear the truth to wipe out the doubt in my mind. Mother took my hand and led me quickly away, looking straight ahead of her. After a while, she said quietly, "Ka-chan, there are people like that in this world. We have to bear it, just like all the other unpleasant facts of life. This is the first time for you, and I know how deeply it hurts; but when you are older, it won't hurt quite as much. You'll be stronger."

Trying to stop the flow of tears, I swallowed hard and blurted out, "But, Mama, is it so terrible to be a Japanese?"

"Hush, child, you mustn't talk like that." Mother spoke slowly and earnestly. "I want you, Henry, and Sumi-chan to learn to respect yourselves. Not because you're white, black or yellow, but because you're a human being. Never forget that. No matter what anyone may call you, to God you are still his child. Mah, it's getting quite warm. I think we had better stop here and get some refreshment before we go on."

I wiped my eyes and blew my nose hastily before I followed Mother into a small drugstore. There I ordered a towering special de luxe banana split, and promptly felt better.

The rest of the day we plodded doggedly through the list without any luck. They all turned us down politely. On our way home, Mother sat silent, while I brooded in the corner of the seat. All day I had been torn apart between feeling defiant and then apologetic about my Japanese blood. But when I recalled the woman's stinging words, I felt raw angry fire flash through my veins, and I simmered.

We found Sumiko sitting up in bed, waiting for us with an expectant smile. Mother swung her up into the air and said gaily, "We didn't find a thing we liked today. The houses were either too big or too small or too far from the beach, but we'll find our summer home yet! It takes time." I set my teeth and wondered if I would ever learn to be as cheerful as Mother.

Later in the evening, Mr. Kato dropped in. Father told him that we were looking for a cottage out at Alki and that so far we had had no luck. Mr. Kato scratched his head, "Yahhh, it's too bad your wife went to all that trouble. That district has been restricted for years. They've never rented or sold houses to Orientals and I doubt if they ever will."

My face burned with shame. Mother and I had walked from house to house, practically asking to be rebuffed. Our foolish summer dream was over.

Somehow word got around among our friends that we were still looking for a place for the summer. One evening, a Mrs. Saito called on the phone. She lived at the Camden Apartments. She said, "My landlady, Mrs. Olsen, says there is a small apartment in our building for rent. She is a wonderful person and has been kind to us all in the apartments, and we're practically all Japanese. You'd like it here."

Mother said to me afterwards, "See, Ka-chan, I told you, there are all kinds of people. Here is a woman who doesn't object to Orientals."

The Camden Apartments was a modest, clean building in a quiet residential district uptown, quite far from Alki.

Mrs. Marta Olsen, a small, slender, blue-eyed woman took charge of the business end of the apartment while her husband and her three brothers were the maintenance men of the large building. Marta said to Mother in her soft Scandinavian accent, "I'm sorry we don't have a place large enough for the whole family."

The modest apartment on the top fourth floor was just large enough to accommodate Mother and Sumiko in the one bedroom while I occupied the sofa in the living room. Father and Henry, we decided, would stay at the hotel, but join us every evening for dinner. Marta assured us that by winter we would be all together in a larger apartment which would be vacated.

Of course, we were grateful for even this temporary arrangement, especially when we found the Olsens to be such warm, friendly folks. Marta and her husband were a middle-aged childless couple; but they apparently looked upon all the children living in the apartments as their own, for they were constantly surrounded by chattering, bright-eyed youngsters. Marta was always busy baking her wonderful butter cookies for them. It was not too long before Sumiko and I were enjoying them ourselves, and Marta and Mother were exchanging their favorite native recipes.

That summer Sumiko and I pretended we were living in the turret of a castle tower. We made daily swimming trips to Lake Washington, surrounded by cool green trees and beautiful homes. But deep in our hearts we were still attached to Alki Beach. We kept comparing the mud-bottom lake and its mosquitoes to the sparkling salt water of Puget Sound, its clean, hot sands and its fiery sunsets.

Mother was more than content with the apartment. Its windows opened up unlimited vistas of beautiful scenery. Straight across we could see a bridge rise up to meet Beacon Hill where on its crest the soft yellow building of the Marine Hospital stood magnificently alone, its soaring clean lines etched sharply against the sky. On clear days we could see the icy beauty of Mount Rainier loom up in its splendor, and in the evenings we watched the brilliant diamond lights of the Rainier Valley Highway strung across the soft blue velvet of the summer night. All this inspired Mother to stand at the bay window at odd hours of the night in a poetic trance. Once she caught a hauntingly beautiful moon-light scene and a *tanka* materialized in her mind, which she interpreted for us:

> *In the spring-filled night*
> *A delicate mauve*
> *Silken cloud*
> *Veils the moon's brilliance*
> *In its soft chiffon mist.*

The words used in *tanka* were quite different from spoken Japanese. *Tanka* was written in five, seven, five, seven, seven accents in five lines, totaling exactly thirty-one syllables, never more, never less. In reciting the poem, it was sung melodiously in a voice laden with sentiment and trembling emotion to give it proper meaning and effect. The expression *nali keli* was often employed in these poems. Whenever we wanted to tease Mother, we added this expression to every sentence we uttered. We nudged each other whenever we caught Mother standing in front of a bubbling rice pot, lost in thought. "Mama, *gohan kogeri nali keli!* The rice scorcheth."

Mother smiled at our crude humor, but we had to admit that there was something in *tanka*, the way Mother used it. With it, she gathered together all the beauty she saw and heard and felt through that window and pulled it into our little apartment for us to enjoy. Sometimes the night was blotted out with heavy fog and we could see nothing. Then Sumiko and I would sit curled on the davenport, reading and listening to the radio while Mother sat in her armchair, mending or sewing, as she listened to the sounds of a fog-bound city. At the end of the quiet evening she would recite to us the *tanka* which she had created.

> *Kiri no yo no*
> *Hodoro ni fukete*
> *Samu zamu toh*
> *Okibe no fune ka*
> *Fue nali kawasu*

The fog-bound night
Ever deepening in somber silence
Tinged with chilling sadness
Could those be ships far off at sea
Echoing and re-echoing their deep foghorns?

On such evenings I felt suddenly old, wondering that I could like such a melancholy poem. It reminded me of the way I had come to feel about my summer experience, half sad and half at peace with the world.

Gradually I learned in many other ways the terrible curse that went with having Japanese blood. As the nations went, so went their people. Japan and the United States were no longer seeing eye to eye, and we felt the repercussions in our daily lives.

International matters took a turn for the worse when Japan's army suddenly thrust into Shanghai. City officials, prominent men and women were interviewed and they all shouted for punishment and a boycott on Japanese goods. People stopped patronizing Japanese shops. The Chinese who were employed by Japanese resigned their jobs, one after another.

I dreaded going through Chinatown. The Chinese shopkeepers, gossiping and sunning themselves in front of their stores, invariably stopped their chatter to give me pointed, icicled glares.

The editorial sections of the newspapers and magazines were plastered with cartoons of hideous-looking Japanese. The Japanese was always caricatured with enormous, moon-shaped spectacles and beady, myopic eyes. A small mustache was perched arrogantly over massive, square buck teeth, and his bow-legged posture suggested a simian character.

When stories about the Japanese Army on the other side of the Pacific appeared in the newspapers, people stared suspiciously at us on the streets. I felt their resentment in a hundred ways—the way a saleswoman in a large department store never saw me waiting at the counter. After ten minutes, I had to walk quietly away as if nothing had happened. A passenger sitting across the aisle in a streetcar would stare at me coldly.

One beautiful Sunday afternoon a carload of us drove out into the country to swim at the Antler's Lodge. But the manager with a wooden face blocked our entrance, "Sorry, we don't want any Japs around here."

We said, "We're not Japs. We're American citizens." But we piled into the car and sped away trying to ignore the bruise on our pride.

Even some of the older Japanese were confused about the Nisei. Whenever a Japanese frieghter crept into the harbor to pick up its cargo of scrap metal or petroleum, a group of angry citizens turned out as pickets in protest. Quite often Nisei college students walked up and down the dock with them, wearing sandwich signs, "Halt the oil and stop the Japs!" It shocked the sensibilities of the community elders. They muttered, "Who do these Nisei think they are? Don't they realize they, too, have Japanese blood coursing through their veins?"

About this time the Matsui's son, Dick, became the talk of the folks of the Tochigi-ken prefecture. Dick had studied electrical engineering through the International Correspondence Course and had just accepted an important job with the Goto firm in Japan. The townfolk buzzed with excitement everytime someone decided to pull up stakes and go to Japan.

I remember one heated argument about Dick's decision at Mr. Waka-matsu's café, where Father had taken me for lunch. Mr. Sakaguchi, hotel manager and one-time president of the Seattle Japanese Chamber of Commerce, and Mr. Sawada, a clothing salesman, joined us.

"I say Dick's a smart lad to be going back to Japan!" Mr. Sakaguchi pounded the table so hard all the coffee cups rattled in their saucers. "Where else could Dicku get a real man's job? Certainly not here!" As he stuck out his lower lip, his round bald head made him look like an octopus.

Mr. Sawada shook his head thoughtfully. "I don't know about that, Sakaguchi-kun. It's Dicku's own decision, but if I were his parents, I would advise him to think twice about it. After all, Dicku's an American citizen; his future is here."

I liked Mr. Sawada. He was a man of gentle humor and understanding. His wife had died many years ago, leaving him with three children to rear. All his life, he worked hard as a salesman. He walked many miles every day on his route and he always walked with firm deliberate footsteps as if he were determined not to show his weariness. Mr. Sawada was one of the happiest and proudest men I knew, for one of his fondest dreams was coming true. His brilliant eldest son, George, was studying medicine.

"A future here! Bah! Words, words!" Mr. Sakaguchi exploded. "How many sons of ours with a beautiful bachelor's degree are accepted into American life? Name me one young man who is now working in an American firm on equal terms with his white colleagues. Our Nisei engineers push lawn mowers. Men with degrees in chemistry and physics do research in the fruit stands of the public market. And they all rot away inside."

Mr. Sawada insisted quietly. "That's why I think our young men should go to the Midwest or East. Jobs, all kinds of them, are open to Nisei, I hear. Take Nagai's son, for example. He took a good civil service job as an engineer in Wisconsin."

"Nagai's boy is one in a million. Most of us don't know a soul out there. You can't just go out there without contacts. I'm telling you, Dicku's the smart one. With his training and ability to use both the English and Japanese language, he'll probably be a big shot one of these days in the Orient." Mr. Sakaguchi continued to prod Mr. Sawada, "Now be frank, Sawada-kun, if you had a good job waiting for you right now in Japan, wouldn't you pick up and leave?"

Mr. Sawada replied firmly, "And leave my children? No, I wouldn't. I've lived here too long. My wife is buried here. All my friends are here. I haven't kept in touch with my relatives in Japan so I'd be a stranger, if I were to return now. Life certainly has its peculiar twists, doesn't it?"

"Indeed!" Father agreed. "After the young ones were born, our roots sank deeper here. This is our children's home, and it has become ours."

When Dick had been offered the attractive job, Mrs. Matsui came to tell us about it. She felt as proud as if the Emperor himself had bestowed a personal favor upon her family. When Mother wondered how Dick would like Japan, a country which he had never seen, Mrs. Matsui said, "Dicku feels that it's the place for him. He would work himself right up to the top without having to fight prejudice."

She said Dick had been developing an intense dislike of America over the years, and she traced it to a certain incident which Dick had never been able to forget. At work one summer at the Pike Public Market, a white man selling vegetables at a nearby stall had shouted at him peevishly, "Ah, why don't all of ya Japs go back where ya belong, and stop cluttering up the joint."

Young and trigger-tempered, Dick had flung back, "Don't call me 'Jap.' I'm an American!"

The man had flung his head back in derisive laughter, and Dick would have torn off his apron and flung himself at him if his friends hadn't held him back.

Mrs. Matsui continued, "Dicku never forgot those words. He said that that was what every white man in this country really thought about us. He refused to go to the university because he said it was just a waste of time and money for a Nisei."

Then Dick had plunged into the correspondence course with fury, determined to be on his own so he would not have to work for a white man. When the agent from Japan approached him, Dick had snatched at the bait.

People of the same mind with Mr. Sakaguchi flatly stated, "What's so terrible about it? It's better for a man to go where he's welcome. You can't waste a man's talent and brains without wrecking his spirit."

On the other hand, young men like Jack Okada, Henry's college friend, were scornful of Dick's decision. "Dick's a fool. He thinks he's going to be kingpin out there with an American education. Those big companies can make use of fellows like him all right, but Dick's going to find himself on a social island. The Japanese hate us Nisei. They despise our crude American manners."

On the day when Dick was to sail for Japan, everyone of the Tochigi-ken prefecture turned out at Smith Cove to give him a send-off. Mother and I represented our family. Confetti and streamers laced the air as hundreds of Japanese milled around on the dock in tight circles, bowing and making their formal farewells. When the ship shuddered, sounding its deep bass horn, we fought our way through the crowd to Dick. Mrs. Matsui was smiling bravely like a samurai mother sending her son off to war. I managed to slide an arm through the crushing wall of bodies and pumped Dick's perspiring hand. He acknowledged my best wishes with an unsmiling face. In the bright sun, his face was drawn and white, making him look young and uncertain, and I wondered if Dick was having a change of heart at the last minute. Another warning horn vibrated through the air. Dick, his arms loaded with gifts and shopping bags full of fruits and packages, fought his way up as the gangplank swung off the dock. It rattled up to the lip of the ship and a sailor walked the deck, vigorously striking a brass cymbal, drowning out all conversation. It was a moment of incomparable confusion and loneliness, the clash of the cymbal mixed with the hurried last-minute farewells and the flowing tears. Another blast of the horn, then from the deck of the ship, the measured strain of "Auld Lang Syne" floated out over our heads. More confetti showered down, colored serpentines snaking swiftly through the air. Everyone was shouting, "*Sayonara . . .* good-by, good-by!"

Mrs. Matsui suddenly burst into tears. Mr. Matsui, standing erect beside his wife, solemnly waved his straw hat at the small figure of his son on the ship, slipping away in the distance. I wanted to flee from Smith Cove. It was no longer the shining shore where the Issei had eagerly landed many years ago, but the jumping-off place for some of their young, looking to Japan as the land of opportunity. We had all felt as Dick had, one time or another. We had often felt despair and wondered if we must beat our heads against the wall of prejudice all our lives.

In the privacy of our hearts, we had raged, we had cried against the injustices, but in the end, we had swallowed our pride and learned to endure.

Even with all the mental anguish and struggle, an elemental instinct bound us to this soil. Here we were born; here we wanted to live. We had tasted of its freedom and learned of its brave hopes for a democracy. It was too late, much too late for us to turn back.

QUESTIONS FOR "WE ARE OUTCASTS" BY MONICA SONE

Talking About the Text

1. In "We Are Outcasts," Sone recounts her experiences as a young girl coming to terms with the realities of prejudice. In what ways does her largely autobiographical piece differ from Peter Rose's essay, "Prejudice"? What does her autobiography give to the readers that an analysis such as Rose's might not be able to offer?

2. What rhetorical and/or literary devices does Sone use to bring us closer to her experiences? Do you find some more effective than others?

Exploring Issues

1. The narrator writes that after being turned away from cottage rentals, her mother said "I want you, Henry, and Sumi-chan to learn to respect yourselves. Not because you're white, black, or yellow, but because you're a human being. Never forget that." Do you find any similarities between this statement and Shelby Steele's assertion (see Reading No. 60, this chapter) that "moral power precludes racial power"?

2. The narrator of "We Are Outcasts" writes, "In the privacy of our hearts, we had raged, we had cried against the injustices, but in the end we had swallowed our pride, and learned to endure." Do you think the private enduring of prejudice by individuals ultimately has consequences for a society as a whole?

3. The conflict that the narrator experiences as a Japanese American living on the West Coast just before the bombing of Pearl Harbor is rooted not

only in racial injustice but also in a coming to terms with ethnic identity. "Even with all the mental anguish and struggle, an elemental instinct bound us to the soil." Discuss what you think the nature of this "elemental instinct" might be.

4. "We Are Outcasts" describes circumstances of racial injustice that occurred over 50 years ago and that were in part caused by the threat of war with Japan. How much have attitudes towards racism changed since that time? Can you think of similar situations or occurrences in more recent times?

Writing Assignments

1. Do some research on the relocation of Japanese Americans to internment camps during World War II. Then write an essay in which you discuss the long-term societal consequences of such an action and what lessons might be learned from it.

2. Sone writes of her experiences with housing discrimination on the West Coast in the 1940s. Do some research on the topic of housing discrimination. Write an essay that explores one particular aspect of this issue, such as current problems, community reactions, emotional and psychological effect on those discriminated against, history of housing discrimination in a specific area, and so on.

Reading 57

It's Ten O'Clock and I Worry About Where My Husband Is

Rosemary L. Bray

Rosemary L. Bray lives in Central Harlem and is an editor for the *New York Times Book Review*. "It's Ten O'Clock and I Worry About Where My Husband Is" was originally published in the April 1990 issue of *Glamour* magazine. As an African American, Bray writes of her fear of white people's fears. She fears "white men in police uniforms; white teen-agers driving by with Jersey plates; thin, panicky middle-aged white men on the subway." Most of all she is afraid that her husband, a tall black man, will cross paths with this fear one night on his way home. Subsequent to the article's publication, *Glamour* was inundated with both positive and negative responses to Bray's article, and in August 1990 the magazine published a follow-up article by Bray, entitled "A Dialogue on Race."

He phoned more than an hour ago, to say he was on his way home. But I have yet to hear the scrape of the iron gate, the rattling keys, so I worry.

Most married women fret about a tardy husband; young black women like myself worry more. For most people in New York—truth be told—the urban bogeyman is a young black man in sneakers. But we live in Central Harlem, where every young man is black and wears sneakers, so we learn to look into the eyes of young males and discern the difference between youthful bravado and the true dangers of the streets. No, I have other fears. I fear white men in police uniforms; white teenagers driving by in a car with Jersey plates; thin, panicky, middle-aged white men on the subway. Most of all, I fear that their path and my husband's path will cross one night as he makes his way home.

Bob is tall—5'10″ or so, dark, with thick hair and wire-rimmed glasses. He carries a knapsack stuffed with work from the office, old crossword puzzles, Philip Glass tapes, *Ebony Man* and *People* magazines. When it rains, he carries his good shoes in the bag and wears his Reebok sneakers. He cracks his knuckles a lot, and wears a peculiar grimace when his mind is elsewhere. He looks dear and gentle to me—but then, I have looked into those eyes for a long time.

I worry that some white person will see that grim, focused look of concentration and see the intent to victimize. I fear that some white person will look at him and see only his or her nightmare—another black man in sneakers. In fact, my husband *is* another black man in sneakers. He's also a writer, an amateur cyclist, a lousy basketball player, his parents' son, my life's companion. When I put aside the book I'm reading to peek out the window, the visions in my head are those of blind white panic at my husband's black presence, visions of a flashing gun, a gleaming knife; I see myself a sudden, horrified widow at thirty-four.

Once upon a time, I was vaguely ashamed of my paranoia about his safety in the world outside our home. After all, he is a grown man. But he is a grown black man on the streets alone, a menace to white New Yorkers—even the nice, sympathetic, liberal ones who smile at us when we're together. And I am reminded, over and over, how dangerous white people still can be, how their fears are a hazard to our health. When white people are ruled by their fears of everything black, every black woman is an addict, a whore; every black man is a rapist—even a murderer.

Charles Stuart understood this fear well enough to manipulate an entire nation. When he said a black man in Boston's Mission Hill district put a bullet through the head of his pregnant wife, who could doubt him? So a city's police force moved through the neighborhood, stopping and strip-searching black men at random, looking for the apocryphal black savage who, it turned out, existed only in Boston's collective imagination. Yet an innocent African-American man, William Bennett, was paraded before the nation for weeks, until Stuart's brother had an attack of conscience and went to the police.

The Stuart case was shameful, but it could have been worse—after all, William Bennett is still alive. When whites' fear of black people is allowed its freest reign, black people can die.

Wasn't Michael Griffith a bum out to make trouble when a teenage posse in Howard Beach chased him onto the Shore Parkway into the path of a car? Wasn't Yusef Hawkins a thug coming to beat up a white man in Bensonhurst when he was surrounded by a gang of teenagers and shot? It doesn't seem to matter that Michael Griffith was a construction worker, that Yusef Hawkins was a student looking for a used car. Someone looked at those two men and saw danger, and so they are dead. And the women who waited for them—who peeked out the front windows and listened for footsteps on the stairs—waited in vain.

So when it's ten o'clock and he's not home yet, my thoughts can't help but wander to other black men—husbands, fathers, sons, brothers—who never do make it home, and to other black women whose fingers no longer rest at a curtain's edge. Even after I hear the scrape of our iron gate, the key in the lock, even after I hear that old knapsack hit the floor of the downstairs hallway and Bob's voice calling to me, my thoughts return to them.

QUESTIONS FOR "IT'S TEN O'CLOCK AND I WORRY ABOUT WHERE MY HUSBAND IS" BY ROSEMARY L. BRAY

Talking About the Text

1. What commentary do you think Bray is making about the nature of stereotypes when she writes, "In fact, my husband *is* another black man in sneakers. He's also a writer, an amateur cyclist, a lousy basketball player, his parent's son, my life's companion"?
2. What does Bray mean when she asserts that white people's "fears are a hazard to our health"? How does fear become hazardous? Can you think of similar examples of this phenomena?
3. Do you find Bray's use of personal experience a persuasive means of exploring issues? Why or why not?

Exploring Issues

1. In "Prejudice," Peter Rose states that "often emotions aroused in the prejudiced person are based upon the stereotypes he or she holds of certain people." How does Bray illustrate this phenomenon in her essay?

2. What connections can you make between Kipling's poem "We and They" in the Peter Rose essay and the way in which fear is portrayed in Bray's essay? Do you think there is any way to eliminate this kind of fear in American society?

Writing Assignments

1. Write a narrative about an incident involving prejudice or discrimination in which you were either a witness or directly involved. How did you feel during and after the incident? What did you learn from the experience?
2. Write a letter to Bray responding to her thoughts and opinions about race relations. Do you feel her fears are justified? What has your experience been?

Reading 58

Across the Lines

Tracy Chapman

Tracy Chapman is a popular singer whose blend of folk music and rhythm and blues is reminiscent of music by Bob Dylan and other singers from the 1960s. In her lyrics, Chapman often addresses themes concerning social injustice, as is the case in the following song taken from her first album, "Across the Lines." In this song, Chapman evokes images of racial strife and of children who were simply in the line of fire.

Across the lines
Who would dare to go
Under the bridge
Over the tracks
That separates whites from blacks

Choose sides
Or run for your life
Tonight the riots begin
On back streets of America
They killed the dream of America

Little black girl gets assaulted
Ain't no reason why
Newspaper prints the story
And racist tempers fly
Next day it starts a riot
Knives and guns are drawn
Two black boys get killed
One white boy goes blind

Little black girl gets assaulted
Don't no one know her name
Lots of people hurt and angry
She's the one to blame

Reading 59

I'm Black, You're White, Who's Innocent?

Shelby Steele

Shelby Steele, an associate professor of English at San Jose State University in California, has published extensively on the subject of race and is the author of a collection of essays entitled *The Recoloring of America*. In the following selection, Steele confronts the issue of power in race relations. Noting distinct differences between the civil rights movement of the fifties and the black power movement of the late sixties and early seventies, Steele asserts that "black power can claim no higher moral standing than white power. . . [and] racial power subverts moral power."

It is a warm, windless California evening, and the dying light that covers the redbrick patio is tinted pale orange by the day's smog. Eight of us, not close friends, sit in lawn chairs sipping chardonnay. A black engineer and I (we had never met before) integrate the group. A psychologist is also among us, and her presence encourages a surprising openness. But not until well after the lovely twilight dinner has been served, when the sky has turned to deep black and the drinks have long since changed to scotch, does the subject of race spring awkwardly upon us. Out of nowhere the engineer announces, with a coloring of accusation in his voice, that it bothers him to send his daughter to a school where she is one of only three black children. "I didn't realize my ambition to get ahead would pull me into a world where my daughter would lose touch with her blackness," he says.

Over the course of the evening we have talked about money, infidelity, past and present addictions, child abuse, even politics. Intimacies have been revealed, fears named. But this subject, race, sinks us into one of those shaming silences where eye contact terrorizes. Our host looks for something in the bottom of his glass. Two women stare into the black sky as if to locate the Big Dipper and point it out to us. Finally, the psychologist seems to gather herself for a challenge, but it is too late. "Oh, I'm sure she'll be just fine," says our hostess, rising from her chair. When she excuses herself to get the coffee, the two sky gazers offer to help.

With three of us now gone, I am surprised to see the engineer still silently holding his ground. There is a willfulness in his eyes, an inner pride. He knows he has said something awkward, but he is determined not to give a damn. His unwavering eyes intimidate me. At last the host's head snaps erect. He has an idea. "The hell with coffee," he says. "How about some of the smoothest brandy you ever tasted?" An idea made exciting by the escape it offers. Gratefully we follow him back into the house, quickly drink his brandy, and say our goodbyes.

An autopsy of this party might read: death induced by an abrupt and lethal injection of the American race issue. An accurate if superficial assessment. Since it has been my fate to live a rather integrated life, I have often witnessed sudden deaths like this. The threat of them, if not the reality, is a part of the texture of integration. In the late 1960s, when I was just out of college, I took a delinquent's delight in playing the engineer's role, and actually developed a small reputation for playing it well. Those were the days of flagellatory white guilt; it was such great fun to pinion some professor or housewife or, best of all, a large group of remorseful whites, with the knowledge of both their racism and their denial of it. The adolescent impulse to sneer at convention, to startle the middle-aged with doubt, could be indulged under the guise of racial indignation. And how could I lose? My victims—earnest liberals for the most part— could no more crawl out from under my accusations than Joseph K. in Kafka's *Trial* could escape the amorphous charges brought against him. At this odd moment in history the world was aligned to facilitate my immaturity.

About a year of this was enough: the guilt that follows most cheap thrills caught up to me, and I put myself in check. But the impulse to do it faded more slowly. It was one of those petty talents that is tied to vanity, and when there were ebbs in my self-esteem the impulse to use it would come alive again. In integrated situations I can still feel the faint itch. But then there are many youthful impulses that still itch, and now, just inside the door of mid-life, this one is least precious to me.

In the literature classes I teach, I often see how the presence of whites all but seduces some black students into provocation. When we come to a novel by a black writer, say Toni Morrison, the white students can easily discuss the human motivations of the black characters. But, inevitably, a black student, as if by reflex, will begin to set in relief the various racial problems that are the background of these characters' lives. This student's tone will carry a reprimand: the class is afraid to confront the reality of racism. Classes cannot be allowed to die like dinner parties, however. My latest strategy is to thank that student for his or her moral vigilance, and then appoint the young man or woman as the class's official racism monitor. But even if I get a laugh—I usually do, but sometimes the student is particularly indignant, and it gets uncomfortable—the strategy never quite works. Our racial division is suddenly drawn in neon. Overcaution spreads like spilled paint. And, in fact, the black student who started it all does become a kind of monitor. The very presence of this student imposes a new accountability on the class.

I think those who provoke this sort of awkwardness are operating out of a black identity that obliges them to badger white people about race almost on principle. Content hardly matters. (For example, it makes no sense for the engineer to expect white people to sympathize with his anguish over sending his daughter to school with *white* children.) Race indeed remains a source of white shame; the goal of these provocations is to put whites, no matter how indirectly, in touch with this collective guilt. In other words, these provocations I speak of are *power* moves, little shows of power that try to freeze the "enemy" in self-consciousness. They gratify and inflate the provocateur. They are the underdog's bite. And whites, far more secure in their power, respond with a self-contained and tolerant silence that is, itself, a show of power. What greater power than that of non-response, the power to let a small enemy sizzle in his own juices, to even feel a little sad at his frustration just as one is also complimented by it. Black anger always, in a way, flatters white power. In America, to know that one is not black is to feel an extra grace, a little boost of impunity.

I think the real trouble between the races in America is that the races are not just races but competing power groups—a fact that is easily minimized perhaps because it is so obvious. What is not so obvious is that this is true quite apart from the issue of class. Even the well-situated middle-class (or wealthy) black is never completely immune to that peculiar contest of power that his skin color subjects him to. Race is a separate reality in American society, an entity that carries its own potential for power, a mark of fate that class can soften considerably but not eradicate.

The distinction of race has always been used in American life to sanction each race's pursuit of power in relation to the other. The allure of race as a human delineation is the very shallowness of the delineation it makes. Onto this shallowness—mere skin and hair—men can project a false depth, a system of dismal attributions, a series of malevolent or ignoble stereotypes that skin and hair lack the substance to contradict. These dark projections then rationalize the pursuit of power. Your difference from me makes you bad, and your badness justifies, even demands, my pursuit of power over you—the oldest formula for aggression known to man. Whenever much importance is given to race, power is the primary motive.

But the human animal almost never pursues power without first convincing himself that he is *entitled* to it. And this feeling of entitlement has its own precondition: to be entitled one must first believe in one's innocence, at least in the area where one wishes to be entitled. By innocence I mean a feeling of essential goodness in relation to others and, therefore, superiority to others. Our innocence always inflates us and deflates those we seek power over. Once inflated we are entitled; we are in fact licensed to go after the power our innocence tells us we deserve. In this sense, *innocence is power*. Of course, innocence need not be genuine or real in any objective sense, as the Nazis demonstrated not long ago. Its only test is whether or not we can convince ourselves of it.

I think the racial struggle in America has always been primarily a struggle for innocence. White racism from the beginning has been a claim of white innocence and, therefore, of white entitlement to subjugate blacks. And in the '60s, as went innocence so went power. Blacks used the innocence that grew out of their long subjugation to seize more power, while whites lost some of their innocence and so lost a degree of power over blacks. Both races instinctively understand that to lose innocence is to lose power (in relation to each other). Now to be innocent someone else must be guilty, a natural law that leads the races to forge their innocence on each other's backs. The inferiority of the black always makes the white man superior; the evil might of whites makes blacks good. This pattern means that both races have a hidden investment in racism and racial disharmony, despite their good intentions to the contrary. Power defines their relations, and power requires innocence, which, in turn, requires racism and racial division.

I believe it was this hidden investment that the engineer was protecting when he made his remark—the white "evil" he saw in a white school "depriving" his daughter of her black heritage confirmed his innocence. Only the logic of power explained this—he bent reality to show that he was once again a victim of the white world and, as a victim, innocent. His determined eyes insisted on this. And the whites, in their silence, no doubt protected their innocence by seeing him as an ungracious trouble-maker—his bad behavior underscoring their goodness. I can only guess how he was talked about after the party. But it isn't hard to imagine that his blunder gave everyone a lift. What none of us saw was the underlying game of power and innocence we were trapped in, or how much we needed a racial impasse to play that game.

When I was a boy of about twelve, a white friend of mine told me one day that his uncle, who would be arriving the next day for a visit, was a racist.

Excited by the prospect of seeing such a man, I spent the following afternoon hanging around the alley behind my friend's house, watching from a distance as this uncle worked on the engine of his Buick. Yes, here was evil and I was compelled to look upon it. And I saw evil in the sharp angle of his elbow as he pumped his wrench to tighten nuts, I saw it in the blade-sharp crease of his chinos, in the pack of Lucky Strikes that threatened to slip from his shirt pocket as he bent, and in the way his concentration seemed to shut out the human world. He worked neatly and efficiently, wiping his hands constantly, and I decided that evil worked like this.

I felt a compulsion to have this man look upon me so that I could see evil— so that I could see the face of it. But when he noticed me standing beside his toolbox, he said only, "If you're looking for Bobby, I think he went up to the school to play baseball." He smiled nicely and went back to work. I was stunned for a moment, but then I realized that evil could be sly as well, could smile when it wanted to trick you.

Need, especially hidden need, puts a strong pressure on perception, and my need to have this man embody white evil was stronger than any contravening evidence. As a black person you always hear about racists but never meet any. And I needed to incarnate this odious category of humanity, those people who hated Martin Luther King Jr. and thought blacks should "go slow" or not at all. So, in my mental dictionary, behind the term "white racist," I inserted this man's likeness. I would think of him and say to myself, "There is no reason for him to hate black people. Only evil explains unmotivated hatred." And this thought soothed me; I felt innocent. If I hated white people, which I did not, at least I had a reason. His evil commanded me to assert in the world the goodness he made me confident of in myself.

In looking at this man I was *seeing for innocence*—a form of seeing that has more to do with one's hidden need for innocence (and power) than with the person or group one is looking at. It is quite possible, for example, that the man I saw that day was not a racist. He did absolutely nothing in my presence to indicate that he was. I invested an entire afternoon in seeing not the man but in seeing my innocence through the man. *Seeing for innocence* is, in this way, the essence of racism—the use of others as a means to our own goodness and superiority.

The loss of innocence has always to do with guilt, Kierkegaard tells us, and it has never been easy for whites to avoid guilt where blacks are concerned. For whites, *seeing for innocence* means seeing themselves and blacks in ways that minimize white guilt. Often this amounts to a kind of white revisionism, as when President Reagan declares himself "color-blind" in matters of race. The President, like many of us, may aspire to racial color blindness, but few would grant that he has yet reached this sublimely guiltless state. The statement clearly revises reality, moves it forward into some heretofore unknown America where all racial determinism will have vanished. I do not think that Ronald Reagan is a racist, as that term is commonly used, but neither do I think that he is capable of seeing color without making attributions, some of which may be negative—nor am I, or anyone else I've ever met.

So why make such a statement? I think Reagan's claim of color blindness with regard to race is really a claim of racial innocence and guiltlessness—the preconditions for entitlement and power. This was the claim that grounded Reagan's campaign against special entitlement programs—affirmative action, racial quotas, and so on—that black power had won in the '60s. Color blindness was a strategic assumption of innocence that licensed Reagan's use of government power against black power.

I do not object to Reagan's goals in this so much as the presumption of innocence by which he rationalized them. I, too, am strained to defend racial quotas and any affirmative action that supersedes merit. And I believe there is much that Reagan has to offer blacks. His emphasis on traditional American values—individual initiative, self-sufficiency, strong families—offers what I think is the most enduring solution to the demoralization and poverty that continue to widen the gap between blacks and whites in America. Even his de-emphasis of race is reasonable in a society where race only divides. But Reagan's posture of innocence undermines any beneficial interaction he might have with blacks. For blacks instinctively sense that a claim of racial innocence always precedes a power move against them. Reagan's pretense of innocence makes him an adversary, and makes his quite reasonable message seem vindictive. You cannot be innocent of a man's problem and expect him to listen.

I'm convinced that the secret of Reagan's "teflon" coating, his personal popularity apart from his policies and actions, has been his ability to offer mainstream America a vision of itself as innocent and entitled (unlike Jimmy Carter, who seemed to offer only guilt and obligation). Probably his most far-reaching accomplishment has been to reverse somewhat the pattern by which innocence came to be distributed in the '60s, when outsiders were innocent and insiders were guilty. Corporations, the middle class, entrepreneurs, the military—all villains in the '60s—either took on a new innocence in Reagan's vision or were designated as protectors of innocence. But again, for one man to be innocent another man must be bad or guilty. Innocence imposes, *demands,* division and conflict, a right/wrong view of the world. And this, I feel, has led to the underside of Reagan's achievement. His posture of innocence draws him into a partisanship that undermines the universality of his values. He can't sell these values to blacks and others because he has made blacks into the bad guys and outsiders who justify his power. It is humiliating for a black person to like Reagan because Reagan's power is so clearly derived from a distribution of innocence that leaves a black with less of it, and the white man with more.

Black Americans have always had to find a way to handle white society's presumption of racial innocence whenever they have sought to enter the American mainstream. Louis Armstrong's exaggerated smile honored the presumed innocence of white society—I will not bring you your racial guilt if you will let me play my music. Ralph Ellison calls this "masking"; I call it bargaining. But whatever it's called, it points to the power of white society to enforce its innocence. I believe this power is greatly diminished today. Society has reformed and transformed—Miles Davis never smiles. Nevertheless, this power has not faded altogether; blacks must still contend with it.

Historically, blacks have handled white society's presumption of innocence in two ways: they have bargained with it, granting white society its innocence in exchange for entry into the mainstream; or they have challenged it, holding that innocence hostage until their demand for entry (or other concessions) was met. A bargainer says, *I already believe you are innocent (good, fair-minded) and have faith that you will prove it.* A challenger says, *If you are innocent, then prove it.* Bargainers *give* in hope of receiving; challengers *withhold* until they receive. Of course, there is risk in both approaches, but in each case the black is negotiating his own self-interest against the presumed racial innocence of the larger society.

Clearly the most visible black bargainer on the American scene today is Bill Cosby. His television show is a perfect formula for black bargaining in the '80s. The remarkable Huxtable family—with its doctor/lawyer parent combination, its drug-free, college-bound children, and its wise yet youthful grandparents—is a blackface version of the American dream. Cosby is a subscriber to the American identity, and his subscription confirms his belief in its fair-mindedness. His vast audience knows this, knows that Cosby will never assault their innocence with racial guilt. Racial controversy is all but banished from the show. The Huxtable family never discusses affirmative action.

The bargain Cosby offers his white viewers—I will confirm your racial innocence if you accept me—is a good deal for all concerned. Not only does it allow whites to enjoy Cosby's humor with no loss of innocence, but it actually enhances their innocence by implying that race is not the serious problem for blacks that it once was. If anything, the success of this handsome, affluent black family points to the fair-mindedness of whites who, out of their essential good-ness, changed society so that black families like the Huxtables could succeed. Whites can watch *The Cosby Show* and feel complimented on a job well done.

The power that black bargainers wield is the power of absolution. On Thursday nights, Cosby, like a priest, absolves his white viewers, forgives and forgets the sins of the past. (Interestingly, Cosby was one of the first blacks last winter to publicly absolve Jimmy the Greek for his well-publicized faux pas about black athletes.) And for this he is rewarded with an almost sacrosanct status. Cosby benefits from what might be called a gratitude factor. His contin-ued number-one rating may have something to do with the (white) public's gratitude at being offered a commodity so rare in our time; he tells his white viewers each week that they are okay, and that this black man is not going to challenge them.

When a black bargains, he may invoke the gratitude factor and find himself cherished beyond the measure of his achievement; when he challenges, he may draw the dark projections of whites and become a source of irritation to them. If he moves back and forth between these two options, as I think many blacks do today, he will likely baffle whites. It is difficult for whites to either accept or reject such blacks. It seems to me that Jesse Jackson is such a figure—many whites see Jackson as a challenger by instinct and a bargainer by political ambition. They are uneasy with him, more than a little suspicious. His powerful speech at the 1984 Democratic convention was a masterpiece of bargaining. In it he offered a Kinglike vision of what America could be, a vision that presup-posed Americans had the fair-mindedness to achieve full equality—an offer in hope of a return. A few days after this speech, looking for rest and privacy at a lodge in Big Sur, he and his wife were greeted with standing ovations three times a day when they entered the dining room for meals. So much about Jackson is deeply American—his underdog striving, his irrepressible faith in himself, the daring of his ambition, and even his stubbornness. These qualities point to his underlying faith that Americans can respond to him despite his race, and this faith is a compliment to Americans, an offer of innocence.

But Jackson does not always stick to the terms of his bargain—he is not like Cosby on TV. When he hugs Arafat, smokes cigars with Castro, refuses to repudiate Farrakhan, threatens a boycott of major league baseball, or, more recently, talks of "corporate barracudas," "pension-fund socialism," and "economic violence," he looks like a challenger in bargainer's clothing, and his positions on the issues look like familiar protests dressed in white-paper formality. At these times he appears to be revoking the innocence so much else about him seems to offer. The old activist seems to come out of hiding once again to take white innocence hostage until whites prove they deserve to have it. In his candidacy there is a suggestion of protest, a fierce insistence on his *right* to run, that sends whites a message that he may secretly see them as a good bit less than innocent. His dilemma is to appear the bargainer while his campaign itself seems to be a challenge.

There are, of course, other problems that hamper Jackson's bid for the Democratic presidential nomination. He has held no elective office, he is thought too flamboyant and opportunistic by many, there are rather loud whispers of "character" problems. As an individual he may not be the best test of a black man's chances for winning so high an office. Still, I believe it is the aura of challenge surrounding him that hurts him most. Whether it is right or wrong, fair or unfair, I think no black candidate will have a serious chance at his party's nomination, much less the presidency, until he can convince white Americans that he can be trusted to preserve *their* sense of racial innocence. Such a candidate will have to use his power of absolution; he will have to flatly forgive and forget. He will have to bargain with white innocence out of a genuine belief that it really exists. There can be no faking it. He will have to offer a vision that is passionately raceless, a vision that strongly condemns any form of racial politics. This will require the most courageous kind of leadership, leadership that asks all the people to meet a new standard.

Now the other side of America's racial impasse: How do blacks lay claim to their racial innocence?

The most obvious and unarguable source of black innocence is the victimization that blacks endured for centuries at the hands of a race that insisted on black inferiority as a means to its own innocence and power. Like all victims, what blacks lost in power they gained in innocence—innocence that, in turn, entitled them to pursue power. This was the innocence that fueled the civil rights movement of the '60s, and that gave blacks their first real power in American life—victimization metamorphosed into power via innocence. But this formula carries a drawback that I believe is virtually as devastating to blacks today as victimization once was. It is a formula that binds the victim to his victimization by linking his power to his status as a victim. And this, I'm convinced, is the tragedy of black power in America today. It is primarily a victim's power, grounded too deeply in the entitlement derived from past injustice and in the innocence that Western/Christian tradition has always associated with poverty.

Whatever gains this power brings in the short run through political action, it undermines in the long run. Social victims may be collectively entitled, but they are all too often individually demoralized. Since the social victim has been oppressed by society, he comes to feel that his individual life will be improved more by changes *in* society than by his own initiative. Without realizing it, he makes society rather than himself the agent of change. The power he finds in his victimization may lead him to collective action against society, but it also encourages passivity within the sphere of his personal life.

This past summer I saw a television documentary that examined life in Detroit's inner city on the twentieth anniversary of the riots there in which forty-three people were killed. A comparison of the inner city then and now showed a decline in the quality of life. Residents feel less safe than they did twenty years ago, drug trafficking is far worse, crimes by blacks against blacks are more frequent, housing remains substandard, and the teenage pregnancy rate has skyrocketed. Twenty years of decline and demoralization, even as opportunities for blacks to better themselves have increased. This paradox is not peculiar to Detroit. By many measures, the majority of blacks—those not yet in the middle class—are further behind whites today than before the victories of the civil rights movement. But there is a reluctance among blacks to examine this paradox, I think, because it suggests that racial victimization is not our real problem. If conditions have worsened for most of us as racism has receded, then much of the problem must be of our own making. But to fully admit this would cause us to lose the innocence we derive from our victimization. And we would jeopardize the entitlement we've always had to challenge society. We are in the odd and self-defeating position where taking responsibility for bettering ourselves feels like a surrender to white power.

So we have a hidden investment in victimization and poverty. These distressing conditions have been the source of our only real power, and there is an unconscious sort of gravitation toward them, a complaining celebration of them. One sees evidence of this in the near happiness with which certain black leaders recount the horror of Howard Beach and other recent (and I think over-celebrated) instances of racial tension. As one is saddened by these tragic events, one is also repelled at the way some black leaders—agitated to near hysteria by the scent of victim-power inherent in them—leap forward to exploit them as evidence of black innocence and white guilt. It is as though they sense the decline of black victimization as a loss of standing and dive into the middle of these incidents as if they were reservoirs of pure black innocence swollen with potential power.

Seeing for innocence pressures blacks to focus on racism and to neglect the individual initiative that would deliver them from poverty—the only thing that finally delivers anyone from poverty. With our eyes on innocence we see racism everywhere and miss opportunity even as we stumble over it. About 70 percent of black students at my university drop out before graduating—a flight from opportunity that racism cannot explain. It is an injustice that whites can *see for innocence* with more impunity than blacks can. The price whites pay is a certain blindness to themselves. Moreover, for whites *seeing for innocence* continues to engender the bad faith of a long-disgruntled minority. But the price blacks pay is an ever-escalating poverty that threatens to make the worst off of them a permanent underclass. Not fair, but real.

Challenging works best for the collective, while bargaining is more the individual's suit. From this point on, the race's advancement will come from the efforts of its individuals. True, some challenging will be necessary for a long time to come. But bargaining is now—today—a way for the black individual to *join* the larger society, to make a place for himself or herself.

"Innocence is ignorance," Kierkegaard says, and if this is so, the claim of innocence amounts to an insistence on ignorance, a refusal to know. In their assertions of innocence both races carve out very functional areas of ignorance for themselves—territories of blindness that license a misguided pursuit of power. Whites gain superiority by *not* knowing blacks; blacks gain entitlement by *not* seeing their own responsibility for bettering themselves. The power each race seeks in relation to the other is grounded in a double-edged ignorance, ignorance of the self as well as the other.

The original sin that brought us to an impasse at the dinner party I mentioned at the outset occurred centuries ago, when it was first decided to exploit racial difference as a means to power. It was the determinism that flowed karmically from this sin that dropped over us like a net that night. What bothered me most was our helplessness. Even the engineer did not know how to go forward. His challenge hadn't worked, and he'd lost the option to bargain. The marriage of race and power depersonalized us, changed us from eight people to six whites and two blacks. The easiest thing was to let silence blanket our situation, our impasse.

I think the civil rights movement in its early and middle years offered the best way out of America's racial impasse: in this society, race must not be a source of advantage or disadvantage for anyone. This is fundamentally a *moral* position, one that seeks to breach the corrupt union of race and power with principles of fairness and human equality: if all men are created equal, then racial difference cannot sanction power. The civil rights movement was conceived for no other reason than to redress that corrupt union, and its guiding insight was that only a moral power based on enduring principles of justice, equality, and freedom could offset the lower impulse in man to exploit race as a means to power. Three hundred years of suffering had driven the point home, and in Montgomery, Little Rock, and Selma, racial power was the enemy and moral power the weapon.

An important difference between genuine and presumed innocence, I believe, is that the former must be earned through sacrifice, while the latter is unearned and only veils the quest for privilege. And there was much sacrifice in the early civil rights movement. The Gandhian principle of non-violent resistance that gave the movement a spiritual center as well as a method of protest demanded sacrifice, a passive offering of the self in the name of justice. A price was paid in terror and lost life, and from this sacrifice came a hard-earned innocence and a credible moral power.

Non-violent passive resistance is a bargainer's strategy. It assumes the power that is the object of the protest has the genuine innocence to morally respond, and puts the protesters at the mercy of that innocence. I think this movement won so many concessions precisely because of its belief in the capacity of whites to be moral. It did not so much demand that whites change as offer them relentlessly the opportunity to live by their own morality—to attain a true innocence based on the sacrifice of their racial privilege, rather than a false innocence based on presumed racial superiority. Blacks always bargain with or challenge the larger society; but I believe that in the early civil rights years, these forms of negotiation achieved a degree of integrity and genuineness never seen before or since.

In the mid-'60s all this changed. Suddenly a sharp *racial* consciousness emerged to compete with the moral consciousness that had defined the movement to that point. Whites were no longer welcome in the movement, and a vocal "black power" minority gained dramatic visibility. Increasingly, the movement began to seek racial as well as moral power, and thus it fell into a fundamental contradiction that plagues it to this day. Moral power precludes racial power by denouncing race as a means to power. Now suddenly the movement itself was using race as a means to power, and thereby affirming the very union of race and power it was born to redress. In the end, black power can claim no higher moral standing than white power.

It makes no sense to say this shouldn't have happened. The sacrifices that moral power demands are difficult to sustain, and it was inevitable that blacks would tire of these sacrifices and seek a more earthly power. Nevertheless, a loss of genuine innocence and moral power followed. The movement, splint·ered by a burst of racial militancy in the late '60s, lost its hold on the American conscience and descended more and more to the level of secular, interest-group politics. Bargaining and challenging once again became racial rather than moral negotiations.

You hear it asked, why are there no Martin Luther Kings around today? I think one reason is that there are no black leaders willing to resist the seductions of racial power, or to make the sacrifices moral power requires. King understood that racial power subverts moral power, and he pushed the principles of fairness and equality rather than black power because he believed those principles would bring blacks their most complete liberation. He sacrificed race for morality, and his innocence was made genuine by that sacrifice. What made King the most powerful and extraordinary black leader of this century was not his race but his morality.

Black power is a challenge. It grants whites no innocence; it denies their moral capacity and then demands that they be moral. No power can long insist on itself without evoking an opposing power. Doesn't an insistence on black power call up white power? (And could this have something to do with what many are now calling a resurgence of white racism?) I believe that what divided the races at the dinner party I attended, and what divides them in the nation, can only be bridged by an adherence to those moral principles that disallow race as a source of power, privilege, status, or entitlement of any kind. In our age, principles like fairness and equality are ill-defined and all but drowned in relativity. But this is the fault of people, not principles. We keep them muddied because they are the greatest threat to our presumed innocence and our selective ignorance. Moral principles, even when somewhat ambiguous, have the power to assign responsibility and therefore to provide us with knowledge. At the dinner party we were afraid of so severe an accountability.

What both black and white Americans fear are the sacrifices and risks that true racial harmony demands. This fear is the measure of our racial chasm. And though fear always seeks a thousand justifications, none is ever good enough, and the problems we run from only remain to haunt us. It would be right to suggest courage as an antidote to fear, but the glory of the word might only intimidate us into more fear. I prefer the word effort—relentless effort, moral effort. What I like most about this word are its connotations of everydayness, earnestness, and practical sacrifice. No matter how badly it might have gone for us that warm summer night, we should have talked. We should have made the effort.

QUESTIONS FOR "I'M BLACK, YOU'RE WHITE, WHO'S INNOCENT?" BY SHELBY STEELE

Talking About the Text

1. What rhetorical effect does Steele obtain by beginning his essay with the dinner party anecdote? Would Steele's essay have been more or less effective if that particular story had not been included?
2. Throughout the essay Steele uses the phrase "seeing for innocence." What does the phrase mean to you in the context of the essay? What meaning(s) do you think Steele assigns to the phrase, and how does it serve the essay as a whole?
3. What difference does Steele see between the civil rights movement of the fifties and early sixties and the black power movement of the mid- and late sixties? According to Steele, how does this difference affect the attainment of racial harmony?

Exploring Issues

1. According to Steele, what relationship does power have to race relations? Do you agree with his position?
2. Steele asserts that

social victims may be collectively entitled, but they are all too often individually demoralized. Since the social victim has been oppressed by society, he comes to feel that his individual life will be improved more by changes *in* society than by his own initiative. . . . The power he finds in his victimization may lead him to collective action against society, but it also encourages passivity within the sphere of his personal life.

Why do you think Steele chooses to separate the individual from society as a whole in the context of race relations? Do you think they can be separated? Why or why not?

3. Steele states, "No power can long insist on itself without evoking an opposing power. Doesn't an insistence on black power call up white power? (And could this have something to do with what many are calling a resurgence of white racism?)" To what extent do you think Steele's opinion is valid? What evidence can you think of that might support or refute Steele's claim?

4. According to Steele, racial power subverts moral power, and in so doing sacrifices true racial harmony. Do you think an insistence on racial power will make racial harmony impossible, or can the two coexist?

5. Steele writes, "We have a hidden investment in victimization and poverty. . . . One sees evidence of this in the near happiness with which certain black leaders recount the horror of Howard Beach and other recent (and highly celebrated) instances of racial tension." How might Rosemary Bray ("It's Ten O'Clock and I Worry About Where My Husband Is") respond to this statement?

Writing Assignment

Steele asserts that "what both black and white Americans fear are the sacrifices and risks that true racial harmony demands." Write an expository essay in which you explore the nature of these "sacrifices and risks." How might we define them? What are their complexities? Use specific examples from either your reading or personal knowledge to support and develop your ideas. You need not feel bound to Steele's notions of sacrifice and risk. Rather, try to develop your own perspective on this issue.

Reading 60

Campus Racism

Walter E. Williams

Walter E. Williams is the John M. Olin Distinguished Professor of Economics at George Mason University. He is also the author of *South Africa's War*

Against Capitalism. In the following essay Williams asserts that the rise in campus racism may not be due to, as many claim, an atmosphere of intolerance created by the Reagan Administration but rather may be the result of current affirmative action policies utilized by college and university admissions offices. He claims that "whatever justification may be given for such a practice, it cannot help but build resentment, bitterness, and a sense of unfair play among whites."

The decade of the 1980s has seen a rise in racial incidents on America's campuses. At Smith College, "NIGGERS, SPICS, AND CHINKS QUIT COMPLAINING OR GET OUT" was painted on a campus building. In a UC Berkeley building, "NIPS GO HOME" was scrawled on the wall. The University of Michigan's Ann Arbor campus radio station featured ethnic jokes aimed at blacks. *The Dartmouth Review,* an independent conservative student newspaper, published an article satirizing black language titled, "Dis Sho' Ain't No Jive, Bro." A leaflet opposing Holocaust studies and a swastika painted on a wall were found at Stanford University. At Philadelphia's Temple University, a White Student's Union was formed. Since 1986, the National Institute against Prejudice and Violence has documented racial incidents on 160 college campuses, including some of the nation's most prestigious. In addition, more and more colleges are becoming the focal point of membership recruitment by the White Aryan Resistance, Skinheads, and the Ku Klux Klan.

Racial incidents have not been a one-sided coin. A black full professor at Dartmouth College frequently uses the term "honky" in his classroom in reference to whites. A black student at Vassar College hurled anti-Semitic insults at a Jewish student which included "dirty Jew," "stupid Jews," and "f------ Jew." At the University of Pennsylvania campus, three black non-students crushed the skull of an Oriental student. On the campuses of Drexel University and the University of Pennsylvania, black non-students have been alleged to systematically seek out white students to extort and rob.

Civil-rights advocates, affirmative-action officials, and politicians see the increase in campus racial incidents as the result of an "atmosphere" created by the Reagan Administration. Their reasoning is that by its attacks on affirmative action, the Administration created a perception of a tolerance for racism. To counteract this "atmosphere," there have been calls for more affirmative-action recruitment programs, mandated Black Studies classes as part of the college curriculum, more "cultural diversity," and more resources devoted to race relations.

Here we might explore the opposite line of causation and ask instead, what role has current campus racial policy played in the build-up of resentment and bitterness, and the consequent rise in campus racial incidents?

Affirmative action in recruitment makes the assumption, implicit or explicit, that a pool of black academic talent exists and that the paucity of blacks enrolled in the nation's colleges, medical schools, and law schools is a result of racial discrimination in admissions. Whether colleges currently engage in discriminatory policies against blacks is a matter for speculation; however, the question of just how large is the pool of black academic talent that meets standard college admissions criteria is not.

Black students score well below the national average on every measure of academic achievement. In 1983, fewer than 4,200 black college-bound high-school graduates, out of 75,400, had grade-point averages of 3.75 (B+) or better, compared to 7,858 out of 36,048 Asians, and 115,722 out of 701,345 whites. That means that 5.5 per cent of black college-bound seniors earned B+ averages, compared to nearly 22 per cent for Asians and 16.5 per cent for whites.

Standard Achievement Test (SAT) scores tell an even more dismal story about college preparation. In 1983, across the nation, 66 out of 71,137 black college-bound seniors (less than a tenth of 1 per cent) achieved 699, out of a possible 800, on the verbal portion of the SAT, and fewer than a thousand achieved scores of 600 or higher. On the mathematics portion of the SAT, 205 blacks had scores over 699 and fewer than 1,700 achieved scores of 600 or higher.

Of the roughly 35,200 Asians taking the test, 496 scored over 699 on the verbal portion (1.4 per cent) and 3,015 on the mathematics. Of the roughly 963,000 whites taking the test, 9,028 scored over 699 on the verbal (just under 1 per cent) and 31,704 scored over 699 on the mathematics.

An important debate wages over just what SAT scores measure and predict, and how reliably they do so. Regardless of the outcome of the debate, the tests do say something about academic achievement in the tested material. Black performance on them has important implications concerning the availability of academically qualified black students for college recruitment.

At some of the nation's most prestigious schools, the SAT scores of the student body are as follows: at Amherst, 66 per cent of the students score above 600 on the verbal and 83 per cent above 600 on the mathematics; at Bryn Mawr, 70 per cent above 600 on the verbal and 70 per cent over 600 on the mathematics; at Haverford, 67 and 86 per cent; at MIT, 72 and 97 per cent. The median student SAT scores for the verbal and mathematics portions are 600 at Brown, Columbia, Cornell, Dartmouth, Duke, Georgetown, Harvard, Oberlin, Princeton, Williams, Yale, and other colleges ranked as most competitive. Student SAT scores at schools ranked very competitive, such as Franklin and Marshall, Lafayette, Brandeis, and Lehigh, range in the high 500s and low 600s.

The black scores on the SAT, compared with the SAT performance of the general student body at the most prestigious schools, suggests that even if these schools made every heroic recruitment effort, it would be impossible to find much more than a tiny handful of blacks who would match the academic characteristics of these schools' average student. In 1983, there were 570 blacks who had combined SAT verbal and mathematics scores above 1,200, compared to 60,400 whites who did. That means, given the paucity of well-qualified blacks, that less-elite schools, among the nation's more than three thousand institutions of higher learning, are quickly left drawing from the lower end of the pool of college-bound black students.

At the graduate-school level, the academic tale is even more gruesome.

The Graduate Record Examination (GRE) is used as a part of the admissions process by most graduate schools. It has three parts, verbal, quantitative, and analytical. In 1983, the mean national GRE scores were 499 on the verbal, 516 on the quantitative, and 522 on the analytical. Black mean scores were well below the national means: 370 on the verbal, 363 on the quantitative, and 363 on the analytical, which translates into a 129-point deficit on the verbal, 153 on the quantitative, and 159 on the analytical. Black performance on the GRE is lower than that of any other ethnic group reported taking the test (American Indians, Mexican-Americans, Asians, Puerto Ricans, Latin Americans, and Whites).

Poor black performance on standardized tests is frequently dismissed as owing to cultural bias of the test. If the charge of cultural bias has merit in the first place, in the sense that a culture-free test could be devised, one would expect cultural bias to be exhibited most strongly on the verbal portion of the test, where there are questions of reading comprehension, language, and litera-ture. A much better performance relative to the national mean would be ex-pected on those parts of the test where cultural bias is minimized—i.e., mathe-matics and analytic reasoning. As it turns out, blacks are closer to the national norm on the verbal portion of the GRE and furthest behind on the quantitative and analytical portions.

The Asian population is more culturally distinct than other reported groups taking the GRE. However, the mean Asian score on the verbal portion of the GRE is 479, just 20 points below the national mean and 109 points higher than blacks. On the quantitative portion of the GRE, Asians' mean score is 575, outscoring the nation by 59 points. On the analytical portion, the Asian mean score is 522, identical with the national mean. Therefore, we might ask: If the examination is culturally biased, how is it that people of a culture far more alien to the American culture score close to the national mean?

Black performance on the GRE also allows us a preliminary assessment of what goes on while blacks are undergraduates. When blacks enter college as freshmen, their SAT scores as a percentage of the national norm are about 80 per cent. After four years of college, those who take the GRE achieve scores that are only 71 per cent of the national norm. Whatever the caveats regarding what tests measure, an unambiguous conclusion is that the achievement deficit of blacks does not diminish during four years of undergraduate training.

The fact that the black achievement deficit does not diminish demands more investigation into the possible reasons. Maybe there is nothing that can be done in the space of four or five years of college to significantly repair pre-college damage. Maybe the pattern of courses chosen by black students are not the most effective in terms of remediation. In any case, much more needs to be done to search for answers to these important questions.

Colleges and universities, under many sources of pressure, have sought to increase their enrollment of black students. If colleges adhered to rigid aca-demic guidelines for admission, most would be frustrated in these efforts. Therefore, academic standards must be compromised. That is, colleges and universities must have one standard for admittance for whites and a lower one for blacks.

Whatever justification may be given for such a practice, it cannot help but build resentment, bitterness, and a sense of unfair play among whites, as it has already in matters of hiring, promotions, and layoffs. Official policy calling for unequal treatment by race is morally offensive whether it is applied to favor blacks or applied to favor whites.

Recently, charges have surfaced about discrimination against Asian-Americans at some of the nation's most prestigious colleges like UCLA, Harvard, Berkeley, and Brown. In 1982, Asians admitted to Harvard had a combined SAT score of 1,467, compared to a combined SAT score of 1,355 for whites. On the average, an Asian had to score over 100 points higher to be admitted than a white. At Brown, between 1983 and 1987, the Asian admittance rate declined, while Asian academic performance (SAT scores and grade-point averages) increased.

Jack Bunzel reports in *The Public Interest* (Fall 1988) that "virtually all American-Indians, Hispanics, and blacks who apply to Berkeley, and meet the minimum UC requirements, are admitted [though it is possible to meet those requirements with a GPA of 2.78]. . . . white or Asian students are rarely accepted by Berkeley without a GPA of at least 3.7 or 3.8." According to Bunzel, for an Asian to have a 50 percent chance of admission to Berkeley, he needs to have an Academic Index score of 7,000, while a score of 4,800 is enough for a black.

The other side of the admittance issue is the graduation issue. According to Bunzel, UC Berkeley figures show that 66 per cent of white students and 61 per cent of Asian students graduate within five years. Only 41 per cent of Hispanics and 27 per cent of blacks graduate in five years. These facts show that affirmative-action programs in college recruitment do not come close to being even a zero-sum game where blacks benefit at the expense of Asians. It is more like a negative-sum game, where everybody is worse off. In other words, Berkeley's affirmative-action program leads to the rejection of Asian and white students with a higher probability of graduation in favor of black and Hispanic students with a significantly lower probability of graduation. Thus, white and Asian students are being sacrificed to the benefit of no one.

This kind of affirmative action is not only inept social policy, it produces personal tragedy. Bunzel relates a story told by Donald H. Werner, headmaster of Westminster School:

UC Berkeley made decisions on two of its students this past year, both Californians. Student A was ranked in the top third of his class, student B in the bottom third. Student A had College Board scores totalling 1,290; student B's scores totaled 890. Student A had a good record of citizenship; student B was expelled last winter for breaking a series of major school rules. Student A was white; student B was black. Berkeley refused student A and accepted student B.

The use of dual standards by college administrators, in an effort to produce "diversity" in the student body, is widespread. Whatever noble goals foster dual standards, one of their side-effects is that of producing racial animosity and resentment. It is easy to understand, though not to justify, how individuals who may never have harbored feelings of racial resentment can come to resent blacks, Hispanics, and other "protected" groups.

Blacks have difficult experiences on campus: high chances of being on academic probation and feelings of alienation from the larger community, which may be manifested in self-segregation, and dropping out of college. Today, there is little evidence of acts of official college racial discrimination against blacks. The bulk of black problems stem from poor academic preparation for college. Continually focusing on affirmative-action programs at the college level, while ignoring the massive educational fraud taking place at the primary and secondary schools blacks attend, means that campus problems will exist in perpetuity. It means most blacks will always need special admission privileges.

Today, many major cities have black mayors, large black representation on the city councils, and many black teachers and principals; in some large cities the superintendent of schools is black. That means blacks have many more policy choices than they had in the past. In the name of future generations of blacks, it is high time that responsible black people stop worrying about what whites are doing to blacks and begin to focus on what blacks are doing to blacks.

QUESTIONS FOR "CAMPUS RACISM" BY WALTER E. WILLIAMS

Talking About the Text

1. Williams supports much of his argument with the use of statistics. To what extent does the use of these statistics help Williams's argument? Do you find certain statistics more convincing than others in this article?

2. Williams reasons that if cultural bias on standardized tests were a legitimate concern, then at the graduate level blacks would perform better on the quantitative section of the GRE than the verbal section, because questions of language and literature would be asked. In fact, he points out that just the opposite is the case. How valid is Williams's line of reasoning? Can you offer any alternative explanations?

Exploring Issues

1. Williams asserts that "continually focusing on affirmative action programs at the college level, while ignoring the massive educational fraud taking place at the primary and secondary schools blacks attend, means that campus problems will exist in perpetuity. It means blacks will always need special admission privileges." Speculate about what Williams means by the term "massive educational fraud." Does it exist, and if so, what is it and what are its origins?

2. Do you agree with Williams that the racial tension that has recently resurfaced on college campuses has resulted more from "resentment and bitterness" about affirmative action practices than from a "tolerance of racism" caused by the Administration's attacks on affirmative action? Why or why not?

3. According to Williams, "it is high time that responsible black people stop worrying about what whites are doing to blacks and begin to focus on what blacks are doing to blacks". To what extent is this assertion valid? To what extent is it feasible?
4. Speculate about the negative and/or positive consequences of ending affirmative action.

Writing Assignments

1. Write an argumentative essay in which you take a stand on the use of affirmative action by university and college admissions officials. Be sure to use specific examples and illustrations to support your opinions.
2. Williams criticizes the use of affirmative action, asserting that "whatever noble goals foster dual standards, one of their side-effects is that of producing racial animosity and resentment." However, he proposes no concrete solutions to the problems of racial inequity in education. Write an essay in which you propose either revisions to the present affirmative action policy or an alternative plan. You may need to do some research in order to develop a strong case for your proposal.
3. Interview students and faculty at your campus about their views on campus racism and prejudice. Do they feel it has increased in recent years? What do they see as potential causes of campus prejudice? What effects do they feel may result from an increase in this sort of behavior? What potential solutions do they think might help alleviate the tension of campus racism and prejudice? Write up your findings in the form of an informative report.

Reading 61

"**The Library Card**"

Richard Wright

Richard Wright was born in Natchez, Mississippi, in 1908 and was raised in Memphis. He educated himself through a disciplined reading program, having attended school formally only until ninth grade. After moving to

Chicago, Wright worked with the Federal Writer's Project. Later he established himself in New York City, where he wrote for the *Daily Worker* and prepared the government-sponsored *Guide to Harlem* (1937). In 1938 he published a series of novellas entitled *Uncle Tom's Children*. However, he is probably best-known for his novel *Native Son* (1940). His later works include *Black Power* (1954), *The Color Curtain* (1956), and *White Man, Listen!* (1957). "The Library Card" is taken from his powerful autobiography, *Black Boy* (1945). In this selection Wright recounts how in the midst of racist oppression he discovered a passion for reading.

One morning I arrived early at work and went into the bank lobby where the Negro porter was mopping. I stood at a counter and picked up the Memphis *Commercial Appeal* and began my free reading of the press. I came finally to the editorial page and saw an article dealing with one H. L. Mencken. I knew by hearsay that he was the editor of the *American Mercury*, but aside from that I knew nothing about him. The article was a furious denunciation of Mencken, concluding with one, hot, short sentence: Mencken is a fool.

I wondered what on earth this Mencken had done to call down upon him the scorn of the South. The only people I had ever heard denounced in the South were Negroes, and this man was not a Negro. Then what ideas did Mencken hold that made a newspaper like the *Commercial Appeal* castigate him publicly? Undoubtedly he must be advocating ideas that the South did not like. Were there, then, people other than Negroes who criticized the South? I knew that during the Civil War the South had hated northern whites, but I had not encountered such hate during my life. Knowing no more of Mencken than I did at that moment, I felt a vague sympathy for him. Had not the South, which had assigned me the role of a non-man, cast at him its hardest words?

Now, how could I find out about this Mencken? There was a huge library near the riverfront, but I knew that Negroes were not allowed to patronize its shelves any more than they were the parks and playgrounds of the city. I had gone into the library several times to get books for the white men on the job. Which of them would now help me to get books? And how could I read them without causing concern to the white men with whom I worked? I had so far been successful in hiding my thoughts and feelings from them, but I knew that I would create hostility if I went about this business of reading in a clumsy way.

I weighted the personalities of the men on the job. There was Don, a Jew; but I distrusted him. His position was not much better than mine and I knew that he was uneasy and insecure; he had always treated me in an offhand, bantering way that barely concealed his contempt. I was afraid to ask him to help me to get books; his frantic desire to demonstrate a racial solidarity with the whites against Negroes might make him betray me.

Then how about the boss? No, he was a Baptist and I had the suspicion that he would not be quite able to comprehend why a black boy would want to read Mencken. There were other white men on the job whose attitudes showed clearly that they were Kluxers or sympathizers, and they were out of the question.

There remained only one man whose attitude did not fit into an anti-Negro category, for I had heard the white men refer to him as a "Pope lover." He was an Irish Catholic and was hated by the white Southerners. I knew that he read books, because I had got him volumes from the library several times. Since he, too, was an object of hatred, I felt that he might refuse me but would hardly betray me. I hesitated, weighing and balancing the imponderable realities.

One morning I paused before the Catholic fellow's desk.

"I want to ask you a favor," I whispered to him.

"What is it?"

"I want to read. I can't get books from the library. I wonder if you'd let me use your card?"

He looked at me suspiciously.

"My card is full most of the time," he said.

"I see," I said and waited, posing my question silently.

"You're not trying to get me into trouble, are you, boy?" he asked, staring at me.

"Oh, no, sir."

"What book do you want?"

"A book by H. L. Mencken."

"Which one?"

"I don't know. Has he written more than one?"

"He has written several."

"I didn't know that."

"What makes you want to read Mencken?"

"Oh, I just saw his name in the newspaper," I said.

"It's good of you to want to read," he said. "But you ought to read the right things."

I said nothing. Would he want to supervise my reading?

"Let me think," he said. "I'll figure out something."

I turned from him and he called me back. He stared at me quizzically.

"Richard, don't mention this to the other white men," he said.

"I understand," I said. "I won't say a word."

A few days later he called me to him.

"I've got a card in my wife's name," he said. "Here's mine."

"Thank you, sir."

"Do you think you can manage it?"

"I'll manage fine," I said.

"If they suspect you, you'll get in trouble," he said.

"I'll write the same kind of notes to the library that you wrote when you sent me for books," I told him. "I'll sign your name."

He laughed.

"Go ahead. Let me see what you get," he said.

That afternoon I addressed myself to forging a note. Now, what were the names of books written by H. L. Mencken? I did not know any of them. I finally wrote what I thought would be a foolproof note: *Dear Madam: Will you please let this nigger boy*—I used the word "nigger" to make the librarian feel that I could not possibly be the author of the note—*have some books by H. L. Mencken?* I forged the white man's name.

I entered the library as I had always done when on errands for whites, but I felt that I would somehow slip up and betray myself. I doffed my hat, stood a respectful distance from the desk, looked as unbookish as possible, and waited for the white patrons to be taken care of. When the desk was clear of people, I still waited. The white librarian looked at me.

"What do you want, boy?"

As though I did not possess the power of speech, I stepped forward and simply handed her the forged note, not parting my lips.

"What books by Mencken does he want?" she asked.

"I don't know, ma'am," I said, avoiding her eyes.

"Who gave you this card?"

"Mr. Falk," I said.

"Where is he?"

"He's at work, at the M——— Optical Company," I said. "I've been in here for him before."

"I remember," the woman said. "But he never wrote notes like this."

Oh, God, she's suspicious. Perhaps she would not let me have the books? If she had turned her back at that moment, I would have ducked out the door and never gone back. Then I thought of a bold idea.

"You can call him up, ma'am," I said, my heart pounding.

"You're not using these books, are you?" she asked pointedly.

"Oh, no, ma'am. I can't read."

"I don't know what he wants by Mencken," she said under her breath.

I knew now that I had won; she was thinking of other things and the race question had gone out of her mind. She went to the shelves. Once or twice she looked over her shoulder at me, as though she was still doubtful. Finally she came forward with two books in her hand.

"I'm sending him two books," she said. "But tell Mr. Falk to come in next time, or send me the names of the books he wants. I don't know what he wants to read."

I said nothing. She stamped the card and handed me the books. Not daring to glance at them, I went out of the library, fearing that the woman could call me back for further questioning. A block away from the library I opened one of the books and read a title: *A Book of Prefaces*. I was nearing my nineteenth birthday and I did not know how to pronounce the word "preface." I thumbed the pages and saw strange words and strange names. I shook my head, disappointed. I looked at the other book; it was called *Prejudices*. I knew what that word meant; I had heard it all my life. And right off I was on guard against Mencken's books. Why would a man want to call a book *Prejudices?* The word was so stained with all my memories of racial hate that I could not conceive of anybody using it for a title. Perhaps I had made a mistake about Mencken? A man who had prejudices must be wrong.

When I showed the books to Mr. Falk, he looked at me and frowned.

"That librarian might telephone you," I warned him.

"That's all right," he said. "But when you're through reading those books, I want you to tell me what you get out of them."

That night in my rented room, while letting the hot water run over my can of pork and beans in the sink, I opened *A Book of Prefaces* and began to read. I was jarred and shocked by the style, the clear, clean sweeping sentences. Why did he write like that? And how did one write like that? I pictured the man as a raging demon, slashing with his pen, consumed with hate, denouncing everything American, extolling everything European or German, laughing at the weaknesses of people, mocking God, authority. What was this? I stood up, trying to realize what reality lay behind the meaning of the words . . . Yes, this man was fighting, fighting with words. He was using words as a weapon, using them as one would use a club. Could words be weapons? Well, yes, for here they were. Then, maybe, perhaps, I could use them as a weapon? No. It frightened me. I read on and what amazed me was not what he said, but how on earth anybody had the courage to say it.

Occasionally I glanced up to reassure myself that I was alone in the room. Who were these men about whom Mencken was talking so passionately? Who was Anatole France? Joseph Conrad? Sinclair Lewis, Sherwood Anderson, Dostoevski, George Moore, Gustave Flaubert, Maupassant, Tolstoy, Frank Harris, Mark Twain, Thomas Hardy, Arnold Bennett, Stephen Crane, Zola, Norris, Gorky, Bergson, Ibsen, Balzac, Bernard Shaw, Dumas, Poe, Thomas Mann, O. Henry, Dreiser, H. G. Wells, Gogol, T. S. Eliot, Gide, Baudelaire, Edgar Lee Masters, Stendhal, Turgenev, Huneker, Nietzsche, and scores of others? Were these men real? Did they exist or had they existed? And how did one pronounce their names?

I ran across many words whose meanings I did not know, and I either looked them up in a dictionary or, before I had a chance to do that, encountered the word in a context that made its meaning clear. But what strange world was this? I concluded the book with the conviction that I had somehow overlooked something terribly important in life. I had once tried to write, had once reveled in feeling, had let my crude imagination roam, but the impulse to dream had been slowly beaten out of me by experience. Now it surged up again and I hungered for books, new ways of looking and seeing. It was not a matter of believing or disbelieving what I read, but of feeling something new, of being affected by something that made the look of the world different.

As dawn broke I ate my pork and beans, feeling dopey, sleepy. I went to work, but the mood of the book would not die; it lingered, coloring everything I saw, heard, did. I now felt that I knew what the white men were feeling. Merely because I had read a book that had spoken of how they lived and thought. I identified myself with that book. I felt vaguely guilty. Would I, filled with bookish notions, act in a manner that would make the whites dislike me?

I forged more notes and my trips to the library became frequent. Reading grew into a passion. My first serious novel was Sinclair Lewis's *Main Street*. It made me see my boss, Mr. Gerald, and identify him as an American type. I would smile when I saw him lugging his golf bags into the office. I had always felt a vast distance separating me from the boss, and now I felt closer to him, though still distant. I felt now that I knew him, that I could feel the very limits of his narrow life. And this had happened because I had read a novel about a mythical man called George F. Babbitt.

The plots and stories in the novels did not interest me so much as the point of view revealed. I gave myself over to each novel without reserve, without trying to criticize it; it was enough for me to see and feel something different. And for me, everything was something different. Reading was like a drug, a dope. The novels created moods in which I lived for days. But I could not conquer my sense of guilt, my feeling that the white men around me knew that I was changing, that I had begun to regard them differently.

Whenever I brought a book to the job, I wrapped it in newspaper—a habit that was to persist for years in other cities and under other circumstances. But some of the white men pried into my packages when I was absent and they questioned me.

"Boy, what are you reading those books for?"

"Oh, I don't know, sir."

"That's deep stuff you're reading, boy."

"I'm just killing time, sir."

"You'll addle your brains if you don't watch out."

I read Dreiser's *Jennie Gerhardt* and *Sister Carrie* and they revived in me a vivid sense of my mother's suffering; I was overwhelmed. I grew silent, wondering about the life around me. It would have been impossible for me to have told anyone what I derived from these novels, for it was nothing less than a sense of life itself. All my life had shaped me for the realism, the naturalism of the modern novel, and I could not read enough of them.

Steeped in new moods and ideas, I bought a ream of paper and tried to write; but nothing would come, or what did come was flat beyond telling. I discovered that more than desire and feeling were necessary to write and I dropped the idea. Yet I still wondered how it was possible to know people sufficiently to write about them? Could I ever learn about life and people? To me, with my vast ignorance, my Jim Crow station in life, it seemed a task impossible of achievement. I now knew what being a Negro meant. I could endure the hunger. I had learned to live with hate. But to feel that there were feelings denied me, that the very breath of life itself was beyond my reach, that more than anything else hurt, wounded me. I had a new hunger.

In buoying me up, reading also cast me down, made me see what was possible, what I had missed. My tension returned, new, terrible, bitter, surging, almost too great to be contained. I no longer *felt* that the world about me was hostile, killing; I *knew* it. A million times I asked myself what I could do to save myself, and there were no answers. I seemed forever condemned, ringed by walls.

I did not discuss my reading with Mr. Falk, who had lent me his library card; it would have meant talking about myself and that would have been too painful. I smiled each day, fighting desperately to maintain my old behavior, to keep my disposition seemingly sunny. But some of the white men discerned that I had begun to brood.

"Wake up there, boy!" Mr. Olin said one day.

"Sir!" I answered for the lack of a better word.

"You act like you've stolen something," he said.

I laughed in the way I knew he expected me to laugh, but I resolved to be more conscious of myself, to watch my every act, to guard and hide the new knowledge that was dawning within me.

If I went north, would it be possible for me to build a new life then? But how could a man build a life upon vague, unformed yearnings? I wanted to write and I did not even know the English language. I bought English grammars and found them dull. I felt that I was getting a better sense of the language from novels than from grammars. I read hard, discarding a writer as soon as I felt that I had grasped his point of view. At night the printed page stood before my eyes in sleep.

Mrs. Moss, my landlady, asked me one Sunday morning:

"Son, what is this you keep on reading?"

"Oh, nothing. Just novels."

"What you get out of 'em?"

"I'm just killing time," I said.

"I hope you know your own mind," she said in a tone which implied that she doubted if I had a mind.

I knew of no Negroes who read the books I liked and I wondered if any Negroes ever thought of them. I knew that there were Negro doctors, lawyers, newspapermen, but I never saw any of them. When I read a Negro newspaper I never caught the faintest echo of my preoccupation in its pages. I felt trapped and occasionally, for a few days, I would stop reading. But a vague hunger would come over me for books, books that opened up new avenues of feeling and seeing, and again I would forge another note to the white librarian. Again I would read and wonder as only the naïve and unlettered can read and wonder, feeling that I carried a secret, criminal burden about with me each day.

That winter my mother and brother came and we set up housekeeping, buying furniture on the installment plan, being cheated and yet knowing no way to avoid it. I began to eat warm food and to my surprise found that regular meals enabled me to read faster. I may have lived through many illnesses and survived them, never suspecting that I was ill. My brother obtained a job and we began to save toward the trip north, plotting our time, setting tentative dates for departure. I told none of the white men on the job that I was planning to go north; I knew that the moment they felt I was thinking of the North they would change toward me. It would have made them feel that I did not like the life I was living, and because my life was completely conditioned by what they said or did, it would have been tantamount to challenging them.

I could calculate my chances for life in the South as a Negro fairly clearly now.

I could fight the southern whites by organizing with other Negroes, as my grandfather had done. But I knew that I could never win that way; there were many whites and there were but few blacks. They were strong and we were weak. Outright black rebellion could never win. If I fought openly I would die and I did not want to die. News of lynchings was frequent.

I could submit and live the life of a genial slave, but that was impossible. All of my life had shaped me to live by my own feelings, and thoughts. I could make up to Bess and marry her and inherit the house. But that, too, would be the life of a slave; if I did that, I would crush to death something within me, and I would hate myself as much as I knew the whites already hated those who had submitted. Neither could I ever willingly present myself to be kicked, as Shorty had done. I would rather have died than do that.

I could drain off my restlessness by fighting with Shorty and Harrison. I had seen many Negroes solve the problem of being black by transferring their hatred of themselves to others with a black skin and fighting them. I would have to be cold to do that, and I was not cold and I could never be.

I could, of course, forget what I had read, thrust the whites out of my mind, forget them; and find release from anxiety and longing in sex and alcohol. But the memory of how my father had conducted himself made that course repugnant. If I did not want others to violate my life, how could I voluntarily violate it myself?

I had no hope whatever of being a professional man. Not only had I been so conditioned that I did not desire it, but the fulfillment of such an ambition was beyond my capabilities. Well-to-do Negroes lived in a world that was almost as alien to me as the world inhabited by whites.

What, then, was there? I held my life in my mind, in my consciousness each day, feeling at times that I would stumble and drop it, spill it forever. My reading had created a vast sense of distance between me and the world in which I lived and tried to make a living, and that sense of distance was increasing each day. My days and nights were one long, quiet, continuously contained dream of terror, tension, and anxiety. I wondered how long I could bear it.

QUESTIONS FOR "THE LIBRARY CARD" BY RICHARD WRIGHT

Talking About the Text

1. Wright begins this selection by referring to an editorial in the Memphis *Commercial Appeal* that denounced H. L. Mencken as "a fool." Who was H. L. Mencken, and why do you suppose Wright had such a keen interest in finding out more about him? How does this anecdote serve the story as a whole?

2. Wright makes use of dialogue in relating his experiences. What effect does this technique have on you as a reader? What do you think the story would have been like without any dialogue?

3. Near the end of this autobiographical story, Wright begins each new paragraph with "I could. . . ." What is the effect of this repetition on your reading? What rhetorical and/or literary purpose does it serve?

Exploring Issues

1. Wright recalls the difficulty he had in taking out a library card so he could read. At one point, the librarian asks "You're not reading these books, are you?" Why do you suppose a library would be a site for discrimination? What might literacy offer to disenfranchised groups or individuals that groups in power might fear?

2. Wright states that "reading was like a drug, a dope. The novels created moods in which I lived for days. But I could not conquer my sense of guilt, my feeling that the white men around me knew that I was changing, that I had begun to regard them differently." Why do you think Wright refers to reading as a "drug, a dope"? What kind of change do you think he was undergoing? Have you ever had a similar experience?

3. Speculate about the relationship between literacy and freedom. What commentary do you think Wright is making about this relationship?

4. Read through some of the essays in Chapter 6, especially those by Rose and Kozol. How are the issues they raise related to some of Wright's thoughts on the power of literacy?

5. At one point in his story Wright says, "I had seen many Negroes solve the problem of being black by transferring their hatred of themselves to others with black skin and fighting them." What might Wright be saying here about the nature of prejudice?

Writing Assignments

1. Wright seems to have undergone a profound emotional change in his passion for reading. Write a personal narrative in which you recount a reading experience that had a significant effect on you. Be sure to be specific about what you read and *how* you were changed by this experience.

2. Brainstorm on Question 3 of the preceding section. Then write an essay in which you explore possible relationships between literacy and freedom. How are they connected? In what ways is each perhaps a consequence of the other? Why might it be important to look at this relationship?

Reading 62

Why Young Women Are More Conservative

Gloria Steinem

Gloria Steinem was born in 1934 in Ohio. Her professional journalism career began with *Esquire* magazine in 1962, and her work subsequently appeared in *Vogue, Glamour, McCall's, Ladies' Home Journal, Life,* and *Cosmopolitan.* She was hired as a contributing editor for *New York* magazine in 1968. Steinem became active in the women's movement during the late sixties and helped found the National Women's Political Caucus and the Women's Action Alliance. In 1972 she launched *Ms.* magazine. The essay we include here is from Steinem's collection of articles entitled *Outrageous Acts and Everyday Rebellions* (1983). As detailed in her cause-and-effect argument, Steinem challenges the assumption that youth is the natural time for rebellion against the status quo. In fact, she questions whether this assumption concerning the effects of youthful protest have really made much of a difference in society's relations of power.

If you had asked me a decade or more ago, I certainly would have said the campus was the first place to look for the feminist or any other revolution. I also would have assumed that student-age women, like student-age men, were much more likely to be activists and open to change than their parents. After all, campus revolts have a long and well-publicized tradition, from the students of medieval France, whose "heresy" was suggesting that the university be separate from the church, through the anticolonial student riots of British India; from students who led the cultural revolution of the People's Republic of China, to campus demonstrations against the Shah of Iran. Even in this country, with far less tradition of student activism, the populist movement to end the war in Vietnam was symbolized by campus protests and mistrust of anyone over thirty.

It has taken me many years of traveling as a feminist speaker and organizer to understand that I was wrong about women; at least, about women acting on their own behalf. In activism, as in so many other things, I had been educated to assume that men's cultural pattern was the natural or the only one. If student years were the peak time of rebellion and openness to change for men, then the same must be true for women. In fact, a decade of listening to every kind of women's group—from brown-bag lunchtime lectures organized by office workers to all-night rap sessions at campus women's centers; from housewives' self-help groups to campus rallies—has convinced me that the reverse is more often true. Women may be the one group that grows more radical with age. Though some students are big exceptions to this rule, women in general don't begin to challenge the politics of our own lives until later.

Looking back, I realize that this pattern has been true for my life, too. My college years were full of uncertainties and the personal conservatism that comes from trying to win approval and fit into the proper grown-up and womanly role, whether that means finding a well-to-do man to be supported by or a male radical to support. Nonetheless, I went right on assuming that brave exploring youth and cowardly conservative old age were the norms for everybody, and that I must be just an isolated and guilty accident. Though every generalization based on female culture has many exceptions, and should never be used as a crutch or excuse, I think we might be less hard on ourselves and each other as students, feel better about our potential for change as we grow older—and educate reporters who announce feminism's demise because its red-hot center is not on campus—if we figured out that for most of us as women, the traditional college period is an unrealistic and cautious time. Consider a few of the reasons.

As students, women are probably treated with more equality than we ever will be again. For one thing, we're consumers. The school is only too glad to get the tuitions we pay, or that our families or government grants pay on our behalf. With population rates declining because of women's increased power over childbearing, that money is even more vital to a school's existence. Yet more than most consumers, we're too transient to have much power as a group. If our families are paying our tuition, we may have even less power.

As young women, whether students or not, we're still in the stage most valued by male-dominant cultures: we have our full potential as workers, wives, sex partners, and childbearers.

That means we haven't yet experienced the life events that are most radicalizing for women: entering the paid-labor force and discovering how women are treated there; marrying and finding out that it is not yet an equal partnership; having children and discovering who is responsible for them and who is not; and aging, still a greater penalty for women than for men.

Furthermore, new ambitions nourished by the rebirth of feminism may make young women feel and behave a little like a classical immigrant group. We are determined to prove ourselves, to achieve academic excellence, and to prepare for interesting and successful careers. More noses are kept to more grindstones in an effort to demonstrate newfound abilities, and perhaps to allay suspicions that women still have to have more and better credentials than men. This doesn't leave much time for activism. Indeed, we may not yet know that it is necessary.

In addition, the very progress into previously all-male careers that may be revolutionary for women is seen as conservative and conformist by outside critics. Assuming male radicalism to be the measure of change, they interpret any concern with careers as evidence of "campus conservatism." In fact, "dropping out" may be a departure for men, but "dropping in" is a new thing for women. Progress lies in the direction we have not been.

Like most groups of the newly arrived or awakened, our faith in education and paper degrees also has yet to be shaken. For instance, the percentage of women enrolled in colleges and universities has been increasing at the same time that the percentage of men has been decreasing. Among students entering college in 1978, women *outnumbered* men for the first time. This hope of excelling at the existing game is probably reinforced by the greater cultural pressure on females to be "good girls" and observe somebody else's rules.

Though we may know intellectually that we need to have new games with new rules, we probably haven't quite absorbed such facts as the high unemployment rate among female Ph.D.s; the lower average salary among women college graduates of all races than among counterpart males who graduated from high school or less; the middle-management ceiling against which even those eagerly hired new business-school graduates seem to bump their heads after five or ten years; and the barrier-breaking women in nontraditional fields who become the first fired when recession hits. Sadly enough, we may have to personally experience some of these reality checks before we accept the idea that lawsuits, activism, and group pressure will have to accompany our individual excellence and crisp new degrees.

Then there is the female guilt trip, student edition. If we're not sailing along as planned, it must be *our* fault. If our mothers didn't "do anything" with their educations, it must have been *their* fault. If we can't study as hard as we think we must (because women still have to be better prepared than men), and have a substantial personal and sexual life at the same time (because women are supposed to care more about relationships than men do), then we feel inadequate, as if each of us were individually at fault for a problem that is actually culture-wide.

I've yet to be on a campus where most women weren't worrying about some aspect of combining marriage, children, and a career. I've yet to find one where many men were worrying about the same thing. Yet women will go right on suffering from the double-role problem and terminal guilt until men are encouraged, pressured, or otherwise forced, individually and collectively, to integrate themselves into the "women's work" of raising children and homemaking. Until then, and until there are changed job patterns to allow equal parenthood, children will go right on growing up with the belief that only women can be loving and nurturing, and only men can be intellectual or active outside the home. Each half of the world will go on limiting the full range of its human talent.

Finally, there is the intimate political training that hits women in the teens and early twenties: the countless ways we are still brainwashed into assuming that women are dependent on men for our basic identities, born in our work and our personal lives, much more than vice versa. After all, if we're going to enter a marriage system that's still legally designed for a person and a half, submit to an economy in which women still average about fifty-nine cents on the dollar earned by men, and work mainly as support staff and assistants, or *co*-directors and *vice*-presidents at best, then we have to be convinced that we are not whole people on our own.

In order to make sure that we will see ourselves as half-people, and thus be addicted to getting our identity from serving others, society tries hard to convert us as young women into "man junkies"; that is, into people who are addicted to regular shots of male-approval and presence, both professionally and personally. We need a man standing next to us, actually and figuratively, whether it's at work, on Saturday night, or throughout life. (If only men realized how little it matters *which* man is standing there, they would understand that this addiction depersonalizes them, too.) Given the danger to a male-dominant system if young women stop internalizing this political message of derived identity, it's no wonder that those who try to kick the addiction—and, worse yet, to help other women do the same—are likely to be regarded as odd or dangerous by everyone from parents to peers.

With all that pressure combined with little experience, it's no wonder that younger women are often less able to support each other. Even young women who espouse feminist goals as individuals may refrain from identifying themselves as "feminist": it's okay to want equal pay for yourself (just one small reform) but it's not okay to want equal pay for women as a group (an economic revolution). Some retreat into individualized career obsessions as a way of avoiding this dangerous discovery of shared experience with women as a group. Others retreat into the safe middle ground of "I'm not a feminist but. . . ." Still others become politically active, but only on issues that are taken seriously by their male counterparts.

The same lesson about the personal conservatism of younger women is taught by the history of feminism. If I hadn't been conned into believing the masculine stereotype of youth as the "natural" time for freedom and rebellion, a time of "sowing wild oats" that actually is made possible by the assurance of power and security later on, I could have figured out the female pattern of activism by looking at women's movements of the past.

In this country, for instance, the nineteenth-century wave of feminism was started by older women who had been through the radicalizing experience of getting married and becoming the legal chattel of their husbands (or the equally radicalizing experience of *not* getting married and being treated as spinsters). Most of them had also worked in the antislavery movement and learned from the political parallels between race and sex. In other countries, that wave was also led by women who were past the point of maximum pressure toward marriageability and conservatism.

Looking at the first decade of this second wave, it's clear that the early feminist activist and consciousness-raising groups of the 1960s were organized by women who had experienced the civil rights movement, or homemakers who had discovered that raising kids and cooking didn't occupy all their talents. While most campuses of the late sixties were still circulating the names of illegal abortionists privately (after all, abortion could damage our marriage value), slightly older women were holding press conferences and speak-outs about the reality of abortions (including their own, even though that often meant confessing to an illegal act) and demanding reform or repeal of antichoice laws. Though rape had been a quiet epidemic on campus for generations, younger women victims were still understandably fearful of speaking up, and campuses encouraged silence in order to retain their reputation for safety with tuition-paying parents. It took many off-campus speak-outs, demonstrations against laws of evidence and police procedures, and testimonies in state legislatures before most student groups began to make demands on campus and local cops for greater rape protection. In fact, "date rape"—the common campus phenomenon of a young woman being raped by someone she knows, perhaps even by several students in a fraternity house—is just now being exposed. Marital rape, a more difficult legal issue, was taken up several years ago. As for battered women and the attendant exposé of husbands and lovers as more statistically dangerous than unknown muggers in the street, that issue still seems to be thought of as a largely noncampus concern, yet at many of the colleges and universities where I've spoken, there has been at least one case within current student memory of a young woman beaten or murdered by a jealous lover.

This cultural pattern of youthful conservatism makes the growing number of older women going back to school very important. They are life examples and pragmatic activists who radicalize women young enough to be their daughters. Now that the median female undergraduate age in this country is twenty-seven because so many older women have returned, the campus is becoming a major place for cross-generational connections.

None of this should denigrate the courageous efforts of young women, especially women on campus, and the many changes they've pioneered. On the contrary, they should be seen as even more remarkable for surviving the conservative pressures, recognizing societal problems they haven't yet fully experienced, and organizing successfully in the midst of a transient student population. Every women's history course, rape hot line, or campus newspaper that is finally covering *all* the news; every feminist professor whose job has been created or tenure saved by student pressure, or male administrator whose consciousness has been permanently changed; every counselor who's stopped guiding women one way and men another; every lawsuit that's been fueled by student energies against unequal athletic funds or graduate school requirements: all those accomplishments are even more impressive when seen against the backdrop of the female pattern of activism.

Finally, it would help to remember that a feminist revolution rarely resembles a masculine-style one—just as a young woman's most radical act toward her mother (that is, connecting as women in order to help each other get some power) doesn't look much like a young man's most radical act toward his father (that is, breaking the father-son connection in order to separate identities or take over existing power).

It's those father-son conflicts at a generational, national level that have often provided the conventional definition of revolution; yet they've gone on for centuries without basically changing the role of the female half of the world. They have also failed to reduce the level of violence in society, since both fathers and sons have included some degree of aggressiveness and superiority to women in their definition of masculinity, thus preserving the anthropological model of dominance.

Furthermore, what current leaders and theoreticians define as revolution is usually little more than taking over the army and the radio stations. Women have much more in mind than that. We have to uproot the sexual caste system that is the most pervasive power structure in society, and that means transforming the patriarchal values of those who run the institutions, whether they are politically the "right" or the "left," the fathers or the sons. This cultural part of the change goes very deep, and is often seen as too intimate, and perhaps too threatening, to be considered as either serious or possible. Only conflicts among men are "serious." Only a takeover of existing institutions is "possible."

That's why the definition of "political," on campus as elsewhere, tends to be limited to who's running for president, who's demonstrating against corporate investments in South Africa, or which is the "moral" side of some conventional revolution, preferably one that is thousands of miles away.

As important as such activities are, they are also the most comfortable ones when we're young. They provide a sense of virtue without much disruption in the power structure of our daily lives. Even when the most consistent energies on campus are actually concentrated around feminist issues, they may be treated as apolitical and invisible. Asked "What's happening on campus?" a student may reply, "The antinuke movement," even though that resulted in one demonstration of two hours, while student antirape squads have been patrolling the campus every night for two years and women's studies have begun to transform the very textbooks we read.

No wonder reporters and sociologists looking for revolution on campus often miss the depth of feminist change and activity that is really there. Women students themselves may dismiss it as not political and not serious. Certainly, it rarely comes in the masculine sixties style of bombing buildings or burning draft cards. In fact, it goes much deeper than protesting a temporary symptom—say, the draft—and challenges the right of one group to dominate another, which is the disease itself.

Young women have a big task of resisting pressures and challenging definitions. Their increasing success is a miracle of foresight and courage that should make us all proud. But they should know that they, too, may grow more radical with age.

One day, an army of gray-haired women may quietly take over the earth.

QUESTIONS FOR "WHY YOUNG WOMEN ARE MORE CONSERVATIVE" BY GLORIA STEINEM

Talking About the Text

1. What common assumption does Steinem question early in her argument?
2. Why do you think she considers it important to challenge this belief?

3. Which audience would be most receptive to Steinem's argument? Which audience would be most angered? Which audience most indifferent? What kind of audience might benefit most from understanding Steinem's claims?
4. If Steinem is addressing college students, what chances is she taking that she will be ignored?

Exploring Issues

1. Examine some of Steinem's reasons supporting her claims concerning the causes of women's conservatism. Judge their relevance as they might apply in your school, community, or workplace.
2. Identify the conflicts Steinem claims female college students face. Compare these conflicts to some of those Belenky et al. identify in their argument in Chapter 6. In what way is the form of protest in a male culture similar to the form of teaching methods in the college classroom that is based on a male model? What is the effect in each instance of this form of protest and teaching?

Writing Assignments

1. Try to find some older female and male students, either in some of your classes or working in other fields at your school. Interview them about their personal and professional aspirations when they were younger and decide if they generally conform to the pattern Steinem claims men and women typically follow. This assignment can also work even if you consider yourself one of those "older" students. Compare and contrast both older and younger views, both male and female.
2. Write a response to Steinem in which you identify one or more of her significant claims. You might want to challenge her views or extend them into aspects of your college experience that she does not consider. You might take, for example, her following statement concerning political activities on campus:

As important as such activities are, they are also the most comfortable ones when we're young. They provide a sense of virtue without much disruption in the power structure of our daily lives.

Can you justify this claim, or is Steinem distorting the real value of past political protests?

Reading 63

Letter from a Friend: A Conservative Speaks Out for Gay Rights

"John Woolman"

"A Conservative Speaks Out For Gay Rights" was published as a letter to William F. Buckley, Jr. in the September 12, 1986 issue of the *National Review*. It was signed simply: "As always, 'John Woolman.' " In his essay "Woolman" discusses a growing concern for the homophobia that he perceives to be running rampant through the conservative movement. Specifically, his letter is a response to a *New York Times* Op-Ed piece in which Buckley suggested that gay persons with AIDS be tattooed and another *National Review* article entitled "The Politics of AIDS," (May 23, 1986) by Joe Sobran. A conservative himself, he takes on Buckley and other conservatives, on the grounds that discrimination of gays could "adversely affect members of previously persecuted ethnic groups."

Dear Bill,

The time has come for me to share with you my theory as to why the Good Lord made human sexuality what it is, whatever that may be. You will be happy, I'm sure, to hear that my theory comes straight out of the natural-law tradition, attempting as it does to ascertain the true meaning of sex by identifying its unique purpose.

Thus the first theory we must reject is the traditional view that the purpose of sex is procreation. The birds, the bees, and the Baptists manage to reproduce themselves in vast numbers without going through all that. Second, I reject the view of the dreaded secular humanists and other subversives that the purpose of sex is simply pleasure. For this we have pot, peanut butter, and Bach and Roll. There must be other items on that list, but too much peanut butter has destroyed my short-term memory, I think.

No, the real reason God made human sexuality whatever it is clearly must be its one absolutely necessary and inescapable function, even, or especially, for celibates: Sex is a lesson in humility. It makes certain that everyone, no matter how otherwise dignified and intelligent, at least once in a lifetime, in thought, word, or deed, will make a complete fool of himself. Having read your *New York Times* Op-Ed piece suggesting we tattoo gay AIDS victims on the tush, and Joe Sobran's *NR* article "The Politics of AIDS" (May 23), I now know that in this, as in so many other ways, you have done much more than the Lord could ever have reasonably expected of you. Now it is my turn, so bear with me, if you will.

Conservatism, from Falwell to *NR* to *Commentary*, appears to have an unseemly obsession with homosexuality, totally disproportionate to its significance as either a phenomenon or a problem compared with the disastrous state of heterosexuality, i.e., divorce, teenage pregnancy, child abuse, rape, wholesale abortion, and congenital venereal diseases that affect far more children than AIDS. Someone once made a remark about getting the beam out of one's own eye before worrying about the speck in someone else's. But what did He know?

You have made major contributions in separating "mainstream conservatism" from the swamp denizens, but *not yet* on this issue. I am particularly disturbed by what I perceive as a total lack of a sense of proportion among conservatives when dealing with this subject. The best example of this that I have seen recently is an article in the May 10 issue of *The Economist* about Pat Robertson:

> There is nothing frightening in the Christian message, he insists. And, indeed everything about Mr. Robertson—his intelligence, friendliness, ordinariness—is reassuring. Then, smiling, he quotes Lloyd George's view: "We might as well legalize sodomy as recognize the Bolsheviks." Mr. Robertson is making the point that America has gone too far on both tracks: turning homosexuals into a privileged class, offering too many concessions to the Soviet Union.

A television evangelist quoting a notorious adulterer equating unauthorized orgasms with Genocide Inc. certainly gives new meaning to the word "queer." *The Economist*'s equation of repealing the sodomy laws with turning homosexuals into a privileged class is an interpretation that is frightening in a different way. I would not for a moment expect Robertson, or you or Joe for that matter, to change his views on sex out of wedlock in general or homosexuality in particular, but for God's sake (and that is not a figure of speech) let's have some common sense. Or should we nuke the gay bars?

I have decided that Sodom is for conservatives what South Africa is for liberals—a focal point of hypocrisy. They are determined to DO THE RIGHT THING, no matter who gets hurt, as long as it is someone else. Unfortunately, conservative rhetoric just about guarantees that everyone will get hurt, including the rhetoricians.

The best way of gaining the missing sense of proportion and seeing the virtues of moderation is to contemplate the actual condition of gays. Morally and politically, sexual orientation is generally not a matter of choice. Can you imagine someone from a traditional American background actually choosing to become a homosexual and thereby become a target of hatred and legal persecution? The literature of homosexuality is replete with accounts of dreaded self-recognition by adults who have never had a homosexual experience, never been "recruited."

The gay rebellion was made inevitable by urbanization, by the vast increase in our knowledge of human sexuality (except among conservatives, who think that carnal ignorance is the cure for carnal knowledge), and by the "sexual revolution" among heterosexuals. It will necessarily continue so long as there are those who are intent on politicizing homosexuality dishonestly.

I would not accuse you of doing so, at least not deliberately. But precisely what effect on gays and gay activists did you think your tattoo suggestion would have? Not to mention your consideration—in an earlier column—of castration as a possible way of dealing with diagnosed AIDS carriers who continue to have sex without warning their prospective partners. This sort of speculation does not engender the needed confidence in the affected community. Will someone who fears he has AIDS be more or less likely to seek testing and treatment if he has been threatened with tattooing and/or castration? A paranoid reaction? Perhaps, but we should remember that homosexuals were the target of mass extermination in our lifetime, and there are those who are advocating it today in America. (One such was invited to testify at the New York City Council meeting at which the gay-rights bill was considered.) Tattooing was a part of that previous program of extermination, too. Considering the response of your friends, is the response from those who don't know you so surprising? I think not. "I'm from *NR*, and I'm here to help you" will now have even less credibility among gays. Another victory for the Left.

But losing votes, or even chasing AIDS carriers away from AIDS clinics, is not the worst effect of hysterical rhetoric. The worst thing about hysterical rhetoric is that it sometimes has its *intended* effect: People believe it. It is possible to frighten people so badly that they will take whatever actions they believe are necessary to protect their children. "Blood libels" usually are of this nature. Jews were said to use the blood of Christian children in rituals. They were also blamed for the Black Plague and were the victims of mass murder. Blaming homosexuals for AIDS, child molesting (most of which is committed by heterosexuals), or the moral decline of the U.S.A. is a blood libel aimed at inciting hatred against gay citizens.

The persecution of homosexuals is deeply rooted in the Judaeo-Christian tradition and in a wide variety of other cultures as well. It also seems to be a part of the human psyche: Boys beat up sissies long before they understand the mechanics of sexuality. The gay subculture, like the speakeasy, "flapper" era of Prohibition, or the so-called "counterculture" of the Sixties and early Seventies, is a culture of rebellion against such persecution. Such rebellions are often childish and self-destructive, but they are also typically American reactions to moral hypocrisy and politicized lying. The persecutors of gays bear significant responsibility for gay militancy and have no right to cite it as an excuse for more persecution.

That observation, unfortunately, brings us to the subject of Joe Sobran and what one might call the politics of homophobia. Joe seems to want AIDS to be both a threat to society *and* something peculiarly homosexual. But really, it can't be both. He warns (threatens?) that even monogamous homosexuals will be blamed for "spreading AIDS." But to whom would they spread it? If it is peculiarly homosexual, then they can only spread it to other homosexuals. If it can be spread by heterosexual or nonsexual contact, then it is not peculiarly homosexual.

Of course the truth is that the overwhelming majority of the people in the world who have AIDS are not homosexual. Homosexuality does not *cause* AIDS, and a homosexual who practices proper sexual hygiene runs a negligible risk of contracting the disease, even if he is extremely promiscuous. Heterosexual transmission from male to female via vaginal intercourse may be less efficient than anal intercourse, but it is clearly established. But if AIDS can be spread by other means, then homosexuals were just the first victims. By indulging in hypocritical condemnation of gays as the cause, we squandered an opportunity to find a cure or vaccine or at least to educate the public before the disease's inevitable spread among heterosexuals. Instead, we are encouraged to blame homosexuals, as though the disease had been caused by them. Very dangerous nonsense.

Equally false is Joe's assertion that the "gay lifestyle" equals promiscuity. This is a variation on what I call "the view from the emergency room": If all we knew about automobiles were learned in a hospital emergency room, we would view them as the greatest menace in human history. The most visible and vocal consumers of alcohol are to be found staggering around the streets. The most visible members of almost any group are not necessarily typical, and this is probably more true of gays than of any other group (for reasons that should be obvious).

The rhetorical purpose of equating homosexuality with promiscuity should be clear: It makes it easier to blame gays for AIDS. But it should be noted that gay *and* straight promiscuity developed during a period in which antibiotics could cure most known sexually transmitted diseases (STDs). The advent of AIDS—and herpes among heterosexuals—was a new risk factor for a population lulled into a sense of false security. The long latency period of AIDS and the recurring nature of herpes meant that by the time the danger was recognized, a large part of the population was already infected. This does not excuse either bad hygiene or bad morals, but when one is sitting in judgment on others, one should consider all the facts. At the practical level, this helps us to understand that AIDS is not the result of some gay death wish but, like most human problems, comes from a mixture of bad judgment and bad luck.

Joe says that "to be gay is to be obsessed with one's homosexuality," but he seems instead to demonstrate that to be conservative is to be obsessed with anyone's homosexuality. Naturally the focal points of the visible gay world— apart from churches, charities, and other civic organizations, which are obviously invisible to conservatives—are bars and baths and similar places that by their nature cater to gays as gays. The problem with generalizing from this is that the same is true of the heterosexual world, if the point is their *sexuality.* There are singles bars, strip joints, even a few bath-type places. There are also numerous prostitution services, e.g., massage parlors, modeling services, etc.

The obvious difference is that homosexuals are a minority whose sexuality is their defining mark, and who must congregate together in order to avoid a hostile environment. A heterosexual can be straight anywhere, but a homosexual can be *safely* gay only in a gay environment.

I was both amused and disturbed by Joe's encounter with the *New York Native,* wherein he discovered that homosexuals have SEX. *Native* publisher Charles Ortleb was probably elected the spokesman for homosexuals in the same election that made Joe the Great Straight Hope. It reminds me of McGovern *v.* Nixon. On this issue, even more than most, we have been stuck with the politics of howler monkeys—he who gets farthest out on a limb and makes the most noise is "spokesman."

Ortleb's idea about the African Swine Fever-CIA connection may be far-fetched, but it did not come from a desire to blame someone else for AIDS, but rather from some very serious questions about the way AIDS research is being conducted. If AIDS is important enough to justify cover stories in *NR*, shouldn't prominent conservatives monitor the quality of the debate and support funding for research?

As to how to combat the further spread of AIDS, many gays support closing baths and other such places. Others, not just gays, oppose closing the baths because they could be used to encourage safer sex practices. (Which position is correct is not the point. Both camps are aware of the problem and are trying to find an effective response.)

The other measures that Joe thinks would be useful, many think would be ineffective or counterproductive. The notion that enforcing the "long dormant laws against sodomy" could be a "health measure" certainly is pernicious nonsense. It would be counterproductive in every way, particularly for contact tracing, which Joe seems to support. It is not possible to regulate that which is absolutely prohibited. Similarly, advice to the anathematized is likely to fall on deaf ears.

Joe's whirlwind tour of Sodom, as seen through the personal ads placed by some especially restless Natives, seeks to create the impression that the practices of a small minority of gays, such as fisting, are not only common but *"standard."* (His emphasis.) This is an ignorant or deliberate misrepresentation of human sexuality. It should be obvious that such extreme practices are quite rare. Nevertheless, I'm sure that the typical reader of *NR* will be misled by this. To paraphrase Joe: Sordid and desperate, such distortions make it impossible for me to idealize conservatism. Of course, I got over that a long time ago, but why would anyone idealize either heterosexuality or homosexuality? All human activity reflects human frailty, especially measuring the frailties of others.

There remains one major question: Will "gay rights" turn the world upside down?

After having terrified the readers of *NR* (or at least having sent them rushing out to buy stock in the makers of Preparation H), Joe announces: "Such is the behavior gay-rights legislation protects. Or rather, such is the behavior gay-rights legislation forbids normal citizens to disapprove." This is untrue. First, these sexual activities are not affected at all by this law. In New York they were and are legal in private. Second, many of these more extreme activities, such as S&M, B&D, AT&T (phone sex) are of no interest to most homosexuals and are also engaged in by some heterosexuals. There are straight publications with advertisements for them, but this inconvenient fact will remain unknown to most *NR* readers. Finally, the law does not in any way forbid anyone to disapprove of such activities or to express that disapproval, except in job or housing discrimination, which rights are already sharply circumscribed in New York City. The stupidity of both the gay insistence on and the conservative objection to this law is that it will have little practical consequence.

The "non-discriminatory curricula" on homosexuality that Joe says will be mandated in public schools may or may not, in fact, be "amoral," if they are simply a factual description of the phenomenon. They could have a strong ethical content and still be "non-discriminatory." This does not in any way deprive parents of their right "to form their children's morals." Parents' rights to communicate with their children at home, in their house of worship, etc. are totally unaffected by this law. Parents of children in New York City public schools have had little control over the curricula anyway. With all the school system's problems, worrying about this is more than a little silly.

The statement that "Gays gain the right to have the city proselytize on their behalf to (desirable?) children" is a blatant violation of the Eighth Commandment. First, a morally neutral description of something does not constitute proselytizing. Or are we to believe that something that we are told draws "the revulsion of the general public" will be irresistible to students if it is described in a "non-discriminatory" way? The parenthetical "desirable?" after "proselytizing" gives the impression that sex-education classes will become shopping malls for homosexual child molesters. This is really a calumny on everyone involved, not just gays.

Now, *are* children sexually "desirable" to homosexuals? All of the evidence is that most child molestation is heterosexual, and most homosexual child molestation is done by someone within the family, not by predatory strangers. A boy is at least as safe with a homosexual man as a girl would be with a heterosexual man, all other things being equal. The overwhelming majority of homosexuals disapprove of pedophilia, and there are frequent letters in the *Native* expressing that point in very strong terms.

The real problems with "gay rights" are very simple. Freedom of association by definition must include the right to be wrong. Even if one believes that it is immoral to discriminate against people for reasons not relevant to the matter at hand, it is also, barring a compelling public purpose, immoral to use force to prohibit that. And state immorality is much more dangerous than personal immorality. Obviously, the same line of reasoning applies to the sodomy laws— hence the desperate attempt to make AIDS uniquely gay. Most importantly, both gay-rights and sodomy laws are counterproductive. The former produce outbursts such as Joe's; the latter produce massive distortions of human sexual behavior.

But though the argument against gay-rights laws is fairly clear, the campaign for them is not mere ideological Mau-Mauing. Gays have legitimate reason to believe they need such laws. Having read Quentin Crisp's *The Naked Civil Servant*, I have concluded that it really takes a lot of courage for effeminate men just to get through life. And I also mean physical courage, since "sissies" are always the targets of bullies of all ages and editorial statuses.

Moreover, the principled argument against gay-rights laws sounds a lot less principled once you ask conservatives if, by the same libertarian logic, they would fight—I mean *fight*—to get sodomy laws repealed. I am not aware of any conservative leaders who have unequivocally called for their repeal. Old friend, from whom I have learned so much about the place of principle in politics, have you ever done so? When even the most principled conservative leaders are uninterested in protecting gays from state harassment, how can conservatives be surprised that some radicalized gays are demanding the same legal privileges that other persecuted groups have attained?

Given our history of racism and our commitment to a multiracial society, we may have no choice, sadly, but to place some restrictions on exercises of freedom of association that would adversely affect members of previously persecuted ethnic groups. It is also sadly true that this has gone much too far with busing and quotas and other forms of "reverse discrimination," all of which understandably cause conservatives to fear that "gay rights" might ultimately lead to busing Hassidic rabbis to Greenwich Village leather bars—such are the inanities of liberalism.

Well, we can't keep the liberals from being inane, and it's a little late to stop the gays from being militant. The question then becomes: What are conservatives willing to do to make gay-rights laws unnecessary? Would television evangelists give up fag-baiting, their favorite fundraising technique? Would Joe forgo the strategy of implying that to tolerate homosexuality is to tolerate anything?

But perhaps giving up a treasured demonology is too much to ask of any person or group that lives its life in the polemical trenches. Here's something easier, then:

While conservatives bloviate about protecting boys from gays, but seldom about protecting girls from straights, it might be appropriate to think about protecting gay kids from the hostile straight world. An effeminate adolescent male from a poor family is often thrown out by his parents, beaten up by his peers, harassed by the law, damned by his church, flunked by his school, raped by the street gangs, mocked by the public, and ignored by conservatives, until the City of New York sets up a special school for his kind. Then, noting the name of an organization for the Protection of Gay Youth, *NR* sarcastically asks, "Protect from whom?" From those who think that, since there is nothing worse than homosexuality, their violence is the wrath of God. Ideas do have consequences.

To end on a more cheerful note, I seem to remember an *Animal Crackers* cartoon in which an elephant was stomping on flowers. "I just don't like pansies," he explained. If *NR* had been equally candid and brief, we would all be better off.

As always,
"John Woolman"

QUESTIONS FOR "LETTER FROM A FRIEND: A CONSERVATIVE SPEAKS OUT FOR GAY RIGHTS" BY "JOHN WOOLMAN"

Talking About the Text

1. Woolman builds his case through a progression of several logically reasoned arguments. Identify some of these and assess their rhetorical force as reasoned arguments. Which arguments did you find particularly strong? Which did you find weak? Why?

2. On several occasions in his essay Woolman uses humor to make his point. For example, he ends his essay with the *Animal Crackers* joke. What rhetorical purpose(s) do you think the humor serves in this essay? Can you find any particular examples in which humor helps Woolman's argument?

Exploring Issues

1. Woolman writes that "the persecutors of gays bear significant responsibility for gay militancy and have no right to cite it as an excuse for more persecution." What connections can you make between this statement and Steele's thoughts on the relationship between the assertion of power by specific races or ethnic groups and race relations? What commentary do you think Woolman is making about the consequences of one group oppressing another?

2. Woolman asserts that "state immorality is much more dangerous than personal immorality." Why do you think Woolman made this statement? What is your opinion of it? Can you think of specific examples that would either support or refute Woolman's claim?

3. Woolman writes, "Given our history of racism and our commitment to a multiracial society, we may have no choice, sadly, but to place some restrictions on exercises of freedom of association that would adversely affect members of previously persecuted ethnic groups." Specifically, to what kinds of restrictions do you think Woolman is referring? What connections do you see between gay oppression and racism or sexism? What differences do you find?

Writing Assignments

1. John Woolman addresses the issue of prejudice and discrimination against gays. As a conservative, Woolman deplores the homophobia that he perceives among other conservatives, most notably William F. Buckley, Jr., to whom Woolman's letter is addressed. Why would prejudice against gays be more pronounced among conservatives than liberals? Is it reasonable for Woolman to expect less prejudice from his fellow conservatives?

2. Write John Woolman a publishable letter in which you respond to his concerns about prejudice and discrimination against gays. Address some of the specific claims Woolman makes and respond to his general aim of attempting to reason with his fellow conservatives. Do you think Woolman will persuade Buckley and others to tone down their rhetoric or to change their opinions? Why or why not? To whom does it matter?

CHAPTER 7: EXTENDED WRITING ASSIGNMENTS

7-1. Read Richard Wright's autobiography, *Black Boy*, in its entirety. Then write a review of the book using the following question as a guide for your review: How effectively and in what ways does *Black Boy* portray racial hatred and injustice? Alternatively, you might choose to read and review *Native Son* or Monica Sone's *Nisei Daughter*, using the same question to guide your review.

7-2. Write a research paper on some aspect of the civil rights movement or the women's movement. Try to narrow your focus by asking a research question that interests you (for example, "Who were the leaders of the movement and how did they affect its development?").

7-3. Read J. Anthony Lukas's "Community and Equality in Conflict" in Chapter 4. Then research the controversial issue of busing public school children. Take a stand on this issue and argue that busing serves to diminish or promote prejudice.

7-4. After reading the articles in this chapter, you probably have a sense of the many forms prejudice can take. Write an essay in which you recount a time when you met prejudice or discrimination. What happened, and what did you learn from the experience?

Chapter 8

Images of Ourselves: the Media and the Arts

*E*ven though we are not always aware of their presence, the media and the arts are constantly with us, sometimes serving as mirrors of our lives and at other times manipulating reality, or at the very least putting it into question. Every day most of us are bombarded by messages, both subtle and overt, from television, radio, musical recordings, billboards, newspapers, books, and magazines, to name only the more obvious forms. Our lives have been and are being shaped for better or worse by media. And as each day passes, the technological capabilities of various media grow more startling. Perhaps more important than those technological advances, however, is the desire each of us has for self-expression in the search for one's identity and media's role in our attempt to realize this goal. As we face the start of a new decade, we might ask the following questions about the role the media and the arts play in our lives: To what extent do the various media serve to liberate and uplift the human spirit? To what extent do they oppress?

The selections in this chapter address these questions from several different vantage points. In the opening essay, "Negative News and Little Else," David Shaw explores both the societal and personal ramifications of a journalism that fails to give a complete portrait of various ethnic minority groups by focusing primarily on crime, poverty, and aberrant behavior. Following Shaw's article, John Leo, in "The Entertaining of America," writes about the potential dangers of an American culture so dominated by "entertainment values" that reality and fiction as presented in various media, especially news media, begin to merge.

Like Leo, Allan Bloom also looks at what he perceives to be hazardous influences from the media on today's youth. In an excerpt from *The Closing of the American Mind*, Bloom discusses his growing concern over a youth culture whose rock music he feels poses a serious threat to the moral education of today's younger generation. Robert Pattison, on the other hand, in "The New Literacy," offers quite a different view of rock music, arguing that this music is a positive form of self-expression. And in "White Boys Dancing," Michael Ventura gives us a provocative analysis of the relationship between class consciousness and rock dancing, claiming that for street kids rock and roll has been an exhilarating and liberating experience. Tipper Gore, in contrast to the more positive images of rock and roll given by Pattison and Ventura, argues against the use of degrading and violent images of women in rock lyrics and films. Similarly, Kenneth W. Goings, in "Memorabilia That Have Perpetuated Stereotypes About African Americans," examines how the popularity of black collectibles such as Aunt Jemima salt shakers helped perpetuate derogatory stereotypes and racism.

The last two essays of this chapter focus on the self-images of the artists themselves. Alice Walker, in "Beauty: When the Other Dancer Is the Self," gives a poignant account of how her search to understand a traumatic childhood event leads eventually to self-discovery. In the final essay, "The Black Writer and the Magic of the Word," John Wideman explores the double bind he and other black artists encounter in trying to express a uniquely African-American experience through mainstream American English.

These essays are by no means exhaustive. Rather, the readings are intended to pique your interest in this area, and we encourage you to look for other essays and articles as a means of furthering your awareness of issues explored in this chapter.

Reading 64

Negative News and Little Else

David Shaw

The following selection, by staff writer David Shaw, originally appeared on the front page of the December 11, 1990, edition of the *Los Angeles Times* as the first column in a series entitled "Minorities and the Press." In "Negative News and Little Else," Shaw critiques the press on its coverage of ethnic minorities, charging that a disproportionate emphasis on crime, poverty, and aberrant behavior gives an incomplete picture of minority groups. In doing so, he looks at the ramifications of this practice on not only the mainstream's perception of these groups but also the self-image of individual minority group members.

Jesse B. Semple—"Simple" to his friends—lived in Harlem, where he often shared with his friend Boyd his wry, homespun observations on the pains and frustrations of life in a racist society.

"The only time colored folks is front page news," Semple once said, "is when there's been a lynching or a boycott or a whole bunch of us have been butchered or is arrested."

Writer Langston Hughes created the fictional character of "Simple" 48 years ago. But there was nothing fictional about Simple's commentary on the American press, and despite substantial improvement in recent years, many journalists of all colors offer disquietingly similar criticisms of their profession today.

Overt racism in the press is rare now, and some newspapers—most notably USA Today, others in the Gannett and Knight-Ridder chains and the Seattle Times—have even tried as a matter of formal policy to include people of color in the mainstream of their daily coverage. But minority journalists (and many of their white colleagues and supervisors) say the overwhelming majority of press coverage still emphasizes the pathology of minority behavior—drugs, gangs, crime, violence, poverty, illiteracy—almost to the exclusion of normal, everyday life.

To some extent, of course, the same criticism can be made of press coverage of whites. News, as defined by the people who write, edit, publish and broadcast it, is about the unusual, the aberrant—about triumphs and tragedies, underachievers and overachievers, it's about the extremes of life, not "normal, everyday" life.

But the press covers a much broader range of white life than of minority life, and critics say the narrow, distorted view of ethnic minorities presented in the press strongly influences how whites—and such white-run institutions as the police, the courts and the school system—perceive and treat minorities. The press thus plays a major role in perpetuating the ethnic stereotypes—and fueling the prejudices and ethnic conflicts—that increasingly polarize our increasingly multicultural society.

Times interviews with more than 175 reporters, editors and publishers from more than 30 newspapers nationwide over the past four months produced a wide range of criticisms of how the press portrays African-Americans, Latinos, Asian-Americans and Native Americans. Among these were: Harmful stereotyping. Ignorance of cultural differences. Use of racially biased or insensitive language. Unfair comparisons between different ethnic groups. A double standard in the coverage of minority politicians. Failure to photograph or quote minorities. Anointing unrepresentative and sometimes irresponsible minority "spokesmen." Automatically lumping together all Latinos or, in particular, all Asian-Americans as a single community, without recognizing the substantial differences in culture and language among the varied elements of those communities.

But no complaint about press coverage was voiced as frequently by minorities (or acknowledged as readily by many whites) as the overwhelmingly negative nature of most stories on people of color—especially blacks and Latinos—and the concomitant absence of people of color from the mainstream of daily news coverage.

Although local television news (with its emphasis on crime and violence) and network news (with its emphasis on public policy) are especially susceptible to these charges, most newspapers aren't much better, the critics say. And yet, only by covering all aspects of minority life can the press give whites a "rounded picture" of society—and give minorities themselves a sense of belonging to that society, says A. Stephen Montiel, a Latino, who is president of the Institute for Journalism Education in Oakland.

Occasionally, newspapers do provide this "rounded picture" by including minorities in their mainstream coverage. USA Today quoted and pictured blacks in a routine story in August on doctor-patient relations. The Seattle Times quoted and pictured an Asian-American couple in a September story on a slowdown in the Seattle housing market. The Miami Herald included Hispanics in a story on Christmas shopping—and illustrated the story with a drawing that showed people of varying ethnic backgrounds.

But these are exceptions. As far as the press is concerned, "We don't exist" in the mainstream of life in this country, says Craig Matsuda, assistant View section editor at the Los Angeles Times.

Indeed, if all one knew about real-life blacks and Latinos in particular was what one read in the newspaper or saw on television news—and in our still largely segregated society, that's where most whites do get most of their information about blacks and Latinos—one would scarcely be aware that there is a large and growing middle class in both cultures, going to work, getting married, having children, paying taxes, going on vacation and buying books and VCRs and microwave ovens.

Only 15% of the poor people in the United States are black, but one would not know that from most press coverage. Nor would one know that most violent criminals, drug-users, prostitutes, drunks, illiterates, high school dropouts, juvenile delinquents, jobless and poor people in this country are neither blacks nor Latino but white. Or that the vast majority of blacks and Latinos are none of the above.

Despite vigorous efforts, even the Detroit Free Press—with several high-ranking black editors and a city population that's more than 70% black—doesn't do as good a job as it should covering blacks as "normal, everyday human beings," concedes the paper's white publisher, Neal Shine.

Thus, while the paper's lifestyle section is officially called "The Way We Live," many blacks call it "The Way *They* Live."

The Free Press has a much better reputation than most for covering blacks, but, "When I'm out in the community covering something, and folks say, 'Well, you work for a racist paper,' it's hard for me to defend" the paper, says Constance Prater, chief of the city-county bureau for the Free Press and president of the Detroit chapter of the National Assn. of Black Journalists.

Blacks at other papers make almost identical comments about their communities and their papers.

Blacks are the largest minority group in the United States, and they have generally been the victims of the worst bigotry here—enslaved, lynched, once officially classified by the U.S. Supreme Court as non-citizens—so it's not surprising that when the press thinks of minorities at all, there's a "historic tendency" to think almost exclusively of blacks, in the words of Leonard Downie, a white, who is managing editor of the Washington Post.

Thus, a New York Times "American Voices" story last month, based on interviews nationwide about the crisis in the Persian Gulf, included a photograph of seven whites and one black but no photos of any other minorities. The story included interviews with 20 "Americans . . . of all walks of life;" not one had an identifiable Latino or Asian-American surname.

That same day, a joint study by the National Commission on Working Women and Women in Film showed that there are about five times as many black characters as Latino, Asian-American and Native American characters combined in prime-time television. The study said there are as many extraterrestrial aliens in prime-time television as there are Latinos and Asian-Americans combined.

"For a long time," says Gerald Garcia, publisher of the Knoxville Journal in Tennessee, "the only minority group that anyone [in the press] . . . had any conscious level about were blacks."

There is some evidence that this is changing, however slowly—especially in cities like Miami, Los Angeles, Chicago and San Francisco and in the Southwest, where there are large and rapidly growing Latino and/or Asian-American populations. But the largely negative press portrayals of blacks and Latinos may be changing even more slowly.

No minority journalist interviewed for this story suggested that these negative portrayals—or the absence of minorities from mainstream press coverage—are the product of a conscious, racist decision by white editors and reporters. In fact, even the most caustic critics of the press acknowledge that most white journalists mean well; it's not the intent but the results that trigger widespread criticism—and those results stem largely from ignorance, insensitivity, the absence of minority journalists from most newsrooms and, more important, the absence of minorities from most editors' offices (which will be the subject of Thursday's story in this series.)

"It's not so much some overt racist plot," says Janet Clayton, a black, who is assistant editorial page editor of the Los Angeles Times. "It has to do with, obviously, who runs newspapers . . . what the values are of those people, the world that they live in. We all bring to the table what . . . our life experience is."

Journalists who have had little exposure to minorities or who have known them only in certain roles tend not to include them in their "everyday thinking," Clayton says, and "if they're not there in your mind, then they tend not be [sic] part of your natural news-gathering process."

Newspapers routinely publish engagement notices ("all of them white"), obituaries ("all of them white") and stories on young, middle-class couples struggling to buy their first homes ("all of them white"), says Ben Johnson, a black, who is assistant managing editor of the St. Petersburg Times in Florida. This coverage of white America, Johnson says, gives readers "some sense of normalcy."

But, he says, that same coverage also gives the impression that "people of color don't buy houses . . . die . . . get married."

Johnson concedes that he may be exaggerating a bit in this characterization of press coverage, but he and others insist that the general, if unwitting message of the white press is that non-white people don't do these "normal" things, don't lead normal lives.

A few newspapers have recently begun trying to correct this imbalance, actively urging social organizations, funeral homes and others in minority communities to send them newsworthy information. But such requests are still relatively rare.

The result: Coverage of minorities continues to be skewed to the negative and the sensational.

The double standard implicit in such coverage is not nearly as blatant as it once was. After all, in our own generation newspapers still routinely identified black crime suspects (but not white crime suspects) by race. Most responsible papers now do that only if it is relevant, and even then they often agonize over it—as the New York Times did this year in making discussion of that subject the lead item in three issues of "Winners & Sinners," its in-house critique of Times coverage.

The discussion was triggered by the failure of the Times to include a racial description of a suspect in a shooting. Mentioning race in a skimpy description—"black male"—would be unfair, but since the paper had identified the suspect as "an unkempt man in his early 30's, about 6 feet tall and 180 pounds, with a moustache and beard," the question was raised, "Can we justify leaving out an element that narrows the field by a huge fraction? The omission itself, however kindly meant, might well seem patronizing—as if we assume that a whole segment of the human race *should* feel stigmatized because one of its number committed a crime."

CRIME SUSPECTS

Careful consideration of the racial identification of criminal suspects is but one example of how the media has changed of late. As recently as the late 1960s—and probably the 1970s in many cities—virtually any reporter covering the police beat knew that if there was a murder in the ghetto or barrio, editors would automatically dismiss it as unworthy of publication—a "misdemeanor homicide" in their lexicon. Now the most enlightened editors struggle to decide which is the worst journalistic sin—publishing a story on a minority murder and contributing to the stereotype of minority communities as violence-prone or not publishing such a story and contributing to the perception that they regard minority lives as worth less than white lives.

But the perception remains that white editors value white lives more highly than minority lives, that "black-on-black violence is not much of an issue until whites are involved," in the words of Bill Sing, an Asian-American who is an assistant business editor at the Los Angeles Times.

This may help explain why most violent crimes in which blacks are the victims still receive far less press attention than do cases in which whites are the victims.

The press swarmed all over the rape and beating of a white woman jogging in Central Park last year; even the Los Angeles Times, 2,500 miles away, put the story on Page 1 six times. The murder of a Utah tourist in a New York subway station this year also received massive press attention.

But two days after the rape in Central Park, a black, off-duty mailman was gunned down in Harlem; about a week later, a black woman, the mother of four, was raped and sodomized at knifepoint, then hurled from the roof of a building, down an open air shaft, three stories to the ground, suffering severe injuries.

Neither of these stories generally received more than passing notice in the news columns of New York's daily newspapers.

JOURNALIST CRITICS

Minority journalists who criticize the press say they are not asking for special treatment—for a kinder, gentler journalism—only for a more comprehensive and comprehending journalism.

"I am the last person in the world who will ever say that the Free Press can or should ignore the negative," says Jacqueline Thomas, associate editor and deputy editorial page editor of the Detroit Free Press.

Some problems may even have been ignored by the paper for too long, she says.

But Thomas, a black, seems uncomfortable with the current boycott of the Free Press by a relatively small group of blacks angry over its "negative" coverage of the city and Mayor Coleman Young, a black.

Some black anger is "justified," Thomas says, because, "We don't do a good enough job in reflecting those things that make Detroit a place some of us want to live in." Thomas says she has "no doubt," however, that much of the criticism of the paper stems from "a fundamental misunderstanding about what our role is."

Some blacks want the paper to be "supportive of black leadership," she says, but "I didn't become a journalist to become a cheerleader for anybody."

Hiawatha Bray, a black reporter at the Lexington Herald-Leader in Kentucky, says much the same thing. But he also says blacks must share responsibility for the negative coverage they receive.

"I get worried and very annoyed that black people would rather sit around complaining about how terrible the media is than saying, 'Well, gee, maybe we better stop our kids from participating in drive-by shootings,' " he says.

Blacks and Latinos do commit a disproportionate share of the nation's crimes and are present in disproportionate numbers on many other indices of social pathology. Minority journalists who criticize the press don't deny these bleak statistics, but they point out that much of this pathological behavior stems in large measure from historic patterns of discrimination, segregation and exclusion.

Moreover, pathology is only part of the story, and yet that's what gets the emphasis in the press.

Most press coverage of minorities in a positive context involves an even narrower range of activity—sports and entertainment, says John Funabiki, director of the Center for Integration and Improvement of Journalism, based at San Francisco State University.

Otherwise, says Felix Gutierrez, vice president of the Gannett Foundation, minority coverage "too often . . . still falls into the predictable categories . . . We're either beset by problems . . . or we're causing problems for the white society . . . The other category of coverage where we're defined as a people are the 'zoo stories'—Chinese New Year, Cinco de Mayo, black history month—basically where they come out and see us in our cultural garb . . . out of the context of our normal daily living."

Covering those stories would be perfectly appropriate, minority journalists say, if their "normal," middle-class existence were covered too.

But the press "doesn't cover middle-class people, period," says Milton Coleman, assistant managing editor in charge of local news coverage at the Washington Post. "Most of us in this newsroom are middle-class; in so many ways, the lives we lead outside the newsroom are rarely covered in the pages of the newspaper because we tend to lean more toward covering policy . . . poverty . . . foreign affairs.

"We're slow, for instance, to get on to covering day care as an issue even though after 3 o'clock or 3:30, the phones in this newsroom ring off the hook—and it's not sources, it's kids calling their parents."

But the problem is "more acute" in minority communities, particularly black communities, says Coleman, who's black.

"In this town, so much of what we would generally regard as news—the bad things—happen to be about blacks," he says. "But a lot of the other news that often gets into the paper about the mainstream or hotsy-totsy people—there aren't a lot of blacks, sometimes, in that news.

"The national news world is a very white world in a lot of ways," Coleman says.

Whites still occupy most of the powerful and visible positions in our society—President, governor, senator, cabinet member, district attorney, Wall Street tycoon, corporate board chairman, network executive, movie mogul, newspaper publisher.

"Most of the big news that the press covers is still made by whites," Coleman says. "If one reads the news pages . . . and tries to get a sense of the community, you get a distorted sense of the black community."

Similar distortions are evident in coverage of other minority communities.

Interestingly, while African-Americans and Latinos object to the preponderantly negative coverage the press give them, Asian-Americans object mostly to coverage that depicts them as a "model minority," largely devoid of the problems besetting other minorities. But some Asian-Americans also share their fellow minorities' complaint that the press sensationalizes much of what it covers in minority communities—the conflict between Korean greengrocers and black customers in several cities being a prime example.

Some critics say the press may occasionally try to overcompensate for its essentially negative portrayal of blacks and Latinos by being too soft on prominent members of those ethnic groups who deserve critical scrutiny. Both the Washington Post and the Los Angeles Times came in for that criticism in their early coverage of Mayors Marion Barry and Tom Bradley, respectively.

But many minorities say the white press has occasionally been too tough on minority politicians, holding them to a stricter standard than white politicians. Some minorities argue that there's a conspiracy in the white establishment— the press included—to discredit prominent black politicians.

Conspiracy, double standard or not, complaints about the misportrayal of minorities in general and the resultant, pervasive public misperception of them is not a simple matter of sensitivity over ethnic image—or of academic journalistic criticism.

The portrayal of many minorities in the press creates a misleading and destructive public impression—even more destructive, in many ways, than that cited in 1968 by the National Advisory Commission on Civil Disorders (popularly known as the Kerner Commission).

"By failing to portray the Negro as a matter of routine and in the context of the total society, the news media have, we believe, contributed to the black-white schism in this country," the commission said.

"If what the white American reads in the newspapers or sees on television conditions his expectation of what is ordinary and normal in the larger society, he will neither understand nor accept the black American."

Indeed, as Marilyn Gist of the University of Washington asks in a study on the negative portrayal of minorities in the press, "To what extent do biased journalistic practices contribute to police practices in the war on drugs or gangs . . . To what extent are the higher rates of incarceration among African-Americans a function of subtle racism among judges and juries—racism perpetuated by media bias?"

Last year, in Boston, Charles Stuart told police that a black man had murdered his pregnant wife and shot him. The media jumped on the story, largely ignoring striking inconsistencies in Stuart's story, and publicly identified several black suspects taken into custody.

Police conducted a massive, invasive search of black neighborhoods and then let it be known that they thought they had a strong case against one of the suspects. A Massachussets state senator later said "I'm positive that [the suspect] . . . would have been charged, convicted and sent to prison for the rest of his natural life" had it not been for one slight hitch: Ten weeks after Stuart's wife was murdered, Stuart apparently leaped to his death from a bridge over Boston Harbor after learning that he had become the prime suspect in the case.

MEDIA BLAMED

Although Boston editors vigorously defend their coverage of the Stuart case, many others were critical of it and blamed the media—in that specific case and in general minority coverage over the years—for having contributed to a climate in which police and public alike automatically assumed the guilt of a black man in the murder of a white.

"The Boston media, including good television stations and a good newspaper, allowed themselves to be duped by stereotypes of who crime victims and perpetrators are," says Tom Morgan, a reporter for the New York Times and president of the National Assn. of Black Journalists.

"This is a continuing pattern throughout the country," Morgan says. "The media are too quick to jump to negative conclusions when it comes to minorities."

Of course, the press is quick to jump to negative conclusions when it comes to almost everyone, as virtually every politician of any color would be quick to point out. Hence former Vice President Spiro Agnew's characterization of the press as "nattering nabobs of negativism," an epithet not noticeably inspired by an abiding sympathy for the plight of the disadvantaged in our society.

But Les Payne, assistant managing editor of Newsday in New York, says media stereotyping of minorities—especially young black males—contributes significantly to the way society treats them, especially in the criminal justice system and on the street.

Whites who killed 16-year-old Yusuf Hawkins in the Bensonhurst section of Brooklyn last year noticed only one thing about their target—"he was black," Payne says.

"He could have been Jamal Payne—my son."

Only one of the seven men ultimately charged in the slaying of Hawkins was held without bail as soon as he was arrested, much as the white defendants in another widely publicized murder of a black in New York—the Howard Beach case—were allowed to remain free on bail, even after they were convicted, pending their appeal. But in the Central Park jogger case, all eight black defendants were denied bail at their arraignment.

Media stereotypes must share the blame for this inequity, Payne and others say.

The media's portrayal of minorities may affect minorities' perceptions of themselves in a way that may be equally damaging.

Most people's self-image derives in part from how they see themselves portrayed in the press, and the negative portrayal of many minorities by the press may be psychologically destructive, Gist says, in transmitting "strong signals . . . to developing minority youth about what they can [and cannot] become."

As David Lawrence, the white publisher of the Miami Herald puts it, "If we show readers only white folks as bankers . . . or chefs, no wonder minorities grow up thinking they can't be those things."

The frustrations and failures engendered by these press messages may help explain not only the pathology of some minority behavior but the resultant social tensions that are growing in many segments of our ever more pluralistic society.

The most notorious racial incidents in recent years—the Central Park jog-

ger case, Bensonhurst, Howard Beach, Tawana Brawley, the black boycott of
Korean grocers—all seem to have happened in New York. That's because the
national media are headquartered in New York. But there have been equally
volatile instances of racial conflict in virtually every major American city, and
unless significant progress is made toward multicultural understanding and
tolerance, critics say the conflict seems likely to increase as minority populations continue to increase.

Minorities now make up about 25% of the nation's population, and the
number is climbing rapidly; since 1980, the percentage of blacks in the population has grown at twice the rate of whites, the percentage of Latinos has grown
at almost six times the rate of whites and the percentage of Asian-Americans has
grown at more than 10 times the rate of whites. Over the next decade, 87% of
the nation's population growth will be among minorities.

"Minorities" are already a majority in such major cities as New York, Chicago, Washington, Detroit, Cleveland, Miami, San Francisco and Los Angeles.

That's one reason why there are now more than 250 black, Spanish-
language and various Asian-language newspapers published in the United
States—most of them providing, among other things, just the kind of mainstream and generally upbeat coverage of their communities that the white press
eschews.

Many minority journalists see this inexorable growth of minority population
as the ultimate answer to the problem of indifferent or insensitive press coverage.

In the 1960s and early 1970s, they say, minorities—and some enlightened
whites—urged the press to give more (and more evenhanded) coverage to minorities because such coverage was the morally and ethically correct thing to do.

With a few notable exceptions, not much really changed.

Then a new argument was mounted, not a moral argument but a journalistic argument: Better minority coverage would make for better—i.e., more
complete, more sensitive and more diverse newspapers.

Again, with a few notable exceptions, not much really changed.

But now, newspaper readership is declining and minority population is
increasing, and the advocates of pluralism in the news columns are mounting a
financial argument: Cover minorities better because they're not going to be in
the minority much longer, and if you don't cover them, they won't read your
papers or patronize your advertisers and you're going to be out of business,
scratching your bald head, wondering what you did wrong.

This is not a new argument, but the new realities of the marketplace have
persuaded more publishers and top editors to listen to it this time.

When the argument was first made, in the mid-1970s, newspapers were
"fascinated with upscale readers" and blinded by the stereotype that said minority readers didn't read or buy, says Jay Harris, a black, who is vice president of
operations for Knight-Ridder newspapers.

A few years ago, Charles Erickson tried to persuade the publisher of a
newspaper in a heavily Latino market to subscribe to his Hispanic Link News
Service, which provides news and commentary on Latino issues.

"Our people wouldn't buy it," the publisher told Erickson. "They're all
illiterate."

Another publisher, Otis Chandler of the Los Angeles Times—now chairman of the executive committee of the Times Mirror Board of Directors—stirred considerable controversy in 1978 when he said in an interview that the black and Latino markets didn't have the purchasing power that Times advertisers required and, further, that it was difficult to get those groups to read the paper because "it's not their kind of newspaper. It's too big, it's too stuffy—if you will, it's too complicated."

Chandler concedes he "shouldn't have used the word . . . 'complicated,' " but he says he was "agonizing over the paper's inadequate coverage of minorities and was groping for explanations." He says he did not mean to imply that "blacks and Latinos are not smart enough to read The Times."

Nevertheless, Frank del Olmo, deputy editorial page editor of The Times, says he still hears complaints in the Latino community about Chandler's remarks and, as Harris says, until relatively recently, most newspapers did think that low education levels and/or language barriers rendered most minorities unlikely readers—and unlikely consumers for their advertisers. So little effort was made to cover them as news subjects—except when their deeds (say, as athletes) or misdeeds (say, as gang members) made them unavoidably "newsworthy" by the standard, white journalist's definition of that term.

"There's a dirty little secret in all newspapers—the advertisers we cater to are not thrilled when you sign up a bunch of readers in some poverty area for home delivery," says Joseph Lelyveld, managing editor of the New York Times.

Lelyveld, a white, says he doesn't know if that attitude "seeped into the newsroom," but he leaves the impression that it is a distinct possibility, particularly from the late 1970s into the early and mid-1980s.

"There was a time when this paper could have been accused of abandoning certain kinds of readers," he says. "We had bumpy times . . . in which it seems to me there was a kind of weariness with poverty issues, city issues. We didn't seem particularly committed to coverage of minorities, especially in our own . . . area."

"We used to give more coverage to Zimbabwe than the Bronx."

The civil rights movement and urban riots of the 1960s sparked widespread journalistic concern about minority coverage—coverable of blacks in particular—that led to a greater sensitivity and commitment which lasted into the 1970s. But during the Reagan/Bush years, a corporate, bottom-line mentality began to take hold at even the best of newspapers, and the revolution "lost its edge," in the words of Ernest Holsendolph, a black, who is about to begin writing a business column at the Atlanta Journal and Constitution after serving as city editor of the paper for a year.

Even when minorities are covered, they are often covered strictly as minorities, not as part of the mainstream.

William H. Gray III (D.-Pa.), majority whip of the U.S. House of Representatives, has long been praised by the press for his political skills and his grasp of a wide variety of issues, but he, too, was "ghettoized" in this fashion. Most stories on Gray in the New York Times, Washington Post and Philadelphia Inquirer early in his congressional career involved black politics or South Africa, according to a study by Linda Williams of the Joan Shorenstein Barone Center on the Press, Politics and Public Policy.

"Apparently, his views were not deemed newsworthy when the subject was not blacks," Williams concluded.

Moreover, Gray's race was often noted in articles that "had nothing to do with the subject of race (especially articles on the budget process) . . . Gray was so often referred to as the 'black Budget Committee Chairman' that a [foreign visitor] . . . might well have wondered if the U.S. House of Representatives had a white budget chairman and a black budget chairman," Williams said.

Similarly, the Los Angeles Times, Washington Post and Chicago Tribune have all referred to August Wilson as a "black playwright;" The Times called him "one of the nation's leading black playwrights." But after winning two Pulitzer Prizes, hasn't Wilson earned the right to be called "one of the nation's leading playwrights," period? After all, no one writes of David Mamet as "one of the nation's leading white playwrights." Doesn't describing Wilson as (merely)a "black playwright" implicitly diminish his achievement?

Lynn Duke, a Washington Post reporter recently assigned to write about race as a regular beat, says this "labeling" makes blacks "appear to be not part of the broader society but a special-interest group."

"The label 'black politician,' 'black writer,' 'black activist' . . . tends automatically to separate that writer, that politician, that activist from the purview of mainstream concerns and makes it a smaller, separate and therefore not as important an issue for the society at-large. . . ."

QUESTIONS FOR "NEGATIVE NEWS AND LITTLE ELSE" BY DAVID SHAW

Talking About the Text

1. Why do you think Shaw chose to begin this article with a quote from Langston Hughes' fictional character Jesse B. Semple—"Simple"?
2. What effect do you think Shaw's profession may have had on how he chose to present the information in his article? What biases might have influenced his writing?

Exploring Issues

1. Shaw states "the press covers a much broader range of white life than of minority life, and critics say the narrow, distorted view of ethnic minorities presented in the press strongly influences how whites—and such white-run institutions as the police, the courts, and the school system— perceive and treat minorities. The press thus plays a major role in perpetuating the ethnic stereotypes. . . ." Can you think of specific examples or instances that might support this claim? To what extent do

you agree with it? What other institutions besides those just listed might be affected by slanted press coverage?

2. Shaw writes that "blacks and Latinos do commit a disproportionate share of the nation's crimes. . . . Minority journalists who criticize the press don't deny the bleak statistics, but they point out that much of this pathological behavior stems in large measure from historic patterns of discrimination, segregation and exclusion." Explore the connection between pathological behavior and historic patterns of segregation and exclusion. To what extent do you think this sort of behavior on the part of ethnic minorities is caused by bigotry and discrimination? What role does the press play in perpetuating this discrimination?

3. To what extent do you agree or disagree with Shaw when he asserts that "the media's portrayal of minorities may affect minorities' perceptions of themselves. . . . [T]he negative portrayal of many minorities may be psychologically destructive"?

4. Both Shaw and John Leo ("The Entertaining of America" in this chapter) make mention of the Charles Stuart murder case in Boston. What connections can you make between the ideas about media coverage Shaw presents in his article and those articulated by Leo?

Writing Assignments

1. Shaw implies that "minority journalists who criticize the press say they are not asking for special treatment—for a kinder, gentler journalism— only for a more comprehensive and comprehending journalism." Choose a major newspaper (e.g., *New York Times, Los Angeles Times, Wall Street Journal, Boston Globe*), and write an essay in which you assess to what extent or degree the journalism and news coverage of that newspaper is "comprehensive and comprehending." Before beginning this assignment, you will need to define for yourself and your audience what "comprehensive and comprehending" journalism might entail. Try the following prewriting activities as a way of starting.

   • Brainstorm with your classmates or by yourself on *the nature of journalism*. What do you think this word means? What should journalism do? What is its function? What is its effect?

   • Ask "Who, What, Where, When, Why" questions about the newspaper you have chosen. Who reads the paper? Why do these people read this paper? What kinds of articles are included in the paper? What features are included in the paper?

   • Interview people connected with the particular newspaper: writers, editors, people who appear in the paper, subscribers.

   • Read articles and critiques written about the newspaper. What have others written about this newspaper? Be careful to get a well-rounded picture. Try not to accept one view without getting the other side of the story.

2. Write an essay in which you explore the level of influence the press has

"in perpetuating the ethnic stereotypes—and fueling the prejudices and ethnic conflicts—that increasingly polarize our increasingly multicultural society." In developing your essay, be sure to incorporate specific examples and details as support for your ideas and claims. You might begin in one of the following ways:

- Look at recent incidents involving racial conflict and ask what role(s) the media played in these incidents. Were both negative and positive influences present? To what extent did the media appear to escalate some of the incidents? Brainstorm on your own, and then ask your classmates for their opinions.
- Interview journalism professionals who might have covered stories involving ethnic or minority groups. If there is a journalism department at your school, interview several of the instructors.

Reading 65

The Entertaining of America

John Leo

John Leo writes on issues of social and political concern, and his work is often anthologized. "The Entertaining of America," originally published in the January 22, 1990, issue of *U.S. News and World Report,* is his commentary on an entertainment value system in American culture that has becme more prevalent in recent years. Leo shows concern for a society where the crime and violence of genuine human tragedy has become the mainstay of the movie industry, and where fiction and reality become increasingly more difficult to tell apart.

I called the confession hot line in New York last week to see what was new in human turmoil. For five or six times the cost of an ordinary phone call, you can now listen in on a great deal of real anguish (and some put-ons) "directly from people who have committed heinous crimes and other unusual acts."

First came the cautionary tale of Nicki, who says she cannot recover from the psychological and physical abuse she suffered while serving as a rock groupie in the '60s. Then a long story of awful sexual abuse told by a teenage girl who said she had murdered a love rival, shot her boyfriend in both legs and then, while on the run, summoned her brother, who raped her. Because the owners of this lucrative service know that private pain in America tends to end up as public entertainment, dialers are urged to "hear it here before you read it in the newspapers or see it on TV."

They are probably right about that. For all we know, agents dial the confession line in search of future properties. Maybe Joe McGinniss calls up looking for yet another mass murderer to write a book with. Or perhaps the titans of tabloid TV, Maury Povich, say, or the hilarious Geraldo, phone in. (Murderous dwarf-tossing lesbian quarterbacks who confess: Growing menace or alternative lifestyle? The next Geraldo.)

We have always turned crime and violence into entertainment, but until recently it never came anywhere near the currently feverish level. Now the murderer or mutilator and the victim or victim's survivors seem to call agents directly from the police station. The recent Stuart case in Boston is probably the all-time champion in generating book and movie ideas: More than a hundred landed on the desks of agents and editors in the first week after Charles Stuart, accused of murdering his wife, committed suicide. At the Little, Brown publishing house, an assistant editor received 10 book proposals on the subject in the first five days. CBS announced last week that it already has a movie in the works.

SOUND-BITE POLITICS

A year ago, Susan Sontag told an interviewer in Boston, "I'm going to say something really crude, because I can't think of a subtler way of saying it." Because Sontag is a high-powered intellectual, treated as an oracle by the press, we can imagine the interviewer sitting expectantly, hoping for dazzling revelation, but instead getting this sensible, almost obvious remark: "I think there has been a decline in the capacity for seriousness—that the society is dominated by entertainment values."

Sontag cited only one example of what she meant: The reduction of politics to bright little sound bites. (George Will says that the TV version of Lincoln's Emancipation Proclamation would have been six words long: "Read my lips: No more slavery.") But politics is just a minor victim of the relentless spread of the amusement industry. Listen to people in the media talk about their jobs and the word *entertainment* comes up all the time. Why did the dreadful info-tainment show "Yesterday, Today and Tomorrow" feature all that reconstructed footage? "People want to be entertained more," said the executive producer. "They want their attention held more." Why did the allegedly factual TV version of Nixon's last days in the White House show the President weeping, when the only two people in the room—Nixon and Kissinger—said it never happened? Because it played better on TV.

STAND-UP EDUCATORS

Many schoolteachers have evolved into entertainers, using magic tricks, rock music or frivolous field trips to win the hearts of students. When challenged, they say they have no choice: The youngsters expect to be entertained. This occurs at colleges, too. A friend who taught at an Ivy League college says "student evaluations of professors have led to a rating system that uncannily resembles TV ratings. Some professors keep their ratings up by preparing Johnny Carson one-liners or taking the class to little picnics or movies."

Each of the major network news shows has had a recent brush with the entertainment ethic. NBC has shamelessly used the "other woman" from the "Today" show, Deborah Norville, as a substitute anchor for Tom Brokaw. Her rating beat Dan Rather's. ABC faked the Felix Bloch spy footage. CBS has never satisfactorily rebutted charges that it used fake combat scenes from Afghanistan. For that matter, sending Dan Rather 8 feet over the Afghan border (the famous Gunga Dan scene of 1980) was highly entertaining, but of no news value at all.

American newspapers are probably going to grow more frivolous, if only because no one can think of any other way to get baby-boomers to read them. Fewer than half of the boomers vote, follow public affairs or read a daily paper. A study by the Knight-Ridder newspaper chain says some way must be found to ovecome the boomers' perception that reading papers is "a complex and unrewarding activity." It does not take a rocket scientist to see that shorter, lightweight journalism is the obvious way to go.

The same pressures are at work in the magazine world. My impression is that there are twice as many celebrity covers as there were a decade ago, and this ranges from traditional service books, such as *Good Housekeeping*, to the radical journal *Mother Jones*, which has adapted to reality by putting Susan Sarandon on the cover. The most dramatic shift is that Time, Inc., inadvertently swallowed whole by Warner, has mutated from an information company with a few amusement properties into an entertainment company with a couple of odd, nonamusement properties. Where all this will end, God knows. As one woman in Boston said of the Stuart case, "I can't wait to see the movie to see how it comes out."

QUESTIONS FOR "THE ENTERTAINING OF AMERICA" BY JOHN LEO

Talking About the Text

1. Leo opens the article with: "I called the confession line in New York last week to see what was new in human turmoil." What effect did this line have upon you as a reader? For what rhetorical purpose do you think Leo might have chosen to start in this manner?

2. Leo cites a variety of examples of personal experiences to support his claims. Which do you think are most persuasive and why?

Exploring Issues

1. Do you agree with Leo when he writes that "private pain in America tends to end up as public entertainment"? Try to cite examples of this phenomenon. What cultural values might be reflected by this sort of entertainment?
2. Look at the last sentence of the article. What does this quote say about the fine line we walk between reality and fiction?
3. Leo quotes an executive producer as saying: "People want to be entertained more. . . . They want their attention held more." Do you agree with the producer? If so, what do you think are the causes of this demand for increased entertainment in all aspects of life? If not, what argument would you use to dispute the producer's statement?
4. What are the potential ramifications of a society dominated by "entertainment values"? What might their effect be on politics? Education? Family? Other social institutions?

Writing Assignment

Keep a journal for one week of at least all encounters with various forms of entertainment media: anything from TV programs to piped music in banks and doctors' offices. Note your feelings at the time of each encounter. Then use your journal as the basis for a paper in which you discuss the role that entertainment media plays in shaping our perceptions of reality. Prewriting questions to consider are:

How many times a day do I encounter each particular entertainment medium?

For whom is this entertainment medium intended?

Who creates and disseminates this entertainment medium?

Am I ever exposed to this form of media without even realizing it?

What effect (emotional, psychological, intellectual) does it have on me (or on others)?

What effect does it have on my factual understanding of events?

Reading 66

Music

Allan Bloom

Allan Bloom is a professor of social thought at the University of Chicago, where he is the co-director of the John M. Olin Center for Inquiry into the Practice of Democracy. His most recent publication is entitled *Giants & Dwarfs*. (1990). He is also the author of the controversial best-seller *The Closing of the American Mind* (1987). The following selection is from that book's chapter on music in which Bloom argues that the moral education of today's youth is being threatened by the influence of rock music.

Picture a thirteen-year-old boy sitting in the living room of his family home doing his math assignment while wearing his Walkman headphones or watching MTV. He enjoys the liberties hard won over centuries by the alliance of philosophic genius and political heroism, consecrated by the blood of martyrs; he is provided with comfort and leisure by the most productive economy ever known to mankind; science has penetrated the secrets of nature in order to provide him with the marvelous, lifelike electronic sound and image reproduction he is enjoying. And in what does progress culminate? A pubescent child whose body throbs with orgasmic rhythms; whose feelings are made articulate in hymns to the joys of onanism or the killing of parents; whose ambition is to win fame and wealth in imitating the drag-queen who makes the music. In short, life is made into a nonstop, commercially prepackaged masturbational fantasy.

This description may seem exaggerated, but only because some would prefer to regard it as such. The continuing exposure to rock music is a reality, not one confined to a particular class or type of child. One need only ask first-year university students what music they listen to, how much of it and what it means to them, in order to discover that the phenomenon is universal in America, that it begins in adolescence or a bit before and continues through the college years. It is *the* youth culture and, as I have so often insisted, there is now no other countervailing nourishment for the spirit. Some of this culture's power comes from the fact that it is so loud. It makes conversation impossible, so that much of friendship must be without the shared speech that Aristotle asserts is the essence of friendship and the only true common ground. With rock, illusions of shared feelings, bodily contact and grunted formulas, which are supposed to contain so much meaning beyond speech, are the basis of association. None of this contradicts going about the business of life, attending classes and doing the assignments for them. But the meaningful inner life is with the music.

This phenomenon is both astounding and indigestible, and is hardly noticed, routine and habitual. But it is of historic proportions that a society's best young and their best energies should be so occupied. People of future civilizations will wonder at this and find it as incomprehensible as we do the caste system, witch-burning, harems, cannibalism and gladiatorial combats. It may well be that a society's greatest madness seems normal to itself. The child I described has parents who have sacrificed to provide him with a good life and who have a great stake in his future happiness. They cannot believe that the musical vocation will contribute very much to that happiness. But there is nothing they can do about it. The family spiritual void has left the field open to rock music, and they cannot possibly forbid their children to listen to it. It is everywhere; all children listen to it; forbidding it would simply cause them to lose their children's affection and obedience. When they turn on the television, they will see President Reagan warmly grasping the daintily proffered gloved hand of Michael Jackson and praising him enthusiastically. Better to set the faculty of denial in motion—avoid noticing what the words say, assume the kid will get over it. If he has early sex, that won't get in the way of his having stable relationships later. His drug use will certainly stop at pot. School is providing real values. And popular historicism provides the final salvation: there are new life-styles for new situations, and the older generation is there not to impose its values but to help the younger one to find its own. TV, which compared to music plays a comparatively small role in the formation of young people's character and taste, is a consensus monster—the Right monitors its content for sex, the Left for violence, and many other interested sects for many other things. But the music has hardly been touched, and what efforts have been made are both ineffectual and misguided about the nature and extent of the problem.

The result is nothing less than parents' loss of control over their children's moral education at a time when no one else is seriously concerned with it. This has been achieved by an alliance between the strange young males who have the gift of divining the mob's emergent wishes—our versions of Thrasymachus, Socrates' rhetorical adversary—and the record-company executives, the new robber barons, who mine gold out of rock. They discovered a few years back that children are one of the few groups in the country with considerable disposable income, in the form of allowances. Their parents spend all they have providing for the kids. Appealing to them over their parents' heads, creating a world of delight for them, constitutes one of the richest markets in the postwar world. The rock business is perfect capitalism, supplying to demand and helping to create it. It has all the moral dignity of drug trafficking, but it was so totally new and unexpected that nobody thought to control it, and now it is too late. Progress may be made against cigarette smoking because our absence of standards or our relativism does not extend to matters of bodily health. In all other things the market determines the value. (Yoko Ono is among America's small group of billionaires, along with oil and computer magnates, her late husband having produced and sold a commodity of worth comparable to theirs.) Rock is very big business, bigger than the movies, bigger than professional sports, bigger than television, and this accounts for much of the respectability of the music business. It is difficult to adjust our vision to the changes in the economy and to see what is really important. McDonald's now has more employees than U.S. Steel, and likewise the purveyors of junk food for the soul have supplanted what still seem to be more basic callings.

This change has been happening for some time. In the later fifties, De Gaulle gave Brigitte Bardot one of France's highest honors. I could not understand this, but it turned out that she, along with Peugeot, was France's biggest export item. As Western nations became more prosperous, leisure, which had been put off for several centuries in favor of the pursuit of property, the means to leisure, finally began to be of primary concern. But, in the meantime, any notion of the serious life of leisure, as well as men's taste and capacity to live it, had disappeared. Leisure became entertainment. The end for which they had labored for so long has turned out to be amusement, a justified conclusion if the means justify the ends. The music business is peculiar only in that it caters almost exclusively to children, treating legally and naturally imperfect human beings as though they were ready to enjoy the final or complete satisfaction. It perhaps thus reveals the nature of all our entertainment and our loss of a clear view of what adulthood or maturity is, and our incapacity to conceive ends. The emptiness of *values* results in the acceptance of the natural *facts* as the ends. In this case infantile sexuality is the end, and I suspect that, in the absence of other ends, many adults have come to agree that it is.

QUESTION FOR "MUSIC" BY ALLAN BLOOM

Talking About the Text

1. Bloom makes several claims about the adverse effects of rock music on the moral education of today's youth? What are some of these claims and how valid are they?
2. Bloom asserts that "the continuing exposure to rock music is a reality, not one confined to a particular class or type of child. . . . It is *the* youth culture. . . ." To what extent is this statement true? To what extent is it a generalization?

Exploring Issues

1. Consider your exposure or lack of exposure to rock music. In what ways have you been affected by it? How might your values and attitudes have been partially shaped by the music?
2. Bloom states that "any notion of the serious life of leisure, as well as man's taste and capacity to live it, had disappeared. Leisure became entertainment." Consider John Leo's article, "The Entertaining of America," in

the context of this statement. What similarities and/or differences do you find?

3. Compare and contrast Bloom's thoughts on culture with those of Pattison and Ventura later in this chapter. Is it possible to categorize youth into one "culture"?

4. Consider the relationship between self-expression and youth culture(s). What are some of the prevalent values and attitudes displayed by the youth culture with which you are most familiar?

Writing Assignment

Write a critical review of Bloom's argument. Whether you agree or disagree with Bloom's claims, consider both the strengths and weaknesses of this piece. Before you begin to write, try some of the following prewriting activities:

Carefully re-read Bloom's essay. As you read, make notes and underline the text for crucial information. Ask yourself which are the most important points. Make comments in the margin that give reasons for why you agree or disagree on certain issues.

List all the strengths and all the weaknesses of the essay. Compare your list with those of your classmates. Discuss differences and similarities.

Discuss with your classmates Question 1 from "Talking About the Text".

Reading 67

The New Literacy

Robert Pattison

Robert Pattison, the author of *On Literacy* (1982), teaches English at Southhampton College. In an excerpt from *On Literacy*, Pattison argues that today's youth have exchanged the values of a rigid and limiting mainstream American literacy for a more vital literacy found in rock lyrics, one that more readily allows for self-expression. As Pattison asserts, "the new literacy is not a by-product of cultural delinquency but a felt need among its users. It has evolution on its side, and its claims will be heard."

The doctrine of correct English in both its practical and quasi-religious aspects has had much to contend with in the last half-century. The natural evolution of language, the introduction and triumph of electronic media, and the democratic process that has increasingly elevated those unskilled in the approved forms of language to positions of popular influence have all worked against it. It survives at all because its benefits for organization outweigh the frustration occasioned by conforming to its restraints. Its continued authority, however, cannot help but give rise to a new, radical literacy, just as occurred in the Roman empire. Then, formal Latin became a written language of imperial power while another literacy, with its roots in the Christian message, grew up beside it and finally absorbed it. We too confront a new, popular brand of literacy, but one that has not yet found a dynamic ideology to give it purpose or direction.

The new popular literacy expresses itself in Americans' almost universal resistance to certain forms of correct English. Correct English, and the mechanical literacy of the middle classes that spawned it, have alienated the writing population just as it was alienated in the Hellenistic age. Today a universal system of mechanical language use according to inflexible rules has helped create two literacies. One is the established literacy taught in schools. The other is a popular literacy keyed to the spoken language of the people. We have one literacy of power and business and another still-forming literacy of popular vigor. This great development reveals itself in small examples. So far as I can judge, for instance, only Americans over forty or those educated in the select few schools that propagate the most exact habits still employ apostrophes with habitual conformity to the established rules. In the population at large, apostrophes to indicate either possession or contraction are an anachronism, and without constant pressure from the educational system, they would have passed out of usage long ago. The *New York Times* now frequently misses the apostrophe in possessives on back pages. Outside New York it disappears on front and back pages. In freshman essays it is nearly extinct. Even threats of corporal punishment could not induce college students to understand the logic or practice the use of the apostrophe. In the evolutionary scheme of the language, the apostrophe is a dodo.

Possessives always vexed writers of English, and the apostrophe is an artificial solution to the problem of distinguishing between contractions, genitives, and plurals. The question of apostrophes is only one example among many. Punctuation, spelling, syntax, and grammar are all slowly suffering an evolution in their popular usage that, unhindered by the restraints of correct English, would soon revolutionize the language.

This revolution, were it to succeed, would have been due in part to sloth. It is easier to ignore apostrophes than to trouble with their correct use. Sloth, while always a potent force for simplification in language, is nevertheless not the only force at work in the formation of a new, popular literacy. The same students who resolutely remain in darkness about the niceties of correct English grammar are as capable of intelligence as any previous generation. They are only selective about what niceties they choose to observe. Months of exercises will not shake their nonchalance about commas, but few are likely to misspell the name Led Zeppelin. The new literacy is not a by-product of cultural delinquency but a felt need among its users. It has evolution on its side, and its claims will be heard.

Heard is the right word, for like its Roman counterpart the new popular literacy is one of the ear more than the eye. The development of electronic media has facilitated its growth, and it finds its readiest means of ideological expression in music. Radio, television, and other sound-carrying electronics systems like tape and record players have been widely blamed for the collapse of literacy. This view is of course highly biased. Literacy from the time of the pharaohs forward has never collapsed but only changed. Those who denounce the new electronic media for corrupting literacy really mean to say that these innovations menace the middle-class literacy approved by the American establishment.

Electronic media are a powerful stimulant to the development of a literacy centered on the spoken word. They threaten established literacy by offering a continuous stream of vernacular raised to the level of popular art—an art without the restraints of correct English. The seemingly disparate programming that fills so much airtime on radio—rock'n'roll and religious revivalism—has in common an appeal beyond the established mechanical literacy. Both reject the prevailing doctrine that language at best suggests but never itself contains truth. American evangelism's alliance with radio and television could have been predicted from the long fundamentalist Christian tradition that emphasizes the enlightening power of the spoken word. Religious revivalism and rock music both assert the primacy of language and the immediacy of its inherent truth:

> I listened and I heard
> Music in the word,

says Peter Townshend's lyric, "Pure and Easy." Though this particular song evokes Eastern mysticism, it shares common ground with the Protestant ministry of the Christian Broadcasting Corporation. Rock and popular religion are alike fed by the desire of the people at large for a literacy that credits the power of language to capture and express the fullness of life.

Established American literacy, with its emphasis on mechanical skills and its assertion of the limitations of language, thwarts man's desire to feel himself fully represented in words. Evangelism and rock seek to provide the satisfaction of full representation in language, one by the traditional message of the living Word, the other by reviving, in the context of new electronic media, the primal appeal of lyric poetry. Rock demands respect as the first art form of the new literacy. Its lyricism is full of vigor and wit. Like the artistic output of any generation, most of it is trite, but its successes are dazzling. The opponents of rock condemn it by the aesthetic canons of the old literacy which it is the point of rock to reject. Implicit in rock is a new set of standards of beauty and language. The best rock is not just imitation Romantic or contemporary poetry. It is a form that asks to be judged by its own new values. Those who venerate the principles of the old print literacy will likely abominate rock, and indeed rock invites their abomination.

Like earlier popular literacies founded on the apotheosis of speech, it scorns formal language structures for the rapture of the Word:

> Don't know nothin' 'bout no Rise and Fall
> Don't know nothin' 'bout nothin' at all.

The new man, like the first Christians, is proud to be *rudis et indoctus,* uncouth and unlearned. This pride is in part the result of the Romantic aspect of current literacy. Words are suspect and counterfeit. Feeling is spontaneous and genuine. The less I know the more real I am. But the new generations of Americans are not without enthusiasm for language. The pride they take in their ignorance of correct English arises from the passion with which they have devoted themselves to a new type of literacy.

Classes of college freshmen, bored by literature anthologies and wary of traditional poetry, can nevertheless recite whole stanzas of The Who's lyrics from memory and discuss them with zeal. Critics of the new literacy claim that memorization is a lost talent among contemporary students, but in fact their memories are fine. Their ability to retain lyrics, commercials, and other forms of oral expression is capacious. Increasingly, however, they resist memorizing dates and literature associated with the established norms of language. They link this kind of memorization with the mechanical view of language against which their new literacy is engaged. Their supposed failure of memory is highly selective, and their ennui is not a response to all literacy, only to the prevailing literacy. Bruce Springsteen (another difficult spelling few students will ever miss) describes the literate man in rock culture:

> the poets down here
> don't write nothing at all.
> They just stand back and let it all be.

The conjunction of incorrect grammar with immediacy in the apprehension of life is no accident in rock lyricism. It is the essence of the new literacy.

The desire for a vital literacy is not new. As we have seen its roots are in the doctrine of the Logos in the early Church, in the popular aspects of the Protestant Reformation. No matter how refined its pedigree, however, this new literacy is not likely to win friends among the adherents of the old. By its nature it follows the early churchmen in finding the man who is *rudis et indoctus* praiseworthy for this nearness to the truth contained in speech. By its nature, it rejects the structures of formal written English in favor of the enthusiasm of the spoken word. The new literacy, however, is not a polar opposite of the old. The two are already inextricable. Television, that scorned object of smug contempt to the guardians of the existing literacy, does not replace reading and writing so much as alter their practice. The experience of the Renaissance with the introduction of print elucidates the process. Then, print did not dislodge the popular literacy of speech and enthusiasm. Instead it blended with it in ways that modified the destinies both of print and of literacy. A recent study of television viewing among American teenagers indicates that those who at an early age watch the most television programming will at a later age read the greatest number of books. Many of us are familiar with the habit of reading while watching television. The man propped up in front of the tv with an open book in hand is an emblem of the new literacy, which is slowly incorporating the mechanics of the old.

We can hear the process at work in expressions like "record library" or "tape library." Television and film strive for literary polish—their concession to established literacy. Authors constantly use tv or radio to promote their work, and script writers dream of publishing novels. Print meanwhile has become the handmaiden of the electronic media. Screenplays are prolegomena to novels. Even avant-garde writing if often little more than transcribed monologue or dialogue. The best selling magazine in America is *TV Guide*. The papers with mass circulation like the *Star* and the *National Enquirer* retail gossip about electronic-media stars.

The new media will not produce a population of non-readers or non-writers. They will, though, change fundamentally the way people regard reading and writing, first, by fostering an attitude toward language that believes in the real, inherent power of the Word and, second, by providing new mechanical means for the expression of literacy.

The new literacy, operating through the electronic media, will compel the established literacy of middle-class authority to become looser and more idiomatic. At the same time the established literacy will assert its claim that it alone provides the social and economic cohesion necessary for a productive society. Each brand of literacy will modify the other while purists of each camp watch in horror at the slow contamination of both. If we are lucky, the resulting mongrel product will be a literacy effective enough to serve the needs of social organization and technological development but sensible enough to maintain rapport with the vitality of spoken language and the need of the population for a sublime sense of language. If we are unlucky, the Edwin Newmans and John Simons will prevail. We will have two literacies, one of authority operating through print and known only to an elect handful of scribes trained at elite universities, the other propagated through electronic media and embodying the people's aspirations for an incarnation of the Word in the daily affairs of life. This second result would represent a severing of the body from the soul of our culture. It would pit class against class as well as literacy against literacy. It would be the end of the American experiment.

QUESTIONS FOR "THE NEW LITERACY" BY ROBERT PATTISON

Talking About the Text

1. Pattison makes use of several generalizations to serve his argument; for example: "Months of exercises will not shake their nonchalance about commas, but few are likely to misspell the name Led Zepplin." What

are some of these generalizations and to what extent do such generalizations serve to strengthen or weaken the rhetorical import of Pattison's claims?

Exploring Issues

1. Pattison writes that "implicit in rock is a new set of standards of beauty and language. The best rock is not just imitation Romantic or contemporary poetry. It is a form that asks to be judged by its own values." Speculate about the nature of these values.
2. Why do you think Pattison makes the claim that "print media has become the handmaiden of electronic media"? Is it an accurate description of the relationship between print and electronic media today? How might writers of other articles included in this chapter comment on Pattison's claim?
3. Pattison asserts that "the new literacy is not a by-product of cultural delinquency but a felt need among its users. It has evolution on its side, and its claims will be heard." What do you think Allan Bloom might say to this statement? What do you think about it?
4. Pattison makes mention several times of modern youth's selective memory. Why do you think it might be easier to remember the lyrics of a rock song or the spelling of a musician's name than certain fine points of English grammar?
5. Pattison writes of different kinds of literacies and their power to either oppress or liberate. What do you think are key qualities of a liberating literacy in which the self is fully represented?
6. To what extent do you think the "new literacy" can coexist with the "established literacy" of middle-class America?

Writing Assignment

Compose a working definition for a "new literacy." You need not directly refer to Pattison's "new literacy," but you should discuss its function and purpose for both self and society. Consider also the thoughts of other writers in this chapter. Some of the following prewriting activities may be helpful as a means of starting.

Brainstorm or cluster by yourself or with classmates on the word *literacy*. What comes to mind when you hear this word? What people, places, things, or ideas do you associate with this word?

Interview friends, classmates, teachers, relatives, co-workers, asking what they think about some of the issues Pattison presents in his essay. Make up an interview guide of questions before you start.

Find Pattison's book *On Literacy* in the library. See what else he has to say on the topic.

Reading 68

White Boys Dancing

Michael Ventura

Michael Ventura is a Los Angeles-based writer, currently a staff writer for *LA Weekly*, and also the author of an essay collection entitled *Shadow Dancing in the U.S.A.*, from which "White Boys Dancing" is excerpted. In this essay, Ventura offers an account of rock and roll's journey out of the slums into mainstream society and analyzes rock and roll's impact on middle-class culture and other societal phenomena such as the civil rights and women's movements.

You can *say* anything, but you can't *move* any way. White people tend to think they know things if they can say them. That's the assumption at the root of our education. It's an assumption that pervades everything in Western life and has long been our standard of superiority. Yet, though pushing forty, there are still some of us who are uncomfortable at parties where people don't dance. What else is a party for?

"Watch a man move," a (white) woman I know once told me, "and you don't need to ask him his life story."

"Can you tell how he'll be in bed?" I asked. And her rap went something like: "It's fun to guess, but naw—too many things enter into *that*. You can tell if he's got *talent*, but talent doesn't mean anything—screwing's like anything else, plenty of people with talent can't *do* much. Dancing—dancing is more how you've lived and where you've been, than how you screw. We're not far enough along yet for screwing to be . . . *representative*, you know? It still says most about our hang-ups. Dancing is what you *might* be when you get to where you're going. Wanna dance?"

The class of white males who've called the shots for so many years, maybe they've *said* it all—but cruise the clubs some night to watch the white boys move. They want to be there—why else would they be there? But the stiffness in the legs . . . feet that seem hardly to move by themselves, as they're hoisted up by the jerky crane of the thigh . . . arms just waggling or moving in half-hearted punchlike jerks, in accompaniment to a kind of hop . . . or flailing arms, with the torso swaying in awkward hula-hoop motions, having no more than a coincidental relation to the music . . . and the face: having to concentrate *so hard* on the little that's going on, and hardly ever smiling . . . and some shake violently, music the merest excuse, as though trying to shake life into atrophied limbs.

Which is, of course, what we're all trying to do. Maybe it's what rock 'n' roll is for.

The descriptions are painful because the process is painful. You've got to call it dancing; what else is there to call it? But if the band weren't playing, if there were no women, no booze, no late-night juices flowing—strip it all away and just watch the middle-class white boys move, and most of what you see is a desperate, rather brave effort to claim their bodies for the first time.

This ain't aerobics. With aerobics and sports the movements themselves may be challenging, but they aren't psychologically threatening. With aerobics you may or may not get healthier, but with aerobics you do not leave the world of white Christianist assumptions for other, entirely different, and possibly revolutionary ways.

For what *happens* when they start playing that music, in whatever dive or fancy joint?

It's an instant environment. One-two-three-rock—and you're there, *in it*. The rules of your culture are changed that instant, done away with. The new rule is: you can move, and you can move any way you want to.

A very new rule, that. Not how dancing was with the twenties' Charleston, the forties' lindy, or white-folk and cowboy dancing taken without much variation from northern Europe. Those dances mimed the patterns of their cultures; specific moves, to specific rhythms, only certain moves allowed, and boy leads girl. But sometime in the fall of 1958, a couple of years after Elvis Presley's "Heartbreak Hotel" had broken the airwaves wide open for rock 'n' roll, a new kind of dancing hit the Italian slums of New York. We didn't know that blacks had been dancing like this for hundreds of years. We didn't know anybody had *ever* danced like this. The first time we saw it in our neighborhood, it was a guy we called "the Weasel"; he was dancing with the memorable Maria Tombino, doing something sexy that looked like fun and was called the slop. In the South it was called the dirty bop, sometimes the sherry bop, and often the nigger bop. It was all the same.

It was the first time we saw people dance without holding hands. With no set step. Which meant that there was no leader. We didn't articulate it that way, that's just the way it was. Weasel was picking up Maria's signals, just like Maria was picking up Weasel's. That came naturally with this kind of dancing. The improvisation, the rhythm, the intensity, the freedom, the equality: *there* was a new culture. There were the only politics that ever held *me*. There was the paradigm for something new in America that could matter.

We were just a bunch of thirteen-year-old kids. We were feeling, not thinking. But the attraction was immense, and soon we were all dancing the slop.

There was something of a slinky shuffle recognizably the slop, but you had your own riff on it or you were nobody. And your face danced as much as your feet. It wasn't the breathless concentrated look of people doing the fifties' version of the lindy (a holding-hands fast-dance that was seen on "American Bandstand"). With the slop faces were playful or bored or tough, a come-on or a come-off-it, sexy-feisty or sexy-deadpan (memories of girls with faces floating as unconcerned as the moon over bodies that undulated, rippled and bumped— and they sure didn't learn to dance that way from their mothers, yet it had somehow been there all along).

After a few months of slopping, everybody was just doing their own no-hands dance. From now on the twist, the monkey, the mashed potato, the swim, and the bump would come and go, but each dance was incorporated into that individual style which was what dancing had become.

You could move any way you wanted.

We didn't know we were doing something new in white culture. We didn't know we were rejecting maybe 3,000 years of patterned white dancing. We'd never seen a ballet with its stiff torsos and tense grace. We didn't know we were taking the principles of Isadora Duncan, Martha Graham, and Merce Cunningham—all the gurus of uptown high art—into the street or that we were getting these principles from the same place they'd gotten them, Africa and the West Indies.

Appropriately enough, the first record that Weasel and Maria slopped to was the flip side of Mickey and Sylvia's "Love is Strange," a tune called "I'm the Monster Rock'n'Roll," in which a gravelly voice growled with great authority, "Ah'm duh mon-ster rock'n'roll, duh louder they scream duh bigger Ah grow," or words to that effect.

On the East Coast the slop-style dancing didn't get out of the slums till around 1961, when the twist caught on. Of course, the twist was as patterned as any kind of traditional dance, but in its excitement well-brought-up suburban children stopped holding hands when they danced, and they didn't start again when the twist wore off. They were dancing like us by then—or trying to. The change was permanent. Each individual dancing with each individual to a music that was their own. Thirty years later, you can go to any rock club anywhere and the dancing is fundamentally the same free-style pattern that began back then. Thirty years have developed infinite varieties, but, except for the brief lapse into disco in the late seventies, what is danced is still individualistic, still free style.

In most cultures that we honor enough to study, the dancing that everyone does—not just the dancing that the few do—has been considered of para-mount, even religious, importance. If our anthropologists had discovered the same sort of change in a non-Western culture, many books would have been written about it by now. Only in a culture like ours, a culture that tries to put everything in its mouth, thinking nothing important unless it can be said—only in such a culture would such a fundamental change go virtually unheralded by the "intelligent" voices of the time.

"The Whole on high hath part in our dancing. Amen. Whoso danceth not, knoweth not what cometh to pass. Amen." So says Jesus in the Gnostic Round

Dance, an early "testament" that the followers of Paul discarded when compiling the "new testament" which codified their authority. Jesus's feeling for dance does not comfort a need for centralized authority. I have also heard it translated, in much better English, as "He who doesn't dance does not know what happens."

Back in Brooklyn we were finding out what happens. Our bodies had been set loose. Still within the limits of the dance floor, yes. For only as long as the music, sure. But for the first time in the world of the Western white there was a *social form* that enabled us to be in our bodies, watch other people be in their bodies, even talk to each other through our bodies. The only limit used to be indecent exposure and that's not really a limit anymore in some places. There wasn't anything you had to learn and there wasn't any standards to scare away the timid. If they were scared, they were scared of the boys, or of the girls, or of their own bodies, but not of the dance itself, because it asked nothing of them but to be danced. Here was an echo, though they didn't know it, of an old saying from Zimbabwe: "If you can talk, you can sing. If you can walk, you can dance." That was rock 'n' roll all the way. For the first time there was an accepted social form of the body that mixed both sexes, as sports never did; wasn't confined to capital-D artistic Dance in the ghetto of "art"; and didn't ape the worst patterns of the culture (like rigid steps and the boy always leads the girl).

It isn't very surprising, when looked at this way, that the rush of excitement generated by this new form of being together would gestate into a youth movement that for the next fifteen years would roll at full momentum, giving tidal-wave force to the civil-rights movement, the antiwar movement, and the feminist movement. All of those would grow like cultures in the petri dish of the unity-of-feeling (not harmony certainly, but unity) that the music and its dancing created. Even now, what is called "pop music" these days is still powerful enough to give young people an environment in which to experiment with life away from the rules and ways of their elders. And we still don't know whether other society-shaking waves may roll out from what they're doing.

This is not to defend the shallow glop that has constituted so much of rock 'n' roll/pop. But the disc jockey Alan Freed knew what he was talking about in the late fifties when he said that this was a music "destined to make history." He should have. His dance show on TV, "The Big Beat," was the first television show in the country on which blacks and whites not only appeared together but danced together—even danced *slow* together. This was before many of our colleges and our lunch counters were integrated. And these weren't carefully selected, acceptable blacks, or whites either. These were street kids. There's good cause to believe that this was the major reason the FBI and the police hounded Freed.

And there is no need to defend rock 'n' roll against those who complain about how loud it is and how much noise it makes. Rock's noise has been necessary to break through the crust of self-consciousness accumulated over these last three thousand years. So that a place long asleep in us would wake.

In the instant environment of rock, the literally deafening noise cancels out the rest of the culture. The culture is based on "In the beginning was the Word," on what can be said, but the music starts and you can't *say* anything. It's too loud to talk by. Either you move or you watch other people move or you watch the performers. There's no way to go but out of the culture and into the beat.

And remember that this music got a lot louder as it was played more and more by suburban WASP kids. The genres of rhythm and blues, rockabilly, and soul music—basically poor-white and black forms, both urban and rural—aren't all that loud. (Certainly they're no louder than a big band of the swing era, and often not nearly as loud.) But WASP families don't scream in their houses. When they argue, things tend to get tensely, unbearably quiet; screaming is taboo. So when their children play music, they play it *loud*.

Once you go out of the society and into the beat, transformations occur. Revelations flash, whether you enjoy them or not. And the culture itself is seen bare in the flash.

Watch the white boys dancing. Most white men of the securer middle classes don't have what they call in rock 'n' roll "the moves." They are singularly graceless. But many of the white women of the same class aren't. They move pretty good, on the whole, especially in comparison with their men. And the people who can *really* move are the street kids—poor whites and Latins as well as blacks—who invent the dances and keep them alive. The mystery, then, is: what do most middle-class white females and most street kids have in common? Because their affinity for the same moves proves that they share something which the white middle-class men don't have.

No matter what level of society a woman's from, her primary awareness right from the first is of her body. She's not necessarily conscious of this, but that doesn't matter. From her earliest memories, what she puts on her body and how it moves is how she's judged. Judged all day, pervasively, no matter how enlightened she and her friends are. Her very survival, the jobs she gets, the people who accept her, is a matter first (and most brutally) of her body. In living rooms, in the girls' room in junior high, in offices, clubs, and while crossing streets, she's looked upon and judged by men, and women, again and again and again, hundreds of times a day. As she learns the dangers of having a female body today and the effects she can produce, she learns to control the signals it sends and receives with a subtlety that is so much a part of her she rarely need think of it. Learning the power of her body, how easily she can be noticed, what a stir she may make in the air as she passes, is fundamental to her knowledge of herself. Whether she likes it or not, this awareness of her body must become so pervasive for her that it ceases to be "awareness." She simply breathes it.

No surprise then that most middle- and upper-class women look graceful on a dance floor, at least when compared to their men. Their men think about their bodies only when hurt, hungry, or horny, or in relation to the mechanics of sports or aerobics. When the music starts, with all its fluidity, they're at a loss, while the women have learned the constant dialogue between a body and its world that is called grace. The difference in the nature of the middle-class male's and female's physical experience is mind-jarring.

But out there on those mean streets, the male experience of the body is as intense as that of the female. Any male growing up on the street is always aware of one overpowering fact: at any moment he may have to fight. The street only asks one question, and asks it again and again, every day: How tough are you? How much can you take? And how do *we* know?

On the street a man's body is an object as much as a woman's. He is always being watched, or feels he is. His moves must be as minutely measured, as delicately shaded as any lady's ever were. At the extreme, your moves can get you killed or save your ass. And on the street, things can get extreme at any moment. You have to show the street, at all times, just how tough you are. And it has to be precise: too much, and somebody a lot tougher than you may feel they have to take you to keep their status; too little, and they take you for sport. You shade your moves for who you're with and where you are, and if you walk around a corner and, like the Springsteen song says, things get real quiet real fast, you shade your moves for what you think your chances are. It's a reflex. And if the girls are watching you, or you want them to watch you, you shade your moves for them. Because boys parade their sex on the street just like women do. Street kids preen. So their repertoire of stances grows. It's not surprising that when the music starts, these boys know how to move.

We are faced with a paradox no liberal will enjoy: danger makes for grace. How to explain to a technocrat that his man-child moves like a constipated aardvark because danger is part of the body's food, and his child has been starved?

So no matter where we dance to rock 'n' roll we're dancing in the street. Just like Martha and the Vandellas once sang. Or as Archie Bell and the Drells put it some twenty years ago, "We not only *sing*, we *dance* just as good as we walk!"

Not just that the toughness of rock comes from the street; or that its dances and its rhythms originate there; or that its greatest innovators and interpreters started poor and tough and streetwise; but this: when rock shouts down the culture, then the music itself is the longest of the mean streets, all sex and quest and provocative moves with a beat, and the beat goes on. A street with enough extremes to keep it interesting; a street, over the last thirty years, with jungle-dense variety; and always the tense dialogues of bodies, even when those bodies don't know what they're saying. A music that inspires the flesh in cities that deny the flesh. And doesn't an empty dance floor feel like a deserted street?

Or say that the music cut a street through the whole society, so that something of what was best in the slums and the tin-roofed shacks made its way out, uptown, and into the suburbs, the small towns, the farms, shaking up everyone, invigorating so many, and giving people who never had it before a chance to find their own body's special grace.

The bitterness is that it's a one-way street, and no gift remotely comparable or life-giving was passed back to the slums.

QUESTIONS FOR "WHITE BOYS DANCING" BY MICHAEL VENTURA

Talking About the Text

1. Ventura uses a very conversational and anecdotal tone to convey his ideas. What effect does this tone have upon you as a reader? Do you think the informal tone is appropriate for the subject matter? Does it help to strengthen or weaken Ventura's arguments?
2. Ventura makes a connection between the musical revolution of rock and roll and other phenomena of the sixties and seventies such as the civil rights, peace, and women's movements. Why do you think he has made this connection, and what effect does the connection have upon you as a reader? How are these events related? What is it about rock and roll that might make it a pivotal force behind some of these other movements?

Exploring Issues

1. Ventura states that the dances of the twenties, thirties, and forties "mimed the patterns of their culture; specific moves, to specific rhythms, only certain moves allowed, and boy leads girl." With the advent of rock and roll, however, all the rules were broken, and a new improvisational freedom and vitality took over. Given this observation, what can we say about the relationship between an artistic medium, such as music, and cultural norms and mores?
2. Ventura makes a distinction between the grace of white, middle-class women and its absence in their male counterparts, finding more similarity between these women and the street kids. How valid are his observations? Do you agree with Ventura's explanation of why white, middle-class women and street kids share this common ground?
3. Ventura writes that "there is no need to defend rock 'n' roll against those who complain about how loud it is and how much noise it makes. Rock's noise has been necessary to break through the crust of self-consciousness accumulated over these last three thousand years. So that a place long asleep in us would awake." Speculate about what exactly is being awakened by this music. What would Allan Bloom say to Ventura's claim?
4. Ventura opens his essay with the statement that "you can say anything, but you can't *move* any way. White people tend to think they know things if they can say them. That's the assumption at the root of our education. It's an assumption that pervades the root of our education. It's an assumption that pervades everything in Western life and has long been our standard of superiority." Do you accept this assumption as something paramount in our culture? What would Pattison say to Ventura? To Bloom?
5. At the end of the essay, Ventura suggests that this music of the street kids is a "life-giving" force that has been shared with society as a whole.

He also notes that nothing comparable has been passed from mainstream society to the slums. In what ways might the "life-giving" force Ventura speaks of be different from what many might see as "life-giving" social programs offered to aid the needy?

Writing Assignment

Ventura states that "it isn't surprising . . . that the rush of excitement generated by this new form of being together would gestate into a youth movement that for the next fifteen years would roll at full momentum, giving tidal wave force to the civil rights movement, the antiwar movement, and the feminist movement." Write an essay in which you explore the political and social ramifications of rock and roll's evolution. You might want to focus your essay by choosing only one or two social or political phenomena as avenues for exploration. Consider trying some of the following prewriting activities.

Brainstorm on your own or with classmates on social or political phenomena you think might be connected in some manner to rock and roll.

Research the history of rock and roll by reading articles and books on the topic.

Interview people who grew up in the fifties, sixties, and seventies. Ask them for their memories of rock and roll at this time. What do they think rock and roll's influence has been? What attitudes and values do they feel have been affected by rock and roll? Make an interview guide before you start.

Reading 69

Tipper Gore

Curbing the Sexploitation Industry

Tipper Gore is co-founder of the Parents' Music Resource Center and has been an influential leader in the cause against violence and sexism in rock

lyrics and other media. In "Curbing the Sexploitation Industry," Gore argues
not for censorship but for rational and intelligent debate on limiting exposure
to "sexploitation" in the media. Her actions are spurred by a concern for
"the fate of the family, the dignity of women, [and] the mental health of
children."

I can't even count the times in the last three years, since I began to express my
concern about violence and sexuality in rock music, that I have been called a
prude, a censor, a music hater, even a book burner. So let me be perfectly clear:
I detest censorship. I'm not advocating censorship but rather a candid and
vigorous debate about the dangers posed for our children by what I call the
"sexploitation industry."

We don't need to put a childproof cap on the world, but we do need to
remind the nation that children live in it, too, and deserve respect and sensitive
treatment.

When I launched this campaign in 1985 . . . I went to the source of the
problem, sharing my concerns and proposals with the entertainment industry.
Many producers were sympathetic. Some cooperated with my efforts. But others have been overtly hostile, accusing me of censorship and suggesting, unfairly, that my motives are political. This resistance and hostility has convinced
me of the need for a two-pronged campaign, with equal effort from the entertainment industry and concerned parents. Entertainment producers must take
the first step, by labeling sexually explicit material.

But the industry cannot be expected to solve the problem on its own.
Parents should encourage producers to cooperate and praise them when they
do. Producers need to know that parents are aware of the issue and are reading
their advisory labels. Above all, they need to know that somebody out there
cares, that the community at large is not apathetic about the deep and lasting
damage being done to our children.

What's at issue is not the occasional sexy rock lyric. What troubles—
indeed, outrages—me is far more vicious: a celebration of the most gruesome
violence, coupled with the explicit message that sadomasochism is the essence
of sex. We're surrounded by examples—in rock lyrics, on television, at the
movies and in rental videos. One major TV network recently aired a preview of
a soap opera rape scene during a morning game show.

The newest craze in horror movies is something called the "teen slasher"
film, and it typically depicts the killing, torture and sexual mutilation of women
in sickening detail. Several rock groups now simulate sexual torture and murder
during live performances. Others titillate youthful audiences with strippers
confined in cages on stage and with half-naked dancers, who often act out sex
with band members. Sexual brutality has become the common currency of
America's youth culture and with it the pervasive degradation of women.

Why is this graphic violence dangerous? It's especially damaging for
young children because they lack the moral judgment of adults. Many chil-

dren are only dimly aware of the consequences of their actions, and, as parents know, they are excellent mimics. They often imitate violence they see on TV, without necessarily understanding what they are doing or what the consequences might be. One 5-year-old boy from Boston recently got up from watching a teen-slasher film and stabbed a 2-year-old girl with a butcher knife. He didn't mean to kill her (and luckily he did not). He was just imitating the man in the video.

Nor does the danger end as children grow older. National health officials tell us that children younger than teen-agers are apt to react to excessive violence with suicide, satanism, drug and alcohol abuse. Even grown-ups are not immune. One series of studies by researchers at the University of Wisconsin found that men exposed to films in which women are beaten, butchered, maimed and raped were significantly desensitized to the violence. Not only did they express less sympathy for the victims, they even approved of lesser penalties in hypothetical rape trials.

Sado-masochistic pornography is a kind of poison. Like most poisons, it probably cannot be totally eliminated, but it certainly could be labeled for what it is and be kept away from those who are most vulnerable. The largest record companies have agreed to this—in principle at least. In November 1985, the Recording Industry Association of America adopted my proposal to alert parents by having producers either put warning labels on records with explicitly sexual lyrics or display the lyrics on the outside of the record jackets. Since then, some companies have complied in good faith, although others have not complied at all.

This is where we parents must step in. We must let the industry know we're angry. We must press for uniform voluntary compliance with labeling guidelines. And we must take an active interest at home in what our children are watching and listening to. After all, we can hardly expect that the labels or printed lyrics alone will discourage young consumers.

Some parents may want to write to the record companies. Others can give their support to groups like the Parent Teacher Association, which have endorsed the labeling idea. All of us can use our purchasing power. We have more power than we think, and we must use it. For the sake of our children, we simply can't afford to slip back into apathy.

My concern for the health and welfare of children has nothing to do with politics: It is addressed to conservatives and liberals alike. Some civil libertarians believe it is wrong even to raise these questions—just as some conservatives believe that the Government should police popular American culture. I reject both these views. I have no desire to restrain artists or cast a "chill" over popular culture. But I believe parents have First Amendment rights, too.

The fate of the family, the dignity of women, the mental health of children—these concerns belong to everyone. We must protect our children with choice, not censorship. Let's start working in our communities to forge a moral consensus for the 1990's. Children need our help, and we must summon the courage to examine the culture that shapes their lives.

QUESTIONS FOR "CURBING THE SEXPLOITATION INDUSTRY" BY TIPPER GORE

Talking About the Text

1. What do you think Gore means by "sexploitation industry," and why do you think she chose this phrase to describe the use of sex and violence in the media? What comes to mind when you hear the phrase?
2. Gore's audience seems to be parents: "This is where we parents must step in. We must let the industry know we're angry." How persuasive do you think her essay is for an audience of parents? How might she revise her essay if she were writing to members of the entertainment industry? What other rhetorical strategies might she need to use?

Exploring Issues

1. Gore is concerned about the violent and degrading images of women found in rock lyrics, films, and soap operas. Are any other groups of people portrayed in similar ways? You might look at the next essay by Kenneth Goings on black memorabilia when considering this question.
2. Besides rock lyrics, films, and soap operas, where else in this society might we find these degrading images of women that concern Gore?
3. Gore says she is "not advocating censorship but rather a candid and vigorous debate about the dangers posed for our children by . . . the 'sexploitation industry.'" Discuss the specific nature of these dangers. Why is Gore so concerned about them?
4. If Gore is not advocating censorship, what is she proposing? How realistic or viable are her suggestions?
5. Gore's essay gets at a fundamental question: How accountable should producers and entertainment artists be for the effects of their material?

Writing Assignments

1. Gore suggests that parents write to record companies expressing their concern about "sexploitation" in rock lyrics. Choose a particular audience (producer, director, artist, or Gore herself) and compose a letter in which you argue your point of view. Before starting your letter, research your audience's attitudes and values toward this issue. Look at the arguments of your particular audience so that you are better able to defend and support your position. If possible, interview a member of that particular audience.
2. Write an argumentative essay in which you take a stand on the issue of labeling "sexploitive" lyrics. Before starting your essay, take some time to assess your feelings by freewriting on the topic for a few minutes.

3. Gore advocates the labeling of recordings that contain potentially problematic material. Write a proposal in which you suggest other methods for curbing the "sexploitation industry." First, brainstorm with classmates or by yourself on potential alternatives.

4. Write an essay in which you take a stand about accountability of entertainment artists and producers to their audiences. You might start by researching cases of criminals who claimed they were incited by various forms of media to perpetrate their crimes: the Hinkley assassination attempt on President Reagan, for example.

Reading 70

Memorabilia That Have Perpetuated Stereotypes About African Americans

Kenneth W. Goings

Kenneth W. Goings is associate professor and chairs the History Department at Rhodes College. He is also the collector of over 200 pieces of black memorabilia. In the following essay from the February 14, 1990, issue of *The Chronicle of Higher Education,* Goings argues that racist and derogatory images of African Americans in housewares, advertising, toys, and lawn ornaments have not only helped to perpetuate stereotypes of African Americans but also serve as "a window into American history."

In Ralph Ellison's great novel *Invisible Man*, the main character, a black person known as Invisible Man, comes across a piece of "early Americana," a "jolly nigger bank," and sees this gross caricature with its black skin, red lips, and white eyes staring up at him from the floor. Enraged at the object and at the insensitivity of his landlady for keeping such an image around, the Invisible

Man inadvertently breaks the bank and tries to sneak the pieces into a neighbor's trash can, but the neighbor stops him. Then he casually tries to leave the bundled pieces along the street, but a good samaritan returns the package to him. Finally, he ends up carrying the pieces with him into his hiding place, underground.

The Invisible Man's attempt to dispose of the broken pieces of the bank is indicative of African America's attempt to throw off racial and gender stereotypes. Every time the stereotypes seem to disappear someone or something brings them back. The something in this case is black memorabilia—often known as black collectibles—which have reflected and perpetuated racial and gender stereotypes about African Americans for years. These objects, produced from the late 17th century to the present, have been almost universally derogatory, with exaggerated racial features that helped "prove" that African Americans were "different" and inferior.

They also have been commonplace, items one might find in any home or yard: housewares (such as Aunt Jemima and Uncle Mose salt and pepper shakers), postcards, advertising cards, toys, lawn ornaments, etc. The everyday nature of these items meant that they were heavily used (the wear and tear on the surviving collectibles attests to this) and that frequency of use reinforced the owners' conscious and unconscious acceptance of the stereotypes. These items of material culture gave a physical reality to ideas of racial inferiority. They were the props that helped reinforce the racist ideology that emerged after Reconstruction.

While collectibles were produced from the late 17th century on, their real significance as icons of racial and gender stereotyping dates back only to the decades immediately after the Civil War, when slavery was no longer a status determiner for African Americans. This was the period from 1880 to 1930, arguably the worst time for black people and race relations in the United States, a time that encompassed the retreat from Reconstruction, the rise of the second Klan, hundreds of lynchings, the Great Migration north, and the race riots during and after World War I. It is during this period that new structures and new routines had to be developed and practiced to create and sustain a "new" or different racial ideology based not on slavery, but on concepts of racial inferiority. Folk-art pieces, sheet music, tourist items, and some housewares dominated this period. Black people, male and female, were portrayed as very dark, generally bug-eyed, nappy headed, childlike, stupid, lazy, deferential but happy. Black women were portrayed in the Jemima/mammy motif: fat, silent, nurturing and taking care of the "masses."

From the 1930's to the early 1960's in the United States, racial attitudes began to relax, to soften. Americans, including African Americans, had fought Nazis and Fascists overseas. It became more difficult, consequently, for whites to hold to the hard racist views of the past. Black collectibles reflect this changed perspective. Items, particularly housewares, became more functional and decorative. The skin tones on the collectibles were brighter, and some of the images of black women were slimmed down. Still, African-American women were generally portrayed as mammies and domestic workers and, increasingly, as the harlot. African-American males were represented as harmless, sexless clowns, not as mature workers, except for the image of the old family retainer, Uncle Mose. Their images emerged on salt and pepper shakers, cookie jars, stringholders, utility brushes, games, toys, and cooking utensils.

The final period, from the 1960's to the present, is somewhat peripheral to the main body of collectibles, much like the late 17th century to the 1880's. The last three decades have seen the most radical changes in race relations and attitudes. African Americans began calling themselves "black." The activism of the civil-rights movement, the resistance to police brutality linked with the assertiveness of the Black Power movement made it almost impossible to portray African Americans as loyal, servile, but happy Aunt Jemimas and Uncle Moses. Americans had only to turn to their television sets: It was obvious that Aunt Jemima and Uncle Mose were out marching, battling police dogs, and burning down Watts. The exaggerated characteristics of the collectibles began to disappear as it became clearly illiberal, if not downright racist, to possess these items. Collectibles became more political: buttons, posters, and bumper stickers abounded. Also, black artists began creating new, more realistic images to replace the distorted images of the past.

To some extent, however, new—albeit more positive—stereotypes simply replaced the old. The militant Angela Davis traded places with Aunt Jemima and Malcolm X attempted to put Uncle Mose to rest.

Black collectibles are a window into American history. As the nation and ideology changed, the image created of black people by white people changed. Black collectibles were props in the slave/racial ideology that has engulfed America from the 17th century to the present. They were the physical manifestation of a culture that continually negated and demeaned African Americans and their achievements. Manufacturers produced the props that gave physical reality to the racist ideology that had emerged, and they did so at a profit. Literally, images of black people were being bought, sold, and used much like the slaves of ante-bellum America.

Perhaps one day, unlike the Invisible Man, African Americans will be able to leave these images in a trash can for keeps.

QUESTIONS FOR "MEMORABILIA THAT HAVE PERPETUATED STEREOTYPES ABOUT AFRICAN AMERICANS" BY KENNETH W. GOINGS

Talking About the Text

1. Goings tells the story of Ralph Ellison's Invisible Man and his inability to rid himself of the broken pieces of a "jolly nigger bank." Why do you suppose Goings chooses to begin his essay with this story? What is its significance to Goings' central theme?

2. Goings develops his essay to a great extent from a historical perspective. How does this perspective serve to guide and structure Goings' argument?

Exploring Issues

1. According to Goings, how does black memorabilia help reinforce racism? In his view, what is the relationship between the physical reality of these objects and ideology?
2. Why do you think the memorabilia took the form of commonplace household items such as salt shakers and lawn ornaments? What is the significance of these items?
3. What is the relationship between black slavery and the retailing of these derogatory images of black people?
4. How does this essay bring to the fore a tension between imagery and reality? How is reality shaped by the images of ourselves we see in various media? What other essays in the chapter have dealt with this issue?
5. Speculate about the relationship between political and/or social reform and the representation of blacks in various media.

Writing Assignment

Do some research on the use in advertising of African-American and African or East Indian characters such as Aunt Jemima and Sambo. Write an essay in which you explore the effect this form of advertising might have had on the perpetuation of racism in the United States. Begin your research with one of the following prewriting activities.

Look through old magazines and newspapers at the library containing advertisements that made use of black characters such as Sambo. Take notes on how these characters are presented and analyze their potential emotional and psychological impact on intended audiences.

Look at advertisements in today's magazines, newspapers, and commercials. Do you find evidence of racism?

Interview people who might remember the use of black characters in advertising from different eras (1930s, 1940s, 1950s). What are their feelings and attitudes toward this form of advertising?

Reading 71

Beauty: When the Other Dancer Is the Self

Alice Walker

Alice Walker is a teacher, novelist, poet, and essayist. Walker is probably best known for her novel, *The Color Purple* (1982); she has also written *Meridian* (1976), a novel of the civil rights movement. *The Temple of My Familiar* is her most recent novel. Her poetry collections include *Once* (1968), *Revolutionary Petunias and Other Poems* (1973), *Goodnight, Willie Lee, I'll See You in the Morning* (1979), and *Horses Make a Landscape Look More Beautiful* (1984).

The following selection has been taken from a collection of essays entitled *In Search of Our Mothers' Gardens* (1983). In this essay, Walker relates a traumatic childhood incident that had a significant influence on her life. Her story, which spans 30 years, tells us how she perceived herself at different times of her life, and in the telling, we begin to see how the artist's work becomes an act of self-discovery.

It is a bright summer day in 1947. My father, a fat, funny man with beautiful eyes and a subversive wit, is trying to decide which of his eight children he will take with him to the county fair. My mother, of course, will not go. She is knocked out from getting most of us ready: I hold my neck stiff against the pressure of her knuckles as she hastily completes the braiding and then beribboning of my hair.

My father is the driver for the rich old white lady up the road. Her name is Miss Mey. She owns all the land for miles around, as well as the house in which we live. All I remember about her is that she once offered to pay my mother thirty-five cents for cleaning her house, raking up piles of her magnolia leaves, and washing her family's clothes, and that my mother—she of no money, eight children, and a chronic earache—refused it. But I do not think of this in 1947. I am two and a half years old. I want to go everywhere my daddy goes. I am excited at the prospect of riding in a car. Someone has told me fairs are fun. That there is room in the car for only three of us doesn't faze me at all. Whirling happily in my starchy frock, showing off my biscuit-polished patent-leather shoes and lavender socks, tossing my head in a way that makes my ribbons bounce, I stand, hands on hips, before my father. "Take me, Daddy," I say with assurance; "I'm the prettiest!"

Later, it does not surprise me to find myself in Miss Mey's shiny black car, sharing the back seat with the other lucky ones. Does not surprise me that I thoroughly enjoy the fair. At home that night I tell the unlucky ones all I can remember about the merry-go-round, the man who eats live chickens, and the teddy bears, until they say: that's enough, baby Alice. Shut up now, and go to sleep.

It is Easter Sunday, 1950. I am dressed in a green, flocked, scalloped-hem dress (handmade by my adoring sister, Ruth) that has its own smooth satin petticoat and tiny hot-pink roses tucked into each scallop. My shoes, new T-strap patent leather, again highly biscuit-polished. I am six years old and have learned one of the longest Easter speeches to be heard that day, totally unlike the speech I said when I was two: "Easter lilies / pure and white / blossom in / the morning light." When I rise to give my speech I do so on a great wave of love and pride and expectation. People in the church stop rustling their new crinolines. They seem to hold their breath. I can tell they admire my dress, but it is my spirit, bordering on a sassiness (womanishness), they secretly applaud.

"That girl's a little *mess*," they whisper to each other, pleased.

Naturally I say my speech without stammer or pause, unlike those who stutter, stammer, or, worst of all, forget. This is before the word "beautiful" exists in people's vocabulary, but "Oh, isn't she the *cutest* thing!" frequently floats my way "And got so much sense!" they gratefully add . . . for which thoughtful addition I thank them to this day.

It was great fun being cute. But then, one day, it ended.

I am eight years old and a tomboy. I have a cowboy hat, cowboy boots, checkered shirt and pants, all red. My playmates are my brothers, two and four years older than I. Their colors are black and green, the only difference in the way we are dressed. On Saturday nights we all go to the picture show, even my mother; Westerns are her favorite kind of movie. Back home, "on the ranch," we pretend we are Tom Mix, Hopalong Cassidy, Lash LaRue (we've even named one of our dogs Lash LaRue); we chase each other for hours rustling cattle, being outlaws, delivering damsels from distress. Then my parents decide to buy my brothers guns. These are not "real" guns. They shoot "BBs," copper pellets my brothers say will kill birds. Because I am a girl, I do not get a gun. Instantly I am relegated to the position of Indian. Now there appears a great distance between us. They shoot and shoot at everything with their new guns. I try to keep up with my bow and arrows.

One day while I am standing on top of our makeshift "garage"—pieces of tin nailed across some poles—holding my bow and arrow and looking out toward the fields, I feel an incredible blow in my right eye. I look down just in time to see my brother lower his gun.

Both brothers rush to my side. My eye stings, and I cover it with my hand. "If you tell," they say, "we will get a whipping. You don't want that to happen, do you?" I do not. "Here is a piece of wire," says the older brother, picking it up from the roof; "say you stepped on one end of it and the other flew up and hit you." The pain is beginning to start. "Yes," I say. "Yes, I will say that is what happened." If I do not say this is what happened, I know my brothers will find ways to make me wish I had. But now I will say anything that gets me to my mother.

Confronted by our parents we stick to the lie agreed upon. They place me on a bench on the porch and I close my left eye while they examine the right. There is a tree growing from underneath the porch that climbs past the railing to the roof. It is the last thing my right eye sees. I watch as its trunk, its branches, and then its leaves are blotted out by the rising blood.

I am in shock. First there is intense fever, which my father tries to break using lily leaves bound around my head. Then there are chills: my mother tries to get me to eat soup. Eventually, I do not know how, my parents learn what has happened. A week after the "accident" they take me to see a doctor. "Why did you wait so long to come?" he asks, looking into my eye and shaking his head. "Eyes are sympathetic," he says. "If one is blind, the other will likely become blind too."

This comment of the doctor's terrifies me. But it is really how I look that bothers me most. Where the BB pellet struck there is a glob of whitish scar tissue, a hideous cataract, on my eye. Now when I stare at people—a favorite pastime, up to now—they will stare back. Not at the "cute" little girl, but at her scar. For six years I do not stare at anyone, because I do not raise my head.

Years later, in the throes of a mid-life crisis, I ask my mother and sister whether I changed after the "accident." "No," they say, puzzled. "What do you mean?"

What do I mean?

I am eight, and, for the first time, doing poorly in school, where I have been something of a whiz since I was four. We have just moved to the place where the "accident" occurred. We do not know any of the people around us because this is a different county. The only time I see the friends I knew is when we go back to our old church. The new school is the former state penitentiary. It is a large stone building, cold and drafty, crammed to overflowing with boisterous, ill-disciplined children. On the third floor there is a huge circular imprint of some partition that has been torn out.

"What used to be here?" I ask a sullen girl next to me on our way past it to lunch.

"The electric chair," says she.

At night I have nightmares about the electric chair, and about all the people reputedly "fried" in it. I am afraid of the school, where all the students seem to be budding criminals.

"What's the matter with your eye?" they ask, critically.

When I don't answer (I cannot decide whether it was an "accident" or not), they shove me, insist on a fight.

My brother, the one who created the story about the wire, comes to my rescue. But then brags so much about "protecting" me, I become sick.

After months of torture at the school, my parents decide to send me back to our old community, to my old school. I live with my grandparents and the teacher they board. But there is no room for Phoebe, my cat. By the time my grandparents decide there *is* room, and I ask for my cat, she cannot be found. Miss Yarborough, the boarding teacher, takes me under her wing, and begins to teach me to play the piano. But soon she marries an African—a "prince," she says—and is whisked away to his continent.

At my old school there is at least one teacher who loves me. She is the teacher who "knew me before I was born" and bought my first baby clothes. It is she who makes life bearable. It is her presence that finally helps me turn on the one child at the school who continually calls me "one-eyed bitch." One day I simply grab him by his coat and beat him until I am satisfied. It is my teacher who tells me my mother is ill.

My mother is lying in bed in the middle of the day, something I have never seen. She is in too much pain to speak. She has an abscess in her ear. I stand looking down on her, knowing that if she dies, I cannot live. She is being treated with warm oils and hot bricks held against her cheek. Finally a doctor comes. But I must go back to my grandparents' house. The weeks pass but I am hardly aware of it. All I know is that my mother might die, my father is not so jolly, my brothers still have their guns, and I am the one sent away from home.

"You did not change," they say.

Did I imagine the anguish of never looking up?

I am twelve. When relatives come to visit I hide in my room. My cousin Brenda, just my age, whose father works in the post office and whose mother is a nurse, comes to find me. "Hello," she says. And then she asks, looking at my recent school picture, which I did not want taken, and on which the "glob," as I think of it, is clearly visible, "You still can't see out of that eye?"

"No," I say, and flop back on the bed over my book.

That night, as I do almost every night, I abuse my eye. I rant and rave at it, in front of the mirror. I plead with it to clear up before morning. I tell it I hate and despise it. I do not pray for sight. I pray for beauty.

"You did not change," they say.

I am fourteen and baby-sitting for my brother Bill, who lives in Boston. He is my favorite brother and there is a strong bond between us. Understanding my feelings of shame and ugliness he and his wife take me to a local hospital, where the "glob" is removed by a doctor named O. Henry. There is still a small bluish crater where the scar tissue was, but the ugly white stuff is gone. Almost immediately I become a different person from the girl who does not raise her head. Or so I think. Now that I've raised my head I win the boyfriend of my dreams. Now that I've raised my head I have plenty of friends. Now that I've raised my head classwork comes from my lips as faultlessly as Easter speeches did, and I leave high school as valedictorian, most popular student, and *queen*, hardly believing my luck. Ironically, the girl who was voted most beautiful in our class (and was) was later shot twice through the chest by a male companion, using a "real" gun, while she was pregnant. But that's another story in itself. Or is it?

"You did not change," they say.

It is now thirty years since the "accident." A beautiful journalist comes to visit and to interview me. She is going to write a cover story for her magazine that focuses on my latest book. "Decide how you want to look on the cover," she says. "Glamorous, or whatever."

Never mind "glamorous," it is the "whatever" that I hear. Suddenly all I can think of is whether I will get enough sleep the night before the photography session: if I don't, my eye will be tired and wander, as blind eyes will.

At night in bed with my lover I think up reasons why I should not appear on the cover of a magazine. "My meanest critics will say I've sold out," I say. "My family will now realize I write scandalous books."

"But what's the real reason you don't want to do this?" he asks.

"Because in all probability," I say in a rush, "my eye won't be straight."

"It will be straight enough," he says. Then, "Besides, I thought you'd made your peace with that."

And I suddenly remember that I have.

I remember:

I am talking to my brother Jimmy, asking if he remembers anything unusual about the day I was shot. He does not know I consider that day the last time my father, with his sweet home remedy of cool lily leaves, chose me, and that I suffered and raged inside because of this. "Well," he says, "all I remember is standing by the side of the highway with Daddy, trying to flag down a car. A white man stopped, but when Daddy said he needed somebody to take his little girl to the doctor, he drove off."

I remember:

I am in the desert for the first time. I fall totally in love with it. I am so overwhelmed by its beauty, I confront for the first time, consciously, the meaning of the doctor's words years ago. "Eyes are sympathetic. If one is blind, the other will likely become blind too." I realize I have dashed about the world madly, looking at this, looking at that, storing up images against the fading of the light. *But I might have missed seeing the desert!* The shock of that possibility—and gratitude for over twenty-five years of sight—sends me literally to my knees. Poem after poem comes—which is perhaps how poets pray.

ON SIGHT

I am so thankful I have seen
The Desert
And the creatures in the desert
And the desert Itself.

The desert has its own moon
Which I have seen
With my own eye.
There is no flag on it.

Trees of the desert have arms
All of which are always up
That is because the moon is up
The sun is up
Also the sky
The stars
Clouds
None with flags.

If there *were* flags, I doubt
the trees would point.
Would you?

But mostly, I remember this:

I am twenty-seven, and my baby daughter is almost three. Since her birth I have worried about her discovery that her mother's eyes are different from other people's. Will she be embarrassed? I think. What will she say? Every day she watches a television program called "Big Blue Marble." It begins with a picture of the earth as it appears from the moon. It is bluish, a little battered-looking, but full of light, with whitish clouds swirling around it. Every time I see it I weep with love, as if it is a picture of Grandma's house. One day when I am putting Rebecca down for her nap, she suddenly focuses on my eye. Something inside me cringes, gets ready to try to protect myself. All children are cruel about physical differences, I know from experience, and that they don't always mean to be is another matter. I assume Rebecca will be the same.

But no-o-o-o. She studies my face intently as we stand, her inside and me outside her crib. She even holds my face maternally between her dimpled little hands. Then, looking every bit as serious and lawyerlike as her father, she says, as if it may just possibly have slipped my attention: "Mommy, there'a *world* in your eye." (As in, "Don't be alarmed, or do anything crazy.") And then, gently, but with great interest: "Mommy, where did you *get* that world in your eye?"

For the most part, the pain left then. (So what, if my brothers grew up to buy even more powerful pellet guns for their sons and to carry real guns themselves. So what, if a young "Morehouse man" once nearly fell off the steps of Trevor Arnett Library because he thought my eyes were blue.) Crying and laughing I ran to the bathroom, while Rebecca mumbled and sang herself off to sleep. Yes indeed, I realized, looking into the mirror. There *was* a world in my eye. And I saw that it was possible to love it: that in fact, for all it had taught me of shame and anger and inner vision, I *did* love it. Even to see it drifting out of orbit in boredom, or rolling up out of fatigue, not to mention floating back at attention in excitement (bearing witness, a friend has called it), deeply suitable to my personality, and even characteristic of me.

That night I dream I am dancing to Stevie Wonder's song "Always" (the name of the song is really "As," but I hear it as "Always"). As I dance, whirling and joyous, happier than I've ever been in my life, another bright-faced dancer joins me. We dance and kiss each other and hold each other through the night.

The other dancer has obviously come through all right, as I have done. She is beautiful, whole and free. And she is also me.

QUESTIONS FOR "BEAUTY: WHEN THE OTHER DANCER IS THE SELF" BY ALICE WALKER

Talking About the Text

1. Walker italicizes key phrases, such as: *I remember, What do I mean? But mostly, I remember this.* Why do you think Walker uses this device? What is the effect of this technique on you as a reader?
2. Walker uses dialogue in several passages in this essay. Why do you think she chose to use direct quotes instead of summary? What rhetorical advantages might the use of dialogue offer?
3. Walker weaves the central incident of her blinding throughout her essay in the form of memories from different ages. Why do you think she structures her essay in this manner? How do the individual memories work together to create a whole?

Exploring Issues

1. Walker is a poet, novelist, and essayist. Given the thoughts she presents in this essay, especially those at the end of the essay, why might one say that the act of writing (or any creative act) is an act of self-discovery?
2. At the end of the essay, Walker relates the story of her daughter saying, "Mommy, there's a *world* in your eye." Why do you think Walker tells us this story? Of what significance is it to the whole essay? What did these lines make you think or feel when you read them?
3. Consider the title of the essay ("Beauty: When the Other Dancer Is the Self") as well as the final lines: "The other dancer has obviously come through all right, as I have done. She is beautiful, whole and free. And she is also me." Walker tells us that this "other dancer" is the self. In your own words, speculate about what she might mean. Have you had any experiences like hers?
4. Read Michael Ventura's essay in this chapter ("White Boys Dancing"). What similarities and differences do you see between what he and Walker say about self-expression?

Writing Assignment

Walker writes about a major event in her childhood that in many respects served to shape her identity. Speculate about key moments or times in your childhood or adolescence that had a significant influence on your life. Then write an exploratory essay in which you describe the event and show how it has had an effect on you. Before writing your essay, brainstorm about childhood memories and their significance for you personally.

Reading 72

The Black Writer and the Magic of the Word

John Wideman

John Wideman is author of the *Homewood Trilogy* and a novel, *Reuben*. In "The Black Writer and the Image of the Word," Wideman looks at the tension between a black writer's two worlds: that of mainstream academic and literary circles, and that of a distinctly African-American heritage. Wideman presented a version of this essay as a speech at the Institute for Advanced Studies in Humanities at the University of Massachusetts at Amherst. The version of the essay reproduced here appeared in the *New York Sunday Times Book Review* on January 24, 1988.

At a certain point in my writing career, after I had done three books, I made a decision. I wanted to reach out to readers that the earlier works had perhaps excluded. I wanted to get everybody's ear. I had in mind a book for people familiar with America, with the technique and history of the novel—a book that audience could appreciate and applaud and relate to the Great Traditions, if there really are such things. But at the same time a book my brothers, sister, aunts, uncles, cousins, mother and father would want to read. And in my mind it became quite clear that I wouldn't be writing down to a black audience. My people's lives embrace the whole range of human experience. In fact, the language they speak, refined and tested by centuries of racial oppression and racial assertion, offers a unique vision of America. So it wasn't a question of condescending to a less educated set of readers, but of becoming more ambitious.

My goal has always been to write as well as anybody has ever written, but I am sure now that for a long time I didn't know what really counted as legitimate subject matter, legitimate language, for such an enterprise. To write the very best, didn't you have to cheat on your past a little, didn't you have to "transcend Blackness"? Didn't you have to prove yourself by grounding yourself outside a black environment like Homewood, the community in Pittsburgh where I was raised?

I was university educated, and as you go through schools like the University of Pennsylvania and Oxford University, you get a value system imposed on you. You don't just guess what the best is, people tell you what the best is. Lessons, styles seep in. As I had grown up, a value system had formed, college attempted to put another in place, and so I was not consciously turning my back on blackness. I was just becoming acculturated, and the acculturation pushed my writing in predictable directions.

When I began to teach literature in college, I taught what I'd learned: books by white authors. Then, about 1967 or 1968, I took a summer and part of a year to develop a course in Afro-American literature. I went from a very superficial acquaintance to an absolute immersion in black literature. Afro-American literature courses have become a special love. And my writing has absolutely been transformed by my study of Afro-American writing and culture.

For seven years between books, I was exploring voice, doing a lot of practicing, studying, "woodshedding," as the musicians would say—catching up. I was learning—relearning may be more accurate—a new language with which to talk about my experience, a language I used in my novel "Damballah": "Hey man, what's to it? . . . ain't nothing to it something to it I wouldn't be out here in all this sun you looking good you into something go on man you got it all you know you the Man hey now that was a stone fox you know what I'm talking about you don't be creeping past me."

Afro-Americans must communicate in a written language which in varying degrees is foreign to our oral traditions. You learn the language of power, learn it well enough to read and write but its forms and logic cut you off, separate you from the primal authenticity of your experience, experience whose meaning resides in the first language you speak, the language not only of words but gestures, movements, rules of silence and expressive possibilities, of facial and tactile understanding, a language of immediate, sensual, intimate reciprocity, of communal and self-definition.

Houston A. Baker Jr. in "The Journey Back," a study of Afro-American writers and culture, speculates on the ex-slave Frederick Douglass's autobiographical narrative: "The voice of the unwritten self, once it is subjected to the linguistic codes, literary conventions, and audience expectations of a literate population, is perhaps never again the authentic voice of black American slavery. It is, rather, the voice of a self transformed by an autobiographical act into a sharer in the general public discourse about slavery." He goes on to ask, "Where in Douglass's narrative does a prototypical black American self reside?"

Does an Afro American necessarily lose contact with an authentic self if he or she decides to tell a story in print, in a second acquired tongue? Are the only options silence or fatal compromise?

For hundreds of years black people have been speaking English. Beginning as a pidgin or trade language on the west coast of Africa, then transformed to a creole as a second generation of Africans was born on American soil, the English that black people speak has a distinct history, intertwined but always systematically in tension with the standard or mainstream variety of English spoken by newscasters and other imaginary Americans. The key word is "systematically."

Since language and culture are symbiotic, if we can begin to describe systematically the kinds and quantity of distance between speech patterns and standard norms, we also will be defining the roots of Afro-American culture. And if we can identify the means Afro-American writers employ to keep the oral roots of black culture alive and kicking in our fiction, we can perhaps find that place in our writing where Houston Baker's prototypical black American self resides.

In simple terms, the "inside" of black speech is just as important as its outside. One highly developed aspect of black speech and Afro-American oral tradition is the means by which its users can signify how they feel about what they're saying. Dual messages are transmitted in a single speech act. Distance between black speech and standard speech always exists, but under various circumstances black speakers acknowledge and use this distance differently. At one end of the continuum measuring this distance between black speech and standard English is bilingual fluency; at the other, silence. Play is the esthetic, functional manipulation of standard English to mock, to create irony or satire or double-entendre, to signify meanings accessible only to a special segment of the audience. Play creates a distinctly Afro-American version of English; the speaker acknowledges to himself and announces to his audience that he's not taking the language of the slavemaster altogether seriously. But the play is serious business. A survival technique, an art form reproducing English in a nonrepresentational fashion, or, if you will, employing what Robert Ferris Thompson, in "African Art in Motion," called the "mid-point mimesis" characteristic of West African sculpture and other arts.

Think of the massive forehead of a Benin mask, how the exaggerated, dominant brow projects cool intelligence, or the elongated, swanlike necks of carved Yoruba female figures, which embody grace, elegance and balance through the calculated distortion of natural proportions. Think of kidnapped Africans learning English during slavery days, improvising, stylizing the master's speech, using it, abusing it, treating it as real, but not too real. If we conceive of the context in which kidnapped Africans learned English during slavery days, clearly the new language would be tainted by the master/slave relationship.

Learning English to survive would have been necessary, but inside the slave's mind a natural resistance, a balkiness, fear, suspicion, even hatred of the new language would condition the learning process. A deep intuitive understanding of the fact that there's no place, no room for me inside this *thing*, this language that is one more cruel weapon my captors wield against me. Recall Caliban's plight. Recall the numb black children nodding in schoolrooms today. The structure of an English pidgin reflects laws of linguistic change, but it also mirrors the dynamics of the social context in which it evolved. The language created in this crucible must not be viewed simply as a clumsy attempt to master the sounds and syntax of English; it should also be seen as a record of the harsh circumstances of its birth, a vehicle captive Africans employed to express their feelings toward English, which is not so much spoken as played with.

The goal of a particular pronunciation is only partially to represent an English sound. The discrepancy between a word in black speech and the *same* word in standard English can function symbolically to stylize, personalize, to appropriate a word. In Charles Waddell Chesnutt's story "Deep Sleeper," originally published in 1887, a character named by his master Secundus after the second Latin ordinal number is known on the plantation as Skundus. If pushed, Skundus' fellow slaves could have learned to enunciate "Secundus" in spite of their inherent laziness, big lips and mental inferiority. The point is they chose not to. They rebaptized Skundus to secure his identity in the black speech community, an identity that slips the yoke and turns the joke back on the pretentious white owner and the dehumanizing number-label he attached to his property.

This process of symbolic abstraction, of creating verbal icons, is basic to black versions of English. Africans took English sounds and with variation in tempo, rhythm, tone and timbre transformed them. Pushing English in the direction of their more tonal African languages, new sense evolved as well as new sounds. Play reinforced a tendency to draw out the music buried within English—rhyme, interpolation of African syllables and words or just plain scat-singing nonsense marked this African stylization of the speech of their captors. The process parallels the magic Billie Holiday performed on the banal tunes and lyrics of Tin Pan Alley. The testimony of contemporary Africans who speak Wes Cos or Kriol or pidgin, West Indian fancy talk, the oral narratives of ex-slaves, contemporary narratives collected from prisons, bars, street corners and the workingplace, as well as rap records and the folk-derived forms of Afro-American music, all testify to the fact that black speech is not simply faulty English but a witness to a much deeper fault, a crack running below the surface, a fatal flaw in the forms and pretensions of so-called civilized language.

The historical, outside approach to defining Afro-American speech emphasizes the *capacity* to speak a second, new language, but what is just as important as capacity is desire and will. And will resides inside an individual. Slaves spoke as much or as little as they chose to speak. In this sense, silence is a logical extreme of play, deadly serious play with standard English, signifying that we ain't playing no more. Pretense is ended. There's nothing more to say. The distance between your version of reality and mine admits no possibility of mutual intelligibility. (Perhaps that's why a black person who's quiet in the company of whites is often perceived by whites as stupid or sullen or dangerous.) Obviously it would not have been to the slave's advantage to reveal to his master his full capacity, whether of language, intelligence or ability to work. The exercise of will, then as today, is a variable difficult to determine from the outside, yet clearly significant if one wishes to understand how, why and when blacks use different registers of English.

A fiction writer is not a slave; he or she is a participant in a literary as well as an oral culture. Most black writers are impressively fluent in a variety of dialects: black, white, genteel, literate and many registers in between. Yet just as the slave's oral pidgin English was English transformed by his original African language and the master-slave relationship, the black writer's English, if examined closely, will reveal its sources in Afro-American culture, a culture that has been generated partly as a response to racism. If he wished to survive, the slave was forced to learn the sounds and syntax of English. If black writers wish to publish, we have to learn the grammars of 20th-century American culture and adjust our literate speech to their constraints: economic, political, moral, esthetic. Whatever individuality, whatever freedom of expression either writer or slave achieves can be illuminated by viewing what they say against the systemic net of restrictions designed to inhibit their voices.

Recall that Billie Holiday's genius flourished in spite of the fact she received only third-rate songs to record, in spite of the fact that her style didn't fit audience expectations, in spite of the simplistic, sentimental lyrics of American popular music, in spite of racism and sexism. The deep structures of African languages survived in the slaves' version of the new language enforced upon them. So too, in the case of Afro-American writing, an authentic prototypical black American self can shine forth in spite of the restrictions imposed upon this voice when it breaks into print.

The terrible thing is that as writers or critics we are forced into certain kinds of choices, choices laden with values the writer doesn't necessarily hold. A critic can argue, "Wideman is a good writer, he uses Afro-American folklore, he knows this or that about his heritage and culture." The critic can make that argument, show it in the work and pat me on the back, but that doesn't get me out of the ghetto. Even if I've accomplished what the critic ascribes to me—and surely that is enough—there is still an implied, invidious comparison "O.K., Wideman does fine with Afro-American stuff, but on the other hand back at headquarters, the real writers are doing thus and so. . . ." To protect ourselves as critics and artists, we are forced to jump back and forth, measure ourselves against an imaginary mainstream, define what we are doing in somebody else's terms. One thing for sure it is a terrible bind.

The historical problem is unavoidably there, and how you solve it creates a sort of "out of the frying pan into the fire" dilemma. There is an Afro-American tradition. There are Afro-American writers working right now, it makes sense to talk about us as a group. It is natural, enlightening, intelligent to approach the work that way, but at the same time, to do so perpetuates the whole wrongheaded notion of looking at things in terms of black and white, and in our culture this implies not simply a distinction, but black inferiority. In academia, Mr. Dewy-Eyed Optimistic (who is really Mr. Turn-Them-Back in disguise) believes that the purpose of Afro-American literature classes is remedial, a fine-tuning of the curriculum, and argues that the millennium will arrive when American literature classes include "Invisible Man." The real challenge of Afro-American culture gets lost. It's not a question of making a little more room in the inn but tearing the old building down, letting the tenants know their losses are such that no one is assured of a place, that the notion of permanently owning a place is as defunct as the inn.

When someone asks if I like being called an Afro-American writer, its almost like asking which of my names I prefer. When I play basketball, some of the young guys at the University gym call me Doc, and I like that. Back in Pittsburgh at Mellon Park playground, some of the old guys call me Spanky;

that's O.K. too. But I don't want other people to call me those names. Names are contextual. They make sense in certain situations, but the same names are insulting in others. Various literary labels are O.K. with me, as long as people don't get confused and call me *out of my name;* that's the important thing.

In the fiction I have published during the last several years, I have been trying to recover some lost experience, to re-educate myself about some of the things I missed because the world was moving so fast. My books returned to Homewood and settled in. I am trying to listen again. Fortunately, my people are kind, compassionate, patient. In contrast to Thomas Wolfe, I can go home again, listen again. There is a basic conservatism in any folk life. Little sayings and phrases that I read in the W.P.A. ex-slave narratives, I'd heard before in my living room. For instance, "Stomp down ugly." When I found that phrase in a slave narrative I cracked up because I had been hearing that my whole life. Afro-American culture is conservative; and it gives you a chance to go back. Writing is a means of preservation for the community, the ethnic group, as well as the individual artist.

Cultures, ethnic groups, nations are fragile, mortal. A whole way of life can disappear. For a long time I'd entertained a secret fear about black people, black culture in the United States. Not the stark 60's paranoia about genocide, but a creeping, exhausting sense that a link was being severed, a connection lost. The main currents of black life had little to do with whatever was unique, special about Africans who had been transplanted to the New World, Africans who'd experienced their Time on the Cross but who'd never lost touch with the old ways, the ancestral spirits that animated Afro-American prayers, music and motion. I had a sense that after all the suffering and struggle, we were losing with a whimper what no one had been able to steal, crush or beat out of us. The melting pot would have its way. Slowly, surely the monoculture would claim us. Black Kens and Barbies would be free at last.

I seldom spoke this fear, both because I didn't want to believe it could happen and because I didn't know exactly how to express what caused me to feel it might happen. Plus, I have a superstition. Naming things can give them life. A former slave being questioned about illness and mortality on slave planta-tions before emancipation declared that people were healthier back then be-cause back then folks didn't know the names of all these diseases they know nowadays. When James Baldwin protested "Nobody Knows My Name," he was complaining about invisibility, the status of nonexistence his color had relegated him to. Of course he was right and wrong. Everybody knew his name. And when they called him "nigger" they tried to manufacture and own him in the same breath.

N. Scott Momaday has pointed out the precariousness of any oral culture, how the tales and ways of Native American people have always been just one generation from extinction. If each generation doesn't learn and pass on the stories and customs, the vitality of ethnic traditions ends. As a fiction writer, a critic and a teacher I am trying to forge bulwarks and bridges, protect and share what is uniquely mine and yours. I depend upon the magic of the word.

QUESTIONS FOR "THE BLACK WRITER AND THE MAGIC OF THE WORD" BY JOHN WIDEMAN

Talking About the Text

1. Wideman recounts personal experiences as a means of developing his thoughts. What overall rhetorical effect does this technique have upon you as a reader?
2. At the end of his essay, Wideman writes that "as a fiction writer, a critic and a teacher, I am trying to forge bulwarks and bridges, protect and share what is uniquely mine and yours. I depend on the magic of the word." He also refers to "the magic of the word" in the title. What effect does this phrase have upon you? Why do you think Wideman chose to title and close his essay with these words? Try to define what Wideman might mean by "the magic of the word."

Exploring Issues

1. Wideman writes of the tension for black writers between the oral traditions of African-American English and the mainstream written traditions of the power elite. What are the inherent difficulties for Wideman in this dichotomy? Can you think of analogous situations in which an artist might feel conflict between the medium of representation and the intended message?
2. Wideman asserts that "oral narratives of ex-slaves, contemporary narratives collected from prisons, bars, street corners and the workingplace, as well as rap records and the folk-derived forms of Afro-American music, all testify to the fact that black speech is not simply faulty English but a witness to a much deeper fault, a crack running below the surface, a fatal flaw in the forms and pretensions of the so-called civilized language." Discuss the nature of this "fatal flaw." To what is Wideman referring?
3. Discuss the nature of language as an art form and its capacity for both representing and shaping identity.
4. Wideman writes that the language of the African-American is a "language not only of words but gestures, movements, rules of silence and expressive possibilities, of facial and tactile understanding, a language of immediate, sensual, intimate reciprocity, of communal and self-definition." What if any, similarities exist between this statement and the thoughts of Michael Ventura in "White Boys Dancing?"
5. Wideman elucidates the double bind of many black writers and artists when he says: "We are forced to jump back and forth, measure ourselves against an imaginary mainstream, define what we are doing in somebody else's terms." Do you think artists of other ethnic groups have a similar experience? Is is possible to clearly define this "imaginary mainstream"?

Writing Assignment

Wideman asserts that "writing is a means of preservation for the community, the ethnic group, as well as the individual artist." Focus on *one* aspect or facet of a particular community or ethnic group with which you are familiar. Observe and consider it carefully. Then write an exploratory essay in which you discuss your observations and analyze their significance for you. You might begin with the following prewriting activity:

> Brainstorm about various communities and ethnic groups to which you belong. Then narrow your focus down to a particular community, group, or segment of community life. Finally, interview people from that community to discover different perspectives.

CHAPTER 8: EXTENDED WRITING ASSIGNMENTS

8-1. After reading all or some of the selections in this chapter, you may now be more attuned to the effects of media on our lives. Return now to the questions asked in the chapter's introduction: To what extent do the various media serve to liberate and uplift the human spirit? To what extent do they oppress? Use the readings in this chapter as well as other pertinent material you may have researched as a basis for a response to either one of both of these questions. Let the following suggested prewriting activities help you to respond:

> Go over your notes from the readings and class discussions. Pick out key ideas that relate to the topic and freewrite on them, as a way to discover subissues you would like to discuss in the essay.

> Make a list of the readings from this chapter (or other readings) that you think are connected to the topic. Go through these readings and look for key ideas or quotes. (Freewrite on the ideas presented in these quotes.)

> Brainstorm on the topic with your colleagues. What do they think about media's role as liberator or oppressor?

8-2. David Shaw asks us to consider how the press may be unfairly representing ethnic minority groups by focusing too much on crime, poverty, and aberrant behavior; Tipper Gore argues for a curbing of violent and sexist images in rock lyrics; Allan Bloom suggests that the moral education of today's youth has been endangered by rock music; and Kenneth Goings explores the relationship between black memorabilia and stereotypes about African Americans. Each author in a slightly different manner comes to the same conclusion: The media has *an effect* on our personal and societal relationships as well as on our own self-perception. Drawing on at least three readings from this chapter, write an essay in which you consider the following question: How accountable should producers or artists of any medium be for the effects of their work on the public and/or the individual? Before writing, interview professionals who work in the various media (journalists, artists, writers, musicians). Ask them for their opinions on the question of accountability. Before interviewing make up some key questions to use.

Chapter
9

Harvesting Our
Differences

W ith this final chapter we attempt to reformulate several themes raised throughout this book, and in so doing, we present some selections that attempt to be restorative. Yet we do not mean "restorative" in the sense of attempting to recapture some previous healthier social condition. Rather, we mean "restorative" to be a reexamination of some of our traditional values that upon reflection might help us to imagine a way our present society might better realize our cherished ideals of freedom and equality. As we approach the twenty-first century and face problems previously undreamed of in the history of the world, it might behoove us to seek out recognizable guides and to reinterpret those ideals that have appeared to us through our history and that beckon us toward our future.

The main theme in this chapter is that we cannot move forward and begin to deal with our conflicts until we face the problem of our own identity. Who are we as individuals? And who are we as a nation? What role does our history play in this search for an identity? And what might be perennial about our condition as a people attempting to do what no other nation has attempted on such a mass scale—to include a wide spectrum of peoples from a diversity of backgrounds and still manage to live, work, play, learn, and grow as one society?

We offer no final solutions; in fact, some selections present further problems, but problems that help us see older ones from new perspectives. Some selections, like that of Kurt Vonnegut, Jr., present us with a satirically dark vision of the future that could conceivably develop from elements believed to be essential to our nation. With a title like "Harvesting Our Differences" we are already claiming that our diversity is our greatest resource and fount of strength and vitality. We just need to learn how to first recognize and then reap our treasures in order that we may all be rich—"rich" not necessarily in the material sense.

In the lead essay, Peter Marin, a contributing editor to *Harper's Magazine*, challenges us to consider what American "culture" really is. He claims that, just as we have always lived in "a moral and spiritual wilderness," so the freedom this brings us is the source of our greatest opportunity as well as of our greatest anxiety. Complementing Marin's essay, the poet Edward Field offers two poems about his grandmothers. Through his dramatic narratives and compelling images, Field reminds us of the sacrifices as well as the horrors endured by past generations in their struggles to reach America. We forget their painful histories at the expense of losing a meaningful connection from our present to their past. Amy Tan succeeds Field with another selection from her exceptional bestselling novel, *The Joy Luck Club*. Here the narrator, Rose Hsu Jordan, embeds one narrative within another as she confesses to her mother that her marriage to an American doctor is failing. Her mother's response triggers the memory of Rose's youngest brother who drowned in the ocean while Rose was assigned the duty of watching out for him.

The fourth selection is by Professor Diane Ravitch, an expert in history and education; her essay on multiculturalism confirms the vitality of our pluralistic society. Yet, Ravitch points out, this pluralism whose advocates "seek a richer common culture" is threatened by a "pernicious" strain that Ravitch calls "particularism." Particularists argue "that no common culture is possible or desirable." Whereas Ravitch views particularists as raising differences above what we all might share in common, to Adrienne Rich individual differences need to be identified, acknowledged, and embraced if people are to discover the self-knowledge of who they are.

Significant turning points in Rich's life are frequently marked by her growing awareness of major political events. One such event was the Civil Rights movement of the sixties. A landmark speech of that movement was Martin Luther King's "I Have a Dream," which he delivered in Washington, D.C., in 1963. We reproduce the written form of that speech here and invite you to consider how King skillfully harmonizes African Americans' struggle for freedom with our national ideals, reminding us of our country's spiritual purposes in the process. After King's speech, another provocative commentary by Michael Ventura challenges us "to remember" what America is really all about. He claims that the "Most Essential Documents" have never been written, and that the series of exchanges between John Adams and Thomas Jefferson reveal a revolutionary (as opposed to a political) impulse that must be "re-created every day in the minds of the people." If our country is failing, according to Ventura, it is due to a failure of the imagination.

From the provocative prose of Ventura we then move to the gentle tone and the exceptional craft and artistry of Eudora Welty. "A Worn Path" is a short story about Phoenix, an elderly grandmother, who makes a frequent but necessary journey to town. Phoenix's passing takes her along a torturous path through the forest in order to secure medicine for her grandson. "A Worn Path" is also a metaphorical journey of the soul, because the lives of our children—our hopes for the future—are in the hands of caretakers like Phoenix who show us what faith, hope, and charity mean when these virtues are embodied in our actions.

Finally, we conclude this chapter and our book with a humorous yet pessimistic glimpse, approximately 100 years into the future. This forward-looking view is provided by Kurt Vonnegut, Jr., who in the year 2081 dramatizes the state of our lives when everybody finally has become equal. However, there is only one drawback: "Equality" is achieved through law and is cruelly enforced by the United States Handicapper General's Office. All differences have been eradicated, though Harrison Bergeron challenges this state of affairs in a solitary act of rebellion witnessed on television by his parents.

Although our book concludes here, we hope that you continue to think about what you have encountered and that you pursue your insights through further reading, writing, and talking to one another.

Reading 73

Toward Something American

Peter Marin

Peter Marin is a contributing editor at *Harper's Magazine.* This essay, as it appeared in *Harper's,* was adapted from Marin's introduction to *The New Americans,* a photo essay by Ulli Stelzer, published in 1988 by New Sage Press. Marin is currently working on a book about homelessness and marginality, entitled *Margins.* In this essay Marin explains how our "culture" is really a composition of the immigrant experience. In America the immigrant is caught between the pull of a past that no longer applies and the yearning for imagined future possibilities but who is without guidance and support for how to achieve that future.

It is a commonplace, I know, to say we are a "nation of immigrants." But that means far more than that we are all descended from foreigners. It also means that the very tenor and nature of American life—its underlying resonance, its deep currents—have been defined in large part by the immigrant experience and, in particular, by the immigrant's experience of displacement and loss. You can find writ small, in individual immigrant lives, the same tensions, ambiguities of desire, contradictions, and struggles that are writ large across almost all of American life and in most American lives.

I am thinking, specifically, about what happens to the traditions and values that previously gave order and meaning to immigrants' lives—the crisis that occurs in terms of *culture*. It is that crisis, I think, that is in an important sense our own, enveloping and involving all Americans—even those of us whose ancestors arrived here long ago.

Culture, after all, is more than the way immigrants (or, for that matter, the rest of us) do things, dress, or eat. It is also more than art, ritual, or language. It is, beyond all that, the internalized and overarching beliefs and systems of meaning that create community, dignify individual lives, and make action significant. It provides a way not only of organizing the world but also of realizing the full dimensions and dignity of one's own existence and the moral relation it bears to the full scheme of earthly and unearthly things.

And it is all of that which is called into question and threatened when immigrants leave one place for another. To put it as simply as I can: immigrants find themselves dislocated not only in terms of space but also in terms of meaning, time, and value, caught between a past no longer fully accessible and a future not yet of use. Inevitably, a sort of inner oscillation is set up, a tension between the old world and the new. The subsequent drama is in some ways more profound, more decisive than the material struggle to survive. It invovles the immigrant soul, if by soul one simply means the deepest part of the self, the source of human connectedness and joy. The great tidal pulls of past and future, of one world and another, create a third and inner work, *the condition of exile*— one in which the sense of separateness and loss, of in-betweenness, of suspension and even orphanhood, become more of a home for the immigrant, more of a homeland, than either the nation left behind or America newly entered.

Perhaps it is easiest to understand all this by looking at the schisms that appear within immigrant and refugee families, the gaps that open up between generations. The parents are for the most part pulled backward toward the values of the past, often struggling to create, in the new world, simulacra of the cultures they left behind. But the children are pulled forward into the vortex of American life with its promise of new sensations, pleasures, experiences, risks, and material goods—most of which have more to do with fashion than with values, and few of which, in the end, can touch the soul, deepen the self, or lead someone to wisdom.

You will note that I said American "life" rather than American "culture." I want to make that distinction clear. For I am not absolutely sure that there really is an American culture—not, at least, in the ordinary sense of the word or in the form of anything that might replace in the heart or moral imagination what immigrant parents left behind. What we like to think of as the "melting pot" often seems more like a superheated furnace that must be fed continuously with imported values and lives, whose destruction creates the energy and heat of American life. And as interesting as that life is, and as liberating or addictive as it can become, in terms of values, America remains even now much what it was when the first Europeans arrived: a raw open space, a wilderness, though today it is a moral and spiritual wilderness rather than a geographical one.

I do not say that mournfully or deploringly. A wilderness, after all, is not empty. It has its own wonders and virtues. It is simply wild, untamed, essentially unknowable and directionless: open to all possibilities and also full of dangers. If you think about it, what one is really talking about here is freedom: the forms it takes in America, and what it costs as well as confers upon us. The ideas of wilderness and freedom have always been intertwined in America. It was the moral neutrality of the wilderness, the absence of preexisting institutions, of culture, if you will, which conferred upon the settlers the freedom they sought. Even while still on their ships, the Puritans claimed to be in "a state of nature" and therefore free of all sovereignty save their own. And now, 300 years later, freedom in America still means essentially *being left alone:* the chance to pursue, undeterred by others, the dictates (or absence) of appetite, will, faith, or conscience.

But that same idea of freedom, which is the real hallmark of American life and perhaps its greatest attraction, also causes immense difficulties for us. For one thing, it intensifies the fragmentary nature of our society, undermining for many Americans the sense of safety or order to be found in more coherent cultures. For another, it makes inevitable social complexity, competition between values, and rapidity of change, which often make the world seem threatening or out of control, inimical to any system of value.

Hence the nostalgia of so many Americans for the past, a nostalgia which exists side by side with perpetual change and amounts, in moral terms, to a longing for "the old country." The fact is that the values and traditions fed to the furnace of American life never disappear altogether—at least not quite. There remains always, in every ethnic tradition, in the generational legacy of every individual family, a certain residue, a kind of ash, what I would call "ghost-values": the tag ends and shreds and echoes of the past calling to us generations after their real force has been spent, tantalizing us with idealized visions of a stability or order or certainty of meaning that we seem never to have known, and that we imagine can somehow be restored.

You can detect the pull of these ghost-values in our political debates about public issues such as abortion, pornography, and "law and order," and in the vast swings in American mores between the adventurous and the conservative. But equally significant and far more interesting are the ways in which these schizoid tendencies are at work in so many of us as individuals—as if we ourselves were (and indeed we *are*) miniaturized Americas.

Let me give two examples. Recently a friend of mine attended a wedding in New England at which two gay women were married in a traditional Jewish ceremony. And I have another friend, an Englishman, who decided after fifteen years in America and a marriage and three children and a divorce, to become a woman. After surgery he turned out to be a carbon copy of the conservative matrons he had seen, as a child, taking tea in his mother's drawing room. When I asked about the children, he said, "I just want to be a mother to them."

There you have it—America! I have not chosen these examples idly, extreme as they may seem. Both are, in essence, attempts to solve the immigrant's dilemma. Both reveal something that seems to me particularly and poignantly American: a combined hunger and innocence in which we ache for both freedom *from* the past and the safety *of* the past at the same time. We are apparently unwilling to sacrifice one for the other. It is as if we are—each one of us, each American—both the immigrant child straining to escape the past and the immigrant parent struggling to preserve it.

The end result, of course, is that we end up much the way our immigrant ancestors did: without a world in which we feel at home. The present itself seems continually to escape us. The good and the true always lie behind us or ahead. Always in transit, usually distracted, we are rarely satisfied or sustained by the world as it is, things as they are, or the facticity of the given, to use a fancy but accurate phrase. We tend to lack the deep joy or the gravid resignation engendered in other cultures by a sense of ease in time: the long shadow cast by lives lived for generations in a loved mode or place. "Home" is for us, as it is for all immigrants, something to be regained, created, discovered, or mourned—not where we are in time or space, but where we dream of being.

QUESTIONS FOR "TOWARD SOMETHING AMERICAN" BY PETER MARIN

Talking About the Text

1. In your own words explain what Marin means when he writes: "Immigrants find themselves dislocated not only in terms of space but also in terms of meaning, time, and value, caught between a past no longer fully accessible and a future not yet of use."

2. Marin distinguishes between American "life" and American "culture." What distinction is Marin making here?

3. Marin writes that "the great tidal pulls of past and future, of one world and another, create a third and inner world, 'the condition of exile.'" Explain further what Marin means by this "condition." How might it apply to nonimmigrants?

4. Try to define that often used but rarely examined abstract term *freedom*. Compare your definition with Marin's when he says that "freedom in America still means essentially 'being left alone.'" What are the similarities? The differences?

Exploring Issues

1. How does this sense of alienation in American life affect families of both immigrants and native-born people? If you have read the chapter on

family life, you might use what you have learned there to help you
elaborate your response further.

2. Marin says that we are "always in transit." How does this affect our lives
   in terms of the family? In terms of education? In establishing and maintaining community? In how we use our resources, build our towns and
   cities, and create the spaces in which we dwell?

Writing Assignments

1. In an expository essay explain American "culture" to someone who has
   just recently arrived in this country. You might highlight what you
   consider the significant and the trivial, the rewarding and the dangerous, about our culture. Use examples from your experience that you
   know your readers your age will understand and probably encounter.
   Your purpose is to explain what, in your view, is most typically "American." In gathering data for this essay, try to interview some immigrants
   who have been in this country only a short time, and find out what
   puzzles them about our culture. Use this information to guide you in
   finding a focus for your essay.

2. Identify problems encountered by new arrivals to this country. Then
   write a proposal to either your city, town, or community leaders recommending ways in which immigrants can be made to feel more at home.

Reading 74

Both My Grandmothers
Edward Field

Edward Field has been writing and publishing poetry since World War II. He
won the Lamont Poetry Award in 1962 for *Stand Up, Friend, with Me*. Field
has wr tten *A Full Heart* (1978) and *Stars in My Eyes* (1979) and edited *A
Geography of Poets* (1979). The following poems about his two
grandmothers appeared in *Variety Photoplays* (1975). We ask that you read
these poems and reflect upon the countless unnamed individuals who

sacrificed so much to get to America. Was their struggle worth it? What happens if we forget why they endured so much to be here?

MY POLISH GRANDMA

Grandma and the children left at night.
It was forbidden to go. In those days
the Czar and his cossacks rode through the town at whim
killing Jews and setting fire to straw roofs
while just down the road the local Poles
sat laughing as they drank liquor.

Grandpa had gone to America first
and earned the money for the rest of the family to come over.
So they left finally, the whole brood of them
with the hired agent running the show,
an impatient man, and there were so many kids
and the bundles kept falling apart
and poor grandma was frightened of him.

She gave the man all the money
but she couldn't round up the kids fast enough for him.
They were children after all and didn't understand
and she was so stupid and clumsy herself,
carrying food for all of them and their clothes
and could she leave behind her pots?
Her legs hurt already; they were always swollen
from the hard work, the childbearing, and the cold.

They caught the train and there was a terrible moment
when the conductor came by for the tickets:
The children mustn't speak or he would know they were Jewish,
they had no permits to travel—Jews weren't allowed.
But the agent knew how to handle it,
everybody got *shmeared*, that means money got you
    everywhere.

The border was the worst. They had to sneak across at night.
The children mustn't make a sound, not even the babies.
Momma was six and she didn't want to do anything wrong
but she wasn't sure what to do.
The man led them through the woods
and beyond they could hear dogs barking from the sentry hut,
and then they had to run all of them down the ravine to the
    other side,
grandma broken down from childbearing with her bundles

and bad legs and a baby in her arms,
they ran all the children across the border
or the guards might shoot them
and if the little ones cried, the agent said he would smother
  them.

They got to a port finally.
Grandpa had arranged for cabin passage, not steerage,
but the agent cheated and put them in the hold
so they were on the low deck looking up at the rich people.
My momma told me how grandma took care of all her children,
how Jake didn't move anymore he was so seasick, maybe even
  dead,
and if people thought he was dead
they would throw him overboard like garbage, so she hid him.
The rich tossed down oranges to the poor children—
my momma had never had one before.

They came to New York, to the tenements,
a fearful new place, a city, country people in the city.
My momma, who had been roly-poly in slow Poland,
got skinny and pimply in zippy New York.
Everybody grew up in a new way.
And now my grandma is dead and my momma is old
and we her children are all scattered over the earth
speaking a different language and forgetting
why it was so important
to go to a new country.

II. MY RUSSIAN GRANDMA

When my father's father went to America
to earn the money for the family to come over later
my grandma had to take care of all six kids alone.

One day coming home from market,
with a baby in one arm and a bag of potatoes in the other,
she was crossing the tracks not paying attention
when she saw the train coming right up on her.
She jumped, dropping potatoes and baby on the tracks
as the train passed over
cutting the child to pieces; and in her grief
she reached under the turning wheels
to pick up the pieces of her baby
and got half her fingers cut off
and a bang on the head that knocked her cold.

Strangers took her to the hospital
where she came to, not knowing who she was or where she
    was—
it was a blessing for her to forget for a while.

But meanwhile the children were left alone.
When their mama didn't come
they huddled in the house afraid and crying,
except my father who went out to beg for food.
He kept them alive for all those terrible months.

And when grandma finally came home from the hospital
with her hands bandaged and anyway useless now
she found them all covered with lice and filthy,
and got to work like a whirlwind
to clean them up as best she could.
But it was too late: the hunger had weakened them
and the lice brought the fever,
and they all died but my father and one girl.

Then with the house half-empty
and in her bitterness and sorrow
my grandma took a lover—who could blame her
for needing a man at such a time?
Perhaps at first he was just a boarder
she took in to help with expenses.
But my father who had taken charge of the family
hated him and tried to throw him out
the way little boys do, so the man beat him,
and my father took to cowering behind the furniture
living such a life of horror and fear
that he still stammers from it.

The money came from America eventually
and grandma and her two remaining children left Russia
    forever.
She would die in the new land of an earache,
my grandma who put sugar in my father's soup to fatten him
    up—
if he got fat she would know he was consoled.

My sister Barbara, being the first girl
born after grandma's death,
should have been named Marsha after her,
according to our traditions
of reincarnating the dead in the living
(as I should have been called Abraham
after my great-grandfather, now unknown to me forever).

Historians aren't writing our histories
so it is up to us to do it for ourselves,
but I know so little: this legend and her name.

Well, before everything is finally lost to us all
I write this remnant down.

Reading 75

Rose Hsu Jordan: Half and Half

Amy Tan

"Half and Half" is from *The Joy Luck Club,* Amy Tan's first novel. In this novel Tan portrays the lives of four Chinese mothers and their American-born daughters. In the following selection the narrator, Rose Hsu Jordan, confronts the seeming inevitability of her doomed marriage by remembering the tragedy of her 4-year-old brother who drowned as Rose was supposed to be watching him. Amy Tan now lives in San Francisco where she works as a free-lance writer. She has also been a consultant to programs for disabled children.

As proof of her faith, my mother used to carry a small leatherette Bible when she went to the First Chinese Baptist Church every Sunday. But later, after my mother lost her faith in God, that leatherette Bible wound up wedged under a too-short table leg, a way for her to correct the imbalances of life. It's been there for over twenty years.

My mother pretends that Bible isn't there. Whenever anyone asks her what it's doing there, she says, a little too loudly, "Oh, this? I forgot." But I know she sees it. My mother is not the best housekeeper in the world, and after all these years that Bible is still clear white.

Tonight I'm watching my mother sweep under the same kitchen table, something she does every night after dinner. She gently pokes her broom around the table leg propped up by the Bible. I watch her, sweep after sweep, waiting for the right moment to tell her about Ted and me, that we're getting divorced. When I tell her, I know she's going to say, "This cannot be."

And when I say that it is certainly true, that our marriage is over, I know what else she will say: "Then you must save it."

And even though I know it's hopeless—there's absolutely nothing left to save—I'm afraid if I tell her that, she'll still persuade me to try.

I think it's ironic that my mother wants me to fight the divorce. Seventeen years ago she was chagrined when I started dating Ted. My older sisters had dated only Chinese boys from church before getting married.

Ted and I met in a politics of ecology class when he leaned over and offered to pay me two dollars for the last week's notes. I refused the money and accepted a cup of coffee instead. This was during my second semester at UC Berkeley, where I had enrolled as a liberal arts major and later changed to fine arts. Ted was in his third year in pre-med, his choice, he told me, ever since he dissected a fetal pig in the sixth grade.

I have to admit that what I initially found attractive in Ted were precisely the things that made him different from my brothers and the Chinese boys I had dated: his brashness; the assuredness in which he asked for things and expected to get them; his opinionated manner; his angular face and lanky body; the thickness of his arms; the fact that his parents immigrated from Tarrytown, New York, not Tientsin, China.

My mother must have noticed these same differences after Ted picked me up one evening at my parents' house. When I returned home, my mother was still up, watching television.

"He is American," warned my mother, as if I had been too blind to notice. "A *waigoren*."

"I'm American too," I said. "And it's not as if I'm going to marry him or something."

Mrs. Jordan also had a few words to say. Ted had casually invited me to a family picnic, the annual clan reunion held by the polo fields in Golden Gate Park. Although we had dated only a few times in the last month—and certainly had never slept together, since both of us lived at home—Ted introduced me to all his relatives as his girlfriend, which, until then, I didn't know I was.

Later, when Ted and his father went off to play volleyball with the others, his mother took my hand, and we started walking along the grass, away from the crowd. She squeezed my palm warmly but never seemed to look at me.

"I'm so glad to meet you *finally*," Mrs. Jordan said. I wanted to tell her I wasn't really Ted's girlfriend, but she went on. "I think it's nice that you and Ted are having such a lot of fun together. So I hope you won't misunderstand what I have to say."

And then she spoke quietly about Ted's future, his need to concentrate on his medical studies, why it would be years before he could even think about marriage. She assured me she had nothing whatsoever against minorities; she and her husband, who owned a chain of office-supply stores, personally knew many fine people who were Oriental, Spanish, and even black. But Ted was going to be in one of those professions where he would be judged by a different standard, by patients and other doctors who might not be as understanding as the Jordans were. She said it was so unfortunate the way the rest of the world was, how unpopular the Vietnam War was.

"Mrs. Jordan, I am not Vietnamese," I said softly, even though I was on the verge of shouting. "And I have no intention of marrying your son."

When Ted drove me home that day, I told him I couldn't see him anymore. When he asked me why, I shrugged. When he pressed me, I told him what his mother had said, verbatim, without comment.

"And you're just going to sit there! Let my mother decide what's right?" he shouted, as if I were a co-conspirator who had turned traitor. I was touched that Ted was so upset.

"What should we do?" I asked, and I had a pained feeling I thought was the beginning of love.

In those early months, we clung to each other with a rather silly desperation, because, in spite of anything my mother or Mrs. Jordan could say, there was nothing that really prevented us from seeing one another. With imagined tragedy hovering over us, we became inseparable, two halves creating the whole: yin and yang. I was victim to his hero. I was always in danger and he was always rescuing me. I would fall and he would lift me up. It was exhilarating and draining. The emotional effect of saving and being saved was addicting to both of us. And that, as much as anything we ever did in bed, was how we made love to each other: conjoined where my weaknesses needed protection.

"What should we do?" I continued to ask him. And within a year of our first meeting we were living together. The month before Ted started medical school at UCSF we were married in the Episcopal church, and Mrs. Jordan sat in the front pew, crying as was expected of the groom's mother. When Ted finished his residency in dermatology, we bought a run-down three-story Victorian with a large garden in Ashbury Heights. Ted helped me set up a studio downstairs so I could take in work as a free-lance production assistant for graphic artists.

Over the years, Ted decided where we went on vacation. He decided what new furniture we should buy. He decided we should wait until we moved into a better neighborhood before having children. We used to discuss some of these matters, but we both knew the question would boil down to my saying, "Ted, you decide." After a while, there were no more discussions. Ted simply decided. And I never thought of objecting. I preferred to ignore the world around me, obsessing only over what was in front of me; my T-square, my X-acto knife, my blue pencil.

But last year Ted's feelings about what he called "decision and responsibility" changed. A new patient had come to him asking what she could do about the spidery veins on her cheeks. And when he told her he could suck the red veins out and make her beautiful again, she believed him. But instead, he accidentally sucked a nerve out, and the left side of her smile fell down and she sued him.

After he lost the malpractice lawsuit—his first, and a big shock to him I now realize—he started pushing me to make decisions. Did I think we should buy an American car or a Japanese car? Should we change from whole-life to term insurance? What did I think about that candidate who supported the contras? What about a family?

I thought about things, the pros and the cons. But in the end I would be so confused, because I never believed there was ever any one right answer, yet there were many wrong ones. So whenever I said, "You decide," or "I don't care," or "Either way is fine with me," Ted would say in his impatient voice, "No, *you* decide. You can't have it both ways, none of the responsibility, none of the blame."

I could feel things changing between us. A protective veil had been lifted and Ted now started pushing me about everything. He asked me to decide on the most trivial matters, as if he were baiting me. Italian food or Thai. One appetizer or two. Which appetizer. Credit card or cash. Visa or MasterCard.

Last month, when he was leaving for a two-day dermatology course in Los Angeles, he asked if I wanted to come along and then quickly, before I could say anything, he added, "Never mind, I'd rather go alone."

"More time to study," I agreed.

"No, because you can never make up your mind about anything," he said.

And I protested, "But it's only with things that aren't important."

"Nothing is important to you, then," he said in a tone of disgust.

"Ted, if you want me to go, I'll go."

And it was as if something snapped in him. "How the hell did we ever get married? Did you just say 'I do' because the minister said 'repeat after me'? What would you have done with your life if I had never married you? Did it ever occur to you?"

This was such a big leap in logic, between what I said and what he said, that I thought we were like two people standing apart on separate mountain peaks, recklessly leaning forward to throw stones at one another, unaware of the dangerous chasm that separated us.

But now I realize Ted knew what he was saying all along. He wanted to show me the rift. Because later that evening he called from Los Angeles and said he wanted a divorce.

Ever since Ted's been gone, I've been thinking, Even if I had expected it, even if I had known what I was going to do with my life, it still would have knocked the wind out of me.

When something that violent hits you, you can't help but lose your balance and fall. And after you pick yourself up, you realize you can't trust anybody to save you—not your husband, not your mother, not God. So what can you do to stop yourself from tilting and falling all over again?

My mother believed in God's will for many years. It was as if she turned on a celestial faucet and goodness kept pouring out. She said it was faith that kept all these good things coming our way, only I thought she said "fate," because she couldn't pronounce that 'th" sound in "faith."

And later, I discovered that maybe it was fate all along, that faith was just an illusion that somehow you're in control. I found out the most *I* could have was hope, and with that I was not denying any possibility, good or bad. I was just saying, If there is a choice, dear God or whatever you are, here's where the odds should be placed.

I remember the day I started thinking this, it was such a revelation to me. It was the day my mother lost her faith in God. She found that things of unquestioned certainty could never be trusted again.

We had gone to the beach, to a secluded spot south of the city near Devil's Slide. My father had read in *Sunset* magazine that this was a good place to catch ocean perch. And although my father was not a fisherman but a pharmacist's assistant who had once been a doctor in China, he believed in his *nengkan*, his ability to do anything he put his mind to. My mother believed she had *nengkan* to cook anything my father had a mind to catch. It was this belief in their *nengkan* that had brought my parents to America. It had enabled them to have seven children and buy a house in the Sunset district with very little money. It had given them the confidence to believe their luck would never run out, that God was on their side, that the house gods had only benevolent things to report and our ancestors were pleased, that lifetime warranties meant our lucky streak would never break, that all the elements were in balance, the right amount of wind and water.

So there we were, the nine of us: my father, my mother, my two sisters, four brothers, and myself, so confident as we walked along our first beach. We marched in single file across the cool gray sand, from oldest to youngest. I was in the middle, fourteen years old. We would have made quite a sight, if anyone else had been watching, nine pairs of bare feet trudging, nine pairs of shoes in hand, nine black-haired heads turned toward the water to watch the waves tumbling in.

The wind was whipping the cotton trousers around my legs and I looked for some place where the sand wouldn't kick into my eyes. I saw we were standing in the hollow of a cove. It was like a giant bowl, cracked in half, the other half washed out to sea. My mother walked toward the right, where the beach was clean, and we all followed. On this side, the wall of the cove curved around and protected the beach from both the rough surf and the wind. And along this wall, in its shadow, was a reef ledge that started at the edge of the beach and continued out past the cove where the waters became rough. It seemed as though a person could walk out to sea on this reef, although it looked very rocky and slippery. On the other side of the cove, the wall was more jagged, eaten away by the water. It was pitted with crevices, so when the waves crashed against the wall, the water spewed out of these holes like white gulleys.

Thinking back, I remember that this beach cove was a terrible place, full of wet shadows that chilled us and invisible specks that flew into our eyes and made it hard for us to see the dangers. We were all blind with the newness of this experience: a Chinese family trying to act like a typical American family at the beach.

My mother spread out an old striped bedspread, which flapped in the wind until nine pairs of shoes weighed it down. My father assembled his long bamboo fishing pole, a pole he had made with his own two hands, remembering its design from his childhood in China. And we children sat huddled shoulder to

shoulder on the blanket, reaching into the grocery sack full of bologna sandwiches, which we hungrily ate salted with sand from our fingers.

Then my father stood up and admired his fishing pole, its grace, its
strength. Satisfied, he picked up his shoes and walked to the edge of the beach
and then onto the reef to the point just before it was wet. My two older sisters,
Janice and Ruth, jumped up from the blanket and slapped their thighs to get the
sand off. Then they slapped each other's back and raced off down the beach
shrieking. I was about to get up and chase them, but my mother nodded toward
my four brothers and reminded me: "*Dangsying tamende shenti,*" which means
"Take care of them," or literally, "Watch out for their bodies." These bodies
were the anchors of my life: Matthew, Mark, Luke, and Bing. I fell back onto
the sand, groaning as my throat grew tight, as I made the same lament: "Why?"
Why did *I* have to care for them?

And she gave me the same answer: "*Yiding.*"

I must. Because they were my brothers. My sisters had once taken care of
me. How else could I learn responsibility? How else could I appreciate what my
parents had done for me?

Matthew, Mark, and Luke were twelve, ten, and nine, old enough to keep
themselves loudly amused. They had already buried Luke in a shallow grave of
sand so that only his head stuck out. Now they were starting to pat together the
outlines of a sand-castle wall on top of him.

But Bing was only four, easily excitable and easily bored and irritable. He
didn't want to play with the other brothers because they had pushed him off to
the side, admonishing him, "No, Bing, you'll just wreck it."

So Bing wandered down the beach, walking stiffly like an ousted emperor,
picking up shards of rock and chunks of driftwood and flinging them with all his
might into the surf. I trailed behind, imagining tidal waves and wondering what
I would do if one appeared. I called to Bing every now and then, "Don't go too
close to the water. You'll get your feet wet." And I thought how much I seemed
like my mother, always worried beyond reason inside, but at the same time
talking about the danger as if it were less than it really was. The worry surrounded me, like the wall of the cove, and it made me feel everything had been
considered and was now safe.

My mother had a superstition, in fact, that children were predisposed to
certain dangers on certain days, all depending on their Chinese birthdate. It was
explained in a little Chinese book called *The Twenty-Six Malignant Gates.* There,
on each page, was an illustration of some terrible danger that awaited young
innocent children. In the corners was a description written in Chinese, and since
I couldn't read the characters, I could only see what the picture meant.

The same little boy appeared in each picture: climbing a broken tree limb,
standing by a falling gate, slipping in a wooden tub, being carried away by a
snapping dog, fleeing from a bolt of lightning. And in each of these pictures
stood a man who looked as if he were wearing a lizard costume. He had a big
crease in his forehead, or maybe it was actually that he had two round horns. In
one picture, the lizard man was standing on a curved bridge, laughing as he
watched the little boy falling forward over the bridge rail, his slippered feet
already in the air.

It would have been enough to think that even one of these dangers could befall a child. And even though the birthdates corresponded to only one danger, my mother worried about them all. This was because she couldn't figure out how the Chinese dates, based on the lunar calendar, translated into American dates. So by taking them all into account, she had absolute faith she could prevent every one of them.

The sun had shifted and moved over the other side of the cove wall. Everything had settled into place. My mother was busy keeping sand from blowing onto the blanket, then shaking sand out of shoes, and tacking corners of blankets back down again with the now clean shoes. My father was still standing at the end of the reef, patiently casting out, waiting for *nengkan* to manifest itself as a fish. I could see small figures farther down on the beach, and I could tell they were my sisters by their two dark heads and yellow pants. My brothers' shrieks were mixed with those of seagulls. Bing had found an empty soda bottle and was using this to dig sand next to the dark cove wall. And I sat on the sand, just where the shadows ended and the sunny part began.

Bing was pounding the soda bottle against the rock, so I called to him, "Don't dig so hard. You'll bust a hole in the wall and fall all the way to China." And I laughed when he looked at me as though he thought what I said was true. He stood up and started walking toward the water. He put one foot tentatively on the reef, and I warned him, "Bing."

"I'm gonna see Daddy," he protested.

"Stay close to the wall, then, away from the water," I said. "Stay away from the mean fish."

And I watched as he inched his way along the reef, his back hugging the bumpy cove wall. I still see him, so clearly that I almost feel I can make him stay there forever.

I see him standing by the wall, safe, calling to my father, who looks over his shoulder toward Bing. How glad I am that my father is going to watch him for a while! Bing starts to walk over and then something tugs on my father's line and he's reeling as fast as he can.

Shouts erupt. Someone has thrown sand in Luke's face and he's jumped out of his sand grave and thrown himself on top of Mark, thrashing and kicking. My mother shouts for me to stop them. And right after I pull Luke off Mark, I look up and see Bing walking alone to the edge of the reef. In the confusion of the fight, nobody notices. I am the only one who sees what Bing is doing.

Bing walks one, two, three steps. His little body is moving so quickly, as if he spotted something wonderful by the water's edge. And I think, *He's going to fall in*. I'm expecting it. And just as I think this, his feet are already in the air, in a moment of balance, before he splashes into the sea and disappears without leaving so much as a ripple in the water.

• • •

I sank to my knees watching that spot where he disappeared, not moving, not saying anything. I couldn't make sense of it. I was thinking, Should I run to the water and try to pull him out? Should I shout to my father? Can I rise on my legs fast enough? Can I take it all back and forbid Bing from joining my father on the ledge?

And then my sisters were back, and one of them said, "Where's Bing?" There was silence for a few seconds and then shouts and sand flying as everyone rushed past me toward the water's edge. I stood there unable to move as my sisters looked by the cove wall, as my brothers scrambled to see what lay behind pieces of driftwood. My mother and father were trying to part the waves with their hands.

We were there for many hours. I remember the search boats and the sunset when dusk came. I had never seen a sunset like that: a bright orange flame touching the water's edge and then fanning out, warming the sea. When it became dark, the boats turned their yellow orbs on and bounced up and down on the dark shiny water.

As I look back, it seems unnatural to think about the colors of the sunset and boats at a time like that. But we all had strange thoughts. My father was calculating minutes, estimating the temperature of the water, readjusting his estimate of when Bing fell. My sisters were calling, "Bing! Bing!" as if he were hiding in some bushes high above the beach cliffs. My brothers sat in the car, quietly reading comic books. And when the boats turned off their yellow orbs, my mother went for a swim. She had never swum a stroke in her life, but her faith in her own *nengkan* convinced her that what these Americans couldn't do, she could. She could find Bing.

And when the rescue people finally pulled her out of the water, she still had her *nengkan* intact. Her hair, her clothes, they were all heavy with the cold water, but she stood quietly, calm and regal as a mermaid queen who had just arrived out of the sea. The police called off the search, put us all in our car, and sent us home to grieve.

I had expected to be beaten to death, by my father, by my mother, by my sisters and brothers. I knew it was my fault. I hadn't watched him closely enough, and yet I saw him. But as we sat in the dark living room, I heard them, one by one whispering their regrets.

"I was selfish to want to go fishing," said my father.

"We shouldn't have gone for a walk," said Janice, while Ruth blew her nose yet another time.

"Why'd you have to throw sand in my face?" moaned Luke. "Why'd you have to make me start a fight?"

And my mother quietly admitted to me, "I told you to stop their fight. I told you to take your eyes off him."

If I had had any time at all to feel a sense of relief, it would have quickly evaporated, because my mother also said, "So now I am telling you, we must go and find him, quickly, tomorrow morning." And everybody's eyes looked down. But I saw it as my punishment: to go out with my mother, back to the beach, to help her find Bing's body.

Nothing prepared me for what my mother did the next day. When I woke up, it was still dark and she was already dressed. On the kitchen table was a thermos, a teacup, the white leatherette Bible, and the car keys.

"Is Daddy ready?" I asked.

"Daddy's not coming," she said.

"Then how will we get there? Who will drive us?"

She picked up the keys and I followed her out the door to the car. I wondered the whole time as we drove to the beach how she had learned to drive overnight. She used no map. She drove smoothly ahead, turning down Geary, then the Great Highway, signaling at all the right times, getting on the Coast Highway and easily winding the car around the sharp curves that often led inexperienced drivers off and over the cliffs.

When we arrived at the beach, she walked immediately down the dirt path and over to the end of the reef ledge, where I had seen Bing disappear. She held in her hand the white Bible. And looking out over the water, she called to God, her small voice carried up by the gulls to heaven. It began with "Dear God" and ended with "Amen," and in between she spoke in Chinese.

"I have always believed in your blessings," she praised God in that same tone she used for exaggerated Chinese compliments. "We knew they would come. We did not question them. Your decisions were our decisions. You rewarded us for our faith.

"In return we have always tried to show our deepest respect. We went to your house. We brought you money. We sang your songs. You gave us more blessings. And now we have misplaced one of them. We were careless. This is true. We had so many good things, we couldn't keep them in our mind all the time.

"So maybe you hid him from us to teach us a lesson, to be more careful with your gifts in the future. I have learned this. I have put it in my memory. And now I have come to take Bing back."

I listened quietly as my mother said these words, horrified. And I began to cry when she added, "Forgive us for his bad manners. My daughter, this one standing here, will be sure to teach him better lessons of obedience before he visits you again."

After her prayer, her faith was so great that she saw him, three times, waving to her from just beyond the first wave. "*Nale!*"—There! And she would stand straight as a sentinel, until three times her eyesight failed her and Bing turned into a dark spot of churning seaweed.

My mother did not let her chin fall down. She walked back to the beach and put the Bible down. She picked up the thermos and teacup and walked to the water's edge. Then she told me that the night before she had reached back into her life, back when she was a girl in China, and this is what she had found.

"I remember a boy who lost his hand in a firecracker accident," she said. "I saw the shreads of this boy's arm, his tears, and then I heard his mother's claim that he would grow back another hand, better than the last. This mother said she would pay back an ancestral debt ten times over. She would use a water treatment to soothe the wrath of Chu Jung, the three-eyed god of fire. And true enough, the next week this boy was riding a bicycle, both hands steering a straight course past my astonished eyes!"

And then my mother became very quiet. She spoke again in a thoughtful, respectful manner.

"An ancestor of ours once stole water from a sacred well. Now the water is trying to steal back. We must sweeten the temper of the Coiling Dragon who lives in the sea. And then we must make him loosen his coils from Bing by giving him another treasure he can hide."

My mother poured out tea sweetened with sugar into the teacup, and threw this into the sea. And then she opened her fist. In her palm was a ring of watery blue sapphire, a gift from her mother, who had died many years before. This ring, she told me, drew coveting stares from women and made them inattentive to the children they guarded so jealously. This would make the Coiling Dragon forgetful of Bing. She threw the ring into the water.

But even with this, Bing did not appear right away. For an hour or so, all we saw was seaweed drifting by. And then I saw her clasp her hands to her chest, and she said in a wondrous voice, "See, it's because we were watching the wrong direction." And I too saw Bing trudging wearily at the far end of the beach, his shoes hanging in his hand, his dark head bent over in exhaustion. I could feel what my mother felt. The hunger in our hearts was instantly filled. And then the two of us, before we could even get to our feet, saw him light a cigarette, grow tall, and become a stranger.

"Ma, let's go," I said as softly as possible.

"He's there," she said firmly. She pointed to the jagged wall across the water. "I see him. He is in a cave, sitting on a little step above the water. He is hungry and a little cold, but he has learned now not to complain too much."

And then she stood up and started walking across the sandy beach as though it were a solid paved path, and I was trying to follow behind, struggling and stumbling in the soft mounds. She marched up the steep path to where the car was parked, and she wasn't even breathing hard as she pulled a large inner tube from the trunk. To this lifesaver, she tied the fishing line from my father's bamboo pole. She walked back and threw the tube into the sea, holding on to the pole.

"This will go where Bing is. I will bring him back," she said fiercely. I had never heard so much *nengkan* in my mother's voice.

The tube followed her mind. It drifted out, toward the other side of the cove where it was caught by stronger waves. The line became taut and she strained to hold on tight. But the line snapped and then spiraled into the water.

We both climbed toward the end of the reef to watch. The tube had now reached the other side of the cove. A big wave smashed it into the wall. The bloated tube lept up and then it was sucked in, under the wall and into a cavern. It popped out. Over and over again, it disappeared, emerged, glistening black, faithfully reporting it had seen Bing and was going back to try to pluck him from the cave. Over and over again, it dove and popped back up again, empty but still hopeful. And then, after a dozen or so times, it was sucked into the dark recess, and when it came out, it was torn and lifeless.

At that moment, and not until that moment, did she give up. My mother had a look on her face that I'll never forget. It was one of complete despair and horror, for losing Bing, for being so foolish as to think she could use faith to change fate. And it made me angry—so blindingly angry—that everything had failed us.

I know now that I had never expected to find Bing, just as I know now I will never find a way to save my marriage. My mother tells me, though, that I should still try.

"What's the point?" I say. "There's no hope. There's no reason to keep trying."

"Because you must," she says. "This is not hope. Not reason. This is your fate. This is your life, what you must do."

"So what can I do?"

And my mother says, "You must think for yourself, what you must do. If someone tells you, then you are not trying." And then she walks out of the kitchen to let me think about this.

I think about Bing, how I knew he was in danger, how I let it happen. I think about my marriage, how I had seen the signs, really I had. But I just let it happen. And I think now that fate is shaped half by expectation, half by inattention. But somehow, when you lose something you love, faith takes over. You have to pay attention to what you lost. You have to undo the expectation.

My mother, she still pays attention to it. That Bible under the table, I know she sees it. I remember seeing her write in it before she wedged it under.

I lift the table and slide the Bible out. I put the Bible on the table, flipping quickly through the pages, because I know it's there. On the page before the New Testament begins, there's a section called "Deaths," and that's where she wrote "Bing Hsu" lightly, in erasable pencil.

QUESTIONS FOR "ROSE HSU JORDAN: HALF AND HALF" BY AMY TAN

Talking About the Text

1. Tan embeds one narrative or story about her brother's death within another narrative about her failing marriage. How does this strategy affect your understanding of the conflict? What might have been the narrative's effect if Tan had just told us about Rose's failed marriage?
2. In what different but complementary ways can we understand the subtitle, "Half and Half"?
3. Note places in the narrative where being Chinese and trying to be American interfere with one another. What results from these conflicts?
4. The sea is frequently used by fiction writers as a symbol for life and death. Apply this interpretation to this story. What are all the possibilities for death and life that arise as a result of Rose's family's experience at the cove?
5. How does Rose's mother try to reconcile "fate" and "faith"? How does Rose attempt such a reconciliation?

Exploring Issues

1. Re-read the lead essay in this chapter by Peter Marin. How might he interpret the conflict in Tan's narrative?

2. In considering some of your responses to Question 2 in the preceding section, look closely at how the narrator describes her relationship to Ted. How does being Chinese cause marital problems for Rose? In what ways do some of Rose's problems with Ted and his mother transcend the fact that she is Chinese?

Writing Assignments

1. Using Tan's narrative as support, write an essay in which you explore the following statement: Faith is often more difficult to follow than a belief in fate. In struggling with this statement, consider what attitudes and actions are available to those who have faith versus those we might deem fatalists.

2. Write an expository essay in which you describe and explain the development of the Rose Hsu Jordan character. In the process analyze closely Rose's relationships to Ted, to Ted's mother, and to Rose's mother. Consider how Rose characterizes her relationship with Ted, including the role each plays. Then consider how Rose deals with various conflicts that arise. Use your fellow classmates as a sounding board to test out your interpretations of these several relationships.

Reading 76

Multiculturalism: E Pluribus Plures

Diane Ravitch

Diane Ravitch is an adjunct professor of history and education at Teachers College at Columbia University. She has written several books, focusing particularly on the history of education. One of her notable contributions has been *The Troubled Crusade: American Education, 1945–1980*. The excerpt reprinted here is taken from her essay appearing in *The American Scholar* in the summer issue for 1990. Ravitch acknowledges that we are a pluralistic culture, and she contends that this fabric is seriously threatened by what she labels "particularism."

Questions of race, ethnicity, and religion have been a perennial source of conflict in American education. The schools have often attracted the zealous attention of those who wish to influence the future, as well as those who wish to change the way we view the past. In our history, the schools have been not only an institution in which to teach young people skills and knowledge, but an arena where interest groups fight to preserve their values, or to revise the judgments of history, or to bring about fundamental social change. In the nineteenth century, Protestants and Catholics battled over which version of the Bible should be used in school, or whether the Bible should be used at all. In recent decades, bitter racial disputes—provoked by policies of racial segregation and discrimination—have generated turmoil in the streets and in the schools. The secularization of the schools during the past century has prompted attacks on the curricula and textbooks and library books by fundamentalist Christians, who object to whatever challenges their faith-based views of history, literature, and science.

Given the diversity of American society, it has been impossible to insulate the schools from pressures that result from differences and tensions among groups. When people differ about basic values, sooner or later those disagreements turn up in battles about how schools are organized or what the schools should teach. Sometimes these battles remove a terrible injustice, like racial segregation. Sometimes, however, interest groups politicize the curriculum and attempt to impose their views on teachers, school officials, and textbook publishers. Across the country, even now, interest groups are pressuring local school boards to remove myths and fables and other imaginative literature from children's readers and to inject the teaching of creationism in biology. When groups cross the line into extremism, advancing their own agenda without regard to reason or to others, they threaten public education itself, making it difficult to teach any issues honestly and making the entire curriculum vulnerable to political campaigns.

For many years, the public schools attempted to neutralize controversies over race, religion, and ethnicity by ignoring them. Educators believed, or hoped, that the schools could remain outside politics; this was, of course, a vain hope since the schools were pursuing policies based on race, religion, and ethnicity. Nonetheless, such divisive questions were usually excluded from the curriculum. The textbooks minimized problems among groups and taught a sanitized version of history. Race, religion, and ethnicity were presented as minor elements in the American saga; slavery was treated as an episode, immigration as a sidebar, and women were largely absent. The textbooks concentrated on presidents, wars, national politics, and issues of state. An occasional "great black" or "great woman" received mention, but the main narrative paid little attention to minority groups and women.

With the ethnic revival of the 1960s, this approach to the teaching of history came under fire, because the history of national leaders—virtually all of whom were white, Anglo-Saxon, and male—ignored the place in American history of those who were none of the above. The traditional history of elites had been complemented by an assimilationist view of American society, which presumed that everyone in the American melting pot would eventually lose or abandon those ethnic characteristics that distinguished them from mainstream Americans. The ethnic revival demonstrated that many groups did not want to be assimilated or melted. Ethnic studies programs popped up on campuses to teach not only that "black is beautiful," but also that every other variety of ethnicity is "beautiful" as well; everyone who had "roots" began to look for them so that they too could recover that ancestral part of themselves that had not been homogenized.

As ethnicity became an accepted subject for study in the late 1960s, textbooks were assailed for their failure to portray blacks accurately; within a few years, the textbooks in wide use were carefully screened to eliminate bias against minority groups and women. At the same time, new scholarship about the history of women, blacks, and various ethnic minorities found its way into the textbooks. At first, the multicultural content was awkwardly incorporated as little boxes on the side of the main narrative. Then some of the new social historians (like Stephan Thernstrom, Mary Beth Norton, Gary Nash, Winthrop Jordan, and Leon Litwack) themselves wrote textbooks, and the main narrative itself began to reflect a broadened historical understanding of race, ethnicity, and class in the American past. Consequently, today's history textbooks routinely incorporate the experiences of women, blacks, American Indians, and various immigrant groups.

Although most high school textbooks are deeply unsatisfactory (they still largely neglect religion, they are too long, too encyclopedic, too superficial, and lacking in narrative flow), they are far more sensitive to pluralism than their predecessors. For example, the latest edition of Todd and Curti's *Triumph of the American Nation,* the most popular high school history text, has significantly increased its coverage of blacks in America, including profiles of Phillis Wheatley, the poet; James Armistead, a revolutionary war spy for Lafayette; Benjamin Banneker, a self-taught scientist and mathematician; Hiram Revels, the first black to serve in the Congress; and Ida B. Wells-Barnett, a tireless crusader against lynching and racism. Even better as a textbook treatment is Jordan and Litwack's *The United States,* which skillfully synthesizes the historical experiences of blacks, Indians, immigrants, women, and other groups into the mainstream of American social and political history. The latest generation of textbooks bluntly acknowledges the racism of the past, describing the struggle for equality by racial minorities while identifying individuals who achieved success as political leaders, doctors, lawyers, scholars, entrepreneurs, teachers, and scientists.

As a result of the political and social changes of recent decades, cultural pluralism is now generally recognized as an organizing principle of this society. In contrast to the idea of the melting pot, which promised to erase ethnic and group differences, children now learn that variety is the spice of life. They learn that America has provided a haven for many different groups and has allowed them to maintain their cultural heritage or to assimilate, or—as is often the case—to do both; the choice is theirs, not the state's. They learn that cultural pluralism is one of the norms of a free society; that differences among groups are a national resource rather than a problem to be solved. Indeed, the unique feature of the United States is that its common culture has been formed by the interaction of its subsidiary cultures. It is a culture that has been influenced over time by immigrants, American Indians, Africans (slave and free) and by their descendants. American music, art, literature, language, food, clothing, sports, holidays, and customs all show the effects of the commingling of diverse cultures in one nation. Paradoxical though it may seem, the United States has a common culture that is multicultural.

Our schools and our institutions of higher learning have in recent years begun to embrace what Catherine R. Stimpson of Rutgers University has called "cultural democracy," a recognition that we must listen to a "diversity of voices" in order to understand our culture, past and present. This understanding of the pluralistic nature of American culture has taken a long time to forge. It is based on sound scholarship and has led to major revisions in what children are taught and what they read in school. The new history is—indeed, must be —a warts-and-all history; it demands an unflinching examination of racism and discrimination in our history. Making these changes is difficult, raises tempers, and ignites controversies, but gives a more interesting and accurate account of American history. Accomplishing these changes is valuable, because there is also a useful lesson for the rest of the world in America's relatively successful experience as a pluralistic society. Throughout human history, the clash of different cultures, races, ethnic groups, and religions has often been the cause of bitter hatred, civil conflict, and international war. The ethnic tensions that now are tearing apart Lebanon, Sri Lanka, Kashmir, and various republics of the Soviet Union remind us of the costs of unfettered group rivalry. Thus, it is a matter of more than domestic importance that we closely examine and try to understand that part of our national history in which different groups competed, fought, suffered, but ultimately learned to live together in relative peace and even achieved a sense of common nationhood.

Alas, these painstaking efforts to expand the understanding of American culture into a richer and more varied tapestry have taken a new turn, and not for the better. Almost any idea, carried to its extreme, can be made pernicious, and this is what is happening now to multiculturalism. Today, pluralistic multiculturalism must contend with a new, particularistic multiculturalism. The pluralists seek a richer common culture; the particularists insist that no common culture is possible or desirable. The new particularism is entering the curriculum in a number of school systems across the country. Advocates of particularism propose an ethnocentric curriculum to raise the self-esteem and academic achievement of children from racial and ethnic minority backgrounds. Without any evidence, they claim that children from minority back-grounds will do well in school *only* if they are immersed in a positive, prideful version of their ancestral culture. If children are of, for example, Fredonian ancestry, they must hear that Fredonians were important in mathematics, science, history, and literature. If they learn about great Fredonians and if their studies use Fredonian examples and Fredonian concepts, they will do well in school. If they do not, they will have low self-esteem and will do badly.

At first glance, this appears akin to the celebratory activities associated with Black History Month or Women's History Month, when schoolchildren learn about the achievements of blacks and women. But the point of those celebra-tions is to demonstrate that neither race nor gender is an obstacle to high achievement. They teach all children that everyone, regardless of their race, religion, gender, ethnicity, or family origin, can achieve self-fulfillment, honor, and dignity in society if they aim high and work hard.

By contrast, the particularistic version of multiculturalism is unabashedly filiopietistic and deterministic. It teaches children that their identity is deter-mined by their "cultural genes." That something in their blood or their race memory or their cultural DNA defines who they are and what they may achieve. That the culture in which they live is not their own culture, even though they were born here. That American culture is "Eurocentric," and therefore hostile to anyone whose ancestors are not European. Perhaps the most invidious implication of particularism is that racial and ethnic minorities are not and should not try to be part of American culture; it implies that American culture belongs only to those who are white and European; it implies that those who are neither white nor European are alienated from American culture by virtue of their race or ethnicity; it implies that the only culture they do belong to or can ever belong to is the culture of their ancestors, even if their families have lived in this country for generations.

The war on so-called Eurocentrism is intended to foster self-esteem among those who are not of European descent. But how, in fact, is self-esteem devel-oped? How is the sense of one's own possibilities, one's potential choices, developed? Certainly, the school curriculum plays a relatively small role as compared to the influence of family, community, mass media, and society. But to the extent that curriculum influences what children think of themselves, it should encourage children of all racial and ethnic groups to believe that they are part of this society and that they should develop their talents and minds to the fullest. It is enormously inspiring, for example, to learn about men and women from diverse backgrounds who overcame poverty, discrimination, physical handicaps, and other obstacles to achieve success in a variety of fields. Behind every such biography of accomplishment is a story of heroism, perseverance, and self-discipline. Learning these stories will encourage a healthy spirit of pluralism, of mutual respect, and of self-respect among children of different backgrounds. The children of American society today will live their lives in a racially and culturally diverse nation, and their education should prepare them to do so.

The pluralist approach to multiculturalism promotes a broader interpretation of the common American culture and seeks due recognition for the ways that the nation's many racial, ethnic, and cultural groups have transformed the national culture. The pluralists say, in effect, "American culture belongs to us, all of us; the U.S. is us, and we remake it in every generation." But particularists have no interest in extending or revising American culture; indeed, they deny that a common culture exists. Particularists reject any accommodation among groups, any interactions that blur the distinct lines between them. The brand of history that they espouse is one in which everyone is either a descendant of victims or oppressors. By doing so, ancient hatreds are fanned and recreated in each new generation. Particularism has its intellectual roots in the ideology of ethnic separatism and in the black nationalist movement. In the particularist analysis, the nation has five cultures: African American, Asian American, European American, Latino/Hispanic, and Native American. The huge cultural, historical, religious, and linguistic differences within these categories are ignored, as is the considerable intermarriage among these groups, as are the linkages (like gender, class, sexual orientation, and religion) that cut across these five groups. No serious scholar would claim that all Europeans and white Americans are part of the same culture, or that all Asians are part of the same culture, or that all people of Latin-American descent are of the same culture, or that all people of African descent are of the same culture. Any categorization this broad is essentially meaningless and useless.

Several districts—including Detroit, Atlanta, and Washington, D.C.—are developing an Afrocentric curriculum. *Afrocentricity* has been described in a book of the same name by Molefi Kete Asante of Temple University. The Afrocentric curriculum puts Africa at the center of the student's universe. African Americans must "move away from an [*sic*] Eurocentric framework" because "it is difficult to create freely when you use someone else's motifs, styles, images, and perspectives." Because they are not Africans, "white teachers cannot inspire in our children the visions necessary for them to overcome limitations." Asante recommends that African Americans choose an African name (as he did), reject European dress, embrace African religion (not Islam or Christianity) and love "their own" culture. He scorns the idea of universality as a form of Eurocentric arrogance. The Eurocentrist, he says, thinks of Beethoven or Bach as classical, but the Afrocentrist thinks of Ellington or Coltrane as classical; the Eurocentrist lauds Shakespeare or Twain, while the Afrocentrist prefers Baraka, Shange, or Abiola. Asante is critical of black artists like Arthur Mitchell and Alvin Ailey who ignore Afrocentricity. Likewise, he speaks contemptuously of a group of black university students who spurned the Afrocentrism of the local Black Student Union and formed an organization called Inter-race: "Such madness is the direct consequence of self-hatred, obligatory attitudes, false assumptions about society, and stupidity."

The conflict between pluralism and particularism turns on the issue of universalism. Professor Asante warns his readers against the lure of universalism: "Do not be captured by a sense of universality given to you by the Eurocentric viewpoint; such a viewpoint is contradictory to your own ultimate reality." He insists that there is no alternative to Eurocentrism, Afrocentrism, and other ethnocentrisms. In contrast, the pluralist says, with the Roman playwright Terence, "I am a man: nothing human is alien to me." A contemporary Terence would say "I am a person" or might be a woman, but the point remains the same: You don't have to be black to love Zora Neale Hurston's fiction or Langston Hughes's poetry or Duke Ellington's music. In a pluralist curriculum, we expect children to learn a broad and humane culture, to learn about the ideas and art and animating spirit of many cultures. We expect that children, whatever their color, will be inspired by the courage of people like Helen Keller, Vaclav Havel, Harriet Tubman, and Feng Lizhe. We expect that their response to literature will be determined by the ideas and images it evokes, not by the skin color of the writer. But particularists insist that children can learn only from the experiences of people from the same race.

Particularism is a bad idea whose time has come. It is also a fashion spreading like wildfire through the education system, actively promoted by organizations and individuals with a political and professional interest in strengthening ethnic power bases in the university, in the education profession, and in society itself. One can scarcely pick up an educational journal without learning about a school district that is converting to an ethnocentric curriculum in an attempt to give "self-esteem" to children from racial minorities. A state-funded project in a Sacramento high school is teaching young black males to think like Africans and to develop the "African Mind Model Technique," in order to free themselves of the racism of American culture. A popular black rap singer, KRS-One, complained in an op-ed article in the *New York Times* that the schools should be teaching blacks about their cultural heritage, instead of trying to make everyone Americans. "It's like trying to teach a dog to be a cat," he wrote. KRS-One railed about having to learn about Thomas Jefferson and the Civil War, which had nothing to do (he said) with black history.

Pluralism can easily be transformed into particularism, as may be seen in the potential uses in the classroom of the Mayan contribution to mathematics. The Mayan example was popularized in a movie called *Stand and Deliver*, about a charismatic Bolivian-born mathematics teacher in Los Angeles who inspired his students (who are Hispanic) to learn calculus. He told them that their ancestors invented the concept of zero; but that wasn't all he did. He used imagination to put across mathematical concepts. He required them to do homework and to go to school on Saturdays and during the Christmas holidays, so that they might pass the Advanced Placement mathematics examination for college entry. The teacher's reference to the Mayans' mathematical genius was a valid instructional device: It was an attention-getter and would have interested even students who were not Hispanic. But the Mayan example would have had little effect without the teacher's insistence that the class study hard for a difficult examination.

Ethnic educators have seized upon the Mayan contribution to mathematics as the key to simultaneously boosting the ethnic pride of Hispanic children and attacking Eurocentrism. One proposal claims that Mexican-American children will be attracted to science and mathematics if they study Mayan mathematics, the Mayan calendar, and Mayan astronomy. Children in primary grades are to be taught that the Mayans were first to discover the zero and that Europeans learned it long afterwards from the Arabs, who had learned it in India. This will help them see that Europeans were latecomers in the discovery of great ideas. Botany is to be learned by study of the agricultural techniques of the Aztecs, a subject of somewhat limited relevance to children in urban areas. Furthermore, "ethnobotanical" classifications of plants are to be substituted for the Eurocentric Linnaean system. At first glance, it may seem curious that Hispanic children are deemed to have no cultural affinity with Spain; but to acknowledge the cultural tie would confuse the ideological assault on Eurocentrism.

This proposal suggests some questions: Is there any evidence that the teaching of "culturally relevant" science and mathematics will draw Mexican-American children to the study of these subjects? Will Mexican-American children lose interest or self-esteem if they discover that their ancestors were Aztecs or Spaniards, rather than Mayans? Are children who learn in this way prepared to study the science and mathematics that are taught in American colleges and universities and that are needed for advanced study in these fields? Are they even prepared to study the science and mathematics taught in *Mexican* universities? If the class is half Mexican-American and half something else, will only the Mexican-American children study in a Mayan and Aztec mode or will all the children? But shouldn't all children study what is culturally relevant for them? How will we train teachers who have command of so many different systems of mathematics and science?

• • •

Particularism is akin to cultural Lysenkoism, for it takes as its premise the spurious notion that cultural traits are inherited. It implies a dubious, dangerous form of cultural predestination. Children are taught that if their ancestors could do it, so could they. But what happens if a child is from a cultural group that made no significant contribution to science or mathematics? Does this mean that children from that background must find a culturally appropriate field in which to strive? How does a teacher find the right cultural buttons for children of mixed heritage? And how in the world will teachers use this technique when the children in their classes are drawn from many different cultures, as is usually the case? By the time that every culture gets its due, there may be no time left to teach the subject itself. This explosion of filiopietism (which, we should remember, comes from adults, not from students) is reminiscent of the period some years ago when the Russians claimed that they had invented everything first; as we now know, this nationalistic braggadocio did little for their self-esteem and nothing for their economic development. We might reflect, too, on how little social prestige has been accorded in this country to immigrants from Greece and Italy, even though the achievements of their ancestors were at the heart of the classical curriculum.

• • •

Particularism can easily be carried to extremes. Students of Fredonian descent must hear that their ancestors were seminal in the development of all human civilization and that without the Fredonian contribution, we would all be living in caves or trees, bereft of art, technology, and culture. To explain why Fredonians today are in modest circumstances, given their historic eminence, children are taught that somewhere, long ago, another culture stole the Fredonians' achievements, palmed them off as their own, and then oppressed the Fredonians.

I first encountered this argument almost twenty years ago, when I was a graduate student. I shared a small office with a young professor, and I listened as she patiently explained to a student why she had given him a D on a term paper. In his paper, he argued that the Arabs had stolen mathematics from the Nubians in the desert long ago (I forget in which century this theft allegedly occurred). She tried to explain to him about the necessity of historical evidence. He was unconvinced, since he believed that he had uncovered a great truth that was beyond proof. The part I couldn't understand was how anyone could lose knowledge by sharing it. After all, cultures are constantly influencing one another, exchanging ideas and art and technology, and the exchange usually is enriching, not depleting.

Today, there are a number of books and articles advancing controversial theories about the origins of civilization. An important work, *The African Origin of Civilization: Myth or Reality*, by Senegalese scholar Cheikh Anta Diop, argues that ancient Egypt was a black civilization, that all races are descended from the black race, and that the achievements of "western" civilization originated in Egypt. The views of Diop and other Africanists have been condensed into an everyman's paperback titled *What They Never Told You in History Class* by Indus Khamit Kush. This latter book claims that Moses, Jesus, Buddha, Mohammed, and Vishnu were Africans: that the first Indians, Chinese, Hebrews, Greeks, Romans, Britains, and Americans were Africans; and that the first mathematicians, scientists, astronomers, and physicians were Africans. A debate currently raging among some classicists is whether the Greeks "stole" the philosophy, art, and religion of the ancient Egyptians and whether the ancient Egyptians were black Africans. George G. M. James's *Stolen Legacy* insists that the Greeks "stole the Legacy of the African Continent and called it their own." James argues that the civilization of Greece, the vaunted foundation of European culture, owed everything it knew and did to its African predecessors. Thus, the roots of western civilization lie not in Greece and Rome, but in Egypt and, ultimately, in black Africa.

• • •

In school districts where most children are black and Hispanic, there has been a growing tendency to embrace particularism rather than pluralism. Many of the children in these districts perform poorly in academic classes and leave school without graduating. They would fare better in school if they had well-educated and well-paid teachers, small classes, good materials, encouragement at home and school, summer academic programs, protection from the drugs and crime that ravage their neighborhoods, and higher expectations of satisfying careers upon graduation. These are expensive and time-consuming remedies that must also engage the larger society beyond the school. The lure of particularism is that it offers a less complicated anodyne, one in which the children's academic deficiencies may be addressed—or set aside—by inflating their racial pride. The danger of this remedy is that it will detract attention from the real needs of schools and the real interests of children, while simultaneously arousing distorted race pride in children of all races, increasing racial antagonism and producing fresh recruits for white and black racist groups.

The rising tide of particularism encourages the politicization of all curricula in the schools. If education bureaucrats bend to the political and ideological winds, as is their wont, we can anticipate a generation of struggle over the content of the curriculum in mathematics, science, literature, and history. Demands for "culturally relevant" studies, for ethnostudies of all kinds, will open the classroom to unending battles over whose version is taught, who gets credit for what, and which ethno-interpretation is appropriate. Only recently have districts begun to resist the demands of fundamentalist groups to censor textbooks and library books (and some have not yet begun to do so).

The spread of particularism throws into question the very idea of American public education. Public schools exist to teach children the general skills and knowledge that they need to succeed in American society, and the specific skills and knowledge that they need in order to function as American citizens. They receive public support because they have a public function. Historically, the public schools were known as "common schools" because they were schools for all, even if the children of all the people did not attend them. Over the years, the courts have found that it was unconstitutional to teach religion in the common schools, or to separate children on the basis of their race in the common schools. In their curriculum, their hiring practices, and their general philosophy, the public schools must not discriminate against or give preference to any racial or ethnic group. Yet they are permitted to accommodate cultural diversity by, for example, serving food that is culturally appropriate or providing library collections that emphasize the interests of the local community. However, they should not be expected to teach children to view the world through an ethnocentric perspective that rejects or ignores the common culture. For generations, those groups that wanted to inculcate their religion or their ethnic heritage have instituted private schools—after school, on weekends, or on a full-time basis. There, children learn with others of the same group—Greeks, Poles, Germans, Japanese, Chinese, Jews, Lutherans, Catholics, and so on—and are taught by people from the same group. Valuable as this exclusive experience has been for those who choose it, this has not been the role of public education. One of the primary purposes of public education has been to create a national community, a definition of citizenship and culture that is both expansive and *inclusive*.

The curriculum in public schools must be based on whatever knowledge and practices have been determined to be best by professionals—experienced teachers and scholars—who are competent to make these judgments. Professional societies must be prepared to defend the integrity of their disciplines. When called upon, they should establish review committees to examine disputes over curriculum and to render judgment, in order to help school officials fend off improper political pressure. Where genuine controversies exist, they should be taught and debated in the classroom. Was Egypt a black civilization? Why not raise the question, read the arguments of the different sides in the debate, show slides of Egyptian pharoahs and queens, read books about life in ancient Egypt, invite guest scholars from the local university, and visit museums with Egyptian collections? If scholars disagree, students should know it. One great advantage of this approach is that students will see that history is a lively study, that textbooks are fallible, that historians disagree, that the writing of history is influenced by the historian's politics and ideology, that history is written by people who make choices among alternative facts and interpretations, and that history changes as new facts are uncovered and new interpretations win adherents. They will also learn that cultures and civilizations constantly interact, exchange ideas, and influence one another, and that the idea of racial or ethnic purity is a myth. Another advantage is that students might once again study ancient history, which has all but disappeared from the curricula of American schools. (California recently introduced a required sixth grade course in ancient civilizations, but ancient history is otherwise *terra incognita* in American education.)

The multicultural controversy may do wonders for the study of history, which has been neglected for years in American schools. At this time, only half of our high school graduates ever study any world history. Any serious attempt to broaden students' knowledge of Africa, Europe, Asia, and Latin America will require at least two, and possibly three years of world history (a requirement thus far only in California). American history, too, will need more time than the one-year high-school survey course. Those of us who have insisted for years on the importance of history in the curriculum may not be ready to assent to its redemptive power, but hope that our new allies will ultimately join a constructive dialogue that strengthens the place of history in the schools.

As cultural controversies arise, educators must adhere to the principle of "E Pluribus Unum." That is, they must maintain a balance between the demands of the one—the nation of which we are common citizens—and the many—the varied histories of the American people. It is not necessary to denigrate either the one or the many. Pluralism is a positive value, but it is also important that we preserve a sense of an American community—a society and a culture to which we all belong. If there is no overall community with an agreed-upon vision of liberty and justice, if all we have is a collection of racial and ethnic cultures, lacking any common bonds, then we have no means to mobilize public opinion on behalf of people who are not members of our particular group. We have, for example, no reason to support public education. If there is no larger community, then each group will want to teach its own children in its own way, and public education ceases to exist.

History should not be confused with filiopietism. History gives no grounds for race pride. No race has a monopoly on virtue. If anything, a study of history should inspire humility, rather than pride. People of every racial group have committed terrible crimes, often against others of the same group. Whether one looks at the history of Europe or Africa or Latin America or Asia, every continent offers examples of inhumanity. Slavery has existed in civilizations around the world for centuries. Examples of genocide can be found around the world, throughout history, from ancient times right through to our own day. Governments and cultures, sometimes by edict, sometimes simply following tradition, have practiced not only slavery, but human sacrifice, infanticide, cliterodectomy, and mass murder. If we teach children this, they might recognize how absurd both racial hatred and racial chauvinism are.

What must be preserved in the study of history is the spirit of inquiry, the readiness to open new questions and to pursue new understandings. History, at its best, is a search for truth. The best way to portray this search is through debate and controversy, rather than through imposition of fixed beliefs and immutable facts. Perhaps the most dangerous aspect of school history is its tendency to become Official History, a sanctified version of the Truth taught by the state to captive audiences and embedded in beautiful mass-market textbooks as holy writ. When Official History is written by committees responding to political pressures, rather than by scholars synthesizing the best available research, then the errors of the past are replaced by the politically fashionable errors of the present. It may be difficult to teach children that history is both important and uncertain, and that even the best historians never have all the pieces of the jigsaw puzzle, but it is necessary to do so. If state education departments permit the revision of their history courses and textbooks to become an exercise in power politics, then the entire process of state-level curriculum-making becomes suspect, as does public education itself.

The question of self-esteem is extraordinarily complex, and it goes well beyond the content of the curriculum. Most of what we call self-esteem is formed in the home and in a variety of life experiences, not only in school. Nonetheless, it has been important for blacks—and for other racial groups—to learn about the history of slavery and of the civil rights movement; it has been important for blacks to know that their ancestors actively resisted enslavement and actively pursued equality; and it has been important for blacks and others to learn about black men and women who fought courageously against racism and who provide models of courage, persistence, and intellect. These are instances where the content of the curriculum reflects sound scholarship, and at the same time probably lessens racial prejudice and provides inspiration for those who are descendants of slaves. But knowing about the travails and triumphs of one's forebears does not necessarily translate into either self-esteem or personal accomplishment. For most children, self-esteem—the self-confidence that grows out of having reached a goal—comes not from hearing about the monuments of their ancestors but as a consequence of what they are able to do and accomplish through their own efforts.

As I reflected on these issues, I recalled reading an interview a few years ago with a talented black runner. She said that her model is Mikhail Baryshnikov. She admires him because he is a magnificent athlete. He is not black; he is not female; he is not American-born; he is not even a runner. But he inspires her because of the way he trained and used his body. When I read this, I thought how narrow-minded it is to believe that people can be inspired *only* by those who are exactly like them in race and ethnicity.

QUESTIONS FOR "MULTICULTURALISM: E PLURIBUS PLURES" BY DIANE RAVITCH

Talking About the Text

1. Ravitch's argument hinges on the distinction between two terms representing important concepts. In your own words explain what Ravitch means by *pluralistic multiculturalism* and by *particularistic multiculturalism*.
2. Ravitch attempts to steer a compromise course between examples of ethnic contributions beneficial to students and those she views as harmful. Evaluate her examples, and analyze the point she is trying to make with each of them.
3. Ravitch says, "One of the primary purposes of public education has been to create a national community, a definition of citizenship and culture that is both expansive and 'inclusive.' " Reflect on some of the problems that might arise as ethnic groups struggle to keep their identity while also struggling to help create a national community and culture.

Exploring Issues

1. Although Ravitch focuses on education, her argument involves the larger issue of ethnic assimilation and separatism. Use her argument to analyze other specific issues related to this larger one. For instance, consider the allocation of public funds for ethnic programs and festivals, for equal opportunity employment, and for affirmative action in our universities.
2. How might Ravitch treat ethnic studies in our colleges?
3. How might Rose, Bechtel, and Belenky et al. in Chapter 6 respond to Ravitch's argument?
4. How might Kit Yuen Quan from Chapter 1 respond to Ravitch's claims against particularists? How might Alice Walker respond?

Writing Assignments

1. Review some of your previous writing you completed in response to selections from Chapter 6. If some of this material is pertinent, draw on it to help you respond to Ravitch's essay. Focus particularly on describing the kinds of citizens Ravitch's curriculum might produce as well as on some of the obstacles her curriculum might encounter.
2. Write a proposal in which you try to solve the problem of how ethnic identities can be maintained on college campuses. As you think about

this problem, be aware of how easy it might be for one group to maintain its identity only in isolation from others.

3. In addition to Ravitch, choose two or three other relevant speakers you have encountered in this book and write a dialogue between them as they address this question: What is best for American education in order to ensure a viable national community?

Reading 77

Split at the Root: An Essay on Jewish Identity

Adrienne Rich

Adrienne Rich is a lesbian, feminist, poet, and an outspoken commentator on a host of social and political issues. She is also a professor of English and feminist studies at Stanford University. This essay is an edited version of the original, which appeared in *Blood, Bread and Poetry: Selected Prose, 1979–85*. In "Split at the Root: An Essay on Jewish Identity," Rich composes her autobiography as a quest to find out who she is. It is a personal journey in which she must recognize and see through the thick screen of prejudice as she struggles to weave together the separate strands of her life.

For about fifteen minutes I have been sitting chin in hand in front of the typewriter, staring out at the snow. Trying to be honest with myself, trying to figure out why writing this seems to be so dangerous an act, filled with fear and shame, and why it seems so necessary. It comes to me that in order to write this I have to be willing to do two things: I have to claim my father, for I have my Jewishness from him and not from my gentile mother; and I have to break his silence, his taboos; in order to claim him I have in a sense to expose him.

And there is, of course, the third thing: I have to face the sources and the flickering presence of my own ambivalence as a Jew; the daily, mundane anti-Semitisms of my entire life.

These are stories I have never tried to tell before. Why now? Why, I asked myself sometime last year, does this question of Jewish identity float so impalpably, so ungraspably around me, a cloud I can't quite see the outlines of, which feels to me to be without definition?

And yet I've been on the track of this longer than I think.

. . .

Sometime in 1946, while still in high school, I read in the newspaper that a theater in Baltimore was showing films of the Allied liberation of the Nazi concentration camps. Alone, I went downtown after school one afternoon and watched the stark, blurry, but unmistakable newsreels. When I try to go back and touch the pulse of that girl of sixteen, growing up in many ways so precocious and so ignorant, I am overwhelmed by a memory of despair, a sense of inevitability more enveloping than any I had ever known. Anne Frank's diary and many other personal narratives of the Holocaust were still unknown or unwritten. But it came to me that every one of those piles of corpses, mountains of shoes and clothing had contained, simply, individuals, who had believed, as I now believed of myself, that they were intended to live out a life of some kind of meaning, that the world possessed some kind of sense and order; yet *this* had happened to them. And I, who believed my life was intended to be so interesting and meaningful, was connected to those dead by something—not just mortality but a taboo name, a hated identity. Or was I—did I really have to be? Writing this now, I feel belated rage that I was so impoverished by the family and social worlds I lived in, that I had to try to figure out by myself what this did indeed mean for me. That I had never been taught about resistance, only about passing. That I had no language for anti-Semitism itself.

When I went home and told my parents where I had been, they were not pleased. I felt accused of being morbidly curious, not healthy, sniffing around death for the thrill of it. And since, at sixteen, I was often not sure of the sources of my feelings or of my motives for doing what I did, I probably accused myself as well. One thing was clear: there was nobody in my world with whom I could discuss those films. Probably at the same time, I was reading accounts of the camps in magazines and newspapers; what I remember were the films and having questions that I could not even phrase, such as *Are those men and women "them" or "us"*?

To be able to ask even the child's astonished question *Why do they hate us so*? means knowing how to say "we." The guilt of not knowing, the guilt of perhaps having betrayed my parents or even those victims, those survivors, through mere curiosity—these also froze in me for years the impulse to find out more about the Holocaust.

1947: I left Baltimore to go to college in Cambridge, Massachusetts, left (I thought) the backward, enervating South for the intellectual, vital North. New England also had for me some vibration of higher moral rectitude, of moral passion even, with its seventeenth-century Puritan self-scrutiny, its nineteenth-century literary "flowering," its abolitionist righteousness, Colonel Shaw and his Black Civil War regiment depicted in granite on Boston Common. At the same time, I found myself, at Radcliffe, among Jewish women. I used to sit for hours over coffee with what I thought of as the "real" Jewish students, who told me about middle-class Jewish culture in America. I described my background—for the first time to strangers—and they took me on, some with amusement at my illiteracy, some arguing that I could never marry into a strict Jewish family, some convinced I didn't "look Jewish," others that I did. I learned the names of holidays and foods, which surnames are Jewish and which are "changed names"; about girls who had had their noses "fixed," their hair straightened. For these young Jewish women, students in the late 1940s, it was acceptable, perhaps even necessary, to strive to look as gentile as possible; but they stuck proudly to being Jewish, expected to marry a Jew, have children, keep the holidays, carry on the culture.

I felt I was testing a forbidden current, that there was danger in these revelations. I bought a reproduction of a Chagall portrait of a rabbi in striped prayer shawl and hung it on the wall of my room. I was admittedly young and trying to educate myself, but I was also doing something that *is* dangerous: I was flirting with identity.

One day that year I was in a small shop where I had bought a dress with a too-long skirt. The shop employed a seamstress who did alterations, and she came in to pin up the skirt on me. I am sure that she was a recent immigrant, a survivor. I remember a short, dark woman wearing heavy glasses, with an accent so foreign I could not understand her words. Something about her presence was very powerful and disturbing to me. After marking and pinning up the skirt, she sat back on her knees, looked up at me, and asked in a hurried whisper: "You Jewish?" Eighteen years of training in assimilation sprang into the reflex by which I shook my head, rejecting her, and muttered, "No."

What was I actually saying "no" to? She was poor, older, struggling with a foreign tongue, anxious; she had escaped the death that had been intended for her, but I had no imagination of her possible courage and foresight, her resistance—I did not see in her a heroine who had perhaps saved many lives, including her own. I saw the frightened immigrant, the seamstress hemming the skirts of college girls, the wandering Jew. But I was an American college girl having her skirt hemmed. And I was frightened myself, I think, because she had recognized me ("It takes one to know one," my friend Edie at Radcliffe had said) even if I refused to recognize myself or her, even if her recognition was sharpened by loneliness or the need to feel safe with me.

But why should she have felt safe with me? I myself was living with a false sense of safety.

There are betrayals in my life that I have known at the very moment were betrayals: this was one of them. There are other betrayals committed so repeatedly, so mundanely, that they leave no memory trace behind, only a growing residue of misery, of dull, accreted self-hatred. Often these take the form not of words but of silence. Silence before the joke at which everyone is laughing: the anti-woman joke, the racist joke, the anti-Semitic joke. Silence and then amnesia. Blocking it out when the oppressor's language starts coming from the lips of one we admire, whose courage and eloquence have touched us: *She didn't really mean that; he didn't really say that.* But the accretions build up out of sight, like scale inside a kettle.

1948: I come home from my freshman year at college, flaming with new insights, new information. I am the daughter who has gone out into the world, to the pinnacle of intellectual prestige, Harvard, fulfilling my father's hopes for me, but also exposed to dangerous influences. I have already been reproved for attending a rally for Henry Wallace and the Progressive party. I challenge my father: "Why haven't you told me that I am Jewish? Why do you never talk about being a Jew?" He answers measuredly, "You know that I have never denied that I am a Jew. But it's not important to me. I am a scientist, a deist. I have no use for organized religion. I choose to live in a world of many kinds of people. There are Jews I admire and others whom I despise. I am a person, not simply a Jew." The words are as I remember them, not perhaps exactly as spoken. But that was the message. And it contained enough truth—as all denial drugs itself on partial truth—so that it remained for the time being unanswerable, leaving me high and dry, split at the root, gasping for clarity, for air.

At that time Arnold Rich was living in suspension, waiting to be appointed to the professorship of pathology at Johns Hopkins. The appointment was delayed for years, no Jew ever having held a professional chair in that medical school. And he wanted it badly. It must have been a very bitter time for him, since he had believed so greatly in the redeeming power of excellence, of being the most brilliant, inspired man for the job. With enough excellence, you could presumably make it stop mattering that you were Jewish; you could become the *only* Jew in the gentile world, a Jew so "civilized," so far from "common," so attractively combining southern gentility with European cultural values that no one would ever confuse you with the raw, "pushy" Jews of New York, the "loud, hysterical" refugees from eastern Europe, the "overdressed" Jews of the urban South.

We—my sister, mother, and I—were constantly urged to speak quietly in public, to dress without ostentation, to repress all vividness or spontaneity, to assimilate with a world which might see us as too flamboyant. I suppose that my mother, pure gentile though she was, could be seen as acting "common" or "Jewish" if she laughed too loudly or spoke aggressively. My father's mother, who lived with us half the year, was a model of circumspect behavior, dressed in dark blue or lavender, retiring in company, ladylike to an extreme, wearing no jewelry except a good gold chain, a narrow brooch, or a string of pearls. A few times, within the family, I saw her anger flare, felt the passion she was repressing. But when Arnold took us out to a restaurant or on a trip, the Rich women were always tuned down to some WASP level my father believed, surely, would protect us all—maybe also make us unrecognizable to the "real Jews" who wanted to seize us, drag us back to the *shtetl*, the ghetto, in its many manifestations.

For, yes, that *was* a message—that some Jews would be after you, once they "knew," to rejoin them, to re-enter a world that was messy, noisy, unpredictable, maybe poor—"even though," as my mother once wrote me, criticizing my largely Jewish choice of friends in college, "some of them will be the most brilliant, fascinating people you'll ever meet." I wonder if that isn't one message of assimilation—of America—that the unlucky or the unachieving want to pull you backward, that to identify with them is to court downward mobility, lose the precious chance of passing, of token existence. There was always within this sense of Jewish identity a strong class discrimination. Jews might be "fascinating" as individuals but came with huge unruly families who "poured chicken soup over everyone's head" (in the phrase of a white southern male poet). Anti-Semitism could thus be justified by the bad behavior of certain Jews; and if you did not effectively deny family and community, there would always be a remote cousin claiming kinship with you who was the "wrong kind" of Jew.

I have always believed his attitude toward other Jews depended on who they were. . . . It was my impression that Jews of this background looked down on Eastern European Jews, including Polish Jews and Russian Jews, who generally were not as well educated. This from a letter written to me recently by a gentile who had worked in my father's department, whom I had asked about anti-Semitism there and in particular regarding my father. This informant also wrote me that it was hard to perceive anti-Semitism in Baltimore because the racism made so much more intense an impression: *I would almost have to think that blacks went to a different heaven than the whites, because the bodies were kept in a separate morgue, and some white persons did not even want blood transfusions from black donors.* My father's mind was predictably racist and misogynist; yet as a medical student he noted in his journal that southern male chivalry stopped at the point of any white man in a streetcar giving his seat to an old, weary Black woman standing in the aisle. Was this a Jewish insight—an outsider's insight, even though the outsider was striving to be on the inside?

Because what isn't named is often more permeating than what is, I believe that my father's Jewishness profoundly shaped my own identity and our family existence. They were shaped both by external anti-Semitism and my father's self-hatred, and by his Jewish pride. What Arnold did, I think, was call his Jewish pride something else: achievement, aspiration, genius, idealism. Whatever was unacceptable got left back under the rubric of Jewishness or the "wrong kind" of Jews—uneducated, aggressive, loud. The message I got was ʰhat we were really superior: nobody else's father had collected so many books, ꞮꞮad traveled so far, knew so many languages. Baltimore was a musical city, but for the most part, in the families of my school friends, culture was for women. My father was an amateur musician, read poetry, adored encyclopedic knowledge. He prowled and pounced over my school papers, insisting I use "grown-up" sources; he criticized my poems for faulty technique and gave me books on rhyme and meter and form. His investment in my intellect and talent was egotistical, tyrannical, opinionated, and terribly wearing. He taught me, nevertheless, to believe in hard work, to mistrust easy inspiration, to write and rewrite; to feel that I *was* a person of the book, even though a woman; to take ideas seriously. He made me feel, at a very young age, the power of language and that I could share in it.

The Riches were proud, but we also had to be very careful. Our behavior had to be more impeccable than other people's. Strangers were not to be trusted, nor even friends; family issues must never go beyond the family; the world was full of potential slanderers, betrayers, *people who could not under-*

stand. Even within the family, I realize that I never in my whole life knew what my father was really feeling. Yet he spoke—monologued—with driving intensity. You could grow up in such a house mesmerized by the local electricity, the crucial meanings assumed by the merest things. This used to seem to me a sign that we were all living on some high emotional plane. It was a difficult force field for a favored daughter to disengage from.

Easy to call that intensity Jewish; and I have no doubt that passion is one of the qualities required for survival over generations of persecution. But what happens when passion is rent from its original base, when the white gentile world is softly saying "Be more like us and you can be almost one of us"? What happens when survival seems to mean closing off one emotional artery after another? His forebears in Europe had been forbidden to travel or expelled from one country after another, had special taxes levied on them if they left the city walls, had been forced to wear special clothes and badges, restricted to the poorest neighborhoods. He had wanted to be a "free spirit," to travel widely, among "all kinds of people." Yet in his prime of life he lived in an increasingly withdrawn world, in his house up on a hill in a neighborhood where Jews were not supposed to be able to buy property, depending almost exclusively on interactions with his wife and daughters to provide emotional connectedness. In his home, he created a private defense system so elaborate that even as he was dying, my mother felt unable to talk freely with his colleagues or others who might have helped her. Of course, she acquiesced in this.

The loneliness of the "only," the token, often doesn't feel like loneliness but like a kind of dead echo chamber. Certain things that ought to don't resonate. Somewhere Beverly Smith writes of women of color "inspiring the behavior" in each other. When there's nobody to "inspire the behavior," act out of the culture, there is an atrophy, a dwindling, which is partly invisible.

I was married in 1953, in the Hillel House at Harvard, under a portrait of Albert Einstein. My parents refused to come. I was marrying a Jew of the "wrong kind" from an Orthodox eastern European background. Brooklyn-born, he had gone to Harvard, changed his name, was both indissolubly connected to his childhood world and terribly ambivalent about it. My father saw this marriage as my having fallen prey to the Jewish family, eastern European division.

Like many women I knew in the fifties living under a then-unquestioned heterosexual imperative, I married in part because I knew no better way to disconnect from my first family. I married a "real Jew" who was himself almost equally divided between a troubled yet ingrained Jewish identity, and the pull toward Yankee approval, assimilation. But at least he was not adrift as a single token in a gentile world. We lived in a world where there was much intermarriage and where a certain "Jewish flavor" was accepted within the dominant gentile culture. People talked glibly of "Jewish self-hatred," but anti-Semitism was rarely identified. It was as if you could have it both ways—identity and assimilation—without having to think about it very much.

I was moved and gratefully amazed by the affection and kindliness my husband's parents showed me, the half *shiksa.* I longed to embrace that family, that new and mysterious Jewish world. It was never a question of conversion—

my husband had long since ceased being observant—but of a burning desire to do well, please these new parents, heal the split consciousness in which I had been raised, and, of course, to belong. In the big, sunny apartment on Eastern Parkway, the table would be spread on Saturday afternoons with a white or an embroidered cloth and plates of coffeecake, spongecake, mohncake, cookies for a family gathering where everyone ate and drank—coffee, milk, cake—and later the talk still eddied among the women around the table or in the kitchen, while the men ended up in the living room watching the ball game. I had never known this kind of family, in which mock insults were cheerfully exchanged, secrets whispered in corners among two or three, children and grandchildren boasted about, and the new laughter-in-law openly inspected. I was profoundly attracted by all this, including the punctilious observance of *kashrut*, the symbolism lurking behind daily kitchen tasks. I saw it all as quintessentially and authentically Jewish, and I objectified both the people and the culture. My unexamined anti-Semitism allowed me to do this. But also, I had not yet recognized that as a woman I stood in a particular and unexamined relationship to the Jewish family and to Jewish culture.

There were several years during which I did not see, and barely communicated with, my parents. At the same time, my father's personali y haunted my life. Such had been the force of his will in our household that fo. a long time I felt I would have to pay in some terrible way for having disobeyed him. When finally we were reconciled, and my husband and I and our children began to have some minimal formal contact with my parents, the obsessional power of Arnold's voice or handwriting had given way to a dull sense of useless anger and pain. I wanted him to cherish and approve of me, not as he had when I was a child, but as the woman I was, who had her own mind and had made her own choices. This, I finally realized, was not to be; Arnold demanded absolute loyalty, absolute submission to his will. In my separation from him, in my realization at what price that once-intoxicating approval had been bought, I was learning in concrete ways a great deal about patriarchy, in particular how the "special" woman, the favored daughter, is controlled and rewarded.

Arnold Rich died in 1968 after a long, deteriorating illness; his mind had gone, and he had been losing his sight for years. It was a year of intensifying political awareness for me: the Martin Luther King and Robert Kennedy assassinations, the Columbia strike. But it was not that these events, and the meetings and demonstrations that surrounded them, preempted the time of mourning for my father; I had been mourning a long time for an early, primary, and intense relationship, by no means always benign, but in which I had been ceaselessly made to feel that what I did with my life, the choices I made, the attitudes I held, were of the utmost consequence.

Sometime in my thirties, on visits to Brooklyn, I sat on Eastern Parkway, a baby stroller at my feet—one of many rows of young Jewish women on benches with children in that neighborhood. I used to see the Lubavitcher Hasidim—then beginning to move into the Crown Heights neighborhood—walking out on *Shabbes*, the women in their *shaytls* a little behind the men. My father-in-law pointed them out as rather exotic—too old-country, perhaps, too unassimilated even for his devout yet Americanized sense of Jewish identity. It took many years for me to understand—partly because I understood so little about class in America—how in my own family, and in the very different family of my in-laws, there were degrees and hierarchies of assimilation which looked askance upon each other—and also geographic lines of difference, as between southern Jews and New York Jews, whose manners and customs varied along class as well as regional lines.

I had three sons before I was thirty, and during those years I often felt that to be a Jewish woman, a Jewish mother, was to be perceived in the Jewish family as an entirely physical being, a producer and nourisher of children. The experience of motherhood was eventually to radicalize me. But before that, I was encountering the institution of motherhood most directly in a Jewish cultural version; and I felt rebellious, moody, defensive, unable to sort out what was Jewish from what was simply motherhood or female destiny. (I lived in Cambridge, not Brooklyn; but there, too, restless, educated women sat on benches with baby strollers, half-stunned, not by Jewish cultural expectations, but by the middle-class American social expectations of the 1950s.)

My children were taken irregularly to Seders, to bar mizvahs, and to special services in their grandfather's temple. Their father lit Hanukkah candles while I stood by, having rememorized each year the English meaning of the Hebrew blessing. We all celebrated a secular, liberal Christmas. I read aloud from books about Esther and the Maccabees and Moses, and also from books about Norse trolls and Chinese grandmothers and Celtic dragon slayers. Their father told stories of his boyhood in Brooklyn, his grandmother in the Bronx who had to be visited by subway every week, of misdeeds in Hebrew school, of being a bright Jewish kid at Boys' High. In the permissive liberalism of academic Cambridge, you could raise your children to be as vaguely or distinctly Jewish as you would, but Christian myth and calendar organized the year. My sons grew up knowing far more about the existence and concrete meaning of Jewish culture than I had. But I don't recall sitting down with them and telling them that millions of people like themselves, many of them children, had been rounded up and murdered in Europe in their parents' lifetime. Nor was I able to tell them that they came in part out of the rich, thousand-year-old Ashkenazic culture of eastern Europe, which the Holocaust destroyed; or that they came from a people whose traditions, religious and secular, included a hatred of oppression and an imperative to pursue justice and care for the stranger—an anti-racist, a socialist, and even sometimes a feminist vision. I could not tell them these things because these things were still too indistinct in my own mind.

The emergence of the Civil Rights movement in the sixties I remember as lifting me out of a sense of personal frustration and hopelessness. Reading James Baldwin's early essays in the fifties had stirred me with a sense that apparently "given" situations like racism could be analyzed and described and that this could lead to action, to change. Racism had been so utter and implicit a fact of my childhood and adolescence, had felt so central among the silences, negations, cruelties, fears, superstitions of my early life, that somewhere among my feelings must have been the hope that if Black people could become free of the immense political and social burdens they were forced to bear, I, too, could become free of all the ghosts and shadows of my childhood, named and unnamed. When "the movement" began, it felt extremely personal to me. And it was often Jews who spoke up for the justice of the cause, Jewish students and civil rights lawyers who travelled South; it was two young Jews who were found murdered with a young Black man in Mississippi: Schwerner, Goodman, Chaney.

Moving to New York in the mid-sixties meant being plunged almost immediately into the debate over community control of public schools, in which Black and Jewish teachers and parents were often on opposite sides of extremely militant barricades. It was easy as a white liberal to deplore and condemn the racism of middle-class Jewish parents or angry Jewish schoolteachers, many of them older women; to displace our own racism onto them; or to feel it as too painful to think about. The struggle for Black civil rights had such clarity about it for me: I knew that segregation was wrong, that unequal opportunity was wrong; I knew that segregation in particular was more than a set of social and legal rules—it meant that even "decent" white people lived in a network of lies and arrogance and moral collusion. In the world of Jewish assimilationist and liberal politics which I knew best, however, things were far less clear to me, and anti-Semitism went almost unmentioned. It was even possible to view concern about anti-Semitism as a reactionary agenda, a monomania of *Commentary* magazine or, later, the Jewish Defense League. Most of the political work I was doing in the late 1960s was on racial issues, in particular as a teacher in the City University during the struggle for open admissions. The white colleagues I thought of as allies were, I think, mostly Jewish. Yet it was easy to see other New York Jews, who had climbed out of poverty and exploitation through the public-school system and the free city colleges, as now trying to block Black and Puerto Rican students trying to do likewise. I didn't understand then that I was living between two strains of Jewish social identity: the Jew as radical visionary and activist who understands oppression firsthand, and the Jew as part of America's devouring plan in which the persecuted, called to assimilation, learn that the price is to engage in persecution.

And, indeed, there *was* intense racism among Jews as well as white gentiles in the City University, part of the bitter history of Jews and Blacks which James Baldwin had described much earlier, in his 1948 essay "The Harlem Ghetto";[1] part of the divide-and-conquer script still being rehearsed by those of us who have the least to gain from it.

By the time I left my marriage, after seventeen years and three children, I had become identified with the Women's Liberation movement. It was an astonish-

---

[1]James Baldwin, "The Harlem Ghetto," in *Notes of a Native Son* (Boston: Beacon, 1955).

ing time to be a woman of my age. In the 1950s, seeking a way to grasp the pain I seemed to be feeling most of the time, to set it in some larger context, I had read all kinds of things; but it was James Baldwin and Simone de Beauvoir who had described the world—though differently—in terms that made the most sense to me. By the end of the sixties there were two political movements—one already meeting severe repression, one just emerging—which addressed those descriptions of the world.

And there was, of course, a third movement, or a movement-within-a-movement: the early lesbian manifestoes, the new visibility and activism of lesbians everywhere. I had known very early on that the women's movement was not going to be a simple walk across an open field; that it would pull on every fiber of my existence; that it would mean going back and searching the shadows of my consciousness. Reading *The Second Sex* in the 1950s isolation of an academic housewife had felt less dangerous than reading "The Myth of Vaginal Orgasm" or "Woman-identified Woman" in a world where I was in constant debate and discussion with women over every aspect of our lives that we could as yet name. De Beauvoir had placed "The Lesbian" on the margins, and there was little in her book to suggest the power of woman bonding. But the passion of debating ideas with women was an erotic passion for me, and the risking of self with women that was necessary in order to win some truth out of the lies of the past was also erotic. The suppressed lesbian I had been carrying in me since adolescence began to stretch her limbs, and her first full-fledged act was to fall in love with a Jewish woman.

Some time during the early months of that relationship, I dreamed that I was arguing feminist politics with my lover. *Of course*, I said to her in this dream, *if you're going to bring up the Holocaust against me, there's nothing I can do.* If, as I believe, I was both myself and her in this dream, it spoke of the split in my consciousness. I had been, more or less, a Jewish heterosexual woman. But what did it mean to be a Jewish lesbian? What did it mean to feel myself, as I did, both anti-Semite and Jew? And, as a feminist, how was I charting for myself the oppressions within oppression?

The earliest feminist papers on Jewish identity that I read were critiques of the patriarchal and misogynist elements in Judaism, or of the caricaturing of Jewish women in literature by Jewish men. I remember hearing Judith Plaskow give a paper called "Can a Woman Be a Jew?" (Her conclusion was "Yes, but . . . ") I was soon after in correspondence with a former student who had emigrated to Israel, was a passionate feminist, and wrote to me at length of the legal and social constraints on women there, the stirrings of contemporary Israeli feminism, and the contradictions she felt in her daily life. With the new politics, activism, literature of a tumultuous feminist movement around me, a movement which claimed universality though it had not yet acknowledged its own racial class, and ethnic perspectives or its fears of the differences among women, I pushed aside for one last time thinking further about myself as a Jewish woman. I saw Judaism simply as another strand of patriarchy. If asked to choose, I might have said (as my father had said in other language): *I am a woman, not a Jew.* (But, I always added mentally, if Jews had to wear yellow stars again, I, too, would wear one—as if I would have the choice to wear it or not.)

Sometimes I feel I have seen too long from too many disconnected angles: white, Jewish, anti-Semite, racist, anti-racist, once-married, lesbian, middle-class, feminist, exmatriate southerner, *split at the root*—that I will never bring them whole. I would have liked, in this essay, to bring together the meanings of anti-Semitism and racism as I have experienced them and as I believe they intersect in the world beyond my life. But I'm not able to do this yet. I feel the tension as I think, make notes: *If you really look at the one reality, the other will waver and disperse.* Trying in one week to read Angela Davis and Lucy Davidowicz;[2] trying to hold throughout to a feminist, a lesbian, perspective— what does this mean? Nothing has trained me for this. And sometimes I feel inadequate to make any statement as a Jew; I feel the history of denial within me like an injury, a scar. For assimilation has affected *my* perceptions; those early lapses in meaning, those blanks, are with me still. My ignorance can be danger-ous to me and to others.

Yet we can't wait for the undamaged to make our connections for us; we can't wait to speak until we are perfectly clear and righteous. There is no purity and, in our lifetimes, no end to this process.

This essay, then, has no conclusions: it is another beginning for me. Not just a way of saying, in 1982 Right Wing America, *I, too, will wear the yellow star.* It's a moving into accountability, enlarging the range of accountability. I know that in the rest of my life, the next half century or so, every aspect of my identity will have to be engaged. The middle-class white girl taught to trade obedience for privilege. The Jewish lesbian raised to be a heterosexual gentile. The woman who first heard oppression named and analyzed in the Black Civil Rights struggle. The woman with three sons, the feminist who hates male violence. The woman limping with a cane, the woman who has stopped bleed-ing are also accountable. The poet who knows that beautiful language can lie, that the oppressor's language sometimes sounds beautiful. The woman trying, as part of her resistance, to clean up her act.

QUESTIONS FOR "SPLIT AT THE ROOT: AN ESSAY ON JEWISH IDENTITY" BY ADRIENNE RICH

Talking About the Text

1. Explain how Rich is "split at the root."
2. Describe how Rich's growing sense of her identity is interconnected to larger social and political events.

---

[2]Angela Y. Davis, *Women, Race and Class* (New York: Random House, 1981); Lucy S. Da-vidowicz, *The War against the Jews 1933–1945* (1975) (New York: Bantam, 1979).

3. Rich's search for identity involves an understanding and attempt to integrate the many parts of her life—being a daughter, wife, and mother; student, teacher, poet, feminist, and lesbian; white and Jewish. How do both prejudice and love affect who Rich is?

4. Rich uses writing to find coherence in her life. Yet she is acutely aware "that beautiful language can lie" and "that the oppressor's language sometimes sounds beautiful." Consider alternate ways that Rich might have written this autobiographical essay, ways that might have been more "beautiful" but less truthful.

Exploring Issues

1. What does Rich mean when she says, "I wonder if that isn't one message of assimilation—of America—that the unlucky or the unachieving want to pull you backward, that to identify with them is to court downward mobility, lose the precious chance of passing, of token existence"?

2. Compare the ways that ethnicity plays an important role in Rose Hsu Jordan's and Arienne Rich's marriages. How does it affect their respective relationships with their parents and in-laws?

3. In what ways might Rich agree with Ravitch's views concerning ethnic identity and particularism? How might Rich disagree with Ravitch?

Writing Assignment

Rich "writes" her life against the background of cultural forces and political events. Write an autobiographical essay depicting who you are in terms of some of these larger cultural, political, social, and economic forces. You might also draw on some of the material you may have developed in Chapter 5 on the family. Perhaps you can view your life and the influences of these larger forces from the perspective of its shaping within the crucible of your family. For instance, consider whether your father's and/or mother's jobs influenced you in certain ways or whether particular social and political events helped shape, challenge, or change your beliefs.

Reading 78

I Have a Dream

Martin Luther King, Jr.

Martin Luther King, Jr., recognized as the foremost leader of the civil rights
movement, was born in Atlanta, Georgia, in 1929 and educated at Morehouse
College, Crozer Theological Seminary, and Boston University. He was
ordained a Baptist minister in 1947 and in 1957 founded the Southern
Christian Leadership Conference. Soon after receiving his ministry, King
became involved in civil rights activities, struggling to achieve racial integration
through nonviolent means. He won the Nobel Peace Prize in 1964. The
speech reprinted here was delivered at the Lincoln Memorial in 1963,
culminating the famous "March on Washington" and commemorating the
100-year anniversary of the Emancipation Proclamation. King's speech places
the struggle for civil rights at the heart of the American dream for all people to
be free and equal. King was assassinated in Memphis, Tennessee, in 1968.

Five score years ago, a great American, in whose symbolic shadow we stand,
signed the Emancipation Proclamation. This momentous decree came as a great
beacon light of hope to millions of Negro slaves who had been seared in the
flames of withering injustice. It came as a joyous daybreak to end the long night
of captivity.

But one hundred years later, we must face the tragic fact that the Negro is
still not free. One hundred years later, the life of the Negro is still sadly crippled
by the manacles of segregation and the chains of discrimination. One hundred
years later, the Negro lives on a lonely island of poverty in the midst of a vast
ocean of material prosperity. One hundred years later, the Negro is still languish-
ing in the corners of American society and finds himself an exile in his own land.
So we have come here today to dramatize an appalling condition.

In a sense we have come to our nation's Capitol to cash a check. When the
architects of our republic wrote the magnificent words of the Constitution and
the Declaration of Independence, they were signing a promissory note to which
every American was to fall heir. This note was a promise that all men would be
guaranteed the unalienable rights of life, liberty, and the pursuit of happiness.

It is obvious today that America has defaulted on this promissory note
insofar as her citizens of color are concerned. Instead of honoring this sacred

obligation, America has given the Negro people a bad check; a check which has come back marked "insufficient funds." But we refuse to believe that the bank of justice is bankrupt. We refuse to believe that there are insufficient funds in the great vaults of opportunity of this nation. So we have come to cash this check—a check that will give us upon demand the riches of freedom and the security of justice. We have also come to this hallowed spot to remind America of the fierce urgency of *now*. This is no time to engage in the luxury of cooling off or to take the tranquilizing drug of gradualism. *Now* is the time to make real the promises of Democracy. *Now* is the time to rise from the dark and desolate valley of segregation to the sunlit path of racial justice. *Now* is the time to open the doors of opportunity to all of God's children. *Now* is the time to lift our nation from the quicksands of racial injustice to the solid rock of brotherhood.

It would be fatal for the nation to overlook the urgency of the moment and to underestimate the determination of the Negro. This sweltering summer of the Negro's legitimate discontent will not pass until there is an invigorating autumn of freedom and equality. 1963 is not an end, but a beginning. Those who hope that the Negro needed to blow off steam and will now be content will have a rude awakening if the nation returns to business as usual. There will be neither rest nor tranquility in America until the Negro is granted his citizenship rights. The whirlwinds of revolt will continue to shake the foundations of our nation until the bright day of justice emerges.

But there is something I must say to my people who stand on the warm threshold which leads into the palace of justice. In the process of gaining our rightful place we must not be guilty of wrongful deeds. Let us not seek to satisfy our thirst for freedom by drinking from the cup of bitterness and hatred. We must forever conduct our struggle on the high plane of dignity and discipline. We must not allow our creative protest to degenerate into physical violence. Again and again we must rise to the majestic heights of meeting physical force with soul force. The marvelous new militancy which has engulfed the Negro community must not lead us to a distrust of all white people, for many of our white brothers, as evidenced by their presence here today, have come to realize that their destiny is tied up with our destiny and their freedom is inextricably bound to our freedom. We cannot walk alone.

And as we walk, we must make the pledge that we shall march ahead. We cannot turn back. There are those who are asking the devotees of civil rights, "When will you be satisfied?" We can never be satisfied as long as the Negro is the victim of the unspeakable horrors of police brutality. We can never be satisfied as long as our bodies, heavy with the fatigue of travel, cannot gain lodging in the motels of the highways and the hotels of the cities. We cannot be satisfied as long as the Negro's basic mobility is from a smaller ghetto to a larger one. We can never be satisfied as long as a Negro in Mississippi cannot vote and a Negro in New York believes he has nothing for which to vote. No, no, we are not satisfied, and we will not be satisfied until justice rolls down like waters and righteousness like a mighty stream.

I am not unmindful that some of you have come here out of great trials and tribulations. Some of you have come fresh from narrow jail cells. Some of you have come from areas where your quest for freedom left you battered by the storms of persecution and staggered by the winds of police brutality. You have been the veterans of creative suffering. Continue to work with the faith that unearned suffering is redemptive.

Go back to Mississippi, go back to Alabama, go back to South Carolina, go back to Georgia, go back to Louisiana, go back to the slums and ghettoes of our northern cities, knowing that somehow this situation can and will be changed. Let us not wallow in the valley of despair.

I say to you today, my friends, that in spite of the difficulties and frustrations of the moment I still have a dream. It is a dream deeply rooted in the American dream.

I have a dream that one day this nation will rise up and live out the true meaning of its creed: "We hold these truths to be self-evident; that all men are created equal."

I have a dream that one day on the red hills of Georgia the sons of former slaves and the sons of former slaveowners will be able to sit down together at the table of brotherhood.

I have a dream that the state of Mississippi, a desert state sweltering with the heat of injustice and oppression, will be transformed into an oasis of freedom and justice.

I have a dream that my four little children will one day live in a nation where they will not be judged by the color of their skin but by the content of their character.

I have a dream today.

I have a dream that the state of Alabama, whose governor's lips are presently dripping with the words of interposition and nullification, will be transformed into a situation where little black boys and black girls will be able to join hands with little white boys and white girls and walk together as sisters and brothers.

I have a dream today.

I have a dream that one day every valley shall be exalted, every hill and mountain shall be made low, the rough places will be made plain, and the crooked places will be made straight, and the glory of the Lord shall be revealed, and all flesh shall see it together.

This is our hope. This is the faith with which I return to the South. With this faith we will be able to hew out of the mountain of despair a stone of hope. With this faith we will be able to transform the jangling discords of our nation into a beautiful symphony of brotherhood. With this faith we will be able to work together, to pray together, to struggle together, to go to jail together, to stand up for freedom together, knowing that we will be free one day.

This will be the day when all of God's children will be able to sing with new meaning.

My country, tis of thee
Sweet land of liberty,
Of thee I sing:

Land where my fathers died,
Land of the pilgrims' pride,
From every mountainside
Let freedom ring.

And if America is to be a great nation this must become true. So let freedom ring from the prodigious hilltops of New Hampshire. Let freedom ring from the mighty mountains of New York. Let freedom ring from the heightening Alleghenies of Pennsylvania!

Let freedom ring from the snowcapped Rockies of Colorado!

Let freedom ring from the curvaceous peaks of California!

But not only that; let freedom ring from Stone Mountain of Georgia!

Let freedom ring from Lookout Mountain of Tennessee!

Let freedom ring from every hill and molehill of Mississippi. From every mountainside, let freedom ring.

When we let freedom ring, when we let it ring from every village and every hamlet, from every state and every city, we will be able to speed up that day when all of God's children, black men and white men, Jews and Gentiles, Protestants and Catholics, will be able to join hands and sing in the words of the old Negro spiritual, "Free at last! free at last! thank God almighty, we are free at last!"

QUESTIONS FOR "I HAVE A DREAM" BY MARTIN LUTHER KING, JR.

Talking About the Text

1. King's powerful speech, delivered at the height of the Civil Rights movement, tries to place the struggle for freedom within a greater national purpose. In so doing he uses a variety of strategies. Identify and consider some of these:

   Fragments or echoes of other well known American texts
   Appeals to both African-American and caucasian audiences
   The use of metaphor
   The use of repetition and parallelism
   Uniting local purpose with the nation's purposes

2. King utilizes an intriguing phrase when he says, "You have been the veterans of creative suffering." What does he mean by "creative suffering"?

Exploring Issues

1. Use Shelby Steele's discussion of African-American and caucasion race relations in Chapter 7 to analyze King's speech. How does King try to harmonize race relations?

2. On the occasion of King's speech, in addition to arguing for civil rights

he was also reaffirming our nation's values. King was attempting to fit the "Negro" struggle into a national system of values. Given what you are learning about such concepts as assimilation, cultural pluralism, and particularism (see Ravitch), if King were speaking today, how might he revise his speech in appealing to the various ethnic and minority groups in America? You might also consider particularly urban problems such as gangs, drugs, and crime.

3. What does King mean by "freedom"? Think about this term both as freedom *from* and freedom *to*. What is involved in being free? How is freedom achieved? Compare your understanding of King's definition with Peter Marin's (in the beginning of this chapter).

Writing Assignments

1. See if you can secure a film of King's original performance of this famous speech (for example, *Eyes on the Prize*). Analyze the differences in its dramatic oral performance versus reading it by yourself as a class assignment. Consider audience reaction, purpose, and context in your analysis.

2. Imitate some of King's techniques and write a speech in which you express your "dream" for confronting and solving a national problem; for example, your dream for improving the environment, for creating ethnic harmony, for ensuring quality education for all, for creating better living conditions, and so on.

Reading 79

"The Most Essential Documents"

Michael Ventura

Michael Ventura lives in Los Angeles where he writes a regular column for the *L.A. Weekly*. This selection is the second one we've included from his collection of essays, *Shadow Dancing in the U.S.A.* Here Ventura challenges each of us not to forget what America is all about. In fact, remembering the essence of what America is assumes an obligation requiring all of us to imagine what the "revolution" continues to mean.

To remember. To re-member. To put the pieces back together. America is being forgotten. America must be remembered.

But can the pieces be put *back* together, or must we imagine them all over again, every generation, every day? Is our failure to *be* America literally a failure of the imagination? Because America was an act of imagination to begin with. There had been nothing like it; there was no model. Our revolutionaries were clearly "imagining things."

In the summer of 1815, former president John Adams, eighty years old, wrote to his friend, former president Thomas Jefferson, seventy-two years old:

> As to the history of the Revolution, my Ideas may be peculiar, perhaps singular. What do We Mean by the Revolution? The War? That was no part of the Revolution. It was only an Effect and Consequence of it. The Revolution was in the minds of the People. . . .

It had been thirty-nine years since the Declaration of Independence—roughly the time from the Second World War to now. Already they felt that their revolution was irrecoverable. A month before, Adams had written to Jefferson: "Who shall write a history of the American revolution? Who can write it? Who will ever be able to write it?

"The most essential documents, the debates and deliberations in Congress from 1774 to 1783 were all in secret, and are now lost forever. Mr. Dickinson printed a speech, which he said he made in Congress against the Declaration of Independence, but it appeared to me very different from that, which you, and I heard."

Ten days later Jefferson wrote back: "On the subject of the history of the American revolution, you ask 'Who shall write it? Who can write it? And who will ever be able to write it?' Nobody; except the external facts. . . .

"Botta [who had written one of its first histories], as you observe, has put his own speculations and reasonings into the mouths of persons whom he names, but who, you and I know, never made such speeches."

I think of the enormous courage of John Adams, who had the courage to struggle for what he thought *should* be, *though he never believed, even as a young man, that the creation of this country would be valued by this country.* In 1787, ten years before he became its second president, he wrote to Jefferson: "Lessons my dear 'sir, are never wanting. Life and history are full . . . Moral Reflections, wise Maxims, religious Terrors, have little Effect upon Nations when they contradict a present Passion, Prejudice, Imagination, Enthusiasm, or Caprice . . . In short my dear Friend you and I have been indefatigable Labourers through our whole lives for a cause which will be thrown away in the next generation, upon the Vanity and Foppery of Persons of whom we do not know the Names perhaps."

To struggle for a nation which you believe beforehand is, because of the nature of humankind, already lost, yet to struggle because of the *beauty* of the nation which you hopelessly imagine—this is an artist's courage more than a leader's. Can you think of another leader who did not nurture the hope that at least some future generation would carry on the struggle and win?

Adams's is not the doctrine of a politician. It is the fire of a revolutionary—a man for whom politics is part poetics. We call them the Founding Fathers to make them safe. To forget them. "Fathers," in that usage, are not dangerous men. But a man who, like Adams, can harbor such disbelief yet fight tirelessly for his belief, is an incredibly dangerous man. What can you do to him? How can you frighten him?

This is a *political* legacy, this attitude that achieves its victories through despising victory, that fights not for gain but because it has imagined something beautiful.

Can this be remembered? Can this piece be put back? Is there the present possibility of a politics that is again a fundamental expression of minds rather than of interests vying for comforts? These are the questions that the politically active are now not asking, but living through. The only answer will be how they live their lives.

Revolutions occur "in the minds of the people." This may be why no fully industrialized nation has ever had a revolution. The major revolutions—in the United States, France, Mexico, Russia, China, and now all over the Third World—all have taken place in agrarian cultures, cultures where the mental processes cannot be outflanked and overwhelmed by technology and media. Ideas have tremendous force in agrarian cultures, once they catch on; whereas in North America or Europe ideas are now lost in the cacophony of media, and the most forceful elements for change are new technologies.

(It is interesting that Marxism only takes root in a society that is *imagining* having industry. Industrialized cultures see quickly that Marxism is too simplistic for a complex socio-economic structure, and either they reject it out of hand or water it down till it cannot be called Marxism except out of sentimentality.)

John Adams did not imagine any "ism," any more than did Zapata. In all their fifty years of correspondence, Adams and Jefferson have no catchword for the balance they sought between individual liberty and mutually beneficial law. They understood that a nation is re-created every day in the minds of the people, and so there are days when it is forcefully and brilliantly a nation, and there are days when it is hardly a nation at all.

Nor would they have criticized Nicaragua's Sandinistas for not holding free elections, for instance, so quickly after their revolution, since the new United States, with no enemies on its borders, no great nations sending money to bring it down, took much longer to hold its first free election. The American Revolution was over in 1781; Washington wasn't elected our first president until 1789, and he was not elected by the people in a free election but by the select, male-only Federal Constitutional Convention. Our Founding Fathers, then, would have shown more tolerance for the ebb and flow of a new nation's often violent struggles, and would have been appalled at our squeaky-clean, pompous image of our own early days. Adams recalled to Jefferson in 1813:

> *You certainly never felt the Terrorism, excited by Genet, in 1793, when ten thousand People in the Streets of Philadelphia, day after day, threatened to drag Washington out of his House [Philadelphia was then the nation's capital], and effect a Revolution in the Government, or compel it to declare war in favour of the French Revolution, and against England? The coolest and firmest minds, even among the Quakers in Philadelphia, have given their Opinions to me, that nothing but the Yellow Fever, which removed Dr. Hutchinson and Jonathan Dickenson Sargent from this World, could have saved the United States from the total Revolution of Government. I have no doubt You was [sic] fast asleep in philosophical Tranquility, when ten thousand People, and perhaps many more, were parading in the streets of Philadelphia, on the Evening of my Fast Day [April 25, 1799, President Adams had called for a fast day, that God "would withhold us from unreasonable discontent, from disunion, faction, sedition and insurrection," so critical was the state of the new union]; When even Governor Mifflin himself thought it his Duty to order a Patrol of Horse and Foot to preserve the peace; when Markett Street was as full as Men could stand by one another, and even before my Door; when some of my Domesticks in Phrenzy, determined to sacrifice their Lives in my defence [sic]; when all were ready to make a desperate Salley among the multitude, and others were with difficulty dragged back by the others; when I myself judged it prudent and necessary to order Chests of Arms from the War Office to be brought through bye Lanes and back Doors; determined to defend my House at the Expence [sic] of my Life, and the Lives of the few, very few Domesticks and Friends within it. What think you of Terrorism, Mr. Jefferson?*

Yet this same President Adams pardoned one John Fries, sentenced to hang for leading an armed rebellion against the federal government's right to tax his land. These men were revolutionaries, not politicians. Having had no illusions about their own day, they surely would have had patience with the Sandinistas, with Allende, with Castro. But what would our politicians and pundits be saying if the same scenes that Adams described of his presidency and of George Washington's were taking place now in the Sandinista capital?

"Shall I tell you what America is?" wrote a reader, Mr. Ernest Kearny, in a letter to the *L.A. Weekly.* "It is an oath. A pledge to its own people and the people of all nations."

The Founding Fathers would have agreed. At the age of eighty, in 1823, three years before they both died on the afternoon of July 4, 1826, the fiftieth anniversary of the Declaration, Jefferson wrote to Adams:

> *The generation which commences a revolution can rarely complete it. Habituated from their infancy to passive submission of body and mind to their kings and priests, they are not qualified, when called on, to think and provide for themselves and their experience, their ignorance and bigotry make them instruments often, in the hands of the Bonapartes and Iturbides, to defeat their own rights and purposes. This is the present situation in Europe and Spanish America. But it is not desperate. The light which has been shed on mankind by the art of printing has eminently changed the condition of the world . . . It continues to spread . . . To attain all this,*

however, rivers of blood must yet flow, and years of desolation pass over. Yet the object is worth rivers of blood, and years of desolation, for what inheritance so valuable can man leave to his posterity?

Adams believed the idea alone worth the trouble; he didn't trust posterity. But Jefferson believed that "the idea of resistance to government is so valuable on certain occasions, that I wish it always to be kept alive. It will often be exercised when wrong, but better so than not to be exercised at all. I like a little rebellion now and then. It is like a storm in the Atmosphere."

But it's no good looking for these men in the past, and it's certainly no good to look for them in the White House. Yet if they are really our fathers, and we are really their children, it might still be possible to look for them in ourselves.

QUESTIONS FOR " 'THE MOST ESSENTIAL DOCUMENTS' " BY MICHAEL VENTURA

Talking About the Text

1. What is significant about the title?
2. Re-read Ventura's first paragraph. What is he saying about memory and history?
3. Ventura writes this essay in the form of a commentary on the dialogue between Jefferson and Adams. Why does he choose to compose his essay in this way? In what sense does the form of the essay contribute to the significance of the title?
4. What does Ventura mean when he writes: "They [Adams and Jefferson] understood that a nation is re-created every day in the minds of the people, and so there are days when it is forcefully and brilliantly a nation, and there are days when it is hardly a nation at all"?

Exploring Issues

1. In what sense might King's speech in the previous selection illustrate Ventura's insistence that Americans need "to re-member"?
2. Ventura cites a letter to the *L.A. Weekly* in which the letter writer claims that America "is an oath. A pledge to its own people and the people of all nations." What are the people's responsibilities as participants in this pledge?
3. How would Peter Marin respond to Ventura's claim that "America was an act of the imagination to begin with"? What might this mean to Amy Tan's characters in "Half and Half"? How would Adrienne Rich interpret it?
4. What would it mean to be a "revolutionary" rather than a "politician" today?

Writing Assignments

1. We think Ventura's essay is provocative and, at the same time, puzzling. Select a passage that provokes, puzzles, or moves you in a particular way and write a response to Ventura exploring your reaction. You might even send this response to Ventura in care of the *L.A. Weekly.*

2. Working in groups, choose two prominent leaders from American history and write a dialogue between them as they discuss the present and future state of America. Your choices may include figures living today.

Reading 80

A Worn Path

Eudora Welty

One of America's greatest literary resources was born in 1909 in Jackson, Mississippi. After receiving her BA from the University of Wisconsin in 1929, Eudora Welty lived and worked in New York for a time before returning to the South. Over her lifetime she has authored an impressive collection of short stories, novels, and essays, for which she has won numerous awards. "A Worn Path" appears in her first book of fiction, entitled *A Curtain of Green* (1941). In this story, the gentle but determined Phoenix reveals a spiritual tenacity as she faithfully endures a repeated journey to town to secure medicine for her injured grandson. If all of us are to reconcile our differences and learn to live together, Phoenix dramatizes the virtues most needed for such a task.

It was December—a bright frozen day in the early morning. Far out in the country there was an old Negro woman with her head tied in a red rag, coming along a path through the pinewoods. Her name was Phoenix Jackson. She was very old and small and she walked slowly in the dark pine shadows, moving a little from side to side in her steps, with the balanced heaviness and lightness of a pendulum in a grandfather clock. She carried a thin, small cane made from an umbrella, and with this she kept tapping the frozen earth in front of her. This made a grave and persistent noise in the still air, that seemed meditative like the chirping of a solitary little bird.

She wore a dark striped dress reaching down to her shoe tops, and an equally long apron of bleached sugar sacks, with a full pocket: all neat and tidy, but every time she took a step she might have fallen over her shoelaces, which dragged from her unlaced shoes. She looked straight ahead. Her eyes were blue with age. Her skin had a pattern all its own of numberless branching wrinkles and as though a whole little tree stood in the middle of her forehead, but a golden color ran underneath, and the two knobs of her cheeks were illumined by a yellow burning under the dark. Under the red rag her hair came down on her neck in the frailest of ringlets, still black, and with an odor like copper.

Now and then there was a quivering in the thicket. Old Phoenix said, "Out of my way, all you foxes, owls, beetles, jack rabbits, coons and wild animals! . . . Keep out from under these feet, little bob-whites. . . . Keep the big wild hogs out of my path. Don't let none of those come running my direction. I got a long way." Under her small black-freckled hand her cane, limber as a buggy whip, would switch at the brush as if to rouse up any hiding things.

On she went. The woods were deep and still. The sun made the pine needles almost too bright to look at, up where the wind rocked. The cones dropped as light as feathers. Down in the hollow was the mourning dove—it was not too late for him.

The path ran up a hill. "Seem like there is chains about my feet, time I get this far," she said, in the voice of argument old people keep to use with themselves. "Something always take a hold of me on this hill—pleads I should stay."

After she got to the top she turned and gave a full, severe look behind her where she had come. "Up through pines," she said at length. "Now down through oaks."

Her eyes opened their widest and she started down gently. But before she got to the bottom of the hill a bush caught her dress.

Her fingers were busy and intent, but her skirts were full and long, so that before she could pull them free in one place they were caught in another. It was not possible to allow the dress to tear. "I in the thorny bush," she said. "Thorns, you doing your appointed work. Never want to let folks pass, no sir. Old eyes thought you was a pretty little *green* bush."

Finally, trembling all over, she stood free, and after a moment dared to stoop for her cane.

"Sun so high!" she cried, leaning back and looking, while the thick tears went over her eyes. "The time getting all gone here."

At the foot of this hill was a place where a log was laid across the creek.

"Now comes the trial," said Phoenix.

Putting her right foot out, she mounted the log and shut her eyes. Lifting her skirt, leveling her cane fiercely before her, like a festival figure in some parade, she began to march across. Then she opened her eyes and she was safe on the other side.

"I wasn't as old as I thought," she said.

But she sat down to rest. She spread her skirts on the bank around her and folded her hands over her knees. Up above her was a tree in a pearly cloud of mistletoe. She did not dare to close her eyes, and when a little boy brought her a plate with a slice of marble-cake on it she spoke to him. "That would be acceptable," she said. But when she went to take it there was just her own hand in the air.

So she left that tree, and had to go through a barbed-wire fence. There she had to creep and crawl, spreading her knees and stretching her fingers like a baby trying to climb the steps. But she talked loudly to herself: she could not let her dress be torn now, so late in the day, and she could not pay for having her arm or her leg sawed off if she got caught fast where she was.

At last she was safe through the fence and risen up out in the clearing. Big dead trees, like black men with one arm, were standing in the purple stalks of the withered cotton field. There sat a buzzard.

"Who you watching?"

In the furrow she made her way along.

"Glad this not the season for bulls," she said, looking sideways, "and the good Lord made his snakes to curl up and sleep in the winter. A pleasure I don't see no two-headed snake coming around that tree, where it come once. It took a while to get by him, back in the summer."

She passed through the old cotton and went into a field of dead corn. It whispered and shook and was taller than her head. "Through the maze now," she said, for there was no path.

Then there was something tall, black, and skinny there, moving before her.

At first she took it for a man. It could have been a man dancing in the field. But she stood still and listened, and it did not make a sound. It was as silent as a ghost.

"Ghost," she said sharply, "who be you the ghost of? For I have heard of nary death close by."

But there was no answer—only the ragged dancing in the wind.

She shut her eyes, reached out her hand, and touched a sleeve. She found a coat and inside that an emptiness, cold as ice.

"You scarecrow," she said. Her face lighted. "I ought to be shut up for good," she said with laughter. "My senses is gone. I too old. I the oldest people I ever know. Dance, old scarecrow," she said, "while I dancing with you."

She kicked her foot over the furrow, and with mouth drawn down, shook her head once or twice in a little strutting way. Some husks blew down and whirled in streamers about her skirts.

Then she went on, parting her way from side to side with the cane, through the whispering field. At last she came to the end, to a wagon track where the silver grass blew between the red ruts. The quail were walking around like pullets, seeming all dainty and unseen.

"Walk pretty," she said. "This the easy place. This the easy going."

She followed the track, swaying through the quiet bare fields, through the little strings of trees silver in their dead leaves, past cabins silver from weather, with the doors and windows boarded shut, all like old women under a spell sitting there. "I walking in their sleep," she said, nodding her head vigorously.

In a ravine she went where a spring was silently flowing through a hollow log. Old Phoenix bent and drank. "Sweet-gum makes the water sweet," she said, and drank more. "Nobody know who made this well, for it was here when I was born."

The track crossed a swampy part where the moss hung as white as lace from every limb. "Sleep on, alligators, and blow your bubbles." Then the track went into the road.

Deep, deep the road went down between the high green-colored banks. Overhead the live-oaks met, and it was as dark as a cave.

A black dog with a lolling tongue came up out of the weeds by the ditch. She was meditating, and not ready, and when he came at her she only hit him a little with her cane. Over she went in the ditch, like a little puff of milkweed.

Down there, her senses drifted away. A dream visited her, and she reached her hand up, but nothing reached down and gave her a pull. So she lay there and presently went to talking. "Old woman," she said to herself, "that black dog come up out of the weeds to stall you off, and now there he sitting on his fine tail, smiling at you."

A white man finally came along and found her—a hunter, a young man, with his dog on a chain.

"Well, Granny!" he laughed. "What are you doing there?"

"Lying on my back like a June-bug waiting to be turned over, mister," she said, reaching up her hand.

He lifted her up, gave her a swing in the air, and set her down. "Anything broken, Granny?"

"No sir, them old dead weeds is springy enough," said Phoenix, when she had got her breath. "I thank you for your trouble."

"Where do you live, Granny?" he asked, while the two dogs were growling at each other.

"Away back yonder, sir, behind the ridge. You can't even see it from here."

"On your way home?"

"No sir, I going to town."

"Why, that's too far! That's as far as I walk when I come out myself, and I get something for my trouble." He patted the stuffed bag he carried, and there hung down a little closed claw. It was one of the bob-whites, with its beak hooked bitterly to show it was dead. "Now you go on home, Granny!"

"I bound to go to town, mister," said Phoenix. "The time come around."

He gave another laugh, filling the whole landscape. "I know you old colored people! Wouldn't miss going to town to see Santa Claus!"

But something held old Phoenix very still. The deep lines in her face went into a fierce and different radiation. Without warning, she had seen with her own eyes a flashing nickel fall out of the man's pocket onto the ground.

"How old are you, Granny?" he was saying.

"There is no telling, mister," she said, "no telling."

Then she gave a little cry and clapped her hands and said, "Git on away from here, dog! Look! Look at that dog!" She laughed as if in admiration. "He ain't scared of nobody. He a big black dog." She whispered, "Sic him!"

"Watch me get rid of that cur," said the man. "Sic him, Pete! Sic him!"

Phoenix heard the dogs fighting, and heard the man running and throwing sticks. She even heard a gunshot. But she was slowly bending forward by that time, further and further forward, the lids stretched down over her eyes, as if she were doing this in her sleep. Her chin was lowered almost to her knees. The yellow palm of her hand came out from the fold of her apron. Her fingers slid down and along the ground under the piece of money with the grace and care they would have in lifting an egg from under a setting hen. Then she slowly straightened up, she stood erect, and the nickel was in her apron pocket. A bird flew by. Her lips moved. "God watching me the whole time. I come to stealing."

The man came back, and his own dog panted about them. "Well, I scared him off that time," he said, and then he laughed and lifted his gun and pointed it at Phoenix.

She stood straight and faced him.

"Doesn't the gun scare you?" he said, still pointing it.

"No, sir, I seen plenty go off closer by, in my day, and for less than what I done," she said, holding utterly still.

He smiled, and shouldered the gun. "Well, Granny," he said, "you must be a hundred years old, and scared of nothing. I'd give you a dime if I had any money with me. But you take my advice and stay home, and nothing will happen to you."

"I bound to go on my way, mister," said Phoenix. She inclined her head in the red rag. Then they went in different directions, but she could hear the gun shooting again and again over the hill.

She walked on. The shadows hung from the oak trees to the road like curtains. Then she smelled wood-smoke, and smelled the river, and she saw a steeple and the cabins on their steep steps. Dozens of little black children whirled around her. There ahead was Natchez shining. Bells were ringing. She walked on.

In the paved city it was Christmas time. There were red and green electric lights strung and criss-crossed everywhere, and all turned on in the day-time. Old Phoenix would have been lost if she had not distrusted her eyesight and depended on her feet to know where to take her.

She paused quietly on the sidewalk where people were passing by. A lady came along in the crowd, carrying an armful of red-, green- and silver-wrapped presents; she gave off perfume like the red roses in hot summer, and Phoenix stopped her.

"Please, missy, will you lace up my shoe?" She held up her foot.

"What do you want, Grandma?"

"See my shoe," said Phoenix. "Do all right for out in the country, but wouldn't look right to go in a big building."

"Stand still then, Grandma," said the lady. She put her packages down on the sidewalk beside her and laced and tied both shoes tightly.

"Can't lace 'em with a cane," said Phoenix. "Thank you, missy. I doesn't mind asking a nice lady to tie up my shoe, when I gets out on the street."

Moving slowly and from side to side, she went into the big builidng, and into a tower of steps, where she walked up and around and around until her feet knew to stop.

She entered a door, and there she saw nailed up on the wall the document that had been stamped with the gold seal and framed in the gold frame, which matched the dream that was hung up in her head.

"Here I be," she said. There was a fixed and ceremonial stiffness over her body.

"A charity case, I suppose," said an attendant who sat at the desk before her.

But Phoenix only looked above her head. There was sweat on her face, the wrinkles in her skin shone like a bright net.

"Speak up, Grandma," the woman said. "What's your name? We must have your history, you know. Have you been here before? What seems to be the trouble with you?"

Old Phoenix only gave a twitch to her face as if a fly were bothering her.

"Are you deaf?" cried the attendant.

But then the nurse came in.

"Oh, that's just old Aunt Phoenix," she said. "She doesn't come for herself—she has a little grandson. She makes these trips just as regular as clockwork. She lives away back off the Old Natchez Trace." She bent down. "Well, Aunt Phoenix, why don't you just take a seat? We won't keep you standing after your long trip." She pointed.

The old woman sat down, bolt upright in the chair.

"Now, how is the boy?" asked the nurse.

Old Phoenix did not speak.

"I said, how is the boy?"

But Phoenix only waited and stared straight ahead, her face very solemn and withdrawn into rigidity.

"Is his throat any better?" asked the nurse. "Aunt Phoenix, don't you hear me? Is your grandson's throat any better since the last time you came for the medicine?"

With her hands on her knees, the old woman waited, silent, erect and motionless, just as if she were in armor.

"You mustn't take up our time this way, Aunt Phoenix," the nurse said. "Tell us quickly about your grandson, and get it over. He isn't dead, is he?"

At last there came a flicker and then a flame of comprehension across her face, and she spoke.

"My grandson. It was my memory had left me. There I sat and forgot why I made my long trip."

"Forgot?" The nurse frowned. "After you came so far?"

Then Phoenix was like an old woman begging a dignified forgiveness for waking up frightened in the night. "I never did go to school, I was too old at the Surrender," she said in a soft voice. "I'm an old woman without an education. It was my memory fail me. My little grandson, he is just the same, and I forgot it in the coming."

"Throat never heals, does it?" said the nurse, speaking in a loud, sure voice to old Phoenix. By now she had a card with something written on it, a little list. "Yes, Swallowed lye. When was it?—January—two-three years ago—"

Phoenix spoke unasked now. "No, missy, he not dead, he just the same. Every little while his throat begin to close up again, and he not able to swallow. He not get his breath. He not able to help himself. So the time come around, and I go on another trip for the soothing medicine."

"All right. The doctor said as long as you came to get it, you could have it," said the nurse. "But it's an obstinate case."

"My little grandson, he sit up there in the house all wrapped up, waiting by himself," Phoenix went on. "We is the only two left in the world. He suffer and it don't seem to put him back at all. He got a sweet look. He going to last. He wear a little patch quilt and peep out holding his mouth open like a little bird. I remembers so plain now. I not going to forget him again, no, the whole enduring time. I could tell him from all the others in creation."

"All right." The nurse was trying to hush her now. She brought her a bottle of medicine. "Charity," she said, making a check mark in a book.

Old Phoenix held the bottle close to her eyes, and then carefully put it into her pocket.

"I thank you," she said.

"It's Christmas time, Grandma," said the attendant. "Could I give you a few pennies out of my purse?"

"Five pennies is a nickel," said Phoenix stiffly.

"Here's a nickel," said the attendant.

Phoenix rose carefully and held out her hand. She received the nickel and then fished the other nickel out of her pocket and laid it beside the new one. She stared at her palm closely, with her head on one side.

Then she gave a tap with her cane on the floor.

"This is what come to me to do," she said. "I going to the store and buy my child a little windmill they sells, made out of paper. He going to find it hard to believe there such a thing in the world. I'll march myself back where he waiting, holding it straight up in this hand."

She lifted her free hand, gave a little nod, turned around, and walked out of the doctor's office. Then her slow step began on the stairs, going down.

QUESTIONS FOR "A WORN PATH" BY EUDORA WELTY

Talking About the Text

1. When we first considered using this short story in this last chapter, we argued about how it would fit into the theme of recognizing and/or reconciling differences. As you can see, we've included it here. What

are some of the "differences" operating in this narrative which Phoenix's journey might be interpreted as attempting to reconcile?

2. Eudora Welty is an accomplished artist who works in the medium of language. Often literary works are analyzed with an assumption that they have a simple surface meaning and further "deeper" meanings. Yet rather than using this depth metaphor, we can begin reflecting on the multiple effects Welty's language might have upon us. In small groups or as a class simply begin talking about the effects this story has upon you.

3. Certainly in understanding these effects you can utilize more traditional heuristics for understanding literature. Consider some of the following: characters, scene, action, conflict, and purpose. You might also examine imagery such as birds, money, the way characters move—walking, dancing, kicking, and so on. Consider the play between sounds and silences, who speaks, and how characters address one another. Consider the role of race relations. What does "charity" mean for instance? "Humility"? Is it significant that Phoenix's grandson swallowed lye? How long will Phoenix continue to make this journey? Why is memory so important?

Exploring Issues

1. Reflect on what you said earlier about fate and faith in the Amy Tan story. Consider this interplay between these two concepts as they apply to "The Worn Path."

2. Remember King's phrase "creative suffering"? How might it apply to Phoenix?

3. Try to read this story first as an allegory for the emancipation of African Americans. Then read it as a reaffirmation of perennial human values. Then try to put the two readings together.

Writing Assignment

In writing about literature, it is often helpful to first simply get in touch with your own reactions. Begin writing a response. Then, depending on how your class discussion progresses, do a more critical evaluation based on what you learn from others and from further readings. Support your interpretations with evidence from the story itself. Show how what you claim can be inferred from the language and from the events in the story.

Reading 81

Harrison Bergeron

Kurt Vonnegut, Jr.

Born in 1922 in Indianapolis, Indiana, Kurt Vonnegut, Jr., served as an
infantry scout in Europe during World War II. As a prisoner of war in
Dresden, Germany, Vonnegut experienced the horrible bombing of that city,
an experience that later was transformed into the novel, *Slaughterhouse-
Five*. As a famous novelist and playwright and through numerous
publications, Vonnegut has provided us, often in a bitingly satiric fashion, a
mirror in which we can see the absurd and frequently tragic situation of our
lives in the twentieth century. This selection is from *Welcome to the
Monkey House* (1961) and dramatizes the radical consequences following
upon our belief that everyone should be equal.

The year was 2081, and everybody was finally equal. They weren't only equal
before God and the law. They were equal every which way. Nobody was smarter
than anybody else. Nobody was better looking than anybody else. Nobody was
stronger or quicker than anybody else. All this equality was due to the 211th,
212th, and 213th Amendments to the Constitution, and to the unceasing vigilance of agents of the United States Handicapper General.

Some things about living still weren't quite right, though. April, for instance, still drove people crazy by not being springtime. And it was in that
clammy month that the H-G men took George and Hazel Bergeron's fourteen-
year-old son, Harrison, away.

It was tragic, all right, but George and Hazel couldn't think about it very
hard. Hazel had a perfectly average intelligence, which meant she couldn't
think about anything except in short bursts. And George, while his intelligence
was way above normal, had a little mental handicap radio in his ear. He was
required by law to wear it at all times. It was tuned to a government transmitter. Every twenty seconds or so, the transmitter would send out some sharp
noise to keep people like George from taking unfair advantage of their brains.

George and Hazel were watching television. There were tears on Hazel's
cheeks, but she'd forgotten for the moment what they were about.

On the television screen were ballerinas.

A buzzer sounded in George's head. His thoughts fled in panic, like bandits
from a burglar alarm.

"That was a real pretty dance, that dance they just did," said Hazel.

"Huh?" said George.

"The dance—it was nice," said Hazel.

"Yup," said George. He tried to think a little about the ballerinas. They weren't really very good—no better than anybody else would have been, anyway. They were burdened with sashweights and bags of birdshot, and their faces were masked, so that no one, seeing a free and graceful gesture or a pretty face, would feel like something the cat drug in. George was toying with the vague notion that maybe dancers shouldn't be handicapped. But he didn't get very far with it before another noise in his ear radio scattered his thoughts.

George winced. So did two out of the eight ballerinas.

Hazel saw him wince. Having no mental handicap herself, she had to ask George what the latest sound had been.

"Sounded like someone hitting a milk bottle with a ball peen hammer," said George.

"I'd think it would be real interesting, hearing all the different sounds," said Hazel, a little envious. "All the things they think up."

"Um," said George.

"Only, if I was Handicapper General, you know what I would do?" said Hazel. Hazel, as a matter of fact, bore a strong resemblance to the Handicapper General, a woman named Diana Moon Glampers. "If I was Diana Moon Glampers," said Hazel, "I'd have chimes on Sunday—just chimes. Kind of in honor of religion."

"I could think, if it was just chimes," said George.

"Well—maybe make 'em real loud," said Hazel. "I think I'd make a good Handicapper General."

"Good as anybody else," said George.

"Who knows better'n I do what normal is?" said Hazel.

"Right," said George. He began to think glimmeringly about his abnormal son who was now in jail, about Harrison, but a twenty-one-gun salute in his head stopped that.

"Boy!" said Hazel, "that was a doozy, wasn't it?"

It was such a doozy that George was white and trembling, and tears stood on the rims of his red eyes. Two of the eight ballerinas had collapsed to the studio floor, were holding their temples.

"All of a sudden you look so tired," said Hazel. "Why don't you stretch out on the sofa, so's you can rest your handicap bag on the pillows, honeybunch." She was referring to the forty-seven pounds of birdshot in a canvas bag, which was padlocked around George's neck. "Go on and rest the bag for a little while," she said. "I don't care if you're not equal to me for a while."

George weighed the bag with his hands. "I don't mind it," he said. "I don't notice it any more. It's just a part of me."

"You've been so tired lately—kind of wore out," said Hazel. "If there was just some way we could make a little hole in the bottom of the bag, and just take out a few of them lead balls. Just a few."

"Two years in prison and two thousand dollars fine for every ball I took out," said George. "I don't call that a bargain."

"If you could just take a few out when you came home from work," said Hazel. "I mean—you don't compete with anybody around here. You just sit around."

"If I tried to get away with it," said George, "then other people'd get away with it—and pretty soon we'd be right back to the dark ages again, with everybody competing against everybody else. You wouldn't like that, would you?"

"I'd hate it," said Hazel.

"There you are," said George. "The minute people start cheating on laws, what do you think happens to society?"

If Hazel hadn't been able to come up with an answer to this question, George couldn't have supplied one. A siren was going off in his head.

"Reckon it'd fall all apart," said Hazel.

"What would?" said George blankly.

"Society," said Hazel uncertainly. "Wasn't that what you just said?"

"Who knows?" said George.

The television program was suddenly interrupted for a news bulletin. It wasn't clear at first as to what the bulletin was about, since the announcer, like all announcers, had a serious speech impediment. For about half a minute, and in a state of high excitement, the announcer tried to say, "Ladies and gentlemen—"

He finally gave up, handed the bulletin to a ballerina to read.

"That's all right—" Hazel said of the announcer, "he tried. That's the big thing. He tried to do the best he could with what God gave him. He should get a nice raise for trying so hard."

"Ladies and gentlemen—" said the ballerina, reading the bulletin. She must have been extraordinarily beautiful, because the mask she wore was hideous. And it was easy to see that she was the strongest and most graceful of the dancers, for her handicap bags were as big as those worn by two-hundred-pound men.

And she had to apologize at once for her voice, which was a very unfair voice for a woman to use. Her voice was a warm, luminous, timeless melody. "Excuse me—" she said, and she began again, making her voice absolutely uncompetitive.

"Harrison Bergeron, age fourteen," she said in a grackle squawk, "has just escaped from jail, where he was held on suspicion of plotting to overthrow the government. He is a genius and an athlete, is under-handicapped, and should be regarded as extremely dangerous."

A police photograph of Harrison Bergeron was flashed on the screen—upside down, then sideways, upside down again, then right side up. The picture showed the full length of Harrison against a background calibrated in feet and inches. He was exactly seven feet tall.

The rest of Harrison's appearance was Halloween and hardware. Nobody had ever borne heavier handicaps. He had outgrown hindrances faster than the

H-G men could think them up. Instead of a little ear radio for a mental handicap, he wore a tremendous pair of earphones, and spectacles with thick wavy lenses. The spectacles were intended to make him not only half blind, but to give him whanging headaches besides.

Scrap metal was hung all over him. Ordinarily, there was a certain symmetry, a military neatness to the handicaps issued to strong people, but Harrison looked like a walking junkyard. In the race of life Harrison carried three hundred pounds.

And to offset his good looks, the H-G men required that he wear at all times a red rubber ball for a nose, keep his eyebrows shaved off, and cover his even white teeth with black caps at snaggle-tooth random.

"If you see this boy," said the ballerina, "do not—repeat, do not—try to reason with him."

There was the shriek of a door being torn from its hinges.

Screams and barking cries of consternation came from the television set. The photograph of Harrison Bergeron on the screen jumped again and again, as though dancing to the tune of an earthquake.

George Bergeron correctly identified the earthquake, and well he might have—for many was the time his own home had danced to the same crashing tune. "My God—" said George, "that must be Harrison!"

The realization was blasted from his mind instantly by the sound of an automobile collision in his head.

When George could open his eyes again, the photograph of Harrison was gone. A living, breathing Harrison filled the screen.

Clanking, clownish, and huge, Harrison stood in the center of the studio. The knob of the uprooted studio door was still in his hand. Ballerinas, technicians, musicans, and announcers cowered on their knees before him, expecting to die.

"I am the Emperor!" cried Harrison. "Do you hear? I am the Emperor! Everybody must do what I say at once!" He stamped his foot and the studio shook.

"Even as I stand here—" he bellowed, "crippled, hobbled, sickened—I am a greater ruler than any man who ever lived! Now watch me become what I *can* become!"

Harrison tore the straps of his handicap harness like wet tissue paper, tore straps guaranteed to support five thousands pounds.

Harrison's scrap-iron handicaps crashed to the floor.

Harrison thrust his thumbs under the bar of the padlock that secured his head harness. The bar snapped like celery. Harrison smashed his headphones and spectacles against the wall.

He flung away his rubber-ball nose, revealed a man that would have awed Thor, the god of thunder.

"I shall now select my Empress!" he said, looking down on the cowering people. "Let the first woman who dares rise to her feet claim her mate and her throne!"

A moment passed, and then a ballerina arose, swaying like a willow.

Harrison plucked the mental handicap from her ear, snapped off her physical handicaps with marvelous delicacy. Last of all, he removed her mask.

She was blindingly beautiful.

"Now—" said Harrison, taking her hand, "Shall we show the people the meaning of the word dance? Music!" he commanded.

The musicians scrambled back into their chairs, and Harrison stripped them of their handicaps, too. "Play your best," he told them, "and I'll make you barons and dukes and earls."

The music began. It was normal at first—cheap, silly, false. But Harrison snatched two musicians from their chairs, waved them like batons as he sang the music as he wanted it played. He slammed them back into their chairs.

The music began again and was much improved.

Harrison and his Empress merely listened to the music for a while—listened gravely, as though synchronizing their heartbeats with it.

They shifted their weights to their toes.

Harrison placed his big hands on the girl's tiny waist, letting her sense the weightlessness that would soon be hers.

And then, in an explosion of joy and grace, into the air they sprang!

Not only were the laws of the land abandoned, but the law of gravity and the laws of motion as well.

They reeled, whirled, swiveled, flounced, capered, gamboled, and spun.

They leaped like deer on the moon.

The studio ceiling was thirty feet high, but each leap brought the dancers nearer to it.

It became their obvious intention to kiss the ceiling.

They kissed it.

And then, neutralizing gravity with love and pure will, they remained suspended in air inches below the ceiling, and they kissed each other for a long, long time.

It was then that Diana Moon Glampers, the Handicapper General, came into the studio with a double-barreled ten-gauge shotgun. She fired twice, and the Emperor and the Empress were dead before they hit the floor.

Diana Moon Glampers loaded the gun again. She aimed it at the musicians and told them they had ten seconds to get their handicaps back on.

It was then that the Bergeron's television tube burned out.

Hazel turned to comment about the blackout to George. But George had gone out into the kitchen for a can of beer.

George came back in with the beer, paused while a handicap signal shook him up. And then he sat down again. "You been crying?" he said to Hazel.

"Yup," she said.

"What about?" he said.

"I forget," she said. "Something real sad on television."

"What was it?" he said.

"It's all kind of mixed up in my mind," said Hazel.

"Forget sad things," said George.

"I always do," said Hazel.

"That's my girl," said George. He winced. There was the sound of a rivetting gun in his head.

"Gee—I could tell that one was a doozy," said Hazel.

"You can say that again," said George.

"Gee—" said Hazel, "I could tell that one was a doozy."

QUESTIONS FOR "HARRISON BERGERON" BY KURT VONNEGUT, JR.

Talking About the Text

1. What is the role of the United States Handicapper General, and why is it needed?

2. When Hazel tries to talk George into removing his handicap bag from around his neck, he replies, "If I tried to get away with it . . . then other people'd get away with it—and pretty soon we'd be right back to the dark ages again, with everybody competing against everybody else." Why is competition associated with being in "the dark ages"?

3. In a futuristic society where everyone "must" be equal, why does the rebel, Harrison Bergeron, declare himself "emperor" instead of president or simply a free man who wishes to free others? Is there a certain ambiguity about this declaration?

Exploring Issues

1. What might both Kurt Vonnegut and Martin Luther King have to say about this line from the *Declaration of Independence:* "We hold these truths to be self-evident, that all men are created equal. . . ."?

2. How might Vonnegut respond to Ravitch's argument against particularism?

3. Vonnegut's short story was published in 1961. Why might women find it offensive? Why might they also find it an affirmation of their individuality?

Writing Assignments

1. From what you have learned so far, write an essay in which you explore possible relationships between being equal and being competitive. In your response, consider whether competition is necessary and valuable or disruptive. Also reflect upon the term *equal.* In what ways are we equal? Unequal? In what fashion might our society balance equality with competition?

2. Write an argument for or against this statement:

   Thinking is a subversive activity.

   Before you begin, however, re-read Vonnegut's tale and note those passages illustrating the consequences of thinking, particularly those moments when George appears to be getting somewhere with his thoughts.

3. Write an essay in which you explore the pros and cons of living in a highly competitive society. Use your own experience and observations as a context for your discussion.

CHAPTER 9: EXTENDED WRITING ASSIGNMENTS

9-1. Write an essay in which you explore the role of memory and history in several of the selections in this chapter. Focus on how memory is used by various writers to help individuals achieve coherence in their lives. Then consider how history as a sort of collective memory is utilized for similar purposes. You might also note, however, the consequences of distorted and incomplete memories and histories.

9-2. By now you are probably familiar with the melting pot theory of assimilation and with cultural pluralism. From what you have learned, invent a metaphor of your own that you believe best describes our present society. This could be an ideal version of what you would like our society to strive toward, or it could represent a more realistic assessment of our current situation. Use specific examples from some of the readings in this chapter to illustrate the realities and the possibilities of various groups and individuals living together.

9-3. Based on your reading in this book, identify one major problem facing our country and try to come up with a solution. You might focus on the family; on education; on our urban and rural environments; on ecology; on problems facing immigrants to this country; on images of different ethnic groups as represented by the media; on self-identity from the perspective of ethnicity, race, gender, and class; on issues dealing with prejudice; or come up with a topic on your own that you have identified through your reading—perhaps one that we have not considered.

9-4. Write a bibliographic essay in which you evaluate and critique a number of selections you have read in this book. Assume that you are writing this to future students who may be reading this same text and that you are offering them your summaries and views on what this book contains.

9-5. Write a recommendation to your instructor on what you think about this book as you used it in your class. What did you like? Dislike? What would you do differently? What selections would you keep or delete? Do you know of some other selections you think should be included?

Credits